THE FEDERAL RESERVE BANK OF CHICAGO
THE INTERNATIONAL MONETARY FUND

THE ASIAN FINANCIAL CRISIS:

Origins, Implications, and Solutions

THE FEDERAL RESERVE BANK OF CHICAGO
THE INTERNATIONAL MONETARY FUND

THE ASIAN FINANCIAL CRISIS:

Origins, Implications, and Solutions

edited by:

William C. Hunter
George G. Kaufman
Thomas H. Krueger

Kluwer Academic Publishers
Boston/Dordrecht/London

Distributors for North, Central and South America:
Kluwer Academic Publishers
101 Philip Drive
Assinippi Park
Norwell, Massachusetts 02061 USA
Telephone (781) 871-6600
Fax (781) 871-6528
E-Mail <kluwer@wkap.com>

Distributors for all other countries:
Kluwer Academic Publishers Group
Distribution Centre
Post Office Box 322
3300 AH Dordrecht, THE NETHERLANDS
Telephone 31 78 6392 392
Fax 31 78 6546 474
E-Mail <services@wkap.nl>

Electronic Services <http://www.wkap.nl>

Library of Congress Cataloging-in-Publication Data

The Asian financial crisis : origins, implications, and solutions /
edited by William C. Hunter, George G. Kaufman, Thomas H. Krueger.
p. cm.
At head of title The Federal Reserve Bank of Chicago. The International Monetary Fund.
Papers presented at a conference held on Oct. 8-10, 1998 at the Federal Reserve Bank of Chicago, and co-sponsored by the International Monetary Fund.
Includes bibliographical references.
ISBN 0-7923-8472-5 (alk. paper)
1. Financial crises—Asia congresses. 2. Asia—Economic conditions Congresses. 3. International finance Congresses. I. Hunter, W. Curt (William Curt) II. Kaufman, George G. III. Krueger, Thomas H., 1956- . IV> Federal Reserve Bank of Chicago. V. International Monetary Fund.
HB3808.A86 1999
332'.095—dc21 99-24642
CIP

Printed on acid-free paper.

Printed in the United States of America

Contents

PART III CAUSES AND IMPLICATIONS OF THE ASIAN CRISIS—THE ROLE OF THE FINANCIAL SECTOR, DOMESTIC POLICIES, AND CONTAGION

PART IV RESPONSE TO THE CRISIS—OVERVIEW AND CASE STUDIES

Acknowledgments

The conference was organized and coordinated by William C. Hunter, George Kaufman, and Vance Lancaster of the Federal Reserve Bank of Chicago, and Thomas Krueger of the International Monetary Fund. At the Federal Reserve Bank, conference arrangements were handled by Ella Dukes, Shirley Harris, and Loretta Novak. They were assisted by Helen Koshy, Kathryn Moran, Surya (Surge) Sen, and Shira Wachtel. Elizabeth Taylor, Gillian Jetson, Hala Leddy, and Barbara Van Brussell assisted in the meeting and travel arrangements. Kathryn Moran, Tom McPheron, and Yvonne Peeples at the Federal Reserve Bank of Chicago assisted in the preperation of the publication of the proceedings.

Preface

The Federal Reserve Bank of Chicago and the International Monetary Fund co-sponsored the conference on *Asia: An Analysis of Financial Crisis*. The conference was held on October 8-10, 1998 at the Federal Reserve Bank of Chicago. The papers in this volume were presented at the conference and encompass a wide range of topics dealing with the ongoing financial crisis in Asia.

The recent disruption of the Asian economic "miracle" has astounded many observers around the world, and has raised questions concerning the stability of the international financial system. The rapid spread of the crisis illustrates how interdependent our economies have become. Global interdependence encourages international cooperation in addressing the Asian crisis in order to promote financial efficiency and stability. Toward this end, the conference brought together more than 230 academics, policymakers and market participants from some 30 countries to gain a better understanding of the elements involved in the crisis and to design appropriate responses for current and future financial crises in the global economy.

The conference addressed the following questions:

- What were causes of the East Asian financial crisis?
- Why was its onset so sudden and unpredicted?
- How effective have international rescue operations been in dealing with the crisis?
- What actions can be taken to prevent future crises?

- How should the international financial system balance the stability gained from a financial safety net against the potential risk of moral hazard?
- Has the opaqueness of Asian financial markets contributed to the crisis?
- Is the Asian crisis a failure of the capitalist experiment or a failure of state-managed capitalism?
- How has financial liberalization and openness to market forces affected the severity of the crisis in each country?

The sessions and roundtables at the conference offered a unique opportunity for such discussion. In addition, three keynote speakers offered their perspective on the crisis. Stanley Fischer, first deputy managing director of the International Monetary Fund (IMF), and Karin Lissakers, executive director for the United States at the IMF, offered behind-the-scenes looks at the decisionmaking of the fund during the crisis. Their candid discussion provided valuable insights into the role of the IMF future crises. Robert Johnson, former investment manager at Moore Capital Management, discussed the difficulties in adapting market solutions in Asian countries.

While the conference participants provided no easy solutions to the ongoing crisis, the conference provided a forum for the reevaluation of current proposals and the dissemination of new ideas. Discussion during the conference promoted a better awareness of the issues involved in international financial crises, which will hopefully serve to improve international responses in the future.

Michael H. Moskow
President
Federal Reserve Bank of Chicago

Michael Mussa
Economic Counselor and
Director of Research
International Monetary Fund

PART I

OPENING REMARKS

Chapter 1

The IMF and the Asian Crisis: A View from the Executive Board

Karin Lissakers
International Monetary Fund

1. INTRODUCTION

I want to look back, and tell you, briefly, how the Asian crisis looked from the perspective of a member of the Executive Board of the International Monetary Fund. Thanks to the IMF's vaunted secrecy, many of you may not even know that there is an Executive Board—24 directors representing 182 member countries—which decides all major fund policies and approves all programs and disbursements of fund resources. Several of my board colleagues are here tonight.

I will also touch on the policy debates which took place in Washington this week during the Annual Meetings of the Board of Governors of the International Monetary Fund and World Bank, but which also included meetings of G-7 and G-10 finance ministers and central bankers and the ad hoc Group of 22 industrial and emerging market countries organized by Secretary Rubin and Chairman Greenspan at the behest of President Clinton. One can discern in these debates, certain common themes with regard to IMF reforms and the new financial architecture more generally.

2. WHAT WE SAW BEFORE THE CRISIS

The IMF has understandably been criticized for not having anticipated and prevented the Asian crisis. The fact that we are in good company offers little comfort; ensuring the stability of the international monetary system is the IMF's job. Our annual surveillance reviews of every member's economic policies and performance, the so-called Article IV consultation, is supposed to provide an early warning of trouble ahead.

Let me describe what we on the board saw in the Asian Article IVs, what I think we overlooked, and what was hidden from view.

The macroeconomic fundamentals in Asia by conventional definition looked strong—low inflation, fiscal balance or surplus, strong private savings, high rates of capital formation, strong export performance, ample foreign direct investment, stable currencies, large foreign exchange reserves, modest debt/GDP ratios. And, not least, the region had achieved a dramatic improvement in standards of living for a significant portion of the population.

As we discussed the Asian performance, some on the board questioned the sustainability of twenty-five to thirty percent or more rates of private credit expansion year after year and wondered about the soundness of the underlying investments. But the weight of opinion was that this had worked well so far, and one could see no obvious reason it could not continue. Dramatic year-on-year growth and investment rates seemed to be the norm for Asia, the standard for "the Asian model."

There were, nevertheless warning signs in Thailand, with a clear indication of overheating. Thailand was developing a classic real estate bubble, and its current account deteriorated sharply, heading for an 8 percent deficit in 1997. The weakening export performance suggested an exchange rate misalignment. However, the IMF's warnings, delivered with mounting intensity over a period of almost two years, fell on deaf ears in Bangkok.

It is fair to say the IMF did not pay sufficient attention to other indicators that were visible at the time, most notably the rapid build-up of foreign, short-term obligations by banks and the nonbank private sector, especially in Korea and Thailand. Although the Bank for International Settlements' data on cross-border bank claims has a long lag, and the coverage is incomplete, there was enough information in the BIS tables, especially on interbank claims on Korea, to hint of the possibility of serious trouble ahead, or at least significant vulnerability.

The IMF obviously pays close attention to exchange rate policies, which are at the center of our surveillance. But in this context, we did not worry enough about the incentives pegged or managed exchange rates given to both borrowers and creditors to accumulate unsustainable cross-border, cross-currency exposures.

3. WHAT WE OVERLOOKED

The IMF has only recently begun to cover systematically the financial sector and banking supervision in its Article IV reviews. As Asian problems were building, we overlooked weaknesses in bank and corporate balance sheets in much of Asia: The fund was unaware of the extraordinary leverage of Korean companies, which in some cases reached a ratio of 600/1 debt to equity; we did not focus on the weak accounting and disclosure practices of banks and nonbanks; or the loose loan loss provisioning and generous rollovers of banks to their key clients.

To the extent these weaknesses posed systemic risks to the financial sector, many of the losses would of course end up on the books of the governments. The losses accumulating on private sector accounts thus constituted contingent liabilities, or quasi-fiscal losses of the public sector. And consequently, the "fiscal fundamentals" in many Asian countries were far less sound than they appeared. The costs of cleaning up the banking systems in Thailand, Korea, Indonesia could go as high as twenty to thirty percent of GDP.

The IMF also underestimated the impact of the Japanese government's contractionary fiscal stance on Japan's fragile economic recovery. In this regard, my U.S. authorities' gloomy predictions were closer to the mark. Obviously, Japan's renewed slump, plus the depth of problems in Japanese banks, which are major creditors in the region, have been a further devastating blow to the crisis countries.

I think we also underestimated the effect of political factors. "Political risk" is unfashionable in the sophisticated financial world of the 1990s. Private sector financial analysts, too, largely discounted the fragility of the political underpinnings of the Asian economies and did not fully comprehend the extent to which rampant corruption was discrediting regimes in the eyes of the people, as well as weakening economies directly, especially in Indonesia.

It is noteworthy that the Philippines, which had gone through a wrenching democratization phase some years back, has fared relatively better in the recent financial turmoil than some of its neighbors. Fortunately, in Thailand and Korea important political transitions took place relatively peacefully shortly after the financial crisis began, and this has undoubtedly helped the economic stabilization effort. Indonesia suffers still from an incomplete process of democratization.

4. WHAT WAS HIDDEN FROM VIEW

We missed other signs of the incipient Asian crisis for the simple reason that they were hidden from view. The IMF did not know of the desperate efforts by some governments/central banks to defend their exchange rates in the summer and fall of 1997. We did not know, because their governments hid the fact that Thailand and Korea had completely exhausted their foreign exchange reserves by time the authorities came to the IMF for help.

We did not know that on May 14, the Thai central bank spent more than $10 billion intervening in the spot, forward, and swap markets. The fund did not know that between May 1 and May 14, Thailand's reserves had dropped from $24.3 billion to $2.5 billion. The facts are laid out in the Thai government's Nukul Commission Report, just published last March (1998). The report makes fascinating reading.

Similarly, the IMF was not told that the Korean central bank had deposited a large part of its foreign exchange reserves with Korean commercial banks to cover the withdrawal of foreign credit lines and foreign bank deposits.

These acts of desperation by the Thai and Korean central banking authorities attest to the severity of the markets' assault on their currencies in the months before the IMF appeared on the scene. Therefore, the charge that the IMF and its adjustment policies are somehow responsible for the steep currency depreciation that followed is patently absurd.

Another important facet that was hidden from view was the extent of hedging of local currency risk by foreign lenders and investors with unhedged Thai, Korean, Indonesian (and Russian) banks and corporations and sometimes the governments themselves, as counterparties. This hedging activity was not limited to the specialized "hedge funds," but was apparently a central feature of the 1990s credit and portfolio investment boom in emerging markets. Now, of course, many of these hedges turn out to offer no protection at all. This aspect was hidden from view because there are limited disclosure requirements for off-balance-sheet transactions.

It is fair to say that derivatives are the black hole of this crisis. We are only now beginning to take its measure, as the losses on these kinds of transactions begin to show up on creditors' balance sheets. As Chairman Greenspan has said, we don't yet fully understand the nature of the global financial contagion. This is particularly true of the role of derivatives and hedging instruments as "vectors" of this contagion, to quote one of tomorrow's panelists, Martin Mayer. Indeed, the speed and virulence of the international financial contagion has caught everyone by surprise, including the IMF.

5. THE IMF'S CRISIS RESPONSE

I will not dwell on the IMF's response to the Asia crisis. You are all familiar with its main elements. I do want to touch on two controversial aspects of the IMF's rescue efforts in Asia. First, we have been criticized for fiscal over—killinsisting on too much fiscal adjustment in the face of recession. I would just say that our fiscal policy recommendations made sense in the context of very high growth and apparent overheating that we saw in Thailand. Once it became evident that we were dealing with a different phenomenon, and that the program countries faced very sharp declines in demand and growth, the IMF quickly adjusted its program conditionality to allow for less fiscal stringency.

The IMF has been more roundly criticized—attacked even—for choosing tight monetary policy over letting exchange rates go. I think it is not telling tales out of school to say this debate has raged inside the fund as well—at the board and among staff. It is still a subject of controversy.

At the very outset, with Thailand, and then Indonesia, we debated heatedly whether high domestic interest rates or steep currency depreciation would do less damage to the economies we were trying to save, given that the private sector had both large short-term debt exposures and large foreign currency obligations.

We chose higher interest rates as the less damaging option. The logic of tightening monetary policy in the circumstance is simple—it raises the cost of getting out while you go about fixing what makes people want to flee the currency in the first place. If you move quickly, a brief period of very high rates should not do major damage to an economy. If, however, you don't put in place credible corrective measures for the underlying problems, the interest rate response obviously will impose a heavy burden on the real economy.

In the event, the Asian crisis countries did not at first follow the monetary trajectory agreed with the fund, but instead pursued an on again, off again, monetary policy that confused investors and undermined the credibility of the whole stabilization effort. Their currencies continued to weaken. Only later as monetary policy firmed and governments moved more decisively on structural problems—which admittedly are not susceptible to a quick fix — have exchange rates recovered, giving scope for monetary easing. Nominal interest rates are now in single digits in Korea and Thailand where inflation also remains subdued.

I have personally come to the conclusion that the argument over tight monetary policy versus letting the exchange rate go is a phony debate in the Asian context. By the time the IMF entered the picture, the vulnerabilities of the corporate and banking sectors in Thailand, Korea and Indonesia to either an interest rate shock or an exchange rate shock were so great that *either* would seriously damage the real economy.

In recent years, access to cheap foreign credit allowed Korean, Thai, and Indonesian banks to sustain the flow of cheap domestic credit to the corporate sector as losses mounted, unrecognized, in their loan portfolios. And the flow of cheap domestic credit and perpetual rolling over of old loans is what sustained the chaebols and many other enterprises even as the marginal rates of return on their investments eroded. One need only look at the return on assets and return on equity of Korean, Thai, and other banks in the region before the crisis hit, to see that this true. The withdrawal of cheap, ample, short-term foreign capital and credit pulled the legs out from under these economies.

In short, it is doubtful the alternative strategy of easy money and letting exchange rates go without any monetary defense would have had a significantly different outcome for these countries, even if events did not play out as expected under the IMF programs. The loss of access to foreign financing would have produced a severe credit crunch even without a deliberate policy to drive up interest rates. Likewise, devaluation by itself would have blown a large hole in Asian balance sheets.

Let me say finally on this point that I agree fully with Mike Dooley's comments today that until losses are allocated and recognized, there will be no recovery. Warehousing bad assets to try to shield asset prices overall will guarantee protracted weakness in these economies. One need only look at Japan.

6. LOOKING FORWARD

There are no magic bullets, no simple formulas for curing what ails the international financial system today. But a number of themes were sounded in Washington this week that point to some corrective measures. These were outlined most clearly in the reports of the G-22's three task forces, which were released during the Bank-fund meetings.

First, we are redefining economic "fundamentals" to encompass the health of the financial and corporate sector, particularly the soundness of banks because of their systemic impact and the fact that they can create contingent claims on the public sector. And it is not enough to point the finger at emerging markets which do indeed have a long way to go before they meet internationally accepted standards of corporate governance and banking supervision. One must also examine the supply side of the equation that led to the current crisis: authorities in the major financial centers also have work to do, as is recognized in the G-22 reports.

Second, there will be an effort to give economic actors fewer places to hide their mistakes, through a general call for greater transparency. There will be a push for central banks to disclose not only gross but net reserves on a regular and frequent basis; for government accounts to be transparent; for banks to be subject to better supervision; and for corporations of all types to be subject to more stringent accounting and disclosure standards. Investment institutions could conceivably be subject to more oversight, as well, or at least more disclosure or reporting.

The IMF should and will become more transparent in its own activities. Jeffrey Sachs wants to be able to critique the IMF's economic policy advice, and I think we should let him. (He has done a lot of critiquing even without full access.) There is growing support among members, as reflected in the G-22 reports, for more public disclosure of IMF policy decisions, agreements with countries on economic programs, and the conclusions of our annual economic consultations. A lot of this information is already available on the IMF's website. I hope there soon will be more.

There is great determination to ensure that private creditors contribute to the resolution of financial crises. This is essential from a practical standpoint; there isn't enough official money to do the job. There is also concern about moral hazard. Measures might include bond covenants or clauses making it easier to organize investor workouts. There have been discussions about establishing more systematic contacts between the IMF and the private financial sector to exchange views on a regular basis, before crises erupt and in order to have channels of communication already well established if they do. However, we must be mindful of the potential insider information problem, given the IMF's access to confidential information from member governments. The IMF is considering ways to clarify its policies with regard to lending into arrears. Even capital controls are getting another look, although these are still regarded with great skepticism and wariness.

More serious consideration is being given to the pace and sequencing of opening capital markets that have been closed for a long time and the need to adequately prepare the financial sector and supervisory framework. Exchange rate regimes have to be looked at carefully in this context.

7. CONCLUSION

How do we deliver this new regime? It is worth pointing out that most of the proposed reforms and solutions, are not economic or financial, but legal/political. Finding global solutions to a global crisis presents a fundamental political challenge: how to reconcile the economic imperatives of global integration with the political reality of independent sovereign states. President Clinton articulated this very clearly during G-22 discussions. There is no simple answer. We are groping for a solution to this political dilemma. The current focus is on voluntary "standards," "codes of conduct," "best practices," in banking supervision; fiscal management; corporate governance; and financial reporting.

International standards, codes of conduct, or best practices may seem like a tame response to a global financial crisis. They certainly aren't the whole answer. But my Indian colleague, Mr. Sivaraman, likes to cite the International Civil Aviation Organization as an example. Under the ICAO's auspices, a large number of countries at different levels of development, acting out of obvious mutual self-interest, have voluntarily adopted common standards for air safety, aircraft inspections, and airport operations. This voluntary regime has been surprisingly effective in reducing the number of air fatalities around the world.

Mr. Sivaraman's example may be particularly apt, for if there is one thing we have all learned over the recent period of severe turbulence, it is that we are all passengers on the same plane.

Chapter 2

The Asian Financial Crisis

Michael H. Moskow
Federal Reserve Bank of Chicago

The Asian financial crisis—the topic has dominated headlines throughout the world. Since July 1997, there have been more than 16,000 articles, journals, and reviews published nationally and internationally on this subject.

An economist always hesitates to make an unqualified prediction, but I think it's safe to say that there will be many thousand more before the subject is exhausted. Throughout this crisis, medical references have been commonplace. Asian economies are "ill" or in "poor health."

The name "Asian flu" has been transformed in the national vocabulary to an economic term. We worry about how contagious it is, and whether it's reached epidemic proportions. Some have called for "economic penicillin" to solve this crisis. Others have said that any solution should be similar to a doctor's approach to a patient—"First, do no harm." That's probably not bad advice for economists and policymakers, as well as doctors. And I think it's useful advice in looking at the Asian crisis. But I hope we can do more than just avoid harm.

I hope we can learn from this event and begin to develop policies to help prevent future crises. In that sense, the Asian crisis represents an opportunity for positive change. And I believe this conference is an opportunity to significantly increase our understanding of what constitutes effective policy.

Our understanding of the Asian crisis has already changed dramatically. When the crisis broke out with the collapse of the Thai baht in July 1997, many believed the damage would be confined to a handful of small Asian economies. Some fourteen months later, it's clear how myopic that thinking was. The crisis has spread to other East Asian countries and to Russia. Just a few weeks ago, Latin America began to encounter serious troubles.

Some claim to have recognized the potential for crisis long before it began. But most experts were taken by surprise by the speed and the timing of the crisis. And the future is highly uncertain. But as Alan Greenspan stated in September, it seems unlikely that the United States can remain an oasis of prosperity.

The international system of capital markets has been radically transformed in recent decades. Today, we have an interdependent, interlinked global financial system with the ability to react to events at incredible speed. This global system has made a substantial contribution to living standards worldwide. But it also responds with brutal speed and efficiency in moving money away from potential risks.

More than ever, financial markets seem to drive developments in the real sector, rather than passively responding to the ebb and flow of real productive activity. In fact, some have characteried the Asian crisis as a virtual decoupling of the financial and real asectors of the economy. The years preceding the crisis were a period of exceptional growth in East Asia. No real macroeconomic distortions were observed.

The economies of the five crisis countries had low inflation, their budgets were generally in surplus, and government foreign debt was declining as a percentage of GDP. During the 1990s, these governments engaged in responsible monetary expansion. The unemployment rates were low. In short, these governments had a good record of managing the real side of the economy.

Instead, the weaknesses seem to have been on the financial side. In the months leading up to the crisis, economic activity was financed increasingly with short-term capital inflows. Short-term capital is "hot money:" It can flow rapidly into countries where expected returns are high; it can flow out just as rapidly.

What precipitated the massive reversal of capital flows we saw in the Asian crisis? Did investors rationally forecast a fall off in economic productivity? Or did investors suffer an exogenous loss of confidence, not triggered by any real economic shocks? Worse yet, did the loss of confidence so damage the business climate that investors' pessimism became self-fulfilling?

This scenario would be the economic equivalent of the tail wagging the dog: real economic activity damaged by a malfunctioning financial sector, rather than the reverse. It remains to be seen whether this characterization of the Asian crisis proves to be the most useful way to think about these events. We have the opportunity to consider the Asian crisis from many different perspectives, in order to better understand its causes and consequences.

I think it's fair to say that there are as many theories about what caused the Asian crisis as there are people at this conference. However, two issues that are likely to be central to understanding the Asian crisis are the distortion of market forces and the resulting moral hazard. If you peel back the many layers of the Asian crisis, you'll find these issues at the core.

Focusing on market forces and moral hazard is important because they are key to *preventing* a bank crisis. The prompt resolution of a banking crisis is important, of course. But regulators tend to focus much of their time and attention preparing to pick up the pieces *after* the crisis. We can spend less time on resolving crises by spending more time on *preventing* them.

Ironically, many point to the turmoil in Southeast Asia as eveidence of a breakdown of capitalism—a failure of market forces. An alternative view is that the crisis resulted from government interference in the normal operation of financial markets. To what extent were dubious investments cheerfully funded by banks as long as the borrower had the right government connection? To what degree was patronage more important than profits? Clearly, these sorts of distortions could subvert the fundamental function of banks as efficient allocaters of credit, and they could undermine the market discipline needed to ensure that financial institutions were properly allocating risk. The weakening of market discipline left these countries susceptible to moral hazard.

Korea, Indonesia, Thailand, and Malaysia among others have strong interlocking relationships between the public and private sectors. Did these relationships carry with them an implicit guarantee of financial institutions? Did lenders assume that their investments were protected by national governments? Did investors in financial institutions exercise insufficient prudence as a result? And were even the more prudent investors unable to make informed choices because of the lack of transparency in Southeast Asian banks? Weakened market discipline is a common thread connecting those countries suffering from economic crisis. They may differ in the way market forces were distorted, but the outcomes were essentially the same.

Now these nations must grapple with the question of how to restore the levels of economic performance that so impressed the world during the years prior to the crisis. Some nations seem to have grown impatient with global markets, and threaten to turn toward isolation. Malaysia imposed currency and stock market controls in an effort to insulate its economy. Russia appears to be reverting to a less market-driven economy.

And even Hong Kong, a bastion of free markets, bought an estimated $15 billion worth of stocks to bolster prices after sell-offs by speculators. Are Asian countries losing faith in free markets. Certainly there's growing anger among some officials, business leaders, and citizens about the crisis. And free markets are an easy target.

But obviously no one can truly "opt-out" of the global financial community. That's no longer a realistic possibility. A return to prosperity for those countries in crisis requires a commitment to market reform. The two are inseparable. I'm sure that market forces and moral hazard are two issues that will feature prominently in our discussion. There are, of course, a number of other important issues that we'll cover during the next three days. Here are just a few of the key questions that we'll be discussing:

What were the causes of the Asian financial crisis and why was its onset so sudden and unpredictable?

- How effective have international rescue operations been in dealing with the crisis?
- How should the international financial system balance the stability gained from a financial safety net against the potential risk of moral hazard?
- How has the opaqueness of Asian financial markets contributed to the crisis?
- Is the Asian crisis a failure of market-oriented capitalism or a failure of state-managed capitalism?
- How has openness to market forces affected the severity of the financial crisis in each country?
- And, perhaps most importantly, what actions can be taken to prevent future crises?

The answers to these questions, and many others we will be discussing will help share the future of public policy related to the international financial system. I am pleased that we have some of the leading experts from the academic, regulatory, and financial services industries to discuss these issues.

PART II

ORIGINS OF THE ASIAN CRISIS

Chapter 3

What Caused the Recent Asian Currency Crises?

Craig Burnside, Martin Eichenbaum, and Sergio Rebelo
The World Bank; Northwestern University, NBER and Federal Reserve Bank of Chicago; Northwestern University and NBER

Abstract: This paper argues that the recent Asian currency crisis was caused by prospective future deficits associated with implicit bank bailouts.

Recent events in Asia have led economists and policymakers to reevaluate the causes and consequences of currency crises. The view favored by many Asian policymakers is that the crises happened because the market expected them to happen. The basic argument is that the economies of the affected countries (Thailand, Indonesia, South Korea, the Philippines, and Malaysia) were fundamentally sound. But at some point in time, speculators came to believe that currency collapses would occur. Based on this belief, investors refused to roll over loans denominated in these currencies. This led to a massive drain on the foreign exchange reserves of the affected countries. Unable to borrow additional reserves at any interest rate or one that was prohibitive because of the effect on their economies, governments capitulated and abandoned fixed exchange rates. In this way, speculators' beliefs became self-fulfilling. Not surprisingly, proponents of this view have argued that the International Monetary Fund should provide the resources required to fend off speculative currency attacks. Indeed some, like Krugman (1998), have gone so far as to suggest that currency controls may be desirable.

The view that the Asian currency crises was a multiple equilibrium phenomenon induced by self fulfilling beliefs can be formalized using dynamic general equilibrium theory. Ruling out such an interpretation of the data is a difficult and subtle task. Rather than trying to do so, we pursue a different objective. Specifically, we present an alternative explanation that attributes the crises to fundamentals: large *prospective* fiscal deficits stemming from implicit government guarantees to failing banking systems.

There is already a large amount of literature that seeks to explain currency crises on the basis of fundamentals. Perhaps the simplest fundamentalist view is that currency collapses reflect monetary and fiscal policies that predate the crises.[1] The idea is that large deficits lead to high growth rates of money and inflation which are incompatible with a fixed exchange rate regime. While this theory has been very useful in explaining a variety of historical episodes, it is not particularly helpful in understanding the recent Asian crises. This is because all of the affected countries had fiscal surpluses or small reported deficits as well as low reported growth rates of inflation (see for example Corsetti, Pesenti and Roubini (1998)).

An alternative fundamentalist view which seems more promising is that large prospective fiscal deficits were the key factor behind the recent Asian currency crises. The basic idea is that markets expected these prospective deficits would be financed, at least in part, by future seignorage revenues. So, *future*, rather than past, monetary policy was the main culprit behind the crises.

The mere fact that governments had to fund future bank bailouts does not imply that a currency crisis was inevitable. After all, markets could have believed that the bailouts would be paid for by cuts in other types of government expenditures or tax hikes. If this were the case, then the banking crises associated with the bailout promises need not have been associated with currency crises. To establish a connection between the two, one must argue that the banking crises caused a change in either past or future monetary policy.

Is the view that the Asian governments would fund bank bailouts by raising taxes and reducing government expenditures credible? In our view it is not. Precisely because banking crises have real causes and consequences, bank failures would be associated with declines in current and future output as well as tax revenues. Massively raising distortionary taxes and cutting government expenditures under those circumstances would be very costly, both politically and socially. To us it seems more credible that governments would attempt to fund the bank bailouts by raising seignorage revenues and obtaining aid from the International Monetary Fund.

In Burnside, Eichenbaum, and Rebelo (1998) we formalize the notion that expected changes in *future* monetary policy can cause a collapse in a fixed exchange rate regime. We do this by studying the dynamics of a speculative attack in a variant of Calvo's (1987) perfect foresight, general equilibrium, small open economy model. The basic argument is as follows. Consider a small open economy that is initially in the steady state of a fixed exchange rate regime. Imagine that at some point in time, people receive information that the present value of current and *future* government deficits will be larger than they initially thought. Then it follows directly from the government's intertemporal budget constraint that the collapse of the fixed exchange rate regime is inevitable. This is because, by assumption, the government has no alternative to funding higher future fiscal deficits than by raising seignorage revenues. But this is incompatible with maintaining fixed exchange rates.

The literature refers to the time of the collapse of the fixed exchange rate regime as the time of a speculative attack. The key result in our paper is that the speculative attack occurs *after* the new information about the rise in the present value of the government deficit arrives, but *before* the new monetary policy is implemented.

Under these circumstances, an econometrician looking at the data would see an exchange rate crisis. But he would not see large fiscal deficits, higher growth rates of money, nor, necessarily, a loss of reserves. If the econometrician were naive, he might even conclude that the attack was a multiple equilibrium phenomenon caused by capricious speculators. But the attack was actually caused by fundamentals: high *prospective* deficits financed by future seignorage revenues.

According to our model, a rise in the present value of government deficits leads inevitably to the end of fixed exchange rates. Even so, the government can delay the date of collapse. But it can do so only at a price: the longer the delay, the higher inflation will be when the collapse does happen. The policy conclusion is straightforward. The government has two options. First it can fix the real problem by fundamental banking and fiscal reforms. Alternatively, it can admit that it does not have the political will to pursue the first option. But then there is no point in delaying the inevitable collapse of the fixed exchange rate regime. The government should float as quickly as possible to minimize the impact on future domestic inflation.

In the remainder of this paper we discuss some of the empirical evidence regarding the three key assumptions in our analysis: (i) foreign reserves did not necessarily play a role in the timing of the attack, (ii) large losses in the banking sector were associated with a large rise in prospective deficits, and (iii) the market knew the banks were in trouble well before the currency crises.

1. FOREIGN RESERVES

Foreign reserves do not play a special role in our discussion of the Asian currency crises. Our basic logic is that whatever their level was prior to the crisis, they were pledged to financing the old level of the deficit. Moreover we assume that governments could always borrow more reserves if they wished, subject to their intertemporal budget constraint. Burnside, Eichenbaum, and Rebelo (1998) discuss the ratio of foreign reserves to the monetary base and M1 in the crisis countries over the period July 1995 to May 1998. Two key facts emerge from our analysis. First, all of the crisis countries had more than enough reserves to buy back the monetary base at the time their currencies collapsed. In fact, in all cases, they could have bought back over ninety percent of M1. Thailand's reserves were actually twice as large as M1 at the time of the collapse. It is true that some of these reserves may have been effectively sold forward. But this strengthens our basic point: the key issue is what the net assets of the governments are, rather than the level of foreign reserves per se.

2. THE SIZE OF THE GOVERNMENT'S IMPLICIT LIABILITIES

Corsetti, Pesenti, and Roubini (1998) provide estimates of loan default rates in Asia prior to the crises. These are summarized in the first columns of Tables 1 and 2, reproduced from Burnside, Eichenbaum, and Rebelo (1998). The key point to note is the sharp difference between default rates in the crisis and non-crisis countries. Using these default rates and data on total credit to domestic enterprises and financial institutions, Burnside, Eichenbaum, and Rebelo (1998) generate a rough estimate of the government's total implicit liabilities stemming from guarantees to the financial sector.

Columns 2, 3 and 4 of Table 1 report total nonperforming bank loans as a percentage of the monetary base, real output and central government revenue, respectively.[2] Table 2 reports the analogue percentages for the liabilities associated with nonbank foreign borrowing.[3] Note that regardless of which measure we use, all of the crisis countries exhibited high levels of total implicit liabilities.

The previous two tables summarize information on default rates and implicit liabilities prior to the currency crises. Burnside, Eichenbaum, and Rebelo (1998) review estimates from J. P. Morgan (1998) regarding the post-crisis situation. Specifically we look at (i) nonperforming loans as a percentage of total loans and GDP in Indonesia, Korea, Malaysia, and Thailand, as of June 1998, and (ii) the amount of capital, as a percentage of GDP, needed to restore bank capital to the eight percent Bank of

International Settlements Capital Adequacy Requirement level. These estimates are summarized in Table 3, reproduced from Burnside, Eichenbaum, and Rebelo (1998).

Notice the dramatic increase in the magnitude of nonperforming loans relative to the pre-crisis estimates. From the perspective of our theory the post-crisis estimates are at least as relevant as the pre-crisis estimates, since these are tied to the current liabilities of the crisis governments.

3. WERE THE BANKING CRISES A SURPRISE?

We now briefly discuss whether private agents anticipated the state of the banking system prior to the currency crises. Corsetti, Pesenti, and Roubini (1998) discuss the fragile state of the financial sectors in the crisis countries prior to the recent speculative attacks. Burnside, Eichenbaum, and Rebelo (1998) construct monthly indices of the market value of the financial and nonfinancial sectors in Korea, Thailand, the Philippines, and Malaysia. These are summarized in Table 4. Note that in Korea, Thailand, and to a lesser extent the Philippines and Malaysia, the value of the financial sectors had been declining well before the currency crises.

For Korea the decline in the banking index from its peak (August 3, 1991) to the date of the currency crisis (October 29, 1997) was sixty-seven percent. The analogue decline in the ratio of the banking index to the manufacturing index was sixty-four percent. In the case of Thailand the decline in the finance index from its peak (January 4, 1994) to the date of the crisis (July 2, 1997) was ninety-two percent. The analogue decline in the ratio of the finance index to the commerce index was eighty percent. In the Philippines, the peak in the finance index took place on February 17, 1997. This series declined by thirty-four percent between this date and the date at which their currency crisis began in earnest (July 11, 1997). The peak to trough decline in the ratio of the finance index to the commerce index was fourteen percent. Finally for Malaysia the peak in the finance index took place on February 25, 1997. This series declined twenty-six percent between this date and the date of the crisis (July 11, 1997). The peak to trough decline in the ratio of the finance index to the industrial index was eight percent.

Based on this evidence we conclude that private agents in these four countries understood the potentially fragile nature of their banking systems. As Burnside, Eichenbaum, and Rebelo (1998) point out, this evidence also suggests that markets anticipated that the government would bail out only depositors and creditors of the banks. Had they anticipated that the banks would be fully insured by the government, the equity value of banks would not have changed, other things being equal.

4. CONCLUDING REMARKS

Absent the political will to raise taxes or cut spending, governments must resort to seignorage revenues to pay for bank system bailouts. In a world of forward looking agents this makes a currency crisis inevitable. The model in Burnside, Eichenbaum and Rebelo (1998) implies that the collapse of fixed exchange rate happens *after* agents learn that future deficits will rise but *before* the government implements its new monetary policy. Under this scenario standard macroeconomic aggregates such as past inflation and fiscal deficits will not be useful in predicting currency crises. In this limited sense our model rationalizes claims that the Asian crises were hard to predict. More importantly our results suggest that empirical work aimed at forecasting currency crises should not look only at past fiscal and monetary policies of governments. It should pay at least as much attention to information that is useful for forecasting future fiscal deficits.

Table 1. Estimated Total Nonperforming Bank Loans

	Nonperforming Loans	Nonperforming Credit		
	% of all loans	% of MB	% of GDP	% of central gov't. rev.
Indonesia	17	129.6	9.4	63.0
Korea	16	454.1	22.1	103.7
Malaysia	16	88.8	23.3	98.3
Philippines	14	84.5	7.8	41.1
Thailand	19	289.6	30.2	176.7
Hong Kong	4	91.6	6.6	33.6
Singapore	4	35.0	4.4	11.8
Taiwan	4	26.8	6.0	50.0

Source: Burnside, Eichenbaum, and Rebelo (1998).

Table 2. Estimated Liabilities from Nonbank Foreign Borrowing

	Nonperforming loans	Nonperforming	Nonbank Foreign Borrowing	
	% of all loans	% of MB	% of GDP	% of central gov't. rev.
Indonesia	17	34.6	2.5	16.8
Korea	16	18.0	0.9	4.1
Malaysia	16	4.1	1.1	4.5
Philippines	14	8.3	0.8	4.0
Thailand	19	12.6	1.3	7.7
Hong Kong	4	8.2	0.6	3.0
Singapore	4	2.6	0.3	0.9
Taiwan	4	0.2	0.0	0.4

Source: Burnside, Eichenbaum, and Rebelo (1998).

Table 3. Post-crisis Estimates of Nonperforming Loans and Recapitalization Requirements

	Indonesia	Korea	Malaysia	Thailand
Nonperforming Loans (% of all loans)	50	30	25	30
Nonperforming Loans (% of GDP)	37.5	49.5	41.3	30
Recapitalization Need (% of GDP)	30	30	22	30

Source: Burnside, Eichenbaum, and Rebelo (1998).

Table 4. Changes in Banking Sector Stock Market Values

	Peak	Crisis	% Decline Banking Index	% Decline Banking Index / Manufacturing Index
Korea	Aug. 3, 1991	Oct. 29, 1997	67	64
Thailand	Jan. 4, 1994	July 2, 1997	92	80
Philippines	Fed. 17, 1997	July 11, 1997	34	14
Malaysia	Feb. 25, 1997	July 11, 1997	26	8

Source: Burnside, Eichenbaum, and Rebelo (1998).

Notes

[1]See for example Krugman (1979.)

[2]Our estimates of nonperforming credit are the product of the percentage of non-performing loans and credit by deposit money banks to the nonbank private sector as of June 1997, as reported in the *International Financial Statistics*. We measured the monetary base as of the end of June 1997. GDP and government revenue were 1997 estimates from the IMF *World Economic Outlook.*

[3]Our estimates of nonperforming foreign borrowing by the nonbank private sector are the product of the percentage of nonperforming loans and foreign credit to the nonbank sector as of June 1997, as reported by the Bank of International Settlements.

References

Burnside, Craig, Martin Eichenbaum, and Sergio Rebelo. "Prospective Deficits and the Asian Currency Crisis." Northwestern University, manuscript, 1998.

Calvo, Guillermo. "Balance of Payments Crises in a Cash-in-Advance Economy," *Journal of Money, Credit, and Banking*, 1987; 19: 19-32.

Corsetti, Giancarlo, Paolo Pesenti and Nouriel Roubini. "What Caused the Asian Currency and Financial Crisis?" New York University, working paper, 1998.

J. P. Morgan. *Asian Financial Markets*, Third Quarter, July 17, 1998.

Krugman, Paul. "A Model of Balance of Payments Crises," *Journal of Money, Credit, and Banking,* 1979; 11: 311-25.

Krugman, Paul. "Saving Asia: It's time to get radical," *Fortune Magazine*, September 1998.

Chapter 4

Origins of the Crisis in Asia

Michael P. Dooley
University of California, Santa Cruz and Board of Governors of the Federal Reserve System

1. INTRODUCTION

It has proven difficult to find a consistent pattern of fundamentals leading up to recent crises in emerging markets. The simple story of a government living beyond its means until the private sector cuts off its access to credit does not seem to fit the Asian tigers. Moreover, the apparent spread of trouble from one emerging market to the next seems unrelated to common problems arising within the individual economies. The inability to understand the disease or its contagion has led many economists and policy-makers to guess that some inherent weakness in private international capital markets accounts for these events. This interpretation has always found a sympathetic audience among policy makers that naturally prefer to believe that the markets are behaving badly rather than the governments they are sometimes called upon to defend. These sentiments have been given very substantial intellectual support by the development of multiple equilibrium models of crises. In these analytic frameworks costly bouts of illiquidity and crisis can be driven by shifts in investors' expectations that are unrelated to economic fundamentals. The paper circulated with my remarks for this conference (Dooley 1997) swims against this stream in that it argues that it is not necessary to abandon a traditional first-generation model of speculative attacks in order to understand recent crises in emerging markets. In my remarks I want to focus on what is at stake in determining which approach better fits the facts.

2. WHY DO WE CARE?

To prevent future crises, we need to understand how and why crises have occurred. If the origins of crises are shifts in expectations, perhaps generated by "contagion," straightforward adjustments in governments' balance sheets and the composition of capital flows might provide a relatively costless and effective defense against future crises. In contrast if the origins of recent crises lie in rational reactions of private investors to incentives created by governments, the origins of crises, and the factors that make crises costly, will be much more difficult to eliminate from the international monetary system.

The multiple equilibrium framework suggests that countries should reduce their vulnerability to shifts in expectations but does not explain why countries have chosen to be vulnerable in the first place. The problem generated by short-term debt, or more precisely debt that is frequently reindexed to market interest rates, is now familiar. Expectations about devaluation in the case of domestic currency denominated debt, or default in the case of foreign currency denominated debt, generates risk premiums on any debt that has to be renegotiated. The rise in spreads in turn increases the real debt service costs of the governments' debt. Even in countries with modest government debt, spreads paid by domestic banks and nonfinancial firms will also rise calling into question the solvency of the banking system. Since the government is expected to step in to support asset values, the line between private domestic debt and the government's debt is blurred. In the end the devaluation or default feared by the private sector becomes the optimal choice for the government confronted by this hostile market environment.

The message from these stories is that governments must insulate their own balance sheets from arbitrary shifts in expectations but this is not nearly sufficient to avoid trouble. Governments must also monitor risks taken on by their banking systems either directly or through nonfinancial firms that can bring the banks down with them. It is very hard to argue with the idea that governments should manage their risks carefully or that vulnerable banking markets are a clear threat to governments' finances. But what I find missing from these stories is a sense of why private investors get into these markets when they know that their own behavior can bring the countries and themselves to ruin.

Moreover, why was there such a general inflow into emerging markets after 1989? The hypothesis that after 1989 investors were too exuberant and then became too sober is dangerously close to a description of the facts that cannot be refuted. Surely there are naive investors but why are there more naive investors at certain times in certain places? For reasons developed below it is important to go deeper into the reasons behind capital inflows and crises.

The alternative "insurance" interpretation is that a change in the comfort level offered to investors by governments after 1989 generated the sequence of capital inflows and crises we have observed. The important implication of this model is that private investors anticipated the crisis and positioned themselves to earn high yields before the crisis and avoid losses at the crisis. For example, this framework suggests that the shift in the composition of capital inflows toward short-term credit to banks in the year or so before recent crises was an endogenous reaction of investors that saw crises coming. Simply put these are the positions the government is most likely to liquidate *without loss during the crisis.*

This, in turn, suggests that policies that merely alter the composition of capital inflows will not delay or prevent a crisis. Investors might prefer short-term claims on banks but if this form of capital flow is cut off they will find another to take its place. Indeed, if there are no short-term claims to be liquidated at the time of crisis, governments' resources can be used to liquidate other claims on the debtor country. The insurance model suggests that even direct investment will be undertaken with the intention of reversing the flow when the crisis comes. Policies that discourage all capital inflows might be effective but would presumably also generate important administrative and efficiency costs for the developing country. Moreover, there is substantial evidence that while control programs have been successful in altering the composition of capital inflows, their ability to limit aggregate private inflows is limited and temporary.

The fact that some investors lost money in recent crises is not sufficient to show that the insurance model is not an important part of the story. We argue below that governments did offer sufficient insurance to allow all the new investors in emerging markets after 1989 to exit without loss during the crises that followed. The fact that some particularly slow investors were left behind does not mean that the important private decisionmakers were also naive about the risks of investing in emerging markets.

3. POLICY CHOICES FOLLOWING CRISES

It is important to think long and hard about preventing future crises but it is even more important today to deal with the residual effects of crises that have already occurred. It is not surprising that alternative interpretations of the origins of crises also have important implications for policies designed to minimize the losses in output that have followed. The multiple equilibrium interpretation suggests that changes in market psychology force vulnerable countries to liquidate assets at fire sale prices. This creates a real economic loss but one that is avoidable. Quick action by a lender of last resort can, in principle, stop the unnecessary and costly liquidation of investments and ensure a quick economic recovery.

The insurance view suggests that avoiding output loss will be much more difficult. There are two reasons for this. First, the crisis is triggered by an accumulation of a real unrecoverable loss in insured domestic banks and corporations in the debtor country. If this loss is not quickly recognized and credibly allocated among creditors, new investment in the debtor country will be discouraged. I suspect that high lending rates in post-crisis economies are due more to lingering contamination of new credits by default risk than to excessively tight monetary policies. Moreover, as long as this overhang is unallocated, a substantial share of new domestic savings will also be lost through capital flight.

The second reason why it will be difficult to avoid losses in output is that creditors understand that their de facto seniority when the crisis comes depends on the cost to the government in not paying them relative to other creditors. It is a fact of life that moral hazard arises from the government's *incentives* to bail out creditors not from the bailout itself. Credits are designed so that negotiations for workouts favor creditors. In particular, creditors try to limit the debtor's ability to withhold payment and then use these resources to retire debt on favorable terms.

In practical terms this means that if an expected bailout is not forthcoming creditors will find it very difficult to renegotiate credits in a way that does not impose considerable economic hardship on the debtor country. My interpretation of the 1982 international debt crisis and the seven years of negotiations that followed is that private creditors had little incentive to restructure debt until the official sector offered substantial subsidies to the agreements (Dooley, 1995).

In contrast, if crises are the result of unexpected shifts in expectations, propagation of declines in output can be truncated by planning ahead so that debts are easily and quickly restructured. New contractual arrangements for cross border lending, for example, changes in risk sharing, voting rules for restructuring and other reforms might be helpful. If the threat of losses in output is an integral part of the reason investors are attracted to the country in the first place, there will be strong resistance to changes in contracts that blunt debtors' incentives to pay.

Finally, there are important differences in interpretations of moral hazard in the two approaches. One view is that international rescue packages have been exogenous shocks to the system that have generated moral hazard. The insurance model suggests that governments bail out investors because the alternative is a debt overhang that generates large costs in terms of lost output. The source of moral hazard in this case is not the bailout per se but the cost of not bailing out. Indeed we argue below that recent capital inflows are largely motivated by government insurance and that insurance determines the structure and consequences of capital inflows and crises. But refusing to honor implicit insurance merely postpones the eventual Brady Plan type restructuring that, given the debt overhang, is the rational policy response.

References

Dooley Michael P. "A Model of Crises in Emerging Markets," NBER, working paper, No. 6300, December 1997.

Dooley Michael P. "A Retrospective on the Debt Crisis," in *Exchange Rate Policy and Interdependence*, Peter Kenan, (ed.), Princeton, NJ: Princeton University Press, 1995.

Chapter 5

Thoughts on the Origins of the Asian Crisis: Impulses and Propagation Mechanisms

Reuven Glick
Federal Reserve Bank of San Francisco

Abstract: The 1997–98 Asian crisis can be explained largely in terms of impulses and amplification mechanisms related to fundamentals, specifically general weaknesses in the financial sector, including relationship lending practices, excessive risk taking, and inadequate financial supervision and regulation. Although elements of illiquidity-based financial panic may also have played a role, it is difficult to determine whether the motivation for the panic was based in a spontaneous shift in creditor confidence or to concern about fundamentals.

1. INTRODUCTION

The 1997 East Asian financial crisis was largely unanticipated. Most of East Asia enjoyed high savings and investment rates, robust growth, and moderate inflation for several decades. Domestic saving and investment rates averaged more than thirty percent of GDP between 1986 and 1996 in Thailand, Indonesia, Korea, and Malaysia—the countries most affected by the crisis—and over twenty percent in the Philippines. Annual GDP growth in these five countries (the "Asian-5") averaged close to eight percent over this period. Net capital inflows to the five Asian economies averaged over six percent of GDP between 1990 and 1996. East Asia's long track record of economic success was one reason that the crisis came as such a surprise. Thus, any successful explanation of the East Asian crisis must also answer the question of *why a system that seemed to work so well for so long could suddenly fail.*

Even the many observers who saw some danger signs in East Asia in late 1996—for example, in the sizable current account deficits, which were as high or higher than those in Latin America in 1994—expected at most a modest downturn. Few thought an Asian crisis would be so large, with domestic asset price and exchange rate collapses, widespread financial sector problems, and a much more severe real decline in economic activity than even the most pessimistic anticipated. The consensus (average) forecast for 1998 GDP (year-over-year) growth for the Asian-5 changed from a robust seven percent in June 1997 to a recessionary –5 percent in July 1998.[1] In contrast to the rapid recovery of Mexico staged in 1996, a turnaround in Asia seems increasingly further in the future. Thus in addition to explaining why the crisis occurred when it did, one must explain *why the crisis has been so severe and prolonged.*

Another way to think about these questions is by analogy to analyses of business cycle fluctuations. Macroeconomists typically interpret economic fluctuations in terms of "impulses" and "propagation mechanisms." Impulses are shocks that get things rolling. Impulses can come from shifts in economic policy or other fundamentals as well as from spontaneous changes in confidence or preferences. Propagation mechanisms are structural features of an economy that amplify and/or prolong the effects of the impulses. A complete understanding of the Asia crisis requires an identification of both the impulse(s) that initiated the crisis, and the propagation mechanism(s) responsible for the ongoing effects.

This paper provides an overview of the origins of the 1997–98 Asia crisis.[2] The roles of macroeconomic and financial fundamentals in the crisis are examined in Section 2. Section 3 addresses the extent to which elements of financial panic may have been involved. Section 4 discusses difficulties in distinguishing confidence shocks associated with panics from changes in fundamentals. Section 5 addresses the roles of domestic financial liberalization and increased foreign capital flows in explaining the timing of the crisis. Section 6 discusses the various propagation mechanisms that amplified and prolonged the effects of the crisis. Section 7 concludes the paper.

2. WHAT WERE THE ROLES OF MACROECONOMIC AND FINANCIAL FUNDAMENTALS IN THE ASIA CRISIS?

Much of the current debate about the origin of the Asia crisis concerns whether it was caused by weak economic fundamentals, or by financial panic unrelated to economic conditions. While the two views are not mutually exclusive, their policy implications vary greatly. If a panic unrelated to fundamentals was the main impulse for Asia's financial crisis, reforms in macroeconomic or financial sector policy are not necessary in planning Asia's recovery. If, however, policy mistakes or other fundamentals were the most important contributors to the crisis, reforms are indeed essential.

2.1 Macroeconomic fundamentals

The traditional fundamentals view of speculative attacks emphasizes the role of various domestic and foreign macroeconomic factors at the root of the crisis. However, as shown in Table 1, most of the macroeconomic fundamentals that drive "first-generation" crisis models (e.g. Krugman, 1979) provided little reason to expect a major crisis in any of the Asian-5 countries. There was no evidence of "bad" government behavior in the form of government budget deficits; budgets were generally in balance or showed surpluses. Though growth in monetary aggregates was fairly high in all of the crisis countries, this cannot be interpreted as providing any evidence of runaway monetary expansion. By emerging country standards, inflation rates were relatively low (below ten percent), and were stable or declining (except for Thailand[3]). Investment rates were high (thirty to forty percent, except for the Philippines) and were generally rising in the years prior to the crisis.

Although there had been some slowdown in real GDP growth in 1996, it still was generally at or above its 1990–94 average rate (except for Thailand). Thus when the crisis began in mid-1997 the Asian-5 victims did not have substantial unemployment nor other apparent incentives to abruptly abandon the pegged exchange rate regimes generally followed in the region in order to pursue a more expansionary monetary policy, as suggested by second-generation crisis models (e.g. Obstfeld, 1994).

Foreign macroeconomic and financial fundamentals also did not apparently play a role in the Asian financial crisis. As Radelet and Sachs (1998b) discuss, international market conditions were generally not unfavorable before the onset of the Asian crisis: U.S. interest rates were low. Growth in the industrial countries, particularly in the United States, was strong, though Japan was an important exception. In addition, world commodity market prices were relatively stable.

However, some indication of increasing Asian vulnerability in the period prior to the crisis is provided by the large and growing current account deficits, slowing exports, and real appreciation of currencies in the region (see Table 1). For quite a while, the current account deficits were viewed as "benign," since they did not result from large fiscal budget imbalances and since the associated foreign capital inflows were used primarily to increase investment (rather than consumption). But in the mid-1990s concerns about the region mounted on several counts:

- Real exchange rates appreciated sharply between December 1994 and early 1997 by fifteen percent or more in Thailand, Malaysia, Indonesia, and the Philippines. The cumulative rate of real appreciation in these countries was more than twenty-five percent between 1990 and early 1997. The exception to this trend is Korea, whose cumulative twelve percent real exchange rate appreciation over this period was much less because it allowed some nominal exchange rate depreciation (though it amounted to over thirty percent between 1987 and 1997).[4]
- Exports slowed in the region. In 1996 Thailand's exports (in dollar terms) fell one percent, after two years of growth above twenty percent; Korea's exports grew by just four percent (down from thirty percent growth in 1995); Malaysia's grew by only six percent (down from twenty-six percent the previous year); while Indonesia's exports grew ten percent, about the same as in the previous three years (but well below the 1990-92 average). Only the Philippines registered significant export growth (of almost twenty percent) in 1996.[5]
- Paralleling the real appreciation and slowdown in exports, the current account deficits in Thailand, Indonesia, and Korea—the three most affected countries—increased by one to two percent of GDP during the 1995–96 period. In 1996, Thailand, the Philippines, and Korea all ran current account deficits of 4.5 percent of GDP or higher, while Indonesia's and Malaysia's deficits were only slightly less at roughly 3.5 percent.

The slowing exports, increasing current account deficits, and growing overvaluation are attributable to a number of factors:

- The sharp appreciation of the U.S. dollar relative to the yen and the European currencies between mid-1995 and mid-1997 led to a worsening of cost-competitiveness in those Asian countries whose currencies were effectively pegged to the dollar.[6]
- The stagnation of the Japanese economy in the 1990s led to a significant slowdown in the growth of Asian exports to Japan. In the months preceding the eruption of the crisis, the slow Japanese economic recovery of 1996 was aborted by a decline in economic activity, partly attributable to an increase in the consumption tax in April 1997.
- Sector-specific shocks caused by apparent overproduction in particular industries, such as semiconductors, caused a significant slowdown of export growth, particularly in Korea and Malaysia, both of which export substantial amounts of electronics products.[7]
- The competitiveness of the several Asian countries also seemed adversely affected by a perceived shift in regional comparative advantage towards China, which competes directly against other firms in the region in textiles, apparel, and electronics.[8] Competitive pressures in the region were further fueled by the devaluation of the yuan in 1994.[9]
- The real appreciation was related to the upward pressure on domestic nontradeables prices from large capital inflows. Also the pegging of currencies against the dollar caused Asian currencies to appreciate along with the dollar against other foreign currencies, such as the yen.

Each of these factors contributed in some part to the export slowdown and current account worsening in the period preceding the crisis. The widespread perception of real overvaluation and the need to adjust current account imbalances affected the credibility of the commitments to exchange rate pegs in many countries and also raised some concern among creditors about the ability of firms in these countries to repay their debts.

However, the perception remained that East Asia was fundamentally healthy, and that a "soft landing" could be successfully implemented through some combination of slower domestic demand and/or gradual nominal exchange rate depreciation.[10] Other emerging market countries, such as Chile and Peru also had current account deficits above four percent of GDP in 1996, while Brazil's deficit was over three percent of GDP. Moreover, the degree of real appreciation of Asian currencies in the 1990s was less than that observed prior to the currency collapse of Mexico—which appreciated almost forty percent between 1988 and 1994. None of the macroeconomic fundamentals suggested that a crisis of the magnitude that occurred was imminent in Asia.

2.2 Financial fundamentals

Another variant of the fundamentals view of financial crises focuses on weaknesses and distortions in financial systems, rather than on macroeconomic imbalances. This variant emphasizes the role of distortions arising from particular structural characteristics of Asian financial systems, often referred to as the "Asian model" of capitalism.

First, Asian countries generally favored *centralized and behind-the-scenes relationships between financial institutions, business, and government for the intermediation and allocation of capital.* The particular financial institutions involved varied from the captive banks of the Korean chaebols to the finance companies of Thailand to government-linked banks in Indonesia, but in general a large share of lending and investment decisions were not made by a decentralized open capital market via arms-length transactions, but rather by personal and business relationships or government influence.[11] In some cases, banks were controlled directly or indirectly by the government or by "Minister's nephews" (Krugman, 1998) and directed credit to politically favored firms, sectors, and investment projects. In other cases, banks were used to finance the operations of affiliated companies. The access of well-connected borrowers or poorly managed firms to credit through such relationship lending implied efficiency concerns in credit allocation were often ignored.

Second, financial institutions and other agents *lacked the incentives to manage risk effectively and bear the full costs of failure.* This was particularly the case with the banking system which, with bond and equity markets relatively underdeveloped, generally carried out financial intermediation in most Asian countries. Banks' risk capital was usually small and owners of banks risked relatively little by lending for excessively risky projects if the projects failed. Depositors of the banks were offered implicit or explicit deposit insurance and therefore did not monitor the lending decisions of banks. The banks themselves were typically given implicit guarantees of a government bailout in the event of adverse financial conditions.[12] The presence of such financial insurance posed a clear moral hazard problem, which distorted the incentives to carry out a proper risk assessment of investment projects.

The financial liability counterpart of the moral hazard problem in investment was the incentive for Asian financial institutions to expand their liabilities excessively, generally by borrowing from abroad.[13] On the international creditor side, the incentive for foreign banks and investors to monitor the repayment potential of domestic banks in Asian countries was lessened to the extent they expected Asian banks would be bailed out by central banks and possibly international financial institutions in the event of financial problems.[14]

The potential for loss in borrowing and lending was increased in most countries by *inadequate financial supervision and regulation.* Capital adequacy ratios and legal lending limits to individual borrowers or sectors tended to be insufficient or poorly enforced. State-owned banks in Indonesia and Korea, for example, were allowed to break many prudential regulations on a regular basis without penalty. Also, in Korea, the widespread use of dummy accounts prevented the enforcement of restrictions against over-concentration of lending. In addition, limited disclosure requirements, inadequate asset classification systems, or unclear definitions of what could be included in capital disguised the extent of nonperforming loan problems. As a result, depositors and regulators had difficulty telling if loans were sound and if bank balance sheets were healthy. This situation led to undetected conflicts of interest and fraud, hindered the governance of financial institutions, and increased the incentives for risk-taking.

Table 2 presents various measures of financial conditions in the Asian-5 countries indicating a lending boom during the buildup to the crisis in 1997. Specifically:

- Deposit-money bank lending to the private sector expanded rapidly in most countries though the 1990s. Between 1990 and 1996, the ratio of bank lending to GDP grew by sixty percent or more in Thailand (from sixty-four percent to 102 percent of GDP) and the Philippines (from nineteen percent to forty-nine percent of GDP), thirty percent in Malaysia (from seventy-one percent to ninety-three percent of GDP), and ten percent in Korea (from fifty-two percent to sixty-two percent of GDP) and Indonesia (from forty-six percent to fifty-five percent).
- Lending growth was as high or higher if increases in nonbank financial claims on the private sector are included, particularly in the case of Korea, where bank and nonbank financial claims grew almost forty percent between 1990 and 1996 (from ninety-eight

percent to 140 percent of GDP). Only in Indonesia did bank and nonbank financial credit to the private sector grow at more modest levels, though this does not take account of significant direct foreign borrowing by domestic private firms.[15]

- Borrowing offshore financed much of the new lending, typically by domestic banks. In Korea, foreign liabilities of (deposit-money) banks more than doubled from four percent of GDP in 1990 to nine percent of GDP in 1996. In the Philippines, foreign liabilities rose from six percent of GDP in 1990 to almost twenty percent of GDP in 1996. The most extreme case was Thailand where foreign liabilities of banks increased to over twenty-seven percent of GDP by 1996.

Table 2 also reports several indicators of the declining quality of loan and investment decisions during this lending boom:

- An increasing share of domestic bank lending was directed to investment in real estate and property and to speculative investment in equities and other financial assets. Real estate exposure prior to the crisis is estimated at thirty to forty percent of bank lending in Malaysia and Thailand, twenty-five to thirty percent in Indonesia, and fifteen to twenty percent in the Philippines and Korea (where real estate loans were also channeled through the chaebols). In some countries, such as Thailand, these investments fueled a boom in asset prices.
- Direct evidence of deteriorating loan quality is provided by the high rate of nonperforming loans in the Asian banking systems at the outbreak of the crisis. In 1997 at the onset of the crisis, non-performing loans were an estimated fifteen percent or more of total bank loans in Thailand, Indonesia, Korea, and Malaysia, and fourteen percent in the Philippines, well above the nonperforming loan ratio of nine percent in Mexico in early 1995 (Caprio and Klingebeil, 1996) and the (average) levels of bank capital in these countries.[16]
- On the macro level, investment efficiency, defined as the inverse of the incremental capital–output ratio (ICOR), or the ratio between investment (as a share of GDP) and changes in GDP, fell between 1990–94 and 1995–96 for Korea, Thailand, and Malaysia, suggesting declining efficiency and falling profitability (though efficiency remained higher than in other developing countries, even in the second subsample).

In the financial fundamentals view, the main problem in East Asia was not macroeconomic imbalances, but rather structural financial system distortions associated with the Asian model of capitalism. From this perspective, the Asian financial crisis was the legacy of bad lending and investment practices that were fostered by the environment of relationship lending, disincentives to fully monitor risk, and inadequate supervision and regulation of domestic financial institutions during the lending boom of the 1990s. These financial distortions in turn led to the buildup of weak bank and nonbank balance sheets and increasingly fragile East Asia financial systems.

Yet, what explains the sudden timing and severity of the crisis?

3. WAS THE CRISIS CAUSED BY A FINANCIAL PANIC?

Contrasting with the fundamentals view of financial crises is the view is that there was nothing inherently wrong with East Asian economies, which historically performed very well and were still exhibiting relatively robust growth even just prior to the crisis. In this alternative view, the Asian crisis mainly involved a sudden interruption in liquidity associated with an arbitrary shift in market confidence, unrelated to economic fundamentals, that disrupted capital flows to Asia.

In this interpretation, the Asia crisis reflected "runs" on domestic financial systems and currencies, that did not necessarily reflect poor fundamentals or policies. As explained in the well-known model of Diamond and Dybvig (1983), even well-managed banks or financial intermediaries are vulnerable to runs, because they traditionally engage in maturity transformation, accepting deposits with short maturities to finance loans with longer maturities. Maturity transformation is beneficial because it makes more funds available to productive long-term investors than they would otherwise receive, while it provides liquidity to savers with unexpected consumption needs. Under normal conditions, banks have no problem managing their portfolios to meet expected withdrawals. However, if all depositors decided to withdraw their funds from a given bank at the same time, as in the case of a run, the bank would not have enough liquid assets to meet its obligations.

What causes such runs? One possibility is that when individual depositors fear that other depositors will withdraw their money for whatever reason, an incentive is created for each to be first in line to make withdrawals before the bank is driven into illiquidity, even though it has the net worth to pay off all creditors in the long run. In this view, changes in depositor expectations about the behavior of other depositors can trigger a run and create a self-fulfilling, individually rational bank panic.[17]

Domestic bank runs, currency crises, and debt crises are all similar to the extent that each process involves creditors trying to unload their holdings of an asset before others beat them to it. In the case of international lending in foreign exchange, a panic can arise from the concern that a country's central bank holds insufficient reserves with which to pay off all short-term foreign exchange claims. In the case of a debt crisis, a financial panic can arise when individual creditors are unwilling to rollover a loan because of the concern that a borrower will be unable to fulfill its debt obligations unless other creditors rollover their loans as well.

Closer integration with world financial markets can increase an economy's vulnerability to runs, particularly if the central bank seeks to peg the exchange rate. In a closed economy, depositors' confidence can be sustained if the government can supply enough liquidity to financial institutions to prevent any losses to depositors. In an open economy, however, that same injection of liquidity can destabilize the exchange rate, and induce a run on the domestic currency. This implies that simultaneously maintaining stability of the financial system and targeting the exchange rate can be incompatible policy objectives. On the one hand, if a central bank chooses to combat a domestic bank crisis by acting as lender of last resort and/or by lowering interest rates, the potential for a run on the domestic currency can be exacerbated if residents turn around and sell the injected domestic funds for foreign exchange reserves. On the other hand, if the central bank raises interest rates and limits liquidity injections to sustain the peg, the bank crisis may go on unabated.[18] Moreover, even allowing flexible exchange rates will not necessarily prevent runs by foreign creditors holding foreign-exchange denominated claims on domestic residents; in such cases there is a potential role for an international lender of last resort.

Table 3 presents several financial indicators for the Asian-5 countries that show an increasing vulnerability to liquidity problems and financial crisis as banks and nonbanks rapidly increased their foreign borrowing in the 1990s.

- Much of the increasing foreign debt of Asian countries was short-term. By mid-1997, the share of short-term foreign debt in total foreign liabilities was more than fifty percent in all of the Asian-5 countries. This implied an increasing dependency on the willingness of creditors to roll over short-term liabilities.

- The ratio of short-term foreign borrowing (cross-border or local foreign currency loans, in dollars) to official foreign exchange reserves was well above 100 percent for Korea, Indonesia, and Thailand by mid-1994. The ratio was below 100 percent for Malaysia, though it increased during the 1990s. (The Philippines had an extremely high ratio in 1990 in the aftermath of the political transition from the Marcos regime and a massive loss of foreign reserves; the ratio fell sharply before rising again.) A ratio greater than 100 percent is not by itself sufficient to trigger a crisis, since it can be sustained as long as foreign creditors are willing to roll over their loans. However, a high ratio, does indicate vulnerability to a crisis. Once something triggers a withdrawal of foreign capital, each foreign creditor has the incentive to demand repayment immediately, since each knows that there is not enough foreign exchange available to repay everyone. The high ratios were clearly unsustainable in the more vulnerable economies when uncertainty spread throughout the region.
- Another indicator of financial vulnerability is the ratio of M2 (in dollar terms) to foreign reserves, reflecting the potential demand for foreign currency by holders of (broad) domestic money. The M2/reserves ratio was 400 percent or higher in all five crisis countries, including Malaysia and the Philippines, ratios similar to that of Mexico prior to the 1994-95 peso crisis.[19]

The rising imbalances between short-term foreign liabilities and official reserves suggest an increasing exposure of the Asian-5 countries to shifts in confidence fostering financial panic.[20] But what might have caused such confidence shocks across Asia? What explains why the effects were greater in some countries than in others?

4. CAN FUNDAMENTALS AND CONFIDENCE SHOCKS BE DISTINGUISHED?

In actuality, it is hard to distinguish between confidence shocks and fundamentals shocks, since confidence is to some extent endogenous and depends on perceptions of fundamentals. Thus it is hard to identify whether a bank run is attributable to a decline in confidence about the likelihood of deposit rollovers by other depositors, or to an adverse shift in fundamentals and an increased recognition a bank has made bad lending or investment decisions reducing its ability to pay out on deposit demands.

Financial systems characterized by capital allocation through relationships and by lax bank regulation, such as in Asia, may have been particularly susceptible to a deterioration in confidence about the quality of investment decisions. If domestic and foreign creditors who had previously been willing to rely on past performance as a predictor of future success suddenly become concerned about investment decisions, the lack of transparent and direct information can seriously weaken market confidence in the quality of those decisions. If the extent of the financial problems faced by individual firms and financial institutions is discovered to be much worse than expected, significant uncertainty will be generated about the extent of the financial problems faced by all domestic banks and firms. Without the information to properly evaluate which banks or other institutions have made good decisions and which have made bad ones, creditors can be induced to withdraw their capital from all institutions indiscriminately. As the perceived extent of financial system problems grow, the implicit or explicit government guarantees of a bailout also lose their credibility, further compounding the problem.

This interpretation also helps explain why it is difficult to identify a single macroeconomic factor behind the crisis in all affected countries. Overvalued exchange rates were perhaps a problem in some countries, but certainly not in all; the slump in the semiconductor industry had a significant impact on Korea, but little effect in Indonesia or Thailand; the current account deficit was large in Thailand and Malaysia, but small in Korea. If, however, the crisis was triggered in each case by a decline in creditors' confidence in the fundamental soundness of the long-term investments backing up their short-term bank deposits, then there would be no necessary reason to expect the same macroeconomic precursors in each case.

Fundamentals also came into play in explaining why the magnitude of the crisis varied significantly across affected countries. In particular, as investors tested financial systems and currency pegs in the region in 1997, those economies with the most vulnerable financial sectors (Indonesia, Korea, and Thailand) experienced the most severe crises. In contrast, economies with more robust and well-capitalized financial institutions (such as the Philippines, Singapore, and Hong Kong) did not experience disruptions of similar magnitude, in spite of slowing economic activity and declining asset values. This suggests that relative structural weaknesses in the financial sectors of the most affected economies played a role in their vulnerability to financial crisis.

Ultimately, the two alternative views of the causes of the crisis—fundamentals versus financial panic—are not inconsistent with each other.

On the one hand, weak macro and/or financial fundamentals are a necessary condition for vulnerability to liquidity and/or speculative crises. On the other hand, a crisis triggered by fundamentals may eventually lead to market overreaction and conditions similar to a pure financial panic.

5. WHY DID THE CRISIS OCCUR WHEN IT DID?

The Asian economies appeared to work well for a long time. Since the structural weaknesses in East Asian financial systems had apparently existed for decades, why did Asian countries not experience any earlier crises of similar magnitude to that of 1997? Of course, lending and investment decisions looked good as long as growth continued. Rapid growth masked much of the extent of risky lending and the weaknesses of the financial sector. For many years, such growth generated cash flows and expectations of future returns that shielded firms incurring losses from the adverse effects of their decisions. Moreover, relationship lending may have worked relatively well at early stages of development because borrowers stood to reap large economic rewards from pursuing available high-return projects (i.e., picking "low-hanging fruit").

However, two developments in the 1990s may be seen as having exacerbated the structural financial weaknesses of Asian economies and increased their vulnerability to a critical level: *domestic financial liberalization* and *foreign capital inflows.*

5.1 Domestic financial liberalization

As financial market liberalization proceeded throughout Asia in the 1990s, the deficiencies of domestic capital and financial markets were accentuated as financial supervision and regulation failed to keep pace. Financial liberalization led to a dramatic increase in the number of financial institutions and their range of activities. In Indonesia, for example, a wide range of financial liberalization reforms in 1988–89 led to a dramatic expansion in the banking sector, with the number of private banks (including foreign and joint venture banks) nearly tripling from seventy-four in 1988 to 206 in 1994. In Thailand, credit expansion by commercial banks was limited by regulation, but financial liberalization in the 1990s led to the emergence of other nonbank intermediaries that were largely unregulated. In Korea, interest rate controls and restrictions on corporate debt financing and cross-border borrowing were reduced. In both Thailand and Indonesia, banks were allowed to finance equity purchases on margin. Domestic financial liberalization permitted greater maturity mismatching between assets and liabilities and increased the potential for illiquidity problems; it also exposed domestic commercial banks to greater competition and increased the pressure on banks to engage in riskier activities as well as allowed banks to evade restrictions on riskier activities.

The rapid growth in bank lending and expansion in financial services was not generally matched by careful regulation and supervision of financial institutions. Some Asian countries did seek to strengthen their supervisory and regulatory infrastructure during the late 1980s and 1990s (partly in response to prior costly banking crises, as in Indonesia and Malaysia), by imposing limits on bank lending, including liquidity requirements and risk-based capital guidelines in keeping with the Basle Accord (although it should be noted that these guidelines did not cover foreign exchange exposure). However, some observers argue that the Basle Accord's risk-adjusted capital ratios of eight percent are too low for emerging markets since they do not take into account the fact that emerging market economies tend to be more vulnerable to shocks (Goldstein and Turner, 1996). Moreover, capital requirements are ineffective as long as accounting standards are inadequate.

Liberalization also gave Asian banks and nonbanks greater access to international financial markets for funds. For example, in Thailand the introduction of the Bangkok International Banking Facility (BIBF) in 1993, with the aim of promoting a regional financial center, allowed for very rapid growth in the number of financial institutions that could borrow and lend in foreign currencies, both on- and offshore; Thai policies gave strong tax-incentives for foreign banks, particularly from Japan, to lend at low rates to Thai institutions through the BIBF. In Korea, financial market reforms in the mid-1990s similarly allowed domestic financial institutions greater freedom in asset and liability management, particularly in borrowing from international finance markets. Regulations limiting corporate borrowing or bond issuance abroad encouraged the channeling of international borrowing through the Korean financial system for onlending to the private corporate sector. In addition, restrictions on long-term capital inflows reduced heavy reliance in short-term foreign borrowing. In Indonesia, although quantitative controls on offshore borrowing by banks were reimposed in 1991, corporations were given greater freedom to borrow abroad for financing trade. In mid-1994 Malaysia lifted reserve requirement restrictions on Malaysian bank borrowing from foreign institutions.

5.2 Foreign capital inflows

The weaknesses of Asian financial system were exacerbated further by large private capital inflows during the 1990s. These inflows were attracted by Asia's successful track record and its opportunities for higher-yielding returns and diversification benefits, propelled initially by low rates in industrial countries and later by very low rates in a stagnant Japanese economy.[21] The inflows were also encouraged by central bank efforts in the region to limit exchange rate changes against the U.S. dollar, which effectively absorbed the perceived risks of exchange rate movements on behalf of investors.[22]

Domestic financial intermediaries, particularly Asian banks played the "spread" by borrowing at low foreign rates and then relending at higher local rates, leading to a buildup of foreign liabilities. Financial sector vulnerability was accentuated by a tendency in countries with pegged exchange rates not to hedge foreign currency borrowing. While the absence of hedging significantly lowered the cost of funds (in the short run), it also created significant heavy exposure of foreign currency loans to the effects of possible exchange rate changes as well as the refusal of creditors to roll over these loans. The short-term maturity of capital inflows also accentuated the mismatch between short-term liabilities and long-term assets of Asian financial institutions and strained their ability to make appropriate risk assessments.

5.3 Impulses and triggers of the crisis

Domestic financial liberalization and the increased volume and volatility of international capital flows combined to exacerbate weaknesses arising from relationship lending and financial guarantees in under-regulated Asian financial markets.[23]

By analogy, the financial system weaknesses may be interpreted as the necessary fundamental elements for creation of an expanding financial market balloon, with domestic financial liberalization and capital inflows as the impulse forces that pumped the balloon up.[24] What then was the trigger—the needle—that pricked the balloon, let all of the air out, and pushed Asia into a full-blown crisis?[25]

Second-generation currency crisis models, liquidity-based financial panic models, as well as other multiple equilibrium models each suggest that in principal anything could be the trigger; any arbitrary piece of information becomes relevant if market participants believe it is relevant. Of course, the Thai baht devaluation in early July 1997 was a major triggering factor for a withdrawal of capital flows from the region by foreign and resident investors. But several earlier events suggest stresses on domestic financial markets were accelerating even before then, and that domestic financial market problems in Asia tended to precede exchange rate crises.[26]

As discussed earlier, macroeconomic fundamentals in 1995 and 1996 in the form of declining international competitiveness and slower export growth adversely affected firm cash flows. In 1996 and early 1997, the asset bubble started to burst in some countries, notably Thailand and Korea. Stock market prices fell sharply in Thailand and Korea during 1996 by forty percent and thirty percent, respectively; in the first half of 1997, Thailand's stock prices fell by another thirty percent. Stock prices in Malaysia and the Philippines also declined by ten to fifteen percent during this period. There were also signs of deteriorating real estate markets beginning in 1996. From 1995 to 1996, the share value of property companies (in local currency) fell by about thirty percent in Korea and fifty percent in Thailand. As equity and real estate and equity prices started to drop, the emergence of wide losses and/or outright defaults in the corporate sectors signaled the low profitability of past investment projects. Sixteen Thai finance companies suspended operations in May 1997. In Korea a string of bankruptcies began in January 1997 with Hanbo Steel (the fourteenth largest chaebol), followed by several other large companies. By mid-1997, eight of the thirty largest chaebols and several merchant banks were effectively bankrupt. In Indonesia, confidence in the banking system had been weakened by revelation of problems of several ailing banks (e.g., Lippo Bank, Bank Yama, and Bank Pacific) in late-1995 and 1996. It also became clear soon after the fall of the baht that neither Indonesian leaders nor authorities could monitor adequately the financial condition of borrowers.[27]

These developments indicate that financial weaknesses, at least in some Asian countries, had reached critical mass and the air was already beginning to leak from the balloon prior to the floating of the baht.

6. WHY WAS THE CRISIS SO SEVERE?

Once a crisis occurs, the effects of the initial impulse(s) may be amplified (or dampened) by various multiplier effects and propagation mechanisms. Understanding the propagation mechanisms at work during the current Asia crisis is important to explaining the severity of the crisis.

6.1 Financial panic

Once the bubble burst, the financial panic story had its place. Domestic investors looked more critically at weaknesses that had been previously ignored or underestimated. In the process, new information amplified concerns about the quality of investments, the magnitude of foreign borrowing, and the stability of the financial system. As the crisis expanded, domestic residents became less willing to hold assets in domestic financial institutions and foreign creditors became less willing to roll over their loans, causing a liquidity squeeze that led to the bankruptcy of Asian financial institutions as well as of the private firms that had borrowed from them. Thus the initial loss in confidence turned into a self-reinforcing creditors' panic. The panic contributed to a downward spiral process whereby once the value of financial assets and real estate declined; agents were encouraged to sell more, further depressing asset prices.

The credibility of government guarantees followed a similar spiral process once it became clear that governments would have to spend a lot of money to bail out financial institutions and their creditors and that there was not enough money. Accordingly, the credibility of government guarantees declined, which led to further drying up of money, which raised bailout costs even further.[28]

However, one need not resort to a pure panic story to understand why the cumulative decline in asset prices and economic activity during the crisis was so large.

6.2 High financial leverage

Large Asian firms tended to finance a high proportion of their investment by bank borrowing rather than by issuing bonds or equity, and to carry relatively large amounts of bank debt relative to equity compared to firms in industrial or Latin American countries.[29] For example, the debt–equity ratio of Korean corporations was almost 450 percent by the end of 1996, three times the U.S. ratio and more than five times that in Taiwan (Bhattacharya et al. 1998). The high degree of leverage together with relatively few liquid assets held by most East Asian firms left the corporate sector very vulnerable to adverse interest rate changes or other cash flow shocks affecting their ability to service debts. For a sample of 300 firms listed on the Thailand stock exchange, Bhattacharya et al. show that even before the crisis, in the first quarter of 1997, half of the Thai firms were unable to service their debts in full from their operating cash flows.[30]

Once the crisis hit, the excessive leverage of nonfinancial business and their resulting debt servicing problems in turn created problems for the lending banks and other financial intermediaries; these problems then spread to other borrowers that relied on these intermediaries for credit. Thus high financial corporate leverage ratios exacerbated the impact of the crisis.

6.3 Collateralized lending and asset prices

Leverage effects also worked through the dynamic interaction of collateralized lending and asset prices. Edison, Luangaram, and Miller (1998) and Kasa (1998), using the framework first developed by Kiyotaki and Moore (1997), show how credit-constrained, leveraged financial markets can generate powerful propagation mechanisms. In this framework, only land can be used as collateral by low-equity, highly-leveraged corporate borrowers ("farmers" in Kiyotaki and Moore nomenclature); creditors limit gross borrowing to the value of this collateral in order to protect themselves from the threat of repudiation. This implies that investment decisions depend on the ability of borrowers to acquire collateral. A key feature of the model is that, because of this credit market imperfection, a temporary shock can generate persistent and large effects on land prices and aggregate activity.

This suggests how for highly-levered, credit-constrained firms, a sudden fall in land asset prices which reduces the value of their collateral means that loans will not be rolled over automatically. Since repayment of loans contracted when asset prices were rising can only be achieved by selling assets, the resulting distress sale of land (or any other collateral assets) causes land prices to fall more, further reducing the collateral value of land. Thus when land prices drop unexpectedly even by just a small amount, the downward spiral of real estate values as the result of such "fire sales" can be quite large, creating the possibility that firm net worth is entirely wiped out and the financial system collapses. In a globally integrated environment, with large capital inflows (as in East Asia), credit market effects can be more pronounced than in closed economies, as capital inflows give financial institutions a larger supply of funds to intermediate.

6.4 Competitive devaluations

Competitive devaluations also played an important role in the unfolding of the currency crisis in 1997 and the magnitude of its impact across countries. While the discussion of Section II suggests that several countries in Asia by early 1997 had overvalued currencies, the extent of this overvaluation is hard to reconcile with the size of the nominal depreciations that occurred after July 1997. Currencies throughout the region lost fifty to eighty percent of their value, well in excess of any estimation of what a devaluation should have been to restore the equilibrium real exchange rate.

One way to explain the magnitude of the nominal devaluation is to view them as the results of competitive devaluations in response to some common shock. Beginning with Thailand, as each country depreciated, markets expected other countries to follow in order to avoid further losses in competition. This in turn fostered further expectations of depreciation in the initial country. In a coordinated response to a common external shock, each country internalizes the negative externality effects of depreciation on its trading partners. Without cooperation, each country's currency depreciates not only to offset the effects of the common shock on the domestic economy, but also to offset the negative impact of the other country's devaluation. Such a "price war" results in much larger cumulative depreciations than if a cooperative equilibrium could have been obtained.[31]

The combination of depreciating yen and yuan against the dollar during the mid 1990s contributed to a loss of competitiveness in the region that can be interpreted as a common shock which contributed to the eventual region-wide currency collapse. As the destination of more than twenty percent of the exports of Thailand, Indonesia, and Malaysia, and more than forty percent of exports of the Philippines, this trade pattern combined with pegs to the U.S. dollar implies that an appreciation of the dollar tended to erode these countries' export competitiveness.[32] Once the Thai baht fell, those countries that tended to compete in the same export markets outside the region, e.g. the U.S., were more likely to be subjected to speculative attacks on their currencies.[33]

6.5 Unhedged foreign liabilities

In an open economy where a significant share of total borrowing takes the form of unhedged foreign currency loans, an unanticipated change in the exchange rate provides another powerful propagation mechanism and channel for amplification. The large unhedged foreign liability position of banks and other financial institutions in Asia magnified the impact of exchange rate changes once the crisis hit. The depreciation in local currencies inflicted large capital losses on banks as the real value of their foreign-exchange denominated liabilities suddenly rose relative to the value of their assets. The scramble of firms and financial institutions to cover their unhedged foreign exchange liabilities as the currencies started to depreciate further weakened currency values.

This propagation channel operated interdependently with other channels, further amplifying their aggregate impact. Efforts by firms and financial institutions to cover their foreign currency liabilities exacerbated the decline in currencies. In some cases borrowers who had not hedged their foreign currency borrowing and had difficulty servicing their debts went bankrupt, worsening the position of lending financial institutions. Falling values of assets used as loan collateral further depressed asset values. Over a longer horizon, as the crisis worsened and economic activity declined in individual countries, its severity was further reinforced through the trade transmission channel.

7. CONCLUSIONS

Much of the current debate about the origin of the Asian crisis concerns whether it was caused by weak economic fundamentals, or by financial panic unrelated to economic conditions. While the two views are not mutually exclusive, their policy implications vary greatly. If a panic unrelated to fundamentals was the main impulse for Asia's financial crisis, reforms in macroeconomic or financial sector policy are not necessary in planning Asia's recovery. If, however, policy mistakes or other fundamentals were the most important contributors to the crisis, reforms are indeed essential.

The traditional fundamentals suggested by first- and second-generation crisis models did not provide much indication of an impending crisis in Asia. Growing current account deficits and somewhat overvalued real exchange rates suggested some need to curtail domestic demand and/or engineer nominal currency depreciation, but did not suggest a crisis of the magnitude that has occurred.

Nevertheless, to a large extent, the Asian crisis can be explained in terms of impulses and propagation mechanisms related to fundamentals, specifically general weaknesses and distortions in the financial sector. These included relationship lending practices, excessive risk taking, and inadequate financial supervision and regulation. The effects of these factors were cumulative and increased the vulnerability of Asia to bad shocks.[34]

Once the crisis hit, various mechanisms magnified its initial impact. These included the effects of excessive leverage, collateralized lending, competitive devaluations, and exposure of unhedged foreign liabilities. Elements of illiquidity-based financial panic may also have played a role. It is important to emphasize, however, the difficulty in identifying whether the motivation for the panic was based in a spontaneous shift in creditor confidence or to changing fundamentals.

Table 1. Macroeconomic Fundamentals in Asian-5 (in percent)

	Indonesia	**Korea**	**Malaysia**	**Philippines**	**Thailand**
1. Capital investment/DP					
Avg. 1990–94	33.6	36.7	36.0	22.7	40.9
Avg. 1995–96	31.4	37.7	42.5	23.1	41.7
2. Government budget/GDP					
Avg. 1990–94	0.4	-0.4	-0.7	-1.4	3.2
Avg. 1995–96	1.7	0.4	0.8	0.4	2.6
3. M2 growth[a]					
Avg. 1990–94	24.4	17.8	19.2	21.0	18.7
Avg. 1995–96	27.2	15.7	22.7	23.7	14.8
4. CPI inflation[a]					
Avg. 1990–94	9.4	7.0	3.8	11.7	4.8
Avg. 1995–96	8.7	4.7	4.4	8.3	5.8
5. GDP growth[a]					
Avg. 1990–94	6.9	7.6	8.7	1.9	9.0
Avg. 1995–96	8.1	8.0	9.0	5.3	7.2
6. Current account/GDPNIA definition					
Avg. 1990–94	–2.5	–1.5	–8.2	–4.5	–7.0
Avg. 1995–96	–3.8	–3.4	–6.3	–4.9	–8.4
7. Real exchange rate appreciation, cumulative					
12/90–12/94	8	9	14	38	11
12/94–3/97	18	2	16	15	16

[a] Average of year-over-year growth rates.

Sources: Data for investment current account, government budget, and inflation from IMF *International Financial Statistics*; data for real exchange rates is from Radelet and Sachs (1998a).

Table 2 Financial Fundamentals in Asian-5 (in percent)

	Indonesia	Korea	Malaysia	Philippines	Thailand
8. Deposit-money domestic bank lending to private sector/GDP					
End 1990	46	52	71	19	64
End 1993	49	54	74	26	80
End 1996	55	62	93	49	102
9. Total domestic lending to private sector/GDP					
End 1990	46	98	111[b]	22	83
End 1993	49	118	111	32	111
End 1996	55	140	142	55	147
10. Deposit-money bank foreign liabilities/GDP					
End 1990	6	4	7	6	5
End 1993	6	4	19	6	11
End 1996	6	9	9	17	27

11. Short-term foreign borrowing[a]/GDP					
mid 1990	NA	7	4	7	7
mid 1994	11	9	11	4	19
mid 1997	17	16	17	10	29
12. Real estate bank loan exposure, 1997	25–30	18–25	30–40	15–20	30–40
13. Nonperforming loans/total bank loans, 1997	17	16	16	14	19
14. Investment efficiency[c]					
Avg. 1990–94	21	20	24	10	20
Avg. 1995–96	25	19	19	25	15

[a]Foreign borrowing from banks in BIS member countries, including borrowing by domestic banks, nonbanks, and public entities.
[b]End 1992.
[c]Defined as GDP growth divided by investment rate of preceding year.
Sources: Bank lending data from IMF *International Financial Statistics*; bank foreign liabilities from Radelet and Sachs (1998a); short-term foreign borrowing from Moreno et al. (1998); real estate exposure and nonperforming loan rates from Corsetti et al. (1998a); investment efficiency from Reisen (1998).

Table 3. Financial Vulnerability Measures in Asian - 5 (in percent)

	Indonesia	**Korea**	**Malaysia**	**Philippines**	**Thailand**
15. Short-term foreign borrowing/ Total foreign borrowing[a]					
mid 1990	NA	68	26	34	58
mid 1994	61	73	59	43	74
mid 1997	59	68	56	59	66
16. Short-term foreign borrowing[a]/ foreign reserves					
mid 1990	NA	115	23	342	54
mid 1994	177	165	26	41	101
mid 1997	174	211	63	86	148
17. M2/ foreign reserves					
End 1990	600	649	291	497	456
End 1993	603	685	209	478	403
mid 1997	616	620	399	487	490

[a]Foreign borrowing from banks in BIS member countries, including borrowing by domestic banks, nonbanks, and public entities.

Sources: Short-term foreign borrowing data from Moreno et al. (1998); M2/reserves data from IMF *International Financial Statistics*.

Acknowledgments: Research assistance by Laura Haworth is gratefully appreciated. The views expressed in the paper are those of the author alone and do not reflect those of the Federal Bank of San Francisco or the Board of Governors of the Federal Reserve System.

Notes

[1]The 1998 growth forecast for Indonesia changed from eight percent to fifteen percent; for Thailand, from six percent to seven percent; for Malaysia, from eight percent to three percent; for Korea from six percent to four percent; and for the Philippines, from six percent to two percent (Consensus Forecasts, *Asia-Pacific Consensus Forecasts*, June 1997 and July 1998).

[2]Other recent surveys of the origins of the Asian crisis include Bhattacharya et al (1998), Corsetti, Pesenti, and Roubini (1998a), Radelet and Sachs (1998a, 1998b), and Reisen (1998).

[3]Even Thailand's inflation rate was declining in 1996 relative to 1995 if measured on a December over prior December basis.

[4]These real exchange rate calculations use the domestic CPI as a proxy for domestic nontradables prices and the foreign WPI as a proxy for foreign-traded goods prices, and define the effective foreign price level as a geometric average of WPI prices for major developed country trading partners based on trade weights of OECD countries excluding Mexico and Korea (see Radelet and Sachs, 1998a, Table 10).

[5]See Radelet and Sachs (1998b, Table 6).

[6]The yen/dollar rate moved from ¥/$ 85 in June 1995 to ¥/$ 127 in April 1997.

[7]Semiconductor prices are estimated to have fallen by as much as 80 percent in 1996 (BIS Annual Report, 1997).

[8]For example, China's share of garment exports of the total from the five crisis Asian economies (Indonesia, Korea, Malaysia, the Philippines, and Thailand) plus itself rose from thirty-seven percent in 1990 to sixty percent in 1996, and its share of electronics exports increased from twelve percent to eighteen percent (Radelet and Sachs, 1998b).

[9]Radelet and Sachs (1998b) argue that, although China's emergence as an exporter may have affected markets for certain products, it had little impact in displacing total exports from the rest of the region during the 1990s. However, this assessment ignores the role of Hong Kong as a transhipper of exports from China to the rest of the world. The market share of Greater China (China plus Hong Kong) in the U.S. grew between 1989 and 1993, mainly at the expense of Korea, Taiwan, and Singapore (though it has not since changed much), while its market share in Japan increased between 1989 and 1996 at the expense of these countries as well as other countries in Southeast Asia (Fernald, Edison, and Loungani, 1998). Radelet and Sachs also argue that the 1994 devaluation of the yuan had a relatively limited impact in the region, since it affected only transactions conducted at the official exchange rate—less than twenty percent of the total by some estimates—and its real effects had been substantially eroded by 1996 through two years of inflation averaging twenty percent compared with an

average of six percent in the Asian-5. However, there are still reasons to believe that the real effects of the yuan depreciation were significant. First, the more market-influenced swap rate affecting the bulk of China's trade transactions had been depreciating over the prior year; the official rate devaluation merely followed this trend. Second, the real exchange rate calculations of Radelet and Sachs (and others) are typically based on domestic CPI measures that certainly overestimate the extent to which domestic price inflation eroded the competitiveness of China's manufactures exports, since much of China's recorded inflation during this period is attributable to a surge in food prices and the ending of price controls on some key commodities that had an extraordinarily high weight in the CPI basket.

[10]In fact, some Asian countries, such as Thailand and even Malaysia to an extent, had sought to restrain domestic demand by raising domestic interest rates prior to the crisis.

[11]In Korea, for example, the government directed allocation of almost half of commercial bank loans over ten years after banks had been privatized.

[12]The system of implicit government insurance blurred the dividing line between public and private liabilities by creating a stock of off-balance-sheet contingent public liabilities that were not fully visible until the financial crisis occurred. Consolidating these contingent liabilities with the on-balance-sheet fiscal budget would have created a much less rosy picture of the overall budget position of most Asian governments prior to the crisis.

[13]McKinnon and Pill (1996, 1998), Krugman (1998), and Corsetti, Pesenti, and Roubini (1998b) model how moral hazard distorts investment and lending decisions. The latter refer to speculative attack models featuring bailout incentives as "third-generation" crisis models.

[14]Dooley (1997) and Krugman (1998) assume that there is an exogenous limit to government resources for funding implicit and explicit financial guarantees. In their frameworks crises can occur when the demand for bailout resources exceeds this limit, analogously to when foreign exchange holdings of monetary authorities are exhausted in speculative attack models.

[15]In most Asian countries there was significant direct foreign borrowing by domestic private corporations. In Indonesia and Malaysia, this direct foreign borrowing exceeded that by domestic banks.

[16]Estimates of the extent of bad loans vary greatly. These figures are based on data from Jardine Fleming, as reported in Corsetti, Pesenti, and Roubini (1998a, Table 24). Official estimates, of course, are typically lower.

[17]Chang and Velasco (1998) extend the Diamond-Dybvig model to analyze liquidity-based financial crises in an open economy framework. Other approaches to explaining the herding behavior of creditors presume asymmetric information among creditors (e.g. Mishkin, 1996) or portfolio managers' excessive sensitivity to small changes in information about economic fundamentals (e.g. Calvo, 1998).

[18]As Dooley (1997) and Chang and Velasco (1998) point out, this interrelation implies that it may be difficult to distinguish whether a financial crisis originates in a run on domestic banks or on the domestic currency.

[19]The corresponding figures in mid-1997 for Argentina, Brazil, and Chile were 358 percent, 367 percent, and 180 percent, respectively.

[20]The role of asset and liability stock imbalances in explaining vulnerability to currency crises was first emphasized by Calvo (1998). The empirical usefulness of these measures for explaining the cross-country spread of crisis has been demonstrated by Sachs, Tornell, and Velasco (1996), Corsetti, Pesenti, and Roubini (1998c), and Tornell (1998).

[21]Somewhat paradoxically, efforts by Asian central banks to sterilize the effects of capital inflow surges on domestic money aggregates raised domestic interest rates and fueled further capital inflows.

[22]Corsetti, Pesenti, and Roubini (1998a) argue that the increase in foreign borrowing was to a large extent an endogenous response to increased domestic capital investment in East Asia and the associated need for financing.

[23]Japan, after which many Asian countries modeled their development strategies, suffers from some of the same financial weaknesses as elsewhere in the region. The current banking problems of Japan, which relative to that in the rest of Asia developed more silently, point out such problems can arise even without the occurrence of capital inflows and the collapse of a currency peg.

[24]Kaminsky and Reinhart (1997) note that in eighteen of thirty-five banking crises in their sample the financial sector had been liberalized some time during the previous five years.

[25]A discrete economic shock is not necessary to precipitate a speculative attack. As first-generation crisis models point out, with forward-looking speculators, smoothly trending fundamentals can generate a sudden speculative attack at a discrete point of time.

[26]Kaminsky and Reinhart (1997) show that banking crises have tended to precede currency crises in emerging market countries.

[27]For example, official statistics on short-term foreign borrowing were initially far below true levels. In early fall 1997, Bank Indonesia placed the country's private foreign debt at about \$55 billion, while private estimates placed the debt burden at over \$100 billion, claiming that short-term offshore borrowing and roughly \$44 billion in offshore bond issues was not included in the official government figures.

[28]Uncertainty about government policy responses to the initial signs of panic may also have contributed to furthering the process (see Radelet and Sachs, 1998a,b).

[29]The preference for bank borrowing was motivated by the lack of developed securities markets in most Asian countries as well as the desire to avoid diluting management control by issuing equity.

[30]The very high debt ratios of the chaebols may also reflect their expectation of government support in the case of adverse outcomes. This was confirmed by events in 1997, when the Korean government encouraged banks to extend emergency loans to some troubled chaebols with difficulties servicing their debts and supplied special loans to banks that did so.

[31]See Huh and Kasa (1997) and Corsetti Pesenti, and Roubini (1998b) for equilibrium models of competitive devaluations.

[32]Bhattacharya et al. (1998) argue that the competitive aspect of the devaluations explains only a small part of the observed depreciations.

[33]See Glick and Rose (1998) for empirical evidence on the role of trade linkages in explaining the cross-country spread of currency crises.

[34]To apply another metaphor, the weaknesses of Asian financial systems can be thought of equivalent to an insect infestation that over time weakens the roots of a tall, outwardly healthy redwood tree (redwoods have shallow root systems). The tree may look fine for a long time, even as it becomes increasingly vulnerable to being uprooted and blown over by a succession of storms. It may in fact survive many windstorms, but at some point in time a windstorm will come along, maybe even a relatively weak storm, which will be sufficient to blow the tree down.

References

Bhattacharya, Amar, Stijn Claessens, Swati Ghosh, Leonardo Hernandez and Pedro Alba. "Volatility and Contagion in a Financially-Integrated World: Lessons from East Asia's Recent Experience," paper presented at the CEPR/World Bank conference "Financial Crises: Contagion and Market Volatility," London, May 8–9, 1998.

Calvo, Guillermo. "Varieties of Capital Market Crises," in *The Debt Burden and its Consequences for Monetary Policy*, Guillermo Calvo and Mervyn King (eds.), London: Macmillan, 1998.

Caprio, Gerald, and D. Klingebeil. *Bank Insolvency: Bad Luck, Bad Policy, or Bad Banking?,* Washington, DC: The World Bank, 1996.

Chang, Roberto, and Andres Velasco. "Financial Crisis in Emerging Markets: A Canonical Model," National Bureau of Economic Research working paper, No. 6606, June 1998.

Corsetti, Giancarlo, Paolo Pesenti, and Nouriel Roubini. "What Caused the Asian Currency and Financial Crisis? Part I: a Macroeconomic Overview," paper presented at the CEPR/World Bank conference "Financial Crises: Contagion and Market Volatility," London, May 8–9, 1998a.

Corsetti, Giancarlo, Paolo Pesenti, and Nouriel Roubini. "What Caused the Asian Currency and Financial Crisis? Part II: Interpreting and Modeling the Crisis," paper presented at the CEPR/World Bank conference "Financial Crises: Contagion and Market Volatility," London, May 8–9, 1998b.

Corsetti, Giancarlo, Paolo Pesenti, and Nouriel Roubini. "Paper Tigers? A Preliminary Assessment of the Asian Crisis," Yale University, mimeo, June 1998c.

Diamond, Douglas, and Philip Dybvig. "Banks Runs, Deposit Insurance, and Liquidity," *Journal of Political Economy* 91: 401-419, 1983.

Dooley, Michael. "A Model of Crises in Emerging Markets," National Bureau of Economic Research, working paper, No. 6300, December 1997.

Edison, Hali, Pongsak Luangaram, and Marcus Miller. "Asset Bubbles, Domino Effects, and 'Lifeboats' Elements of the East Crisis," paper presented at the CEPR/World Bank conference "Financial Crises: Contagion and Market Volatility," London, May 8–9, 1998.

Fernald, John, Hali Edison, and Prakash Loungani. "Was China the First Domino? Assessing Links Between China and the Rest of Emerging Asia," Board of Governors of the Federal Reserve System, International Finance Discussion Paper, No.604, March 1998.

Glick, Reuven, and Andrew Rose. "Contagion and Trade: Why Are Currency Crises Regional?," paper presented at the CEPR/World Bank conference "Financial Crises: Contagion and Market Volatility." London, May 8–9, 1998, and CEPR discussion paper, No. 1447, August 1998.

Goldstein, Morris, and Philip Turner. "Banking Crises in Emerging Economies: Origins and Policy Options," *BIS Economic Papers*, No. 46, 1996.

Huh, Chan, and Kenneth Kasa. "A Dynamic Model of Export Competition, Policy Coordination and Simultaneous Currency Collapse," Federal Reserve Bank of San Francisco, Center for Pacific Basin Monetary and Economic Studies, working paper, No. PB97-08, 1997.

Kaminsky, Graciela, and Carmen Reinhart. "The Twin Crises: the Causes of Banking and Balance-of-Payments Problems," Board of Governors of the Federal Reserve System, International Finance Discussion Paper, No. 544, 1997

Kasa, Kenneth. "Borrowing Constraints and Asset Market Dynamics: Evidence from the Pacific Basin," Federal Reserve Bank of San Francisco, Center for Pacific Basin Monetary and Economic Studies, working paper, No. PB98-05, 1998.

Kiyotaki, Nobuhiro, and John Moore. "Credit Cycles," *Journal of Political Economy,* 105: 211–248, 1997.

Krugman, Paul. "A Model of Balance of Payments Crises," *Journal of Money, Credit, and Banking,* 11: 311–325, 1979.

Krugman, Paul. "What Happened to Asia?," Massachussetts Institute of Technology, mimeo, January 1998.

McKinnon, Ronald, and Huw Pill. "Credible Liberalizations and International Capital Flows: The Overborrowing Syndrome," in *Financial Regulation and Integration in East Asia*, Takatoshi Ito and Anne Krueger (eds.), Chicago: University of Chicago Press, 1996.

McKinnon, Ronald, and Huw Pill. "The Overborrowing Syndrome: Are East Asian Economies Different?," in *Managing Capital Flows and Exchange Rates: Perspectives from the Pacific Basin*, Reuven Glick (ed.), Cambridge, U.K.: Cambridge University Press, 1998.

Mishkin, Frederic. "Understanding Financial Crises: A Developing Country Perspective," National Bureau of Economic Research, working paper, No. 5600, 1996.

Moreno, Ramon, Gloria Pasadilla, and Eli Remolina. "Asia's Financial Crisis: Lessons and Policy Responses," *Asia: Responding To Crisis*, Asia Development Bank Institute, 1998.

Obstfeld, Maurice. "The Logic of Currency Crises," *Cahiers Economiques et Monetaires,* Banque de France, 43:189–213, 1994.

Radelet, Steven, and Jeffrey Sachs. "The Onset of the East Asian Financial Crisis," Harvard Institute for International Development, mimeo, March 1998a.

Radelet, Steven, and Jeffrey Sachs. "The East Asian Financial Crisis: Diagnosis, Remedies, and Prospects," *Brookings Papers on Economic Activity,* No. 1, 1–90 1998b.

Reisen, Helmut. "Domestic Causes of Currency Crises: Policy Lessons for Crisis Avoidance," OECD Development Centre, technical paper, No. 136, June 1998.

Sachs, Jeffrey, Aaron Tornell, and Andres Velasco. "Financial Crises in Emerging Markets: the Lessons of 1995," *Brookings Papers on Economic Activity,* No. 1, 147–217, 1996.

Tornell, Aaron. "Common Fundamentals in the Tequila and Asian Crises," Harvard University, mimeo, July 1998.

Chapter 6

Origins of the Asian Crisis: Discussion

Roberto Chang
Federal Reserve Bank of Atlanta

Abstract: The fundamental views on the causes of the recent Asian crisis have clearly emerged: a "bad policy" view and a "financial panic" view. I discuss these perspectives, their implications for public policy, and outline challenges for the bad policy camp.

In order to obtain a proper perspective on the papers in this session, it is useful to review the dominant views on emerging markets crises before and after the Mexican crisis of 1994. In so doing, my discussion will overlap somewhat with Reuven Glick's. However, my emphasis will be different and will inevitably reflect my work with Andrés Velasco on the subject.

1. EARLIER VIEWS ON EMERGING MARKETS CRISES

Before the 1994 Mexican crisis, a dominant view had arisen from the seminal paper by Paul Krugman (1979). Its central tenet was that a fixed exchange rate system eventually had to be abandoned if a government had limited reserves and ran a persistent fiscal deficit. Hence, this "first generation" view saw a balance of payments crisis as the predictable outcome of inconsistent macroeconomic policy.

While useful in other episodes, the "first generation" view is clearly inadequate to explain recent events. Both Mexico before 1994 and the Asian countries that went into crisis last year had been posting small fiscal deficits or even surpluses.

A "second generation" view was proposed by Maurice Obstfeld (1994). Obstfeld argued that governments may not *have to* abandon fixed exchange rates; however, they may *choose* to do so if the social cost of defending fixed rates, particularly in terms of unemployment, becomes too large. An interesting implication of Obstfeld's hypothesis is that crises may be driven by market expectations. Expectations of devaluation may increase the interest rate and unemployment levels needed to defend an exchange rate. The government may decide to devalue as a consequence, confirming expectations.

Obstfeld's work stimulated a new flurry of research on crises. Unfortunately for this view, neither the Mexico before its 1994 crisis nor Asian countries before their recent crisis exhibited a particularly weak macroeconomic picture. Hence the "second generation" view also seems inapplicable to recent crises.

2. RECENT VIEWS: BAD POLICY VERSUS FINANCIAL PANIC

Given this state of affairs, economists have been led to develop new approaches to financial crises that can explain what happened in Mexico and, more recently, in Asia. While hundreds of papers on the subject have been written recently, two camps have clearly emerged: a *bad policy* camp and a *financial panic* camp.

Bad policy advocates follow the "first generation" view in asserting that, ultimately, crises are the inevitable outcome of misguided government policy. However, they need to solve the puzzle of why policy imbalances were not apparent from conventional measures of monetary or fiscal policy. Their answer has been to argue that Asian policies were "really" bad but, at the same time, were obscure enough so that their effects did not show up in conventional measures. While not manifest, the damage on the economy accumulated over time, which eventually led to a crisis and a policy reversal.

What kind of policies fit such a description? Implicit liability insurance is the leading candidate. It has been argued that Asian governments guaranteed domestic private liabilities, in spite of the fact that such guarantees encouraged domestic borrowers to take socially costly actions (such as investing in excessively risky projects or simply stealing funds). This strategy, it is said, "succeeded" for a while, because the government had enough funds to keep it going. The "insurance fund" had a limit, however, which was eventually reached. At that point, private agents understood that further borrowing would not be guaranteed and, in an "attack," creditors exchanged existing private liabilities for the government insurance fund.

The story just described was developed first by Michael Dooley and is detailed in his contribution to this conference, which is an outgrowth of Dooley (1997). Other important papers in the bad policy camp are Mc Kinnon and Pill (1996), and Krugman (1998) although, in my opinion, Dooley (1997) is still the most compelling statement of that view. The contribution by Craig Burnside, Martin Eichenbaum, and Sergio Rebelo also belongs to this camp, although its primary focus is to explain when an exchange rate peg will be abandoned after a financial crisis, not to explain the crisis itself.

The opposite position is that the Asian crisis was the result of a *financial panic*. Those in this camp argue that economic fundamentals in Asia, including government policies, may not have been entirely satisfactory yet did not warrant a crisis. Instead, the cause was that international creditors, fearing a crisis, suddenly refused to roll over credit to Asian countries. As a consequence, these countries had to scramble for short term funds, which resulted in costly liquidations, asset price collapses, domestic bank runs, and credit crunches.

A key policy implication is that the Asian crisis *did not need to happen*: if foreign lenders had not panicked, Asian financial systems would not have had to endure the 1997 credit shock, and the costly disruption of the system would have been avoided, justifying the optimistic expectations. Hence, for financial panic advocates, market expectations were key to the Asian crisis.

While the emphasis on the role of market expectations resembles Obstfeld's (1994) views, the financial panic view postulates very different mechanisms. In particular, Chang and Velasco (1998a,b) have shown that the key condition for a small country to be prone to financial panics is *international illiquidity.* A country's financial system is internationally illiquid if its potential short-term obligations in hard currency exceed the hard currency liquidation value of its assets. If holders of the short-term liabilities of the financial system lose confidence and attempt to redeem their holdings, the system will become bankrupt, making the confidence loss self fulfilling, if and only if it is internationally illiquid.

In other words, financial panic advocates argue that the root of the Asian crisis was a maturity mismatch: short-term international liabilities were far greater than short-term assets. Evidence in favor of this view has been provided in Chang and Velasco (1998c) and Radelet and Sachs (1998). To illustrate, consider Table 1, taken from Chang and Velasco (1998c). In the table, the short-term liabilities of Korea, Indonesia, Malaysia, the

Philippines, and Thailand are proxied by their short-term borrowing from BIS reporting banks; their short-term assets are proxied by the level of their international reserves. The bottom panel of the table shows that the ratio of short-term debt to reserves far exceeded unity in June 1997 in Korea, Indonesia, and Thailand. This means that if, as it was the case, international bankers had refused to roll over credit, these countries would have not had enough reserves to meet their immediate obligations. Also, while the debt-reserves ratio was below one in Malaysia and the Philippines, it had more than doubled since 1994.

A crucial question for the financial panic camp is then: how did Asian countries become internationally illiquid? Financial liberalization appears as the main culprit. As documented by Chang and Velasco (1998c), the Asian countries affected by the recent crisis had enacted sweeping reforms designed to make their financial systems more market oriented. These reforms are beneficial in principle, but may also have exacerbated international illiquidity; this is indeed one consequence of the theory put forward in Chang and Velasco (1998b).

The distinction between the bad policy view and the financial panic view is not only an academic matter. It is in fact a crucial issue because the two perspectives have very different implications for public policy. To be concrete, consider the issue of whether there should be an international lender of last resort. If we believe the bad policy camp, the answer is clearly negative. In fact, if we take Dooley's analysis literally, such a facility only makes problems worse, since access to international credit would only induce governments to keep lending for ill-fated purposes. On the other hand, if one believes that crises are caused by financial panics, one must conclude that the existence of an international lender of last resort would be of great help. Depositors and international creditors would be reassured that their short-term claims would be ultimately honored, and hence they would have no reason to panic.

Needless to say, I believe that the financial panic view is more promising than the bad policy view. The former is consistent with a wide array of evidence, and its theory has been developed in a much greater level of detail; I refer you to my papers with Andrés Velasco for demonstration of these assertions. But my role here is to discuss the papers in this session, and hence I will conclude with some further comments on them and on the bad policy view.

3. CHALLENGES TO THE BAD POLICY VIEW

What obstacles must advocates of the bad policy view overcome if they are to gain the upper hand in the current debate? I think that the main challenge is to make that view more believable both in the theoretical sense and in the empirical sense. Theories developed by the bad policy camp often assume policies that are too contrived to be believable. The model in the paper by Burnside, Eichenbaum, and Rebelo, for example, does not "work" unless very strong and arguably unreasonable assumptions are imposed on the availability and timing of taxes, and the actions of monetary authorities.

The policies postulated in Dooley's contributions are more intuitively plausible. However, it is unclear why a government would stick to those policies. More generally, the bad policy camp needs to find some explanation of why the bad policies are implemented. Is it because of politics? Concerns about redistribution? Time inconsistency? Answers are needed to lend credibility to the bad policy position. In addition, without them we can say little or nothing about the desirability or possibility of reforms.

Finally, advocates of the bad policy view should bite the bullet and present supporting empirical evidence. In spite of the attention this view has received, I have yet to see one compelling piece of data supporting it. It is not enough to show that countries were corrupted and that their financial system were distorted. A lot of emerging economies suffer from comparable levels of corruption and financial distortions, but were not attacked recently as one would expect if the bad policy evidence were valid. Also, while corruption and financial distortions in Asia have presumably been present for decades, the Asian crisis countries had performed remarkably well up to last year. If corruption and financial distortions are the cause, why then did it take so long for these countries to go into crises?

Ultimately, the bad policy view can succeed only if can present valid evidence that matches the predictions of its theory. I believe this will be a formidable task, partly because bad policy theories are constructed so that policy effects are not manifest in standard measures of monetary or fiscal imbalances. But I want to encourage "bad policy" believers to try. This effort can only contribute to a richer debate, the outcome of which has key implications for world welfare.

Table 1 Asian-5: Short-Term Debt vs Reserves

Short-Term Debt (millions of US$)	Indonesia	Korea	Malaysia	Philippines	Thailand	Total
Jun-90	10,360	15,528	1,761	3,019	7,026	37,694
Jun-94	18,882	34,908	8,203	2,646	27,151	91,790
Jun-97	34,661	70,182	16,268	8,293	45,567	174,91

International Reserves (millions of US$)	Indonesia	Korea	Malaysia	Philippines	Thailand	Total
Jun-90	4,693	14,642	8,114	948	11,882	40,279
Jun-94	10,915	21,684	32,608	6,527	27,375	99,109
Jun-97	20,336	34,069	26,586	9,781	31,361	122,133

Debt to Reserves Ratio	Indonesia	Korea	Malaysia	Philippines	Thailand	Total
Jun-90	2.208	1.061	0.217	3.185	0.591	0.936
Jun-94	1.730	1.610	0.252	0.405	0.992	0.926
Jun-97	1.704	2.060	0.612	0.848	1.453	1.433

Source: BIS, IMF and Chang and Velasco (1998c).

References

Chang, Roberto, and Andrés Velasco. "Financial Fragility and the Exchange Rate Regime," NBER, working paper, No. 6469, 1998a.

Chang, Roberto, and Andrés Velasco. "Financial Crises in Emerging Markets: A Canonical Model," NBER, working paper, No. 6606, 1998b.

Chang, Roberto, and Andrés Velasco. "The Asian Liquidity Crisis," Federal Reserve Bank of Atlanta, working paper, No. 98–11, 1998c.

Dooley, Michael. "A Model of Crises in Emerging Markets," NBER, working paper, No. 6300, 1997.

Krugman, Paul. "A Model of Balance of Payments Crises," *Journal of Money, Credit, and Banking,* 11, 311–325, 1979.

Krugman, Paul. "What Happened to Asia?," Massachussetts Institute of Technology, mimeo, 1998.

Mc Kinnon, Ronald, and Huw Pill, "Credible Liberalizations and International Capital Flows: The Overborrowing Syndrome," in *Financial Deregulation and Integration in East Asia*, T. Ito and A. Krueger (eds.), Chicago: University of Chicago Press, 1996.

Obstfeld, Maurice. "The Logic of Currency Crises," *Cahiers Economiques et Monetaires,* 43 189–213, 1994.

Radelet, Steve, and Jeffrey Sachs. "The Onset of the Asian Financial Crisis," Harvard Institute for International Development, mimeo, 1998.

PART III

CAUSES AND IMPLICATIONS OF THE ASIAN CRISIS —THE ROLE OF THE FINANCIAL SECTOR, DOMESTIC POLICIES, AND CONTAGION

Chapter 7

Precarious Credit Equilibria: Reflections on the Asian Financial Crisis

Joseph R. Bisignano
Bank for International Settlements

1. INTRODUCTION

This paper examines some of the origins of the current East Asian financial crisis. Its focus is on the role of moral hazard and the weakness of prudential regulation and supervision in countries following financial deregulation and capital flow liberalization. While major differences exist among the Asian countries currently in crises, there are important similarities between the micro-financial vulnerabilities which eventually led to earlier crises in Latin America, Japan, and the Nordic countries. These similarities are illustrated with reference to Korea, Sweden, and Chile.

We begin in section two by considering the imbedded moral hazard problems in highly concentrated bank-dominated systems. Emphasis is placed on the pervasive role of government in influencing private market credit allocation decisions, in part by providing incentives for the private sector to exploit implicit government guarantees, and on the repeated absence of efficient financial oversight following financial deregulation. Moral hazard is also considered to have contributed to the overborrowing syndrome in East Asia, as it had in Latin America during the 1980s. Given the limited financial transparency in East Asia, it is surprising that, instead of the credit rationing we might have expected in such an environment, we observed large foreign capital inflows, much of it intermediated by banks.

Section three considers a few parallels between East Asia and earlier financial crises in Chile and Sweden with regard to the retarded evolution of the prudential regulatory and supervisory functions following deregulation.

This retarded evolution has been observed in a number of countries since the early 1980s. Attention is also drawn to the difficulty markets may have in evaluating the quality of emerging-market banking systems. This section includes a review of Harberger's 1985 study of the Chilean financial crisis of 1981–84 and the role played by the deficiency of financial oversight. Mention is made of opportunities to exploit government guarantees and "inefficient contracts" designed to secure financial stability in the absence of adequate prudential regulation and banking supervision. Because of the deficiencies of corporate governance, transparency, and less than adequate attention to supervisory oversight, the financial crisis of East Asia is to a degree a case of self-inflicted wounds.

Section four considers the problem of the underproduction of information in the financial systems of emerging market economies and the use of implicit government guarantees to substitute for this deficiency. The credit market in these countries, relying heavily on short-term international capital flows, can be thought of as possessing a "precarious equilibrium," in which foreign flows continue when the implicit guarantee is credible but suddenly revert to extreme credit rationing when the implicit guarantee is undermined by the threat of potential widespread financial illiquidity or insolvency. The last section draws a few conclusions.

2. ECONOMIC DEVELOPMENT AND MORAL HAZARD

2.1 Embedded moral hazard in bank-dominated systems

As noted earlier by Andersen (1993) and Huh and Kim (1994), a frequently ignored aspect of the rapid growth of many East Asian countries was the general absence of well-developed financial markets. (The obvious exceptions are Hong Kong and Singapore.) This is not uncommon. In the early stages of economic development an efficient, market-based financial system has often been thought to be of second order importance to economic growth. The banking system typically dominates the intermediation process, often with little-disguised intervention by the government, and usually with widespread implicit stability guarantees. For example, between 1970 and 1990 the net bond financing of corporations in the five Eastern Asian countries for which data exists was less than ten percent.[1] Several countries in East Asia grew at surprisingly rapid rates of growth without the benefit of well-developed financial markets but with a major participation of government in providing implicit guarantees.[2]

The large role played by governments in developing economies in choosing specific industries for development and in directing and subsidizing credit to them is well known.[3] In East Asia, Korea and Japan in the past have relied heavily on directed credit programmes to promote specific industries. Selective credit allocation was also used in Indonesia, Malaysia, and Thailand.[4] This pattern of selective investment and credit allocation has frequently retarded and masked the need for the development of the micro-credit analysis structure in the banking industry and appropriate official supervisory oversight. The financial history of Japan should not be forgotten. Successful industrial development programs in Asia often went hand-in-hand with an underlying weakness in the quality of credit analysis. When financial deregulation took place, it was often without the concurrent development of an efficient prudential regulation and supervisory structure. In many regards the East Asian experience was typical of developing economies' financial system evolution.

In the mid-1980s Suzuki (1986) pointed to the dangers of what he referred to as "socialism in financial markets" in Japan. By this he meant the artificially low interest rate policy used in the promotion of investment/export-led growth in the early stages of post-war Japanese industrial development and, between mid-1970 and early-1980, the high degree of public financial intermediation fostered by continued cheap financing by government intermediaries.[5] Suzuki warned of three problems which were likely to result from the heavy role of government in financial intermediation. The first was the harm it would cause to the allocation of financial capital. Excessive public intermediation would hamper the growth of private credit institutions, with real investment being based not on the efficiency of capital but on the basis of nonmarket determined public policy objectives. Secondly, the continued growth of public intermediation would potentially undermine the effectiveness of monetary policy. And lastly, it threatened to reduce fiscal discipline, as nonmarket loan criteria would gradually lead to a deterioration in the quality of the loan portfolio of public intermediaries. Developing country governments' intermediation role have often also included partly shielding the private sector from foreign exchange risk by stabilising exchange rates. Although the nature of "public intermediation" was less apparent in many cases, these potential problems have all come to pass in East Asia. The problem for many developing countries has been when and how best to remove the government from its large direct or indirect intermediation role, how to encourage the development of a market-based credit screening and monitoring culture, and how to regulate and supervise a system of private intermediation.

In the early stages of economic development it may be the case that government intervention in investment decisionmaking and credit extension is desirable and welfare improving, given serious informational asymmetries, the absence of well-organized financial markets and the size of required infrastructure investments. Because of the frequent absence of well-defined property rights, of an efficient legal system to enforce contract compliance and bankruptcy proceedings, and of transparent accounting and disclosure standards, it is hardly surprising that the banking system typically grows more rapidly than financial markets with tradable debt and equity contracts.[6] Banks are typically thought to be more efficient than securities markets in resolving agency problems in an environment of severe information asymmetries.

In some regards the banking systems in developing countries incorporate some of the aspects of legal and accounting systems by having access to deposit histories and by relying on long-term relationships, the need for loan renewal and collateral requirements to enforce contract compliance and information disclosure. It also frequently carries with it government stability guarantees and enforcement mechanisms, given the need for banks to fund long-term loans with short-term deposits. One aspect of the moral hazard problem in young financial systems emanates from this close government–corporate banking sector link, the weakness of "arms length" financial relationships. In addition, for any economy to function the system requires a reliable payments system. This reliability results from the requirement that banks hold deposits with the central bank and from the central bank assurance that liquidity will be maintained in times of stress. Hence, there is at the core of the financial system of developing economies an intrinsic insurance-based moral hazard problem: the need to assure an often poorly informed public of the stability of banking intermediaries with predominantly nonmarketable information-idiosyncratic loans, where there are often few alternatives to bank credit. The pervasiveness of the moral hazard problem related to the banking system can be seen in sovereign credit ratings. Standard and Poor's, for example, considers banking sector liabilities as contingent liabilities of sovereigns.[7]

Compounding the intrinsic moral hazard problem in developing economies is the weakness of the "bankruptcy threat" for many large firms and banks, potentially weakening financial discipline and encouraging excessive risk taking. This is a particular problem when political connections reduce manager concern with failure and particularly where firms directly control banks. For example, following privatization, new "groupos," large conglomerates, emerged in Chile in the early 1970s. Unlike earlier family-centered, conservative groupos, the new ones were aggressive, highly leveraged, and organized around one or more banks. By 1979 they controlled the equity of more than eighty percent of all private banks, and almost seventy percent of the equity of firms listed on the stock exchange. Even without direct government direction of investment and credit because of their size, the groups and their banks appeared to rely on implicit government guarantees. As described by Le-Fort (1994), the banks acted as agents of the group of engaging in risky investment activity despite extremely low capital positions. Confronting difficulty and facing insolvency in 1982, there was the expectation of a "discriminatory bailout." As a result of excessive leverage and large foreign currency borrowing, the two largest groupos went bankrupt in 1983. The government then took over five banks, among which included the two largest private banks, owned by important conglomerates.[8] Direct government control or ownership was not necessary for banks to behave as if government support was assured.

Suzuki's lament over the excessive degree of public intermediation in Japan as late as the early-1980s illustrates how difficult it is, even for advanced industrialized countries, to extricate the role of government in the banking system. Since his writing, events in Japan have illustrated how vulnerable a large, well-capitalized banking system can be to the dangers posed by moral hazard, even after the government has retreated from direct intervention in the financial system. We should also recall that a major difference between Japan's high-growth period without a major banking crisis and the current banking crises in East Asia is that Japan's earlier success took place during a time of limited international capital mobility. The moral hazard potential was there but was arguably kept manageable by the limited access of Japanese firms and banks to foreign short-term capital.

Moral hazard problems in developing economies may also be heightened by their success at achieving rapid real growth and rising standards of living. We saw this in Chile in the 1980s and in Mexico in the 1990s. Early "catch up" economic growth produced by a mobilization of domestic labor and capital resources, particularly in high savings rate countries, may be misinterpreted as efficiency gains.[9] Nothing blurs economic vision like success, particularly when its origins are misunderstood, resulting in a postponement of necessary policy adjustment to the new environment.

The combination of government protection of banks and large enterprises, directed investment allocation, a lack of efficient credit screening and monitoring technology, and a misinterpretation of the sources of rapid economic growth, has been the source of intrinsic moral hazard risks in many developing countries. Park (1998), for example, argues that moral hazard problems played a major part in precipitating the Korean financial crisis. The general opinion was that the Korean government would not allow commercial banks and merchant banking corporations to fail. Unlike commercial banks, who were subject to supervision by the central bank, merchant banks were much more loosely regulated and under the control of the Ministry of Finance. The moral hazard problem may also have influenced the behavior of foreign institutions lending to Korean banks, many of whom may have believed that repayment was implicitly guaranteed by the government, similar to what is thought to have contributed to the banking crisis in Chile in the early 1980s.[10]

Government protection of domestic banks in East Asian countries can also be observed in banking competition policy and in the responses to previous banking crises. Most of these countries, with the exception of Hong Kong, Singapore and Indonesia, have had until recently quite rigid restrictions on both foreign and domestic entry into the banking industry. Most of the expansion in the banking industry came through the granting of licenses for branches of existing banks. The World Bank reports that entry restrictions were preferred to high capital standards "to encourage prudent behavior" because this provided governments with "a more discretionary tool to influence the behavior of the banks".[11]

We observe the umbrella of implicit guarantees of the banking systems in East Asia in government treatment of weakened institutions. Although only Korea and Thailand had explicit deposit insurance programs, all other countries in Eastern Asia have had implicitly insured deposits.[12] Up to 1993 only Hong Kong and Thailand closed the doors of insolvent intermediaries. What is curious in retrospect is the statement by the World Bank that "because of tougher prudential supervision and better economic growth, the costs of bank rescues in East Asia have been lower than in many other economies."[13]

An indication of the pervasiveness of implicit government guarantees of financial intermediaries in many developing countries is the repeated occurrence of limited improvement in the supervision of financial intermediaries immediately before or after rapid financial deregulation and the privatization of state enterprises. Deregulation frequently has been followed by the rapid growth of little regulated nonbank financial intermediaries, a major credit expansion, large rises in asset prices, followed by severe credit problems, if not crises.[14] This pattern was observed in Argentina after the rapid deregulation in 1978 and in Chile beginning in 1974 with the reduction in reserve requirements, the entry of the "financieras," new nonbank financial intermediaries, and later the privatization of nationalized banks.[15] In Venezuela, prior to 1989 the banking system consisted of a variety of specialized banks which were members of financial groups, largely outside of the supervisory reach of the

Superintendency of Banks. As Garcia-Herrero (1997) reports, between 1989 and end-1993, when the Venezuelan banking crisis exploded, the supervisory and regulatory structure was left basically unchanged due to delays in adopting the financial reform program that was to complement the country's macroeconomic program.

The financial deepening in Korea took place in the less-regulated/supervised nonbank financial intermediary sector, which was also covered by widespread implicit government guarantees. The Korean Deposit Insurance Corporation was established only in June 1996 because, in the view of its president, "Korean financial institutions were virtually immune to failure because the government implicitly guaranteed the solvency and liquidity of financial institutions through the central bank's function as the lender of last resort." [16]

Following the 1991 financial reform, in which most short-term lending rates of banks and nonbank intermediaries were deregulated, as well as those on a variety of money and capital market investments, competition intensified. It increased further in 1993 when lending rates were further liberalized. This was followed by deposit rate liberalization in 1994. Although initially slow and cautious during the 1980s, financial deregulation in Korea was later followed by the rapid growth of three types of nonbank financial intermediaries, investment and finance companies, mutual savings intermediaries and merchant banking corporations.[17] They all were provided with the ability to pay higher interest rates than banks, as well as greater management autonomy. This was done in order to attract funds from the unregulated money market. As a result, they quickly grew to compete strongly with commercial banks and eventually outgrew them in size: non-commercial bank intermediaries share of total "deposits" grew from thirty-seven percent at end-1980 to sixty-eight percent by June 1995.

Some of the more aggressive Korean institutions attempting to profit from the new liberal financial environment were merchant banks, who were permitted to engage in foreign exchange business after 1994. They quickly developed a serious maturity mismatch. By 1997 over seventy percent of their funds raised were short-term, while almost ninety percent of their investments were long-term, many placed in high risk investments in Southeast Asia, Russia, and Latin America. In addition, according to official sources, they were improperly supervised, with the quality of their assets poorly examined.

Another Asian example of deficiencies in regulation and supervision following financial deregulation is the Indonesian experience during the late 1980s. Indonesia introduced a number of liberalizing measures during the 1980s which were further enhanced with the PAKTO program in 1988. The result was the rapid entry and growth of private banks. Between 1978 and 1995 the number of banks almost doubled and the number of bank branches more than tripled. According to the Asian Development Bank, the regulatory and legal structure was simply unable to manage a much more diversified and competitive banking system.[18] For one thing, there was a deficiency of banking supervisors and auditors. In consequence, there was a serious decline in the standards of credit evaluation, supervision and portfolio quality. Large bank losses followed.

Further expanding the moral hazard umbrella has been the treatment of weak or failing banks in developing countries. With few exceptions the government was there to catch the falling. Even where the banking system was largely in the private sector, banks were bailed out. At the onset of the Venezuelan banking crisis in late 1993 approximately ninety percent of deposits were in private banks. Given the oligopolistic structure of the industry, with the six largest banks holding fifty-two percent of all banking assets, and with these held by just a few individuals, the ability of the supervisory authorities to effect anything other than a complete coverage of all depositors was seriously limited.[19]

In East Asia we have observed similar cases of highly concentrated banking systems, inadequate prudential regulation and supervision, implicit government guarantees, and imprudent lending resulting in financial crises and the need for large government assistance. Major government support was provided to financial institutions in Malaysia in 1985-1988, in Thailand 1983-1987, and in the Philippines between 1981 and 1987, to cite just a few examples.

A number of studies conducted by the International Monetary Fund and the World Bank in recent years on the origins of banking crises in developing economies since the early 1980s point to the weakness of prudential regulation and supervision. Where attempts were made to strengthen them they were often only made after a crisis and insufficient to prevent the next crisis. While in several cases the trigger was a major external shock, it is remarkable how many crises had contributing factors which could have been prevented by effective prudential regulation and supervision. And behind these factors has been a major source of vulnerability of banking systems in both developed and developing countries, the simple lack of independence of the financial supervisory authorities.

2.2 Moral hazard and excess borrowing

In recent years a number of authors have argued that emerging market economies are often subject to an "overborrowing syndrome" resulting from moral hazard. The source of the moral hazard is sometimes attributed, as in McKinnon (1991) and McKinnon and Pill (1996 and 1998), to explicit or more commonly implicit deposit insurance. Illustrations have been given of a number of Latin American episodes of rapid and excessive debt and investment buildup followed by financial crisis and collapse.

A difficulty with many of these arguments is that we have no good discriminating mechanism to select among alternative candidates giving rise to the moral hazard. It may be best to simply conclude, as the Bank of Korea has in the review of its financial crisis, that, "... moral hazard was prevalent among all economic actors including enterprises, financial institutions, workers, and depositors."[20] The assumed prevalence of moral hazard in Korea suggests that the true origins of the financial crisis are much deeper and more widespread than simply deposit insurance. It suggests that the roots of the crises in Asian emerging market countries are similar to those currently facing Japan, that being the incentive and information structure of the financial system and the system of corporate governance which encourages highly leveraged enterprises and intermediaries.

Regarding the role of information, we know from the theory of agency that an optimal "first-best" sharing of investment risk cannot be achieved when the agent and the principal are risk averse and there is limited information.[21] Second-best solutions can be found to reduce the costs of agency by improving the public disclosure of accounting information. In this light, consider the recent Bank of Korea explanation of the causes of its financial crisis:

> "If one thing had to be pointed out as the primary cause of the financial crisis, it would be the country's loss of confidence in the eyes of institutional investors, a loss primarily due to inadequate transparency. First, there was a loss of accounting transparency. ... It was difficult to grasp the actual status of firms. ... Their profits were often overstated by internal transactions among them. ... In the case of financial institutions, the scale of bad loans was underestimated. Figures for banks' nonperforming loans were announced by supervisory authorities, but they were underestimated by excluding substandard loans. ... Thus, banks' apparent soundness was based on unreliable figures.

> ... The lack of transparency, one of the weakest points of the Korean economy, was nothing new, and had grown up as a tradition during the thirty odd years of rapid growth. ... However, international investors did not have a full recognition of its seriousness."[22]

Here we have a puzzle. If we lean on our traditional models of lending in a world of severe information asymmetries between borrowers and lenders, we do not arrive at what has been observed in Asia, the so-called overborrowing syndrome. The now-classic Stiglitz–Weiss (1981) model, where banks face potential borrowers with projects of the same expected return but different riskiness, but are unable to differentiate between different risk classes of borrowers, leads not to excess borrowing but to less than "optimal" lending. The "equilibrium" in such a loan market should be one of credit rationing. Recognizing that raising the loan interest rate or increasing collateral requirements is likely to attract riskier borrowers and chase away good ones, as a protective device the bank resorts to restricting credit availability. Furthermore, we would expect credit rationing in a market in which loan repayment is not enforceable and where borrowers may choose not to repay when the cost of default is less than the required repayment.[23] Credit rationing could be desirable in a world of limited transparency even for "good borrowers," since with fewer defaults average lending rates would not need to incorporate a large default risk premium. Moreover, the banking system would likely be more stable, as aggregate bank profitability would be expected to improve.

We are then faced with the obvious question: If the quality of information on potential borrowers was so questionable in many of the Asian crisis countries, why was so much lent? Indeed, why in recent years were foreign lenders so willing to provide billions of dollars of credits to Asian borrowers in a world with severe information problems?

Three arguments might be given to explain the over-borrowing syndrome, which could just as well be called the over-lending syndrome: competition, long-term relationship banking, and moral hazard. The first hypothesis, related to the supply of credit, would rely on competitive forces in the financial industry, particularly like those in Korea, which saw the aggressive entry of lightly regulated noncommercial bank intermediaries. New entrants into the banking industry may not find it profitable to attract competitors' borrowers by offering lower interest rates, since lower rates will be matched for good borrowers but not for bad. Instead, both new and old intermediaries may compete by oversupplying credit at the prevailing interest rate.[24] We saw this behavior in the earlier Nordic banking crisis. This problem was likely magnified by the increased liberalization in East Asian financial markets occurring during a period of low interest rates in the major industrial countries, abundant international credit availability and the aggressive search for returns by banks and institutional investors in the major financial centers.

Alternatively, an oversupply of credit may result from the dominance of relationship banking over securities markets. This may be the case where major lending decisions are partly centralized, as they have been in some developing countries, or "encouraged" by political pressure. Where long-term relationship lending predominates and lender sunk costs have been paid in developing the relationship, the threat of a cutoff of lending may be an idle one, causing the borrower to undertake riskier projects than it would if the threat were credible. On the other hand, where lending is noncentralized, as in securities markets, the borrower may be held on a "shorter credit leash," the cutoff threat more credible and overborrowing less likely.[25]

A third possible explanation for the overborrowing/lending syndrome is moral hazard, as argued earlier. The recent frank discussion by the Bank of Korea, noting that Korean financial institutions "depended on government control and protection over a long period of time," gives us some insight into the depth of the problem. "The business style of Korean banks was usually to make loans to large enterprises and to those who were able to offer collateral such as real estate, without thoroughly screening their investment plans."[26]

The pattern of passing the ultimate credit risk "upstream" to the government is reminiscent of the "danger of financial socialism" Suzuki (1986) noted in Japan, which would ultimately harm the efficient allocation of resources. Like Japan, several East Asian countries relied on mutual risk-sharing arrangements with related firms and intermediaries and implicitly with the government to crank up corporate leverage much higher than observed in most Western economies.

Hanging the story of excess borrowing in East Asia on deposit insurance thus seems a narrow argument. Banking competition with recent entrants into the newly deregulated financial system, the pervasiveness of relationship lending in a culture of mutual risk sharing and widespread moral hazard are all likely to have contributed to the "overborrowing syndrome" in several East Asian countries.

3. FINANCIAL STRUCTURE EVOLUTION WITH LIMITED OVERSIGHT

3.1 Excess momentum and excess inertia in financial development

Evident in East Asia and a recurring problem in many developing countries has been the retarded evolution of the prudential regulatory and supervisory function, particularly after the relaxation of constraints on intermediation and the privatization of state-owned enterprises. What appears to occur is "excessive momentum" on the part of the private sector to exploit new profit opportunities and holes in the regulatory/supervisory structure and "excess inertia" on the government's side in putting in place a rigorous financial oversight function. Further inertia is seen in the frequent reluctance of regulators to force financial intermediaries to make adequate provisioning and to write off bad loans resulting from rapid credit growth soon after deregulation. The consequence has often been a combination of financial opportunism and moral hazard leading to excessive credit growth, asset price bubbles, and financial collapse. The crisis is frequently more severe when domestic firms and banks have access to foreign capital.

The recent experience of several East Asian countries is reminiscent of the growth expectations and financial excesses seen in Chile during the late 1970s and early 1980s.[27] In the Chilean experience, considered later, we saw the contribution to excessive borrowing of each of the factors mentioned earlier: relationship lending, wherein Chilean large conglomerates owned banks; aggressive competition, often from nonbank intermediaries; and embedded moral hazard. As argued by Edwards and Edwards (1987), because of the degree of moral hazard in the banking system, depositors had little incentive to try to discriminate between sound and unsound banks. Similarly, Park (1998) has argued that implicit guarantees eliminated the incentive for foreign lenders to analyse carefully the credit quality of Korean banks.

The excessive growth optimism in Chile during the late 1970s, and the lack of efficient bank loan screening and monitoring are not significantly different from the conditions which preceded the recent East Asian financial crises. The current problems of Korean banks, for example, were to some extent anticipated in the work of Huh and Kim (1994). They attempted to determine whether Japan or Korea, both with heavily bank-centred financial systems, had the more "efficient" banking system by examining the bad loan rate for each country.[28] They argued that the more privately owned Japanese banking system, with substantial business loan monitoring by the main bank, was more efficient than the Korean model, where the government earlier had a major ownership in the banking system, and where "bankers were treated as civil servants" and "performance was evaluated on their compliance to the government guidelines rather than their efficient management of assets and liabilities" (p. 25). They suggest that Korean banks were earlier required by the government to understate nonperforming loans and to keep them on their books rather than taking write-offs or make loan loss provisions.

The examples of Chile and Korea facing endemic moral hazard problems and liberalization without sufficient supervision should not be taken to suggest that it is primarily developing/emerging market countries which have faced such problems. The inertia of governments in adopting adequate regulatory and supervisory systems before financial deregulation has occurred with surprising frequency in a number of industrial economies. While different in many regards, the deregulatory process, rapid credit growth, and resulting banking crisis in Sweden from 1991 to 1994 share a number of similarities to the crisis in East Asian.

For many years the Swedish banking system had been tightly regulated with the specific objective of avoiding banking failures. Between 1945 and 1983 no new private bank was created. While some inefficiencies were apparent, the confidence in the banking system was sufficient for a prominent Swedish economist to suggest in 1986 that "the idea of a run on a bank or a bank collapse is out of the question."[29] For many years there was an extensive system of formal and informal contracts between banks and industrial firms, with commercial banks replacing "market relations to their industrial clients with coordination, monitoring, and hierarchical control."[30] Long-term relations between banks and large firms were traditional in Sweden, the most notable being that between the Wallenberg Group and Stockholm's Enskilda Bank. Often relationships were cemented by a firm having only one bank.[31]

As Ingves (1997) has stated, "the financial institutions were clearly not prepared to handle financial liberalization." An easy bank life of credit rationing in Sweden gave way to intense competition, with banks struggling for market share and survival. Not unlike the state of financial oversight in some emerging market countries, the Financial Supervisory Authority (FSA), according to Ingves, "lacked the competence and the instruments to make assessments of the financial risks and other important developments pertaining to the financial institutions. ... Most importantly, guidelines for internal controls and the proper management of various risks were inadequate."

Similar to some Asian countries, the overregulation of the Swedish banking industry until the 1980s spurred the development of a largely unregulated financial sector. Constraints on the intermediated sector encouraged the growth of a non-intermediated (direct finance) sector. While the banking system was weighing under the burden of heavy liquidity ratios, requiring them to hold large quantities of public sector bonds, the non-banking financial sector grew rapidly. Finance houses sidestepped lending regulations, overreaching their original purview of leasing and factoring with heavy lending to small- and medium-size enterprises. The less-regulated finance company sector engaged in highly leveraged mortgage lending, helping to fuel a boom in real estate prices. When the collateralized asset bubble burst the finance companies fell, taking with them some of their banks. Between early 1988 and October 1990 fifty percent of Swedish finance companies went out of business. This is similar to the behavior of nonbank intermediaries in Thailand and Korea.

True, the extreme corporate leverage encouraged by implicit government guarantees in Korea was absent in the Swedish banking crisis. Nonetheless, the process of financial liberalization which saw the removal of bank liquidity ratios to control bank lending, a loss of bank lending business to the unregulated nonbank financial sector, and the elimination of constraints on bank deposit and loan rates contributed to a decline in the quality of credit screening and monitoring and a major banking crisis. As was the case in the East Asian and Chilean examples cited, the Swedish banking crisis was in part the result of insufficient supervision and prudential regulation of both banking and nonbank financial intermediaries.[32] The financial supervisory technology necessary to survive in a deregulated environment was in many cases simply not there.

3.2 Market assessment of banking system health: The weakness of market discipline

The previous sections suggest that the underlying weakness of several East Asian countries' banking systems were in some regards not unlike the vulnerability seen in the past in Latin American countries and several industrial countries once financial liberalization took place. The delayed evolution of the financial supervisory and prudential regulatory functions appear time and again, ignored during periods of prosperity and growth and only addressed once severe financial crisis emerges.

This lack of attention to improved financial oversight is surprising given the difficulty the market has in evaluating the quality of banking assets and the risk this poses to financial stability. In addition to the potential threat to stability presented by a new competitive financial environment, the difficulty the market has in assessing the quality of banking institutions adds another potential weakness.

Evidence that markets have considerable problems in evaluating the quality of banking institutions is available in the study by Randall (1989) on the ability of investors and security analysts to identify the quality of U.S. bank holding companies in the 1980s, before these institutions come into difficulty. Randall presents evidence to suggest that both the equity market and bond rating agencies were unable to identify the credit problems of large U.S. bank holding companies until it was too late. His evidence casts considerable doubt on the ability of market discipline alone to limit the credit risk intermediaries take on.

Consider the equity market assessment of the quality of banks in East Asian countries before the recent crisis. Bank shares in Indonesia and Malaysia consistently performed better than their respective overall equity index during the 1990s, then fell precipitously in 1997. In Thailand both the overall index and the bank share index increased strongly during the 1990s and fell together from 1997. Only in Korea did it appear that the equity market may have been signalling some weakness in the banking system.

It is also noteworthy that a survey of country risk seen in the eyes of leading banks, conducted by the *Institutional Investor*, failed to signal major problems in East Asia immediately before the financial crises. (Between seventy-five and 100 banks are asked to rate countries on a scale of 0 to 100; they are not allowed to rate their own country. The responses are weighted by the *Institutional Investor* according to the individual bank's worldwide exposure and the sophistication of its country risk analysis.)[33] Among the downgrades between March 1996 and March 1997 stood Thailand, Taiwan, Malaysia, and South Korea in that order, but with only Thailand displaying a large negative revision. Indeed, the overall international investment climate in the eyes of banks was quite sanguine. In March 1997, the global average country credit risk rating rose to its highest level since September 1986. The picture was bright enough for the *Institutional Investor* survey writer to conclude that for many countries "they are turning back the clock to an earlier era, when international finance seemed highly promising and less risky, when everyone knew Walter Wriston was right when he implied that countries do not go broke."[34]

3.3 Harberger redux

Thirteen-year-old Harberger (1985a and 1985b) makes good reading in the shadow of the East Asian crisis. His finger allocating the blame for the Chilean crisis of 1981–1984 pointed in several directions and his strongest criticism was reserved for policymakers. It rests with their failure to enforce "rigorous vigilance" over the behavior of Chilean banks.[35]

It pays to note how many similarities there are between the Chilean experience of the early 1980s and the current East Asian crisis. After a large downturn in 1975 partly due to fiscal tightening, real GDP increased by almost eight percent for the next five years. Growth weakened, but only modestly, in 1981. Chile fixed its exchange rate in 1979 at thirty-nine pesos to the dollar. Harberger argued, however, that the Chilean peg of the dollar was not the fundamental source of the crisis.

A central vulnerability was the banking system. After 1973 a large number of Chilean firms were returned to the private sector, many sold at auction. A good number were in weak financial condition. As banks began to accumulate bad loans they were extremely reluctant to take write-offs because of the damage it could bring to their capital position and hence to their competitiveness. Much of the credit demand during the 1975–1982 period was artificial, used to roll over debt, with the effect of crowding out legitimate credit demands and keeping real interest rates high. When eight financial institutions got into trouble in 1981, four of which were banks, they were bailed out; both depositors and other creditors were made whole. This was in keeping with the bailout of Banco Osorno several years earlier. Harberger argued forcefully that these earlier bailouts were the argument used by the international banking community to request a bailout of almost the entire banking industry when the crisis hit its peak in January 1983. The government then provided guarantees for all foreign debts of the Chilean banking system. By 1985 more than seventy percent of the banking system was controlled by the government.

Before the crisis Chile was viewed as the "darling" of the international banking community, much as several Asian countries were recently. With this darling status came an inflow of foreign capital. Earlier regulations on capital inflows—for example, on the amount and maturity of Chilean bank borrowing from foreigners—were relaxed in 1980, leading to a large inflow of capital in 1981. Few argued against this relaxation. Harberger also points his finger at the "zeal" of international bankers lending to Chile, who appeared to ignore the risk in Chilean bank portfolios. For a time Chilean bankers were borrowing at 62.5 basis points above LIBOR in the international interbank market.

Observing the questionable quality of the assets on the books of Chilean banks, the size and cost of their borrowing from abroad, one might have expected the Chilean Superintendency of Banks to step in. This did not occur with any force. Had Banco Osorno not been bailed out, Harberger suggests that both Chilean banks and the international banking community might have acted more cautiously.[36] His final lament in 1985 might be applied with equal force to the current difficulties of East Asia. "Few who have witnessed the banking disasters of Chile, Mexico and Argentina ... can doubt that the supervision of banks is indeed a most serious and important responsibility of economic policy." (p. 248).

Harberger's admonishments regarding dangerous moral hazard precedents and lax bank supervision have been repeatedly ignored by governments pushing to deregulate their financial systems. The excessive momentum to deregulate has often met with considerable inertia to seriously improve prudential regulation and supervision of aggressively competitive banking systems. The recent review of the Nordic banking crisis by IMF economists highlights the "little emphasis" the Nordic countries put on reinforcing regulatory oversight of the financial system after deregulation.[37] Indeed, in some cases the quality of the regulatory oversight of the banking system worsened after deregulation. The supervisory officials in Finland and Norway reduced on-site bank examinations, emphasizing supervision by documentation. In Norway and Sweden more attention was paid to the status of capital market improvement and less to the quality of bank risk management in the newly deregulated environment.

Thirteen years after Harberger's assessment of "what went wrong in Chile?," we now have the question being asked of East Asia. The response might be the same, that "Chile could well not have found herself in a bad problem, starting in mid-1981, had the banks been better regulated." And in fact it is. The Bank of Korea now admits that "no strict examination was carried out on the scale of nonperforming loans of the nonbank financial institutions, whose business conditions were no better and often worse than the banks."[38]

It is incorrect to suggest that all the countries currently enmeshed in financial crisis in East Asia had completely inefficient systems of prudential regulation and supervision. After earlier crises a number of countries had attempted to restructure and strengthen their financial oversight function. However, even where major improvements in bank supervision and regulation have occurred doubt may remain about the ability of financial intermediaries to sustain a sudden external shock. For example, after Argentina put in place its currency board monetary arrangement in 1991, it strengthened its bank regulation and supervision. This included a reorganization of bank supervision at the central bank, the adoption of a US-like "CAMEL" rating system for banks, and reinforced capital standards. Nonetheless, problems with provincial banks remained and were well known. When the Mexican devaluation occurred it took only the liquidity problems of a small bond trader to incite financial panic.[39]

It is not a wasted effort to recall the number of banking crises since 1980 which have had inadequate prudential supervision as an underlying cause. According to a World Bank review of banking crises, inadequate prudential regulation played a leading role in: Hong Kong, 1982–83; Japan, 1991; Chile, 1981–93; Philippines, 1981–87; Turkey, 1982–85; United States, 1979–89; to name just a few.[40] The weakness of financial oversight in East Asia was well known. In 1992 the IMF drew attention to the rapid growth and modest regulation of nonbank financial intermediaries in Korea.[41] In 1995 it pointed to the absence of adequate regulation and supervision in the APEC developing countries.[42] At the same time, some remained uncritical of the quality of banking supervision in East Asia. As recently as 1996, Stiglitz (1996, p. 258) suggested that with the exception of Indonesia, central banks in East Asia had performed a "good job" of supervising commercial bank loan portfolios.[43]

3.4 Short-term capital flows and financial immaturity

The history of financial development since the 1970s provides enough examples of financial liberalization, rapid credit growth, and asset price booms, followed by asset price collapse, for us to understand some of the origins of financial crisis. One of the triggers has been the result of a large reversal in international short-term capital flows. In the East Asian crisis we have seen a reversal of private capital flows for the five countries in difficulty of the order of $109 billion between 1996 and 1997, from a net inflow of $97 billion to a net outflow of around $12 billion (Institute of International Finance estimate). Such reversals have at times been in response to a rapid change in perceptions regarding the health of the financial system and the ability of the government to come to its aid.

A financial system with severe moral hazard problems may provide a put option to owners of financial intermediaries, particularly if they are large and politically well-connected. It presents an opportunity for individual initiatives in the financial system to prosper from success, while having losses shouldered by the government in the event of failure. Equity holders in some financial systems are able to exploit the weak information and control position of creditors and financial authorities. The incentive is for the intermediaries to take on greater risk than it might otherwise.

The regulatory, information and corporate control conditions in a number of developing financial systems often make intermediaries prime candidates for exploitation, or, as some have called it, "looting" or "go-for-broke" investment strategies.[44] There are a number of reasons such behavior may arise, many having to do with a macroeconomic objective of the government which permits private market participants to exploit a particular government vulnerability. In some cases it involves the government's desire to fix or stabilize some particular price (e.g. the exchange rate) or provide a blanket guarantee to insure stability because of severe information asymmetries in the financial system (e.g. deposit insurance). As developed by Akerlof and Romer (1993), the incentive for looting occurs because the government establishes an inefficient contract which private market participants attempt to exploit, such as non-risk-based deposit insurance. The frequently cited example of this behavior is that of the management of a number of saving and loan associations in the United States during the 1980s.

The incentive for intermediaries to exploit new opportunities provided by a more liberalized financial system are enhanced once a country has access to international capital markets. It is difficult to judge when a country is "mature" enough to permit it access to foreign capital. But it is clear what the incentive is. As Akrasansee (1998) has stated in the case of Thailand, "The argument is very simple. International capital is cheap." Despite several previous crises originating in part with large foreign short-term capital inflows, during the 1990s most emerging market countries have been reluctant to heed Harberger's (1985a) lesson from the Chilean experience of the 1980s, that some flexible restrictions on capital inflows may be desirable.[45] The near-term advantages of foreign borrowing, even for countries with high saving rates, usually outweigh the distant risk of capital flight.

Encouraged by large Thai interest rate differentials over foreign rates, large short-term capital flooded into Thailand in recent years, much of it through the Bangkok International Banking Facilities (BIBFs). Established in 1993 the BIBFs were composed of forty-five banks, thirty-four of which were foreign. They provided private institutions with ready access to foreign short-term financing at favourable rates. According to BIS statistics, total gross international claims of foreign banks on Thailand grew from almost $23 billion in 1992 to $70 billion in 1996. A fixed exchange rate meant that market participants faced no exchange risks, at least until the crisis erupted.

Thai officials admitted that their capital markets were seriously underdeveloped, with little depth in the equity market and an almost nonexistent long-term bond market.[46] The high level of private market confidence after several years of strong real growth appeared to relax concern regarding foreign indebtedness, although the Bank of Thailand was clearly worried about the large sums of foreign capital being funnelled into the real estate sector.

Thailand was not alone in availing itself to plentiful foreign capital. Several East Asian countries increased by large amounts their international indebtedness. The shift in the composition of external financing from foreign equity investment to bond and especially foreign bank financing increased the vulnerability of these countries, particularly as much of the foreign bank financing was short-term and foreign currency denominated. What is notable in the financing patterns of East Asian countries is the large amount of interbank borrowing. For example, in 1996 sixty-five percent of Korea's gross foreign bank debt was interbank.[47] The size of the short-term foreign funding in East Asia and the underdeveloped nature of their capital and money markets suggested a vulnerability of these countries to an international liquidity squeeze.

For many of the five East Asian countries currently in difficulty dependence on short-term foreign funding was a relatively recent phenomenon. The reasons for the resort to such enormous amounts of foreign financing differ by country. In Malaysia, for example, one contributing factor may have been the government's attempt to build a regional financial center. In addition, the ready availability of foreign short-term borrowing contributed in some cases to "the development of get-rich-quick, casino mentality which led to the diversion of resources from productive activities toward speculative ones," according to Piei and Ariff (1998).

In Korea the relaxation of controls on foreign borrowing in the 1990s took place without adequate supervision, particularly of merchant banks.[48] Unable to raise long-term capital because of inadequate credit ratings, merchant banks raised short-term foreign capital to fund long-term investments, resulting in a serious maturity misalignment. At one point sixty-seven percent of their borrowing was short-term and ninety-five percent of their lending long-term. Moreover, the Foreign Exchange Management Law restricted long-term foreign borrowing, while few restraints were placed on raising funds short-term.

Not unlike the earlier Nordic and Chilean banking crises, foreign capital inflows intermediated through the banking system were used to fuel a boom in asset prices, particularly in equity and real estate. Rising asset prices increased the value of collateral, inducing further lending by banks. The underdevelopment of local capital markets made hedging of long-term lending difficult. Further exposing the banks in several countries was the limited degree of bank portfolio diversification. The old cycle was repeated, this time in East Asia.

Certainly excessive lending for real estate and equity investment was not the only cause of the crisis in East Asia. Nonetheless, together with interconnected lending it was a feature shared with many earlier banking crises. A generic vulnerability has been the excess leverage in economic systems with long histories of government guarantees and poor corporate control in both financial and nonfinancial sectors. The availability of low cost foreign short-term financing provided additional resources for further exploitation of the inefficient contracts the government had with the private sector.

The dynamic mechanism which increases leverage in newly liberalized financial systems often derives from the endogeneity of credit limits. Real assets used as collateral increase credit limits as their market value rises. This can spark the beginning of an asset price bubble, as financial liberalization first relaxes credit constraints, leading to a demand for fixed assets, such as real estate, whose higher market price raises collateral values, further increasing credit availability, borrowing, and asset prices.[49] This dynamic multiplier of credit lines and asset values can become all the more rapid the poorer the quality of credit screening by intermediaries and the greater the number of new underinformed lenders, some entering as a result of capital account liberalization.

Bank funded property and equity provide lucrative private opportunities to increase the vulnerability of the government's guarantee of the liabilities of financial institutions. The difficulty of determining the fundamental value of property and equity investments, particularly for an economy with poor accounting, auditing and disclosure standards in a stage of rapid development, further stimulates bank lending based on current market collateral values. In a competitive environment, with banks having been recently released from lending and funding constraints, the incentive to finance such investments often proves irresistible.

It is not a purely academic question to ask whether international lending to some East Asian countries contributed to a run-up in corporate debt which had the characteristics, in the technical sense, of a "rational Ponzi game."[50] (Modern usage of this term does not refer to fraudulent behavior, just as asset price bubbles do not.) At the end of 1997, for example, the thirty largest Korean conglomerates had an average debt–equity ratio of 519 percent, compared with 86 percent in Taiwan, 193 percent in Japan, and 154 percent in the United States.[51] The Ponzi game characteristic is the perpetual rolling over the debt by additional borrowing. In modern parlance, the game is rational in the sense that each loan has positive net present value for the borrower. For this to be possible requires a continuous flow of new lenders into the market.

That a string of new international lenders would enter such a market is understandable when a country has grown rapidly for several years and where borrowers have for a long time enjoyed a considerable degree of government protection, as The Bank of Korea suggests large enterprises enjoyed in Korea.[52] The heavy government protection of banks is said to have emboldened Korean banks to borrow short-term and invest long-term in Southeast Asia and other emerging markets. It is somewhat of an exaggeration to claim that the East Asian crisis is different from earlier crises because of the heavy concentration of problem debt in the private sector. In some cases private debt with strong implicit government guarantees might just as well be considered quasi-sovereign obligations. In retrospect, it may not be such a surprise that international bank lending to Korea rose to such high levels in just a few years. At mid-1997, gross international claims by foreign banks on Korea totalled $104 billion, of which $68 billion was international interbank debt. As detailed by O'Connell and Zeldes (1988), to understand the ability to sustain Ponzi game credit equilibria in the international lending market it is necessary to focus on the conditions in the *lenders*' economies.[53] These conditions were such that liquidity was ample, interest rates were low, and one lender, the United States, was itself in a state of economic "euphoria" given several years of rapid growth.

4. PRECARIOUS CREDIT EQUILIBRIA

4.1 Reluctant disclosure and government risk sharing

If the East Asian financial crisis has taught us anything, it has taught us to be suspicious of any confidence we have in thinking we know what factors contribute to financial stability. It has taught us that sound macroeconomic fundamentals are not sufficient to prevent major banking crisis. Indeed, it should make us redefine what we consider to be "fundamentals" capable of sustaining a financial system through unexpected domestic and foreign asset price shocks. We have also learned that Goldsmith (1982) was off the mark when, in an attack on Minsky, he referred to financial crises as "a childhood disease of capitalism, not an affliction of old age." East Asia currently presents us with an example of a mature economy, Japan, suffering from a similar rude reversal of fortunes as five economies in much earlier stages of financial development, and partly for similar reasons. Here we focus briefly on the role of information in providing resiliency to a financial system.

Many of the banking crises of recent vintage have had as a contributing factor the absence of sound corporate governance of enterprises and intermediaries, whose components include rigorous accounting, auditing, and disclosure requirements and efficient prudential regulations and supervision. Given their deficiency in some countries, we should first ask what the motives are for their underproduction. Secondly, we need to understand why depositors, in particular international lenders, were content to place funds with intermediaries whose behavior was so difficult to monitor.

In several of both recent and past financial crises there has been evidence of wilful misrepresentation of the financial status of nonfinancial and financial enterprises. The inefficiency of external auditing and poor public disclosure is often observed even if intentional misrepresentation is not. The recent surprise failure of two large Japanese institutions, for example, recently increased the public loss of confidence in accounting, auditing and disclosure systems in Japan, creating credit risk concerns in the interbank market.[54] Inadequate transparency has also been singled out as a primary cause of financial crisis in Korea.[55] Financial crises are often first information crises.

Part of the blame for the lack of transparency of the financial status of some intermediaries rests with the regulators themselves.[56] As elsewhere, government regulators of emerging market countries are not infrequently pursuing more than a single objective, two of which are to assist with government macroeconomic objectives and desired credit allocations and to protect favored financial intermediaries or sectors from aggressive competition, foreign institutions or capital markets.[57] The underproduction of external information is often used as a protective device by financial and nonfinancial enterprises (against take-over, to secure favourable credit conditions), sometimes with the consent of regulators. Moreover, when intermediaries come under attack, opacity is sometimes used as a means of hiding their vulnerability in order to reduce the costs of restoring stability.

It would be naive to believe that depositors are completely unaware of this lack of transparency, or are completely uninformed of the quality of banking supervision and regulation.[58] They are likely aware that both intermediaries and regulators may have strong motives to delay provisioning and costly loan write-offs. We have seen this in developed countries as well. To compensate for deficiencies in external transparency, governments may extend both explicit and implicit guarantees to creditors. Limited transparency and government guarantees have permitted some nonfinancial firms to sustain, for a time, extraordinarily high debt–equity ratios and some banks to borrow heavily in the international interbank market from lenders with little knowledge of the quality of their loan portfolios or their off-balance-sheet positions. Government creditor guarantee systems thus can for a time stabilize an inherently "underinformed" financial system as long as the guarantee is credible. This credibility may be weakened, sometimes abruptly, if the market realizes that the local authorities are increasingly concealing information.

No doubt some corporate governance structures in the past have worked well with modest external disclosure. Business information in a number of countries is closely held inside interdependent industry–bank networks cemented by large cross-shareholdings and systems of mutual risk sharing.[59] In some cases government regulators are part of this inside information network. However, this lack of transparency can at times result in an overreaction of doubtful creditors, particularly where information is difficult to verify.

The crisis in East Asia is in many ways a crisis of corporate control and information structure. The underproduction of public information may have been an element in their stability, both economic and political, as long as any excesses of the participants were not great enough to threaten the solvency of strategic members of the group, particularly banks, or threaten the credibility of the government's implicit guarantees. This weakness of public information and corporate governance structures in several East Asian countries contributed to the "overinvestment" by industrial firms and the "interconnected lending" by banks we now frequently see reference to.[60] It also contributed to weak prudential oversight, to the ability of banks to delay provisioning and to overstate their capital positions.[61] The lack of transparency is now making more difficult the restoration of confidence.

4.2 Unstable risk preferences and capital flow volatility: a stylized characterization

The Asian crisis illustrates once again that the incentives for the private sector of emerging market countries to build up large foreign currency exposures have not been matched by the incentives for governments to improve the transparency and rigorous oversight of their financial systems.[62]

An important question is why we did not earlier observe greater foreign lender "equilibrium credit rationing" in East Asia, as we might have expected given the information problems which existed and the potential unenforceability of some international claims. The factor which might help to explain this phenomenon is the role played by implicit government guarantees to lenders.[63] The problem of asymmetric information in international credit markets appears to be ignored when a government's implicit guarantee is credible but amplified when, for some reason, the ability of the government to satisfy the implicit guarantee becomes doubtful.[64] The deficiency of international borrower transparency, underemphasized in good "states of the world," can lead to a rapid exit of foreign lenders when either the guarantee is brought into question or the foreign lending institution itself is in difficulty and needs to retrench by calling in loans. The international banking market works surprisingly smoothly in one instance, given the information gaps, but suffers from extreme credit rationing in another, as if lenders cannot distinguish between good and bad borrowers.[65] The result can be market failure and the rapid disappearance of liquidity.

The international interbank market might be thought of as having a "precarious credit equilibrium," where at some point lenders may feel they hold potentially legally unenforceable claims, mistrust the quality of public information on the borrower and question the credibility of any government guarantees.[66] Lending banks are also aware that as the capital position of poorly supervised borrowing banks weakens there may be strong incentives for them to take on additional risk.

This stylized characterization of the international banking market as one having severe asymmetric information problems combined with implicit government guarantees for large institutions is obviously an oversimplification. But there is an element of truth in the story.[67] The international interbank market is in some regards similar to the foreign exchange market when the government has a fixed exchange rate commitment. The government is not attempting to stabilize a relative price but a quantity, the liquidity of the banking system. The credibility of the implicit commitment to assist a banking sector in difficulty depends on how large the problem is perceived to be. The lack of transparency makes this evaluation difficult.

Guttentag and Herring (1985) earlier raised the issue of official implicit guarantees when considering how the international interbank market avoided disruption from several major shocks which occurred between the 1974 Herstatt crisis and the run on Continental Illinois several years later. Their "suspicion" was that the stability was less the result of the quality of credit evaluation and monitoring of banks in the interbank market but more the implicit guarantees provided by official institutions.[68]

Foreign lenders no doubt are aware of the conflicting incentives of the government, banks and their regulators in the borrower countries and the potential for misrepresentation of the depth of a bank loan problem. The difficulty of verifying the quality of information on borrowers may significantly increase perceptions of credit risks, leading in extreme cases to the equivalent of a bank run. Hence, we might observe a sudden sharp adjustment in lender risk preferences, from modest risk aversion to a widespread flight from risk and a search for safe assets. This appears to be occurring in East Asia.

What is surprising in retrospect is the size and speed with which foreign claims on private institutions grew in East Asia, in spite, in many cases, of limited transparency on the financial status of borrowers. Even when there were signs of potential vulnerability we still observed large short-term capital inflows into several East Asian countries. Korea again provides an example: international interbank claims on Korea continued to grow rapidly between 1994 and 1996 when Korean bank profitability was weakening and bank share prices declining.

The precarious nature of the credit equilibrium in Asian countries was also the result of the conditions of the lending countries over the past several years, as described in the latest Annual Report of the Bank for International Settlements.[69] The earlier increase in international portfolio investor risk preferences, sometimes described as a greater "appetite for risk," was encouraged by the relatively easy monetary policies in the major industrial economies, reflected in low interest rates and abundant liquidity. This liquidity was directed at the high growth countries of East Asia, as well as the equity markets in the industrial countries. Spreads on U.S. dollar sovereign international bonds over U.S. Treasury yields fell dramatically for Latin American issuers from 1995 through mid-1997 and remained very small for Asian borrowers. They have recently dramatically increased.

The picture painted here is one of an earlier abundance of international liquidity and of declining risk aversion of international lenders confronting investment opportunities in high growth Asian emerging market countries. What may have brought these two together was the assumption, based on the past behavior of governments, of large implicit credit guarantees for the banking systems of borrowing countries. The impression that these guarantees could not be sustained led to an enormous exodus of foreign short-term capital. We are now observing the second leg of what is here described as a precarious credit equilibrium, a major international investor flight from risk.

5. CONCLUSION

In 1985 Carlos Diaz-Alejandro stated that "the financial history of Latin America remains to be written." Thirteen years later we can reply that it has been, but no one was reading it. During the early 1980s economists talked of the "Chilean miracle" and of its "remarkable fiscal performance," similar to the euphoria over the "Asian miracle" and Asia's solid macroeconomic fundamentals. In both cases extreme optimism was followed by sudden dismay and financial disarray. The discussion has now changed dramatically, as we attempt to understand why so many were so slow to learn from earlier crises. The financial crisis of East Asia is different from the Chilean crisis of the early 1980s in that an unsustainable exchange rate policy, with the exception of Thailand, was not an obvious trigger for the crisis. Aside from this difference, many of the elements that eventually brought Chile to the brink are similar to those which have seriously weakened Korea, Thailand, Malaysia, Indonesia, and the Philippines, all factors which contributed to a "significant microeconomic misallocation of credit."

In searching for an understanding of the origins of the Asian crisis we need to study carefully both the demand and supply sides of emerging economy financial markets and ask what elements contributed most to the misallocation of credit and the liquidity crisis. This paper has focused on the contribution of government guarantee induced moral hazard problems to the behavior of large borrowers and lenders in recently deregulated financial systems. We have emphasized the immature nature of some of these systems, their bank domination, and their underlying structural vulnerability. The weaknesses in financial transparency, corporate governance, and prudential regulation and supervision in a high-growth environment led to excessive credit creation, an asset price boom, and large foreign currency exposure. Banking systems intermediating enormous short-term capital inflows took on risks they could not properly manage. As in several previous crises, a serious vulnerability was the loosely regulated behavior of aggressive nonbank financial intermediaries. We have tried to emphasie that this pattern of behavior was by no means unique to East Asia, nor the resulting crises. Countries which have significantly deregulated their financial systems have often been slow to improve market-driven corporate governance and credit screening and monitoring structures which might contribute to their financial stability. They have also been slow to reinforce the prudential regulation and supervision of bank and new nonbank financial intermediaries.

On the supply side attention has been drawn to the precarious credit equilibrium in international banking markets, in which there appears to be a surprising lack of desirable credit rationing in the face of major deficiencies in borrower transparency, which can during stress periods lead to severe credit rationing and a liquidity crisis. Foreign lenders may have relied excessively on implicit government guarantees in extending large credits to

East Asian borrowers. This too is behavior we have earlier observed in Latin American crises. Many investors were aware that the financial transparency of individual enterprises and intermediaries was wanting in East Asian countries. Moreover, there was plenty of available evidence pointing to the serious deficiencies of banking supervision and prudential regulation. Few appeared to heed these signs.

Finally, we should ask whether it is desirable to take more seriously McKinnon's (1991) suggestion that the international capital market should move in the direction of its late-nineteenth century status where international capital flows were intermediated much less by banks and presented less of a danger to domestic and international financial systems.

Acknowledgments: The views expressed in this paper are those of the author and in no way represent an official view of the Bank for International Settlements. My thanks to Bob Aliber, Chris Bennett, Florence Béranger, Henri Bernard, João Cabral dos Santos, Charles Freeland, Steve Kamin, Jean-Marie Kertudo, and Hoil Oh for helpful comments and assistance.

Notes

[1]World Bank (1993), p. 224.

[2]See Goldstein and Turner (1996). In 1994 between sixty-four percent and ninety-one percent of financial intermediation in Indonesia, Malaysia, and Thailand was bank intermediation. Before 1983 eighty percent of bank deposits in Indonesia were in state-owned banks. McKinnon (1991) emphasizes the danger of the combination of moral hazard and financial repression, with real interest rates below a loan-rationing equilibrium.

[3]This story for East Asia is described in World Bank (1993). Even loans from foreign banks came under the influence of the government. For example, in 1986 when foreign banks were given access to the Bank of Korea's rediscount facilities for export financing and commercial bills they were required to devote a percentage of their lending to "priority sectors." See Layman (1988).

[4]See Stiglitz and Uy (1996) and Folkerts-Landau et al. (1998) on directed credit allocation in East Asia. The latter reports that policy loans amounted to almost half of commercial bank lending in Korea in 1990, ten years after banks were privatized.

[5]Suzuki (1986), pp. 17–25.

[6]See Stiglitz (1991) on the role of government in promoting economic development and the dominance of banks over securities. Rojas-Suárez and Weisbrod (1995) emphasize the large role of banks in Latin America. Cho (1986) argues that government intervention in credit markets may be desirable when equity markets are absent and some borrowers, because of information asymmetries, would be unable to obtain finance. However, he admits that forced lending is often inefficient and subject to political corruption.

[7]Standard and Poor's (1998a).

[8]See Edwards (1995), chapter four for an interesting discussion of the Chilean groupos.

[9]See Krugman's (1994) interpretation of Asia's economic miracle as a myth.

[10]This argument is made by Greenspan (1998), who suggests that creditor banks in the international interbank market may have expected claims on banks in emerging market countries to be protected by a safety net. Hence interbank claims may have been considered to be sovereign lending.

[11]World Bank (1993), p. 215.

[12]Deposit insurance was introduced in Korea only in 1996.

[13]World Bank (1993), p. 215.

[14]Lightly regulated finance companies played a big role in undermining financial stability in Thailand and earlier in Sweden. Such institutions were often owned or funded by banks, as they were in Sweden, engaging in activities banks were restrained from conducting.

[15]See Edwards and Edwards (1987), Edwards (1995), Rojas-Suárez and Weisbrod (1995), Sundararajam and Baliño (1991), and Garcia-Herrero (1997). Note that financial liberalization in Korea did not immediately lead to a major expansion in credit growth as seen in most countries following deregulation. On this point see W-A. Park (1996).

[16]J-S. Park (1998).

[17]Y-C Park (1996) provides an overview of the financial liberalization experience in Korea.

[18]See Dickie (1997).

[19]Garcia-Herrero (1997).

[20]Bank of Korea (1998), p. 11.

[21]See Barnea, Haugen, and Senbet (1985).

[22]The Bank of Korea (1998), pp. 9–10. Similarly, Thailand has admitted having difficulty in negotiating with foreign investors in seeking to recapitalize its banking system because of information disclosure problems. See Bank of Thailand (1998), pp. 65–66. Poor accounting standards were known to exist in many of the APEC developing countries. For example, an IMF study in 1995 found an absence of standards to ensure consistency in financial accounting by banks in Indonesia and a limited ability of auditors to inspect company accounting documents in the Philippines. See Folkerts-Landau et al. (1995).

[23]Such a model is considered in Jaffee and Russell (1976). The bank may ration credit in order to insure that the cost of default remains greater than the repayment. Implicit government guarantees would tend to reduce the cost of default. Allen (1983) extends the

Jaffee–Russell result by considering an endogenous cost of default, this being the exclusion from the loan market. If this threat is credible credit will be rationed. An ample supply of alternative credit sources and implicit government credit guarantees would reduce the potential cost of default, and reduce the likelihood of credit rationing.

[24]See Stiglitz and Weiss (1981), p. 409.

[25]This point is rigorously made by Dewatripont and Maskin (1995). Miller (1998) offers the advice that Southeast Asia and China should follow the U.S. example and shrink their banking industry, calling banking a "disaster-prone nineteenth century technology." Instead, they should rely on market alternatives to bank loans.

[26]The Bank of Korea (1998), p. 12.

[27]See Edwards and Edwards (1987), chapter three.

[28]Weinstein and Yafeh (1998) argue that close bank–firm relationships in bank-centered financial systems benefit banks more than it does firms. In the case of Japan they show that main bank clients did not grow faster nor were more profitable than firms without main bank ties.

[29]Jonung (1986), p. 116. See Englund (1990) on financial deregulation in Sweden.

[30]Lindgren (1990), p. 264.

[31]It should be mentioned that historically the large banks in Sweden have had quite good systems of credit analysis and loan performance monitoring.

[32]Drees and Pazarbasioglu (1998) provide a good overview of financial liberalization in the Nordic countries.

[33]See Shapiro (1997) for a discussion of country risk ratings before the East Asian crisis.

[34]ibid., p. 201.

[35]Harberger's arguments were not ignored by everyone in East Asia. Park (1991) repeats Harberger's claim that the Chilean crisis could have been avoided with better banking regulation. Velasco (1991) provides a comprehensive overview of the Chilean liberalization and crisis between 1975 and 1985. He argues that the interlocking ownership arrangements between firms and banks were the root source of the excessive loan growth and the ultimate financial collapse in Chile.

[36]The Chilean experience of the 1980s has not been forgotten—at least in Chile. Le-Fort (1994) argues that three conditions made the Chilean financial system vulnerable and potentially subject to crisis: (1) implicit deposit insurance made depositors (domestic and foreign) ignore portfolio risk; moreover, the government did not regulate and supervise banks because the authorities felt this should be left to the market; (2) excessive growth optimism deflected concern with levels of indebtedness; and (3) some of the major banks were members of large conglomerates, their capital was marginal and the banks were used to grant loans to enterprises within the conglomerate, at rates and conditions to the disadvantage of the bank. Some of these conditions also existed in Asian countries currently in crisis. In the 1986 Chilean banking law reform, the Superintendency of Banks and Financial Institutions was

required to publish in the press each year the condition of individual banking institutions. Another major change in banking law was in the requirements for bad loan provisioning.

[37]See Drees and Pazarbasioglu (1998).

[38]Bank of Korea (1998), p. 10.

[39]See Garcia-Herrero (1997) for details.

[40]World Bank (1993), pp. 249–251.

[41]Bisat, Johnston, and Sundararajan (1992), p. 55.

[42]Folkerts-Landau et al. (1995).

[43]Stiglitz (1996, p. 272) suggests that it was "remarkable" that East Asian governments took action to address financial market failure, "such as prudential regulation," at an earlier stage of development than that seen in industrial countries.

[44]Akerlof and Romer (1993) provide a simple model of looting and go-for-broke strategies, together with several interesting examples. Krugman (1998a) picks up on this theme to analyze the Asian financial crisis.

[45]Krugman (1998b) is one of the few academics to consider the potential desirability of exchange controls to permit lower interest rates in East Asia. Governor Gramlich (1998) of the Federal Reserve admits to there being "occasional instances" when some capital flow restrictions may be justified.

[46]Akrasanee (1998).

[47]See Bank for International Settlements, sixty-eighth Annual Report, Chapter VII, for a discussion of financial intermediaries and the Asian crisis. Much of this analysis reflects the work of Philip Turner.

[48]See Kim and Rhee (1998).

[49]A model of the dynamic interaction between credit limits and asset prices is presented in Kiyotaki and Moore (1997).

[50]See O'Connell and Zeldes (1988) on rational Ponzi games.

[51]Bank of Korea (1998), p. 12.

[52]The Bank of Korea (1998) suggests that it was "an unwritten law" that "conglomerates will never go broke" (p. 11).

[53]See O'Connell and Zeldes (1988), pp. 445–446. The perpetual rollover of debt "equilibrium" requires that the growth rate of the lending country exceeds the rate of growth of debt of the borrowing country.

[54]Fukao (1998) suggests that the mistrust of the internal auditing systems in Japan is causing concern over the execution of the fiduciary responsibilities of some intermediaries.

[55]Bank of Korea (1998), p. 9.

[56]Kane (1998) emphasizes the incentive conflicts of government regulators. Kane (1991) considers an incentive-based theory of financial regulation.

[57]Calomiris (1998) quotes a former Chilean finance minister who describes how the superintendency of banks was restrained from providing an independent judgement of bank exposure to foreign exchange risk because of its potential conflict with macroeconomic policies.

[58]Folkerts-Landau et al. (1995) pointed specifically to the weak supervisory and regulatory infrastructures in several of the APEC countries.

[59]Fukao (1998) reports that at the end of September 1997 Sanwa Bank, Tokai Bank, and Sakura Bank each held a 4.8 percent share in Toyota Motors, equal to thirty-seven percent, seventy-nine percent, and forty percent of the respective capital of these banks (at Toyota's share price of 12 February). Japanese law prohibits banks from owning more than five percent of the shares of one domestic company, but does not restrict the total amount of stock that is owned.

[60]In some cases banking reforms to correct these problems were made more difficult due to banks being owned by or closely related to business conglomerates, as in Indonesia. See Nasution (1995).

[61]See Bank for International Settlements (1998), pp. 118–121.

[62]Korea, for example, known for having followed a gradual pace of financial liberalization, saw gross foreign bank claims on Korea rise from $28.7 billion in 1990 to $100 billion in 1996, of which two-thirds were interbank claims. (BIS statistics.) Net foreign debt grew by thirty-three percent per year from 1994 to 1997, twice as fast as between 1979 and 1985, when Korea last experienced serious financial difficulty. Kim and Rhee (1998), p. 21

[63]Diaz-Alejandro (1985, p. 8) conjectured that after the bailout of Banco Osorno in 1977, partly because of the authorities' concern with the possible impact of its failure on foreign lending to Chile, foreign creditors interpreted lending to the Chilean private sector as guaranteed by the state.

[64]The credibility of government implicit guarantees is obviously difficult to judge. One measure might be, for example, Standard & Poor's sovereign "contingent liability estimates," representing the potential peak of gross problematic assets in the financial system as a percentage of domestic credit to the private sector and nonfinancial public enterprises in the event of a worst-case recession. See Standard & Poor's (1998b).

[65]Recall that the early models of imperfect information credit markets, such as Jaffee and Russell (1976), emphasized the potential unstable nature of these markets and the possibility of their collapse. McKinnon (1991), chapter ten, has argued that in the past both implicit guarantees in the debtor countries and deposit insurance and official export–import banks in the creditor countries caused both borrowers and lenders to ignore or underestimate normal credit risks.

[66]Niehans (1985) questions the assumption of legal enforceability of claims in international credit markets.

[67]The story in many ways is not new. Diaz-Alejandro (1985) emphasized the role of implicit guarantees and poor banking supervision in the Chilean financial crises of the early 1980s. Dooley (1997) develops a similar theme, relating private capital flows to the government's implicit or explicit insurance of intermediaries.

[68]Federal Reserve Governor Ferguson (1998) has also drawn attention to the role of the implicit safety net in attracting foreign bank creditors to Asia and to the lax standards for transparency and disclosure. Once such moral hazard risk exists they may be difficult to remove. For example, up to 1979 the Argentinean central bank fully insured all depositors at its own cost. In November 1979 the central bank dramatically changed the insurance scheme, providing only limited coverage, with institutions not required to join. The new insurance system is said to have altered perceptions of bank risk, but only when failure of large institutions occurred. In fact, Balino (1991) suggests that some institutions (state banks and branches of foreign banks) which chose not to participate in the new deposit insurance programme were still thought to have de facto insurance. See also Nam (1995).

[69]Bank for International Settlements (1998), chapter seven.

References

Akerlof, George A., and Paul M. Romer. "Looting: The economic underworld of bankruptcy for profit," *Brookings Papers on Economic Activity*, No. 2, 1993.

Akrasanee, Narongchai. "Recent financial and economic crisis in Thailand," paper prepared for the Conference on Asian Crisis, co-organized by Asia-Europe Foundation and the Centre d'Etudes Prospectives et d'Informations Internationales, Paris, May 11–12, 1998.

Alchian, Armen. "Uncertainty, evolution and economic theory," *Journal of Political Economy*, June 1950.

Allen, Franklin. "Credit rationing and payment incentives," *Review of Economic Studies*, 1983.

Andersen, Palle Schelde. "Economic growth and financial markets in selected Asian countries," in *Finance and the International Economy*, Vol. 7, *The AMEX Bank Review Prize Essays*, Richard O'Brien (ed.), Oxford University Press, 1993.

Balino, Tomas J.T. "The Argentine banking crisis of 1980," in *Banking Crises: Cases and Issues*, V. Sundararajan and Tomas J. Balino (eds.), International Monetary Fund, 1991.

Bank for International Settlements, Sixty-Eighth Annual Report, June, 1998.

Bank of Korea. *Financial System in Korea*, 1995.

Bank of Korea. "Financial Crisis in Korea: Why it happened and how it can be overcome," Research Department, research paper, July 1998.

Bank of Korea. "Asset price inflation and monetary policy: the case of Korea," country paper for the EMEAP's asset pricing study, July 1998.

Bank of Thailand. *Annual Economic Report 1997*, 1998.

Barnea, Amir, Robert A. Haugen, and Lemma W. Senbet. *Agency Problems and Financial Contracting,* Englewood Cliffs, NJ: Prentice-Hall, 1985.

Bisat, Amer, R. Barry Johnston, and V. Sundararajan. "Issues in managing and sequencing financial sector reforms: lessons from experiences in five developing countries," International Monetary Fund, Washington, DC, working paper No. 92/82.

Bisignano, Joseph. "Towards an understanding of the changing structure of financial intermediation: An evolutionary theory of institutional survival," Société Universitaire Européenne de Recherches Financières, Amsterdam, SUERF Studies, No. 4, 1998.

Calomiris, Charles W. "The IMF's imprudent role as lender of last resort," *The Cato Journal* 1998.

Caprio, Gerard, Jr. "Safe and sound banking in developing countries: We're not in Kansas anymore," The World Bank, Policy research working paper, No. 1739, March 1997.

Cho,Yoon. "Inefficiencies from financial liberalisation in the absence of well-functioning equity markets," *Journal of Money, Credit, and Banking,* 1986.

Dewatripont, M., and E. Maskin. "Credit and efficiency in centralised and decentralised economies," *Review of Economic Studies*, 1995.

Diaz-Alejandro, Carlos F. "Good-bye financial repression, hello financial crash," *Journal of Development Economics*, September/October 1985.

Dickie, Paul M. "Toward resilient financial systems," in *Creating Resilient Financial Regimes in Asia: Challenges and Policy Options,* Priya Basu (ed.), proceedings of an Asian Development Bank Seminar, Manila, April 29, 1996, Hong Kong: Oxford University Press, 1997.

Dooley, Michael P. "A model of crises in emerging markets," NBER, working paper, No. 6300, December 1997.

Drees, B., and C. Pazarbasioglu. "The Nordic banking crisis: pitfalls in financial liberalization?," International Monetary Fund, Washington, DC, occasional paper, No. 161, 1998

Edwards, Sebastian. "Public sector deficits and macroeconomic stability in developing countries," in *Budget Deficits and Debt: Issues and Options,* a symposium sponsored by the Federal Reserve Bank of Kansas City, Jackson Hole, Wyoming, August 31–September 3, 1995.

Edwards, Sebastian, and Alejandra Cox Edwards. *Monetarism and Liberalisation: The Chilean Experiment,* Chicago: The University of Chicago Press, 1987.

Englund, Peter. "Financial deregulation in Sweden," *European Economic Review* 1990.

Ferguson, Roger W., Jr. "Themes in international bank supervision," speech delivered to the Federal Financial Institutions Examination Council, International Banking Council, Arlington, Virginia, July 20, 1998.

Folkerts-Landau, David, Garry J. Schinasi, Marcel Cassard, Victor K. Ng, Carmen M. Reinhart, and Michael G. Spencer. "Effects of capital flows on the domestic financial sectors in APEC developing countries," in *Capital Flows in the APEC Region* IMF occasional paper, No. 122, Moshin Khan and Carmen Rheinhart (eds.), Washington, DC: International Monetary Fund, 1998

Fukao, Mitsuhiro. "Japanese financial instability and weaknesses in the corporate governance structure," Keio University, Tokyo, Faculty of Business and Commerce, discussion paper, No. 9801, May 1998.

Garcia-Herrero, Alicia. "Banking crises in Latin-America in the 1990s: Lessons from Argentina, Paraguay, and Venezuela," International Monetary Fund, working paper, No. 97/140, October 1997.

Goldsmith, Raymond. "Comment," in *Financial Crises: Theory, History and Policy,* Charles P. Kindleberger and Jean-Pierre Laffargue (eds.), Cambridge University Press, 1982.

Goldstein, Morris, and Philip Turner. "Banking crises in emerging economies: origins and policy options," BIS economic papers, No. 46, October 1996.

Gramlich, Edward. "World capital flows: let's fix the system, not abandon it," remarks at the Carnegie Bosch Institute, University Centre of at Carnegie Mellon, Pittsburgh, September 15, 1998.

Greenspan, Alan. "Remarks at the thirty-fourth Annual Conference on Bank Structure and Competition," Federal Reserve Bank of Chicago, May 7, 1998.

Guttentag, Jack, and Richard Herring. "Funding risk in the international interbank market," in *International Financial Markets and Capital Movements: A Symposium in Honor of Arthur I. Bloomfield*, W.J. Ethier and R.C. Marston (eds.), *Essays in International Finance*, No. 157, Princeton University, September, 1985.

Harberger, Arnold C. "Observations on the Chilean Economy, 1973-1983," *Economic Development and Cultural Change*, April 1985a.

Harberger, Arnold C. "Lessons for debtor country managers and policymakers," in *International Debt and the Developing Countries*, Gordon W. Smith and John T. Cuddington (eds.), Washington, DC: The World Bank, 1985b.

Huh, Chon, and Sun Bae Kim. "Financial regulation and banking sector performance: a comparison of bad loan problems in Japan and Korea," *Economic Review*, Federal Reserve Bank of San Francisco, No. 2, 1994.

Ingves, Stefan. "Experiences from the Swedish bank crisis 1991 to 1994: With a view to strengthening future financial stability," paper presented at the conference Managing Systemic Risk, London, December 3–4 1997.

International Monetary Fund. *World Economic Outlook: Interim Assessment*, December 1997.

Ito, Takatoshi. "Japan and the Asian economies: A "miracle" in transition," *Brookings Papers in Economic Activity*, No. 2, 1996.

Jaffee, D., and T. Russel. "Imperfect information, uncertainty and credit rationing," *Quarterly Journal of Economics,* 1976.

Jonung, Lars. "Financial deregulation in Sweden," *Skandinaviska Enskilda Banken Quarterly Review,* 1986.

Kane, Edward J. "Financial regulation and market forces," *Schweizerische Zeitschrift für Volkswirtschaft und Statistik*, September 1991.

Kane, Edward J. "Offshore financial regulation competition: A force for modernisation and for crisis," paper prepared for the Conference on Financial Modernization and Regulation, Federal Reserve Bank of San Francisco, September 1998.

Kim, In-June, and Yeongseop Rhee. "Currency crisis of the Asian countries in a globalised financial market," paper presented at the Bank of Korea conference on "The implications of globalization of world financial markets," June 22–23, 1998.

Kiyotaki, Nobuhiro, and John Moore. "Credit cycles," *Journal of Political Economy*, April 1997.

Krugman, Paul. "Financial crises in the international economy," in *The Risk of Economic Crisis,* Martin Feldstein (ed.), Chicago: The University of Chicago Press, 1991.

Krugman, Paul. "The myth of Asia's miracle," *Foreign Affairs*, November/December 1994.

Krugman, Paul. "What happened to Asia?," *PK Home Page*, January 1998a.

Krugman, Paul. "Saving Asia: it's time to get radical," *Fortune*, September 7, 1998b.

Layman, Thomas A. "Monetary policy and financial reform in Korea," in *Monetary Policy in Pacific Basin Countries,* papers presented at a Conference Sponsored by the Federal

Reserve Bank of San Francisco, Hang-Sheng Cheng (ed.), Boston: Kluwer Academic Publishers, 1988.

Le-Fort, Guillermo. "The financial system and macroeconomic stability: The Chilean experience," in *Financial Sector Reforms, Economic Growth, and Stability: Experiences in Selected Asian and Latin American Countries*, Shakil Faruqi (ed.), EDI Seminar Series, The World Bank, 1994

Lee, In Ho. "Korean financial crisis: a price for a miracle," paper presented at the CEPR/ESRC/GEI Conference, World Capital Markets and Financial Crises, University of Warwick, July 24–25, 1998.

Lindgren, Hakan. "Long-term contracts in financial markets: Bank–industry connections in Sweden, illustrated by the operations of Stockholms Enskilda Bank, 1900-70," in *The firm as a nexus of treaties*, Masahiko Aoki, Bo Gustafsson and Oliver E. Williamson (eds.), Sage Publications, 1990.

Lowe, Philip. "The impact of financial intermediaries on resource allocation and economic growth," Reserve Bank of Australia, research discussion paper, No. 9213, December 1992.

McKinnon, Ronald. "The order of economic liberalisation: Lessons from Chile and Argentina," *Carnegie-Rochester Conference Series on Public Policy*, Vol. 17, Autumn 1982.

McKinnon, Ronald I. *The order of economic liberalisation: financial control in the transition to a market economy*. Baltimore: The Johns Hopkins University Press, 1991.

McKinnon, Ronald and Huw Pill. "Credible liberalization and international capital flows: The 'overborrowing syndrome," in *Financial Deregulation and Integration in East Asia*, Takatoshi Ito and Anne O. Krueger (eds.), Chicago: The University of Chicago Press, 1996.

McKinnon, Ronald, and Huw Pill. "The overborrowing syndrome: Are East Asia countries different?," in *Managing Capital Flows and Exchange Rates: Perspectives from the Pacific Basin*, Reuven Glick (ed.), Cambridge University Press, 1998.

Miller, Merton H. "The current Southeast Asia financial crisis," *Pacific-Basin Finance Journal*, August 1998.

Nam, Sang-Woo. "Korea's financial markets and policies," in *Financial sector development in Asia*, Shahid N. Zahid (ed.), Asian Development Bank, 1995.

Nasution, Anwar. "Financial sector development in Indonesia," in *Financial sector development in Asia*, Shahid N. Zahid (ed.), Asian Development Bank, 1995.

Niehans, Jurg. "International debt with unenforceable claims," Federal Reserve Bank of San Francisco, *Review*, Winter 1985.

O'Connell, S. A. and S. P. Zeldes. "Rational Ponzi games," *International Economic Review,* 1988.

Park, Jong-Suk. "The nature and role of deposit insurance in Korea," paper presented at the International Conference on Deposit Insurance, Federal Deposit Insurance Corporation, September 8–11, 1998.

Park, Won-Am. "Financial liberalization: the Korean experience," in *Financial Deregulation and Integration in East Asia*, Takatoshi Ito and Anne O. Krueger (eds.), Chiago: The University of Chicago Press, 1996.

Park, Yung Chul. "What have we learned from the Korean financial crisis?," Korean Institute of Finance, paper prepared for the CEPII conference on the Asian Crisis, Paris, May 11–12, 1988.

Park, Yung Chul. "East Asian liberalization, bubbles, and the challenge from China," *Brookings Papers on Economic Activity,* No. 2, 1996.

Park, Yung Chul. "Financial repression and liberalization," In *Liberalization in the Process of Economic Development*, Lawrence B. Krause and Kim Kihwan (eds.), Berkeley: University of California Press, 1991.

Piei, Mohd Haflah, and Mohamed Ariff. "Crisis and lessons of the Asian Crisis: Malaysian Perspective," Malaysian Institute of Economic Research, paper, May 1998.

Radelet, Steven, and Jeffrey D. Sachs. "The East Asia financial crisis: diagnosis, remedies, prospects," *Brookings Papers on Economic Activity*, No. 1, 1998.

Radelet, Steven, and Jeffrey Sachs. "The onset of the East Asia financial crisis," Harvard Institute for International Development, mimeo, March 30, 1998.

Randall, Richard A. "Can the market evaluate asset quality exposure in banks?," *New England Economic Review*, Federal Reserve Bank of Boston, July/August 1989.

Rojas-Suarez, Liliana, and Steven R. Weisbrod. "Financial fragilities in Latin America: The 1980s and the 1990s," *Occasional Paper No. 132*, International Monetary Fund, 1995.

Shapiro, Harvey, D. "How high is up?," *Institutional Investor*, March 1997.

Standard & Poor's. "Sovereign credit analysis: New environment after Asian crisis," *Standard and & Poor's Credit Week*, February 18, 1998a.

Standard & Poor's. "Global financial system stress: leading indicators signal pressure in sixteen countries," *Standard and & Poor's Credit Week*, September 16, 1998b.

Stiglitz, Joseph E., and Andrew Weiss. "Credit rationing in markets with imperfect information," *American Economic Review*, June 1981.

Stiglitz, Joseph E. "Governments, financial markets, and economic development," NBER, working paper No. 3669, April 1991.

Stiglitz, Joseph E., and Marilou Uy. "Financial markets, public policy, and the East Asian miracle," *The World Bank Research Observer*, August 1996.

Sundararajan, V., and Tomas J. T. Balino. "Issues in recent banking crises," in *Banking Crises: Cases and Issues*, V. Sundararajan and Tomas J.T. Balino (eds.), International Monetary Fund, 1991

Suzuki, Yoshio. *Money, Finance, and Macroeconomic Performance in Japan,* New Haven, CT: Yale University Press, 1986.

Velasco, Andrés. "Financial crises and balance of payments crises: A simple model of the Southern Cone experience," in *International Trade, Investment, Macro Policies and History: Essays in Memory of Carlos f. Diaz-Alejandro,* P. Bardhan, A. Fishlow and J. Berhman (eds.), Amsterdam, North-Holland, 1987.

Velasco, Andrés. "Liberalization, crisis, intervention: the Chilean financial system, 1975-85." in *Banking Crises: Cases and Issues*, V. Sundararajan and Tomas J.T. Balino (eds.), International Monetary Fund, 1991.

Weinstein, David E., and Yishay Yafeh. "On the costs of a bank-centred financial system: Evidence from the changing main bank relations in Japan," *Journal of Finance*, April 1998.

World Bank. "The East Asian miracle: Economic Growth and Public Policy," *World Bank Policy Research Report*, Oxford University Press, 1993.

World Bank. "Global development finance: Analysis and summary tables," Washington, DC, 1998.

Chapter 8

Causes and Implications of the Asian Crisis: An Indonesian View

J. Soedradjad Djiwandono
Bank of Indonesia

1. INTRODUCTION

As it has been said by many, the Asian crisis stands out as one of the major crises of the century, especially for those economies which are experiencing the turmoil. The impact of the crisis has been so devastating that even pessimists acknowledge that it has been worse than their expectations. Indonesia, together with Thailand and South Korea, has been suffering more than others have. And it is certainly indisputable to argue that, among the three, the Indonesian case is the worst. In terms of the decline in economic growth, depreciation of the currency, social dislocation, and other problems, Indonesia has undoubtedly suffered the most.

I will discuss the causes and implications of the crisis, the role of the financial sector, and domestic policies as they have been unfolding in Indonesia with a view to the Asian context. By offering an assessment of how the crisis has been unfolding, the policy responses by the monetary authority, and reactions from the market players, one could get a clearer picture of the crisis facing the Indonesian economy and the contagious process impacting the Asian economies.

2. THE CRISIS

There have been so many conferences and writings on the Asian crisis, discussing the causes, the implications, as well as lessons to be learned from it, and one could be sure that studies about the crisis and its implications will continue in the years to come. This is due to the fact that despite the attention that it received, the crisis has been going on for a period longer than people thought. And the effects have been more devastating than most of us expected. There have even been signs recently that it could be developing into a global crisis.

Current views on causes of the crisis could be separated into two catagories. First, those who view the origin of the crisis as domestically grown, arising from practices of crony capitalism and weak financial structures plus inept macro policies. Second, those who view the contagion process triggered by a shift in the market sentiment, in other words external factors, as the origin of the crisis. It is my view that the Indonesian crisis came from a combination of contagion from outside the national economy on the one hand and weak domestic economic and financial structures on the other. The contagion factor of the crisis was emanating from a sudden change in market sentiment in the region that led to a shock in the currency markets of the region. This led to paniced selling of local currencies for dollars. The shift in market sentiment was demonstrated by the rapid downgrading process of the region's sovereign credit ratings and, in the media, the disappearance of the term "Asian miracle" to be replaced by "crisis," or "meltdown." But, the most telling was the Institute of International Finance's publication on capital flows for Thailand, Malaysia, Indonesia, the Philippines, and South Korea, which showed a dramatic shift from inflows of $93 billion in 1996 to outflows of $12 billion in 1997, or a change of capital flows of $105 billion in a single year. For Indonesia, the reversed capital flows of last year were estimated to reach $22 billion, from inflows of $10 billion to outflows of $12 billion

Confronted with the contagion effects, the Indonesian economy, which had been suffering from inefficiency in the real sector (a high cost economy suffering from crony capitalism) and a weak financial system—banking in particular—could not cope with the shock. The domino effect of the weakening rupiah adversely affected the financial sectors, and on into the real sectors of the national economy. Thus, a combination of severe external shocks, triggered by changes in market sentiments, and financial real-sector structural weaknesses had caused a contagions process that ultimately severely damaged the whole economy.

The contagion process has been working not just across geographical or national borders. Within a country, it trespasses all aspects of lives, from economic to social and political. As I observed, in Indonesia the spread from economic crisis to a social and political crisis was also through a contagion process, which was facilitated by inherent weaknesses in our social and political systems.

A more careful study on the causes of the collapse of the Indonesian economy over the past year has to be conducted. However, it seems clear that a combination of political and economic forces, both external as well as domestic, had been at work such that when a contagion effect from the Thai baht devaluation hit the rupiah, the Indonesian economy was already collapsing.

But, how did the crisis develop? Basically, the Indonesian crisis originated from an ordinary currency problem, when rupiah suffered from sudden pressure in July of last year, after the floating of Thai baht in early July 1997. However, after a process of policy responses by the government and reaction from the market, the problems spread rapidly and deeply to effect all sectors of the national economy, before finally impacting politics.

The process of how the crisis developed in Indonesia could be described as followed:

- It started with market pressure on the rupiah as part of the contagion effects from imbalances in the currency markets in the region. Facing such pressure in the currency market, the government, based on its exchange rate management policy of a managed float with creeping depreciation, which relied on the mechanism of intervention bands which had been adjusted continuously since 1994, took the decision to further widen the bands from eight percent to twelve percent on July 11, 1997—the day the Philippine peso was floated.
- The market reaction to Bank Indonesia's move was in contrast to its past pattern. Previously, every time the BI intervention bands were widened (five times from 1994 to 1997) an appreciation of the rupiah usually followed. However, this time the rupiah rapidly depreciated instead. When the spot rate crossed the BI-selling rate, some intervention in the currency market was exercised. This intervention began with forward sales of dollars in the beginning, and later progressed to spot sales. The pressure on the rupiah was not abating, however, despite market intervention by the central bank.
- Bank Indonesia floated the rupiah on August 14, 1997. Intervention in both the forward and spot markets was continued. To support the

currency intervention, monetary tightening, through monetary and fiscal means, was conducted.

- After Bank Indonesia intervened in the market several times and exercised monetary tightening, the problems started to spread to include the banking sector. The Indonesian banking industry started to experience distress. And, as the problems continued, confidence in the banking sector started to decline. The banking sector experienced the familiar process of *flight to quality and flight to safety*. A crisis of confidence started to appear, through the weakening of the rupiah, tiering of the interbank money market, and a loss of confidence from bank depositors and creditors.
- After some time, the real sector started to feel the impact since banks reduced their lending and lending rates rose dramatically. The banking sector experienced a *crisis,* especially after the closing of the sixteen insolvent banks. Thus, starting from currency shocks and the rupiah crisis, through to banking distress and a banking crisis, the final result was a total economic crisis.[1]
- The impact of the economic crisis on politics and society almost became self-fulfilling. When economic recession became a reality, social unrest broke out everywhere and public confidence in the government and the national leadership was gone.

3. DOMESTIC POLICIES

The initial policy response to the currency problem was prompt. It started with an immediate step to widen the central bank intervention bands in the foreign exchange market, soon after the Thai baht was floated early in July 1997. However, a completely different reaction came from the market. On previous occasions, every time Bank Indonesia widened the intervention bands—five times since 1994—the rupiah was appreciated. In fact, previously the dollar spot rates followed closely the buying rates of Bank Indonesia. But, this time, the rupiah depreciated after the bands were widened. The spot rate of the dollar not only broke through the mid-rate, but it also broke through the central bank's selling rate. The latter prompted Bank Indonesia to intervene in the market. It could now be said that what happened in July 1997 was definitely different from previous periods of pressure in the currency market. It was, to be sure, a contagion effect in progress.[2] This is "the wake up call" argument for the Asian crisis. Investors basically believed that Southeast Asian economies had similar weak conditions such as crony capitalism practices and weak financial systems. In this condition, a shift in market sentiment leads investors to follow their "herd instinct" that tells them to move their capital out of Asia.

Faced with persistent pressure on the rupiah, the government intervened in the foreign exchange market, first by selling dollar forward, and later, in the spot market. When these efforts could not strengthen the rupiah, Bank Indonesia discarded the managed floating exchange system, and floated the rupiah freely in mid-August 1997. These were done with the support of monetary tightening through drastic increases in interest rates, administrative intervention, as well as fiscal tightening. But, partly due to the monetary and fiscal tightening, the weak banking sector started to suffer from distress. In fact, a sizeable bank (Bank Dannamon) had suffered from a run in late August 1997.

Realizing the fact that the problem had spread to the banking sector, in early September 1997 the government launched a broad economic policy initiative, which encompassed not just monetary and fiscal measures, but also deregulation steps in the real sector. This was a precursor of an IMF-supported program, which came later, at the end of October 1997.

The IMF-supported program was introduced through a letter of intent with a Memorandum on Economic and Financial Policies (MEFP), submitted to the fund on October 31, 1997. The program was comprised of a package of policies for economic reform in the real sector and financial restructuring to be supported with prudent monetary and fiscal policy. The monetary and fiscal measures were comprised of standard programs of macroeconomics management to cope with exchange rates and other monetary variable issues together with fiscal ramifications.

The core of the program was comprised of a comprehensive policy package to deal with insolvent and weak banks and the financial infrastructure, including the strengthening of banking supervision, and to overcome structural rigidities in the real sector of the economy. Thus, a framework was put in place for a comprehensive policy to restore confidence and arrest the decline of the rupiah. In essence, the program was built around three areas:

- A strong macroeconomics framework designed to achieve an orderly adjustment in the external current account, incorporating substantial fiscal adjustments as well as a tight monetary stance,
- A comprehensive strategy to restructure the financial sector, including early closing of insolvent institutions, and
- A broad range of structural measures which also improve governance.

Initially, the implementation of the program received a positive response from the market, the external market in particular. The closing of sixteen insolvent banks and joint intervention in the currency market by Bank Indonesia, together with the Monetary Authority of Singapore and the Bank of Japan, were welcomed by the (external) market and resulted in the strengthening of the rupiah, temporarily stabilized it at a stronger rate—from 3,900 rupiah to 3,200 rupiah to the dollar.

However, the domestic reaction to the closing of banks was the reverse of what was expected. It was ironic that a step, which was designed to return confidence to the banking sector, instead resulted in the collapse of confidence, which plunged the banking sector into chaos. The banking sector has suffered from a "flight to safety and to quality" since then. Many banks lost their deposit base, the inter bank money market suffered from compartmentalisation, and since January 1998, letters of credit issued by Indonesian banks were not accepted abroad. The problems of confidence in the national economy basically involved three areas: the rupiah exchange rate which was weakening dramatically against the dollar, the banking sector which was losing its deposit base as well as creditors, and the business sector that was unable to repay foreign debts.

After some flip-flop implementation of the IMF-supported program with a record four letters of intent in seven months, coupled with social unrest spearheaded by continuous students' demonstrations, the confidence problem shifted from not just an economic problem but to a problem of national leadership as well. When Suharto was still in power the overriding question was his sincerity in implementing the difficult reform program. Actually, the market—the foreign market—lauded the closing of sixteen insolvent banks in particular. But domestically the closing of banks was badly received. It even caused further loss of confidence in the banking system. However, when some political intervention by the government was suspected on the execution of bank closures, the foreign market started to react negatively also. This had basically transformed the banking sector from a state of distress into a crisis when market confidence was almost completely lost.

The negative reaction to the implementation of the reform program was more pronounced when a reversal was announced to postpone big government projects. At about the same time there was a reappearance of monopoly practices and some other inconsistencies in the implementation of the program for restructuring the real sector. This was how market confidence evaporated in the government's commitment to the program for economic restructuring. As a result, the rupiah's downward slide was not just difficult to stop, but the economic crisis was rapidly shifting into a total crisis in a downward spiral. President Suharto had to pay dearly for not addressing the problem head-on by resigning in humiliation on May 21, 1998.

In five months after his unexpected elevation as the new president, Dr. Habibie has been surprising many people as a national leader who has been trying very hard to do and say things that are politically correct. He has been making positive steps in human rights and scoring some points in strengthening the rupiah. But, has he been successful in eliminating the loss of confidence in the national leadership to be able to lead the government and the nation to implement the national program for restructuring economic and political lives in Indonesia? At this point the answer is no.

Despite the good publicity that President Habibie has been receiving so far, the market has not been impressed with his leadership. In fact, statistics on maroeconomic indicators have shown a gloomier picture in terms of GDP growth prospects, the inflation rate, the budget deficit, and the situation with regard to food and other basic commodities. The rupiah has been strengthening somewhat, possibly due to some encouraging news recently about the $8 billion loan for fast disbursement from the CGI. But, the bad news from Japan and its implication for Asia and the still unclear government position about some social issues seem to have caused lukewarm attitude of the market so far. Investors and creditors keep saying that they still want to wait for the return of social and political stability first before they are willing to invest in or lend to Indonesia. They trust the long-term potential but are waiting for some time before resuming their activities in Indonesia. In other words, despite the positive public reception to some statements or steps that President Habibie has recently made, questions are still being raised, if not on whether he is sincere, on whether he is able to deliver.

4. NOTES ON THE ROLE OF THE BANKING SECTOR

It has been stated above that in the Indonesian case, the crisis which came out in the beginning as a currency problem due to an external shock, through a contagious effects triggered by a shift in the market sentiment, became a fully blown crisis involving economic, social and political crisis. Weak economic structure and unsound financial system facilitated the economic contagion.

Indeed, it has been conjectured that banking soundness is vital for a sustainable macroeconomic management of a national economy. Despite the continuous competition from other financial intermediaries as a result of the globalisation process, the banking sector still plays a dominant role in a national economy, particularly in developing countries. The condition of the banking sector generally reflects the status of the financial sector as a whole. Thus, there is an overriding concern over bank soundness.

According to the IMF Executive Board, efforts to strengthen the banking system should be guided by the following principles: [3]

- The soundness of a bank is first and foremost the responsibility of its owners and managers; yet the soundness of a banking system is a public policy concern;
- Bank soundness is crucially linked to sound macroeconomic policies;
- A framework for sound banking must include structures to support internal governance and market discipline, as well as official regulation and supervision; and
- International Cupertino and coordination can play an important role, not only in strengthening the global financial system, but also in improving the soundness of the national banking system.

Let me summarize how bank restructuring was conducted in Indonesia with a view to the principles mentioned before. Prior to the current banking crisis, the most recent experience of dealing with problematic banks was the closure of Bank Summa, a sizable bank, at the end of 1992. A significant number of banks, including a major portion of the seven state banks and some provincial governments' development banks were faced with serious problems of nonperforming loans, partly as an implication of a step in the monetary policy to deal with the overheating of the economy in 1991–1992. The IMF classified the condition of the Indonesian banks in its study as a system experiencing significant problems.[4] The closing of Bank Summa was a distressing experience for Bank Indonesia, since it took a long time to resolve. However, over the course of time, conditions improved as shown by the national average of nonperforming loans, which declined from twenty-five percent of total lending in 1993 to twelve percent in 1995.[5]

The banking crisis was preceded by a short period of distress when, due to a process of erosion of confidence, banks lost their deposits' base. In addition, the interbank money market functioned poorly, suffering from compartmentalization. Weak banks had to rely on Bank Indonesia's facility for liquidity to keep afloat. Confidence was completely lost when "flight to quality" was rampant and a substantial number of banks were confronted with bank runs within a short period of time. Strangely, in the Indonesian experience, this phenomenon happened following the closure of the sixteen banks in early November 1997, a step which was originally designed to boost confidence in the banking system. Individually, a bank confronted with problems of mismatched liquidity could easily become insolvent during a period of crisis. For the banking sector, the problem changed from a distress to a crisis.

When currency crisis spread to inflict the national economy, the government's efforts to address the banking problems were combined with other policies and treated as a part of the adjustment policies for stability and sustaining growth. But, this treatment was more explicit in the IMF supported programs, from the first letter of intent in October 1997 to the most recent one in September 1998.

The Indonesian government asked for a three-year standby loan from the IMF, which was processed through an emergency procedure.[6] The loan was SDR 7.3 billion, and together with those provided by the World Bank and the Asian Development Bank (ADB), the total amount was $18 billion. This amount, plus $5 billion of Indonesia's own reserves set aside for balance of payments support, made a total of $23 billion available to be drawn. And together with bilateral participation in a second line of defence, the total amount of the package amounted to $43 billion. This is what popularly known as the Indonesian bail out.[7]

Basically, the IMF-supported program was comprised of a comprehensive policy package to deal with insolvent banks, and to overcome structural rigidities in the economy, supported by prudent fiscal and monetary policy. The financial restructuring program, which had been put together with technical assistance from the IMF, the World Bank, and the ADB to restore public confidence in the financial system, was comprised of five parts, namely:

- The closure of sixteen insolvent banks, which was executed on November 1, 1997.
- The establishment of proper procedures and policies to deal promptly with weak but viable financial institutions, so that they can be placed quickly on the road to recovery; some banks were to be put under intensive supervision by BI.
- The resolution of specific problems of state and regional development banks.
- The strengthening of the institutional, legal and regulatory frameworks for banking operations to ensure the emergence of a sound and efficient financial system; this program includes the modification of such laws as the central bank law, the law on bank liquidation, and the bankruptcy law.

- The establishment of Indonesia Bank Restructuring Agency (IBRA), after the second letter of intent.

The program of banking restructuring was part and parcel of a comprehensive program that comprises both the real and financial sectors, supported by prudent fiscal and monetary policy.

If we look at what was put into the program, one could argue that the right steps were taken to address the Indonesian crisis. But, why is Indonesia's IMF-supported program showing negative results thus far? In comparison with the implementation of other IMF-supported programs, the Indonesian case is definitely the worst, particularly when one compares the rate of currency depreciation, growth prospects, inflation, and the development of other variables in the respective countries.

5. CONCLUDING NOTES

Based from my assessment on what have been unfolding in Indonesia, the followings are some lessons to be learned for future efforts to address banking sector problems:

- Some lessons from financial liberalization policies in Indonesia, which were primarily adopted in the late 1980s and 1990s, are in order. The Indonesian experience underlines the argument that banking liberalization has to be done in coordination with the improvement of the financial infrastructure, including strict prudential measures and supervision, adequate disclosure, governance, legal protection, and market discipline. Proper sequencing is very good, but different original condition may require different sequence. Furthermore, it is impossible to move backward or to retract once a path of liberalization is adopted.
- Lessons from the past crises are still valid here, namely that *the sooner the better* and *the problems are usually worse than expected.*[8] In the Indonesian experience, an IMF study for Bank Indonesia in 1996 showed the number of problem banks and cost for their restructuring, both were much smaller than the estimated magnitudes in the IMF supported program. Basically, the sooner the problems are identified or recognized and the sooner they are properly addressed, the smaller the cost involved and thus, the better the chances for success.

- On banking soundness as a requisite for sustainable monetary policy, I would argue that the Indonesian experience supports the contention. It is even plausible to suggest that the linchpin of the crisis is the weak banking system, which has constrained the monetary authority in conducting monetary policy and banking supervision as well as facilitating a payment system. I think the inclusion of banking soundness, as an explicit objective of monetary policy, as argued by Guitian, should be seriously considered.[9] However, I cannot help but note that, even though there has been an increasing awareness of the close link between banking soundness and macroeconomic policy, partly due to the socialization campaign by the IMF and others, it has not been adequate to prepare monetary authorities and market players in developing countries to cope with the crisis. And this lack of preparation has resulted in devastating impacts, especially in Thailand, South Korea and Indonesia. The sooner must have been the better.
- In an effort to create a sound banking system by implementing a program that combine bank restructuring and monetary management, we have to be very cautious about the fact that we are working with different variables in terms of their time frame. Monetary policy deals with variables, which have short time lag, even though it has long term implications. To adopt a tight or lose monetary policy is a short-run issue. Furthermore, it deals with macroeconomic variables. Bank restructuring is, however, a long-term problem. It deals with problems of efficiency, management, supervision, regulation, law enforcement, banking ethics, etc., which are long terms and microeconomic issues. I do not want to imply that because they are long-term problems a country has more time to address them. The point I would like to raise is that we have to be extra careful in designing and implementing a program that combines monetary policy and banking reform. They are very closely related, and yet they are problems of different nature.
- The Indonesian experience also teaches us that, when public expectation is fragile, the closure of insolvent banks, a must for creating a sound banking system, could have an adverse result. A step, which was originally intended to regain public confidence, resulted in a further loss of it. Liquidation of banks should be done when the economy is not in distress, when public expectation is not fragile. This is, of course, easier said than done. However, it remains true: the sooner the better, and the later the costlier.

Notes

[1]Experts distinguish between banking distress, when a number of banks suffer an insolvency problem, even though not a liquidity problem, and banking crisis. Banking crisis is defined as a situation in which a significant group of banks have liabilities exceeding the market value of their assets, leading to runs and other portfolio shifts, collapse of some banks, and government intervention. Read V. Sundararajan and Tomas J.T. Balino, (eds,) *Banking Crisis: Cases and Issues*, Washington DC : IMF, 1991, p. 3.

[2]The impact of the Mexican crisis in January 1996 and the strengthening of the yen in April 1996 occasioned the previous external shocks. In both instances, the rupiah was weakened substantially, but it recovered within days, after Bank Indonesia's intervention.

[3]Carl-Johan Lindgren et al., *Bank Soundness and Macro-economic Policy,* Washington, DC: IMF, 1996, p. 5

[4]Carl-Johan Lindgren et al., ibid., p.26.

[5]On the main issues confronting Indonesia in coping with banking system management and banking reform prior to the present crisis, see David C.Cole and Betty Slade, *Building a Modern Financial System: The Indonesian Experience,* New York: Cambridge University Press, 1996. I also wrote a paper "The Banking Sector in Emerging Markets: The Case of Indonesia" published in Charles Enoch and John H.Green (eds.) *Banking Soundness and Monetary Policy,* Washington, DC: IMF, 1997, pp. 335–352.

[6]In the preparatory discussions, my preference was for a 'precautionary arrangement' instead of a full-fledged stand-by arrangement, partly because of my concern about the possible problems arising from the conditionalities of a stand-by loan.

[7]Some questions have been arising on the exact amount available to be drawn, what was actually the $5 billion of Indonesia's own reserve, what was the second line of defence, etc. These have to be clarified for the records.

[8]See Andrew Sheng, *The Crisis of Money in the 21st Century,* City University of Hongkong, guest lecture, April 21, 1998.

[9]See Manuel Guitian, "Banking Soundness: The Other Dimension of Monetary Policy," in *Banking Soundness and Monetary Policy,* Charles Enoch and John H.Green (eds.), pp. 41–62. See also Richard N. Cooper in his comment on Steven Redelet and Jeffrey D.Sachs, "The East Asian Financial Crisis: Diagnosis, Remedies, Prospects," in *Brookings Papers on Economic Activity*, Vol. 1, 1998.

Chapter 9

The Korean Banking Crisis: Picking up the Pieces

William C. Hunter
Federal Reserve Bank of Chicago

As is well known, the industrial policy of the Korean government during the 1970s gave rise to the *chaebol* groups, i.e., large family controlled industrial conglomerates. These companies, unlike traditional Korean companies, focused on the production and export of products in heavy industries such as industrial machinery, electronics, chemicals, autos, and shipbuilding. During this time, Korean commercial banks were instructed to allow easy credit access (at favorable loans rates) to the firms in these industries. This policy required additional sources of funding that the existing commercial banks were unable to meet. Subsequently, the government established specialized banks to fill the gap. Toward the latter part of the 1970s, policy loans, i.e., loans which supported government programs and aimed primarily at the *chaebol* companies, accounted for nearly eighty percent of domestic credit extended during that period. During this same period, tightly regulated non-bank financial institutions were introduced into the economy in an effort to diversify financing sources and to attract funds into the organized market. The development strategy bolstered the expansion of existing firms into targeted sectors through preferential access to bank credit at below-market rates. These firms not only expanded rapidly into many areas of specialization but also into many which were not explicitly targeted by government policy. As a result, these firms grew into internationally recognized economic conglomerates and dominated the Korea economy. These firms also held equity investments in the commercial banks.

Although the economy was growing at a rapid pace under this strategy, some government policymakers recognized that privatization and deregulation of the banking sector was imperative. Market mechanisms provide banks with the incentive to exert self-discipline to effectively allocate financial resources, which is necessary to sustain economic growth.

The government began to re-privatize the banking system near the end of the 1970s and undertook an additional series of financial reforms in the early 1980s. With revisions to the General Banking Act in 1982 and the launch of a new five-year economic plan in the early 1980s, direct government controls over banking practices were eased, and permissible banking activities were expanded. For example, permissible banking activities were expanded to include a wide variety of fee driven non-interest income activities including sales of commercial bills and government and public bonds under repurchase agreements. The government also had a stated goal of eliminating policy preference loans in the banking sector and further steps were taken to liberalize interest rates.[1]

Further reforms were announced when the General Banking Act was revised again in 1991 and 1994. These revisions gave commercial banks further autonomy in their business activities and management. For example, banks were allowed to act as leading underwriters for government and public bonds. In 1991, a four-stage plan for the full liberalization of interest rates was announced to effectively set the price mechanism of interest rates. Through interest rate deregulation, the competitiveness of domestic financial services industry could be strengthened to cope with continued global financial liberalization.

As is evident from the recent collapse of the Korean banking system, the liberalization initiatives were, in a large sense, proven ineffective. With a growing number of large corporate failures and mounting domestic debt, Korean banks are currently bearing the consequences of widespread corporate insolvency. As such, much of the country's current economic crisis can in part be traced to the failure of the financial reforms to take effect and to the collusive links among the Korean government, the *chaebol*, and the privatized banking industry (the so-called crony capitalism).

Immediately following the collapse of the Korean economy, the country's unemployment rate reached its highest level in thirty-one years and during the first half of 1998, the country's GDP shrunk 5.3 percent—the largest drop in Korean history. This situation is not expected to improve dramatically in the near term. Against this backdrop, the short-term prospects for the Korean banking sector appear dire indeed. Most bank stocks are now trading well under $1 per share and twelve small merchant banks and five small commercial banks were closed by the Korean government following the imposition of the IMF rescue package. With nonperforming loans approaching as much as forty percent to fifty percent of GDP and expected to rise further before falling, future prospects for the Korean economy depend significantly on the ability of the government to recapitalize and restructure the banking and financial systems. The prospects also depend on the country's ability to break the collusive links among government officials, the *chaebol*, and the banking industry.

The government officially began its major bank-restructuring program in early 1998 and has committed to complete a significant amount of the needed restructuring of the financial sector by the end of 1998. As of October, of the twenty-six commercial banks in existence at the end of 1997, two banks—Korea First Bank and Seoul Bank—have been nationalized and are being prepared for sale to foreign investors. Twelve banks that failed to meet the eight percent Bank for International Settlements (BIS) capital adequacy standard at the end of 1997 were asked to submit rehabilitation plans and were subjected to asset quality diagnostic reviews. The plans of five of these twelve banks were deemed infeasible and these banks had their licenses suspended and are in the process of being acquired by five banks deemed be stronger (with the addition of public support) under purchase and assumption transactions. The remaining undercapitalized banks received conditional approval to operate and most are currently in the process of seeking merger partners. The nine healthy banks not involved in mergers, including the five involved in purchase and assumption transactions, continue to operate under strict supervision to insure that they do not become distressed.

It should also be noted that several banks deemed to be most healthy have been identified as lead banks in corporate restructuring for the sixty-four large chaebol groups deemed to be in financial distress. These banks include: Commercial Bank of Korea, Cho Hung Bank, Hanil Bank, Korea Exchange Bank, and Bank of Seoul. These banks have created internal workout units which will address their *chaebol* bad loan problem. These bank workout units will be assisted by external financial advisors retained under the World Bank's technical assistance loan.

Of the many interesting questions one might ask regarding the Korean banking system restructuring effort, one involves the question of the relative economic performance of the banks that have been designated as lead or acquiring banks in the restructuring (either by government fiat or voluntarily) during the period prior to the crisis. While such factors as the level of nonperforming loans and other accounting ratios were undoubtedly key in determining which banks were designated as lead banks, it is interesting to see whether these banks had the most effective management and were the more efficient producers of intermediation services during the period prior to the crisis. To this end, the results of a recent study (Hao et al., 1998) examining the efficiency of the private Korean banks between 1985 and 1995 are informative.

This study begins by estimating the level of efficiency of each bank in the sample. Rather than concentrating on traditional scale and scope analysis of productive efficiency, the study concentrates on management efficiency. Recent research in banking indicates that ineffectiveness in managing resources accounts for a significantly higher percentage of costs compared to scale and scope efficiencies. Furthermore, instead of comparing the operating performance of the sample banks with a set of superior-operated banks by using financial ratios, the study uses production theory and econometric procedures to extract information on managerial efficiency.

The stochastic frontier approach was used to calculate a measure of production efficiency for each bank in the sample. This approach uses a parametric technique to estimate the characteristics of "best-practice" banks. These best-practice banks represent institutions which produce their financial products and services at the lowest cost using the most efficient mix of productive inputs or factors of production. Individual bank efficiency indices were measured by computing the deviations of costs from the cost frontier estimated from the sample data. This inefficiency factor captures both allocative inefficiencies from failing to react optimally to relative prices of inputs, and technical inefficiencies resulting from employing excessive amount of the inputs to produce outputs. In this framework, systematic deviations of cost from the frontier or best-practice levels are associated with poor management. Random deviations are attributed to uncontrollable factors that affect total costs, such as weather, luck, labor strikes, or machine performance.

To calculate each bank's efficiency index, we first fitted a stochastic frontier cost function to characterize the efficient frontier for the sample banks. Total costs included all labor costs, physical capital expenses, and allocated interest expenses. Three output quantities were included in the cost function: total loans and securities, demand deposits, and fee income. The prices of inputs used in the production of bank assets were the wage rate, interest for borrowed funds, and the price of physical capital. The cost function also included equity capital for each bank. It was used to adjust for increased costs of funds due to financial risk. Using this methodology, the most efficient bank in the sample had efficiency score of 1.0 and the least efficient bank had a score of 0.

The banks included in the sample along with their efficiency scores are presented in Table 1.

The grand mean efficiency score for the sample was 0.866 with a standard deviation of 0.082. The highest efficiency index in the sample was 0.9734 while the lowest index was 0.5267. The mean efficiency index is well within the range estimated for other countries, including the U.S. Studies that have used stochastic econometric methodologies have found efficiency on the order of twenty to thirty percent in U.S. banking. The average bank in

Table 1

Bank Name	Average Efficiency	Standard Deviation	Minimum	Maximum
Cho Hung Bank	0.9080918	0.0205754	0.8823058	0.9494293
Kookin Bank	0.8496247	0.0941274	0.6705332	0.9577079
Hanil Bank	0.8516210	0.0459996	0.7726563	0.9092797
Korea First Bank	0.8230604	0.0807017	0.6737905	0.9371849
Commercial Bank of Korea	0.8707437	0.0510245	0.7851077	0.9523536
Bank of Seoul	0.9342483	0.0364389	0.8675867	0.9716806
Shinhan Bank	0.9191186	0.0447135	0.8254023	0.971082
Korea Exchange Bank	0.7571875	0.1322026	0.5758239	0.9323697
KorAm Bank	0.9063666	0.0647956	0.7561179	0.9614145
Daegu Bank	0.9114072	0.0407867	0.816541	0.9516561
Pusan Bank	0.8446082	0.049014	0.7587563	0.9282293
Kwangju Bank	0.8729311	0.0674226	0.7088932	0.9589421
Chungbuk Bank	0.7643886	0.1130081	0.5266924	0.9281676
Chung Chong Bank	0.8763645	0.0631293	0.7626339	0.9589659
Kangwon Bank	0.8523274	0.0680208	0.7240866	0.9351441
Kyungki Bank	0.8551051	0.070452	0.7589281	0.9637721
Kyongnam Bank	0.8573998	0.0794825	0.7167567	0.9663202
Jeonbuk Bank	0.8777808	0.0693247	0.7300003	0.9612096
Bank of Cheju	0.9304448	0.0383638	0.8485234	0.9734144

our sample would have increased its efficiency level about 13.4 percent had it been able to operate on the efficient frontier.

Regarding the disposition of the banks included in the original sample, as of September 1998, two of these banks—Korea First Bank (average efficiency score of 0.823) and Bank of Seoul (average efficiency score of 0.934)—were nationalized. The Commercial Bank of Korea (average efficiency score of 0.871) and the Hanil Bank (average efficiency score of 0.852) are merging on a voluntary basis. The Kookim Bank (average efficiency score of 0.85) acquired the Dae Dong Bank, a failed bank not included in our original sample. The Kookim Bank has subsequently become involved in a merger transaction with Korea Long-Term Credit Bank. Two banks—Chung Chong Bank (average efficiency score of 0.876) and Kyungki Bank (average efficiency score of 0.855)—have been closed and sold in purchase and assumption transactions with banks not in our sample. Two banks—Shinhan Bank (average efficiency score of 0.919) and KorAm Bank (average efficiency score of 0.906)—are acquiring failed banks in purchase and assumption transactions. KorAm is acquiring Kyungki Bank, one of the failed banks in our sample.

Regarding the question of the lead bank's managerial capacity to restructure the acquired banks, it appears from this study that the lead banks identified by the Korean officials were on average more efficient than the banks being acquired or closed during the pre-crisis period. In addition, most of the lead banks typically were among the set of banks that exhibited improving efficiency scores after the 1991 deregulation. Thus, on the basis of these results, it appears that the management of these banks may be the most qualified to lead the restructured banking institutions.

It should be noted that the impact of *chaebol* bankruptcies on the Korean banking sector cannot be overstated. For example, the failure of Korea First Bank (average efficiency score below the sample average) can be traced directly to the failure of its key *chaebol* borrowers: Kia motors, Hanbo Iron and Steel, Sammi, New Core, Sinho, and Tongil. Similarly, the Bank of Seoul (average efficiency among the highest in the sample) was brought down by the failure of its main *chaebol* customers: DaeNong, ChungGu, HanshinGongYoung, and Jindo.

In conclusion, although the process of rationalization of the Korean banking sector seems reasonable from a bank performance perspective, one might question the decision of the Koreans to merge some of the best performing banks into one organization reducing the number of competitively viable institutions in the market. Given the importance of a competitive banking sector to the process of economic growth and development it could be argued that the most efficient banks should be merged only with less efficient ones, thereby preserving the maximum number of competitor banks in the system. Although some Korean analysts argue that Korea needs a few large globally competitive banks, to compete in international markets and to serve Korea's large multinational corporations, this argument ignores the negative consequences which would follow from a more concentrated domestic banking industry (for example, the proposed merger between the Commercial Bank of Korea and the Hanil Bank would control almost fifty percent of the country's banking assets). Clearly, the possible adverse consequences of such a high level of concentration deserves careful evaluation.

Note

[1]Beginning in 1984, banks were permitted to vary their lending rates within a limited range depending on the creditworthiness of borrowers and to increase competition, openness, and efficiency, the government further lowered both entry barriers for bank and nonbank financial institutions and restrictions upon foreign bank branches. New commercial banks and investment and mutual savings companies were established as a result of the policy change. Discriminatory restrictions were also reduced to allow for equal treatment between foreign and domestic banks. Foreign banks were able to access the central bank rediscount window for financing and to engage in trust activities.

Reference

J. Hao, W. C. Hunter, and W. K. Yang, "Deregulation and Efficiency: The Case of Private Korean Banks," Federal Reserve Bank of Chicago, working paper, November 1998.

Chapter 10

Asian Currency Crisis

Desmond Lachman
Salomon Smith Barney

1. INTRODUCTION

The Asian currency crisis that began in July 1997 with the devaluation of the Thai baht shows little sign of abating. Indeed, the very poor state of the domestic economies in the region, which as yet show no real signs of improving, would suggest that this crisis is likely to deepen in the period ahead and that it could spread further to countries that have so far not felt the full force of the crisis. This would make one think that we may very well only be at the end of the beginning of this crisis rather than at the beginning of its end. As such, in attempting to draw any definitive conclusions about this crisis, I find myself much in the position of Chou en Lai, the former Chinese premier who, when asked in 1979 about his opinion of the French Revolution some 200 years before, replied that it was too early to draw definitive conclusions.

The depth and global ramifications of the crisis will certainly make it a subject that will be long analyzed by scholars. As a market participant, I offer the lessons that I would draw from this crisis with some humility. In doing so, I would distinguish between (a) those lessons that relate more to the original causes of the crisis and (b) those lessons that relate more to the way in which this crisis is playing itself out and that pose a risk to the global system. I regard these latter lessons as the more pressing, since they might guide us in how to prevent the crisis from deepening.

2. LESSONS RELATED TO THE ORIGIN OF THE CRISIS

By now there seems to be common ground as to the main lessons that are to be drawn relating to what might have caused the crisis. These include the following:

- An excessive reliance on short-term external borrowing by the banking system at the time that bank regulation was lax;
- A excessive degree of corporate borrowing in foreign exchange that was not hedged;
- An undue reliance on fixed exchange rate regimes and a pegging to the wrong currency given the countries' trade and investment patterns;
- A mode of corporate finance that relied too much on bank borrowing as opposed to equity financing or bond financing; and
- An insufficiently regulated banking system that allowed over-investment in the property sector or in poor bank lending practices to large corporations.

The recognition of these weaknesses is likely to result in changes in the global financial architecture that might prevent the recurrence of future crises. Thus, one might find support for some form of inward capital controls, prudential limitations on bank borrowing from external banks, better bank supervision, etc. While all this is well and good for the long run, this would not seem to address the more immediate and pressing problems where more basic lessons have to be learned as to how can one set the basis for an early recovery from the present sharp downturn in these economies.

3. LESSONS IN THE PROCESS OF BEING LEARNT

Perhaps the more fundamental lessons from the Asian crisis are still in the process of being learned. These relate to the appropriate policy response to the massive economic and financial dislocation that is being experienced on a regional basis to a degree that has not been experienced in recent memory. In this respect, I would distinguish between:

a) The cyclical dimension of the crisis that is being marked by a collapse in domestic demand and by contractions in output ranging from some 7 percent in Korea, 8-10 percent in Thailand, and some 15-20 percent in Indonesia;
b) The absence of any sign of recovery in these economies in terms of real indicators of activity. Particularly striking in this regard is the continued sharp decline in the US dollar value of imports of the order of 45 percent on a twelve month basis and the absence of any sustained export growth in US dollar terms despite the sharp devaluations of the currencies;
c) The deflationary tendencies that these economies are beginning to display in a forward looking sense despite the very large depreciations in their currencies; and
d) The very large private sector debt overhangs that are crippling the corporate sectors of these economies and that are impeding the proper functioning of these economies' banking sectors. The early resolution of this debt situation will be essential if there is to be any recovery in these economies.

These features would suggest that three lessons are yet to be learnt from this crisis:

a) How to set macroeconomic demand management policies for a more deflationary environment where output is in a downward spiral and where signs of inflation are all but non-existent. Specifically, we may yet be learning that when output is contracting and inflation is all but absent in a forward looking sense it might not make much sense to keep interest rates high in real terms in order to prevent a further depreciation of the currency. In this respect, one might wish to adopt a more Canadian style approach to policy that aims at ensuring that there is an adequate but not excessive degree of monetary stimulus to the system through an adequate combination of exchange rate and interest rate levels;
b) Likewise, one may question whether fiscal stringency is the most appropriate budgetary approach in countries whose budgets are being impacted by dwindling tax bases and whose economies are sorely lacking for want of aggregate demand. This is all the more so the case for countries which have had sound past records of fiscal policy management and whose public debt levels are presently relatively low; and
c) More fundamentally from the point of view of ever getting these economies to recover one may question whether more radical solutions

> need to be found to solving the corporate debt and banking sector problems of these countries. In this respect, at this stage one must wonder whether traditional bankruptcy workout procedures, even if properly implemented, can possibly be a swift enough approach to deal with countries where gearing ratios are often 500 percent and where corporate debt to GDP ratios are frequently over 200 percent. As the sad experience of Japan attests, failure to face these problems head on in a decisive manner could condemn Asia to the lost decade sort of experience that characterized Latin America in the 1980s.

I would venture to add that it is the rapid learning of these lessons that is more pertinent than pondering about how to avoid the next crisis, if we are not to have Asia continuing to pose a threat to the global economy in the period ahead.

Chapter 11

Causes and Implications of the Asian Crisis

Flemming Larsen
International Monetary Fund

Earlier speakers have already identified a number of *internal factors* that appear to have played an important role in the buildup to the Asian crisis. I will, therefore, first discuss the role of the *external environment* and then briefly address the implications of the crisis for Asia's near-term growth prospects.

Few economies have benefited as much from globalization as the countries of southeast and east Asia. It is, therefore, a tragic twist of fate that these countries should become the victims of a financial crash brought on by a sudden shift in global financial market sentiment. Work has been underway during the past year at the IMF and by many others to try to identify the main causes of the crisis, but arriving at a full understanding of the forces that produced the Asian crash of 1997–98 will, of course, require extensive further diagnosis. At this stage, my preliminary conclusion is that the crisis resulted from the interaction between, first, external events largely beyond the control of the countries concerned, and second, a number of serious shortcomings of the "managed development models" characteristic of many Asian economies.[1] These models or approaches to economic policies have been widely credited for the region's earlier successes and the notion of an "Asian Miracle," but the crisis has cast doubt on at least some of their features.

The role of the external environment can best be appreciated from a flow of funds perspective. Typically, cross-border flows of funds are quite sensitive to cyclical divergences among the major countries and regions. This has also been the case in the 1990s. At the beginning of the decade, virtually all of the major countries experienced successive economic downturns. These downturns occurred for quite different reasons, which had an important bearing on the shape of the subsequent recovery.

In the United States, the economy recovered very quickly and has subsequently enjoyed an exceptionally long and strong expansion. In the United Kingdom, where the recession was much deeper than in the United States, the subsequent recovery was also very strong. In both the U.S. and the U.K., the output gaps that had emerged earlier in the decade had been eliminated by 1997.

In sharp contrast, the pickups after the recessions in Japan and the major continental European countries were unusually sluggish: In Germany and France, for example, growth has only been above potential twice (in 1994 and 1998) during the past seven years, and in Japan only once (in 1996) since 1992, and the Japanese economy has now fallen back into an even deeper recession than in the early 1990s.

These large cyclical divergences between the U.S. and the U.K. on the one hand and continental Europe and Japan on the other, which gave rise to procyclical movements in exchange rates, also resulted in a sharp widening of current account imbalances. Japan's surplus surged to over $130 billion in 1993-94 and the future euro area's surplus exceeded $110 billion by 1997. The counterpart to these large surpluses were large, mainly private, capital flows from Japan and Europe not only into the United States but also into many emerging market countries, especially those in Asia. Of course, not all capital flows to emerging market countries originated in Japan and Europe; U.S. investors also contributed. But the large **net** movements of capital into emerging market countries from the early 1990s until 1997 clearly could not have occurred in the absence of these large surpluses. In my view, this was an absolutely critical element in the buildup to the Asian crisis, which is often being ignored.

While these capital flows were not exceptionally large from the perspective of the originating countries, they were very large from the perspective of the recipients. And large capital inflows are rarely sustainable. As it has happened so often in past episodes of large-scale movements of capital into developing countries, the tide will eventually turn. It can turn as cyclical conditions normalize in the originating countries, raising expected returns on investments at home. Or the capital flows can decline, or even be reversed, if investors eventually decide that the returns abroad (in emerging markets) are no longer worth the risk, for example, if perceptions of countries' fundamentals change.

Which explanation fits the Asian episode? By 1996 there had been some signs that the global upturn was gaining momentum. In the United States, economic slack had been substantially absorbed and concerns about overheating became more prominent. In Japan, there was a sudden (albeit short-lived) burst of dynamism, and in continental Europe, activity seemed to be picking up. Indeed, expectations in financial markets seemed to suggest that interest rates in the industrial countries were likely soon to begin to head upwards.

In the event, however, although international cyclical conditions had begun to change, revised perceptions about the fundamentals of the emerging Asian economies were unquestionably much more important in triggering the virulent crisis. Other speakers have discussed some of the most critical factors that led to the changed assessment of fundamentals and the contagion that ensued; I need not repeat their conclusions, which I broadly share, including the role the capital inflows played in exacerbating problems of overheating and imprudent borrowing and lending.

At this stage, many aspects of the crisis remain unresolved, including the reasons for the unexpectedly severe compression of output, and the likely shape of recovery.

Regarding the reasons for the depth of the downturn in activity, the fact that it is a regional crisis, and that so many economies are affected, clearly plays an important role. All of these countries had benefited greatly from the rapid expansion of intra-Asian trade during the past decade or so. And now with much of the region in recession, the strong intra-regional trade links are working in reverse. That Japan, Hong Kong SAR, and Singapore are also in recession both reflects and contributes to the compression of output in the economies at the center of the crisis.

A more controversial issue is whether the depth of the downturn may also reflect the possibility that the fundamentals of the crisis afflicted countries may have been in worse shape than has been generally recognized. There is, I believe, considerable evidence in support of this hypothesis: The very high rates of capital accumulation characteristic of these countries, appear to have been associated with declining efficiency of new investments and falling rates of return; the volume of problem loans in the banking systems had been rising already before the crisis (although lack of transparency meant that these problems were not visible); and there were mounting signs of overcapacity in industry and in the construction sector, and property market bubbles had begun to burst well before the crisis broke.

When one adds up the evidence, it becomes clear that these economies were facing the likelihood of at least a business cycle downturn, and perhaps also a slowdown in trend growth, **even in the absence of the financial crisis.** The problem was that these strains and imbalances had been ignored for too long by domestic and foreign investors and banks, and by decision-makers across the region. The failure to read the writing on the wall was probably due to the familiar reluctance to quarrel with success: There was a widespread belief at home and abroad that the Asian Miracle would continue and that these countries were somehow immune to business cycle fluctuations.

Because of the exuberant expectations that existed both within and outside the region, the shock to investor sentiment when the crisis hit was particularly severe. And when investors opened their eyes to the more problematic features of Asia's impressive growth record, they suddenly became aware of the potential (and need) for a cyclical correction and also began to question of the sustainability of underlying growth trends. The Asian Miracle suddenly lost its shine.

Looking ahead, what can the region expect and how supportive will be the external environment these countries will be facing during the period ahead?

We have seen very large contractions in economic activity: by almost ten percent on average for the worst afflicted countries. With output probably still falling in the final quarter of 1999, it may appear that the downturn will never end. What are the forces that will gradually emerge to support a turnaround and ignite recovery? There are in fact three such forces that are likely to generate at least a moderate pickup in growth during 1999:

- First, the turnaround in financial market confidence, which is being aided by the implementation of reforms and restructuring measures and large-scale international financial assistance.
- Two, both monetary and fiscal policies have become very supportive in all cases, which has been made possible by the return of confidence and by the low levels of public debt in most cases.
- Three, competitive positions remain very strong despite the rebound in exchange rates, which should help stimulate exports.

At the same time, questions remain about the health of financial systems and about corporate indebtedness. Frameworks are being put in place to facilitate the needed consolidation, restructuring, and recapitalization. While the decline in interest rates and rebound in exchange rates are substantially facilitating the task of restructuring, the full resolution of these problems will necessarily require some time.

Uncertainties also remain about the external environment. An early pick up in Japan is particularly critical to support recovery elsewhere in Asia. And the containment of financial pressures and contagion in other regions will also have a bearing on Asia. In the wake of the Russian crisis, major uncertainties remain about investors' and banks' appetite for emerging market risk and thus about the levels and terms of capital flows to emerging markets during the period ahead. There is some reason for optimism that strong preemptive actions by Brazil to forestall a financial crisis will allow the international community to help erect a firewall against further contagion. But it is too soon to conclude that the crisis is over.

Note

[1]Some of the work by the IMF on the causes of the crisis has been published in recent issues of the *World Economic Outlook* (December 1997, May 1998, and October 1998). See also background study for the "*World Economic Outlook* by Nicholas Crafts," East Asian Growth before and after the Crisis, IMF, working paper, No. 98/137, October 1998.

Chapter 12

The Yen and Boom–Bust Cycle in East Asia

Kazuo Ueda
Bank of Japan

Abstract: One of the key determinants of the boom–bust cycle in East Asia was the sharp appreciation of the yen against the dollar between the mid-1980s and the mid-1990s, and its subsequent depreciation. Real investment and speculative financial capital in and into East Asia responded too much to the yen movements.

1. INTRODUCTION

I would like to start by saying that the economic crisis in East Asia since 1997 has not been an "Asian" crisis, but resembles a typical domestic financial crisis with some international aspects added on.

As in a domestic banking crisis, East Asian countries borrowed heavily short term and invested long term. Investments went to domestic businesses, and to some extent, assets markets. Investment and assets markets booms were at least partially excessive. Upon seeing signs of excesses, providers of funds to the economies started withdrawing funds, turning booms into busts and delivering devastating blows to domestic financial systems. Unlike in some other currency crises, domestic macroeconomic policy was not a main driving force. Crises spread from one country to another, exhibiting the feature of self-fulfilling contagion. During the process, East Asian currencies depreciated sharply. This added to the severity of the crises by increasing the burden of foreign currency denominated debt.

Interestingly, many financial panics in the then emerging economies such as Australia, Argentina, Italy and the US in the late nineteenth & early twentieth. centuries shared such characteristics except that exchange rates were mostly fixed under the gold standard. (See, for example, Goodhart & Delargy (1988).)

In this sense, I believe that it is misleading to emphasize too much "Asian" aspects of the current crisis.

2. THE YEN AND EAST ASIAN GROWTH

Having said that there are common elements between the East Asian economic crisis and some previous crises, I would like to turn to pointing out features specific to the East Asian crisis. As they say, all unhappy people have some special things to worry about. Needless to say, I do not intend to produce a complete set of special features of the Asian crisis.

I will point out just one such feature, i.e., the role played by medium-term fluctuations in the yen-dollar rate. Specifically, the yen appreciated sharply in the mid- to late-1980s and again in the mid-1990s. Correspondingly, Asian currencies depreciated against the yen, not just in nominal terms, but in real terms. The attached chart shows the ratio of Japanese producer price index to East Asian producer price index (Jap. PPI/Asian PPI).[1] Between the mid 1980s and the late 1980s, East Asian price competitiveness went up by about fifty percent. The increased price competitiveness produced a massive relocation of production units within Asia, especially from Japan to East Asia. During the process fixed investment in Asia relative to Japan rose sharply. In fact, the chart shows that the real exchange rate, Japan's foreign direct investment to Asia (FDI), and Asian growth (growth) are very highly correlated.[2] In this sense, the movements in the yen, its appreciation between 1985 and 1995 had a decisive impact on Asian growth.

Things were OK until 1995 when the yen reversed its course and started to depreciate drastically. As can be seen from the figure, the competitive edge Asian economies had gained during the 1985-1995 period mostly disappeared by early 1997.

With hindsight, we know that the yen was overvalued in 1995, that real depreciation of the Asian currencies had to be at least partially corrected, and that real investment and associated assets markets booms in Asia were excessive.

Unfortunately, Asian and multinational firms that were carrying out investment projects, Asian and non-Asian investors and financial institutions that were providing the funds did not realize the excesses. I hasten to add that a significant portion of FDI into Asia was doing the right thing. Only those that came at the last stage and short-term speculative flows associated with these generated excesses.

In short, the sharp appreciation of the yen between 1985-1995 and its subsequent correction seem to have been one of the driving forces of the boom and bust cycle in East Asia.

3. IMPLICATIONS

The boom and bust cycle would have been less volatile had Asian investment and assets markets responded less to the yen-dollar movements, or had the appreciation of the yen in 1995 been milder. In this sense, the two bubble-like episodes are related. This suggests that market failures played a role and that one failure led to another. How we could address these failures, I am sure, will be discussed elsewhere in this conference.

Even with a bubble in the course of the yen, the Asian crisis would have been more moderate had Asian currencies been partially pegged to the yen.

The story I have told is somewhat at odds with a standard view about the linkage between Japan and East Asia. The view holds that, for example, Japan's share in Asian exports (13.1 percent in 1996) is smaller than that of the US (19.3 percent). Hence, real exchange rates between Japan and East Asia are not as important as I have argued. My stance here has been that they have been a bit more significant. The most important component of Asian exports, electric machinery, competes worldwide with Japanese products. Moreover, the linkage I have emphasized turns on trade and exchange rate effects on investment and growth. Through this mechanism, the two regions seem to have been more closely inter-related than a linkage by exchange rate and trade alone may suggest.

Notes

[1]East Asia refers to Asian NIES, ASEAN, and China. The weights were determined by the shares in Japan's foreign trade in 1990. For the growth rate series, the weights reflect GDP shares as of 1990.

[2]In the chart, Asian growth (scale left) and FDI (scale right) are in growth rates over year earlier. The real exchange rate (scale left) is the level of an index with differences over year earlier corresponding to rates of change.

Reference

Goodhart, C., and R. Delargy. "Financial crises: Plus ca change, plus c'est la meme Chose," *International Finance,* Vol. 2, 1988.

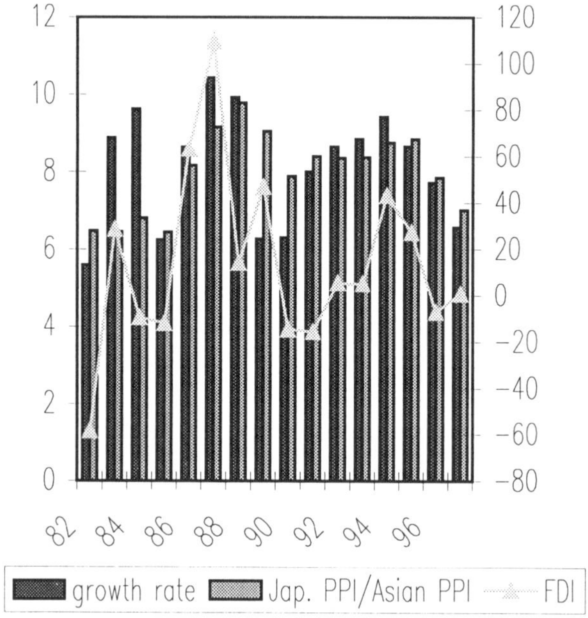

Graph 1 Intereactions between Japan and East Asia

Chapter 13

Causes and Implications of the Asian Crisis: The Role of Financial Sector, Domestic Policies and Contagion

Chaiyawat Wibulswasdi
Former Governor, Bank of Thailand

1. INTRODUCTION

Time does not permit me to touch on all issues relating to the causes and implications of the Asian Crisis. Therefore, I will confine myself to some observations as to how the situation has been aggravated into a deeper and more prolonged crisis than initially envisaged, and thus turned out to be extremely difficult to resolve.

In my remarks, I will basically draw on experiences with which I am familiar, namely the case of Thailand. Most of the issues are, nonetheless, relevant to other cases as well.

2. CAUSES OF THE CRISIS

Let me start with a note on the causes of the crisis. I can be very brief at this point as it has already been well documented and in fact will be covered by many other speakers in this Conference. In my view, the important factors that contributed to the crisis, in order of development, include:

1. Overreliance on foreign capital by the Asian emerging economies;
2. Weakness of the financial system;
3. Inappropriate macroeconomic policy responses to external problems and pressures;
4. Sudden shift in foreign investors' confidence, and overreactions in some cases, which led to contagion; and
5. Vicious circle of the interactions between the banking crisis and weakening real economies, which led to a deeper and deeper recession.

3. RESOLUTION

A particular observation that I would like to draw your attention is that in the process of solving the problems that emerged in a country or a group of countries, a number of practical issues have arisen in the implementation of corrective policies and measures that were difficult to deal with. Therefore, the problems may not have been addressed in time or in some cases even deteriorated.

Among the important areas of crisis solution that I would like to discuss are (1) the reform of the financial sector; (2) the shift in macroeconomic policies; (3) the restructuring of the real economies; and (4) external factors outside the control of the authorities.

3.1 Reform of the financial sector

To correct the weaknesses in the financial sector, which were perhaps the most significant cause of the crisis, the strategy and set of policies are somewhat familiar. Among them are the closure of unviable financial institutions and the strengthening of the remaining institutions through recapitalization and improvement of asset quality. The action needs to be both decisive and comprehensive in order to quickly restore public confidence in the soundness of the banking system.

However, in practice, there are several obstacles to the implementation of desirable policy measures. Let me cite two specific examples.

First, on the closure of unviable institutions, while various options are available as regards implementation depending on the circumstances and the legal framework, there are some cases where the legal framework for banking supervision in a particular country does not allow an immediate intervention by the authorities to close troubled financial institutions. In Thailand, temporary measures, e.g., suspension of operations, had to be resorted to while the process of legal amendment was taking place. Such temporary measure was certainly not an optimal solution to the prevailing problem. On the contrary, it prolonged the problem and led to continued loss of confidence or even panic. The problem was further compounded by the deterioration of asset quality as a result of weakening economic activities, thus pushing more institutions into insolvency. As the solution was delayed, instability in the financial sector persisted and precipitated a fast deterioration of the real sector when the remaining financial institutions tried to protect themselves or took a defensive approach that led to a sharp curtailment of credit and subsequent problems in the real economies.

Another example is the recapitalization of financial institutions. While the need for recapitalization is clearly recognized, implementation at the time of an unstable financial environment is extremely difficult. Domestic sources of capital become scarce due to the reduction of wealth as well as the declining equity market. At the same time, foreign capital is not forthcoming, even without any restriction on foreign ownership, as the majority of investors adopt a wait-and-see attitude so long as the financial situation in the recipient country remains unstable.

These two examples illustrate the difficulties in taking immediate or timely actions to address financial sector weaknesses that partially accounted for the deepening and prolonging of the crisis.

3.2 Shift in macroeconomic policies

When the economy drifts into a recession, it is accepted that tight macroeconomic policies need to be relaxed to prevent a deeper recession.

On the fiscal side, some degree of relaxation is a natural process because tax revenue cannot be collected anyway and the shortfall contributes to a fiscal deficit. There are instances, however, when even a conscious effort to increase government spending to help stimulate the economy cannot be implemented immediately due to bureaucratic operational constraints. Often, government agencies need time to draw up a new activity program and actual disbursement of funds will lag even further. In this regard, a fiscal stimulus may not be as strong and effective as designed.

The shift in a monetary policy stance is more controversial. Tight monetary conditions and high interest rates are needed at an initial stage of the crisis in order to help stabilize foreign exchange markets. The difficult part in policy decision is how temporary this restrictive stance should be. When a satisfactory degree of stability in exchange markets is achieved, monetary policy should be eventually relaxed and interest rates allowed to decline to help relieve pressure on both financial institutions and corporate borrowers.

There are criticisms that tight monetary policy has been maintained for too long which acted to aggravate the problem and that relaxation has come too little and too late. It is indeed easy to assess the situation ex post, i.e., with the benefit of hindsight. For policymakers, the timing of a decision to shift the monetary policy stance early is not crystal clear and involves risks in both directions. If relaxation comes too soon, there is a risk of creating instability in exchange markets, which is undesirable. On the other hand, if relaxation comes too late, i.e., only after exchange rates have really been stabilized, there is a risk of exacerbating financial sector problems and recession. Therefore, the timing for the shift in monetary policy is always controversial and one cannot win both ways.

3.3 Restructuring of the real economies

At the initial phase, problems in the real sector were attributed mainly to the factors pertaining to the financial sector, e.g., the lack of credit availability and high debt servicing burden due to high interest rates and depreciating currencies. As the crisis persisted, however, other factors pertaining to the real sector itself started to exert their impacts, namely, the rising cost of production, the weakening demand for products from both external and domestic sources, and the decline in world commodity prices which adversely affected commodity exports. These explain why the real economies have deteriorated so fast and the prospect of recovery has drifted further away.

It is essential that actions be taken to resolve the real sector and financial sector problems simultaneously in order to break the vicious circle. This is not a matter of shifting macroeconomic policies only, but an action at the micro level is also essential. In the context of an industrial economy, it may sound unconventional and undesirable for the government to interfere with the functioning of market mechanisms and get involved with the problems at the sectoral level. In developing countries, on the other hand, there is scope for government involvement in the restructuring or rationalization of the corporate sector. There are several programs designed by international development organizations, such as the IBRD and ADB, for this purpose. Recently, the authorities in several countries have started to engage in the corporate debt restructuring process.

Notwithstanding the recognition of the need for real sector restructuring and the scope for government involvement, the process of policy implementation remains very difficult as the legal system, institutional framework, and infrastructure are not always readily available and the solution is most often sector-specific. Moreover, the completion of such process is long-term in nature and thus may delay other actions needed to accelerate economic recovery.

3.4 External factors

As part of the solution, the countries in crisis still need the resumption of foreign capital to help improve liquidity, recapitalize weak financial institutions and corporations, and stabilize exchange rates. Of course, it is desirable to obtain a better pattern and quality of capital inflows this time, i.e., more of long-term rather than short-term capital. However, the process of capital reflows has been slow so far, thus prolonging the crisis. This is understandable since once confidence has been lost, it is difficult to be regained in a short period of time. The wait-and-see or cautious approach seems to be adopted as foreign investors would prefer to see the economy bottoming out before starting to reinvest. At present, this seems like a moving target, as evidenced by the continued downward revisions of the WEO forecast or successive downward revisions of the recessionary trend in countries under fund programs. External financial assistance needed is slow to come and not contributing enough to the solution of the crisis situation.

4. CONCLUDING REMARKS

To conclude my observations regarding the delays in crisis resolution, I would like to note some common features that seem to emerge:

1. Some crisis solutions are long-term in nature, or take time to accomplish; thus, one should not expect any quick outcomes, for example from financial sector reform and industrial restructuring.

2. The countries in crisis are not prepared for quick implementation due to institutional, legal, and infrastructural constraints. This is because in good times or booming period, the weakness in the system is masked by superficial success and the authorities fail to lay appropriate groundwork to avert any possible crisis.

3. Economic management of the crisis situation is often complicated by political uncertainties. Political factors serve as both the cause and the effect of the crisis. Therefore, political stability and political will to implement necessary and painful adjustments are yet another key to the solution of the crisis.

PART IV

RESPONSE TO THE CRISIS—OVERVIEW AND CASE STUDIES

Chapter 14

Asian Crisis: Causes and Remedies

Bijan B. Aghevli
International Monetary Fund

First, let me tell you a fable:

Once upon a time and far away, a litter of little tiger cubs was born. And foreigners came from far and wide to admire the cubs, and comment upon the growth potential in their sturdy limbs and the irresistible allure of their shiny coats. The keepers were proud of their small charges, and set up open zoos with no restrictions and invited everyone to come. Foreign visitors rushed in bearing a formula of milk fortified with vitamins and growth hormones for the cubs, and clamored for the privilege of filling their bowls which, fashioned for a trickle, cracked and leaked under the sudden surge. The cubs grew at an astounding rate, and newspapers and scholarly journals marveled at the miracle of their growth. Before long, the cubs were tigers, and still they grew until they burst out of their flimsy cages and roamed unfettered through the streets, howling for the surfeit of milk and hormones on which they had come to depend. Seeing the tigers at such close range, the visitors began to criticize their less-than-perfect coats, their tendency to purr, their unorthodox values. The food, which had flowed like a river, began to dry up. The keepers, in their confidence that the flow was endless, had not repaired the bowls to safeguard the milk they still had, and watched helplessly as the tigers sickened and gnashed their teeth. Then the IMF doctors were called in to wean the tigers off their rich diet and offer alternative lifestyles. As the tigers limped back into their shattered cages, a rowdy crowd of professors gathered to denounce the cruelty of international civil servants in white coats.

This story serves to remind us that the Asian-crisis countries, which include Indonesia, Korea, Philippines, Malaysia, and Thailand, have indeed had an impressive record of economic performance over the past three decades: very high rates of growth, relatively low inflation rates, especially during the 1990s, macroeconomic stability and strong fiscal positions, very high rates of saving, open economies, and high export orientation.

It is therefore not too surprising that no one really predicted this crisis. That is not to say that we, at the IMF, did not in our work with these countries point out some of the underlying problems, but we did not really predict the crisis, certainly not of such magnitude. The real question then is, what went wrong? Now that the crisis has unfolded, it is, of course, much easier to identify the problems. In fact, there is a general consensus on the causes of the crisis, in sharp contrast to the diversity of views on the appropriate remedies.

To a large extent, these countries were victims of their own success. What do I mean by that? Because of their success throughout the early 1990s, all of these countries went through a denial stage when the first signs of the problem emerged. We have all heard the arguments why the problems which existed in Latin America in the 1980s did not really apply to the Asian countries because they did not suffer large government deficits and public debt, rapid rates of monetary expansion, and structural impediments. Consequently, these countries did not deal in earnest with the emerging problems until it was too late in the game.

The Thailand story is very telling in this regard, particularly since this was the first case, which started the whole process of contagion. The problems in Thailand started in 1996. I know for a fact that we gave the authorities a very strong warning on the emerging problems in early 1997, but it was very difficult to convince them that there were serious problems lurking behind the scenes. We were not, of course, in a position to give a public warning, lest we actually precipitate the crisis by our warning.

And, we were not aware of the full extent of potential problems at the time, because, as is generally known by now, the baht was initially supported by heavy intervention in the forward market. So we were looking at a level of international reserves, which, indeed, seemed quite comfortable, not knowing that pretty much all of the international reserves had already been committed in the forward market. This process went on until mid-1997, when the authorities realized that usable reserves had been all but depleted. At that stage, the authorities came to the IMF, and we had to negotiate a program under tremendous time pressure. Similarly, we were not aware that Korea's foreign exchange reserves had been all but depleted until we were called to the scene and had to put together an adjustment program in a matter of two weeks.

The underlying causes of the crisis are well identified by now. The most important element was the dynamic relationship in the capital markets. On the external side, substantial funds were available at relatively low interest rates, reflecting the paucity of investment opportunities in Europe and other developing countries. So the funds shifted into the fast growing Asia region, in retrospect, recklessly. All the investors in the industrial countries thought that this was a fantastic opportunity. And, in the early stages, as in all boom cycles, stock and real estate prices shot up, attracting even more funds. No one seemed worried.

At the same time, the whole process of borrowing from abroad and allocating the resources domestically was being undermined by a very weak banking system that had not kept pace with the rest of the economy. There were also serious problems of governance and transparency that interfered with efficient allocation of funds.

Another factor was a fixed exchange rate policy that encouraged investors to borrow dollar-denominated debt at very low interest rates with the false security that there was no the exchange rate risk. The rigidity of exchange rate was an issue, which was of concern to the IMF. In most of these countries, we were advocating more exchange rate flexibility which, during this period, would, in fact, have resulted in an appreciation. But a more flexible exchange rate policy would have removed the security of an implicit guarantee and would have eliminated the one-way bet that may have motivated excessive reliance on foreign financing.

There were also a number of factors contributing to a weakness of exports in these countries in mid-1990s. These included: the depreciation of the U.S. dollar against the yen since mid-1995; the devaluation by China, and then NAFTA.

In the meantime, the substantial capital inflow was naturally absorbed through a widening of the current account deficits. And, critically, much of this borrowing was done at short term, amplifying vulnerability.

In hindsight, it's clear that there was a big accident just waiting to happen, and it was just a question of what was going to trigger it. Once the Thai crisis broke in the middle of 1997, the Asian countries were all vulnerable. And the markets, not having reacted to the underlying problems for a long time, overreacted as everyone thought. If this can happen in Thailand, it is bound to happen in the rest of Asia too. Market participants looked at the problems Thailand was facing—weak financial and corporate sectors, large current account deficit, and large external debt, particularly short-term—and realized all of these countries shared these problems to varying degrees. As creditors withdrew funds from the region, the Thai crisis spread to the Philippines, Indonesia, and Korea.

Let me now turn to the adjustment phase and the role of the IMF. I will briefly outline the main elements of IMF programs, which have a fair bit in common, although there are also differences. In addition to their traditional focus on monetary and fiscal policies, IMF programs with the Asian countries also included important structural reforms, as the root cause of the problem in all of these countries was essentially structural.

The immediate issue in all of these countries was to provide adequate financing to deal with the liquidity crisis that was created by the sharp withdrawal of funds and the collapse of the currency. Thus, the main, common element of all of these programs was for the fund to provide substantial resources, much larger than usual. At the same time, we sought to arrange for additional funds from other countries in the region, as well as the G-7, to both substitute for the withdrawing capital inflows and give confidence to the market.

Given that the Asian crisis was initially manifested in the collapse of the currencies, it is not surprising that the formulation of monetary policy was considered to be a key element of all of the programs. Ironically, fund programs have been criticized from both sides of the spectrum: some have held the view that interest rates should have been raised more to defend the currency, while others have advocated vociferously that the rise in interest rates was the main source of subsequent problems.

Frankly, it's very difficult to see how interest rates can be reduced in the middle of a currency crisis. A number of academics have made the point that, in a recession, the orthodox policy would be to lower interest rates and allow the exchange rate to slide to boost economic activity. For example, one commentator has observed that "we cheerfully let the dollar slide from 240 yen to 140, from three Deutsche marks to 1.8; the Fed even helped the process along by cutting interest rates." But this observation overlooks an important fact: the dollar decline was spread over a period of one and half years, while the drop in the won from less than 1000 per dollar to nearly 2000 took place in only one month. In such an extreme situation, the first priority has to be to stabilize the exchange rate before a vicious inflationary cycle sets in. Once domestic prices begin to skyrocket, the monetary tightening required to reestablish price stability would be extremely costly.

The strategy pursued in these countries was to raise short-term interest rates to arrest the deterioration in the exchange rate, and then gradually reduce it as the exchange rate stabilized. Here, I would like to point out an important fact that has been lost in the debate. Contrary to the prevailing conventional wisdom, the initial rise in interest rate in the Asian countries was quite moderate and short lived: in Thailand, short-term rates rose to a peak of twenty-five percent and, in Korea, to thirty-five percent, and they stayed at these peaks for only a few days before declining rapidly to their precrisis level. Furthermore, taking into account the impact of sharp exchange rate depreciation on inflationary expectations, the increase in interest rates was significantly lower in real terms than in nominal terms. Real interest rates (based on the consensus forecast of inflation as a measure of inflationary expectations), which were in the range of seven to eight percent before the crisis, rose to short-lived peaks of twenty-to twenty-five percent before dropping sharply. In both countries, real rates were above 15 percent for only two months, and they are presently about zero. At the same time, both the won and the baht appreciated substantially after the initial crisis, vindicating the approach adopted in these countries.

By contrast, Indonesia's earlier efforts to stabilize the rupiah turned out to be futile. Indonesia's experience, however, is the exception that proves the rule. During the first week of the program, the authorities engaged in unsterilized intervention and allowed short-term interest rates to double to thirty percent. As a result, the rupiah appreciated sharply. But within two days, contrary to understandings with the fund, Bank Indonesia was instructed to cut interest rates back to their initial level. The subsequent liquidity expansion, together with strong signals from the highest levels of the government that commitments under the IMF program would not be fulfilled led to the subsequent plunge of the rupiah. The resulting high inflation has necessitated much higher interest rates to reestablish financial stability. The adjustment cost would have been drastically smaller had the government persevered with the original program in November 1997.

To be sure, the weakness of the banking and corporate sectors in the Asian countries did constrain the scope for raising interest rates. However, while many critics of fund programs have pointed to the adverse impact of higher interest rates on domestic borrowers, they have neglected to take into account the impact of exchange rate depreciation on holders of external debt. A precipitous drop in the exchange rate raises the corresponding burden of external debt on the banking and corporate sectors to an intolerable level and undermines financial stability. Thus, the trade-off between exchange rate depreciation and interest rate increase shifts drastically in the presence of exchange rate overshooting. The negative impact of the exchange rate depreciation is particularly pronounced for Indonesia, Korea, and the Philippines, which have a relatively higher ratio of external debt to domestic credit.

I should also underscore that the liquidity squeeze in these countries was not just a consequence of high interest rates, as the banks have been reluctant to roll over their credits, given their large nonperforming loans and the weak position of the corporate sector. It is instructive to note that credit squeeze has not been alleviated even as interest rates in Korea and Thailand have fallen to well below their precrisis levels. An even clearer example of this phenomenon is Japan, where short-term interest rates have been essentially zero for some time, while the economy has been facing a credit crunch.

On fiscal policy, the budgetary positions of these countries were strong initially. The original fiscal targets envisaged a small surplus to help external adjustment and provide a cushion for financing the substantial cost of financial sector restructuring. However, as the economic conditions deteriorated, the initial fiscal targets were adjusted to allow for the working of automatic stabilizers and to finance additional social spending to protect the poorer groups. In fact, given the fiscal conservatism of these countries, in some cases we found ourselves in the unusual position of trying to convince them to undertake additional fiscal expansion. The fiscal targets in all of these countries now show substantial deficits. Thus, the criticism that the fiscal contraction under the fund program led to the economic contraction in the Asian countries is largely misplaced.

We could, of course, be faulted for having missed the depth of the recession initially. This is a fair point but I would note that there was no systematic bias in our growth forecasts, as they were broadly in line with the consensus forecast. It is perhaps too early to be definite about why every one missed the severity of the recession, but I would offer a few tentative explanations. First, we have learnt that when boom-bust cycles are superimposed on a very weak financial system and highly leveraged corporate sector, the amplitude and duration of the cycle is much more pronounced. We have seen this also in the case of Japan. Second, up until mid-1997 it had appeared that Japan was finally pulling out of its prolonged recession. But these hopes were dashed as the Japan's economy plummeted, exacerbating the depth of recession in the Asian countries, which had close links with Japan. Finally, the impact of concurrent crisis in the Asian countries adversely affected general confidence and led to a sharp contraction of domestic demand, which far exceeded initial expectations.

Let me now turn to the structural elements of the programs, the most important elements of which were financial sector reform and corporate restructuring. In the case of Indonesia, there were also additional reforms designed to improve governance and signal to the market that resources would not continue to be channeled to connected groups.

The role of structural reforms in these countries has also been a point of debate. Some have argued that the fund should have focused only on macroeconomic policies, rather than structural reform, which is a medium-term process. But I would note that the main source of the problems in all of these countries was structural—the weakness of the financial and corporate sectors as well as governance and transparency issues. And, as the situation got worse, markets focused intensely on these problems. So the argument that "these problems were always there, why do we have to worry about them now" does not hold. Markets were worrying, and if these programs did not give assurance that important initiatives were being put in place, it would be very difficult to regain investor confidence. That is not to say that the structural problems could be solved overnight, but a critical mass had to be done up-front to instill confidence that the governments recognized the size of the problem and were committed to correcting it.

In addition, and this was particularly relevant in the case of Indonesia, the authorities themselves were keen to take advantage of the crisis to push through important reforms. The economic team in Indonesia was ultimately undermined by the connected parties who were threatened by the proposed reforms, and this led to the change in government. But the fund could hardly press the economic team to abandon its reform ambitions, lest they incur the wrath of connected parties. The myth that the IMF pushed unpopular reforms on the Asian countries is just that. Domestic support for IMF reforms was, in fact, strong and, ironically, criticisms were voiced mainly by outsiders.

A case in point is the closure of sixteen banks in Indonesia, which has often been cited by critics as a major mistake. The extremely weak position of Indonesia's financial system was widely known even before the fund program was negotiated. In fact, the authorities had already identified seven banks to be closed before the arrival of fund mission in Jakarta in late October, 1997. There was concern, however, that closing only seven banks and leaving some of the other ones which were in even worse shape would be counterproductive, particularly as some of the excluded bankrupt banks were known to belong to connected parties. Given the shortage of expert manpower to undertake the complex task of closing banks with many branches, a decision was reached together with authorities to close sixteen banks, which clearly had negative net worth. At the same time, a limited guarantee was extended to small depositors.

In retrospect, it would have probably been better to have given a blanket guarantee to minimize the subsequent runs on banks, but the decision to limit the guarantee also took into account moral hazard considerations. In any event, the resulting run on banks was quite manageable had it not been for two serious problems. First, the owners of two of the closed banks who were related to the president refused to accept the authority of the minster of finance and attacked him publicly. This episode undermined confidence in the government's commitment to push through the reform program, and started the subsequent capital flight. Second, Bank Indonesia proceeded to provide unchecked liquidity to banks well in excess of what was needed to accommodate the shift of deposits into currency. This unconditional provision of liquidity fueled the ongoing capital flight and set the stage for the collapse of the rupiah in early December when President Soeharto became ill. The problem with the closing of banks was therefore what it revealed about the lack of commitment by the government to follow through with reforms, rather than faulty program design. Had these banks not been closed, the original program would still have failed given the political problems, and the fund would then be criticized, probably by the same critics, for not having dealt with the fundamental structural problem which gave rise to the crisis in the first place.

The next question is, where do we stand now? In Korea and Thailand, the situation has turned around quite significantly. I wouldn't say the crisis is over, but certainly these countries have turned the corner. Exchange rates have appreciated considerably, and interest rates have already declined to below precrisis levels, which will allow investment to start and growth to resume. But having said that, a very difficult period is still ahead. Much like the patient who is going to feel worse for a period after the surgery before he starts to recover. The important task now is to manage the situation carefully so that unemployment problems do not get out of hand and undermine the programs. Both of these countries will emerge from the crisis considerably healthier as long as they maintain their resolve to carry through with their financial and corporate sector reforms.

The case of Indonesia, however, has proved to be much more complicated because of the volatile interaction of political and economic problems. As you know, the new government of President Habibie renegotiated the program in June and the IMF has just concluded the third monthly review of the EFF. This program aims to reverse the serious economic deterioration which has occurred in that country, prevent inflation from spiraling out of control, and extend the social safety net, so as to cushion the impact of the crisis on the poor. I am optimistic that Indonesia's bold reforms will take hold gradually, as long as the political situation is not allowed to get out of hand.

The success of the reform programs of the Asian countries will depend importantly on the external environment. Here, unfortunately, we are all aware of recent deepening of the crisis in Russia and its repercussions in Latin America. So far, the impact of this latest crisis on the Asian countries has been relatively limited. One favorable factor is the continuing strength, albeit gradually weakening, of the economies of the United States and Western European countries. On the other hand, the situation in Japan is worrying, particularly given its critical importance for the region. It is essential that Japan moves expeditiously to rehabilitate its financial system and to provide adequate fiscal stimulus to kick-start its economy so as to ensure that the prospective recovery of the crisis countries is not jeopardized.

Before concluding, let me just say a few words about what lessons are to be learned and what we can do to avoid such crises in the future. I should first emphasize that we will not be able to avoid crises. As long as we have financial markets, we will continue to have boom and bust cycles. A better question is, what can we do to limit vulnerability.

First, we need better information to monitor the situation and act in a timely fashion. Had we known how weak the financial systems in these countries were, something could have been done much earlier. Similarly, had we known how rapidly international reserves were falling in Thailand and subsequently in Korea, policy adjustments could have been made before absolutely the last moment.

Second, in all of these boom-bust cycles—and this is not unique to developing countries, we have also seen it in the industrial countries—the financial sector plays a very critical role. It is essential that appropriate prudential and supervisory procedures are in place and banks are in a position to assess risk. There's nothing wrong with taking large risk in the hope of larger returns. But, then you should know that's what you are doing. So financial sector reforms are extremely important.

Third, one very important lesson we have learned is that it is a mistake to have a fixed exchange rate unless you are really prepared to do what it takes. What I mean by that is, in addition to sound macroeconomic policies, you also need to have a healthy banking system and a strong reserve position, which can withstand a defensive rise in interest rates to fend off speculators. But there are not many countries that can hold onto a fixed exchange rate when things go wrong.

Fourth, and this is an issue which is being debated actively, is the capital market liberalization. One common theme has been that Asian countries should not have liberalized their capital market so early. To my mind, however, the problem was not that the capital account was liberalized, but that the sequencing was wrong and liberalization was only partial. What I mean by that is that most of these countries liberalized short-term capital inflows before foreign direct investment, rather than the reverse, which is the appropriate sequencing. Furthermore, while capital inflows were liberalized, the financial system remained closed to competition from outside. Thus, the combination of partial liberalization of the capital account in the presence of structural rigidities led to a channeling of external funds without due regard to risk and contributed to the ensuing crisis.

Would it then be appropriate to impose capital controls now to deal with the problem? But this would be like closing the door after the proverbial horse has bolted. Furthermore, capital controls are much less effective in stemming outflows than inflows. It would bc much more effective to move boldly to deal with the underlying problems in the financial and corporate sectors and to create the right environment for the resumption of capital inflows that can be used productively. After all, let's not forget that these countries' access to foreign capital in the past contributed significantly to their rapid growth. Even if output in the Asian countries declines by, say, ten percent, these countries would still have an impressive growth average over the last twenty years. What is important is that, when the capital market is opened, there is an appropriate sequencing so that the financial system is capable of channeling capital into productive investment.

Finally, IMF resources need to be replenished by the quota increase currently being considered by its members to ensure it is in a position to continue to perform its function effectively.

Chapter 15

Korea's Financial Sector Reforms

Stijn Claessens, Swati Ghosh, and David Scott
World Bank

Abstract: Korea has made great strides in its financial sector reforms, but many challenges remain. Most importantly these concern the deep links between corporate and financial sector reforms and the large fiscal resources required to resolve the current under capitalization of banks. This paper draws on work of other World Bank colleagues, in particular Ira Lieberman and Bill Mako. It also draws on information from the Korea government, in particular, *Korean Government's Economic Reform Progress Report*. Helpful comments were received from Jose De Luna Martinez and participants in the conference, *Asia: An Analysis of Financial Crisis*, Chicago, October 8-10, 1998, jointly organized by the Federal Reserve Bank of Chicago and International Monetary Fund. The opinions expressed are the authors' own, however, and do not necessarily reflect those of the World Bank. For comments, please contact Stijn Claessens, e-mail: CClaessens@worldbank.org, fax: (202) 522-2031.

1. THE DEVELOPMENT AND ONSET OF THE CRISIS

1.1 Underlying problems

Difficulties in the corporate and financial sectors have been at the core of Korea's financial crisis. The incentive framework for the financial sector did not lead to an efficient allocation of resources or promote the institutional development of financial institutions that adequately appraise risks. Poor credit culture and the lack of adequate risk analysis and management were two main weaknesses. Following a long period of government control, liberalization measures in the late-1980s and 1990s were mostly half-hearted and often not backed up by improvements in the supervisory and disclosure framework. Merchant banks, for example, were allowed to operate under more liberal capital adequacy requirements than commercial banks while they are inherently more risky. Prudential rules and their applications had fallen behind international best practices and differences existed between the treatment of various related financial instruments and institutions. Supervision of financial institutions was weak, scattered over various government agencies, and mostly focused on compliance with rules, rather that on assuring soundness and proper management. Especially in the area of dealing with troubled financial institutions there was a legal and institutional vacuum. Despite steps to increase openness, such as those negotiated with the Organization for Economic Cooperation and Development (OECD), Korea's financial system remained protected from foreign competition, with a low share of foreign investment in capital markets and limited foreign ownership of financial institutions. Earlier reform plans, such as those suggested by a presidential financial reform commission in early 1997, failed to gain enough political support.

Adding to the financial sector problems were difficulties in the corporate sector and its competitiveness. Major corporations (chaebols) had undertaken ambitious expansion and diversification drives in the last few years, including numerous overseas investment projects. The expansion drives were funded with very aggressive borrowings from Korean commercial and merchant banks, often short-term. Banks relied mainly on collateral in the allocation of credit and relatively little attention was paid to the earnings performance and cash flow generation, or the corporates' ability to repay. The chaebols generally supplied guarantees to their affiliates and subsidiaries to secure loans. The Korean stock market is thinly capitalized, and chaebols have traditionally raised little in new equity. The government often supported this expansion and directed chaebols into specific lines of business.

The policy of aggressive, leveraged expansion worked well as long as the economy and exports expanded vigorously and returns on new investment exceeded the cost of capital. In recent years, however, all measures of financial performance among the thirty largest chaebol worsened—free cash flow, return on equity, profit margin, and debt coverage ratio—while their debt/equity ratios continued to rise. Rapid wage increases, a result of a highly unionized and strong labor force, often outstripped productivity growth. Declining demand and falling prices for Korean exports—particularly in semiconductors, chemicals, shipbuilding and steel markets—

in part associated with a depressed Japanese economy and weakened yen, further weakened profitability in the last years.

The low internal profitability fuelled large borrowings in the last few years, from both domestic and foreign sources, and debt-equity ratios rose to over 30 percent by 1996. The very complex system of cross guarantees from affiliates within the group, as well as personal guarantees, allowed loss-making affiliates to continue to borrow from banks and drain financial resources from healthier affiliates. Serious problems began to surface starting early in 1997 and drew attention not only to the weakness of many conglomerates, but also to banks closely related to the business groups. On January 23, 1997, Hanbo Iron and Steel, Korea's second largest steel maker, was unable to honor its promissory notes and was forced to file for bankruptcy. The collapse of Hanbo was followed in quick succession by a series of other business failures. Key financial ratios deteriorated further and by end 1997, the debt/equity ratio of the thirty largest chaebols reached an average of 500 percent (600 percent if the debt of their financial subsidiaries is included). This compares with an industrial country norm of below 200 percent, and is four times the Taiwanese ratio. Total corporate debt is currently estimated to be on the order of $500 billion (or more than 150 percent of GDP at current exchange rates), of which around ninety percent is domestic.

1.2 Spillovers and initial policy responses

Following the devaluation of the Thai Baht—which had heightened investor sensitivity—investor concerns about Korea grew in the face of mounting evidence of difficulties in the corporate and financial sectors especially the liquidity positions of merchant banks. In response, the government announced on August 25, 1997 that it was committed to providing financial support to commercial and merchant banks and that it would ensure repayment of foreign debt liabilities of Korean financial institutions. It also announced that all financial institutions would be required to submit restructuring plans to be implemented over a period of three to five years. The market, however, remained unsatisfied and the failure of the National Assembly to pass important bills to institute financial reforms further weakened investor confidence. On November 19, the government announced another set of policy measures to deal with the growing financial crisis.[1] Once again, these measures did little to calm the markets, and when it was announced that the daily exchange band had been widened to plus/minus ten percent and that there would be no more intervention on the foreign exchange market, the Korean Won began a free-fall in late November/early-December, reaching a low of almost 2,000 won/dollar. In the end, the Korea crisis became a triple crisis—balance-of-payments, banking and corporate crisis.

2. EARLY POLICIES TO DEAL WITH THE FINANCIAL CRISIS

2.1 Financial sector

Restoring confidence and expediting the resolution of troubled financial institutions was the most urgent priority in the first few months. While there was no significant loss of confidence among depositors, also as there was a general guarantee in place, financial distress was widespread. Significant improvements in the framework for the financial sector, many of which had been proposed earlier by the Presidential Reform Committee and which had been debated but not enacted in Parliament, were passed in late December.

2.2 Resolution of financial institutions

The government first had to deal with the troubled merchant banks, and it closed ten in the first weeks of January. Two major commercial banks (Korea First Bank and Seoul Bank) had run up substantial nonperforming loans (NPLs). The government imposed substantial losses on the owners of these banks, injected public resources to stabilize their capital position, and assumed ownership control. The government plans to privatize these two banks in the near future. The role of the Korean Asset Management Corporation (KAMCO) in restoring bank portfolios was initially large as it bought substantial amounts of NPLs from many banks in December and early January. Commercial banks which did not meet the eight percent BIS capital adequacy ratios as of end-1997 (12 out of 25) were asked to provide recapitalization and rehabilitation plans.

2.3 Supervision and legal reforms

A new supervisory structure was enacted late December, consolidating various supervisory functions—covering banks, nonbank financial institutions (NBFIs) and capital markets—in one body (Financial Supervisory Board, FSB and Financial Supervisory Committee, FSC) under the direct supervision of the prime minister. The Bank of Korea (BOK) Act was amended to provide for greater independence of BOK in setting monetary and credit policy. Barriers between financial service providers were lowered to increase competition within the financial sector and enhance stability. Prudential rules for merchant banks were tightened and harmonized with other financial institutions. Legal changes were made to consolidate and improve depositor protection schemes and to enhance the powers of the deposit insurance agency to undertake examinations of financial institutions, and intervene in and resolve troubled financial institutions.

2.4 Financial services and capital account liberalization

The government went beyond the WTO Financial Services Agreement of December 1997, and liberalization measures agreed earlier with the OECD, and opened up more to foreign entry in the financial sector. For capital account transactions, the IMF-program included, among others, full liberalization of foreign exchange transactions over time, no limits on foreign investment in local bonds and short-term money markets, and no limits on foreign banks and brokerage houses to establish subsidiaries. The government also made general changes in the liberalization of the foreign direct investment regime, and issued clarifying guidelines governing foreign investment in financial institutions, including through mergers and acquisitions.

2.5 Corporate sector

Given the very high levels of debt to banks (the top thirty chaebols account for over sixty percent of bank lending), the problems of the banking sector have been very closely linked to those of the corporate sector. With the onset of the economic crisis in late 1997 and the spike in interest rates in 1998, five major groups worth about $20 billion in assets quickly failed, unable to pay their debts. Moreover, it soon became apparent that eighteen of the largest thirty groups were at risk of bankruptcy, with combined liabilities of about $75 billion. Not surprisingly, a series of syndicated emergency loans were provided by major banks to a number of major groups at risk, totaling some 2.5 trillion won. The problems of the largest groups quickly spread to SMEs, which often operate as satellites of the major groups. Also a complex system of payments from the big to small firms via promissory notes, traditionally discounted at banks, adversely affected the liquidity of the latter, as the terms of the notes were extended from an average of 30–60 days to 90–180 days and discounting rates rose from 12–30 percent. Moreover, exporting SMEs found it difficult to finance imports of needed raw material and other inputs.

2.6 Corporate sector reforms

A number of acts passed late 1997 and on February 14, 1998 provided for many changes in the framework for corporate transactions. These included permitting takeovers of non-strategic companies by foreign investors without government approval and raising the foreign stock ownership ceiling; accelerated introduction of consolidated financial statements and requirements for audit committees; and strengthening minority shareholders' rights. The Composition and Reorganization Acts were revised to induce a more expedited process for financial restructuring by fixed deadlines, promoting expertise of the courts by creating a separate administrative body, and strengthening the creditors' role by allowing creditor committees. New cross guarantees were prohibited and all existing guarantees would need to be unwound by the year 2000.

2.7 Macroeconomic stabilization

Macroeconomic stabilization aimed—in the first instance—at restoring exchange rate stability, rebuilding international reserves and containing potential inflationary pressures resulting from the economic shocks. This initially involved a relatively sharp tightening of monetary policy (benchmark interest rates rose from twelve to thirty percent), as well as some fiscal tightening. The program restored exchange rate stability, with the currency strengthening from a low of near 2,000 won/$ to about 1,300–1,400 won, and over the past few months Korea has seen a significant improvement in its external reserves position. Output has fallen very sharply, however, and is expected to register negative growth of seven percent in 1997. And although greater stability in the foreign exchange market and the subsiding of inflationary pressures in recent months have led to an appreciable decline in nominal interest rates, real lending rates are still above those before the crisis, especially for SMEs.

As often in financial crises, macroeconomic developments and corporate and financial sector distress have reinforced each other. Given the very high leverage of Korean corporates, corporate financial positions, and consequently also the health of the portfolios of creditor financial institutions, have been particularly vulnerable to interest rate spikes.[2]

Compounding the effect of higher interest rates has been the depreciation of the won, albeit now stabilized, the plunge in domestic demand and the only slowly growing external demand (in value terms), which has further lowered firms' profitability. Corporates' financial difficulties, in turn, led to a cutback in demand for (and supply of) new lending. NPLs increased rapidly, and, including those classified as nonperforming on a precautionary basis, amounted to almost nine percent of all bank loans in March 1998, compared to less than one percent in 1995. Banks, in the face of rising NPLs and the need to restructure and recapitalize, have resorted to loan recalls and higher spreads.

3. FINANCIAL SECTOR RESTRUCTURING PROGRAM

Avoiding systemic risks, and restoring solvency of financial institutions, while keeping fiscal costs manageable, have been the main goals of the financial sector reform program. The government was also committed to conclude many aspects of the first phase of its bank-restructuring program by the end-of-September. As of end-of-September, a number of non-viable financial institutions—including sixteen merchant banks, two securities companies, and one investment trust company—have been closed, while the operations of other troubled financial institutions, including insurance companies, have been suspended. In total, ninety-four financial institutions had their operations suspended or were closed as of the end of September. Table 1 provides an overview of the financial sector restructuring progress to date.

3.1 Commercial banks restructuring

Korea has relatively concentrated banking, with the six largest banks accounting for more than fifty percent of the banking system. Korean banks are also large relative to GDP: assets of the six largest banks account each for about ten percent of GDP, compared to less than five percent for the largest bank in most other OECD-countries. Dealing with the large commercial banks has been a central part of the restructuring strategy. Of the twenty-six commercial banks in existence at the end of 1997—which includes sixteen national banks and ten regional banks—two as noted were taken over by the government and recapitalized in December. The government has initiated the privatization of these banks, with the objectives of attracting foreign capital and expertise into the system. Twelve commercial banks that failed to meet capital adequacy standards at end-1997 were asked to submit rehabilitation plans and subjected to asset quality diagnostic reviews. The FSC announced on June 28 that the rehabilitation plans of five of the twelve banks were deemed infeasible. These five banks had their business licenses suspended and have since been acquired by five stronger banks under purchase and assumption (P&A) transactions, with public support to ensure that the acquiring banks would not be weakened.

Table 1. Financial Institutions Suspended or Closed (as of September)

	Total No. of Institutions (end-1997)	License Revoked	Suspended	Subtotal
Commercial Banks	26	—	5	5
Merchant Banks	30	16	—	16
Securities Companies	34	2	4	6
Insurance Companies	50	—	4	4
Investment Trust Companies	8	1	1	2
Mutual Savings and Finance Companies	230	1	21	22
Credit Unions	1,653	12[1]	27	39
Leasing Companies	25	—	—	—
Total	2,063	32	62	94

Note: 1) Bankruptcy.
Source: MOFE, Korea.

The remaining seven undercapitalized banks received conditional approval. These include four large banks that account for more than one third of total commercial bank assets (Cho Hung, Commercial, Hanil Bank, and Korea Exchange Bank). Banks were instructed to submit revised implementation plans containing proposed management changes, cost reductions, capital increases, and measures taken to limit the accumulation of nonperforming assets. Currently, six large banks, including both conditionally approved banks and other banks, are, on a voluntary basis, proceeding with mergers so as to increase their scale economies and efficiency. Of these, the agreed merger of Commercial Bank of Korea and Hanil Bank is the largest. Other conditionally approved banks not involved in merger deals are taking rehabilitation actions, such as disposing of NPLs, inducing new equity capital, and streamlining business operations. The nine healthy banks not involved in mergers, including the five receiving banks involved in P&As, are being reviewed for their financial soundness and management practices.

3.2 Nonbank financial institutions

The FSC is applying basically the same scheme with regard to the restructuring of NBFIs. Self-rehabilitation under the initiative of major shareholders is being encouraged, but is closely monitored by the FSC. If self-rehabilitation steps are deemed inadequate, the institutions will either be subject to corrective actions or face closure. Of the thirty merchant banks at the end of 1997, sixteen troubled merchant banks have had their licenses revoked and have been undergoing resolution procedures. The remaining fourteen merchant banks will be monitored for the implementation of rehabilitation plans and achievement of capital adequacy targets. Securities firms, insurance companies, leasing companies, and investment trust companies have had to submit rehabilitation plans, followed by review by the FSC and, if necessary, resolution through closure. The first round of restructuring was completed in September, and some NBFIs had their licenses revoked.

3.3 Supervision and regulations

The FSC, formally established in April 1998, is an integrated financial supervision body, and all financial institutions will be supervised by the FSC. The four existing supervisory agencies (Banking Supervisory Authority, Securities Supervision Board, Insurance Supervisory Board, and the Non-Bank Financial Institution Supervisory Authority) are expected to be fully integrated into the FSB by end-1998. With the consolidation of supervisory organizations, supervisory arrangements for commercial banks will be extended to all NBFIs. The FSC will also be granted powers to enforce supervisory actions against specialized and development banks, and prudential rules applied to commercial banks will be extended to other type of banks.

Since December 1997, the regulatory framework is being strengthened to conform more closely to international norms. Changes have been made in rules for mark-to-market accounting, disclosure of NPLs, asset classification criteria, and foreign exchange liquidity and exposure criteria. On July 1, a number of additional prudential regulations and reporting requirements were announced: loan classification and provisioning,[3] accounting and disclosure of trust accounts, and short-term foreign borrowing and foreign exchange exposures. Limits on connected lending that apply to commercial banks will be extended to merchant banks, and full disclosure will be required of such lending. To reduce large exposures, single borrower and group exposure limits for commercial banks will be reduced over time, with a phased reduction of exposures in excess of these limits. Deposit insurance consolidated in KDIC and the present general protection will be narrowed.[4]

3.4 Fiscal support

Public support is being provided through purchases of NPLs by KAMCO and recapitalization and depositor protection by KDIC. During late 1997 to early 1998, public support consisted of the reinforcement of commercial banks' capital through the subscription by the government of subordinated debt issued by these banks the assumption of impaired loans from some commercial banks by KAMCO; equity injections amounting to three trillion Won to recapitalize Korea First and Seoul Bank; and payments to the depositors of the fourteen merchant banks that were closed through KDIC. Support has since been provided to the five banks involved in the recent P&A transactions—through purchases by KAMCO of NPLs and a put-back option, and KDIC capital injections. For other banks that merge as part of their rehabilitation plan, the government is will bring these banks' capital adequacy ratio up to at least ten percent (in the case of mergers between weak banks) and up to those of sound banks (in the case of mergers between sound and troubled banks). Government will support stand-alone banks (i.e., those that are not merging as part of their rehabilitation plans) by matching new equity contributions (under the condition of sufficient operational restructuring efforts).

At the end of September, the government has budgeted in total sixty-four trillion won or fourteen percent of GDP for financial sector restructuring, of which approximately thirty-eight trillion won has already been spent. The sixty-four trillion won is to cover equity injections, purchases of bad assets from commercial and merchant banks, purchase of subordinated debt from commercial banks, recapitalization of commercial banks and expenditures on depositor insurance for all commercial banks.[5] Fiscal resources are being mobilized largely by issuing public bonds. These interest costs are estimated to be 3.6 trillion won for 1998 and eight to nine trillion won for 1999.

3.5 Strategy

The strategy for restructuring financial institutions is to provide government support in addition to private recapitalization efforts. The latter have been limited, however, with total domestic private equity raised by commercial banks in 1998 equal to $0.6 billion and foreign capital equal to $0.7 billion. NBFIs have attracted another $0.7 billion in foreign capital, but the total raised is still much less than total government resources committed, about $6 billion. Recapitalization with government resources has led to significant government ownership; the government now controls banks which assets are about a third of total bank assets, or, put differently, banks which assets' size is equal to about fourty percent of GDP. This effective nationalization of a substantial part of the banking system raises the question of interim governance. The government will have to assume the responsibilities of ownership, including contracting with experienced senior managers to undertake restructuring, until sale to strategic investors with sufficient capital and expertise to manage banks. This privatization will be difficult, however, given the lack of domestic, qualified capital, and the reluctance, so far, of foreign investors to provide resources. Deteriorating global conditions have made this task even more difficult. A substantial period of time may thus elapse before re-privatization.

Nevertheless, the importance of foreign know-how to help strengthen Korea's financial sector can not be understated. Korea, as many other Asian countries, had before this crisis limited the entry by foreign financial institutions. Empirical evidence for Asia—and other countries—suggested that this slowed the banks' institutional development and led to more costly financial services provision. It was then recognized that, going forward, Asian countries could benefit from accelerating the opening up. These benefits are even larger today as there is not only a severe shortage of bank capital, but also an even greater need for the introduction of foreign expertise to help in the restructuring of the corporate sector and in enhancing the quality of the financial sector in general. Formally, most East Asian countries have opened up considerably. In practice, there are many barriers still to be overcome to make it attractive enough for foreign investors to come in.

The strategy for NBFIs centers on the rationalization of the industry in a market-based manner. In the context of NBFI resolutions, only explicitly government-guaranteed liabilities will be covered. In exceptional cases, and in the context of a comprehensive restructuring plan, support may be provided to NBFIs if failure of these institutions poses a systemic risk.

4. CORPORATE FINANCIAL RESTRUCTURING

4.1 Status

The needed corporate restructuring involves both financial and operational restructuring. Overextended chaebols need to restructure their balance sheets, increase equity and the maturity profile of their debt. Reducing debt/equity ratios is also essential to reduce vulnerability to future financial shocks. The longer-term process of operational restructuring will need to include improved corporate governance, product line rationalization, increases in productivity, and a fundamental change in corporate strategies and culture, focusing on profitability and liquidity versus aggressive expansion at virtually any cost.

The approach to restructuring has differed for the top five chaebols versus the other chaebols, six through sixty-four. The top five (Hyundai, Samsung, LG, Daewoo, and SK) are generally considered to currently have a better cash flow position than the other chaebols. They have more access to external financing, particularly through capital markets, and have the ability to sell off some of their foreign assets acquired during their expansion. Some of this better liquidity position derives perhaps from their size—they may be considered too big to fail—and thus raises issues of its own. SMEs, as noted, have been more affected by credit crunch directly and indirectly through links with chaebols. Separate government programs are adopted for these firms.

4.2 Policy actions to date

The immediate focus of restructuring efforts has been on restructuring the "non-top five" chaebols. In principle, all methods of financial restructuring are contemplated. In practice, market conditions and deadlines of the reform program encourage initial emphasis on debt restructuring, including debt/equity conversions. Subsequent emphasis is likely to be on asset sales, foreign investment, and new equity infusions. Among the non-top five chaebol in distress, some owners appear willing to give up control, and restructuring efforts have been addressing the issue of cross guarantees. Size, cross-ownership and cross-guarantees are insulating the top five chaebol to a larger degree from change. The government is responding with Fair Trade Commission actions against improper intra-chaebol transactions, statutory reductions in cross guarantees, more careful standards for future lending, and pressures for banks to exit from non-viable chaebol affiliates. This process is expected to take time. In the mean time, the risk is that cross—guarantees both postpone the reckoning for non-viable affiliates and continue to compromise the financial health of the whole group.

Supportive macroeconomic policies, involving the gradual easing of monetary policy—with due regard to maintaining exchange rate stability—and more expansionary fiscal policy are being pursued. In addition, changes have been underway in accelerating the role of banks in corporate restructuring, the enabling environment, the framework for corporate restructuring, and the role of capital markets.

4.3 Commercial banks

The government has opted so far for bank-led voluntary corporate debt workouts for the non-top five chaebols. Hence the recapitalization and restructuring of banks is a central element in the strategy for corporate financial restructuring. Eight major creditor banks, identified as lead banks, are to take the responsibility for negotiating workouts. Each of the banks has formed a workout unit. Policy measures are being implemented to strengthen incentives to undertake debt restructuring.

4.3.1 Curtailing emergency or rescue loans to corporates

Emergency syndicated loans to troubled debtors, which had the effect of delaying restructuring, will be curtailed in the future. Fresh capital will be provided to financially distressed but viable companies only in the context of the workout process, and subject to guidelines. Only in exceptional cases, can corporations not in the process of a workout, but due to be restructured, be provided with new loans.

4.3.2 Tightening prudential limits

The government has adopted a schedule for over time tighter prudential limits on connected lending and large exposures by banks, which will place further pressures on banks to undertake corporate debt workouts. This is especially relevant for the larger chaebols where exposures are currently above the (future) lending limits.

4.3.3 Reducing cross guarantees

The FSC is encouraging banks to reduce cross-guarantees through the workout process, and is proposing market-based approaches to unwind these guarantees, such as exchanging the guarantees for equity or warrants.

4.4 The enabling environment

An integral element has been changes in the legal and regulatory environment to remove impediments to corporate restructuring, encourage the infusion of new equity into the system and facilitate debt/equity conversions. Regulations governing foreign ownership in listed stocks have been changed (it now allows 100 percent foreign ownership); the M&A regime has been liberalized (it now allows hostile takeovers by foreigners); tax incentives, e.g. on asset sales, have been introduced; the real estate market has been opened to foreigners; financial disclosure and reporting have been strengthened; and insolvency procedures have been improved. Changes have also been made to the labor law, which now allows layoffs and measures to improve labor market flexibility. These measures will not only complement financial restructuring, but are also needed to improve the efficiency of corporates over the medium term.

The stock of corporate debt is so large, that sustainable debt/equity ratios cannot be achieved over a reasonable time frame only through the flow of new equity, asset sales and retirement of debt. In addition, stock adjustments in the form of conversion of debt into equity will be necessary. In the first instance, the banking law has been changed to allow banks to hold up to fifteen percent of their equity in a corporation (and no more than 100 percent of their equity in total). Since banks can hold only so much equity, however, and may moreover be ill-prepared to manage equity, equity will need to be unloaded over time. So far, indications are that the supply of equity capital is insufficient to allow an off-loading of equity over a reasonable period of time.

4.5 Voluntary framework

The FSC has developed an out-of-court framework for corporate workouts. This framework, within which banks, NBFIs and corporates will undertake workouts, utilizes so-called London Rules, which basically call for extra-judicial resolution of problem debtors. A Corporate Restructuring Accord (CRA) has been signed by some 200 Korean banks and NBFIs, which commits them to follow agreed workout procedures. In the event that financial institutions cannot agree on a workout strategy among themselves or the lead bank and the debtor cannot reach agreement, an arbitration committee, the Corporate Restructuring Coordination Committee (CRCC), has been created to resolve differences. If a CRA signatory fails to comply with an approved workout agreement or the CRCC arbitration decision, the CRCC has the power to impose penalties. The FSC will monitor the workouts agreed under the CRA to ensure consistency with the guidelines issued for the workouts.

4.6 Capital markets

Capital markets development is another important component. Deeper capital markets will help shift corporate finances away from debt and associated risk thus far carried by the banking system. A new regulatory framework, providing greater independence to market institutions, is being put in place. The FSC will accord securities market agencies increased authority to regulate and supervise their members. Prudential rules for securities markets activities are also being strengthened, including standards for risk management, adoption of mark-to-market accounting, and use of credit rating. Improvements in financial disclosure and minority shareholder rights will further support securities market development by enhancing investor confidence.

To develop a more liquid and active bond market the government is developing a clear, comprehensive funding strategy, including financing of the financial sector restructuring costs. The strengthening of the institutional investor base, being supported through changes in the legal and regulatory framework, allow the establishment of mutual funds and other corporate restructuring vehicles.[6] Improvements in the management of pension system reserves are also underway.

4.7 Role of KAMCO

A bridge bank has assumed distressed assets from merchant banks and KAMCO has bought NPLs from commercial banks (as of the end of September, 37 trillion won was purchased by KAMCO at a cost of 17.2 trillion). KAMCO will have to restructure these loans and has a number of tools at its disposal to restructure loans: asset-backed securities; loan portfolio sale; asset sale; and M&A or direct investment. Potentially, KAMCO can be an important actor in the corporate restructuring process.

4.8 Support for SMEs

The government has adopted a special program for SMEs caught in the wake of the financial crisis. As a first step, the government decided to rollover the debts of the SMEs by extending working capital maturities. It has also provide liquidity to finance working capital needs of SMEs, to discount promissory notes, and to provide trade finance for critical imports. The scope of corporate workout programs is being expanded to include SMEs. Creditor banks have evaluated the financial status of approximately 22,000 SMEs with outstanding loans of one billion won or more, and have classified about 13,000 of these as viable, and candidates for workout programs. A special task force unit within each bank is reviewing the feasibility of rehabilitation plans and will devise specific measures and schedules for workout programs.

4.9 Corporate governance improvements

Important changes in the corporate governance framework have been adopted. Transparency and accountability in corporate governance are being facilitated by: consolidated financial statements required from 1999; domestic accounting practices conforming to international standards; representation requirement for class action suits was drastically relaxed from one percent to 0.01 percent in May;[7] restrictions on institutional investors' voting rights were eliminated in June; and all listed companies are required to appoint outside directors from 1998.

4.10 Strategy

The current approach to corporate restructuring can best be described as bank-led, in a "market-based" environment, enhanced by an out-of-court process. The main function of creditor banks will be to drive the operational restructuring process, reduce the level of debt to appropriate levels, and, if necessary, provide new money for working capital purposes. The government does not plan to intervene directly in the restructuring process. All types of restructuring tools are in principle at the banks' disposal.[8] The presumption is that banks will to try to bring in genuine new equity from strategic investors to take over some of the (converted) loans. Some additional sticks and carrots to accelerate restructuring are in place. In particular, the recapitalization of banks will provide a carrot as it allows for debt rescheduling and debt relief. The recapitalization of the banking sector, together with the change in the banking law which now allows banks to hold more equity, means that banks can convert loans into equity as part of the restructuring package. The CRA is a stick as it sets processes and deadlines and allows the imposition of penalties. And the revamped bankruptcy code is a stick to encourage voluntary agreements while maintaining payment discipline.

5. CHALLENGES

The Korea government realizes the enormity of the task ahead. Several areas are of particular challenge: the size of the problem; the fiscal resources required; the tight links between bank and corporate restructuring; and the credit crunch.

5.1 Size of the problem

Measured by assets, commercial banks and the entire financial system represented 171 percent and 344 percent of GDP, respectively, at the end of 1997. According to official estimates, as of the end of June 1998, estimated total NPLs of all financial institutions, broadly defined to include loans classified as "precautionary", was 136.0 trillion won, or 21.8 percent of total outstanding loans, up from 13.3 percent at the end of 1997 (Table 2). Due to the tightened loan classification standards effective July 1, 1998, and continued economic decline, a substantial portion of precautionary loans are likely migrate to the "substandard" category before the end of this year. Furthermore, the quality of some of the precautionary loans may deteriorate over the course of corporate restructuring process. In light of this, the government expects core NPLs, i.e., loans more than three months overdue, to peak at 100–120 trillion won by the end of this year, or about 25 percent of GDP. Including possible migration of precautionary loans will raise this number further.

Table 2. Nonperforming Loans (end of period)

Nonperforming Loans (unit: trillion won)

	Dec. 1997	March 1998	June 1998	Dec. 1998(e)
Precautionary	42.8	57.7	72.5	—
Substandard Or below (A)	43.6	59.6	63.5	100–200
Bank	31.6	38.8	40.0	—
NBFI	12.0	20.8	23.5	—
Total Loan (B)	647.4	668.7	624.8	—
Precautionary and below/Total loans(%)	13.35	17.54	21.77	

Note: (e) Denotes estimated figures.
Source: MOFE, Korea.

Currently the private sector already estimates higher NPLs, thirty percent of GDP or more, with some estimates of fifty percent of GDP or more by the end of the year. Analysis of corporates' financial positions also suggests higher figures. For a sample of large Korean firms, under current exchange and interest rates, total liabilities exceed assets for 40 percent of corporates, i.e., 40 percent of firms are technically insolvent.[9] Extrapolating this sample, non-performing bank loans could be 24.8 percent of GDP, and non-performing assets (including all forms of credit) 64.2 percent of GDP. The latter is probably a more appropriate measure in case of Korea given the large trust-account activities and the many capital markets instruments which are guaranteed by banks, but which are not captured in the first figure.

5.2 Fiscal resources

The estimates of NPLs suggest that the final fiscal costs will likely be sizably higher than 75 trillion won. At least 125-150 trillion won may be a more realistic assessment, or approximately 30-35 percent of GDP. Assuming that the government would want to restore bank solvency quickly and finance the costs primarily by the issuance of government bonds, the stock of public debt would jump sharply. This raises the issue whether the stock of public debt would rise to too high levels, and, related, whether the annual financing costs would become unsustainable. Given Korea's very low initial public debt levels—10.7 percent of GDP in 1997, financial restructuring costs of thirty-five percent of GDP would still result in levels of public debt that are lower than or comparable to other countries.[10]

Such higher public debt also appears sustainable. Taking the mid-range of current estimates—150 trillion won—and using a simple debt sustainability calculation, reasonable medium term growth and real interest rate projections suggest that this initial debt/GDP of fourty-six percent can be brought down to about twenty percent of GDP over a decade by running primary surpluses on the order of four percent—five percent of GDP. Although Korea has run relatively high primary surpluses in the past, it might not be necessary to run this level of primary surpluses as stabilizing debt/GDP might suffice. Primary surpluses on the order of only 1.4 percent of GDP would already stabilize Korea's debt/GDP at fourty-six percent.[11] Thus, there might not be a great urgency to run large primary surpluses. And, in any case, it needs to be assured that the way in which the primary surplus would be generated (by taxes, cut in expenditures, privatization proceeds, etc.) is the most efficient in restoring growth. Indeed, given the current macroeconomic downturn and need for higher social expenditures, it might be more appropriate to postpone running significant primary surpluses, and achieve the decline in debt/GDP on a more gradual path. In fact, the decline in debt/GDP could probably be phased over a even longer period: if debt/GDP were brought down to only thirty percent in the next ten years (requiring average primary surpluses of under four percent of GDP), Korea's public debt ratio at the end of the period would still be comparable to that of other many countries.

5.3 Links between corporations and the financial system

Korea is following by-and-large a voluntary, bank-led corporate restructuring strategy (with supportive measures to encourage corporate restructuring). This approach has benefits. It signals clearly to the market that the financial sector problems are being addressed. Since the government has already guaranteed the liabilities of banks, it formalizes some of its responsibility and thus creates clarity. It mitigates, in appearance at least, any direct government involvement in corporate restructuring. And, provided it is accompanied by substantive changes in the corporate governance of and operations of banks, it can amount to an up-front investment that may lead to lower ultimate costs as the moral hazard of bailouts may be avoided.

Yet, a bank-led approach has risks given the large exposures of banks, especially for the top five chaebols, the tight historical links, the lack of credit culture, and especially the lack of debt restructuring skills and experiences. Several specific risks can be identified. For one, recapitalization of banks in advance of substantial progress on debt restructuring has risks: many countries have gone through recurrent recapitalizations because the overhang of bad debts was not adequately dealt with and eliminated. Concurrent reforms—covering the governance of banks, the prudential and supervisory framework, and the role of markets in disciplining banks—are also necessary. Banks will also need enhanced technical capacity and institutional capacity to deal with the restructuring of a large number of corporates and a large magnitude of corporate debt. Related banks will need to enhance their institutional capacity to manage and dispose of equity holdings (if banks end up with large amounts of equity holdings that they can not dispose off quickly, banks' portfolios may become unstable and perverse incentives may result). Furthermore, it has been questioned whether banks would be strong enough vis-à-vis corporates. It has been argued, partly because of "too big to fail" reasons, as well as because of the social and political consequences associated with restructuring, that banks will not be able to hold their own vis-à-vis the chaebols. This may result in not deep enough corporate financial and operational restructuring plans and a larger ultimate fiscal cost. The risks are that restoration of corporations' competitiveness, and thereby economic growth, will not be attained.

Most notably, it is not clear whether this approach will achieve fundamental changes in the way corporates are controlled. The shortage of equity in the system will mean that current shareholders can not be completely be diluted, as otherwise the government will own much of the corporate sector. It might also be necessary to retain the current owners as they have important managerial skills. Leaving the current shareholders too much in control of corporations, however, risks a repeat of vulnerable financial structures and inefficient investments. Going forward, alternatives may be necessary which achieve both good short-term and medium-term outcomes. Certainly, the government needs to continue to set the rules of the game, and let corporates, banks and third parties negotiate without direct interference. It is also essential that adequate safeguards are built in, market-based principles are accepted at the political and operational level, as much as possible the current institutional structure is used, private involvement is maximized, and no new mechanisms for financial support to corporates are created. Lastly, it should aim to achieve, over time, a better corporate financing and governance structure.

One proposal which has been put forward is to have corporates "apply" to a process in which they can have their debt restructured provided they undertake the necessary operational restructuring. Corporates can be encouraged to submit themselves to this process by instructing all banks to stop lending to corporates with debt-servicing problems or by greatly increasing the provisioning requirements for loans to such corporates. The corporate then needs to provide an operational and financial restructuring plan to a committee of creditor banks and other independent members. Various consultants and staff would support the committee. The plan should indicate the savings achieved through operational restructuring, sell-off of assets, the contribution in new equity, and the degree of financial restructuring and relief sought and through what modalities. If an acceptable plan can not be agreed, the corporate is due for the standard bankruptcy process.

In many ways, this is akin to the current process for corporate restructuring. The key additional feature of this approach would be to introduce to the workouts not just banks and corporations, but directly (new) private investors and a party representing government interests. The government could be represented by a privately managed fund (possibly with private-sector equity interest) and would negotiate as a potential equity investor in the restructured corporation. Financial relief provided by creditor banks would be mainly lengthening maturities and interest relief, and some (limited) debt–equity swaps. Creditor banks might also provide working capital, but only under strict conditions (for example, highly collateralized). The private investor and the government fund would take over some loans from creditor banks and swap these claims for equity. The bank could be compensated for losses these on loans, through cash, a claim on the fund or a government bond.

All this requires participation by of the private sector, by putting up capital and being heavily involved in management of the fund. One way would be to make the fund jointly owned (private and public) with private shareholders the ultimate claimholder. This would ensure those private shareholders in the fund, which have to make the final decision on the viability of financial restructuring, face the right incentives. Public resources would only be provided at the point when all parties—creditor banks, other creditors, new private investors, and the private shareholders in the fund—have reached agreement with the corporation.

This could lead to deeper capital markets. As an equity holder, perhaps the largest one, the fund(s) would have responsibility to ensure that enterprises are properly managed. But the government should not be a permanent corporate owner. It should dispose of its holdings—through sales to strategic or portfolio investors—as quickly as it can at realistic prices. This may be difficult, however, given the limited supply of (domestic and foreign) capital. Options include making an equity distribution to taxpayers, or transferring the shares to an institution to be held in trust for the public's benefit. Or the public could be encouraged to buy shares on advantageous terms (for example, with a small down payment and the balance paid over an extended period). This would lead to deeper capital markets, with attendant benefits in terms of improved corporate governance, better risk diversification, and better price signals.

5.4 Credit crunch

Availability of credit has emerged as one of the main issues. As of the second quarter of 1998 the nominal growth of domestic credit to the private sector was only nine percent yoy—as compared to a growth of twenty-one percent yoy in the second quarter of 1997. As in other financial crises, the slowdown in credit is likely attributable to a mixture of supply and demand factors: banks' lending capacity, in part affected by deteriorated capital adequacy positions and tighter prudential regulations, may play a role on the supply side, while the drop in aggregate demand (domestic and external), weakened balance sheets of corporations and increased risk (perceptions) may play a role on the demand side. Whether there is a credit crunch, i.e., whether there is excess demand for credit at prevailing lending rates, is unclear.

The minimum eight percent capital adequacy ratio, tightened provisioning and other prudential requirements, and more rigorous enforced standards could have affected the supply of loanable funds. Analysis based on reported data through May suggests that deposit money banks' capacity to lend remains higher than the volume of domestic credit extended to the private sector. Analyzing deposit money banks' lending capacity in aggregate suggests that banks have capacity to lend. This is not to say, of course, that individual banks may not be constrained in making loans. It is also likely that reported figures underestimate the true capacity of banks to lend. Many banks may realize that their real capital adequacy position is much weaker, and are therefore holding back lending to the private sector in an effort to restore (risk-weighted) capital positions. And, even if currently not the case, banks' capacity to lend could become a constraining factor in the future.

Historically, domestic credit to the private sector has often tended to be supply-constrained. Currently, however, it appears that demand for credit, or lack thereof, has become the determining factor.[12] The fact that many of the financing schemes for SMEs are currently still underutilized would appear to corroborate these findings. Of course, given the distribution of credit, there may be borrowers with unsatisfied credit demand—i.e., there may be particular borrowers or sectors that currently face a credit crunch. It has been reported, for example, that an increasing share of lending has gone to the largest chaebols, thus skewing the lending. Moreover, the tightening of credit and higher interest rates contributed to corporate sector distress early on, and may therefore have also contributed to lower credit demand. Since SMEs are heavily dependent on bank financing, any credit crunch that occurred in the early stages of the crisis would have disproportionately affected them.[13]

This importance of demand factors reflects in part that at current (or any) interest rates, many corporates are not creditworthy or cannot borrow. To a large extent, these high lending rates are reflecting a large risk premium (which in turn is related to the problems in the financial and corporate sector). This suggests that a (further) loosening of credit would not necessarily lead to larger extension of credit. Put differently, high lending rates are reflecting the financial/corporate sector problems and general uncertainty in the economy as opposed to tight monetary policy. In addition to progress in financial and corporate sector restructuring, macro-policies that help re-ignite the economy, and thus improve earnings prospects of corporates, might be the best course to bring down risk premiums and hence lending rates.

5.5 Other challenges

Asset problems are not just large in banks; many NBFIs, most notably insurance companies, have significant asset problems. In addition, management and corporate governance in these institutions needs to be improved. While the government has committed itself not to provide any resources for the restructuring of NBFIs,[14] the risk is that some of the problems in the NBFIs will spill over into the banking system, in part as there are many cross-ownership, financial and other links.

The external financing situation has improved significantly. Foreign exchange reserves have been restored to levels almost equal to short-term debt outstanding. A large debt service hump, from claims rescheduled in early 1998 as well as previous claims, exists, however, for 1999. Extending the maturity of financing will thus remain an important issue.

Social consequences of reform have included a rapid rise in unemployment, now above eight percent, up sharply from below three percent pre-crisis. Opposition to restructuring from labor unions has become an important factor in affecting the speed of corporate restructuring. Observers have also drawn attention to the serious competitiveness problems in some sectors, notably cars and electronics. The depreciation of the won has alleviated some of this, but global import demand and a possible rise in protectionism in import demand may not allow rapid export responses. In any case, the operational restructuring process will likely be long and intense, and the risk of lost value is great if firms can not maintain sufficient investments in plant and equipment, and acquire the necessary inputs. Accelerated restructuring will be necessary to make firms creditworthy again.

There is little disagreement that in the medium, the role of capital markets in financing of corporations will need to increase. Which model of corporate governance will emerge, and what the role of capital markets will be in the oversight of corporations, is much more unclear. Lastly, the degree of independence and authority of supervisors and restructuring agencies and the speed of their institutional development will be important. Clearly, Korea has the capacity, with the help of technical assistance, to develop over time a good and independent supervisory system, but it will require adequate political support.

6. CONCLUSIONS

Korea has made great strides in its financial sector restructuring and reform. Nevertheless, the challenges are large and the process of corporate restructuring has just started in earnest. Large amounts of fiscal resources will be needed to deal with the extensive repair of banks' and corporations' balance sheets. The operational restructuring of corporations will require a long time, and adequate external resources will need to be available. To achieve long-lasting solutions, the process of restructuring will need to be more decentralized so as also to limit the political backlash and develop a larger support base for the reforms. This will require bringing in other agents and investors. Further foreign direct investment can be beneficial as part of this process.

Notes

[1]This included increased funding for the Korean Asset Management Corporation (KAMCO) to enhance its capacity to deal with distressed assets; incentives to promote merger and acquisition among financial institutions and rules that mandated the restructuring and exit of nonviable institutions; increased funding for the new consolidated Deposit Insurance Corporation; further liberalization of capital account transactions; and enhanced disclosure standards and loan classification requirements.

[2]The interest coverage (or the ratio of operating income before interest and taxes to net interest payments) of Korean corporations had already been declining progressively and was about 135 percent at end-1997—by comparison, interest coverage ratios range between 250–450 percent in other OECD countries. For every one-percentage-point increase in domestic interest rates, interest coverage in Korea falls by about 3–4 percentage points.

[3]Until July, loans more than six months overdue were classified as nonperforming. This has been changed to more than three months overdue.

[4]All deposits made until July 31 are fully protected until the year 2000. Under a revised deposit protection law, for deposits made after August 1, 1998, only the principal will be guaranteed until 2000 if the amount exceeds W20 million (both principal and interest will be guaranteed for smaller deposits).

[5]Some specialized banks (KDB, KEXIM, IBK and KCGF) will also receive support.

[6]Corporate restructuring vehicles (CRVs) are expected to play an important role in purchasing and/or managing converted equity. The CRVs, e.g. trusts or mutual funds, might operate by purchasing converted equity from banks, managing converted equity for a fee, or purchasing debt and converting it to equity. Such CRVs would be privately owned and managed. The government has reviewed the tax and regulatory regime to remove any barriers that may exist to the establishment and operation of such vehicles.

[7]Recently, a court ruling was handed down in favor of minority shareholders in a suit against the management of the Korea First Bank. The executives were held responsible for lending money in defiance of the shareholders' objections. This unprecedented ruling is expected to open the door for other suits.

[8]While the government has improved the enabling environment for enterprise restructuring, there are still some issues related to the process of restructuring to be resolved, e.g., what is the seniority status of various claims, what are the exact tax and regulatory implications of debt restructuring, how long can banks keep equity on their books, how will this equity be valued, etc., which will have to be resolved, mainly as the restructuring process evolves on a case-by-case basis. There may also be a need for a separate approach for small debtors. These issues are not discussed here.

[9]Stijn Claessens, Simeon Djankov and Giovanni Ferri, 1998, "Corporate Distress in East Asia: Assessing the Impact of Interest and Exchange Rates Shocks," World Bank, mimeo, September. They also find that in the post-crisis scenario, forty-nine percent of Korean firms are illiquid, that is their interest payments exceed their earnings.

[10]The average (central government debt/GDP ratios for high-income countries was around sixty percent, while that of OECD was fifty-four percent in 1995.

[11]These calculations assume a medium-term, real growth rate of output of five percent of GDP and real interest rates of around eight percent. While real interest rates have traditionally been relatively high in Korea, so has the rate of growth-which averaged around 7.5 percent per annum during 1990–96. Therefore the calculations above may well overestimate the primary surpluses required.

[12]Preliminary analysis through the first quarter of 1998. Swati Ghosh, 1998, "Korea: Credit Crunch or Lack of Demand?," World Bank, mimeo, September.

[13]See Ilker Domac and Giovanni Ferri, 1998 "The Real Impact of Financial Shocks: Evidence from Korea," World Bank, mimeo, for evidence that the credit channel is particularly operative for SMEs.

[14]In the context of NBFI resolutions, only explicitly government-guaranteed liabilities will be covered. In exceptional cases, and in the context of a comprehensive restructuring plan, support may be provided to NBFIs if failure of these institutions poses a systemic risk.

Chapter 16

Whither Thailand?

Yoshihiro Iwasaki
Asian Development Bank

Thailand is where it all began. With some luck, Thailand may be among the first to emerge from crisis. To see why, it is necessary to trace the origins and examine the dynamics of the crisis.

1. THE ONSET OF THE CRISIS

As a consequence of financial liberalisation, capital account opening, and an easing in global liquidity conditions, Thailand was the recipient of large inflows of international capital for much of the 1990s. These capital inflows fed a spurt in investment that helped to underpin strong economic growth. Booming growth was accompanied by a widening current account deficit and an appreciation of the real effective exchange rate. In the normal course of events, these imbalances would have been self-correcting. But lurking beneath the surface of Thailand were structural weaknesses that not only frustrated the normal adjustment process, but which ultimately proved the undoing of Thailand's financial and corporate sectors.

An important reason why international capital was attracted to Thailand was that it had undertaken significant steps to liberalize its banking and non-banking financial sectors. But while market liberalization proceeded apace, measures to promote supervision, corporate governance, market discipline and financial stability had not been pursued with commensurate vigor. The upshot of this was that Thailand's financial system did not have the capacity to channel efficiently funds (whether domestic or foreign) from savers to borrowers. Weak prudential regulation and inadequate supervision of banks let vulnerability build-up. Cracks in financial sector governance meant that regulations were often treated cavalierly, or just plain ignored. Markets were unable to discipline effectively wayward banks because reliable and timely information about their activities was often unavailable. Besides, the credit boom that financial liberalization spawned provided a smokescreen of profitability behind which accumulating vulnerabilities on balance sheets were difficult to spot.

At a macroeconomic level, apparently strong fundamentals masked a lack of policy coherence. There was too much reliance on monetary policy to attempt to "cool" domestic demand in a context where a pegged exchange rate limited the freedom of the Bank of Thailand. A comparatively tight monetary policy and pro-cyclical fiscal policy was particularly problematic in a context of expanding global liquidity. The resulting misalignment of baht and world, particularly yen, interest rates, created the opportunity for arbitrage gains on cross-currency trades. A "guarantee" of a stable nominal exchange rate encouraged domestic banks and nonbank financial institutions (NBFIs) to borrow abroad and to on-lend in domestic markets at higher interest rates. Equally, it attracted foreign capital to baht currency deposits. Attempts by the domestic monetary authorities to sterilize the monetary consequences of capital inflows served only to put further upward pressure on domestic interest rates, and invited yet further capital inflows.

The crisis in Thailand was eventually triggered by a loss of credibility of the pegged nominal exchange rate regime. To some degree, the loss of confidence was the result of adverse external events, including a cyclical downturn in world trade, and a sharp appreciation of the dollar against the yen. But, critically, growing weaknesses in the balance sheets of Thai financial institutions also served to undermine the currency peg. As local asset prices fell in response to slowing demand growth, the quality of financial institutions' asset portfolios quickly deteriorated. In committing its support to illiquid and in some cases insolvent financial institutions, the Bank of Thailand was effectively forced to abandon the use of domestic interest rates to defend the currency peg. Higher interest rates would have served only to deepen financial distress and were incompatible with the expansion of liquidity that support for troubled institutions entailed. Attempts by the authorities to directly defend the currency peg through intervention in foreign exchange markets quickly bled reserves. Faced with the increasing likelihood of default, the Thai authorities let the Baht float on July 2, 1997, and withdrew support for distressed nonbank financial institutions.

2. THE DYNAMICS OF CRISIS

In response to Thailand's balance of payments problems, the international financial community, led by the IMF, agreed an assistance package of $17.1 billion with the government of Thailand at the end of August 1997. The Asian Development Bank has now committed nearly $1.8 billion to this package.

The conditions that accompanied the initial IMF-led program emphasized measures to stop financial hemorrhaging, steps to strengthen fiscal balances, a new framework for monetary policy, and structural reforms to strengthen Thailand's private sector. Essentially, these were the same measures that had worked reasonably well in stabilizing exchange rates and the balance of payments in crisis situations elsewhere, and, particularly, in Mexico only two years before. The hope was that once stabilization had been achieved, interest rates would come down, and exports would quickly lead the real economy out of recession. Alas, this was not to be. Thailand was different from Mexico, and Asia was different from Latin America.

With the benefit of hindsight, there is now little doubt that the initial macroeconomic framework and targets set under the August IMF program misread some key features of Thailand's crisis. First, the program underestimated the depth of the structural difficulties that beset Thailand's banking and financial system. Second, the program aimed at fiscal targets that were much too tight in a context where the economy had already suffered a massive deflationary shock. Third, the program did not anticipate the extent to which the region would become mired in financial turmoil, and the economic downdraft that this would cause. Even by late August of 1997, few foresaw the economic devastation that was about to be unleashed on the region. Despite massive hikes in real interest rates, the Thai baht continued to depreciate against the dollar and asset prices continued to spiral downwards. The Thai economy fell quickly into deep recession.

The dynamics of Thailand's crisis quickly became destabilizing. As demand dipped, bank's nonperforming loans mounted, and bank capital was eroded. In an attempt to shore-up their capital, distressed banks responded by curtailing their lending even to creditworthy borrowers. Some debtors, who had expected loans to be rolled over, now found that they had to liquidate assets in extremely depressed markets to meet their obligations. Others found it increasingly difficult to service their obligations in an environment where interest rates had risen sharply, and real incomes were shrinking. As banks curtailed credit, illiquid but viable businesses began to perish, and with them the jobs and incomes of workers. Exporters who had been expected to lead the recovery were starved of working and trade capital.

Those who were lucky enough to retain their jobs found their real incomes being eroded through accelerating inflation.

At the root of these difficulties lay a massive coordination failure. As each bank (rationally) attempted to restore its capital adequacy, the collective actions of banks led to a credit crunch that served only to impair further the capacity of borrowers to service their obligations. The end result was that the nonperforming loans and bad debts that the banking system as a whole carried began to expand quickly, and bank balance sheets and the real economy came under even greater stress.

Caught by the severity of the economic slowdown, the failure to arrest the depreciation of the baht, a worsening regional situation, and mounting troubles in financial and corporate balance sheets, the IMF program was modified in late November 1997. Measures were announced to accelerate the needed recapitalization of banks. The ADB and the World Bank had also begun working hard to mitigate the adverse social impacts of the crisis through assistance for the social sector. However, the twin pillars of tight fiscal and monetary policy remained in place. By year's end, real GDP had shrunk by –0.4 percent, the first decline in income for over a decade. Unemployment had risen sharply, and consumer price inflation was accelerating. The government's budget balance, which had traditionally been in surplus, moved sharply into deficit. Asset markets were hemorrhaging. The crisis was putting Thailand's social achievements at risk. If there was a bright spot it was that import compression had been so severe that Thailand's balance of payments position had quickly strengthened. Thailand's current account deficit had fallen to two percent of GDP, from nearly eight percent one year earlier, and was in surplus for the last quarter of the year.

As 1998 approached, the depreciation of the baht seemed to be relentless. In response, to the depreciating baht, monetary policy was further tightened. Interbank interest rates peaked in January and February of 1998. The baht reached also reached its nadir in February. By late February of 1998, it was clear that fiscal targets would be breached. The IMF program was then modified to permit some fiscal easing, but tight monetary policy was maintained to support the baht. In the context of a tight liquidity squeeze, selective measures were introduced to attempt to ease credit constraints for exporters. The focus on financial sector reform and restructuring continued, as did measures to buttress the social safety net. Meanwhile the situation of the banking and corporate sector continued to deteriorate as demand and incomes shrank further. Manufacturing production collapsed.

By the middle of this year, the baht had stabilized, and indeed had begun to appreciate. In response to this, monetary policy was gradually eased, and interbank interest began to fall from the peaks attained at the beginning of the year. While the authorities remained committed to supporting the baht through monetary policy, the baht has proven resilient to lower domestic interest rates. The current account has also continued to strengthen, and official foreign exchange reserves have stabilized at around $26 billion. This gives cover for a multiple of 1.5 Thailand's short-run maturing (one year) debt. External debt may contract by around $10 billion to around $80 billion by year's end. Other hopeful indicators are that there has been robust growth in export volumes, suggesting that trade credit difficulties may have been easing.

However, there can be little doubt that enormous difficulties remain in Thailand. GDP is expected to shrink in real terms by about seven percent this year. Gridlock in the real economy is causing severe social distress and pain. Real economic recovery has been hampered by distress elsewhere in the region, and by the more general flight from emerging markets. Despite some improvement in its financial situation, the spread on Thai debt in international markets is now around 800 basis points, up from 475 basis points at the end of 1997. Thailand's stock market has fallen by more than half over the course of this year. The fragile nature of Thailand's banking system still hinders the needed resumption in credit growth, and the difficulties of working-out corporate debts continues to cast a shadow over bank balance sheets.

3. STRUCTURAL REHABILITATION AND REFORMATION

Thailand has reached a critical juncture in its crisis. While much will depend on what happens in the regional and global economy, much, too, will depend on Thailand's capacity for domestic renewal. The severity of Thailand's difficulties, and those elsewhere in the region, are a reflection of their stock rather than flow characteristics, and of underlying structural weaknesses. It is these structural problems that now must be worked out. The Thai authorities have rightly been praised for the foresight of their macroeconomic policies, and as a result now enjoy enhanced credibility. They must now use this credibility to good effect.

The balance sheets of Thailand's banks and corporations are seriously impaired. The overhang of debt in Thailand is a major factor blocking the economic recovery of the real sector. Since bank balance sheets are increasingly being burdened by nonperforming and bad loans, banks are reluctant to extend credit to liquidity starved businesses. Some estimates suggest that bad debt as a percentage of financial assets could be as high as thirty-five percent.

The government of Thailand has been alert to these difficulties for some time. At the outset of the crisis, the Bank of Thailand acted quickly in an attempt to restore stability to the banking system, within the broader context of the IMF-led emergency assistance program. The Bank of Thailand set capital adequacy targets. Banks that could not meet these standards were intervened (including six banks and twelve financial institutions). Loan-loss provisioning standards were gradually tightened. Regulations that restricted foreign direct investment in banks were relaxed, and markets were invited to resolve the situation of distressed banks. However, in a context of a rapidly deteriorating economy, these measures were insufficient to rehabilitate bank balance sheets. Only a small number of private banks were able to raise new capital, and most banks' financial position continued to deteriorate along with the severe contraction in economic activity.

In response to continuing difficulties in the banking and corporate sector, a second recapitalization and restructuring plan has now been introduced. The plan has four pillars. First, the plan aims to catalyze private sector resources to facilitate bank recapitalization through offering the carrot of matching public funding support (for Tier 1 capital). Second, it seeks to extend public financial assistance to banks balance sheets (for Tier 2 capital) conditional on acceptable restructuring arrangements for the corporate debt on their balance sheets. Third, it makes provision for the establishment of private asset management corporations, to whom tax privileges would be extended. Fourth, the plan outlines a resolution strategy for banks that have been earlier intervened, and announces measures to be taken in newly intervened banks and finance companies. Mergers are to be accelerated and both private and foreign investment in the intervened banks is to be encouraged.

Thailand's approach to restructuring and recapitalization is commendable in a number of important ways. Significant steps have been taken to mobilize private capital, bailouts have been avoided, and the risks of moral hazard largely mitigated. Taxpayer resources will only be available for recapitalization if strong conditions are met, including the dilution of the equity of existing owners or their agreement to tough debt restructuring arrangements, or both. Institutional arrangements for the implementation of the restructuring and recapitalization process are clearly assigned and credible. The government has also taken firm measures to ensure disclosure of the information that private sector investors need to make intelligent investment decisions. Prudential regulation and supervision has been strengthened and a number of important reforms that should contribute to a more efficient banking system have been undertaken. There is a clear recognition by the Thai government of the important developmental role that the banking system plays, and their support for the banking system has focused clearly on the broader significance of rectifying financial and banking sector distress.

In its recent announcement, the government of Thailand has also reaffirmed that the costs of its earlier guarantees will be fiscalized. In addition, to support the second phase of the bank-restructuring program, the government has sought authority for the issuance of $300 billion in government bonds to support Tier 1 and Tier 2 capital of banks. While these commitments have been made in a context of a comparatively low overall level of government debt to GDP, they will entail breaching IMF targets for the fiscal deficit. It is estimated that the costs of servicing new bond debt may increase the deficit to four percent in the current fiscal year. But, on the other hand, if viable banks are not nursed back to health, lending will not resume, and Thailand's recession may deepen. The loss of fiscal revenue that this would entail would also certainly mean that deficit targets would be breached.

A particularly welcome feature of Thailand's approach to restructuring is its intention to tackle banking and corporate difficulties within an integrated approach. The two are intertwined. In other respects, the approach taken to corporate restructuring, is market-based with the role of government being one of incentive facilitation. In this capacity, government is making important changes in the legal framework on foreclosure and bankruptcy, and on secured lending. The government is also eliminating tax disincentives that work against debt restructuring. All these measures are expected to be promulgated in October of 1998.

4. WHITHER THAILAND?

Perhaps, with some justification, it can be argued that when confronted by a financial rather than macroeconomic crisis, prolonged tight monetary policy may not have the beneficial effects that are expected. While we shall never know the counterfactual, stabilizing the baht proved to be an extremely painful experience. Maybe interest rates should have been raised much further and much sooner, to add credibility to the defense of the baht. But, maybe, hiking interest rates heightened risks, lowered expected returns, encouraged capital outflows and so pushed the baht lower. It is important that we learn the answers to these puzzles sooner rather than later, and that these answers influence the design of future policies.

But for Thailand, this debate is now somewhat academic. Its macroeconomic course was chartered along comparatively "orthodox" lines, and the balance of payments stabilization phase of its crisis seems to be drawing to an end. In going forward, it would seem Thailand is prepared to let fiscal balances take up slack demand, partly because Thailand still enjoys a low ratio of debt to GDP. The most recently agreed target for its fiscal deficit is three percent of GDP, which seems likely to be breached given the estimated fiscal costs of bank recapitalization. The monetary authorities would, however, be extremely reluctant to give up recent gains on baht without first again tightening policy.

On the structural side, the government of Thailand has shown that it is prepared to act quickly and decisively. When Thailand emerges from the crisis it will have a much more robust and efficient financial sector than it had before it began. Improved institutional capacities and governance will eventually make Thailand an even more attractive place to do business in. In the medium-term, much will depend on the resolution of Thailand's banking and corporate sector problems.

Now that the baht has stabilized and domestic interest rates have come down, there is a glimmer of hope that growth of output may accompany the benefits of structural reforms in 1999. In recent months, there have been some signs of some stabilization in the output of Thailand's manufacturing sector, and agricultural output should pick up with better weather conditions and favorable movements in relative prices. If Thailand begins its recovery in 1999, it will, in no small measure, be due to the clarity of vision and collective wisdom of its economic leadership.

Acknowledgment: The views expressed in this paper are those of the author, and do not necessarily represent the official view of the Asian Development Bank.

Chapter 17

Comment on "Asian Crisis: Causes and Remedies"

Richard J. Herring
University of Pennsylvania

The IMF has been barraged by criticism from all sides—from debtor countries and creditors, from the left and from the right, for doing too much and for doing too little. Some want the IMF abolished. Others want it to have greatly augmented resources. In the face of such pervasive and sweeping criticism one perversely wonders if the IMF may not have been doing something right after all. Aghevli makes the case that it has.

The international financial markets did not foresee the outbreak of the crisis. But the IMF got it partly right. The fund saw that Thailand was headed for a crisis. Indeed the classic signs had been apparent for at least a year—slowing export growth, a currency appreciating in real effective terms, a growing current account deficit financed by short-term capital inflows, rapid domestic credit growth, and a banking system decapitalized by the collapse of a real estate bubble. Unfortunately, the fund was unable to persuade the government to take corrective action and it failed to anticipate that other Southeast Asian countries would be vulnerable to contagion from the crisis in Thailand. The collapse of the Thai baht led investors to ask which other countries were also vulnerable. They first focused on countries that competed with Thailand in export markets—Indonesia, the Philippines, and Malaysia. And then, investors pondered which countries shared the vulnerability of Thailand and Indonesia to a crisis because of a weak financial sector. Like Thailand, Korea had a decapitalized banking system with large short-term foreign-currency-denominated liabilities and it too succumbed. The IMF did not predict a crisis of such magnitude, as Bijan Aghevli admits, and did little to prevent it.

I largely agree with Aghevlis' assessment of what went wrong, although I would place a greater emphasis on the weakness of the financial and corporate sectors. Excessive exchange rate rigidity was clearly part of the problem, but there were deeper structural problems as well. If an overvalued exchange rate had been the only problem, a quick depreciation should have restored equilibrium. But the exchange rate crisis interacted with an already weakened banking system. This was the Achilles' heel of the Asian miracle. The Asian model of development emphasized high savings channeled through a protected banking system to highly leveraged firms with close ties to the banks and the government. The Asian Tigers achieved remarkable, sustained growth rates for three decades with this model. But it proved inadequate for the complexities of a modern industrial economy competing in world markets. Insulation from market discipline—competition from other financial institutions and the threat of corporate takeover—has meant that a significant amount of investment had been unproductive. Examples include the creation of a car industry in Indonesia, still more steel mills in Korea, but most of all commercial real estate bubbles. A real estate bubble undermined the creditworthiness of banks before the foreign exchange crisis in each of the most seriously affected countries. Banks thought they had good real estate collateral and, indeed, relied on it rather than credit analysis for many corporate loans. And when the financial system was liberalized to permit banks to finance this kind of investment partly with short-term foreign borrowing the countries' vulnerability to a foreign exchange crisis grew.

With the benefit of hindsight, a darker side of the Asian miracle is apparent. High leverage and the lack of transparency raise concerns about solvency of firms and their bank lenders when a shock occurs. Lack of external audits and consolidated accounts make firms opaque to their lenders and the public. Weak accounting practices and minimal disclosure standards make it difficult to distinguish sound firms from unsound firms and exacerbate credit rationing. The cooperation between business and government, which some Western observers found so attractive, begins to look more like collusion, cronyism, and corruption. Concern over the soundness of the financial system and the ability of the government to make good on implicit guarantees led to capital flight and when governments ran out of reserves to support the exchange rate, they turned to the Fund.

As Aghevli reports, the IMF responded with massive loans to countries in order to mitigate the collapse of the exchange rate conditional upon (1) tighter fiscal policy, (2) tighter monetary policy, and (3) structural reform of the financial and corporate sector. The fund has been heavily criticized on all three aspects of these programs. The fiscal targets gave rise to the charge that the IMF was applying a one-size-fits-all policy, originally developed for fiscally profligate Latin American countries, to fiscally conservative Asian countries. The fund was undoubtedly correct that restructuring costs facing governments will be huge—probably well over twenty percent of GDP in the most seriously affected countries. Indeed, the market's recognition of the magnitude of these future claims on taxpayers may have contributed to capital flight. But the depth of the crisis was surely not an appropriate time to start paying for the clean up, particularly at a time when Japan was in recession and growth had virtually halted in the other ASEAN countries. To its credit, the IMF quickly reversed course and eased fiscal conditions.

The IMF's insistence on higher interest rates has been bitterly contested. Critics charge that higher interest rates are devastating to highly leveraged financial systems already encumbered by massive nonperforming loans. And, of course, they are correct. But what is the alternative? A plummeting exchange rate is also punishing on an economy with substantial unhedged foreign exchange liabilities. Moreover, it risks setting off a burst of inflation that will require still greater monetary austerity in the future. To my mind, the decisive argument is that higher interest rates are necessary to halt capital flight. They signal the authorities' intent to stabilize the exchange rate and make clear to domestic residents that they cannot convert their liquid assets into foreign currency and still maintain control over other domestic assets. Moreover, higher interest rates can be reversed (and, indeed, have been in Korea and Thailand) with less disruption than an excessive depreciation of the exchange rate. Unfortunately, once a crisis erupts, hard choices are inescapable.

Feldstein and others have criticized the IMF's insistence on structural reform of the financial sector as an unwarranted intrusion into institutional arrangements that are properly a matter of national choice. They would prefer that the IMF tend to its macroeconomic knitting and not meddle in structural and institutional reforms. But, it is hard to imagine a sustainable recovery that does not address the underlying problems of corporate governance, bankruptcy procedures, disclosure practices, financial supervision and regulation. I think that the emphasis on structural reform is crucial, but it is an enormously ambitious agenda that surely demands close cooperation with the World Bank.

Finally, I would like to raise a concern about the IMF programs that Aghevli does not address—the risk that a country's access to the IMF engenders moral hazard. This has two aspects: moral hazard vis-à-vis borrower governments and vis-à-vis foreign investors. Does access to the IMF undermine incentives for countries to undertake needed structural reform? It is certainly true that no country approaches the IMF lightly. The kind of medicine that the IMF asks the government to administer will usually revive the economy in the long run, but is usually fatal to the government that administers it. Indeed, governments in Thailand, South Korea and Indonesia fell shortly after administering IMF remedies. Nonetheless, the fundamental rationale for IMF assistance is that it will make adjustment less painful than it would otherwise be. Because short-run elasticities are always lower than longer-run elasticities, financing permits adjustment to take place in a way that is less disruptive to the home country and the rest of the world. Those who emphasize perverse incentives for borrower governments note that Chile, which did not have access to the fund during the 1980s, took much more effective reforms than Mexico, which has had a series of IMF programs for the last two decades. (See Meltzer's contribution to this volume.) They also note that Taiwan, which no longer belongs to the IMF, has pursued policies that largely insulated it from the Asian crisis. But even if one doubts the importance of the moral hazard problem vis-à-vis governments, the impact of IMF programs on international investors still deserves attention.

To be sure, not all foreign investors benefit from IMF stabilization programs. Usually equity investors and most bondholders suffer heavy losses when a country experiences a foreign exchange crisis. But short-term lenders, especially short-term interbank lenders have often been protected. This pattern was set in the 1995 Mexican bailout where all holders of Mexican Tessobonos were guaranteed. It was repeated most explicitly in the case of South Korea where IMF funds flowed through the central bank to Korean banks to foreign banks with breath-taking speed. Earlier this year an agreement was negotiated with bank creditors to South Korea in which the bank creditors agreed to reschedule their interbank claims for a three year term at the U.S. Treasury bill rate plus 250 basis points in return for a government guarantee. The IMF likes to boast that this is bailing-in the banks rather than bailing them out. Yet it surely appears to reward short-term lending which contributed to South Korea's vulnerability to a foreign exchange crisis. The broader problem is that investors who believe they will benefit from an implicit guarantee in the event of a crisis have no incentive to monitor or discipline the borrower. This may contribute to making the whole system more vulnerable to crises.

Ironically, international capital adequacy rules also provide incentives for bank lenders to keep their maturities short. Bank lenders to banks in Thailand and Indonesia were required to hold only one-fifth as much capital against their short-term claims as against their claims with a maturity greater than one year.

How could this perverse incentive be corrected? Several policy changes are possible. Borrower countries could discourage short-term foreign borrowing by making use of controls on short-term capital inflows like Chile. In addition, borrower countries could discourage short-term foreign borrowing by eliminating the tax deductibility of interest payments on short-term foreign debt. The Basle Committee could eliminate the favorable treatment given to short-term interbank claims. And the IMF could require that countries enact legislation that would impose a haircut on short-term creditors who attempt to withdraw during a crisis. (See Litan's contribution to this volume.)

Of course, the first rule of policy changes should be "Do no harm." Would such measures make matters worse? One cannot dismiss fears that harsh treatment of creditors would worsen contagion. But neither can one dismiss concerns that increasing IMF resources without ameliorating the moral hazard problem will only succeed in increasing the frequency and severity of crises.

References

Economist Newspaper, Ltd., The. 1998, "Will China be next?," *The Economist,* October 24–30..

Economist Newspaper, Ltd., The. 1997, "Fragile, handle with care," *The Economist,* April 12.

Herring, Richard, and Anthony Santomero. 1995, "The Role of the Financial Sector in Economic Performance," Financial Institutions Center, working paper, No. 95–08.

World Bank, The. 1989, "Why does finance matter?," *World Development Report 1989.*

Chapter 18

The East Asian Financial Crisis: A Year Later

Yung Chul Park
Korea University

One year after the crisis erupted in Thailand and spread to other countries in the region, East Asia is littered with idle plants, insolvent financial institutions, loan defaults, and bankrupt businesses, both large and small. All of the countries hit by the currency attack are now in deep recession. GDP growth in these countries will collapse in 1998 with no prospects for early recovery. The total volume of foreign capital inflows into these countries has dwindled to a trickle and will not likely exceed the level of 1997. Similarly the real exchange rates, which depreciated sharply in 1997, are not likely to change significantly for some time to come. The stock markets in the region remain depressed and show little sign of recovery.

Thailand, Indonesia, and Korea are expected to generate large "recession surpluses" on their current accounts, ranging from two percent of GDP in Indonesia to eight percent in Korea in 1998. It was expected that after the IMF programs were initiated the patterns of adjustment in these countries would follow a "V" shaped recovery, but with the passage of time, it appears that the performances are more likely to resemble the letter "L" with long drawn-out floors. Unlike Mexico in 1994 and 1995, the East Asian countries are going to suffer a deep, sharp shock with long-lasting effects. The East Asian recovery has been further frustrated by the ongoing recession and financial crisis in Japan, which is no longer able to play the role of locomotive in the region.

Thailand, Indonesia, and Korea have been implementing IMF rescue and restructuring plans. In all three countries, the major components of the IMF programs include: a macroeconomic policy framework based on fiscal tightening and monetary contraction aimed at stabilizing the nominal exchange rate; financial, corporate, and labor market restructuring; and market deregulation and opening, including the financial sector.

Although still ongoing, it is fair to ask whether these policies have been effective. The IMF programs were designed to reestablish financial market confidence by stabilizing the exchange rate. In this regard, the contractionary monetary and fiscal policy was necessary and to some extent successful in calming the foreign exchange markets in earlier stages of the crises, but it has also exacted a heavy cost, as we shall discuss later in this section. The IMF places emphasis on structural reforms as a crucial element of its rescue programs in restoring financial market confidence. To signal their determination, the crisis countries were asked to take decisive actions by closing or suspending nonviable financial institutions and following a strict time table of longer-term reforms for the financial markets, corporate governance system, and domestic market liberalization and opening.

In earlier stages of the crisis, the IMF program for Korea stood out as the most successful of all the similar programs applied to countries in East Asia. A wide range of measures for financial market opening, suspension of a number of failing merchant banks, and most importantly, the Korean government's commitment to restructuring of financial institutions saddled with huge burdens of nonperforming loans and high-leveraged and poorly managed large conglomerates were well received and widely considered appropriate by foreign financial market participants and multilateral institutions alike. This favorable response no doubt helped Korea to reschedule $24 billion in short-term foreign liabilities at banks into longer-term loans in early February 1998.

This rescheduling was followed by the successful floating of $4 billion in sovereign bonds in April 1998. These two events were regarded as the turning point in Korea's adjustment in the crisis and signs of a quick recovery, resembling the pattern of the Mexican adjustment. However, the Korean economy has since sunk deeper into recession, and perhaps for this reason, foreign creditors' confidence has yet to be restored, as evidenced by Korea's borrowing cost premium of 500 basis points or more over LIBOR.

Soon after the restructuring plan was announced in Korea in early 1998, reports began to surface that the levels of nonperforming loans and corporate debts were much higher than expected. The total of nonperforming loans at banks was estimated to be more than 100 trillion won ($70 billion), much more than expected, and the volume of corporate debts was estimated at almost twice the size of Korea's annual GDP. The dismal state of affairs at Korean corporations and financial institutions naturally raised uncertainties in the minds of foreign creditors as to whether Korea would be able to mobilize enough resources domestically to pay off these debts.

In the meantime, high nominal interest rates and a credit crunch further deepened the recession. Since most Korean firms are highly leveraged, the high cost of credit increased their debt service burden so greatly that a growing number of both large and small firms—some of which would be completely viable under normal circumstances—have been closing down their operations. The unemployment rate at the beginning of May 1998 was more than twice that of a year earlier, and the GDP growth forecast for 1998 has been revised downward yet again to -5 percent. The current account has been generating a huge surplus almost entirely because of the collapse in imports.

Contrary to initial expectations, the real exchange rate depreciation and domestic recession have not improved the prospects for a boom in Korea's exports. Exporters have been hampered by the limited availability of supplier credit and by the unwillingness of foreign banks to accept Korean banks' letters of credit. The limited availability of import credits has also made it costly for exporters to import parts, components, and other industrial materials needed to produce export goods.

What has gone wrong in Korea and the other crisis countries in East Asia following an IMF program? By and large Korea's experience with restructuring typifies the kinds of predicaments these countries are facing, although they would, of course, differ in detail.

Foreign lenders including major international banks have yet to resume new lending. They are even reluctant to restore trade credit facilities, largely because they are uncertain about the outcomes of the restructuring plans of these countries. Their position has been that they would not return to East Asian financial markets unless they are convinced of the success of the restructuring efforts mounted by these countries or at least until they see some positive signs that the restructuring program is working. The IMF has been monitoring the process of restructuring in these countries and has on many occasions expressed its satisfaction with the progress they have made. The IMF's endorsement, however, seems to have done little in the way of building up foreign creditors' confidence in these countries. Perhaps, as Radelet and Sachs (1998b) point out, the IMF may be "poorly placed to rally market confidence in the short run." Given the intense criticism directed at IMF programs, the majority of foreign lenders may have little confidence that the IMF programs are really the best for the crisis countries in East Asia.

More importantly, there is no consensus on what constitutes a successful restructuring, that is, the scope, speed, and an optimal path of adjustment, a successful reform of banks, corporations and labor markets would require. There are also no widely accepted indicators or criteria by which one could judge whether a restructuring program is progressing as planned. Foreign market participants cannot be lumped into a single group of homogeneous lenders. Instead, they include a large number of commercial and investment banks, insurance companies, bond market dealers, and fund managers of all types with diverse business backgrounds, and different investment strategies and interests. It is hard to imagine that as a group they could reach a consensus on a restructuring program which they believe help these East Asian countries to find a way out of the current crisis. Different individual lenders are likely to have different views on the appropriate scope and speed of any restructuring plan and to react differently to the side effects of a crisis. Some creditors may not believe these crisis countries would survive or have the will to follow the restructuring plan through the end. In some quarters of creditors, the side effects may be viewed as the sign of a mismanaged and hence unsuccessful restructuring. In particular, small lenders have been sensitive to the market disruption and instability that inevitably occur during the restructuring process.

Moreover, the dilemma of the collective action problem that played a role in causing the crisis also serves as a serious roadblock to the restructuring process. Individually, some foreign creditors probably believe that the IMF program is the best alternative for the crisis countries to restore market confidence in East Asia. They may also realize that restructuring is a protracted process often marked by backslidings and relapses and often detracted by the adversely affected groups such as labor unions. They also likely know that the resumption of lending and the restoration of export and import related credits is crucial for speeding up the restructuring process. However, few individual creditors will make a move if other creditors do not lend as well.

The reluctance of foreign creditors to restore trade credit facilities and to extend new loans to these countries creates a serious dilemma of a non-cooperative game. Their reluctance to normalize the credit flows into these countries certainly hampers and possibly jeopardizes the entire restructuring program. In fact, the longer creditors wait until they see tangible results of restructuring, the less likely they are to see the results they want to. The reason for this is that the restructuring plan cannot be engineered successfully unless corporations and banks are able to obtain trade credits and new loans from international financial markets. International creditors know this, but they demand the evidence that the restructuring plan is moving in the right direction before extending their loans. And different lenders demand different pieces of evidence. As a result, the catch 22 situation continues in East Asia.

Individual lenders also know the pitfalls of the non-cooperative game that both they and East Asian countries are locked in. However, individual lenders would not take an initiative by making new loans unless other lenders are prepared to do the same. As in the case of a self-fulfilling crisis, the problem of collective action in international capital markets could possibly derail the IMF guided restructuring plans.

Chapter 19

Removing Financial Bottlenecks to Labor Productivity in Thailand

Robert Townsend
University of Chicago and Federal Reserve Bank of Chicago

1. APPROACH

1.1 Background

The National Institute of Health (NIH) and the National Science Foundation (NSF) in the U.S. have been funding through the National Opinion Research Center (NORC) and the University of Chicago a large socio-economic/institutional survey in Thailand which serves as a major input for this paper. The funding was received and the surveys designed prior to the crisis with the goal of understanding and analyzing the structural underpinnings of Thai growth at that time. A particular goal was the evaluation of the role of various kinds of financial institutions, both informal and formal, running the gamut from the family and networks of friends and relatives to finance companies and commercial banks. In designing the study, a particular concern was the observation that prior growth was associated with increasing inequality and apparent financial deepening. Increasing inequality had long been a concern of the Thai government, and to some extent financial deepening, or at least targeted credit through a particular set of institutions, has been promoted as a partial remedy. In summary it was thought important at the time of the design of the project to understand the role that these various financial and social institutions were playing in growth, inequality, and financial deepening.

Clearly the crisis has made this research project more important than ever for three reasons:

First, because our initial survey was completed by the end of May 1997, and because the crisis was severe and in large part unanticipated, we now have baseline or benchmark data available which tell us what conditions were like in semi-urban and rural areas prior to the crisis, that is, prior to the abrupt economic changes which are now taking place. Indeed, a resurvey of thirty-three percent of the original sample was funded graciously by the Ford Foundation. This will tell us how socioeconomic conditions have changed, that is, what the impact of the crisis has been on households and small businesses both in areas close to Bangkok and areas in the relatively poor Northeast. We will also see from the resurvey the role that informal and formal financial institutions are playing in buffering if not exacerbating aggregate if not idiosyncratic shocks. This evaluation of the role of the various financial institutions is consistent with the initial design of the project, though, of course, we too did not envision such severe shocks.

Second, we can see from the precrisis data if there are barriers to productivity associated with the precrisis financial structure. This provides a basis for a discussion of altered financial sector policies to facilitate economic recovery and promote growth in the medium term. Basically, the data show that even if there had been no crisis, substantial improvements in labor productivity would have been attainable through financial sector reform. That is, financial sector reform would have improved growth and attenuated increasing inequality in the medium term. With the advent of the crisis and the apparent need to place the Thai economy on a more secure footing, reforms of the financial sector would now seem to be more important than ever.

Third, the extraordinary database of this project combined with the latest advances in economic theory can help us think through financial sector reforms, which might mitigate the possibility of future crisis. That is, the project may provide helpful suggestions for the regulation of financial companies, commercial banks, and other financial institutions and provide guidance for the formulation of monetary and macro policy. The focus is less on recapitalization, as important as that may be, and more on medium and long-term regulation; portfolio diversification, the documentation and the monitoring of procedures in lending, incentives and liability, and public disclosure.

Related, in June 1998, we began implementation of a continuing month by month survey of a subset of our original sample. The information from this ongoing survey can be used in monitoring the process of transition and recovery and thus might help the Thai government to evaluate the economic, social, and monetary policies it is implementing.

1.2 Sample selection and methodology

We proceeded by imaging from theory what the true story underlying Thai growth with inequality and financial deepening might have been, or more formally, by writing down and simulating a variety of economic models. This generated a list of variables crucial to telling whether a particular story or model has any validity, and this list formed the basis for the questionnaires and the field research. The theories under consideration included models with liquidity constraints in human capital formation, in occupation choice, and in input financing; models of growth with costly investment in financial infrastructure; and models which take into account private information and incentives and thus deal with the details of financial contracting and possibilities for regulatory/monetary reform.

The institutions under consideration are national level institutions (commercial banks, finance companies, insurance companies, and the government savings bank); county or village-level institutions (rice banks, production credit groups (PCGs), rotating credit associations, and local indigenous funds); informal institutions (money lenders, traders, shopkeepers, and networks of family and friends); and interactions among these.

The initial NIH and NSF funded baseline survey covered the provinces of Lopburi and Chachoengsao, both relatively near Bangkok. Part of Lopburi coincides with the fertile rice bowl of Asia, an area also suited for cultivating other profitable cash crops, and part of Chachoengsao contains an important industrial corridor making its way to the formerly booming eastern seaboard. The survey also covered the provinces of Buriram and Srisaket in the Northeast. Srisaket is perhaps the poorest province in Thailand, and Buriram provides an example of a "transition" province as one moves closer toward Bangkok. The gain from this deliberately chosen contrast is evident. Indeed, our survey data confirm that average wealth, income, and consumption cover both the extremes of Thailand's semi-urban and rural areas as well as of areas in between. Roughly, wealth, consumption, and income are rank-ordered, from low to high; Srisaket, Buriram, Lopburi, and Chachoengsao.

Of course there would be other ways to generate this contrast, that is, other ways to choose provinces. We used the following method. Within the central and northeast areas, provinces were chosen because at least one amphoe[1] in each province was selected by the Thai Socioeconomic Survey (SES)[2] from 1976–1992. We thus have a baseline history of each province that we can use to better understand the retrospective and contemporary data of our own survey.

Within each province, twelve tambons[3] were selected in a stratified random sample, the stratification ensuring an ecologically balanced sample, that is, ensuring an unbiased selection of the various diverse areas even within a province, see Binford, Lee, and Townsend (forthcoming).[4] In particular, the stratification was used in Srisaket, Buriram, and also Chachoengsao to ensure the inclusion in the sample of two upland if not partially forested tambons. Data on reflectants and a factor analysis confirmed that in Srisaket, the southern tier tambons looked substantially different from the rest, at least from the point of view of satellite imagery. Buriram is similar in the same respect. Chachoengsao was known to contain heavily forested regions on its eastern border. Landsat images from Lopburi, on the other hand, displayed no evident pattern, and there the selection of the twelve tambons was entirely random, that is, not stratified at all.

Within each tambon, four villages were selected at random. This clustering made the logistics of these ambitious surveys a little bit easier and was consistent with the goal of evaluating the various financial institutions. That is, it was hoped that within the relatively small area of a tambon, there would be relatively little ecological or environmental variation, at least from one village to the next, while prior experience suggested relatively large variation in informal and formal institutions from one village to the next.

Within each village, we selected fifteen households entirely at random. We got soil samples from one plot of each of the first ten of these households to measure natural productivity of the environment, and there was a short questionnaire to accompany the household soil sample. We also got the history, procedure, and records of all village or tambon level financial institutions, and we interviewed up to two joint liability groups of the Bank for Agriculture and Agricultural Cooperatives (BAAC) if the BAAC functioned in that village. Finally, we interviewed the headman or key informant of each village to get the village history, with dates, and to get general contemporary information. In summary, then, we have precrisis socioeconomic and financial data on 2,880 households, 606 small businesses, 192 villages, 161 local financial institutions, 262 BAAC borrowing groups, and soil samples of 1,880 agricultural plots. For the sake of clarity below we refer to this as our own initial baseline survey.

The Ford Foundation funded a resurvey of four of the original tambons of each of the four provinces. The four tambons of each province were selected at random from the original survey, from a list of twelve. Within each resurvey tambon we have, of course, selected the same villages and the same households that were interviewed in the initial survey, with a successful reinterview rate of about ninety-four percent We also resurveyed the headman and the local financial institutions. The resurvey began in mid-April of 1998, and was completed by the end of May. This time frame is deliberately chosen to be identical with the period in which the initial survey was conducted, one year later. Again, for clarity, we refer to this below as our resurvey data.

We have also deliberately selected one tambon in each province from the original twelve which displayed minimal ecological variation, according to the analysis of the soil data (nitrogen, acidity, cat-ion exchange capacity) and which simultaneously displayed maximal institutional variation. We have designed a monthly survey to get more exact data for the institutional evaluation, beginning with a census (in May), then continuing with the collection of baseline information (replicating in part the resurvey questions) in June and July, and then with monthly sampling beginning in August. We hope to continue this monthly survey for up to two years. We thus end up with forty-two of the original sample for the resurvey and the possibility of tracking diverse areas of the Thai economy through crisis, transition, and hopefully growth. We call the monthly surveys our own "micro" survey data, but at the time of writing we have nothing yet to report.

Some words of caution are in order. The results reported below are still preliminary. Indeed, we have pressed hard to use the data to get results which can be helpful now, today, to Thai policymakers, but this is not a substitute for carrying out the longer term and more exacting analysis. Second, the results of the resurvey are even more preliminary. We report here on ninety-percent of the data and are in the process of the second round double blind computer entry. We hope to have available a more complete summary soon. Third, and on the other hand, we do have the capacity to generate reports on specialty topics (e.g. savings, borrowing and informal lending, the scope of village institutions, the role of the BAAC borrowing groups, and other reports) at the request of government, private or international agencies.

2. RESULTS

2.1 Liquidity and financing constraints

The first story of Thai growth starts with the notion that internal credit markets are relatively poor and that to finance or to expand entrepreneurial business activities, one needs to accumulate wealth. Those in the labor force with talent or high productivity may wish to change occupations, from subsistence labor to entrepreneurship for example, or to expand the size of existing businesses. But in the absence of credit, only the relatively wealthy can do so. Initially, wages are relatively low, while those able to finance themselves in business make extraordinary profits, contributing to high and rising inequality. Over time, the economy accumulates real physical capital, giving rise eventually to increasing wages. The fruits of growth trickle down slowly to the poor. An example of a formal model in this vein is Bernhardt and Lloyd-Ellis (1993).

In this context, the spread of intermediation—as with increased lending on the part of the BAAC, the spread of commercial bank branches, the establishment of village-level production credit groups, or other past policy interventions—has an important role to play. Households and businesses with access to this intermediation can choose occupations and scale without constraints. That is, only talent or ability will matter, not initial or accumulated wealth. This will not only be more efficient for the households and businesses themselves, it will also be associated with high levels and high growth of national income. (see Moloche and Townsend (forthcoming) for numerical simulations).[5]

This model of Thai growth does receive substantial support in the SES data of the National Statistics Office and in our own survey data. As shown by Hyeok Jeong (1998) in his University of Chicago dissertation, structural shifts have been important for long run average income growth. That is, shifts of the population from unskilled to increasingly educated, from agricultural to industry, and from rural to urban areas account for thirty-seven percent of the household income growth in Thailand from 1976 to 1994. In semi-urban and rural areas, shifts from agriculture and wage labor into entrepreneurship are of particular importance in explaining the growth of average income, even more so than in urban areas. But industrialization and education shifts have also contributed to rising inequality in rural areas, as the relatively few who do move into the associated high income groups benefit the most and as the gaps between groups have widened. Particularly impressive is the role of financial deepening in rural areas, accounting for twenty-two percent of growth and thirty-five percent of the increased inequality, roughly consistent with the model.

The precrisis data show that in 1997, about twenty-one percent of the households of the survey own businesses (see Jeong and Townsend, 1998). Though most use family labor only, twenty-three percent hire up to five workers, and a handful of rural enterprises have up to twenty employees. Clearly, the potential for growth and employment is there, but the ability to start these businesses depends primarily on accumulated savings, not on credit. For example, seventy-two percent of the assets used to start a business were financed with cash, only 2.7 percent came from private gifts, 2.4 percent from the BAAC, and 2.3 percent from commercial banks, with the rest in residual categories. Thus the story of poor credit markets carries a lot of weight in the actual data. The credit numbers are somewhat higher for nonasset startup costs, but still the BAAC finances only 15 percent of the total.

Indeed, fifty-three percent of precrisis household businesses say they would make more profits if they could expand (by borrowing). The most constrained are shop owners and the least are shrimp farms, with traders around the average. More formal but very preliminary logistic regressions show that a business is more likely to be constrained in scale the lower is wealth and the lower is access to commercial credit. No doubt related, the ability to become an entrepreneur in the first place is facilitated by wealth and access to commercial bank credit, and, also revealing perhaps, by high BAAC/Coop credit. This provides direct evidence for the micro underpinnings of the model. These tests are being done as in earlier literature, e.g., Evans and Jovanovic (1989), Feder (1988), and Benjamin (1992).

Only 125 out of 2,880 households had loans from commercial banks at the time of the precrisis survey. For a data summary see Kaboski and Townsend (1998). Commercial banks do lend 36.3 percent of their own total to business, but by account purpose this is only eight percent of the business credit market. The BAAC does finance the bulk of pesticide, herbicide, and fertilizer but also provides some business loans, amounting to 17.4 percent of its own total and by account thirty-five percent of the business credit market. But overall, the rural credit market is seen as limited, with family and neighbors themselves the largest providers of housing and loans for the purchase of consumer durables.

2.2 Risk, diversification, and financial deepening

A second story for Thai growth with inequality and financial deepening takes a modern financial markets point of view, emphasizing diversification and the optimal allocation of risk bearing. In this model (see Greenwood and Jovanovic, 1989), the construction of financial infrastructure is costly. That is, there are fixed costs to expansion and marginal costs for ongoing use. Relatively low wealth and high fixed costs can keep some of the population cut off from access to financial institutions, except perhaps for access to local support systems, e.g., those connected to remittances and migration (see Paulson 1994). These households and small businesses must diversify across activities, keeping average productivity low. As wealth accumulates slowly, reinvestment of savings is low and growth is also slow. In contrast, relatively wealthy households enter the financial system, at either the village, regional, or national level. A combination of mutual funds for savings and equity or return-contingent borrowing allows them to diversify financial risk. In the end, they specialize in production and occupations, choose higher productivity activities (even if these involve high risk), and have higher income growth (see Townsend and Ueda (forthcoming)[6] for numerical simulations).

The relevance of this model to Thailand is reinforced by the SES and initial survey data. To be noted first is that there is much risk involved not only with investments financed by foreign capital inflows but even within the domestic financial system more generally. But there are also ample, and perhaps unrealized, possibilities for diversification. For example, from 1988–90, some amphoes in the northeast had growth of 114 percent but others had shortfalls of –77 percent (see Figure 2 in Townsend, *Journal of Economic Perspectives*, 1995). As summarized in Table 1 from Townsend (1995), we regressed growth in income on time, regional, and community type fixed effects. We found that there are common components in income growth for farmers, especially in the central plains and northeast, but the residual variance remains high and is in principle diversifiable. There are also few fixed effects of any kind for entrepreneurs, suggesting that idiosyncratic, uncorrelated, and diversifiable risk is enormous. In our own initial survey data, households name the worst and the best year in the last five. In a preliminary regression with that year as the dependent variable, we find tambon-specific fixed effects, suggesting great variation from one tambon to another in the timing of bad and good years. Likewise, a typical tambon in the survey, Hua Chang in Srisaket, shows that even within a tambon, the four villages and sixty households of the initial survey are not usually having a bad year at the same time (see Figure 1). In sum, there appear to be possibilities for diversification at virtually all geographical levels, even at the local scale.

Some of the financial institutions under consideration do take actual households and businesses in the right direction, which is toward an optimal allocation of risk bearing as predicted by the model. In his University of Chicago dissertation, using SES amphoe level data on income and consumption and Community Development Department (CDD) data on access to financial institutions, Anant Chiarawongse (1998) shows that the ability of an amphoe to insure itself against idiosyncratic, amphoe-specific income shortfalls is enhanced by the intensity of BAAC involvement and, to a lesser extent, by the presence of commercial banks. In our own initial retrospective survey data, very preliminary results show that the likelihood of having to reduce consumption expenditures in a bad year is lessened in the northeast by being a member of a production credit group, while in the central plains and near Bangkok, it is lessened by being a member of a women's group. Wealth also buffers consumption (see also Pawasutipaisit (1997) which uses data from the pretests of the survey instruments).[7]

In the absence of explicit or implicit insurance, economists predict that people will borrow and lend to smooth, as in Zeldes (1989) and especially, Paxson (1992) using the Thai SES data. If there are credit limits, people may save even more (see Deaton 1989). Indeed, according to the initial survey, the dominant motive for saving across all types of savings accounts is precaution for emergencies (55 percent), followed by 13.8 percent for bequests, 10.6 percent for old age, and eight percent for children's education (see Seiler and Townsend 1998). The point is that other methods for the reallocation of risk appear missing. This can have an adverse impact on the availability of long-term savings, presumably for the financing of industry and other productive enterprises.

One should also understand that the informal systems may be playing an important and previously unmeasured buffering role. Though exceptional, in Buriram there is more in value in rice storage than in all other accounts combined. Table 2 summarizes these and other results. Households do complain on occasion about inability to access financial institutions, even for purposes of saving.

2.3 Optimal financial contracts and procedures with private information and incentive problems

The third story of Thai growth takes the realistic point of view that optimal insurance and credit contracts are constrained by private information and incentive problems (see Aghion and Bolton 1994, Ma and Smith 1996, and Piketty 1994). The poor in particular may be constrained in their access to credit because the costs of monitoring a borrower's project by a bank is high or because repayment of principal plus interest is so large relative to profits after repayment that the borrower has little incentive to be diligent and to work hard. Initially, then, as with the earlier models, growth proceeds unevenly, with the poor depending on their limited wealth or only limited, imperfect financing. Further, there will not be full insurance, even for those with access to the financial sector, precisely because it is difficult for the bank to verify underlying conditions or because borrowers must be given an incentive to work hard, to benefit in good times and be penalized in bad, to bear responsibility for their actions. That is, borrowers, and nonborrowers, of course, will be exposed to risk and will experience fluctuations.

Still, this story alone does not rationalize any degree of unequal growth or limited insurance. The overall outcome depends on three factors: the technology of production and capital accumulation, risk aversion, and a prior information structures. For example, if labor and capital inputs are highly complementary, then there is a tendency for the poor to get more credit, even more than the relatively rich, precisely because in equilibrium they are working hard, providing much labor on their own project (see Lehnert, 1998). That is, credit finances capital inputs, these are particularly productive when labor effort is high, and the poor at low relative wealth work hard, (though obtaining less consumption). Similarly, the higher the degree of risk aversion, the greater the degree of insurance. It is rare indeed that insurance is precluded entirely. Related, bank verification and monitoring costs may be substantial, but schemes with limited probability verification usually dominate simple, noncontingent debt. Depending on the role of these three factors, the second portfolio story of Thai growth should not lead us too far astray.

The more general implication of this model is that, with information and incentive problems, the implicit or explicit nature of credit/insurance arrangements and the procedures which banks and financial institutions actually use can make large differences in the ability to access credit. In the medium to long term, they can make a difference in the degree of overall growth and the extent of inequality. Therefore, it is crucial to ask how we can identify inefficiencies that can be remedied. The literature on mechanism design teaches us various lessons in this respect.

First, sorting and screening of customers by offering a variety of incentive compatible contracts is highly desirable. For example, risk averse customers will prefer high interest rates in return for some flexibility in repayment. Similarly, allowing cosigners to take on liability for a defaulting borrower's nonrepayment can induce customers to sort into diligent groups ex ante, taking advantage of what they know about one another (see Becker and Murphy, 1994; Ghatak, 1998; and Rai, 1997).

Second, banks may not only assign the level of credit or credit financed inputs, but also restrict customers away from other lenders, if they can do so. In effect, the lender takes a more active role in managing the enterprise and looks more like a holder of equity. Similarly, optimal contracts are long term contracts (see Townsend, 1982; and Green and Oh, 1991). Competition for the provision of loan contracts should take place ex ante, in a market for long term contracts, so to speak, not ex post, after an understanding is entered into, as this undercuts the ability to monitor the use of credit (Prescott and Townsend, 1984). This may give the appearance of segmented markets, as in Siamwalla et al. (1990) for Thailand and Aleem (1990) for Pakistan, but it does not mean that markets are inefficient or exploitative.

Third, and related, customers can be given the option of reporting difficulties which occur after a loan is granted, but before repayment is due. A financial institution can then reschedule loans, for example, by giving the borrowers the option of repaying even more in present value terms in return for paying less now (see Prescott 1995).

Fourth, simple debt contracts which require repayment of principal and interest, except in the event of bankruptcy, may not allow the bank to take on sufficient risk and to benefit in good times, and may give borrowers adverse incentives (see Lehnert, Ligon, and Townsend, 1998).

Fifth, it is sometimes optimal for individual borrowers to pool funds, risk, and available labor, in effect acting as a single group or client in their relation with the outside bank. This is especially true when internal information and monitoring possibilities are good, when individual project returns are not too correlated so there is much internal risk to share, and, surprisingly, when individual clients do not have similar wealth.[8] The more general point is that there can be an optimal degree of financial hierarchy.[9] Moving upward from the bottom of the hierarchy to the ultimate market or lender, such an hierarchy can encompass: cosigners of any individual loan, explicit borrowing groups, cross-village assistance, cross-regional intermediation through a centralized lender or market, and ultimately perhaps the central bank. Still, there is not a uniform formula prescribing the optimal degree of hierarchy, not a fixed rule which is independent of preferences, technologies, and a priori information structures. The degree of hierarchy, the degree and stages of joint liability, and whether or not one should use borrowing groups depends on the underlying environment. When the project returns of individual clients are highly correlated, for example, both banks and customers are better off if the banks compare project returns across these clients to decide whether or not to make exceptions (see Holmstrom, 1982).

Sixth, and related, financial institutions such as banks can be viewed themselves as clients or agents in their relationship to each other and to the central bank. Banks may provide loans to each other or enter into contingent risk agreements, and the central bank may provide liquidity or act as a lender of last resort (see Holmstrom and Tirole, 1998; and Townsend, 1989). But the optimal degree of this implicit, if not explicit, insurance depends on the ability of banks to monitor or verify one another, and of the Central Bank to monitor the banks in close coordination with the Office of Supervision. Similarly, depositors or note holders of these banks, though adverse to risk, should be given at least some degree of risk and should bear some degree of liability if the bank's portfolio goes bad (see Chari, 1989; Diamond and Dybvig, 1983; and Wallace, 1988). A lesson from the theory of incentives is that it is an error for the Central Bank to underwrite ex ante too much of the risk of a given troubled financial institution, bailing out ex post depositors, note holders, and other banks if not the holders of equity. Taxes to achieve fiscal balance, or inflation taxes otherwise, fall upon the public in unmeasured and ill-documented ways. Incentives might also be improved by greater disclosure.

There is some support from pretests, field research leading up to the surveys of this project and the preliminary data that more finely tuned incentive contracts can make a difference in access to credit and thus to productivity and growth with lessened inequality.

First, the typical experience with the funds of a successful Production Credit Group is that there are risk contingencies implicit in the repayment agreement. In a given year, one can find that ten to twenty percent of borrowing clients have not paid back loans, but virtually all will do so by the end of the second year. The headman or committee usually know the adverse condition which triggers the slow payment, or at least are confident, and correctly so, that ultimate repayment is forthcoming. An exception occurs when a truly poor or very unlucky client fails to repay some or all of the loan, but even here these terms are often accepted by the committee not as a willful default but as a need for insurance or welfare, sometimes paid by an explicit fund collected from all ex ante.

The BAAC has similar, though not officially documented, provisions in its loan contract and collection procedures. At certain times, much of the staff in a BAAC branch office will be out in the field verifying actual circumstances of client borrowers who have communicated in advance the existence of difficulties. About fifty-five percent of group heads in our initial survey say that, in the past, they have informed the BAAC of potential difficulties and the vast majority claim this has been helpful to all. Though overall BAAC operational costs are high, ultimate repayments are good and the BAAC covers most of its costs. An ongoing project with Jacob Yaron of the World Bank will document better how the implicit insurance system works.

More generally, the BAAC uses joint liability groups for small borrowers without formal collateral, and the project will document the precise degree to which customer sorting, internal monitoring, and internal risk sharing are playing a role (see Ahlin, Sakuntasathien, and Townsend, 1998). For example, as regards screening, virtually eighty-eight percent of the BAAC group members in our survey have a near relative in the same BAAC group, and thirty-nine percent of the groups claim there was someone who wanted to join who was screened out. They also acknowledge, however, that the BAAC goes beyond character and relationships to look at income, assets, and credit history. As regards monitoring, if one member announces he cannot pay the BAAC, eighty-four percent of the groups say there is an investigation. Only ten percent say they have actually paid off another member's loan, but there is much internal borrowing and lending, and this can accomplish much the same thing. 98.5 percent of members do verify that loans would otherwise be cut off for all members.

Less formal and therefore less evident groups may also be working in the way theory predicts. It is evident in the survey data, for example, that the general degree of help and assistance through networks of friends and relatives is extraordinarily high. With eighty-one percent and eighty percent of Chachoengsao and Srisaket households sharing meals outside the household, seventy-five percent and ninety percent sharing labor, fifty-nine percent and seventy-five percent sharing equipment, and eighty-seven percent and seventy-seven percent sharing money. Note that informal networks remain high even in the central area. Certainly, most clients have loans from multiple sources. More specifically, some borrow from the formal sector and then onlend to others. As for the reverse, it is well known from the work of Siamwalla et al. (1990) that not a small number of BAAC clients borrow from an informal source to pay off a BAAC loan. Our own initial survey confirms that moneylenders are indeed a huge escape hatch. We add to this that the informal loan and insurance market in a village does not necessarily consist of stereotypical money lenders only but is much deeper, again with a variety of loan types and differing relationships. The general point is that finance and insurance from the informal sector can be a good thing, especially if it is thought about in tandem with the formal sector. This might also give one pause in uniformly condemning the relationship commercial banks have with their customers or of customers with each other, though these practices deserve and require measurement and documentation.

As noted, commercial banks have lent relatively little to the households and small businesses investigated in our initial semi-urban and rural survey. The average ratio of collateral value to loan value is thirty to one as reported by customers, though commercial banks say they will lend up to sixty to eighty percent of collateral value. One can draw the hypothesis, to be checked carefully in the survey data, that relative to the BAAC and village funds, banks are less actively involved in monitoring and in explicitly assuming the risk of client enterprise. But again, some of these practices are implicit, if as yet poorly documented.

2.4 Impact of and response to the crisis: resurvey results

The economic crisis and agro-climatic shocks have not hit Thailand's semi-urban and rural areas uniformly (see Pawasutipaisit, Sakuntasathien, and

Townsend, forthcoming).[10] Table 3 displays the number and percent of households responding that the last twelve months period was worse in terms of income than the year before. Within the central region there is great variety, with Lopburi having fifty-five percent of households claiming lower income than the year before the crisis, and forty-one percent claiming so in Chachoengsao. Even within Lopburi there is variety, with one of the four tambons showing only twenty-five percent having lower incomes. There is more uniformity in Chachoengsao, where the income of virtually half of households has remained unchanged over the two years in question. An even greater contrast is afforded by a comparison of Buriram and Srisaket in the Northeast. While sixty percent of households had a bad income year in Buriram, only thirty percent had so in Srisaket. Within Srisaket, there is variety across tambons as well. More generally, and consistent with the notion that ex ante diversification might have been possible, we note that for eleven percent and twenty-two percent of households in Chachoengsao and Lopburi, respectively, and seventeen percent and thirty-nine percent in Buriram and Srisaket, respectively, the post-crises year was a relatively *good year*. Ironically, this fact lowered the sample size for some of the results reported below.

Related, a large amount of measured variety is revealed by histograms plotting per capita income growth over the two-year period. For those claiming that last year was a worse year, income growth varies from –150 percent to +150 percent. Consistent in a way with their earlier answer, however, this distribution is shifted to the right for those claiming to have had a better year, with some mass in the far right tail. We note, of course, that any such histogram should not be taken literally as the income data of any given household are noisy, we but not the households converted income to per capita terms, and absolute and relative prices have changed, making real welfare comparisons delicate.

One can attempt to paint a picture of the causes of these ups and downs by decomposing nominal household income into its various sources, then adding up over households. There are modest shifts: remittances are down from 14.1 percent to 12.1 percent of the total, and wages and salaries are down from 35.5 percent to 29.7 percent. In contrast, business income and farm income are up from 5.4 percent to 6.8 percent and 38.3 percenet to 39.6 percent, respectively. There is variation by province, however. For example, business income increased from 5.7 percent to 11.9 percent in Lopburi, while farm income declined there. The histograms of the percentage changes of the various income components are also revealing the underlying variety. While remittances, and to some extent also wage and salary income, have much mass in the negative range, farm income is more uniformly distributed.

Stratification by the bad year versus good year responses restores some order. In Lopburi, Srisaket, and Buriram, those who claim to have had a good year are typically those with a larger percentage of income from farm sources, while in Chachoengsao, those in business and with wage and salary income are those who have had a good year.

The initial survey and resurvey offer mixed evidence for the negative picture of a large number of unemployed industrial workers returning to villages. Household size is quite stable, with a relatively large number of households experiencing no change. Positive and negative changes roughly balance out. A related question is whether households had returning those members who had previously migrated. Though 11.82 percent of households say yes, an even larger number report increased outmigration, namely 18.42 percent. Thus net outmigration would seem to be positive. Net outmigration is the largest in the northeast, especially in Srisaket, with 12.95 percent of households receiving at least one member and 23.66 percent losing one member. Unfortunately, due to the lack of benchmark panel data, we do not know if this is peculiar to the crisis or due to chronic outmigration.

Interviews with the headman of each of the survey villages do, on the other hand, reveal some increased unemployment. Out of sixteen villages in each province, seven and nine villages in Chachoengsao and Lopburi, respectively, and fourteen and fifteen in Srisaket and Buriram, respectively, have a headman reporting increased unemployment. Only one headman in Lopburi reported less unemployment. At the same time, headmen report increases and decreases in work in factories, namely two and nine, respectively, in Chachoengsao; six and one in Lopburi; two and twelve in Srisaket; and one and five in Buriram, with the rest of the sixteen headmen reporting no change. New factories near one survey village were reported in Lopburi and Buriram, and no nearby factories were shut down. Similarly, the results on work in construction vary across villages with activities in this sector going up in some and down in others. The number of households involved in livestock is down, especially in Srisaket, while the number of households growing crops has increased in Chachoengsao. Results are mixed for Lopburi.

The impact of agro-climatic shocks is the dominant reason cited by households for having had a bad year (see Table 4). Drought is the dominant response in all four provinces, with the percentage of households giving this reason ranging from forty-seven percent to seventy-one percent. An exception is Srisaket with 31 percent. Floods are also mentioned by twenty-four percent of households in Srisaket and pests by ten percent in Chachoengsao. Six to seven percent of households report to have worked fewer days, with the exception of Lopburi, were nineteen percent do so. Low output prices, high input prices, educational expenses, and illness are additional factors mentioned by some. The latter reasons are given even more often when households are asked for secondary causes. It should be emphasized that these adverse events can be quite serious for households experiencing them.

An average of twenty-two percent of the households report having established new businesses over the past twelve months, ranging from a low of seventeen percent in Lopburi to a high of thirty-one percent in Chachoengsao. For those who run existing businesses, a comparison of the last twelve months with the year before reveals that output is down for forty-two percent to fifty-eight percent of the household businesses. Though value of output is up eighteen percent to forty-three percent, profitability is down for thirty-two percent to forty-three percent across provinces. There are, however, a minority who report increased output and increased profitability. Apart from that, few complain about quantity, quality, or wages of workers and few complain about changes in credit. This does not presume they had credit in the first place, however.

Response strategies to these problems, which are crucial to understanding potential impact, vary across households and regions. Households reporting a relatively low-income year were asked how they responded. Their first unsolicited response is emphasized and recorded in Table 5. Then, after prompting, households were asked to rank-order their three most important responses. These are recorded with equal weight in Table 6.

"Reducing consumption" is the most common unsolicited response among households in the central region. It also shows up as the most important rank-ordered response in not only Lopburi and Chachoengsao, but also in Buriram. Surprisingly, however, reducing consumption does not show up as a dominant rank-ordered response in Srisaket.

"Working harder," and, to a lesser extent, "migration" and "finding additional jobs" are frequently reported unsolicited responses. However, as a rank-ordered response, "working harder" moves from the second most common response in the central areas to the third and fifth most common response in Buriram and Srisaket, respectively.

Finally, "reducing productive inputs" is a relatively uncommon response in all provinces except Chachoengsao, where it shows up as fourth most important.

In summary, there seems to be a direct impact of the agro-climatic shocks, if not the economic crisis, on consumption, work, and productive-inputs. The overall impact on consumption, work, and inputs is largest in the central region, consistent with the notion of an inverse correlation between real impact and the level of "development." On the other hand, a very preliminary pooling of four provinces reveals that drops in income show up at a positive but low value as drops in consumption. The elasticity is 0.14.

One naturally wonders how households and small business have managed to buffer so well, at least on average. We can group responses into various categories in this regard.

The first category is the self-insurance category. For example, "use of rice in storage" is a typical unsolicited response in the Northeast, and after reflection it shows up as the first and second most common rank-ordered response in Srisaket and Buriram, respectively (recall the earlier discussion on the use of rice and other savings as buffer stocks).

Similarly, "use of financial savings" is a typical unsolicited response, showing up as the third most frequent rank-ordered response in both provinces of the central area, and fourth in Srisaket. "Selling jewelry, land, or livestock" is quite common as an unsolicited response, too. As a rank-ordered response, "selling jewelry" is the fifth most common in Lopburi and "selling livestock" is the third and fourth most common in Srisaket and Buriram, respectively. Direct evidence on the use of land is mixed. Fewer households sold land in the last twelve months than in the year before, but the headmen note land sales in two to four of the sixteen villages of each province.

"Use of formal credit" varies with the institution used. "Got help from the BAAC" shows up in unsolicited responses quite often, except in Lopburi. It is, in fact, the second most common rank-ordered response in Srisaket and the fifth most common in Chachoengsao. Notably, none of the other *formal* credit institutions show up at this level as playing a significant role, not ag-coops, commercial banks, nor village organizations.

"Informal help and assistance" does rival the BAAC, however. "Help from relatives" is a common unsolicited response in all four provinces, and it shows up as the fourth most common rank-ordered response in Lopburi. Similarly, "money lenders" are mentioned in the northeast for not a small number of households, and also in Lopburi, and this is the fifth most common rank-ordered response in Buriram. "Help from nonrelatives" is mentioned in unsolicited responses in Lopburi.

The initial survey and resurvey also ask direct questions about help and assistance from friends and relatives and attempts to gauge the strength of informal networks. A striking pattern emerges. "Help among relatives in the form of meals received or given" is up relative to the year before the crisis, but "exchange of equipment and money" are down. "Labor exchange" is unchanged. With respect to "help among nonrelatives," the outcome is different: there is no change in shared meals, and labor exchange is down. Otherwise, Lopburi is confirmed as a place where networks are important; help in the form of money among relatives *and* nonrelatives actually went up.

Ongoing analysis hopes to better document the consumption, work, and production impact of recent adverse shocks, portraying possible differences in self insurance, formal credit and informal community response across regions. Needless to say, this goal is very consistent with the initial design of the project.

3. POLICY RECOMMENDATIONS

3.1 Commercial banks

Because commercial banks are relatively inactive in the semi-urban and rural areas of Thailand, especially on the lending side, every effort should be made to remove obstacles. Commercial banks should be free to set their own on-lending rates, with a premium for agriculture and small business if they view the risks and costs to be high. The Bank of Thailand should reconsider its use of minimum retail rates, MRR, with uniform markups. This does not preclude the prevention of monopsonistic inefficiencies. Related, the new foreclosure law should create a legal and social climate under which penalties and stigma are attached to nonperformance and default on the part of borrowers. Commercial banks should enter into clearly understood and explicit contracts with farmers and small businesses, contracts that allow rollovers and adjustments to external shocks. Thus, loans affected by such shocks would not be counted as nonperforming loans per se, but increased provisioning might be necessary, depending on analysis of the historical data. Related, documentation of customer screening, communication, and direct disclosure should receive much more emphasis in regulatory changes, as should more conventional levels of loan diversification, through investment into a diversified portfolio of agricultural assets, avoiding excessive concentration in real estate. The overall presumption should be full public disclosure of procedures and portfolios. Finally, interactive research should continue to explore actual or potential barriers in lending to agriculture and small business by commercial banks.

3.2 Bank for agriculture and agricultural cooperatives

The BAAC charter should be modified to allow lending to business, health, and housing, dropping all references to percentage ceilings of any such activities and leaving behind the idea that only farm households are the real targets of BAAC lending. Any implicit or explicit understanding that the

BAAC and commercial banks should not compete with one another should be dropped insofar as ex ante competition is concerned, while long-term multi-period contracts should be respected. Related, the BAAC should charge customers competitive on-lending rates, covering the costs of such loans with a reasonable margin. Concessionary sources of funds, at below market rates, should be priced internally at market rates, and if certain target groups receive concessional on-lending, the subsidy to them should in turn be made explicit. Contractual arrangements for risk mitigation and procedures for internal communication and monitoring should be made even more explicit, again for reasons of clarity and to avoid the appearance of nonperforming loans. A full array of savings and insurance instruments should be offered at market rates. Full disclosure should be maintained, and the issue of BAAC equity (or profits sharing) to BAAC loan officers, customers, and farmers in general should be encouraged.

3.3 Village funds

Production credit groups (PCGs) and other indigenous funds should also be studied as a potential vehicle for the expansion of Thai rural credit. Indeed, cooperative movements were the starting points for the contemporary financial grants of Germany and Japan, and there is no reason in principle why a similar development could not take place in Thailand. A first step is to gain a better understanding of the successes and failures of PCGs, and of the great institutional and socioeconomic variation over villages within a tambon. This is part of the ongoing research project. New PCGs might be established, or existing PCGs expanded and connected one to another. Tambon or amphoe level associations should be designed with an awareness of the possibility of increased risk diversification, that is, by maintaining local provisions for "insurance" and incentive compatible welfare, and extending these to larger areas. Standardization, formalization, and uniform accounting need not rule out these provisions. The government savings bank might lend to community groups, but only as the rating system is put into place.

3.4 Tiered lending

An alternative to direct lending by banks or by the BAAC would be the use of PCGs and other village organizations as second tier lending and saving institutions. In that spirit, greater accessibility by those in rural and semi-urban areas to mobile bank vans, ATM's, and other facilitators might be promoted if these can be made self-funding by user fees at appropriate fixed and marginal costs.

3.5 Bank of Thailand

The financial system should move toward full and complete disclosure of portfolios and lending procedures, substantially altering laws requiring secrecy. The central bank should make explicit the rules for limited deposit insurance with liability clearly delineated in advance.

3.6 Information systems

The Thai government should consider a two-pronged strategy to make full use of improved information systems in the formulation of economic and social policy. One prong would work toward connecting the many pieces of useful socioeconomic information that are currently scattered across various Thai ministries. The second prong would envision the collection of additional useful information through repeat surveys. In this way, data and candidate models can be used to track the evolution of the economy and be available for monetary, regulatory, and other policy evaluation on a systematic basis.

Table 1: Common Region, Year and Community Type Effects in Income and Consumption Growth Rates

**=significant at 5% level, *=significant at 10%

	F test for:	Different Occupation Groups: All Households		All Farmers		Rice Farmers		Entrepreneurs		Different Measures of Income and Consumption: All Income	No In Kind	Wages	Food
		Y	C	Y	C	Y	C	Y	C	Y	Y	Y	C
1	N: 75-81											*	
2	N: 81-86												
3	N: 86-88						**						
4	N: 88-90									*	**	**	
5	N										**	**	
6	NE: 75-81											**	
7	NE: 81-86												
8	NE: 86-88			**					**		*		*
9	NE: 88-90	**	**	**	**	**	**	**	**	**	*		**
10	NE		**	**	**		**		**			*	**
11	C: 75-81												
12	C: 81-86												
13	C: 86-88			**		*	**						
14	C: 88-90			**		**							
15	C			**		**							
16	S: 75-81												
17	S: 81-86												
18	S: 86-88												
19	S: 88-90	**	**	*						**			
20	S												
21	B: 75-81												
22	B: 81-86												
23	B: 86-88			*									
24	B: 88-90		**	**									**
25	B			**									

Notes: This table presents the results of F-tests for the joint significance of dummy variables for common fixed effects. The dependent variables are demeaned income (Y) and consumption (C) growth rates. Where the division is by occupation, consumption is equal to expenditures on food, clothing, shoes, and tobacco; and income is equal to wages, profits from farming, entrepreneurial income and income-in-kind. A * indicates that the test is significant at the 10% level, ** indicates significance at the 5% level, N = North, NE = Northeast, C = Central, S = South, B = Bangkok. Reproduced from Townsend, Journal of Economic Perspectives.

Table 2: Percent of Savings by Institution/Region

	Chachoengsao	Lopburi	Buriram	Srisaket
Commercial bank	66.76	72.10	23.24	14.50
Ag coop	04.18	3.27	.70	2.72
BAAC	18.58	5.92	5.87	32.72
PCG	0.31	7.48	.33	3.12
Rice bank	0	0	6.63	1.01
Rice storage	5.42	2.43	47.61	38.62

Table 3: General comparison between this year and last year (from household resurvey)

Province:	Chachoengsao	Lopburi	Buriram	Srisaket
Last year is worse than the year before	86 (41%)	114 (55%)	133 (60.2%)	67 (30%)
Last year is better than the year before	23 (11%)	46 (22%)	50 (22.6%)	70 (31.4%)
Unchanged income	101 (48%)	48 (23%)	38 (17.2%)	86 (38.6%)
# of households	210	208	221	223

Table 4: Reason for Bad Income—% of Households

Province:	Chachoengsao	Lopburi	Buriram	Srisaket
Flood	1.16	.88	.75	23.58
Drought	62.79	47.37	70.68	31.34
Pests	10.47	1.75		
Other reason low crop yield	2.33	1.75	7.52	4.48
Low price of output	9.30	7.02	3.01	8.96
High input price	2.33	2.63	1.50	4.48
Education expense higher	1.16		.75	1.49
Need extra money for ceremony		.88		
High investment costs	1.16	3.51	2.26	4.48
Expenses due to illness		3.51	1.50	1.49
Building expenses higher			2.26	1.49
Death in family				
Worked fewer days	5.81	19.30	7.52	5.97
Bad year for household business	2.33	3.51	.75	5.97
Money gambling				
Unable to repay debts		.88		
Other	1.16	7.90	1.50	5.97

Table 5: Response to Bad Year—Unsolicited Responses (from household resurvey)

Provinces:	Chachoengsao	Lopburi	Buriram	Srisaket
Direct Impact:				
Reduce consumption	25(22.5)	46(32.8)	14(12.5)	5(7.3)
Reduce productive inputs	11(9.9)	3(2.1)	5(4.5)	1(1.3)
Work harder	16(14.4)	28(20.0)	13(11.6)	9(13.0)
Migrate	8(7.2)	0	1(0.9)	3(4.3)
Do additional job	12(10.8)	6(4.3)	22(19.6)	9(13.0)
Self-Insurance:				
Use/sell rice in storage	1(0.9)	0	11(9.8)	10(14.5)
Use savings	2(1.8)	6(4.3)	7(6.3)	2(2.9)
Sell jewelry/land/ livestock	10(9.0)	10(7.1)	4(3.6)	5(7.2)
Formal Organization:				
Borrow from BAAC	9(8.1)	1(0.7)	11(9.8)	8(11.6)
Borrow from Agri.Coop.	2(1.8)	2(1.4)	0	0
Borrow from Commercial Bank	0	0	0	0
Borrow from village organization	1(0.9)	3(2.1)	1(0.9)	2(2.9)
Informal Mechanism:				
Borrow/help from relatives	6(5.4)	16(11.4)	12(10.7)	5(7.2)
Borrow/help from nonrelatives	2(1.8)	7(5)	1(0.9)	0
Borrow from supplier	3(2.7)	4(2.9)	0	1(1.4)
Borrow from moneylender	1(0.9)	7(5)	10(8.9)	7(10.1)
Special:				
Help from government	2(1.8)	1(0.7)	0	2(2.9)
Help from temple	0	0	0	0
Number of Households	111	140	112	69

Note: Number in parenthesis is percent

Table 6: Rank-Ordered Responses

Province	Most Important Response				
Chachoengsao 86 Households	Reduce consumption (65%)	Work harder (33.7%)	Use savings (32.5%)	Reduce productive inputs (18.6%)	Borrow from BAAC (16.3%)
Lopburi 114 Households	Reduce consumption (65%)	Work harder (45.6%)	Use savings (29.82%)	Help from relatives (21%)	Sell jewelry (15.8%)
Buriram 133 Households	Reduce consumption (36.8%)	Use/sell rice in storage (36%)	Work harder (31.5%)	Sell livestock/ equipment (26.3%)	Borrow from money lender (21.8%)
Srisaket 67 Households	Use/sell rice in storage (44.7%)	Borrow from BAAC (28.3%)	Sell livestock (28.3%)	Use savings (26.8%)	Work harder (23.8%)

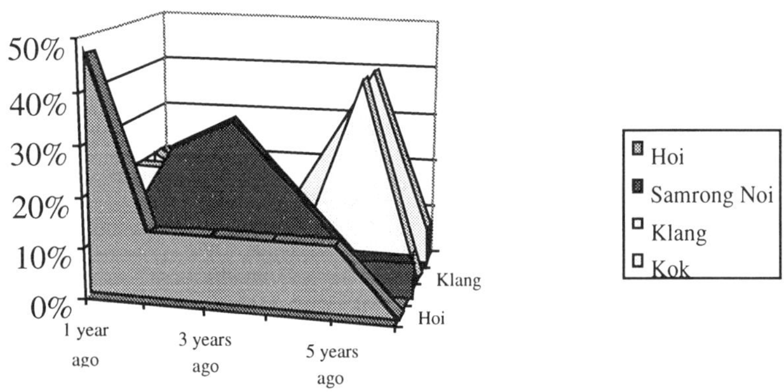

Figure 1. Distribution of worst income years across villages in Tambon Hua Chang (Sisaket)

	1 year ago	2 years ago	3 years ago	4 years ago	5 years ago	no changes
Hoi	47%	13%	13%	13%	13%	0%
Samrong Noi	7%	27%	33%	20%	7%	7%
Klang	20%	20%	13%	7%	40%	0%
Kok	20%	13%	0%	20%	40%	7%

Notes

[1]Amphoe = Thai word for district.

[2]This household survey is conducted every two years by the Thai Government's National Statistical Office (NSO).

[3]Tambon = Thai word for subdistrict.

[4]For further information on this research, please contact Robert Townsend at the University of Chicago, or his coauthors Tae Jeong Lee or Michael Binford.

[5]For further information on this research, please contact Robert Townsend at the University of Chicago, or his coauthor Guillermo Molochee.

[6]For further information on this research, please contact Robert Townsend at the University of Chicago, or his coauthor Kenichi Veda.

[7]For a larger literature on risk sharing, see Altonji, Hayashi, and Kotlikoff (1992), Altug and Miller (1990), Cochrane (1991), Deaton (1994), Mace (1991), Paulson (1994), and Townsend (1994), and on production see Morduch (1990).

[8]See Holmstrom and Milgrom (1990), Itoh (1991), and Prescott and Townsend (1996).

[9]See Bond (1998) Diamond (1984), and Krasa and Villamil (1992).

[10]For further information on this research, please contact Robert Townsend at the University of Chicago, or his coauthors Anan Pawasutipaisit or Sambat Sukuntasathien.

References

Aghion, Philippe, and Patrick Bolton. 1994, "A Theory of Trickle Down & Development," manuscript, October.

Ahlin, Christian, Sombat Sakuntasathien, and Robert Townsend. 1998, "BAAC Group Lending," project notes.

Aleem, Irfan. Imperfect Information, 1990, "Screening and the Cost of Informal Lending: A Study of Rural Credit Markets in Pakistan," *World Bank Economic Review*, September.

Altonji, J., F. Hayashi, and L. Kotlikoff. 1992, "Is the Extended Family Altruistically Linked? Direct Tests Using Micro Data," *American Economic Review*, 82: 1177–1198.

Altug, Sumru, and Robert Miller. 1990, "Household Choices in Equilibrium," *Econometrica*, 58: 543–570.

Becker, Gary, and Kevin Murphy. 1994, "Optimal Social and Private Sorting Among Categories When the Composition of Members Matters," working paper, October.

Benjamin, Dwayne. 1992, "Household Composition, Labor Markets, and Labor Demand: Testing for Separation in Agricultural Household Models," *Econometrica.*

Bernhardt, Dan, and Huw Lloyd-Ellis. 1993, "Enterprise, Inequality and Economic Development," December.

Bond, Philip. 1998, "Costly Communication and Institutions," University of Chicago, dissertation.

Chari, V. V. 1989, "Banking without Deposit Insurance or Bank Panic Lessons from a Model of the U.S. National Banking System," Federal Reserve Bank of Minneapolis, *Quarterly Review*, Summer.

Chiarawongse, Anant. 1998, "Consumption Insurance and Financial Intermediaries," University of Chicago, dissertation.

Cochrane, John. 1991, A Simple Test of Consumption Insurance," *Journal of Political Economy,* 99: 957–976.

Deaton, Angus. 1989, "Saving in Developing Countries: Theory and Review," *In Proceedings of the World Bank Conference on Development Economics.*

Deaton, Angus. 1994, *The Analysis of Household Surveys: Microeconomic Analysis for Development Policy*, Research Program in Development Studies, Princeton University, April, chapter on risk-sharing in Cote d-Ivoire.

Diamond, Douglas. 1984, Financial Intermediation and Delegated Monitoring,"*Review of Economic Studies,* 51.

Diamond, Douglas, and Philip Dybvig. 1983, "Bank Runs, Deposit Insurance and Liquidity," *Journal of Political Economy.*

Evans, David, and Boyan Jovanovic. 1989, "An Estimated Model of Entrepreneurial Choice Under Liquidity Constraints," *Journal of Political Economy*, August.

Feder, Greshon. 1988, *Land Policies and Farm Productivity in Thailand,* World Bank.

Feder, Greshon, et al. 1991, "Credit's Effect on Productivity in Chinese Agriculture," World Bank.

Ghatak, Maitreesh. 1998, "Screening by the Company you Keep: Joint Liability Credit Contracts and the Peer Selection Effect," University of Chicago, mimeo.

Green, Edward, and Soo-Nam Oh. 1991, "Contracts, Constraints and Consumption," *Review of Economic Studies,* 58: 883–899.

Greenwood, Jeremy, and Boyan Jovanovic. 1989, "Financial Development, Growth and the Distribution of Income," *Journal of Political Economy*.

Holmstrom, Bengt. 1982, "Moral Hazard in Teams," *Bell Journal of Economics*, 324–40.

Holmstrom, Bengt, and Paul Milgrom. 1990, "Regulating Trade among Agents," *Journal of Institutional and Theoretical Economies,* 146, 85–105.

Holmstrom, Bengt, and Jean Tirole. 1998, "Private and Public Supply of Liquidity," *Journal of Political Economy,* 106.

Itoh, Hideshi. 1991, "Incentives to Help in Multi-agent Situations," *Econometrica* 59, 611–36.

Jeong, Hyeok. 1998, "Decomposition of Growth and Inequality in Thailand," University of Chicago, dissertation.

Jeong, Hyeok, and Robert Townsend. 1998, "Household Businesses and Their Financing," project notes.

Kaboski, Joseph, and Robert Townsend. 1998, "Borrowing and Informal Lending in Rural Thailand," project notes.

Krasa, Stefan, and Anne Villamil. 1992, "Monitoring the Monitor: An Incentive Structure for a Financial Intermediary," *Journal of Economic Theory,* 57(1). June 197–221.

Lehnert, Andreas. 1998, "Solow Growth Models and Moral Hazard," University of Chicago, dissertation.

Lehnert, Andreas, Ethan Ligon, and Robert Townsend. 1998, "Liquidity Constraints and Incentive Contracts," *Macroeconomic Dynamics*.

Ma and Bruce Smith. 1996, "Credit Market Imperfections and Economic Development: Theory and Evidence," *Journal of Development Economics,* 48(2), March, 351–387.

Mace, Barbara. 1991, "Consumption Volatility: Borrowing Constraints or Full Insurance," *Journal of Political Economy,* 99: 928–956.

Morduch, Jonathan. 1990, "Risk, Production, and Saving: Theory and Evidence from Indian Households," Harvard University, manuscript.

Paulson, Anna. 1994, "Insurance Motives for Migration: Evidence From Thailand," University of Chicago, dissertation.

Pawasutipaisit, Anan. 1997, "A Study of Risk Sharing and Institutions in Village Thailand," Thammasat University, dissertation.

Paxson, Christina 1992, "Using Weather Variability to Estimate the Response of Savings to Transitory Income in Thailand," *American Economic Review*, March.

Piketty, Thomas. 1994, "The Dynamics of Wealth Distribution and the Interest Rate with Credit Rationing," October, manuscript.

Prescott, Edward S. 1995, "Communication in Models with Private Information: Theory, Applications, and Computation," University of Chicago, dissertation.

Prescott, Edward C., and Robert Townsend. 1984, "Pareto Optima and Competitive Equilibria with Adverse Selection and Moral Hazard," *Econometrica*, January.

Prescott, Edward S., and Robert Townsend. 1996, "The Boundaries and Connectedness of Economic Organizations," working paper.

Rai, Ashok. 1997, "Efficient Audit Mechanisms to Target the Poor," University of Chicago, dissertation.

Siamwalla, Amar, et al. 1990, The Thai Rural Credit System: Public Subsidies, Private Information and Segmented Markets," *World Bank Economic Review*, September.

Seiler, Edward, and Robert Townsend. 1998, "Saving in Rural Thailand," project notes 1998.

Townsend, Robert. "Optimal Multiperiod Contracts and the Gain from Enduring Relationships under Private Information." Journal of Political Economy 90(6), December 1982, 1166–1186.

Townsend, Robert. 1989, "Currency and Credit in a Private Information Economy," *Journal of Political Economy,* 97(6), December, 1323–1345.

Townsend, Robert. 1994, "Risk and Insurance in Village India," *Econometrica*, 62(3), May, 539–591.

Townsend, Robert. 1995, "Consumption Insurance: An Evaluation of Risk-Bearing Systems in Low-Income Economies," *Journal of Economic Perspectives,* 9(3), Summer, 83–102.

Townsend, Robert. 1995, "Financial Systems in Northern Thai Villages," *Quarterly Journal of Economics*, November, 1011–1046.

Wallace, Neil. 1988, "Another Attempt to Explain an Illiquid Banking System: The Diamond-Dybvig Model with Sequential Service Taken Seriously," *Quarterly Review*, Federal Reserve Bank of Minneapolis, 1988.

Zeldes, Stephen. 1989, "Consumption and Liquidity Constraints: An Empirical Investigation," *Journal of Political Economy.*

PART V

CONTAINING THE RISKS OF FUTURE CRISIS—STRENGTHENING THE REGULATORY FRAMEWORK

Chapter 20

What's Wrong With The IMF? What Would Be Better?

Allan H. Meltzer
Carnegie Mellon University

The International Monetary fund (IMF) and the World Bank were created in 1944 reflecting the experience of the 1920s and 1930s. The fund's tasks were to adjust current account imbalances and manage the exchange rate system. The bank's main tasks were to lend for the reconstruction of Europe and eliminate the alleged bias against lending to developing countries.

Whatever may have been true in the 1940s, the international financial system has found other means of solving the problems that the fund and the bank were supposed to solve. Changes in exchange rates are now one common means of adjusting current account imbalances. Leading countries including the United States, Japan, Britain and the European Union allow their currencies to float. Within Western Europe there will soon be a common currency with a single central bank in place of fixed but adjustable exchange rates.

Many of the problems or international financial crises of recent years arose because there is too much lending, especially short-term lending, to developing countries, not too little. Recent history gives good support to the proposition that, if a country adopts market-oriented policies of privatization and deregulation, opens its trade to competition in foreign markets and by foreigners in domestic markets, and carefully controls its budget, foreign lenders and investors are willing to finance development.

Yet, the international financial system is crisis-prone. Latin America in the 1980s, Mexico in the 1990s, and Asia and Russia now are well-known examples of deep, pervasive financial crises that have been costly to the public in the countries with financial problems, their trading partners, and, often, much the rest of the world. The past fifteen years have seen ninety serious banking crises, most of them followed by deep recessions. More than twenty of these crises produced direct losses to the developing country exceeding ten percent of its gross domestic product. In half of these cases, including several Asian countries now, losses exceed twenty-five percent of gross domestic product. Caprio and Klingabiel (1996, 1997); Calomiris (1998). These losses, relative to GDP, are far larger than the cost of the U.S. saving and loan problem to U.S. taxpayers.

The frequency and severity of recent international financial problems in a period of growth, economic progress, and low inflation should raise a series of questions. Why is there so much financial fragility? Is the current set of international institutions appropriate for current conditions? Have international financial arrangements and institutions adapted appropriately to the changes in the world economy? Is it time to agree upon new arrangements? What set of international financial arrangements will serve the world well for the next decades?

I do not pretend to have complete answers to all of these questions. I believe they are questions that economists and policymakers must ask and try to answer. This paper attempts to start that discussion. After pointing to what I believe are some of the failures of current arrangements, and their lack of fit with current problems, I propose some changes. I concentrate on the IMF, although there is now substantial convergence in the activities of the bank and the fund. I omit discussion of policy errors, for example in Asia in 1997. All policymakers err at times. The important issue, I believe, is not judgmental errors but structural flaws that support and encourage financial fragility.

1. ORIGINS AND RATIONALE FOR THE FUND AND THE BANK

Planning for postwar international monetary cooperation began before the United States entered the war. The lend-lease agreement, under which Britain and others obtained military supplies and equipment on "credit", provided that the United States could waive postwar repayment if the British agreed to eliminate trade "discrimination." The term was not further defined, but the objective it expressed included elimination of the prewar system of imperial preference that bound its empire to Britain and favored British exports to its colonies.

As negotiations of postwar arrangements proceeded, trade issues faded into the background, and financial issues moved to center stage. By September 1941, Keynes had developed a proposal for an international currency union as part of the British contribution to discussion of postwar arrangements. With minor adjustments, Keynes's proposal became the

British government proposal in April 1943, when formal bilateral discussions began (Meltzer (1988, pp. 236–37).)

Keynes visited the United States in the fall of 1941 and may have discussed his plan informally. In December, a week after the United States entered World War II, Secretary Morgenthau asked Harry Dexter White to "prepare a memorandum on the establishment of an inter-Allied stabilization fund" as the basis for postwar international monetary arrangement. Blum (1967, v. 3, pp. 228-29).[1] Morgenthau's diary suggests that he had a vague idea about expanding the 1936 Tripartite Pact to avoid competitive devaluations.

Keynes (1923) developed the basic analytic problem. Each country acting alone can achieve either stable prices or a fixed exchange rate but not both. To achieve both there must be international cooperation or agreement. The classical gold standard was one such agreement. Keynes (and others) had recognized earlier that the gold standard required deficit countries to bear the cost of adjustment, required pro-cyclical monetary policies, and was inflexible and costly for a country with downward wage rigidity. Like White, and many others, he considered the inflexibility of the gold standard, the distribution of gold, and the monetary policies of the surplus countries, mainly France and the United States, as leading causes of the great depression. The aim was to avoid a return to the classical gold standard while retaining enough of its features to solve the coordination problem while making the arrangement acceptable to prospective surplus and deficit countries.

Both Keynes's and White's plans and the Bretton Woods agreement imposed costs on surplus countries that would neither expand imports nor lend to deficit countries. The justification was elimination of an externality. By forcing adjustment on surplus countries, deficit countries would be spared higher interest rates and contraction. This would benefit surplus countries and others, since their exports and incomes would be maintained. If the surplus countries could be made to lend to the deficit countries, fluctuations in economic activity would be damped. Both surplus and deficit countries would gain. Of course, this could work only if the imbalance was temporary. Persistent imbalances required a change in exchange rates, with the consent of the IMF.

Both Keynes and White limited their proposals for the IMF to the financing of current account deficits. To the extent that financing of capital flows was discussed, it was the proposed Bank for Reconstruction and

Development (later the World Bank) that would be responsible. White explained privately why the U.S. favored an international bank.

> "Many of the loans will be risky and there will be some losses. This is one of the reasons why we insisted that the bank be an international bank rather than to take the risks ourselves. We felt that the benefits would be world-wide and that other countries should be at risk." H.D. White to the Board of Governors and Reserve Bank Presidents, Board Minutes (March 2, 1945, p. 17)

There were two reasons for the proposed bank. One is risk sharing, a reason that continues to be used. This is a distributive, not an efficiency argument. The second is the benefit to the world economy. This claim reflected the belief that economic development was hindered by risk averse lenders who restricted the supply of capital and charged premium rates. The supply of capital to developing countries was believed to be sub-optimal. The proposed bank would remove the capital market restriction.

Although the argument was not developed more carefully, it was widely accepted. The experience of the 1930s, when there were sizeable defaults by developing countries, was taken as evidence that lenders would be restrictive in the future.

The international system did not evolve as planned. Experience showed that many of the beliefs and conjectures on which it was based proved to be wrong. The United States did not return to its interwar policies. Instead of large, persistent surpluses, and high tariffs, it ran small surpluses or deficits on current account and worked to reduce tariffs globally. Loans and transfers added to the dollar claims held by foreigners. By 1951, the U.S. gold stock started a fall that, with a few brief interruptions, continued until the U.S. suspended gold sales in August 1971.

During its early years, when the U.S. had its largest current surpluses, the fund had a very modest role in the international payments system. The Marshall Plan redistributed part of the U.S. surplus, and the European Payments Union cleared payments imbalances for the inconvertible European currencies. Historians describe the early years as a period in which the status of the fund and even its survival were in question (Presnell (1997, p. 229), James (1996)).

The fund became more active in the mid-1950. For a few years, the new system functioned smoothly. Membership increased; more countries drew on the fund's resources, and the amounts drawn increased. The fund specialized in making relatively small, short-term loans. Since repayment was usually prompt, the fund recycled its resources (James (1996)).

This period was followed by a series of crises or disturbances affecting key currencies, first the pound, then the dollar. By 1968, the U.S. gold stock had fallen so far that a de facto restriction on gold convertibility was in place. The fixed but adjustable rate system limped through the next two years. In mid-1971, convertibility ended formally with the closing of the gold window.

If the original plan had been implemented, the IMF would have ceased to exist in 1973 when the fixed but adjustable rate system officially ended. The Bretton Woods system left capital account lending to the World Bank. The fund no longer had a reason for being.

2. RECENT HISTORY

In the 1970s and 1980s, the fund took an important role in capital account lending to "recycle" the revenues of oil producing countries after the oil price rise. Its role as advisor to developing countries on macroeconomic adjustment increased. This advice was tied to lending; the fund made loans to ease the burden of adjustment to the structural and macroeconomic reforms it advocated.

Edwards (1989, p. 78) summarizes the results of an internal IMF study by Mohsin Khan of these policies and actions. "Khan found that fund programs had a statistically nonsignificant effect on the balance of payments, a nonsignificant effect on inflation, a significant positive effect on the current account, and a significantly negative effect on output." In other words, the fund's programs moved the current account toward balance by reducing output, income, and imports. The conditions for IMF assistance required countries to control inflation, but the condition was not met in many countries. IMF research found no significant effect of its programs on inflation.[2]

Beginning in the summer of 1982, the fund greatly expanded lending to countries experiencing capital outflow. It continued to lend during the years of financial distress known as the "Latin American debt crisis." This was a major extension of its capital market program. The size of loans and the time to repayment increased. Many countries became permanently indebted to the fund.

The fund's main function in the 1980s was lending money to debtor countries to pay interest on their outstanding debts to the fund and commercial banks. As part of these arrangements, commercial banks also increased their loans to indebted countries. Most of this was an accounting operation to avoid recognizing defaults. The result was that Latin American debt rose, the creditor banks were protected, and the debtor countries continued to suffer under a rising debt burden and falling per capita income.

IMF programs postponed recognition of losses by U.S. and other international banks at the expense of living standards in Latin America. By the end of the decade, as part of so-called Brady adjustments, banks accepted part of their losses, workout agreements were reached for the remaining debt, and growth resumed in Latin America.

Latin American loans were made under the IMF's conditional lending program under which governments agreed to follow stabilizing policies. As before, the problem was enforcement against sovereign governments. The IMF's main threats were to cancel the loan program or withhold payments. In a preview of what was to happen in Russia and Asia, the threats usually proved to be empty. The main reasons are of interest because they show some principal flaws in the system.

First, the IMF becomes committed to the "success" of the program. Cancellation is seen as a failure. Governments understand that the IMF is reluctant to withhold funds or cancel programs. Hence the threat loses force.

Second, IMF officials are judged partly on their contacts with high officials of borrowing governments. Critical reports by an IMF task force reduce the welcome the IMF team can expect on its next visit. The finance minister is "too busy." Failure to meet with principal officials is treated as a "failure," harmful to the IMF official's career. Borrowing governments recognize this power, so they are able to restrain criticism and prevent or delay information from reaching the IMF's top management.[3]

The Latin American program was a model for subsequent capital market programs. The next large financial crisis was in Mexico in 1994–95. Again, the IMF, with assistance from the U.S. Treasury, protected foreign banks and financial institutions by allowing them to avoid portfolio losses. Although many of the foreign commercial banks had made loans in 1994 at interest rates of twenty percent per annum or more, they were not required to bear the risk that they had undertaken. Instead the IMF loaned money to Mexico at below market interest rates. Again, the international bankers were spared, while the economy suffered a severe recession.

The IMF and the U.S. Treasury claim success in Mexico. A principal reason, I suspect, is that the loans by the IMF and the U.S. Treasury were repaid. Much of the repayment was effected by the Mexican government borrowing in capital markets at higher rates of interest, surely not an improvement from the standpoint of Mexican economic welfare.

The welfare losses to Mexicans were much larger than the increased interest payments. Chart 1 shows Mexico's per capita real GDP in U.S. dollars. The striking feature of the chart is that per capita income in 1997 was only slightly higher than in 1973. In a period of rising world real incomes, Mexican income was highly variable but stagnant. Meanwhile debt per capita rose by a factor of three or four so, after twenty-five years, with income unchanged on average, taxes for debt service were much larger and Mexican disposable income per capita was smaller.

The IMF, the bank, and the U.S. Treasury are not responsible for all of the problems that Mexico experienced. Oil price changes and mistaken policies of the Mexican government made large contributions. To the extent that IMF support contributed to the durability of mistaken policies and to the burden of the debt, the IMF must bear some responsibility. Mexico is far from the success that IMF and U.S. Treasury officials proclaim. The IMF did not foresee the Mexican crisis partly because the Mexican government did not provide information, partly because of the incentives within the IMF discussed above.

One promising feature of the Mexican program was a new departure on which better arrangements can be built. Mexico gave a lien against Mexican oil revenues to guarantee repayment of its U.S. government loan. Use of collateral to support borrowing is a helpful step, but it raises a question about why oil revenues could not have been used to guarantee private lending without subsidies from the IMF.

A bad feature of the Mexican program was its contribution to the belief that international banks had a safety net not available to investors in equities or purchasers of real assets in foreign countries. The message implicit in these actions was clear to bankers and investors. Between 1990 and 1996, capital flows to emerging markets rose from $60 billion to $194 billion. After 1995, with Mexican experience in mind, portfolio investment declined, but bank lending increased.

In the past twenty years, the IMF has introduced two new loan facilities. One is the Extended Structural Adjustment Facility (ESAF). The other is the Structural Transformation Facility (STF) to assist former members of the communist block, including Russia and states of the former Soviet Union. Both facilities extend the conditional lending procedures in new directions without correcting the flaws.

ESAF offers medium-term loans at an interest rate of 0.5 percent with repayments up to ten years. The borrower agrees to make structural adjustments such as fiscal reform, privatization, and trade liberalization. "A recent IMF-World Bank study concludes that the results of ESAF loans have been largely negative in terms of reducing budget deficits and inflation and mixed in terms of producing external viability and promoting per capita growth." (Quoted in Mikesell (1998, p. 31)).

The STF has contributed to transformation in several former communist countries. The bulk of its funds—and other IMF–World Bank loans—have gone to Russia where policy mistakes, misjudgments, and corruption have prevented successful transformation. When oil and commodity prices fell in 1998, lenders began to question Russia's ability to service its large outstanding debt.

A principal policy mistake in Russia is neglect of the necessary conditions for transformation to a capitalist economy. The conditions include structural reforms that increase transparency of business and government reports and statistics, establish private property, a commercial code, accounting standards, and enforcement through the rule of law. Some commercial and industrial property has been privatized, often in deplorable ways, but ninety percent of agricultural land remained under state or collective controls in 1997. And federal law does not permit the sale of agricultural land. In contrast, China began its more successful reform program by introducing long-term leases that had many features of private ownership of agricultural land.

The above structural reforms, if adopted, would have provided a Hayekian infrastructure. A structure of this kind introduces incentives that direct resources to efficient uses. Capitalism is more than trade at market prices. Successful capitalism is a set of institutions that provides incentives compatible with economic development, efficient use of resources and enforcement of contracts. These features of successful capitalist countries are missing in Russia and many countries of the former Soviet Union. The IMF has shown little interest in encouraging these reforms.

Corruption and mismanagement are widespread in Russia. Published estimates in 1997 suggested that capital flight was about $2 billion per month with a total of $150 billion from Russia since the breakup of the USSR (Jenkins (1998, quoting *Global Finance*). A report by the director of the chamber of accounts of the Russian Federation gives some specific examples.[4] (Sokolov (1998)).

1. Parliament appropriated $150 million to build planes for sale to India. An audit showed that none of the funding reached the enterprise.
2. Parliament appropriated funds to aid Chechnya after the war ended. The total bill was $3 billion. The audit found documentation for $2

billion, less than $150 million reached Chechnya. No record of the remainder was found.

3. $30 million of a World Bank loan was allocated to compensate victims of bank frauds and pyramid schemes. Audits showed that after several years, not a single victim had received payment.
4. The government issued debt to finance a large fraction of its payments. Forty-five percent of state revenues in 1998 went to pay interest on the debt. "This means no money is left to pay workers or to support education, public health" or other government services. (ibid)

These criticisms were made before recent crises drove interest rates above a 100 percent annual rate. The IMF did not publicly condemn these improper and corrupt practices. We now know that the IMF was aware of the problems of inadequate accountability and corruption. It failed to enforce the conditions of its loans and the most elementary standards of accountability and performance.

IMF, U.S. and German government policies encouraged banks and financial institutions to believe that a Russian default on its debt would be avoided. IMF and U.S. actions had prevented lenders from taking losses in Mexico. If Mexico was critical to the stability of the United States, the reasoning went, surely Russia was more critical. On this reasoning, interest rates of 40 percent, 50 percent or 100 percent seemed to be a gift to international lenders—default premiums without comparable default risk.

Moral hazard arises when the private risk to the lender is less than the risk borne by society. This was clearly the case, ex ante and ex post in Mexico and in Asia. Banks and other lenders did not experience the large losses borne by ordinary citizens and owners of equity and real assets. Ex ante, banks and financial institutions that made loans to Russia believed that they would be spared losses also. The $22 billion loan promised by the IMF, World Bank and others in July seemed to confirm this view for a time.[5] Inability of the Russian government to fulfill its commitments soon raised doubts, followed by capital outflow.

Moral hazard lending to Russia, encouraged by the bailout of foreign lenders to Mexico, permitted Russia to finance large, unbalanced budgets by borrowing externally. The result is a much larger financial problem for international lenders and possibly for economies in several countries. The IMF continued lending despite the Russian government's failure to meet the loan conditions. The IMF continued to lend when the Russian government "reduced its deficits" by not paying soldiers, miners, and others. Again, the

IMF was committed to "success." The government understood that, so "conditionality" failed.

The IMF's mistake was to establish the STF and undertake structural reform. It had no prior experience and no special competence. The lessons it had learned, mainly in Latin America, concerned macroeconomic adjustment of market economies. It was slow to recognize that structural transformation involved the development of a Hayekian infrastructure. And it refused to learn a main lesson of its own past experience—sovereign governments cannot be compelled to implement programs that they do not favor. Policy changes will not be implemented unless they are supported by local political institutions and their leaders.[6]

3. IMF ERRORS AND RESPONSES

The IMF had more success in the 1960s when it limited its efforts to helping countries with current account deficits. As its scope expanded, its record became ambiguous or worse. In this section, I will comment on three errors or problems: (1) undertaking structural transformation lending and advice in Russia, (2) moral hazard, and (3) the ambiguous effects of IMF (and bank) lending. These errors, and the IMF's responses, lead to recommendations for reform.

There was no previous experience on which to base transformation policies in Russia. Primarily for political and military reasons, there was intense interest in Europe and the U.S. to transform Russia into a more democratic, market economy. The G-7 governments either were unwilling, or believed they were unable, to obtain funding for the transformation from their parliaments. The IMF agreed to accept responsibility. In doing so, it moved far beyond its competence.

Even if its advice had been well-founded, the IMF had little scope for enforcing Russian commitments. Like most borrowers, Russian officials understood that the IMF and the G-7 had a stake in reform and transformation. The fund could threaten to withhold payments. It did, on occasion, delay payments. As in many previous experiences, however, the fund did not want the program to fail.

Governments in Russia (and other countries) understand that the fund's commitment to "success" weakens its ability to enforce threats. The IMF was unwilling to call attention to widespread corruption, failure to implement reforms, and cynical maneuvers to reduce reported budget deficits by failing to pay civil servants, coal miners, soldiers, and others.[7]

Russia differed from other countries in many ways, but the IMF's failure in Russia was not unique. The IMF also tolerated corruption in Indonesia. In Korea, Indonesia, and elsewhere, it tolerated fragile financial systems used to subsidize projects favored by government officials or their political supporters. A main question about these and other failures is whether the IMF lending delayed reform both directly by lending and by encouraging private capital inflows. These additional resources may have contributed to reform, but they also permitted bad policies to continue.

No single answer can be given for all countries. There may be countries where IMF loans helped reform politicians to make changes that would have been delayed or avoided. It seems clear, however, that IMF lending, and the private capital flows that followed, permitted unbalanced budgets, fragile financial systems, government subsidies to specific programs through banking systems, and corruption to continue longer and at higher levels.

Much has been written about moral hazard in Asian lending. I want to distinguish two separate problems. First is the effect of IMF policies toward Mexico and Russia on private lenders. The second is the decision to delay reform knowing that IMF lending, at low interest rates, is available in a crisis.

IMF officials minimize the role of moral hazard in Asia. A typical statement is that no government pursues policies that lead to the loss of output, employment and living standards experienced by Mexico, Thailand, Indonesia, Korea, and others. (Fischer (1998, p. 5)) calls "far fetched" the idea that policymakers will take excessive risks because the IMF can help.

This defense shows little understanding of the way the financial problem develops. Ministers of finance do not set out to generate a crisis. At each critical decision point, however, they often decide to allow an additional increase in short-term foreign borrowing rather than adopt policies that would avoid the crisis. A common example from Mexico, Korea and others is the decision to offer exchange guarantees to foreign lenders who are reluctant to renew loans. The guarantees may sometimes be followed by stabilizing policies, but in many countries, they are not. Rather, they postpone and enlarge the subsequent crisis.

This behavior is understandable. The crisis is not a "sure thing." As always, there are risks both ways. A government that adopts restrictive policies early runs the risk that parliament will not approve, that the opposition will claim the policies were unnecessary, and that voters will support the opposition.

This behavior is not unique to developing countries, and it does not occur only in countries that borrow from the IMF. The U.S. government delayed responding to the saving and loan problem for many years. The arguments were similar at the time. Japan delays a solution to its banking problems. The finance minister who chooses delay may be proved right. Even if he is wrong, a crisis may not occur during his term of office. IMF loans, at subsidized rates, are available.[8] A timely loan may require some retrenchment, but all countries that go to the IMF do not have a crisis.

It is sufficient for moral hazard that the existence of subsidized loans from the IMF modifies the finance minister's evaluation of the costs he faces. The very large increase in the number of countries experiencing large crises in recent years suggests that a change of this kind has occurred. Perhaps the severity of the crises in Indonesia, Thailand, Korea, and Russia will change future behavior. I believe that institutional reform is desirable even in this case.

A more problematic defense compares the IMF's rescue packages for international banks to the rescue of some of the passengers on the Titanic.[9] The comparison is inapt. There is no important difference between individual and social losses when a ship like the Titanic sinks. There was no learning by other ships or their captains as a result of the rescue. In the Mexican and Asian crises, there are large differences between the losses borne by international banks and the losses to the Mexican, Thai, Indonesian, Korean, and other populations. Bankers learned that the IMF and the U.S. Treasury would lend to reduce losses to large banks and financial institutions.

The IMF and U.S. Treasury loans to Mexico permitted the Mexican government to honor most of the exchange guarantees on the dollar-guaranteed bonds called Tesobonos. By asking member governments subsequently for a large quota increase, the IMF furthered the belief that similar commitments by governments in Asia, Russia or elsewhere would be honored. If the IMF was not planning large future rescues of banks and lenders, why was a large increase in funding, about $80 billion, needed?

The IMF is not responsible for all the errors that governments make. Nor is it responsible for all the errors made by lenders and borrowers. At issue is whether IMF lending increases the risks in the international financial system. By minimizing the moral hazard problem, the IMF avoids recognizing that it is part of the problem. Its behavior encourages too much short-term lending by financial institutions and too few losses on risky loans.

The third problem is that the effects of conditional lending are ambiguous. Lending may encourage reform, for example by reducing transition costs and strengthening the position of reform proponents. But, lending also may delay reform by permitting governments to continue inappropriate policies. The IMF lacks adequate mechanisms for enforcing desirable change and avoiding retrograde actions.

IMF officials have not proposed effective programs for strengthening the international financial system. Some hint at the possibility of restricting short-term capital movements. (Fischer (1998, p. 7)). Other suggestions include improved supervision or more timely information.

One need not oppose the suggestions for improving information and supervision. They may be helpful, but they are insufficient. Studies from Benston (1973) to Berger et al. (1998) show that banking supervisors and regulators rarely foresee failures. With modern financial instruments, a banker can change portfolio risk as soon as the examiner leaves the bank. Moreover, there are better alternatives. Based on experience with large-scale failures and moral hazard, some countries have reduced their reliance on supervision and regulation. Recent practice in New Zealand, Chile, the United States and elsewhere now relies more on capital and market-based incentives to increase safety and soundness.[10]

4. SUGGESTIONS FOR REFORM

The IMF was created to assist in adjustment of current account imbalances in a world with fixed exchange rate and widespread capital account restrictions. The World Bank was given responsibility for capital transfers on the presumption that government programs were needed to compensate for a sub-optimal volume of development lending.

The conditions under which these institutions were founded are no longer with us. It is time to consider the institutions and arrangements useful for current and expected future conditions. I believe there are structural flaws in the current system, in part because it developed as a response to specific problems and without attention to the longer-term effects of the changes that were made.

To encourage discussion of these issues, this section offers some tentative proposals to improve the functioning of the international financial system by increasing efficiency and reducing moral hazard. My aim is to open discussion of arrangements that maintain capital flows and international lending, while reducing the frequency and depth of financial panics and the losses to countries and their citizens. The proposed system seeks to reduce moral hazard and avoid both subsidies to lending and regulatory restrictions or taxes that prohibit types of lending. There are seven proposals.[11]

1. Increased reliance on fluctuating exchange rates. Many of the exchange rates may be "dirty floats," but I believe experience has shown that capital mobility, fixed exchange rates, price stability, and full employment are rarely compatible. Rogoff (1998) shows that, in recent years, few countries have been able to maintain a fixed exchange rate for six years or longer. Floating exchange rates shift costs to lenders who withdraw their capital and raise the price borrowers pay for large capital inflows. Plus, they reduce inflows and outflows.
2. Improved management of capital flows. Central banks can manage their exchange rate systems to maintain price or economic stability. If a capital inflow threatens stability, the central bank can (1) permit the exchange rate to appreciate, (2) sterilize the inflow by selling domestic securities, or (3) do some of each. Similarly, the central bank can offset capital outflow by allowing the exchange rate to depreciate or by buying domestic assets.
3. Increased reliance on competition in local banking markets. Many producers of goods or services diversify risk in their international operations by locating facilities in many countries. The Coca-Cola Company has expanded internationally since the 1930s. It prospered despite wars, inflation, and many local or regional crises. The company has learned to manage the risk inherent in an internationally diversified company and has provided a model that others have followed. Many countries do not permit banks to follow this model. They prevent international banks from competing in local markets. International banks are limited to making mainly dollar (yen or D-mark) loans to local banks. If international banks held portfolios of local assets and issued local currency liabilities, country risks would be part of a diversified international portfolio. Diversification would reduce the cost of bearing risk. Competition would work to improve local banking practices.
4. Increased size and diversification. Many countries are too small to achieve optimal diversification of financial assets. Loans to a few

industries dominate portfolios of local banks.[12] Suboptimal diversification has been a principal cause of bank failures throughout U.S. history. Admission of foreign banks to local markets should be accompanied by rules for bank capital that prevent international banks from leaving in a crisis. There are different ways to sustain commitment to the country. All involve greater losses from withdrawing than from remaining, hence capital or asset holdings denominated in local currency.

5. Establish an international lender of last resort. More than a century ago, Bagehot (1873) explained that a financial system requires a lender of last resort to assist financial institutions in a liquidity crisis. Unlike the IMF and many country central banks, Bagehot distinguished between liquidity and solvency and provided rules that separated the two. He required the borrower to offer marketable assets as collateral for a loan, and he required the lender to charge a penalty rate on all such loans. The collateral requirement separates insolvent from illiquid banks. The penalty rate eliminates subsidies, reduces moral hazard and reduces reliance on the lender. Most of the time the lender of last resort would be idle. Markets would function, and borrowers would offer collateral. This means that they would hold such collateral, or they could not get assistance.
6. Enforcement of the collateral requirement has stabilizing dynamic properties. Central banks could borrow from the international lender of last resort only on the presentation of internationally traded assets, so they would be induced to hold such assets. They would lend to domestically chartered banks, in the event of bank runs. The international lender of last resort would be barred by statute from making loans without receiving marketable collateral (at a price below last market price). A foreign government that wished to circumvent collateral requirements to assist a developing country would have to obtain an appropriation through its legislature.
7. Development lending would be done through the capital markets. Experience has shown that, if a country opens its markets, controls spending and budget deficits, reduces inflation, and deregulates and privatizes, capital comes. International financial institutions are no longer needed for development lending. A modest role for redistributive lending to reduce poverty would remain.

The combined effect of fluctuating exchange rates, diversified international banks, capital requirements, and a Bagehotian lender would reduce reliance on short-term capital flows and the crises that occur when several international lenders simultaneously fail to renew their loans. A Bagehotian lender of last resort reduces moral hazard.

At the organizational meeting of the IMF and World Bank, Keynes argued against locating these institutions in Washington. His concern was that they would be overly influenced by U.S. domestic politics and the pressures generated by domestic interest groups. It is not known whether such pressures would be dampened by locating the lender of last resort outside the U.S. I believe it is a subject worth more study.

Finally, what should be done about assistance to Russia? This is primarily a political question, and it should be treated as a political issue. Parliaments should be asked to appropriate transfers, perhaps in exchange for warheads and missiles, as was done in Ukraine. There is a possible collective benefit that has little relation to international development lending. Mixing the two was a mistake that is now apparent to all.

Chart 1: Mexico Per Capital GDP, Converted to Real U.S. Dollar Equivalent on Market Exchange Rate Basis

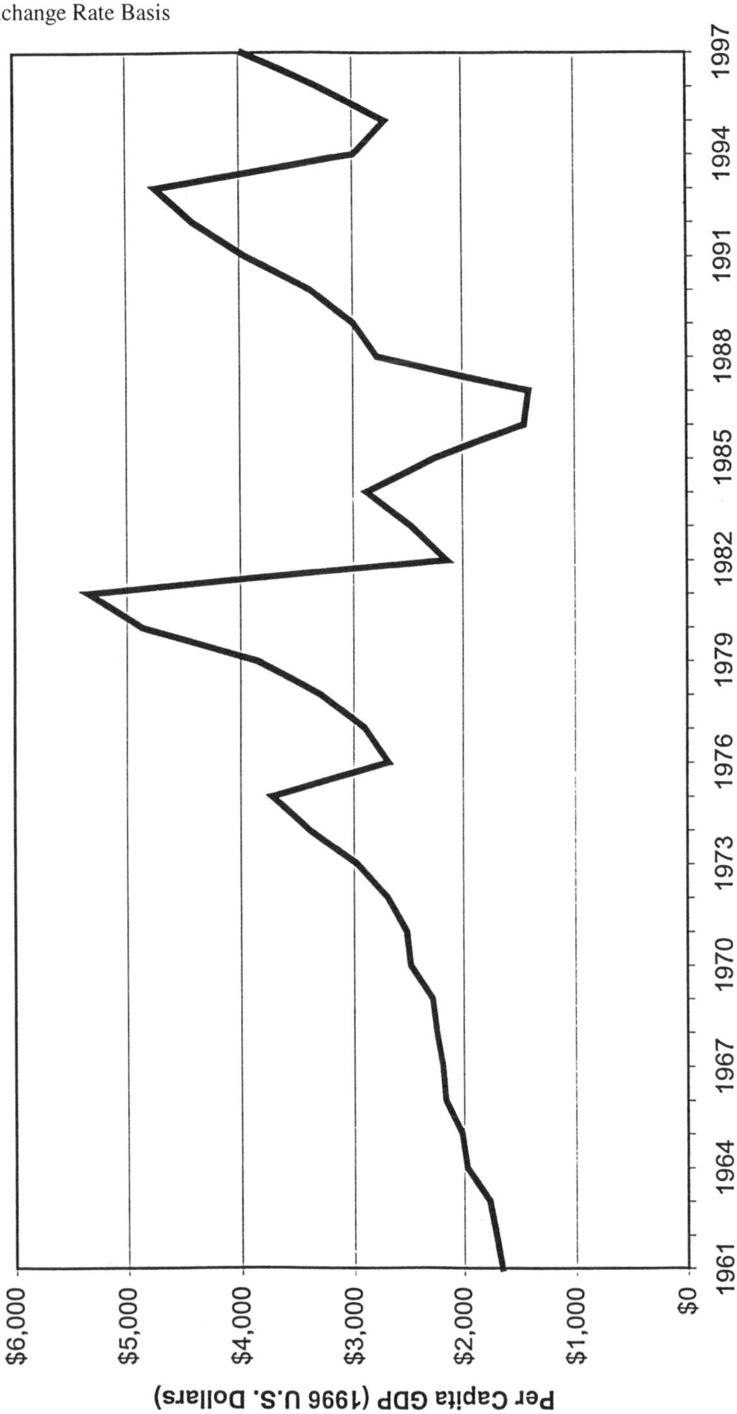

Acknowledgment: I am grateful to Bennett McCallum and Charles Calomiris for helpful discussions.

Notes

[1]White was Director of Monetary Research and later Assistant Secretary of the Treasury. The U.S. proposal that became the basis of the International Monetary Fund is often referred to as the White Plan. Keynes's plan called for a clearing union to adjust current account balances of debtors and creditors. White envisaged a permanent fund that could lend to debtor countries.

[2]I believe there is a likely reason for failures in some cases and success in others. Success requires support by domestic political leaders and local institutions. For an example in Mexico, see Calomiris (1998).

[3]This partially explains why the IMF's management is often slow to recognize emerging problems. The two reasons also help to explain why the IMF tolerated corruption in Indonesia, Russia, and elsewhere.

[4]The Chamber of Accounts is the Russian equivalent of the General Accounting Office. Venyamin Sokolov is a director of the chamber.

[5]IMF promised $11.2 billion in 1998 and $2.6 additional in 1999. This lending was an addition to $1.3 billion committed earlier. The World Bank promised $6 billion over the two years. Japan committed $1.5 billion. The U.S. did not contribute this time. The proposal called for tax increases in Russia. The Russian government proposed a sales tax, despite estimates that more than 50 percent of Russian exchanges are barter exchanges. The government also planned to exchange up to $45 billion of short-term ruble debt for longer-term dollar denominated debt.

[6]Cavallo (1998) draws the same conclusion from his experience as Argentina's finance minister. "If this [committed local leaders] doesn't exist, the IMF should stay out rather than attempt to force a government to implement a program it doesn't believe in." (ibid., p.1) Cavallo argues that the IMF's main role should be to audit the programs developed domestically and, by improving some, help reforming countries to borrow in the capital markets. He adds that in 1995 he felt compelled to accept advice he considered incorrect to get IMF approval so that bankers would resume lending.

[7]One may also question the rationale for some "reforms". In a country where fifty percent or more of all transactions are reported to be barter exchanges, increasing the sales tax is an odd reform to propose.

[8]The IMF has recently raised its lending rates to Korea, a constructive step.

[9]This argument was used by Michael Mussa at the June Brookings Conference (and perhaps elsewhere.) It was repeated by First Deputy Managing Director Stanley Fisher at the American Enterprise Institute's World Forum in June. The author was present on both occasions.

[10]Meltzer (1995) reviews a large literature on safety and soundness issues in developing countries.

[11]Earlier versions are Meltzer (1998a) (1998b).

[12]Close relationships between industrial conglomerates and banks in Asia add to this problem. The problem would arise in many Asian countries even if the relationships ended.

Reference

Bagehot, Walter. 1873, *Lombard Street,* London: Scribners, Armstrong, Reprinted 1962, Homewood: Richard D. Irwin.

Benston, George J. 1973, "Bank Examination," *Bulletin of the Institute of Finance,* New York: Graduate School of Business Administration, New York University, May, entire issue.

Berger, Allen, Sally Davies, and Mark J. Flannery. 1998, "Comparing Market and Supervising Assessments of Bank Performance: Who Knows What When?," Board of Governors of the Federal Reserve System, Finance and Discussion Series, 1998–32.

Blum, John M. 1967, *From the Morgenthau Diaries: Years of War,* Boston: Houghton Mifflin.

Board of Governors of the Federal Reserve System. 1945, "Minutes," unpublished..

Calomiris, Charles. 1998, "The IMF's Imprudent Role as Lender of Last Resort," *Cato Journal*, winter, 275–94.

Caprio, G., and D. Klingabiel. 1996, "Bank Insolvency: Bad luck, bad policy, or bad banking?," in *Annual world Bank Conference on Development Economics,* M. Bruno and B. Pleskoric (eds.), Washington: The World Bank.

Cavallo, Domingo. 1998, "Good Information, Bad Advice," *Forbes Global*, Internet, March 31.

Edwards, Sebastian. 1989, "What Does the International Monetary fund Really Do? Reply to Goldstein," *Carnegie-Rochester Conference Series on Public Policy*, 31, autumn, 77–82.

Fischer, Stanley. 1998, "The Asian Crisis Countries and International System Improvements," *Berlin,* New York: The Trilateral Commission, 3–7.

James, Harold. 1996, *International Monetary Cooperation Since Bretton Woods,* Washington: International Monetary Fund.

Jenkins, Jr., Holman W. 1998, "Russia a Deadbeat? Funny the Banks Never Mentioned It," *The Wall Street Journal*, September 2, A19.

Keynes, John Maynard. 1923, *A Tract on Monetary Reform,* Vol. 4 of *The Collected Writings of John Maynard Keynes,* London: Macmillan and St. Martin's Press for the Royal Economic Society, reprinted 1971.

Meltzer, Allan H. 1988, *Keynes's Monetary Theory: A Different Interpretation*. Cambridge: Cambridge University Press.

Meltzer, Allan H. 1988, *Sustaining Safety and Soundness: Supervision, Regulation and Financial Reform,* Washington: The World Bank.

Meltzer, Allan H. 1998a, "Asian Problems and the IMF," Joint Economic Committee, February 24, reprinted, *Cato Journal*, 17 winter, 267–274.

Meltzer, Allan H. 1998b, Financial Structure, Saving and Growth: Safety Nets, Regulation, and Risk Reduction in Global Financial Markets, presented at First International Conference, Bank of Korea, June.

Mikesell, Raymond F. 1998, "The Future of the Bretton Woods Institutions," *Jobs and Capital*, 7 Spring, 27–33.

Presnell, L. S. "What Went Wrong? The Evolution of the IMF 1941-1961," *Banco Nazionale del Lavoro Quarterly Review,* 50, June, 213–37.

Rogoff, Kenneth S. 1998, "The Risks of Unilateral Exchange Rate Pegs," presented at the First International Conference, Bank of Korea, June.

Sokolov, Venyamin. 1998, "The Virus in Russia," *New York Times*, June 1.

Chapter 21

Containing The Risks of Future Crises: Strengthening the Regulatory Framework

Tom de Swaan
Board of the ABN AMRO Bank, N.V.

As we learned on the first day of this conference, the causes of the Asian crisis are manifold. Judging from the fact that financial systems in many of the countries involved in the crisis came to the brink of collapse or in some cases actually collapsed, I think it is fair to conclude that failing banking supervision plays a major part in explaining the crisis. The events in Asia have once again proven that exposing poorly regulated and supervised financial systems to huge global capital flows is a hazardous act.

It was precisely for this reason that last year, when I had the honor of serving as its chairman, the Basle Committee on Banking Supervision formulated, in conjunction with supervisors in emerging markets, the twenty-five "Core Principles for Effective Banking Supervision." The principles were approved by the G-7 countries last year and are now about to be implemented in individual countries around the world, because it is believed that strengthening banking supervision worldwide can contribute to preventing calamities like we have witnessed lately in Asia and Russia.

Effective banking supervision is, in my opinion, extremely important for ensuring global financial stability. But implementing the principles of the Basle Committee can only be accomplished in an environment that actually can enforce them. For how effective is supervision if supervisors have no means to enforce their regulations in banks, or can be overruled by governments at any time? How can supervisors judge banks' credit and investment policies when there is no adherence to accepted accounting principles and when private property laws are ill-defined?

So apart from the *principles* for banking supervision, I would also like to discuss with you today the *preconditions* which should be met for supervisors to be able to do their work properly. Although preconditions are mentioned in the document of the Basle Committee, they may have remained somewhat underexposed until now. In some circles, the committee was criticised for devoting too little attention to the preconditions that should be in place to successfully implement the core principles, mentioning them only in the introduction and hardly elaborating on them. In response to those criticisms, I would like to point out that supervisors in general, and the Basle Committee in particular, are not the right parties to criticise in this respect. Clearly, supervisors cannot claim the authority to prescribe the preconditions I would like to discuss with you today. Having moved to the private sector, however, I feel more at liberty to do so. I would like to end my contribution today by discussing the means we can employ to persuade governments to implement both the principles and the preconditions.

Part of the cause of the Asian crisis lies with banks and other financial institutions that were taking too much risk by funding short-term, mostly in dollars, and investing in long-term, mostly high-risk property projects, in many cases generating local currency income. Moreover, ill-managed government influence on investment decisions was rather common in most of the afflicted countries.

As supervisors were, and in many cases still are not politically independent and had little formal enforcement mechanisms, they were in a weak position to prevent government influence on the banks. Capital requirements were apparently too low, which contributed to excessive risk-taking by the management and owners of the financial institutions. Supervision of the credit process and the quality of the investment portfolio, of provisions, of the interest rate, liquidity and exchange risks of the funding and of asset and liability management was clearly failing, given the events that led up to the crisis. In many cases, the financial institutions formed part of industrial conglomerates, inducing connected lending without proper credit assessment. The absence of information systems to show those concentration risks, and the absence of limit systems, hampered the work of the supervisors. There was a lack of transparency, partly because there was no authority able to enforce it. Coordination with other supervisors was lacking. As a result, problems did not become visible until it was already too late for many corrective measures. The banking system was left with a large share in nonperforming loans, which at present squeezes further credit.

Banking supervision in Asia thus shows major shortcomings if we compare it with the Basle Committee principles. Consequently, there were no warning systems in place which would have helped the authorities to take timely action and thus possibly prevent many of today's problems. However, it is unlikely that simply introducing the principles today would be enough to prevent financial instability in the future. Supervisors do not operate in a vacuum. As I said, certain preconditions need to be in place for supervision to be able to function properly.

In the "Core Principles for Effective Banking Supervision," five preconditions are said to be essential for properly functioning banking supervision. They are:

1. Sound and sustainable macroeconomic policies;

2. A well-developed public infrastructure;

3. Effective market discipline;

4. Procedures for efficient resolution of problems at banks; and

5. Mechanisms for providing an appropriate level of systemic protection (or public safety net).

What is meant by each of these five points and how do they relate to what happened in Asia?

1. If *macroeconomic policies* are such that they undermine the stability of the financial system, banking supervisors are faced with a virtually impossible task. Is economic policy to blame for the Asian crisis? With hindsight, it is not too difficult to put the finger on some sore points. In all crisis-hit countries, pegging the currency to the dollar was part of the economic policy. Although banking supervision was insufficient, capital flows were liberalised. There was no supervision of foreign capital inflows, especially short-term capital. The fixed peg to the dollar required high domestic interest rates, so that companies turned abroad for their funding. Supervisors did not put caps on open currency positions of banks and other financial institutions, or did so only to a limited extent. The fixed dollar exchange rate made them believe that the currency risk was small, so they didn't bother to hedge their positions.

This was, of course, a gross miscalculation. When the dollar appreciated strongly against both the European currencies and the Japanese yen, while the Japanese economy grew weaker and weaker, the Asian countries were confronted with an erosion of their competitiveness and a deterioration of their current accounts. The peg to the dollar had to be abandoned; the devaluation that followed caused massive financial problems and a reversion of short capital streams.

These macroeconomic events are another part of the explanation of the Asian crisis, but there are more, quite fundamental factors that lay at the root of things. These will be addressed in the review of the rest of the preconditions.

2. Under the heading of a *well-developed public infrastructure*, we combine things like a well-developed legal system and the existence of, and adherence to well-defined accounting rules. The latter should be ensured by independent auditors, declaring that financial statements give a fair view of the financial situation of companies. There should be effective supervision of banking (as described by the principles) and of other financial markets, and there should be a secure and efficient payment and clearing system for the settlement of financial transactions. If these facilities are not provided for, legal security is undermined, which can easily lead to destabilisation of financial systems.

   In many Asian countries, accounting principles hardly comply with internationally accepted standards, which greatly complicates the risk assessment of an investment. There are no serious penalties for publishing inaccurate information. We also find ample examples of deficiencies in the legal system, such as the absence of well defined private property laws, bankruptcy laws, standard contracts, and the possibility of seizing collateral.

Financial markets are another part of the public infrastructure. They are mostly underdeveloped in the Asian countries, as pension funds, insurance companies, and mortgage banks only play a minor role. The funding of the economic process relies on debt rather than equity. The stability of foreign funding could also be helped by the existence of well-functioning domestic capital markets. It would encourage foreign capital to take the form of more stable equity and bond investments rather than volatile short-term, foreign currency bank lending.

3. *Effective market discipline* requires that sufficient, transparent, and reliable information is available for all market participants. In Asia, there was a clear lack of information that would enable depositors and supervisors to judge the financial health of banks. The fact that long-term property investments were funded with short dollar liabilities, for example, was not visible to outsiders. The lack of

information thus led to an unintentional increase in high-risk investments. Conversely, a lack of information can lead to a run on banks when the public for some reason loses faith in the financial system, even if the panic is just based on rumors and the banks in question are basically sound.

A properly functioning market mechanism should also prevent investors and bank managers from being safeguarded against the negative consequences of their decisions. The conviction that the government would bail them out in the case of large losses led financial institutions in Asia to take excessive risks, which lay at the root of the financial crisis.

Governments influencing commercial decisions—whether to support government policy or to favor certain groups—also led to wrong investment decisions and increased the problems in the Asian financial sector. The same goes for relations between financial institutions and companies that are far too close. The chaebols in South Korea, the finance companies in Thailand and government-linked banks in Indonesia are all examples of institutions that make decisions on the basis of relationships or government influence, rather than on sound commercial considerations. China, which also has a massive banking problem but has been able to skirt around the edges of the storm until now, is another distinct example in this respect. (The problem is closely related to the political system and therefore requires wide-ranging reforms.)

4. The *prompt and orderly exit* of institutions that are no longer able to meet supervisory requirements is a necessary part of an efficient financial system. Muddling through often makes things worse.

5. Putting into place a *public safety net* or deposit insurance system can induce people to keep their savings with banks. It stabilizes the financial system by preventing negative developments at one bank from contaminating other, possibly healthy institutions. However, such guarantees always bear the risk of distorting market signals. This distortion works both ways. Bank managers' appetite for risk tends to increase if they perceive that they are implicitly backed by government guarantees. The Thai finance companies, government-linked banks in Indonesia and chaebol-controlled banks in South Korea, but also the saving and loan companies in the U.S. are clear examples. On the other hand, a comprehensive safety net reassures bank depositors and reduces the need to assess the safety of the banks with which they deposit their money.

To prevent distortion of market signals as far as possible, the system should insure depositors only to a maximum percentage, so that they still bear some risk of their own, and/or a maximum amount, so that only small depositors are fully protected. The risk appetite of banks can be limited by leaving the responsibility of a guarantee system with the banks through a contribution system, with no recourse on government funds.

We have now looked at the preconditions, which should ensure an environment in which banking supervision can function effectively. Implementing these in the countries that are presently struggling to overcome financial instability will prove to be a hard and lengthy process, because we are talking about true political and social reforms. And these may not even be sufficient. What if laws are well formulated and recorded, but the courts are corrupt? Then there will still be legal insecurity.

We may therefore need to formulate more fundamental conditions if these preconditions are to be effective and financial systems to be stable in the long run. A stable government is essential for sound and sustainable macroeconomic policies. Indicators like the (in) equality of income distribution, the "tolerance level" in a society (for example with respect to religion), standards of health care and education and the existence of an effective social security system are probably factors which influence stability in the longer run. A true division of powers and independent judges are prerequisites for legal security and the fair settlement of disputes.

In spite of the fact that the Asian countries showed many deficiencies in these respects, foreign investors were more than willing to invest their money and profit from the high growth rates that were so common in these countries for many years. Yet, one of the lessons we may have to learn from the Asian crisis and present conditions in Russia is that the risks of investing in a country that fails to put the basic conditions for stability in order are higher than we were recently inclined to think.

The countries in Asia that are troubled by the crisis are developing various measures to deal with financial instability, mostly in conjunction with the IMF. There is one element of short-term crisis management I would like to discuss with you in some more detail, which is the establishment of capital controls. In this connection, it should be recognized that in many countries, many de facto forms of capital control are already in place through the system of supervisory regulation. Limits on foreign exchange exposures, or regulations that limit the admission of foreign banks, are examples of supervisory measures that also have the effect of capital control. Nevertheless, the tightening of capital controls recently announced in Malaysia runs (somewhat) counter to existing trends.

The liberalization of capital streams offers some distinct advantages above maintaining restrictions. More funds will flow into the country and the pricing will be relatively low (as investors can fairly easily withdraw). Moreover, a liberalized capital market is usually judged to be a positive point in the general assessment of countries.

As a result of capital controls, the influx of foreign capital is very likely to dry up. As in the longer term, countries will want to attract foreign capital again; capital controls can only be a short-term solution. We are probably talking about months rather than years. And even if they are maintained only for a short period of time, investors may remain reluctant to re-enter the market for a prolonged period.

Therefore, capital controls should only be used as a means to restore calm, in order to support the currency and reestablish stability. In order to be effective, they should be accompanied by complementary measures aimed at putting more fundamental matters in order. Apart from that, capital controls can only be useful under certain conditions. In the first place, the economy to which they are applied should be reasonably small for the restrictions to be sustainable. Second, public infrastructure should be developed enough to allow for proper checks on compliance with the directives. In the present situation Russia, for example, could never effectively introduce capital controls because it would be impossible to arrange adequate surveillance of compliance.

However, one can question whether it was wise to expose the underdeveloped banking systems in the Asian countries to the rapid exchange liberalization of the sophisticated financial markets in the developed countries.

Clearly we should recognize that neither the preconditions nor the supervisory systems were in place to set the stage for balanced and healthy development of the financial systems in the Asian countries over the last decade.

Fixing the problems in Asia and safeguarding international financial stability in the longer term requires wide-ranging legal, infrastructural and educational changes. How do we bring them about?

First and foremost this is the responsibility of the countries in question. No external force, be it the market or the IMF, can enforce change without the political will and very substantial efforts of the Asian countries themselves. In this respect, it is encouraging that a country like Indonesia is now making serious efforts to change its banking and bankruptcy laws. Less encouraging are the very slow developments in Korea, where the intended efficiency measures to be taken by the chaebols so far seem to have yielded little progress.

The markets can play a beneficial role. Risks should translate more directly and effectively into spreads. For example, spreads over Libor of the bonds of the ABN AMRO Bank "Global Limited Recourse Debt Issuance Program" show that in September 1997, the Indonesian country risk was priced in the capital market at no more than sixty basis points over US Treasury. When troubles began last year, the spread rose gradually to some 110 bp. However, when the full extent of the crisis became visible, the spread rose to 1,400 bp by mid-October, at least clearly showing that risks had been seriously underestimated before. Another part of the market mechanism is the role of the rating agencies. Unfortunately we have to recognize that their original reaction to the crises did not alleviate the problems. The rating agencies continue to improve their ability to assess country risks, increasing the weighting of conditions that determine financial stability in the ratings.

Foreign supervisors can put "peer pressure" on their colleagues that have less well-developed supervisory systems. Pressure on supervisors could also come from *foreign banks* that have to compete with domestic banks subject to less strict supervision. One could even argue that banking supervision in emerging markets should in fact be stricter than in industrialized countries. Emerging markets are more volatile and therefore riskier, and banking problems often have a larger negative impact upon emerging economies, because there is no developed capital market.

The *IMF*, and other international financial institutions, can and have made their loans conditional on the implementation of reforms. However, in an acute crisis situation the IMF, too, will prefer reestablishing short-term stability over demanding long-term political reforms. We must also, in view of past experience, question the likelihood of international consensus on action to be taken against countries that fail to implement reforms. This may therefore be a long and not very efficient way of realising the objective of financial stability.

Finally, markets should be aware of the fact that if fundamentals are wrong in a country, sooner or later the bomb may explode, and markets should act on that knowledge, thus forcing countries to act.

As Jerry Corrigan recently said in a speech "It is virtually impossible for a country to escape from a financial crises without incurring a substantial decline in economic activity. Like it or not, that is the reality.

Given the hardships that such a substantial decline entails, it is vital that public and private institutions cooperate with the countries in question to help them to set their houses in order.

Chapter 22

Banking Fragility, Effectiveness, and Regulation in Less-Developed Countries

George J. Benston
Emory University

Abstract: Banks in less-developed countries can offer borrowers a stable source of loans, deposits secure from loss, and competitive provision of financial services. These objectives can be achieved by a regulatory system based on adequate required capital and structured early intervention and resolution that permits unrestrained entry and costless (to taxpayers) exit of domestic and foreign banks.

Alan Meltzer begins his critique of the IMF by observing that "[t]he frequency and severity of recent international financial problems in a period of growth, economic progress, and low inflation should raise a series of questions." The first of these is "Why is there so much financial fragility?" The other questions are directed to the ability of international institutions, particularly the International Monetary Fund, to deal with this situation. The balance of his article provides answers to those questions, with which I largely agree. Because he does not analyze or answer the first question (probably so that I would have something about which to write), I concentrate on it. I begin by outlining the problem—bank failures in less-developed countries. I then describe three features that, I assume, less-developed countries want their banking systems to have: (1) maintenance of banks as sources of funds for borrowers; (2) protection of depositors against loss of their funds; and (3) enhancement of competition among bank providers of financial services. I propose and describe a system of banking regulation that would enhance these objectives at almost no potential cost to domestic taxpayers or the IMF.

1. THE PROBLEM

Judging from recent history, the banking systems in Asian countries, as well as countries in South America and Europe, appear to be fragile.[1] Banks in these countries have experienced losses sufficient to render many of them insolvent.[2] Because many of these countries are relatively small and are not served by many banks, the failure of several banks is sufficient to cause considerable economic distress. Were it not for implicit, as well as explicit, government-provided deposit insurance, the banks would have experienced runs, which probably would have disrupted these countries' payments systems. Depositors as well as stockholders and other creditors would have lost their investments. Further, were it not for government policies that allow insolvent banks to remain open by explicitly or implicitly guaranteeing deposits, borrowers who depend on banks for funds would have had their loans called or been unable to obtain promised or expected funds.

Deposit insurance and forbearance by governments, though, is costly. When depositors believe that they are protected from loss and, as a result, bankers do not fear runs on their banks, ex ante bank owners have incentives to maintain lower levels of capital and take greater risks—the well-known moral hazard effect. Ex post, after their banks have incurred losses that reduce capital, the owners of these weak and insolvent banks would forbear from raising more capital and would continue to pay dividends as long as their governments did not resolve them. Because these banks often are poorly supervised, they might be tempted to make even riskier, negative-present-value loans and investments, since they would have little or nothing to lose and much to gain. The cost of government-provided deposit insurance and forbearance by governments in closing insolvent banks and their failure to deal effectively with weak banks are borne by taxpayers and, possibly, by the IMF.

Some people have pointed to inadequate regulation and supervision of banks as the reason for their recent and past apparent fragility. However, I suggest that a major cause for banks' losses and insolvencies is regulations imposed by governments that have restrained banks from diversifying effectively, and supervision by government agents that has directed loans towards rather than away from excessively risky loans and investments. Banks in many Asian countries have been required or pressured into making loans to businesses and individuals favored by the government in power. These loans often are made at less than market rates and in amounts that are excessive, particularly considering the low level of the borrowers' stockholder equity. In addition, the fixed exchange rates maintained by several of these countries have encouraged banks to borrow foreign currency at low rates of interest and lend or invest the funds in domestic currency at nominally high interest rates. If the fixed exchange rate were maintained, this would be a riskless arbitrage. But, disparities in exchange and nominal interest rates cannot be maintained. The result, therefore, is subsidized borrowing and importing which, eventually, must lead to a devaluation of the local currency. Banks and other borrowers, then, must repay their foreign-currency denominated loans with the depreciated domestic currency.[3]

An additional dysfunctional aspect of bank regulation is that it restrains entry of both domestic and foreign banks in order to protect favored domestic banks from competition. As a result, consumers are disadvantaged and the banking system is more fragile. As Meltzer points out, this situation is exacerbated in small countries, because domestic banks are unable to diversify their investments adequately. These banks invest in domestic businesses, both because they have a comparative disadvantage in lending and investing in other countries and because their banking supervisors encourage, if not require, them to support favored domestic enterprises.

The problems can be solved by a relatively easy-to-implement capital requirement and a system of structured early intervention and resolution. I first outline the assumptions underlying the proposed solution.

2. DESIRABLE FEATURES OF A BANKING SYSTEM FOR LESS-DEVELOPED COUNTRIES[4]

I assume that less-developed countries want their banking systems to have three basic features or objectives: (1) banks should be maintained as sources of funds for borrowers; (2) depositors should be fully guaranteed by the government against loss; and (3) there should be competition among providers of lending and deposit services. Achievement of these goals will safeguard both the banking system and most individual banks from collapse, save for the negative effects of substantial macroeconomic shocks imposed by incompetent government policies or very bad fortune (e.g., natural disasters and war). If the proposed bank regulatory system were adopted, the three goals and stability of the banking system can be achieved without costs being imposed on taxpayers. It should be noted that I am assuming that the objective of a country's banking system should *not* be to increase the wealth of government-favored projects, enterprises, or people. Indeed, if adopted, the proposed system would make this goal very difficult to achieve.

3. BORROWERS AND BORROWING FACILITIES SHOULD BE PROTECTED

Unlike the situation in developed and large countries, consumers and businesses in several Asian countries do not have many alternative sources of funds. In these countries, the failure of several banks or a large bank could result in the premature recall of outstanding loans. Also, loan demands would not be met until other lenders expanded or entered the market. This situation probably would impose financial costs on the failed banks' former borrowers, their customers and employees. These costs could result in their bankruptcy. This is an externality that should be mitigated, as long as the cost of the "cure" does not exceed the benefits therefrom.

To look ahead, costly disruption of borrowing facilities can be avoided efficiently by implementing policies that reduce (indeed, virtually eliminate) the possibility that banks will become insolvent and have to be closed and by reducing barriers to entry of additional institutions that could offer alternative sources of loans.

4. DEPOSITORS SHOULD BE FULLY GUARANTEED AGAINST LOSS OF THEIR FUNDS

4.1 Arguments against deposit insurance

Good arguments can be made against government-provided deposit insurance. Similar to the situation facing creditors generally, depositors could assess the risk to which their funds are subject and place their funds in prudently managed and adequately capitalized banks and/or demand compensation for the risk that they might incur. Depositors' concerns, in turn, provide bankers with strong incentives to maintain their depositors' confidence, thus avoiding both the need to pay depositors high rates of interest and the possibility of substantial and rapid depositors' withdrawals (runs). Thus, the moral hazard cost of deposit insurance could be avoided. Furthermore, the central bank could use open market operations to offset runs to currency that otherwise would result in a multiple decrease of the nation's money supply and bank credit. Although runs that result in bank failures could disrupt the payments system, the system could be protected by rules requiring collateral coverage of liabilities, payments only for good funds, and netting of obligations.

4.2 Arguments for deposit insurance

Nevertheless, three important reasons support the provision of government guarantees to depositors: efficiency—government's comparative advantage in providing people with a safe and convenient payments and saving medium; the political reality that elected governments will not permit depositors to absorb losses; and enhancement of competition by giving privately owned banks the same advantage as government-owned banks. Whether the deposit insurance should cover all or a portion of deposits is considered in the last part of this section. I conclude that 100 percent coverage of deposits is best.

4.3 Efficiency—government's comparative advantage in providing "safe" depositories

A country's economy is enhanced when the means of effecting claims over resources at a point in time (via a circulating medium) and over time (via savings) is efficient. In the past, notes issued by banks were the principal means of making payments. At present, demand deposits largely serve this function. Checks are less costly for people to use and accept, when they do not have to be concerned about the solvency of the bank on which the checks are drawn. Consequently, people would be more likely to use checks, if they did not have to worry about the solvency of banks.

Banks also provide a convenient means for people to save for investment and future consumption. This vehicle is particularly valuable for people with relatively small amounts of resources, because the transaction costs of depositing and withdrawing savings is much less than that incurred for most other investments, such as stocks and bonds. However, people might underuse banks and, hence, engage in less saving than is optimal, if they have to incur the cost of determining and monitoring the extent to which their funds might be lost should a bank fail. Rather than each individual having to make this assessment, a government could offer deposit insurance. In general, then, it would be socially beneficial for a government to insure deposits, if the costs of this insurance (including direct costs imposed on banks and the cost of monitoring and administering the scheme) were less than the costs that individual depositors would have incurred.

4.4 Political reality—deposit insurance will be provided

Even if, on the average, the benefits of government-provided deposit insurance did not exceed its cost, experience indicates that elected governments almost never allow depositors to incur losses as a result of bank failures. In the United States, for example, from the enactment of federal-government-provided deposit insurance in 1933 through 1991 (when the Federal Deposit Insurance Corporation Protection Act—FDICIA—was enacted), almost all depositors in banks, savings and loan associations, and credit unions were protected from loss of their funds, often by the assumption of their deposits by another bank or thrift. FDICIA now emphasizes limiting coverage, in fact as well as in law, to $100,000 per account. Banks and thrifts that failed in Canada, Australia, Japan, and Western Europe have been merged into solvent banks, usually at the request of governments, thereby protecting depositors. Governments (e.g., Mexico) often have protected depositors by nationalizing banks. Other governments have exchanged bad loans for government bonds, to avoid having to close insolvent banks. Only a few exceptions stand out. Australia and some other countries have imposed some costs on depositors by requiring them to take government bonds in payment for their deposit balances. The United Kingdom limits deposit insurance to seventy-five percent of £20,000, a limit which has been maintained in two failures. The United Kingdom recently increased coverage to ninety percent. Argentina has allowed some depositors to take losses; however, most depositors were protected by mergers and by central bank assistance supported by pension fund purchases of obligations, and Argentina has now adopted deposit insurance. The European Union has even mandated deposit insurance for countries (e.g., Denmark) that have not had not needed deposit insurance.

Governments protect depositors from loss for several reasons. First, the banking systems in most countries have many depositors. These people comprise a large voting block that might incur specific personal losses compared to taxpayers generally, who rarely understand that they will bear the cost of paying off depositors in failed banks. Second, large depositors often exercise strong political pressure to be bailed out. Examples outside of Asia include Chile under General Pinochet (despite prior assurances to the contrary), the United States prior to enactment of FDICIA, and the possibility that the United Kingdom would have protected depositors in Barings had the bank's liabilities not be taken over by a Netherlands bank. Third, large banks and groups of institutions often exercise strong political pressure to prevent being closed. Examples include the U.S. savings and loans associations and farm-state banks. Fourth, the public and legislators fear bank runs and economic collapse. Although, central banks could take offsetting actions, people who want to be protected from loss can exploit this fear.

4.5 Private vs. government-owned banks

Although a government could provide banking facilities directly, via government-run banks or postal savings, the cost to the economy is likely to be greater than if these facilities were provided privately. Government enterprises tend to be inefficient, and they are subject to misallocation of resources as the result of political pressures. Privately owned banks also have greater incentives to determine present and potential customer demands and to develop and adopt efficient innovations, processes, and services.

Nevertheless, several countries, including Asian countries, have government-owned banks and postal-savings systems. These institutions offer depositors 100 percent deposit insurance, because it is not conceivable that they would be permitted to fail with losses imposed on depositors. Hence, privately owned banks are at a comparative disadvantage. Government insurance of deposits for all domestically chartered depositories would, at least, tend to put privately operated banks on an equal footing.

4.6 Limited vs. full deposit insurance coverage

A good case can be made to limit deposit insurance to relatively small deposit amounts. The cost to holders of these accounts of individually assessing and monitoring the risk of loss tends to exceed the benefits they might achieve. Holders of large deposit balances, though, could make these judgements, thereby reducing the moral hazard that otherwise would plague deposit insurance.

However, rather than monitor their bank's activities, holders of large deposit balances could arrange to transfer their funds almost instantly to another bank, if it appears that their bank might be or might become insolvent. These depositors could accept higher interest payments for deposits placed in a risk-prone bank and incur the cost of monitoring the bank sufficiently to decide when to run. It is likely that they could transfer their balances before the bank is closed. Thus, if the bank does get into financial trouble, the cost will be borne primarily by depositors who are neither fully insured nor sufficiently aware of the bank's condition. Many people would consider this to be "unfair," which might lead the government to extend insurance protection, ex post. Furthermore, from the experience of many countries, runs by large depositors tend to result in government intervention and an extension of deposit insurance. For example, in 1984, when it was rumored that the authorities might have to close the Continental Illinois Bank, the Federal Deposit Insurance Corporation extended protection to all creditors of the bank and its holding company to forestall runs both at Continental and at apparently similar large banks. Although FDICIA (1991) imposes conditions designed to avert such "too big to fail" extensions of deposit insurance coverage, there has been no occasion, as yet, to put these provisions to the test.

A more important reason for my conclusion that Asian and other governments should provide 100 percent deposit insurance coverage is that subordinated debt with remaining maturity of at least two years can be more effective than legally uninsured deposits for reducing the moral hazard cost of deposit insurance (as is explained below). However, it is vital that the insurance is limited to genuine deposits. This can be done by defining deposits as liabilities that can be withdrawn only at face value (par) and that bear interest at no more than the market rate on government obligations of the same maturity. The later requirement is suggested to constrain risk-prone banks from readily obtaining funds.

In addition, deposit insurance should be available only to institutions that meet the capital, reporting, and prudential requirements presented below. These requirements, if implemented, should limit the direct and indirect costs of deposit insurance to a very small amount.

5. COMPETITION AMONG PROVIDERS OF DEPOSIT AND LENDING SERVICES

It is a truism of economics that entry with few constraints usually is necessary and sufficient for competition to be effective. Consumers benefit when new suppliers enter a market and vie for their trade. New entrants usually must offer better products and services to businesses and consumers to overcome the cost to these potential customers of shifting their accounts from their present bank. Thus, it is likely that new entrants will have developed preferable (to consumers) alternatives that established suppliers either cannot provide or may not want to provide. Collaterally, the mere possibility that other suppliers may enter their market gives established suppliers strong incentives to please their customers and to innovate effectively.

However, completely unregulated entry of banks when their deposits will be covered by government-provided deposit insurance is likely to be costly. Opportunistic or dishonest people might establish banks that invest in excessively risky assets or engage in self-dealing or fraud, because they do not have to be concerned about monitoring by depositors to whom risk-reflecting interest would have to be paid. In addition, existing banks that cannot successfully compete might fail and their depositors would have to be bailed out, with the cost borne by taxpayers or other banks and their customers. If it is likely that the exit of existing banks will impose costs on taxpayers or other banks, it also is likely that government officials will heed existing bankers' self-interested demands for restraints on entry. Hence, the essential issue, to which I now turn, is how inadequate or unfortunate banks can exit without imposing costs on the implicit or explicit deposit insurance fund or taxpayers and without greatly disrupting their borrowers and other customers.

The regulatory structure now described both permits the banking authorities to allow essentially unrestrained entry and 100 percent deposit insurance. Concomitantly, this structure substantially reduces (almost to zero) the probability that existing banks would exit in a manner that imposes substantial costs on borrowers and depositors.

6. PROPOSED SYSTEM OF BANK REGULATION AND SUPERVISION

The proposed system consists of four elements. One is a *capital requirement*, which effectively deals with the moral hazard problem. The second is a structured early intervention and resolution (SEIR) rule for determining when a bank's capital is inadequate and what steps first may and then must be taken by the banking authorities, which would effectively deal with the banking authority's agency problem. The third is limited prudential reporting and examination that enables the authorities to determine that the capital requirement is being met. The fourth is permitting, indeed, encouraging, the entry of foreign banks that are chartered and supervised in countries with strong capital and prudential requirements.

6.1 Capital requirement

The proposed capital requirement, if adopted and implemented, would ensure that institutions offering insured deposits have strong incentives not to take excessive risks and sufficient resources to absorb losses that might be incurred. The banking authorities also will have both the incentive and the means to ensure that the capital requirement is being met.

The proposed capital requirement has two elements: (1) the amount of capital relative to assets (both on and off the balance sheet) should be equivalent to the ratio that banks would hold if their deposits were not covered by government-provided insurance; and (2) subordinated (explicitly uninsured) debt that cannot be redeemed until the authorities can act should be both counted as part of capital and be required. Of course, the effectiveness of any capital requirement depends on the extent to which economic capital can be measured meaningfully. I conclude this subsection by outlining the measurement problems and suggesting solutions to those problems.

6.1.1 Capital-to-assets ratio

A required minimum ratio of capital to assets is necessary to overcome the moral hazard incentive of bankers to operate with low capital, given government insurance of deposits. Without such a requirement, opportunistic bank owners may be tempted to take excessive risks—risks they would not take if they paid the full cost of decisions that turn out badly. Even though some (perhaps most) bankers would not act opportunistically, the capital requirement is necessary for two additional reasons. One is that bankers may misperceive the extent to which they might incur loan losses and other costs, perhaps because economic conditions and their recent experience have been favorable. The other is that capital provides a cushion to absorb losses, whether expected or not.

Capital is the total claim by equity holders and creditors on a bank's resources that is not insured by the government and, hence, is at risk. It should be sufficient to absorb almost all of the losses that a bank might incur, so that these losses are not imposed on the deposit insurance fund or taxpayers. "Almost all" is specified, because there could be instances of massive fraud and severe economic downturns that deplete an unusually large proportion of a bank's assets. These risks are insurable. The amount of capital, though, would not be risk weighted, as is the procedure employed for the Basle international capital standard. My objection to the Basle risk weights is that they necessarily are crude (the risk categories are very wide—all commercial loans are weighted equally), the measurement is incomplete (covariances of cash flows are not accounted for), and the weights and categories are subject to political pressures (all residential mortgages are given lower weights than other consumer loans, even though fixed-interest mortgages are subject to greater interest-rate risk). Rather, the required ratio should be sufficiently high to discourage bankers from taking excessive risks and to cover the costs of the risks they do take. Furthermore, as is discussed later, the interest that banks must pay to private investors in the banks' subordinated debt is the equivalent of a risk-adjusted deposit-insurance premium.

Some bankers might object to a higher-than-present capital requirement, because capital is more costly than deposits. Indeed, capital is more costly, but for only two reasons. One is that deposits are government-insured and the insurance is under-priced. The proposed capital requirement is designed to eliminate this under-pricing. The other results from the income tax statutes present in many countries that permit companies to deduct against taxable income payments to debt holders, but not payments to equity holders. Consequently, debt (which includes deposits) is less costly than equity. Avoidance of this situation is one reason for permitting banks to meet their capital requirement with subordinated debt. In effect, they would simply be substituting a portion of their insured deposits with uninsured debt, both of which offer the same tax advantages.

6.1.2 Subordinated debt

Subordinated debt is, by definition, explicitly uninsured. It must be issued in large denominations, so that people will not confuse it with certificates of deposit and claim they thought it was government insured. To be included in capital, subordinated debt also must not be directly or indirectly repurchased or redeemed by a bank and must have a remaining maturity of at least two years, to allow authorities to act before it may be redeemed. These requirements are imposed to prevent holders of subordinated debt from "running" to avoid taking losses that the bank might incur.

In addition to being available to absorb losses, subordinated debt offers several advantages over equity. This source of capital serves as a means of imposing risk-determined deposit insurance premiums on banks, because, similar to the situation faced by corporations whose debt is not government insured, the risks perceived by debt holders are reflected in the interest rates that the bank must pay to get subordinated debt holders' funds. Unlike equity holders, subordinated debt holders do not benefit when the risks result in high net profits, while they might lose if the cost of the risks exceeds the equity. The interest rates required on new debt and reported on traded debt, therefore, provide the banking authorities with early warning signals of the risks taken by banks as perceived by investors. The difficulty or ease experienced by banks in refunding maturing debt also provides an early warning. Consequently, there is reason to require banks to have a substantial portion of their capital provided by subordinated debt, preferably debt that must be refunded continuously.

The authorities should recognize a serious possible limitation of subordinated debt. The benefits it provides from risk-reflecting interest rates and early warning signals would be limited or lost if equity holders were permitted also to hold subordinated debt, directly or indirectly. Furthermore, should a bank have incurred losses that absorbed its equity capital, its subordinated debt holders would be, in effect, equity holders. They then would have the same incentives as equity holders to take excessive risks.

Some bank owners, particularly those whose banks are small, might argue that it is difficult for them to find purchasers of subordinated debt. However, they could obtain funds from insurance companies, pension funds, and investors who otherwise would purchase the bonds of other corporations. Bankers who cannot find investors who would be willing to put their funds at risk should not be permitted to operate institutions that hold government—guaranteed deposits.

6.1.3 Measurement of capital—problems and solutions

Mismeasurement of Capital Generally

Capital should be measured as the difference between the economic market values of a bank's assets and liabilities (other than subordinated debt that serves as capital). Because these values are rarely readily available or even precisely measurable, the amount of capital to which a capital requirement usually applies is accounting (book) capital. (An exception is securities and similar financial obligations that, under US generally accepted accounting principles, must be reported at market or current values, although the balance sheet numbers are not changed from historical-costs if the securities will be held to maturity.) Traditional accounting procedures tend to both under- and over-state capital (relative to economic values). Understatements of capital result from inflation; reported fixed asset values usually are not increased to account for changed price-levels and long-term liabilities that were sold before an inflation was expected are not reduced to their present values. In addition, intangible assets, such as business development, employee training, goodwill, and charter value, are not capitalized and recorded as assets. Since these understatements result in greater economic- than book-value capital, there is a regulatory advantage.

Accounting (book-value) capital tends to be overstated as a result of changes in interest rates that decrease the present value of assets more than the present value of liabilities (duration imbalances) and when loans that might not be repaid as contracted are not adequately written down. The overstatement resulting from interest rate changes could be corrected by requiring banks to use current interest rates to determine and record the present values of restructured loans and fixed-interest obligations.

The overstatement of capital that results from understating allowances for bad loans is more important and more difficult to solve. Understatement of loan loss allowances (reserves) has been found at banks in many countries, both developed and underdeveloped, as documented by Goldstein (1997, pp. 16–18.) Three factors appear to be responsible. First, bankers may deliberately understate the allowance to avoid reducing their reported capital. They can do this by not recognizing seriously delinquent loans as uncollectible until the borrower has formally been declared bankrupt. This practice can be reduced by constructing explicit rules that specify when loans must be reported as nonperforming (e.g., when they are sixty or ninety days past due) and when they must be reserved against and written off. Even then, bankers can adopt an often-costly procedure of lending more funds to delinquent borrowers so that they can keep interest and principal payments current (a practice called "ever-greening"). Only bank examinations or audits by independent public accountants can detect this subterfuge. Second, the banking authorities often permit or even direct bankers to forbear from writing down bad loans. They do this to avoid having to recognize publicly banks' weaknesses and insolvencies, which would require the authorities to take politically difficult actions, including requiring weak banks to obtain more capital and resolving insolvent banks. Third, the loan loss allowance may have been reasonably recorded, ex ante, but is inadequate, ex post, when business conditions unexpectedly changed. The proposal outlined below is designed to deal with all three situations.

6.1.4 Economically meaningless capital at closely held or controlled banks

The owners of closely held or controlled banks, which are common in less developed and small countries, have both the incentive and opportunity of evading the capital requirement by fulfilling it with economically misstated assets. They can do this by "paying" for their bank stock with substantially overvalued assets (such as undeveloped land and shares in companies that are not publicly traded or that are controlled) or with loans from their banks or related banks. Consequently, purchasers of banks stocks should be required to pay for their shares in cash. They should not be allowed to borrow from their own bank, directly or indirectly, at any time. Nor should they be allowed to borrow from another bank, if their bank has deposited funds with that bank.

Direct loans to stock holders in banks are easy to detect and, in most countries, are not permitted. However, bank owners can avoid a self-lending prohibition with reciprocal borrowing, wherein two unrelated parties (A and B) mutually fund their capital contributions to banks that they control with loans from the other's bank. Assume that party A becomes bankrupt and cannot pay his loan at all to bank B. That bank would become insolvent, if its capital were less than the amount of the loan. With bank B insolvent, party B might not be able to repay her loan to bank A. This, in turn, could result in Bank A becoming insolvent.[5] A similar situation is described by the Governor of the Central Bank of Ecuador, Augusto de la Torre. He explains:

> We in Ecuador have found that business groups that own industrial companies and banks have actively used offshore jurisdictions to generate fictitious capital increases. Domestic deposits have been transformed into accounting capital (as opposed to real capital) by circulating them around the various Caribbean jurisdictions and others where similar practices prevail. A striking example is a bank in which the Ecuadoran authorities intervened. [F]rom the end of 1994 until the beginning of 1996 [t]he owners [of this very rapidly growing bank] had created fictitious capital by transferring deposits to offshore centers and then using those deposits to lend to the bank's shareholders, who in turn had used those funds to increase the bank's capital. (de la Torre, 1997, p. 79)

Rules can and should be established to prohibit evasion of the requirement that bank owners provide capital represented by meaningfully valued assets. Bank examiners and independent external auditors can uncover the mismeasurement of bank capital, and they should be specifically charged with this task. For example, they should closely examine all large loans to determine the recipients and the reason for and (if possible) disposition of deposits in other banks. These examinations should be preceded by an analysis of the holdings and relationships among a bank's capital holders (equity and subordinated debt). Closely held and rapidly growing banks should be examined particularly carefully.

Therefore, I conclude that capital can be measured meaningfully, although probably imperfectly. That is one reason that a higher ratio of capital to assets is recommended. Before discussing the ways in which bank reporting and prudential examination can be effective for assuring that the measurements are likely to be accurate, I describe the proposed rules that specify when and how the banking authorities should act to ensure that the capital requirement is maintained.

6.2 Structured early intervention and resolution (SEIR)

SEIR was proposed in 1988 by Benston and Kaufman and was substantially adopted by the United States in 1991 as part of the Federal Deposit Insurance Corporation Improvement Act (FDICIA). It provides incentives for and imposes requirements on the banking authorities to act expeditiously and responsibly. Together with the capital requirement, the result should be almost no depositor bailouts.

Four capital zones or trip wires (or traunches) are established that define first when the authorities, at their discretion, may act and when they must act. The ratios suggested here are higher than those specified in FDICIA, which are too low, even for the United States. The ratios should be higher for less-developed countries for the reasons enumerated by Rojas-Suárez and Weisbrod (1995), derived from their studies of Central and South American countries and by Goldstein (1997), who reviews bank failures in many developing countries: [6]

1. Financial data often are not reliable;

2. Arms-length relationships between borrowers and banks often are not present;

3. The legal environment makes it difficult for banks to gain possession of collateral in the event of default; and

4. National economic policies often have been destabilizing, resulting in sharp downturns in economic conditions and losses in the values of bank assets.

The four capital-to-assets-ratio zones and the pre-specified actions by the authorities are as follows.

6.2.1 Adequately capitalized banks

These are banks with capital-to-assets ratios approximately equal to those of firms without government-provided deposit insurance (perhaps twenty percent); they would be subject to minimum supervision that is limited to determining that the bank was reporting its financial numbers correctly and was not being managed fraudulently or recklessly.

6.2.2 First level of supervisory concern

Includes banks with capital-to-asset ratios below, say, twenty percent, but above, say, twelve percent; they would be subject to increased regulatory supervision and more frequent monitoring. The authorities would require a business plan for quick recapitalization and, could, at their discretion, impose such sanctions as restricting growth, prohibiting dividend payments, and restraining payments for services provided by related companies.

6.2.3 Second level of supervisory concern (inadequate capitalization)

If the bank does not bring its capital-to-assets ratio back into compliance, the authorities *must* impose additional and harsher sanctions, including prohibition of dividend payments and interest payments to subordinated debt holders and restrictions on growth and on transfers of funds to related entities.

6.2.4 Resolution

Should a bank's capital-to-assets ratio falls below a predetermined point (say, five percent), the authorities *must* resolve the bank quickly through sale, merger, or liquidation. Rather than permit this to happen, an economically solvent bank most likely would voluntarily raise its capital-to-assets ratio into compliance, liquidate, or sell out to or merge with another institution.

6.3 Prudential reporting and examination

6.3.1 Reporting requirements

The banking authorities should regularly monitor the activities of institutions with government-insured deposits to determine whether or not the capital requirement is being complied with and to provide an early warning of possible problems that warrant closer examination and may require supervisory intervention. The requirement outlined should impose low costs on the institutions, because they surely would be maintaining and reviewing most of the information for purposes of internal management and oversight by their boards of directors.

Deposit-insured institutions should submit monthly and annual reports to the banking authorities. The annual reports should be audited and attested to by independent external auditors (certified public accountants) who are approved by the banking authorities. All directors of the bank should sign the reports. To the extent feasible, assets and liabilities should be stated at current (present or market) values. Delinquent and nonperforming loans should be clearly defined (e.g., payments over due by more than thirty or sixty days or where additional loans are made to enable payments to be met). Loans to related parties should be identified as such, as should the total amount of loans made to an associated group.

In addition, the authorities should conduct regular field audits to check that the reports are correct. These audits should be directed towards and limited to concerns about the measurement and adequacy of capital. Additional examinations should be made where the monthly reports or other information indicates substantial growth or possible exceptionally risky operations. Banks owned or controlled by a few persons or groups should be more closely monitored and examined. The direct cost of these examinations should be charged to the banks examined.

6.3.2 Prudential regulations

Self-dealing must be prohibited. This includes all loans to stockholders, subordinated bondholders, and bank managers and to parties related to them, whether personal or business. An exception, however, could be made for loans made to parties who have but a small interest in the bank (e.g., ownership of less than five percent of total capital). Loans to one or a related group of borrowers should be limited to a percentage of capital (perhaps fifteen percent). Additional, so-called prudential regulations that limit the activities in which banks can engage, are not required and are likely to be detrimental both to banks and consumers, because they tend to limit competition rather than actually reduce the risks in which banks might engage.

6.4 Foreign banks

Gavin and Hausmann (1997) point out that, to achieve a competitive market for banking services, less-developed countries must meet several conditions. These include a stable macroeconomic environment, effective bank regulation conducted by experienced, well-trained people, and judicial enforcement of contracts. In addition, in some countries relatively few domestic investors may be willing to meet the capital requirements that should be imposed on banks with government-insured deposits. Gavin and Hausmann propose opening domestic markets to foreign banks. These banks can bring an additional source of funds and services to consumers. Not only will they tend to offer better products to consumers, as would a domestic new entrant, but they often bring with them improved procedures and products that were developed in their home countries. Foreign banks generally find it desirable to hire local people. Hence, they also can provide training for people who might leave to work for domestic banks or to establish their own banks. In addition, because foreign banks are diversified geographically, they are less subject than are domestic banks to domestic macroeconomic changes.

Consequently, I suggest that banks owned by foreigners that are chartered and supervised in countries with strong capital and prudential requirements should be encouraged to open branch offices in less-developed countries. These banks should be required to insure their deposits either from their home country funds or from other sources, such as collateral or insurance policies written by reputable and secure companies. The local banking authorities, therefore, would only have to determine that these banks could fully meet deposit withdrawals by domestic depositors. Otherwise, there should be no restraints on the repatriation of funds by foreign banks to their home countries. Domestically chartered subsidiaries of foreign banks should be treated in the same manner as are other domestically chartered banks.

7. CONCLUSION

Goodhart et. al (1998, Chapter 7) review banking crises in the Nordic countries, the United States, Japan, Argentina, Chile, and Mexico, from which they draw "three basic principals" with which, they say, "good banking crisis management must begin." The system of bank regulation and supervision proposed above fulfils their principals:

- "Ensure that parties responsible for the crisis bear most of the costs of restructuring"—the capital requirement together with the reporting requirement should prevent owners of banks from taking excessive risks that imposed deposit insurance costs on taxpayers or on other banks;
- "Prevent problem banks from expanding credit to delinquent borrowers"—the structured early intervention and resolution (SEIR) procedures together with the reporting and prudential requirements should prevent this from happening;
- Avoid financing the programme with inflation by making the restructuring programme a high priority"—the capital requirement that includes subordinated debt and SEIR should prevent restructuring from becoming necessary.

Better yet (I believe), the solution, if adopted, would largely prevent crises from occurring, would enhancing competition by permitting relatively free entry, and would not impose costs on banking customers and taxpayers as a result of bank failures.

The proposed system can be implemented without disrupting present banking systems or banks that are well capitalized. Undercapitalized banks will be affected, but this is as it should be. Owners of some undercapitalized banks might prefer to merge with or be acquired by other banks, thereby relieving the banking authorities from later having to intervene and possibly resolve them. With entry unrestrained (except for capital and reporting requirements), consumers will not be disadvantaged from mergers and acquisitions that reduce the number of competitors.

Notes

[1]See Benston and Kaufman (1995) for a comprehensive review of studies of banking fragility, which concludes that although banks are fragile, banking systems are not unstable.

[2]See Goldstein (1997, pp. 3-21), Lindgren, Garcia, and Saal (1996), and Goodhart et. al (1998) for a comprehensive review of studies on the causes and effects of recent banking crises in many countries.

[3]This situation might be dealt with by legislation that must be adopted by a country as a requirement for it to be eligible for an IMF loan. The legislation would require a mandatory reduction ("haircut") in the principal amount of loans made to domestic banks that are denominated in a foreign currency, if these loans are withdrawn after IMF assistance is announced. This proposal is detailed in Shadow Financial Regulatory Committee's Statement 145 (May 4, 1998) and outlined in Robert Litan's comments in this voume.

[4]An earlier version of much of the following materials was presented at an InterAmerican Development Bank conference in Buenos Aires, Argentina in August 1997 and is published in Spanish (Benston, 1998.)

[5]This illustration is derived from Rojas-Suárez and Weisbrod (1997, pp. 46-49), who point to several instances in South American where this was found to have occurred.

[6]Goldstein (1997) describes similar problems present in less developed countries.

References

Benston, George J. 1998, "Ingreso y Retiro de Bancos in América Latina y el Caribe: Preocupaciones por la Polítaca Publica y Propuesta de Soluci6n," *Superbancaria*, Superintendencia Barcaria de Colombia, Marzo, 25–36

Benston, George J., and George G. Kaufman. 1988, "Risk and Solvency Regulation of Depository Institutions: Past Policies and Current Options," Monograph Series in Finar and Economics, Salomon Center, New York University Graduate School of Busin Administration, monograph -1.

Benston, George J., and George G. Kaufman. 1995, "Is the Banking and Payments System Fragile?," *Journal of Financial Services Research*, 9: 209–240.

de la Torre, Augusto. 1997, "Comment," in *Safe and Sound Financial Systems: What Works for Latin America*, Liliana Rojas-Suárez (ed), Washington, DC: Inter-American Development Bank, 79–81.

Gavin, Michael, and Ricardo Hausmann. 1997, "Make or Buy? Approaches to Financial Market Integration," in Liliana Rojas-Suárez (ed)., *Safe and Sound Financial Systems: What Works for Latin America*, Washington, DC: Inter-American Development Bank, 133–162.

Goldstein, Morris. 1997, *The Case for an International Banking Standard*, Washington, DC: Institute for International Economics, 1997.

Goodhart, Charles, Philipp Hartmann, David Llewellyn, Liliana Rojas Suárez, and Steven Weisbrod. 1998, *Financial Regulation: Why, how and where now?*, London and New York: Routledge (in association with the Bank of England).

Lingren, C.–J., Gillian Garcia, and M.I. Saal. 1996, *Bank Soundness and Economic Policy*, Washington, DC: International Monetary Fund.

Rojas Suárez, Liliana, and Steven R. Weisbrod. 1995, *Banking Crises in Latin America: Experiences and Issues*, Washington DC: Inter-American Development Bank, September.

Rojas Suárez, Liliana and Steven R. Weisbrod. 1997, "Towards an Effective Financial Regulatory and Supervisory Framework for Latin America: Dealing with the Transition," in *Safe and Sound Financial Systems: What Works for Latin America,* Liliana Rojas-Suárez, (ed.), Washington, DC: Inter-American Development Bank, 35–74.

Shadow Financial Regulatory Committee. 1998.

Chapter 23

Comments on "What's Wrong with the IMF" and "Containing the Risks"

Anil K. Kashyap
University of Chicago and Federal Reserve Bank of Chicago

Abstract: I review the arguments made by the two authors and emphasize the importance of ill-defined property rights as a central problem in precipitating crises. I also argue that the unfortunate handling of the failure of Long-Term Capital Management provides some lessons for crisis management in developing countries.

I found the papers by de Swaan and Meltzer to be quite interesting and provocative. In my comments I aim to accomplish three things. First, I identify the main points of agreement among the two papers. Next, I discuss the two main points of disagreement between the two authors. Finally, I make a couple of observations about the current crises and what we can conclude about their implications for future crises.

1. POINTS OF AGREEMENT

At first glance one might read the de Swaan paper as suggesting that there are five preconditions that are needed in order for a rescue operation to be mounted and for banking supervision to be able to do its job. On the other hand, it appears that Meltzer believes that the current system is badly broken and that even if these conditions hold that it is doubtful that the combination of an IMF and domestic regulators can prevent crises. Superficially, this might lead one to conclude that the two authors completely disagree about what needs to be done. In fact, I think there is strong agreement between both authors that the establishment of property rights and an elected and accountable government are of central importance.

The paramount importance of the rule of law, together with the development of a legitimate, honest government is most easily seen by reviewing the preconditions put forward by de Swaan. He starts out by arguing that it is essential that a country have good macro policy. Both he and Meltzer argue that fixed exchange rates constituted bad macro policy for many of the Asian countries now facing crises. But, why do countries choose fixed exchange rates in the first place? A key factor is that in most cases you can't trust anyone to make monetary policy. So the decision to tie the hands of the monetary authority is really just an admission that you do not have a capable set of government officials that can be counted on to act responsibly.

De Swaan's second precondition is good public infrastructure. The essence of public infrastructure is a functioning government and legal system.

His third and fourth preconditions are effective market discipline and procedures for efficient resolution of problems at banks. The presence of a well-functioning legal system together with a set of honest civil servants does not guarantee that these conditions will exist in a country. However, their absence makes it virtually impossible for markets to operate and for workouts to be done on an orderly basis. Thus, four of de Swaan's five preconditions really can only occur when the legal system and the government are sound—I return to discussing his last precondition for effective banking supervision below.

These same factors are also important for understanding why both authors argue you can't cram down programs on elected governments. Why would the international community want to force some sort of adjustment program on an unwilling government? The outsiders must believe that the government is either incompetent, not capable of telling good choices form bad, corrupt, having different goals than the public, or impotent, being too weak to do the right thing. All three of these diagnoses imply that the international community doubts the quality of the government or strength of the legal and political system.

Finally, there is the issue of "hot money." Much of the discussion at the conference has focussed on the potentially destabilizing aspects of large short-term capital flows (i.e. hot money). I think of hot money as a direct consequence of bad infrastructure. As Rajan and Zingales (1998) observe, if the ability to enforce property rights is doubtful, and one wants to lend in such an environment, then it is natural to structure the lending so that you can get your money back quickly without having to go through the legal system. While making the lending callable on short notice offers imperfect protection for lenders it surely beats long-term contracting.

This perspective suggests that hot money is more of symptom than a cause of problems. Moreover, it follows that capital controls are unlikely help deal with the hot money problem. If the lending is being done on a short-term basis because the legal system is shaky, imposing rules that outlaw short-term lending without fixing the basic imbalance in the legal system seems pointless. So once again we are led back to the importance of the infrastructure, legal institutions, human capital and the like.

If one accepts that these factors are the key to setting up sustainable policy and avoiding crises it makes me wonder about the role of the IMF. I think even the most ardent defenders of the fund would concede that it was not designed to provide this kind of technical assistance. It does not have much a track record in trying to do this and does not recruit professionals that specialize in these issues. If we agree that these factors are essential for good policy even in large, relatively developed countries, then I believe we need to consider whether the IMF needs to be downsized and/or replaced by an organization with a different mandate and set of experts. I welcome an active debate on whether the return to investing so much money on macroeconomic stabilization efforts is as high as the return to investing in political and legal infrastructure.

2. POINTS OF DISAGREEMENT

There is one significant point of disagreement among the authors. It boils down to differences of opinion about how the IMF's existence changes the type of market discipline and public safety net that we will observe. Essentially, de Swaan believes that market discipline and a public safety net can coexist with the IMF, and Meltzer believes that cannot.

I believe that the concerns raised by Meltzer about the incentives of bureaucrats and regulators are very important. Indeed, the recent lesson from the workout arranged by the Federal Reserve for Long-term Capital Management (LTCM) appears to provide decisive evidence about the problems created by regulators. Let me review the three most relevant facts about the LTCM rescue.

First, many observers, including me, believe that an outright failure of LTCM could have been very disruptive to capital markets throughout the world. Accordingly, I applaud the Federal Reserve Bank of New York's decision to convene a meeting to bring together many the major parties in the case. Setting up the meeting was a wise decision.

The second key piece of information was that a private group led by Warren Buffett offered to take over LTCM and assume its liabilities. No one disputes that Buffet made a credible offer to acquire the firm and that if his group had succeeded that disruptions to the public markets would have been prevented. It appears that the Buffett bid may effectively wiped out the partners at LTCM. Even if this is true it should be of no concern to the Federal Reserve.

Finally, and most significantly, the Fed continued to encourage an alternative workout arrangement (that ultimately took place) after the Buffett bid was turned down by the LTCM management. The arrangement that was eventually consummated did protect the markets. In a technical sense the deal was also purely private since no federal money was put up. I believe that everyone also agrees that the presence of the Fed-orchestrated rescue coalition at least partially helped the LTCM management avoid having to accept the Buffett offer.

The Fed decision to not completely pull out of the scene once the Buffett offer surfaced is lamentable in several respects. First, even if the eventual non-Buffett deal included no promises or official money from the Fed, it certainly appears that arms were twisted. Appearances in these situations matter, because the next crisis will depend partly on what type of risks people believe they might be insured against. Even if the Fed did nothing improper, there have been many rumors to the contrary which feed the perception that a large, politically well-connected firm was given a break.[1] This can only serve to encourage other firms, perhaps some time from now when the exact facts of the LTCM case are long-forgotten, to believe that a bailout will be available.

More significantly, the fact that Mr. Buffett's group was thwarted at least partially because of the coordinating efforts of the Fed will act as deterrent for the private sector to help out in future crises. The incentive to put together a bid is completely undermined if there is a reasonable possibility that the government (or official international organizations) will offer the distressed firm a better alternative. If one worries at all about moral hazard, there should a strong presumption that if a private group is willing to provide a backstop that they should be permitted to do so—regardless of whether the private deal is ruthless in the way it treats the distressed firm.

The disturbing thing about the LTCM case is that it occurred in the United States where presumably all of the conditions identified by de Swaan are in place. It is amazing that a private sector offer was even an option. If the U.S. authorities are unwilling to risk letting the market handle one of these situations it seems very unlikely that any other major country will either. Moreover, it seems hypocritical to have U.S. officials criticizing "crony-capitalism" in other countries in light the failure to let the private agents deal with the LTCM crisies. In short, there was a perfect opportunity to see how a private workout could proceed and it was squandered.

In light of this evidence I do not see why should expect the IMF to be able to avoid the same temptation that seems to have overcome the Fed in the LTCM case. In this sense, I agree with the basic Meltzer argument that marginal changes to the current system are unlikely to be very successful.

3. LESSONS FROM THE CURRENT CRISES

It seems unlikely that we will ever be able to definitely sort out the role of moral hazard in the current crises in Asia and Russia. IMF officials are no doubt correct in saying that governments do not consciously pursue reckless policies because they know the IMF will bail them out. The costs to the countries of accepting the conditions of the official rescue packages are clearly large and politicians are often not pleased with the terms of the package. However, whether or not the lenders to many of these countries extend credit on the belief that a bailout may be possible is much more difficult to prove. If there is moral hazard problem it is clearly on the lender side.

Under this assumption it is hard to say how to answer the final question posed by Meltzer: "What should we do about Russia?" This is a much more political question than an economic one. Certainly we want the lenders who put up money to experience some losses. Looking back at how Russia has been handled, I believe we would have been better off if the IMF had never been called upon to lend to Russia. The case for lending was always somewhat political—we cannot let the second major nuclear superpower implode. This concern is the only reason that Russia still commands so much attention.

If explicit foreign aid had been offered instead of IMF money I believe we would have avoided setting some bad precedents. The way the money was sent to Russia can only serve to confuse other countries about what role the IMF and economics plays in the allocation of financial support. It is only counterproductive to let Russia continually default on the promises made to the IMF. If for the short-run at least we are destined to have an organization like the IMF making emergency loans to countries, let us avoid relying on tortured explanations that use on bad economics to justify certain lending programs.

If for political reasons we decide Russia too important to fail then we should admit this. If we make such an admission we will then have to live with the bad incentives that such policy might create. But, at least we will avoid sending the IMF in to work on political problems. This conclusion brings me back to the central point of agreement between de Swaan and Meltzer, that looking ahead devoting more resources to building political and legal infrastructure is highly desirable.

Acknowledgment: The views expressed herein are entirely my own and not necessarily endorsed by the Federal Reserve Bank of Chicago or the Federal Reserve System.

Note

[1]Importantly if the Fed governors believed that the nationalization of LTCM was needed to protect the financial system they have the authority proceed. Of course, in this case the partners at LTCM would be wiped out and the full details of what the Fed saw as the risks would be made public.

Reference

Rajan, Raghuram, and Luigi Zingales. 1998, "Which Capitalism? Lessons from the East Asian Crisis," *Journal of Applied Corporate Finance*.

Chapter 24

Commentary on "What's Wrong with the IMF" and "Containing the Risks"

Carl-Johan Lindgren
International Monetary Fund

The reasons for the Asian financial crisis clearly are manifold. However, Meltzer pays little attention to the complexities of the recent developments in Asia but rather focuses his presentation excessively on the IMF, its origins and its role in Eastern Europe and in Mexico. As the issues raised by Prof. Meltzer will be the focus of other sessions, they will not be commented upon here, except to state that his analysis seems biased and often misinformed. Nevertheless, one can agree with most his conclusions, except with the proposal for an international lender of last resort with strict collateral rules—the proposal is simply not practical or feasible. A better and proven mechanism for providing countries with liquidity in systemic crisis situations could be facilities such as commercial standby credit lines and remunerated high reserve requirements held abroad, like as those recently used in Argentina.

My commentary will focus on the presentation of de Swaan, who points out the need for strengthening banking supervision to help prevent banking crisis. He also stresses certain preconditions for supervisors to do their work properly, and suggest that the focus has been too much on the Basle Core Principles for Effective Banking Supervision and not enough on their preconditions, which include sound and sustainable macroeconomic policies, a well-developed public infrastructure, effective market discipline, procedures for effective resolution of problem banks, and mechanisms for providing systemic protection.

I could not agree more with de Swaan's points. In fact, in the IMF we have for some time analyzed the broader setting and the preconditions for effective banking supervision and for stable and efficient banking systems and have come to the same conclusions.[1] Our efforts have aimed at increasing the awareness and improving the understanding of financial sector problems and their solutions both among our own staff as well as among national policymakers. Below I will discuss the five areas of preconditions raised by de Swaan, and what efforts are being made in the IMF and elsewhere to deal with them. But before doing so, it is necessary to stress the limitations of regulations and the essential role played by bankers.

Prudential *regulations* have been under review internationally in recent years and are now being reexamined by the Basle Committee on Banking Supervision (BCBS) and other international bodies in view of the experiences of the recent crises. Such reviews include not only the rules for managing market risks, but also for loan valuation and capital adequacy, disclosure, consolidation, market exit, etc. The focus is not only on rules and practices for borrowers and borrowing banks but also those for lenders and creditor banks in more mature markets. There is a renewed awareness that large short-term capital flows make banking systems more vulnerable, and a search is under way for new policies and institutional arrangements aimed at making banks and banking systems less vulnerable. While all this work to strengthen the regulatory framework is under way, there also is a sobering realization that prudential rules and supervision alone cannot achieve safe banking and banking systems.

Systemic banking problems always have their origin, at least in part, in *bad banking*. This is typically manifested in a combination of poor corporate governance, lending to related parties, directed credit to uncreditworthy borrowers, excessive risk-taking or concentration, lending without proper credit analysis, excessive reliance on collateral, typically on the assumption that favorable economic conditions and assets price increases will continue forever. The new international emphasis on better risk management by banks and more effective supervision can be expected to help, especially if assisted by market developments. Hopefully, the examples of the massive losses incurred in the ongoing banking crisis cases around the world will lead banks and other market agents to be more cautious in the future. Improved monitoring by shareholders, market analysts, rating agencies, and auditors will also be needed.

Let me now comment on de Swaan's five areas of preconditions:

1. Sound and sustainable macroeconomic policies are crucial for sound banking. At the same time, sound banking is crucial for successful macroeconomic policies and performance. In the IMF, we have for some time been studying and stressing the importance of this dual relationship, the power of which has been amply demonstrated by the recent Asian crises.[2] We are still at

an early stage of understanding exactly how it works but it is reassuring to see that a lot of research has started on the subject. Banks are highly leveraged and tend to be forcefully affected by major macroeconomic policy shifts or disturbances. The recent crises cases have shown the dangers of excessive short-term foreign borrowing and of maturity and foreign exchange mismatches, not only in the banking sector but also in the nonfinancial sector, as well as the complex links between bank and real/corporate sector restructuring. In order to better foresee and more effectively deal with future financial sector disturbances, the IMF is substantially strengthening the emphasis on financial sector issues in the surveillance of economic policies in the context of its regular consultations with all its member countries.

2. A well-developed *public infrastructure* must include—in addition to competent bankers and macroeconomic policymakers—a proper framework of banking and other laws (including laws on ownership, contracts, collateral and negotiable instruments, foreclosure, and bankruptcy), a reliable judicial system and general respect for the law, proper registries for property and collateral, and payment and settlement systems, proper accounting and auditing practices implemented by competent professionals, as well as foreign exchange, money, and capital markets. Regarding the latter it should be noted that markets often become segmented and can seize up when problems emerge—markets often work the least when they are needed the most. And this applies even to the largest markets—we only need to look at Japan. In addition, and perhaps most importantly for official oversight, it is essential to ensure a supervisory body with autonomy, authority, and professional competence. Such a body must coordinate its work closely with other financial supervisors nationally and internationally. Reforms in these areas already are supported by various international, regional, and bilateral efforts.

The remaining three preconditions have been identified by various international groupings as areas in which standards, principles and best practices are missing. An international effort is to fill these "gaps" to help prevent future problems or deal with them effectively when they occur. These efforts include not only the IMF and the World Bank but also the BCBS which has established several subgroups to deal with the "gaps."

3. The key to effective *market discipline* is transparency of banking data. The recent crises have shown that banking data often are grossly misleading, and that disclosure of poor data works against effective market discipline. Without reliable data, neither depositors nor creditors, existing or potential shareholder nor official oversight will work as intended. Some improvement could be found through improved loan classification and provisioning rules, more disclosure of qualitative information, and more alert auditors and market analysts. But it is unlikely that changes in banks loan values and accordingly their capital adequacy can be anticipated without analysis of macroeconomic policies and corporate profitability by supervisors as well as by other economic agents involved.
4. Early *exit* of unviable institutions is key to keeping a banking system sound. The development of efficient procedures for dealing with individual problem banks is crucial. This goes beyond the introduction of a prompt corrective action (PCA) framework, which is often undermined due to the problems of loan valuation/capital adequacy mentioned above. There is a need to develop graduated responses to deal with individual problem banks and to strengthen administrative procedures rather than involvement of the courts, in view of the need for speed and efficiency to preserve asset values in banks. There is also a need to study optimal exit arrangements in systemic situations to minimize the disruptive effects of different bank resolution strategies on the real economy; such effects will be different depending on the relative size of the banking system in the economy.[3] Bank exit policy also has a cross-border dimension, an area that so far has benefited relatively little from international cooperation and harmonization.

5. Systemic protection or *official safety nets* mainly consist of deposit insurance and lender of last resort (LOLR) facilities. Deposit insurance should be explicitly limited to small depositors to contain moral hazard. But it needs to be recognized that deposit insurance can deal only with individual problem banks, not with systemic problems, and cannot prevent contagion. Also, experience shows that small depositors typically do not run; large institutional investors are the ones that do. The more difficult part of designing a safety net is the design of a proper LOLR facility. While in principle a LOLR should only lend to solvent banks against collateral and at a penal rate, in practice insolvency can seldom be separated from illiquidity and the use of prime collateral in cases of existing insolvency is likely to be contested by other creditors, especially if the LOLR is privy to supervisory information. It should be noted that in cases of systemic banking problems there are typically no private sector solutions; only government intervention can ensure the continued operation of a core banking system so essential for economic activity. Moral hazard is often mentioned as the major cause for excessive risk-taking by banks and major banking problems; however, the power of herd mentality and inflated market expectations should not be disregarded.

Core principles are relatively easy to proclaim but their implementation is a much slower more tedious process. The implementation of the preconditions for a sound banking system and effective banking supervision is an even more complex and longer-term process. While the focus of IMF adjustment programs necessarily is on the short term, it should be stressed that the organization has gone to unprecedented efforts to make sure that fundamental medium-term structural reforms are not being forgotten. Such measures should be in place and tested before crisis occurs. Unfortunately, it is inherently difficult to make any reforms when economic times are good and there are no apparent problems. Also, countries typically consider themselves to be unique and are reluctant to learn from others' mistakes. Crises provide a window of opportunity to get things done. National authorities and international bodies should take advantage of that window by being prepared to implement necessary reforms as rapidly and thoroughly as possible.

Notes

[1]Folkerts-Landau, D., and C-J. Lindgren, 1998, "*Toward a Framework for Financial Stability*; IMF.

[2]Lindgren, C-J., G. Garcia, and M. Saal, *Bank Soundness and Macroeconomic Policy*; IMF.

[3]The effect of closing and liquidating a sizable portion of a banking system would be quite different in Russia or Mexico, where banking system assets account for twenty and fifty percent of GDP, respectively, than in Thailand or Japan where they count for 200 or over 300 percent, respectively.

PART VI

EARLY WARNING INDICATORS, TRANSPARENCY, AND MARKET RESPONSE

Chapter 25

Improving Transparency in Asian Banking Systems

Jerome S. Fons
Moody's Investors Service

Abstract: Many banking systems exhibit very poor transparency, including those of the crisis affected countries in Asia. Calls to increase transparency may prolong the crisis by further harming investor confidence and should wait until confidence returns and the banking systems stabilize.

1. INTRODUCTION

There is a perception that credit ratings are driven by financial accounting inputs and that ratings map into well-established ratios or other performance measures. This may hold to a certain extent in the U.S. or other developed countries with advanced reporting and regulatory controls. However, where transparency is weak, rating analysts must rely on soft data sources. Indeed, the lack of transparency in many parts of the world forces analysts to base opinions on criteria obtained through indirect means.

Subjective data are typically much more scarce and costly to acquire. Moreover, it is natural, under certain circumstances, to interpret vague assurances, or a "trust us" attitude, with a grain of salt. Where transparency is lacking, our experience has taught us to favor a conservative view of the situation. We are willing to trust the source of soft data as long as the data is confirmed by other sources or subsequent developments. But if we feel misled or lied to, that trust is broken and credibility may be damaged for a very long time.

This paper examines the role that poor transparency has played in the East Asian financial crisis. Our focus is on the banking systems of the affected countries. We argue that weak transparency increases funding costs, especially in times of financial distress. Yet transparency can only help prevent a financial crisis and should not be seen as a cure for systems already under stress. Poor transparency is typically found in societies characterized by unchecked economic power or those with corrupt business practices. Deep-seated cultural differences suggest that it may be many years before changes in transparency can occur.

2. THE EAST ASIAN CRISIS

The meltdown in currency, bond and equity markets, over the past year or more has contributed to massive credit rationing for East Asia, particularly by foreign creditor banks. (Figure 1) A permanent solution to the East Asian financial crisis will require a restoration of interbank confidence in the region's banks, which, in turn, will require credible transparency, massive restructuring, and state-financed recapitalization. Vague, or unrealistically broad guarantees, half-hearted support measures, and minor improvements in transparency will not be enough to induce interbank creditors to reopen credit lines voluntarily; there will be too much uncertainty. Interbank creditors will demand solvency and transparency.

Figure 1 Credit Rationing in Asia

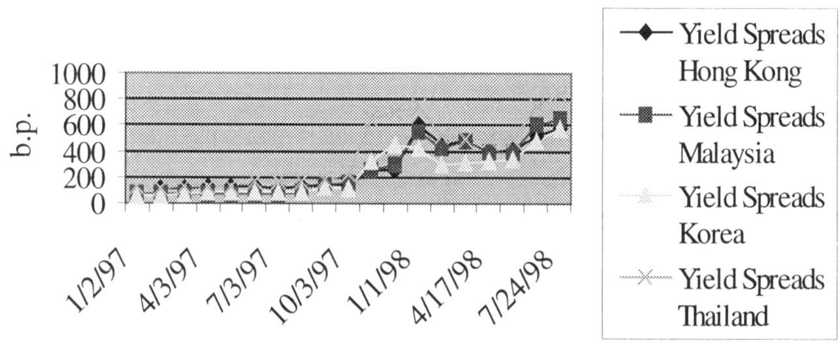

The roadblock in the way of such measures is that transparency is revealing insolvency, further shaking creditor confidence, wiping out existing shareholder claims and endangering nondepository creditors (e.g., subordinated bondholders). Since some of these banks have undergone recent capital-raising operations, foreign investors have been further injured and credibility has taken another major blow. On top of this, revelation of insolvency is likely to bring to light managerial corruption and incompetence, requiring the dismissal of the existing managers, if not their arrest and trial. This is a powerful disincentive for bank management to come clean about asset quality.

The best way that credible transparency can be achieved is if arms-length bank examination and loan classification policies are adopted and conducted by independent and incorruptible bureaucrats. This is a part of the various IMF plans, but very difficult to actually achieve in societies without a tradition of independent, authoritative, and incorruptible civil servants. Consequently, it seems very unlikely to us that transparency and solvency can be achieved in the near term and, therefore, it will be a challenge to restore interbank confidence within the next few years.

A critical factor here is the central role of banks in the financial equation: the debtor banks who act as the countries' principal credit-takers, and the creditor banks who act as the countries' principal credit providers. *The restoration of credit availability will be decided not by the debtor countries, the IMF or creditor governments, but rather as a result of private, autonomous decisions made by individual bank credit departments about other bank obligors.*

3. TRANSPARENCY DEFINED

The dictionary provides several definitions of transparency, most having to do with light. Definitions applicable to a financial context include: easily understood or detected; obvious; guileless (free of deceit, cunning or craftiness); candid; open. In other words, fully revealing the true financial picture of a bank or firm. Transparency insures that reported financial data reflects reality. If there is a change in the financial status of a reporting entity, full transparency requires that that change be reflected accordingly and instantaneously to all concerned.

Transparency is not about cultural differences. Yet it is clear that certain cultures naturally resist attempts to improve transparency. Or worse, they wait until there is a crisis to make the change. At times, this exacerbates the problem and causes the crisis to deepen. As we argue below, transparency fosters confidence and trust as well as better economic decision making. Confidence and trust reap benefits of lower overall funding costs and higher profits.

As banks push beyond the basic, sound banking practice of engaging in short-term, self-liquidating lending, the need for transparency increases. Balance sheets stacked with long-term commitments, margin lending and direct equity investments are most vulnerable to economic disruptions. The weaker the transparency for such banks, the greater the likelihood that they may be trying to hide bad news and the larger the premium they must pay to attract funds. Where local laws permit poor transparency, managers of these institutions intuitively weigh the costs of improved transparency against the benefits of reduced funding costs.

4. EXAMPLES OF POOR TRANSPARENCY

We have encountered many examples of poor transparency throughout the world. The list below, while not exhaustive, provides a flavor of the issues faced by analysts trying to uncover the true financial status of debtors:

- Delays in financial reporting or the absence of quarterly and semi-annual updates;
- Lax accounting practices, especially those relating to loss and impairment definitions of financial assets;
- No consolidation of the financial results of related companies, and conversely, the lack of separate corporate entity financial statements;
- Complex corporate structures, lack of clear ownership interests and hidden related party lending;
- Continuing accrual of interest for problem loans;
- Undisclosed derivatives activity, such as forward contracts; likewise, missing footnotes;
- Lack of independent outside auditors and audit committees;
- Lack of timely information about material events when they occur and/or the poor distribution of information that is made public; and
- Restrictions on the freedom of independent third parties to voice opinions of financial issues.

5. TRANSPARENCY IN BANKING SYSTEMS

Accounting transparency is vital to the health of a banking system. Without transparency, diseased banks, which are insolvent in an economic sense, are certified healthy in an accounting sense and are therefore allowed to survive and risk contaminating the entire banking system. With transparency, the diseased banks are naturally cut out of the system, reducing capacity and allowing the remaining banks to operate profitably. But if diseased banks are kept alive because of opaque accounting methods or regulatory forbearance, the strong banks will often grow weak.

When otherwise healthy banks become infected due to delays in resolving sick banks, the costs of returning the system to health inevitably rise. If the disease has spread throughout the banking system, the direct costs of restoring individual banks to health may be only a small part of the total bill. As diseased banks are recognized by market participants, despite the efforts of officials to hide the problems, the entire banking system can be penalized through increased funding costs or outright credit rationing. The banks, infected or otherwise, will face pressures to restrict growth or even shrink lending operations. Asset prices may decline, liquidity may dry up, and loan quality at all banks may suffer, depending on the perceived difficulties facing the banking system. Moreover, business activity will likely stall and unemployment could rise. The bailout costs in such a situation may become a significant portion of the country's wealth.

At least until recently, it is our opinion that most Asian banks have played lip service to accounting transparency. Although many banks provide negligible detail and wholly implausible "headline" financial results, many have gone through the motions of providing excruciating detail about all of their activities. This might be referred to as nominal accounting transparency. While the banks may have followed the letter of the regulations when it came to classifying problem loans, they did not fulfill the spirit of the regulations. For example, many banks book additional loans to weak borrowers as current and performing. In a strict accounting sense, the loans *are* performing. Yet, because these loans have been made to borrowers who have already defaulted, and are therefore weak, in an economic sense, the loans should be classified as being of doubtful quality.

This is one of the key lessons being learned today in Asia as those countries try to restore international confidence to banking systems badly shaken by massive bad debt problems incurred as a result of asset bubbles and poor underwriting practices. The true extent of problem loans at many Asian banks is still not officially recognized. The risk now is that the situation has been made worse by banks that grew their loan books by extending new loans to insolvent borrowers in order to help them make payments on their existing loans.

To a certain extent, inaction on the part of authorities to deal with the banking mess in Asia reflects an unwillingness to see firms fail. There appears to be a cultural bias against failure, contrary to the capitalist model practiced in the West. Our textbooks tell us that the deliberate restraint of the invisible hand will lead to a misallocation of scarce resources. Inefficiencies will be allowed to persist and growth is stifled. In Asian banking systems there are no winners and no losers. Management is not held accountable for mistakes and misdeeds go unpunished.

Asia's banking system problems have in turn contributed to a sustained regional decline in asset prices, particularly real estate and commodities, which despite low interest rates in some countries, continue to weaken. Other fallout from the ongoing banking crisis are falling currencies, depressed equity prices, a flight to financial asset quality, stagnant economies and rising unemployment, all of which serve to lengthen the period before recovery can occur.

Transparency could also be said to be lacking when it comes to official policy regarding the protection of bank creditors. The deepening banking crisis in Japan, for example, has caused various officials to make vague or even conflicting statements about the treatment of different claims in the event of a bank closure. Lacking historical precedents, there is much uncertainty about how small depositors versus large depositors might fare. Or how authorities might treat foreign depositors, interbank claims, senior unsecured bondholders, subordinated bondholders or preferred stockholders. Mindful that each situation would likely be unique, a consistent, authoritative statement would go far in restoring confidence. Blanket guarantees, while perhaps helpful from a systemic risk perspective, can lead to moral hazard issues. Moreover, such guarantees could be seen as being insupportable in light of available resources.

6. HOW MIGHT ONE MEASURE TRANSPARENCY?

Because there is no universally accepted definition of transparency and the concept itself remains somewhat subjective, a quantitative measure of a transparency is extremely difficult to prepare. We turn instead to the results of a readily available survey, which attempts to quantify the perceived degree of corruption in a large number of countries. The surveys are conducted by Göttingen University and Transparency International, a non-governmental organization whose mission is to curb corruption. The organization was founded in 1993 and is headquartered in Berlin. Each country is ranked, based only on the perceptions of business people that participated in the surveys, on a scale of one to ten. A perfect 10.00 would be a totally corruption-free country. There had to be at least four responses for a country to be included in the corruption index.

Why use a corruption index as a measure of transparency? Intuitively, there is a strong relationship between corruption within a country and the transparency of its bank accounting standards. Many social systems are characterized by economic power concentrated in the hands of government officials, the military, or business interests. Lacking appropriate checks and balances, such power often begets corruption and/or political interference. Such practices provide very strong incentives to obfuscate the picture being presented to outside parties. Self-dealing, related party lending, and questionable loans to politicians and friends are not the sort of laundry that banks want aired publicly. Thus, corrupt regimes are most likely to favor poor transparency.

Figure 2 is a ranking of fifty-two countries (or special regions) by their 1997 TI Score. The country having the lowest perceived corruption, with a corruption score of 9.94, is Denmark. Nigeria, with a perceived corruption score of 1.76, is seen as the most corrupt country on the list. In the appendix, we list each country and score alphabetically. Three East Asian names, Singapore, Hong Kong, and Japan, rank above the median score as being regarded as having relatively low corruption. Conversely, Taiwan, Malaysia, South Korea, Thailand, the Philippines, China, and Indonesia are well below the median.

Moody's bank financial strength ratings (BFSRs) provide investors with an indication of a financial institution's ability to withstand stress. In nearly all of the countries now experiencing problems, average system-wide BFSRs have been among the lowest in the world. Moody's introduced its bank financial strength ratings in 1994 to serve the interbank deposit and lending market. Today, Moody's has over 854 BFSRs for banks in sixty-three countries. Our strategy has been to assign BFSRs to all banks holding a deposit rating. Multilateral and national development banks are current exceptions to this rule, however, because of their special role in facilitating economic growth.

BFSRs are intended to provide investors and cross-border interbank lenders with a measure of a bank's intrinsic safety and soundness on an entity-specific basis. Thus, unlike traditional bond or deposit ratings, BFSRs are assigned to issuers, not specific debt issues. Also unlike debt ratings,

Figure 2 Transparency International Corruption Perception Index

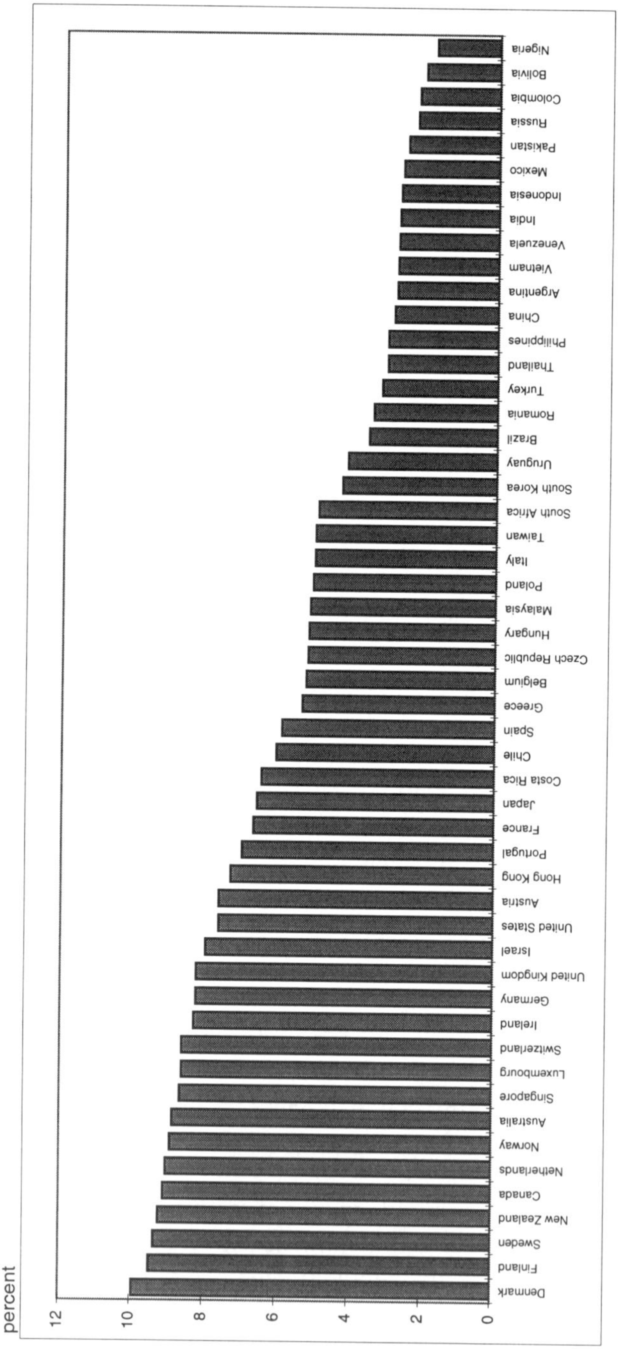

BFSRs are not intended to measure the risk of credit loss, or expected loss. Hence they do not replace bond and deposit ratings.

BFSRs assess a bank's credit profile by excluding factors related to country risk concerns, regulatory support mechanisms, ownership, or membership in a banking group. Instead, they are opinions of the stand-alone risk of a bank enterprise and address aspects of risk familiar to regulatory examiners. In particular, we evaluate the bank's capital adequacy and quality. We also look at the quality of the bank's assets. Typically this would entail an estimate of the loss content of the loan portfolio or losses on equity shareholdings, if any. We try to assess the professionalism of management by asking questions about bank strategy and risk control mechanisms. We also look at the profitability of the bank and the strength of its franchise. And we consider the liquidity position of the bank by estimating its capacity to meet maturing obligations, as well as the bank's sensitivity to adverse interest rate or exchange rate movements.

Also shown in the appendix, we matched the average financial strength rating across banks within each country to its corresponding corruption score. The ratings were those in effect as of August 3, 1998. Five countries of the fifty-two TI-rated countries did not have banks with Moody's-assigned financial strength ratings. For the remaining forty-seven countries, we construct below a scatterplot showing the corruption index (the horizontal axis) against Moody's average BFSR for that country.

As Figure 3 indicates, the two series are in fact significantly correlated. A regression of the corruption index on average BFSR yields an adjusted R^2 of 0.53. The sign of the relationship also conforms with intuition: countries perceived as being less corrupt have stronger banks, on average.

Moody's also provides country ceiling credit ratings for each country on the TI list except Nigeria. Also using the August 3, 1998 date, we show in the appendix the country ceiling long-term debt ratings for each country. These represent the highest foreign currency rating an issuer might receive where the obligor is subject to the sovereignty of a particular government. Such ratings are based upon the default risk for medium and/or long-term debt obligations issued by a national government (denominated in a foreign currency), either in its own name or with its guarantee. Put differently, it represents the "foreign currency transfer risk" associated with investing in a particular country. In cases where there is no particular debt obligation outstanding, a country ceiling rating could still be issued based on an assessment of risk posed by a national government if it were to issue a foreign currency obligation. We consider such obligations to represent the lowest foreign currency default risk within a country. The reason: a national government, through its ability to mobilize foreign currency assets within its own domain, has almost by definition the best ability to obtain foreign

Figure 3 Corruption Index Against Average BFSR

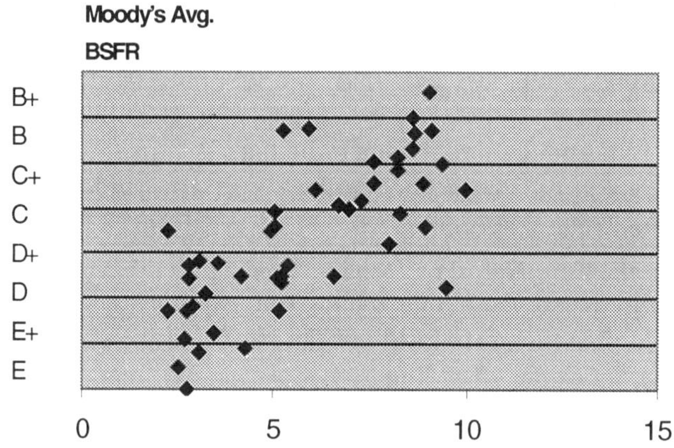

exchange of any issuer within the country. For instance, governments may, and often have, imposed foreign exchange controls.

We repeat the above exercise and plot below TI's corruption index against Moody's country ceiling ratings. The series do appear correlated, with higher-rated countries receiving better scores in the area of corruption. Regression results bear out this observation and indicate an even higher statistical relationship with an adjusted R^2 of 0.71.

These two comparisons help support the hypothesis that increased transparency, all else equal, will yield lower overall credit risk. Although we have admittedly used a very narrow definition of transparency, the relationship is strong enough to consider. The question then becomes: is the potential improvement in credit standing worth the risk of increased disclosure?

7. WHY SOME BANKS (AND EVEN SOME REGULATORS) MAY NOT WANT TRANSPARENCY

The positive aspects of transparency have been weighed against the costs throughout the history of banking. Debilitating panics and runs encouraged a form of secrecy surrounding financial conditions fully sanctioned by regulators. Today there still persists an attitude among banks and their regulators that somehow the average citizen is incapable of acting rationally on sophisticated financial data. Even in developed countries, bank examination results (such as CAMEL ratings) are kept out of the public

Figure 4 Corruption Index Against Sovereign Rating

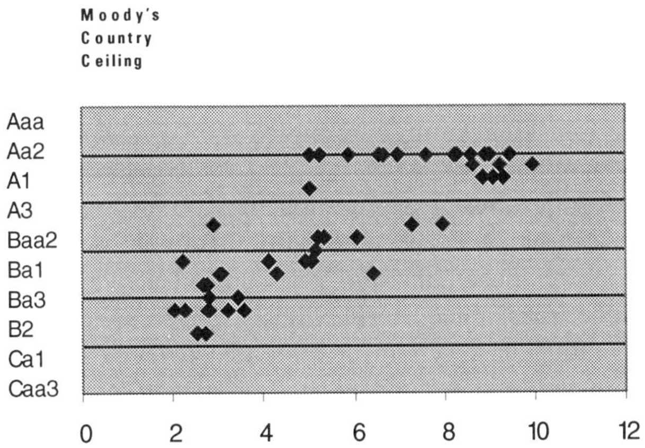

domain. Regulators may favor such secrecy to deflect public criticism arising from the failure to resolve or close a troubled bank. While improved transparency is advocated as a means of improving market discipline, regulators clearly fear the consequences.

There are several reasons why certain banks would favor poor transparency. Chiefly, it costs money to institute timely, accurate and detailed accounting systems. Resources that might be more profitably employed elsewhere are relegated to a reporting function. Statements must be formatted to international standards and outside auditors must be hired to opine on the quality of reporting. Many banks in developing countries are small and the costs of complying with transparent reporting practices may be significant.

Also of concern, transparency restricts management's ability to engage in self-dealing. Loans to subsidiaries, politicians, family and friends may be interpreted in a harsh light when subject to international scrutiny. Lending of this type often finds its way into such speculative activities as stock market or real estate purchases. Such lending could also be used to prop up inefficient or corrupt business activities. In many cultures, it is expected that a loan officer would receive a "gift" for making a loan to certain borrowers. These activities may be difficult to hide under a fully transparent system of reporting. Banks have a large incentive not to reveal such activities as they may subject managers to civil or criminal legal action.

Fully transparent reporting may also reveal competitive strategies or vulnerabilities where a bank holds a large unhedged position in some asset or currency. State-owned banks may not want transparency to reveal policy lending or loans to finance a project considered to be a state secret. State-owned banks in many countries without well developed capital markets are used as instruments of economic policy. They direct funds to targeted industries in order to gain a foothold in international markets. Moreover, they can subsidize loss making entities or projects for broader political purposes.

When confronted with unusual or questionable activity on a bank's part, market discipline can be swift and potentially disruptive to the entire banking system of a country. Indeed, there may develop a Catch 22 situation when trying to introduce transparency to previously closed systems. First, assume that banks operating in a system of poor transparency have been poorly managed and have hidden fundamental problems in their loan portfolio. As long as the region or economy seemingly prospers, the market (i.e., investors and interbank lending officers) will not mind the poor transparency. Once problems surface, however, investors may begin to lose confidence. They may suspect that there are bigger problems lurking beneath the surface but they don't know.

While officials may encourage increased transparency as a means of easing the banking system's ensuing credit crunch, increased transparency would instead reveal the true state of the banks and/or the inadequacy of regulator's plans to deal with the banking crisis. Investor fears may be confirmed and confidence may fall further. The credit crunch could deepen and the economy, along with the quality of bank assets, would be further compromised. A vicious cycle might develop until the entire system has virtually collapsed. The irony is that efforts to improve transparency in fact worsen the situation.

Transparency is a preventive measure, which must be introduced when confidence is rising and market reaction is likely to be benign. Just as one would not prescribe physical exercise to a patient in an intensive care ward—however proper such advise may be for a healthy person—transparency can only be introduced when a banking system is free from stress.

8. CONCLUSION

We have argued that poor transparency has played a key role in the East Asian financial crisis. We discussed examples of poor transparency, and noted a correlation between credit risk and a quantitative measure of corruption. We suggest that weak transparency increases funding costs, especially in times of financial distress, but note that transparency can only help prevent a financial crisis and should not be seen as a cure for systems already under stress. Poor transparency has been associated with societies characterized by unchecked economic power or those with corrupt business practices. Cultural and other barriers suggest that it may be many years before changes in transparency can occur.

Appendix

As of 8/3/98 Country	TI Corruption Perception Index	Moody's Avg BFSR	Moody's Avg BFSR	Moody's Sov. LT Rating
Argentina	2.81	2.44	D	Ba3
Australia	8.86	4.54	C+	Aa2
Austria	7.61	4.57	C+	Aaa
Belgium	5.25	5.71	B	Aaa
Bolivia	2.05	NA	NA	B1
Brazil	3.56	2.79	D+	B1
Canada	9.1	5.70	B	Aa2
Chile	6.05	4.40	C	Baa1
China	2.88	1.83	D	A3
Colombia	2.23	3.50	C	Baa3
Costa Rica	6.45	NA	NA	Ba1
Czech Republic	5.2	2.33	D	Baa1
Denmark	9.94	4.40	C	Aa1
Finland	9.48	2.25	D	Aaa
France	6.66	4.07	C	Aaa
Germany	8.23	4.84	C+	Aaa
Greece	5.35	2.71	D+	Baa1
Hong Kong	7.28	4.18	C	A3
Hungary	5.18	2.50	D+	Baa2
India	2.75	1.75	D	Ba2
Indonesia	2.72	0.00	E	B3
Ireland	8.28	3.90	C	Aaa
Israel	7.97	3.20	D+	A3
Italy	5.03	3.92	C	Aaa
Japan	6.57	2.47	D	Aaa
Luxembourg	8.61	5.33	C+	Aaa
Malaysia	5.15	1.75	D	Baa2
Mexico	2.66	1.10	E+	Ba2
Netherlands	9.03	6.57	B+	Aaa
New Zealand	9.23	NA	NA	Aa1
Nigeria	1.76	NA	NA	NA
Norway	8.92	3.60	C	Aaa
Pakistan	2.53	0.50	E+	B3
Philippines	3.05	2.82	D+	Ba1
Poland	5.08	2.44	D	Baa3
Portugal	6.97	4.00	C	Aaa
Romania	3.44	1.25	E+	Ba3
Russia	2.27	1.73	D	B1
Singapore	8.66	5.67	B	Aa1
South Africa	4.95	3.50	C	Baa3
South Korea	4.29	0.89	E+	Ba1
Spain	5.9	5.74	B	Aaa
Sweden	9.35	5.00	C+	Aa2
Switzerland	8.61	6.00	B	Aaa

Appendix (cont'd)

As of 8/3/98 Country	TI Corruption Perception Index	Moody's Avg BFSR	Moody's Avg BFSR	Moody's Sov. LT Rating
Taiwan	5.02	3.60	C	Aa3
Thailand	3.06	0.82	E+	Ba1
Turkey	3.21	2.13	D	B1
United Kingdom	8.22	5.15	C+	Aaa
Uruguay	4.14	2.50	D+	Baa3
United States	7.61	5.05	C+	Aaa
Venezuela	2.77	2.71	D+	B1
Vietnam	2.79	NA	NA	B1

Chapter 26

Early Warning Indicators of Financial Crises

Morris Goldstein
Instiute for International Economics

1. INTRODUCTION

My aim in this paper is to discuss early warning indicators of financial crises. I plan to do that in three steps.

First, I will suggest *why* one might be interested in early warning indicators.

Second, I will highlight a number of the *results* that come out of existing empirical studies (drawing in part on some ongoing joint work with Carmen Reinhart).[1]

And third, I will outline a few avenues for *further work* in the future.

Because Graciela Kaminsky is also contributing to this volume, and because she has done a great deal of work in this area—much of it with the same coauthor—I will try to avoid undue overlap by emphasizing different points.

2. WHY DO EARLY WARNING STUDIES MATTER?

Why might one be willing to spend resources on finding early warning indicators of banking and currency crises?

I think there are two key reasons. First, there is strong evidence that *banking and currency crises are extremely costly to the countries in which they originate* (as well as posing significant spillover risks to other countries). According to the IMF's tally, there have been over sixty-five developing-country episodes during the 1980–95 period when the banking system's capital was completely or nearly exhausted.[2] The public-sector bailout costs of resolving banking crises in developing countries during this period has been estimated to be at least $250 billion.[3] In more than a dozen of these banking crises, the public-sector resolution costs amounted to ten percent or more of GDP.[4] In the latest additions to the list of severe banking crises, the cost of bank recapitalization for the countries most affected in the ongoing Asian financial crisis is expected to be huge—on the order of thirty percent of GDP for both Thailand and South Korea and twenty percent of GDP for Indonesia and Malaysia.[5]

In addition to the enormous fiscal costs, banking crises also exacerbate declines in economic activity. Illustrative of the magnitude of output losses, an IMF (1998) study, drawing on a sample of thirty-one developing countries, reports that it typically takes almost three years for output growth to return to trend after the outbreak of a banking crisis and that the cumulative output loss averages twelve percent.

The costs of currency crises have likewise been shown to be significant. Mexico's peso crisis was accompanied in 1995 by a decline in real GDP of six percent—its deepest recession in sixty years. During the ERM crises of the fall of 1992 and summer of 1993, on the order of $150 billion was spent on official exchange market intervention in the fruitless effort to stave off the forced devaluation and/or floating of ERM currencies. In emerging Asia, consensus forecasts for 1998 growth issued just prior to the crisis (that is, in May/June 1997) generally stood in the six to eight percent range. These forecasts have now been subject to unprecedented downward revisions in the midst of the currency, banking, and debt crises enveloping these economies. The consensus 1998 growth forecasts are now about –15 percent for Indonesia, –5 to –6 percent for South Korea, Thailand, and Malaysia, –3 percent for Hong Kong, and about zero for East Asia as a whole.[6] And like banking crises, currency crises too seem to exhibit contagious behavior. One recent study found that a currency crisis elsewhere in the world increases the probability of a speculative attack by about eighth percent, after controlling for economic and political fundamentals in the country concerned.[7]

The more costly it is to clean up after a financial crisis has already occurred, the greater the returns to identifying reliable early warning indicators that can prompt corrective policy action.

The second reason for the increased interest in early warning indicators of financial crises is that there is *accumulating evidence that two of the most closely watched "market indicators" of default and currency risks—namely, interest rate spreads and changes in credit ratings—frequently do not provide much advance warning of currency and banking crises.*

Empirical studies of the 1992–93 ERM crisis have typically concluded that market measures of currency risk did not point to the specter of significant devaluations of the weaker ERM currencies before the fact.[8] In the run-up to the Mexican crisis, market signals were again muted or inconsistent. More specifically, measures of default risk on tesebonos (dollar indexed Mexican government securities) jumped up sharply in April 1994 (after the Colosio assassination) but stayed roughly constant between then and the outbreak of the crisis.[9] From April 1994 on, market measures of currency depreciation on the peso usually were beyond the government's announced rate; nevertheless, this measure of currency risk fluctuated markedly and the gap between market expectations and the official rate was widest in the summer of 1994 when the attack came with most ferocity only in late December.[10]

The preliminary evidence now available similarly suggests that the performance of interest rate spreads and credit ratings was likewise disappointing in the run-up to the Asian financial crisis. Examining interest rate spreads on three-month offshore securities, one study found that these spreads gave no warning of impending difficulties (i.e., were either flat or declining) for Indonesia, Malaysia, and the Philippines and produced only intermittent signals for Thailand.[11] A recent analysis of spreads using local interest rates for South Korea, Thailand, and Malaysia found similarly little indicator or growing crisis vulnerability.

Sovereign credit ratings (on long-term, foreign currency debt) issues by the two largest international ratings firms were even less prescient in the Asian crisis. There were almost no downgrades for the most severely affected countries in the eighteen-month run-up to the crisis. As the *Economist* [1997, p. 68] put it, "in country after country, it has often been the case of too little, too late." Looking at a larger sample of cases, a recent OECD study was unable to find consistent support for the proposition that sovereign credit ratings act more like a leading than a lagging indicator of market prices (i.e. of interest rate spreads).[12]

If interest rate spreads and credit ratings only blow the whistle on financial crises once in a while, then there should be strong interest in any other indicators that the data suggest would do a better job.

3. SOME RECENT FINDING

Enough for motivation. What do the early warning exercises usually show?

First, within the sample period, and much like the leading-indicator analyses of business cycles—you do find that there *are recurring patterns in the run-ups to banking and currency crises*. Crises don't just come out of the blue. The better leading indicators seem to anticipate correctly somewhere between 50–100 percent of banking and currency crises.[13] Of course, they also send false signals, with even the best ones sending one false signal for every three to five correct signals.

Second, when monthly data are examined, *banking crises typically turn out* (again, within the sample period) *to be harder to predict than currency crises*. Part of that, I think, reflects the fact that it's harder to identify the duration of banking crises, particularly as regards the end of the crisis. Also, the indicators exercise is pretty much restricted to macro variables and to proxies for the onset of financial liberalization. You can't pick up institutional weaknesses in banking systems with available time-series data (see section 4).

Third, there is wide *variation in performance across leading indicators*, with the best performing indicators displaying noise-to-signal ratios and conditional probabilities that are two to three times (or more) better than those for the worst-performing ones. In addition, the group of indicators that shows the best (in sample) explanatory power also seem, on average, to send the most persistent and earliest signals. Lead times are usually somewhere between ten to eighteen months.

Fourth, when the "signals approach" to forecasting crises is employed and when the in-sample tests are conducted on monthly data, *what works well in anticipating banking crises are appreciation of the real exchange rate (relative to trend), a decline in equity prices, a rise in the (M2) money multiplier, a decline in real output, a fall in exports, and a rise in the real interest rate.*[14] When annual data are used as a supplement to the monthly tests, the best of the pack seem to be a high ratio of short-term capital flows to GDP and a large current account deficit relative to investment. When a "regression approach" to explaining past banking crises is utilized (instead of the signals approach), (an increase in) world or "northern" interest rates usually winds up at or close to the top of the class.

Fifth, *turning to currency crises, the best of the monthly indicators (from the signals approach) are: appreciation of the real exchange rate (relative to trend), a decline in equity prices, a fall in exports, a high ratio of broad money (M2) to international reserves, a low ratio of international reserves by itself, and excess narrow-money (M1) balances*. A recession just misses the top group. Among the annual indicators, the two best performers are both current-account indicators, namely, a large current-account deficit relative to both GDP and investment. The regression format identifies many of the same leading indicators, as well as finding some support for the inflation rate, world commodity prices, and a decline in (incoming) foreign direct investment.

Sixth, we found that *changes in sovereign credit ratings* (at least those produced by Moody's and *Institutional Investor* magazine) *performed considerably worse than the better leading indicators of economic fundamentals* in anticipating both currency and banking crises in emerging economies. In addition, we could find no support, in our sample, for the view that rating changes have led financial crises rather than reacting to these crises. In a similar vein, we found that interest rate spreads (i.e. foreign/domestic real interest rate differentials) were not among the best-performing group of leading indicators. While we had data only for a sub-sample of countries and while we need to test this proposition further, our results suggest that if you are looking to "market prices" for early warning of crises in emerging economies, you should focus on the behavior of real exchange rates and of equity prices—not on credit ratings and interest rate spreads.

Seventh, like Kaminsky (1998), we have performed some out-of-sample tests looking at the January 1996–June 1997 period and the January 1996–December 1997 period. For the Asian crisis countries, the model does quite well (with the exception of Indonesia).

For example, suppose we look at currency crises over the 1996 to mid-1997 period. The ordinal vulnerability rankings among our group of twenty-five sample countries were as follows (with "1" being the most vulnerable):

1. Czech Republic
2. Thailand
3. South Korea
4. Greece
5. South Africa
6. Colombia
7. Turkey
8. Philippines
9. Malaysia.

The countries estimated to be the least vulnerable were Mexico, Venezuela, Argentina, Peru, and Indonesia.

For the somewhat longer January 1996 to December 1997 period, Czech Republic, Thailand, Korea, Greece, Philippines, South Africa,

Colombia, Turkey, and Malaysia again emerged as highly vulnerable to currency crises.

Overall, I would regard these ordinal country rankings as encouraging. Most of the countries actually experiencing crises were estimated to be highly vulnerable and there were few misclassifications as well at the low vulnerability end of the spectrum. The one Asian crisis country where the model does poorly is Indonesia, which is ranked twenth-fifth and twenty-third place in the two out-of-sample tests. This may reflect the fact that (owing to data limitations) our set of indicators does not include a variable that picks up liquidity and currency mismatches among nonfinancial corporations. In addition, some of the best performing indicators overall—namely real exchange rate overvaluation, equity prices, and low international reserves, were *not* flashing in Indonesia's case.

The out-of-sample results for banking crises are decent, but not as impressive as the currency predictions.

My conclusion is that these kinds of forecasting models are useful for making coarse distinctions between, say, the six or seven countries ranked as most vulnerable and the six or seven countries ranked as least vulnerable. In other words, these models can serve as a useful first screen.

4. SUGGESTIONS FOR FURTHER WORK

Finally, let me offer some suggestions for how we could improve these kinds of models.

(a) An obvious extension would be to bring *cross-country contagion* into the model. At the simplest level, you could include as an independent indicator the number of crises that had taken place in the region or in the world over the past "x" months.

Now, you might say, I could improve on that by accounting for the fact that a crisis in country A is more likely to make country B vulnerable than a crisis in country C.

The difficulty is that there are *many channels of contagion*.

One is straightforward *bilateral trade and investment flows*. The more I export to you and the more my banks lend to you, the more vulnerable I am when you have a crisis.

A second channel is the *dynamics of competitive devaluation*. As one country after another in the region devalues, the countries that have not devalued suffer a loss of competitiveness that makes them more vulnerable. Here we also want to compare competition in third-country markets.

Channel number three for contagion is *perceived similarities in country vulnerabilities*—what I've labeled (in the context of the Asian financial crisis) the "wake-up call."[15] When Thailand falls, it wakes up investors to the reality that many other Asian emerging economies have similar vulnerabilities, e.g. weak financial sectors, large current account imbalances, appreciated real exchange rates etc. They then reassess creditworthiness in the region, and write down other Asian economies with similar vulnerabilities.

Yet another contagion channel operates via the *induced effects of a crisis on demand and prices for primary commodities.* For example, the Asian crisis has exacerbated the weakness in oil prices and as such has increased the vulnerability of oil producers (Russia, Ecuador, Mexico, Venezuela, and Norway).

The *liquidity and margin call channel* also should be taken into account. As financial firms mark to market their losses on some emerging market securities, their efforts to meet margin calls and to stay within value-at-risk targets induce sales of other emerging market economy securities—including those with relatively good creditworthiness and relatively high liquidity.

Finally, a *perceived regime shift* can be an instrument of contagion. For example, the unilateral and discriminatory nature of the recent Russian debt rescheduling/default, cum the relatively mild criticism of it by the G-7 countries and the IMF, may have convinced investors that more debt rescheduling by other emerging economies would be in the offing, and that the risks of investing in emerging economies as an asset class had undergone a sharp upward shift. This, in turn, would increase interest rate spreads for all emerging market borrowers.

Modeling cross-country contagion is therefore going to be a real challenge—but one that will need to be addressed.

(b) A second improvement would be to bring *institutional characteristics of weak banking systems* into the forecasts of banking crises. There is a strong presumption that such institutional features as weak accounting, provisioning, and legal frameworks, policy-directed lending, the ownership structure (government ownership, foreign ownership, etc.) of the banking system, high levels of connected lending, and incentive-incompatible official safety nets, matter for vulnerability. Yet it is only very recently that these factors have begun to enter the empirical literature.[16]

The main constraint on making better use of these institutional banking variables is that one can't of course get high frequency measurements of them; indeed, for some of them (e.g., the share of government ownership or the share of foreign banks in total banking assets), it's proven difficult to get annual data that is less than two or three years old. This means that such institutional variables have to be introduced as zero-one dummy variables in a time-series context. There should be more scope to take advantage of such factors in cross-section work, that is, in explaining cross-country differences in the incidence of banking crises over long-time periods. To my mind, such work should be encouraged as a companion to the high frequency time-series studies since the former would help us to obtain a better picture of which institutional characteristics of emerging market banking systems seem to increase crisis vulnerability and which do not.

The third and final set of improvements goes under the heading of *methodological refinements*. Here I would emphasize three suggestions.

First, we need to learn more about the relative performance of the signals approach and the regression approach. In a very useful recent paper, Berg and Patillo [1998] do out-of-sample tests on currency crises, where they compare the signals approach to two regression-based models by Frankel and Rose [1996], and Sachs et al [1996]. The signals approach wins, but they also find that (i) you could obtain better results by dropping the threshold restrictions from the signals approach, that is, just letting the indicators enter linearly; and (ii) that while the signals approach does better than the others, the signals model does not do well in forecasting currency crisis in 1997. In my work with Reinhart, the signals model does better for 1996 and 1997 than Berg and Patillo find. We need further work on these out-of-sample tests.

Second, the work Kamisnky [1998] is now doing on the best way to construct a "composite indicator" is important and should be expanded. In a similar vein, it would be useful to test whether the *interaction* of indicators (e.g. the real interest rate in conjunction with the debt stock, rather than just the real interest rate alone) shows any promise.

Finally, we need to find out *whether the different forecasting models of crises* now available in the official and private *sectors produce robust ordinal rankings of country vulnerabilities*, that is, can we get from the models a reasonable consensus about "whose next."

All of this should yield fertile ground for future work on early warning of banking and currency crisis.

Notes

[1]See Goldstein and Reinhart (1999, forthcoming).

[2]Lindgren et al. (1996).

[3]Honohan (1997).

[4]Caprio and Klingebiel (1996).

[5]Eschweiler (1998).

[6]See IMF (1998) and Eschweiler (1998).

[7]See Eichengreen et al. (1996).

[8]Rose and Svensson (1994).

[9]Leiderman and Thorne (1996).

[10]Obstfeld and Rogoff (1995).

[11]See Eschweiler (1997).

[12]Larrain et al (1997).

[13]See Kaminsky and Reinhart (1996) and Goldstein and Reinhart (1999, forthcoming).

[14]See Kaminsky and Reinhart (1996) for an explanation of the "signals approach" methodology.

[15]See Goldstein (1998).

[16]See, for example, Demirguc-Kunt and Detragiache (1997).

References

Berg, Andrew, and Catherine Patillo. 1998, "Are Currency Crises Predictable? A Test," International Monetary Fund, working paper, July.

Caprio, Gerard, and Daniela Klingebiel. 1996, "Bank Insolvencies: Cross-Country Experience," World Bank, unpublished.

Demirguc-Kunt, Ashli, and Enrica Detragiache. 1997, "The Determinants of Banking Crises: The Evidence from Developed and Developing Countries," International Monetary Fund and the World Bank, unpublished, May.

Eichengreen, Barry, Andrew Rose, and Charles Wyplosz. 1996, "Contagious Currency Crises," NBER, working paper, No.5681, July.

Eschweiler, Bernhard. 1997, "Did the Market See the Asian Crisis Coming?," paper presented at World Bank Conference on The Asian Crisis, Washington, DC, (October 4).

Eschweiler, Bernard. 1998, "Asian Financial Markets," Singapore: JP Morgan, (July 17).

Goldstein, Morris. 1986, "The Asian Financial Crisis: Causes, Cures and Systemic Implications. Policy Analyses in *International Economics,"* No. 55, June.

Goldstein, Morris, and Carmen Reinhart. *1999, Forecasting Financial Crises: Early Warning Signals for Emerging Markets* Policy Analyses in International Economics. Washington: Institute for International Economics forthcoming.

Honohan, Patrick. 1997, "Banking System Failures in Developing and Transition Economies: Diagnosis and Prediction." Dublin: University College, unpublished.

International Monetary Fund, 1996, *World Economic Outlook,* Washington: International Monetary Fund, October.

Kaminsky, Graciela, and Carmen Reinhart. 1996, "The Twin Crises: The Causes of Banking and Balance of Payments Problems," Board of Governors of the Federal Reserve System and the International Monetary Fund, International Finance, discussion paper, No. 544,

Larrain, Guilermo, Helmut Reisen, and Julia von Maltzan. 1997, "Emerging Market Risk and Sovereign Credit Ratings." OECD, technical papers, No. 124, April.

Leiderman, Leonardo, and Alfredo E. Thorne. 1991, "The Mexican Crisis and Its Aftermath: What are the Main Lessons?," in *Private Capital Flows to Emerging Markets After the Mexican Crisis* Guillermo Calvo, Morris Goldstein, and Eduard Hochreiter (eds), Washington: Institute for International Economics.

Lindgren, Carl-Johan, Gillian Garcia, and Mathew Saal. 1996, *Bank Soundness and Macroeconomic Policy,* Washington: International Monetary Fund.

Obstfeld, Maurice, and Ken Rogoff. 1995, "The Mirage of Fixed Exchange Rates," *Journal of Economic Perspectives*, Vol. 9, pp. 73–96.

Rose, Andrew, and Lars Svensson. 1994, "European Exchange Rate Credibility Before the Fall," *European Economic Review*, pp. 1185–1216.

Sachs, Jeffrey, Aaron Tornell, and Andres Velasco. 1996, "Financial Crises in Emerging Markets: The Lessons from 1995," *Brookings Papers on Economic Activity*, Vol. 1, Washington: Brookings Institution.

Chapter 27

The Asian Crises: A New Breed or Déjà Vu?

Graciela L. Kaminsky
George Washington University

Abstract: This chapter summarizes the discussion and findings in Kaminsky and Reinhart (1998a, 1998b, and 1998c), Kaminsky, Lizondo, and Reinhart (1998), and Kaminsky (1998) who examine eighty currency crises from twenty countries during 1970–1997.

The spectacular collapse of several Asian currencies in 1997 and the globalization of the so-called Asian flu into a major epidemic engulfing countries in Europe, Africa, and most of all in Latin America have rekindled the eternal question of whether these crises could have been avoided. Naturally, for governments to adopt preemptive measures, it is necessary to detect the symptoms of crises early on. This brings up the question of the possibility of constructing an early warning system to help monitor countries that are likely to be the subjects of speculative attacks against their currencies.

Naturally, if financial panics had been at the core of the Asian crises and the worldwide waves of turbulence in 1997–1998, it would have been impossible to predict let alone avoid them. This is because, according to this view, the trigger of financial crises is a sudden shift in market expectations and confidence, unrelated to macroeconomic fundamentals. The only hope at controlling or at least lessening the severity of these speculative attacks would be to introduce "sand in the wheels" of international capital markets.

In contrast, if these crises were the result of an unsustainable deterioration in macroeconomic fundamentals, it can be argued that it is possible to construct a warning system that will pinpoint poor domestic policies or unusually adverse external shocks. Yet, alerting about upcoming currency crises would prove to be an impossible task if, as some have claimed, the nature of crises is changing. If the Latin American debt crisis is the result of irresponsible fiscal finances, the 1992–1993 ERM crises are of a self-fulfilling nature and triggered by rumors unrelated to market fundamentals, and the Asian crises are the product of moral hazard behavior by banks, the hopes of constructing an early warning system are dashed to pieces because trying to forecast an upcoming crisis would be like shooting at a moving target. An essential ingredient to make this task possible is that crises should be of a similar nature or at least follow a certain pattern.

This chapter builds on the view that many of the features and antecedents of the Asian crises are common to a substantial number of crisis episodes in the past, such as the Debt crisis in the early 1980s or the ERM crises in 1992–1993. Moreover, it shows that, in fact, the Asian crises are preceded by the same signs of distress observed in the Latin American economies at the onset of the Debt crisis. This evidence that common factors preceded crises as far apart in distance and time as the Debt crisis and the Asian crises suggests that it is in fact possible to construct an early warning system to help monitor whether a country may be slipping into a potential crisis.

1. ON THE CAUSES OF CURRENCY CRISES: LITERATURE REVIEW

The currency crises of the 1970s, 1980s, and the 1990s have generated a prolific and still-growing literature on balance-of-payments problems. This section briefly reviews this literature to pinpoint the triggers of past episodes of crises and to examine the possible sources of vulnerability of the Asian economies at the beginning of the 1997–1998 crises.

Many of the theories of currency crashes emphasize that extended credit is at the core of these crises. Still, the source of extended credit varies across models. For example, Krugman (1979), inspired in the Latin American currency crises of the 1970s, focuses on the monetization of the government deficit. In a similar vein, but this time focusing on the currency crisis in Chile in 1982, Diaz-Alejandro (1985) highlights that difficulties in the banking sector can give rise to a balance-of-payments crisis and argues that if central banks finance the bailout of troubled financial institutions by printing money, we have the classical story of a currency crash prompted by excessive money creation. More recently, McKinnon and Pill (1994) and Kaminsky and Reinhart (1998a) stress the role of financial liberalization and foreign capital inflows channeled through domestic banks, deposit insurance, moral hazard, and overlending. In this approach, currency crises occur as an economy enters a recession that follows a prolonged boom in economic activity fueled by credit creation and surges in capital inflows. The cycle of overlending is exacerbated by implicit or explicit deposit insurance, poor supervision, and moral hazard problems in the banking sector. Crises are accompanied by an overvaluation of the currency, weakening exports, the bursting of asset price bubbles, and overall banking fragilities.

Stimulated by the EMS collapses in 1992 and 1993, other models of currency crises have stressed government officials' concern on, for example, unemployment. Governments are modeled facing two targets: reducing inflation and keeping economic activity close to full employment. Fixed exchange rates may help in achieving the first goal but at the cost of a loss of competitiveness and a recession. With sticky prices, a devaluation may restore competitiveness and help in the elimination of unemployment, thus prompting the authorities to abandon the peg during recessions.

Whether crises have a fiscal origin `a la Krugman or a banking problem á la Diaz-Alejandro or countercyclical government policy as in Obstfeld (1996), speculative attacks can become more severe when foreign debt has reached "dangerous" levels and there is a bunching of maturing loans, that is, when foreign debt is concentrated at very short maturities. In this case, monetary policy tightenings in industrial countries can fuel sudden reversals of capital flows leaving emerging markets scrambling for liquidity. Problems mount even further in the presence of capital flight with gross inflows of capital only financing domestic residents investments overseas. This phenomenon of coexistence of inverse and offsetting capital flows, with domestic residents often choosing to invest their savings in international capital markets at the same time that they are seeking external finance has been an important feature during the debt crisis.

2. QUANTIFYING THE SIGNS OF DISTRESS

To examine whether the Asian crises are of a new breed, I examine the behavior of twenty-one macro and financial indicators at the onset of the Asian balance-of-payment problems in 1997 and compare to their behavior in Latin America at the start of the Debt crisis in 1982.[1]

The indicators used to capture the overborrowing cycles include the M2 multiplier, the ratio of domestic credit credit to nominal GDP, and an indicator of domestic and external financial liberalization.[2] Increases in any of these indicators might signal possible financial sector problems. Problems can compound in the presence of bank runs, which are captured by the growth rate of bank deposits (in real terms). Loose monetary policy is captured by "excess" real M1 balances. Current account problems are captured using the following indicators: exports, imports, the terms of trade, and the real exchange rate, with increases in imports and real appreciations of the domestic currency and the deterioration of exports and the terms-of-trade signaling potential problems in the current account. The capital-account indicators are foreign exchange reserves of the central bank, M2/reserves, domestic foreign real interest rate differentials, world interest rates, foreign debt (as a percentage of foreign exchange reserves), capital flight (which is captured using deposits of domestic residents in BIS banks), and short-term foreign debt (as a percentage of total foreign debt). Reserve losses and increasing interest rate differentials are signals of future problems in the capital account. The ratio of M2 (in dollars) to foreign exchange reserves in dollars is used to examine to what extent the liabilities of the banking system are backed by international reserves. High foreign debt concentrated at short maturities and capital flight can complicate the external outlook for the domestic economy. Finally, high world real interest rates can anticipate capital outflows from emerging economies and currency attacks. I include output, stock prices (in dollars), domestic real interest rates, and the ratio of lending-to-deposit interest rates to capture growth slowdown, with declines in output, stock-market crashes, high real interest rates and lending-to-deposit interest rates ratio signaling impending crises. Finally, a banking crisis indicator is also used to characterize the start of currency crises.

Naturally, not every real appreciation of the domestic currency anticipates a crisis, nor does every single boom in credit markets. In previous work (with Carmen Reinhart), we conclude that an indicator can provide an early warning of future crises only when its behavior departs significantly from its behavior in tranquil times. That is, for an indicator to give a signal of an impending crisis this indicator has to exhibit "anomalous" behavior on the eve of a crisis.[3]

An assessment of the degree of fragility and the sources of distress of the four Asian countries at the onset of the 1997 crises is provided. I quantify, crisis by crisis, the number of the twenty-one indicators showing "unusual" behavior in the twenty-four-month period prior these crises.[4]

With the exception of Indonesia, all the Asian countries show a severe state of distress with about sixty-five percent of the indicators flashing red lights. These currency crises are the paradigm of a typical financial crisis with the onset of these crises occurring as the economies enter a marked slowdown in growth after a prolonged boom in economic activity fueled by rapid credit creation. This dramatic surge in credit is, in large part, explained by heavy capital inflows and partly by the reform of the financial system, which is accompanied by drastic reductions in reserve requirements. Overall, the explosive growth in these countries comes to an end with a real appreciation of the domestic currency and the corresponding loss of export markets and in the midst of financial fragilities.

For example, short-term capital inflows to Thailand amount to seven-tenths percent of GDP in each of the years 1994–1996, with the growth rate of credit to the nonfinancial private sector over 1990–1995 being more than twenty-three percent. While in the early 1990s, output growth rates increase to almost nine percent fueled in part by easy credit, the explosive growth in Thailand comes to an end with the real appreciation of the domestic currency and the corresponding loss of exports markets (the annual growth rate of exports falls from a peak of thirty percent per year in 1994 to about zero in 1996). Financial fragilities are also evident, with runs against major banks starting to occur in as early as May 1996. Finally, the sharp increase in interest rates in 1997 to defend the baht puts the nail in the coffin of the already defunct banking sector. Overall, seventy-five percent of the indicators for which there is available data were exhibiting "anomalous" behavior.

The boom–bust cycle in lending is also evident in the Philippines, fueled as in Thailand by capital inflows but also by a dramatic reduction in reserve requirements. Bank credit increases by forty-four percent a year in 1995–96. As in Thailand, the rapidly expanding credit is an important contributor to the rally in stock and real estate markets, with a four-fold increase in prices in both markets. As in other countries in the region, foreign currency exposure increases in the Philippines in the 1990s through foreign borrowing to finance domestic lending, with foreign borrowing concentrated at short maturities. Consumer lending also increases and fuels a surge in consumption, leading to a deterioration of the current account, which is accentuated by the real exchange rate appreciation of the domestic currency. The loss of competitiveness anticipates a future decline in growth and also contributes to a substantial deterioration of the quality of banks' assets, further reducing the odds of survival of many individual financial institutions. Overall, in the Philippines, about fifty percent of the indicators are signaling the increased vulnerability of the economy in the two years prior to the collapse of the peg in July 1997.

Malaysia has a number of features in common with Thailand. It is also affected by the slowdown in the region, though to a much smaller degree. It also has current account deficits similar in magnitude to those in Thailand in the period 1990–1995, although in 1996 the outlook of the external sector improves somewhat with the current account/GDP ratio declining to –5.3 percent (In Thailand the current account/GDP ratio in 1996 is still –8.0 percent). Moreover, Malaysia as Thailand accumulates debt rapidly in the 1990s, with capital inflows fueling a stock and real estate market boom, with prices increasing about 300 percent in the early 1990s. Malaysia is also suffering from financial fragilities as a result of the high degree of leverage of the economy (Malaysia has one of the highest credit-to-GDP ratio in the world) and the large exposures to the property and stock markets. For Malaysia, about sixty percent of the indicators are showing signs of distress at the onset of the crisis.

Indonesia, however, looks somewhat different. While it is still true that, as the other countries in the area, it is exhibiting banking fragilities[5] and short-term debt sharply exceeds available foreign exchange reserves (about 1.7 times the stock of foreign exchange reserves of the country), the current account deficit is not deteriorating as fast—only reaching 3.5 percent of GDP in 1996, the slowdown in growth is not yet evident, and the real exchange rate does not appreciate as much as in the other countries in the region. Only very few indicators (less than twenty percent) are showing signs of strains in the economy in the months prior to the crisis. While the degree of distress in the domestic economy in the months prior to the crisis cannot explain the meltdown of the rupiah and of the economy as a whole in 1998, the flurries of financial crises in 1997 do add a severe element of instability as Indonesia and the other countries in the region are left scrambling for liquidy when Japanese banks—the major lenders to the region—pull out rapidly across the regions after the major losses suffered in the wake of the Thai crisis.[6]

For comparison, the same catalogue of macro fragilities for four Latin American economies during the debt crisis in the early 1980s again show signs of distress are widespread. For example, in Argentina, the failure of major banks in March 1980 results in a sharp increase in central bank lending to the financial system, with the growth rate of credit to the private sector increasing two-fold from the end of 1980 to the end of 1982. As in Asia, the collapse of the banking sector is preceded by a lending boom, fueled by capital flows in the late 1970s, which in turn trigger a consumption boom, a current account deficit, and a sharp appreciation of the domestic currency.[7] The next domino in this crisis is Chile. Again financial fragilities are at the heart of the currency crisis with the usual pre-crisis symptoms of a credit boom, leading to consumption booms and current account deficits.[8] The resolution costs of the banking crises in these two countries amounted to about forty percent of GDP. The Mexican and the Uruguayan crises in 1982 shared similar problems. Overall, more than ninety percent of the indicators were showing signs of abnormal behavior.[9] Thus, while far apart in time and distance, the crises in Latin America and Asia suggest a common pattern and the possibility of constructing a warning system pointing déjà vu sources of fragility.

As shown in Kaminsky (1998), the signals issued by each indicator can be combined into a unique measure of the likelihood of balance-of-payment problems. Interestingly, the probabilities of currency crises for Thailand and the Philippines increase from a low of twenty percent in 1995 to about 100 and seventy percent, respectively, in 1997. For Malaysia, the probabilities of currency crises also increase almost reaching about seventy percent by the time the crisis erupts. Only the crisis in Indonesia remains unexplained by the composite indicator, which ignores the role of international bank lending.

3. CONCLUSIONS

I have examined the main culprits behind the 1997 Asian crises and compared the onset of these crises to that of other currency crises, such as the Debt crisis episode. The analysis suggests that many of the features and antecedents of the crises in Asia are common to previous crisis episodes in Latin American, and as shown in Kaminsky and Reinhart (1998a,b,c) are also common to the crisis episodes in Europe and elsewhere. We can only conclude that the Asian crises are of a new breed if we ignore the multiple lessons that history offers. The results presented also indicate that overall, crises are preceded by a common pattern of multiplying fragilities in all sectors of the economy, which can be used to anticipate when a country is likely to be subject to serious speculative attacks.

This chapter has focused on a specific early warning system for currency crises, which basically highlights poor domestic economic policy, either public or private, as the trigger of crises. I have examined, however, that the frailty of an economy can be exacerbated by currency crises in other countries. For example, Indonesia falls prey of a liquidity crunch when Japanese banks recall their loans from all Asian countries after suffering major losses with the devaluation of the Thai baht. Future work on early warning systems should combine the information on the domestic economy with that of possible spillover effects from other countries in crisis. Finally, work in this area should also assess the state of political instability and perhaps include information on the nature of the political institutions, which has been shown to help in understanding, for example, the sources of economic growth.

Acknowledgment: I thank Ian Anderson for superb research assistance.

Notes

[1]See Kaminsky (1998) for a description of the indicators and the sources of the data.

[2]This is a dummy variable equal to zero when the domestic financial sector is regulated and there are restrictions to capital account movements and is equal to one when controls both in the domestic and external front have been lifted.

[3]For a detailed description of the methodology used to classify what is considered "anomalous" behavior in an indicator and what is not, see Kaminsky and Reinhart (1998a).

[4]Part of this table is reproduced from Kaminsky and Reinhart (1998a).

[5]The beginning of banking crisis in Indonesia can be dated to November 1992 when a large bank (Bank Summa) collapses and triggers runs on three smaller banks.

[6]The reversal was in fact quite pronounced, from capital inflows to the region of $50 billion in 1996 to an outflow of $21 billion in 1997. See, Kaminsky and Reinhart (1998c) for detailed discussion on world and regional financial links and their effects on the odds of currency crises.

[7]For example, real domestic credit increases at about 50 percent in 1979 while real private consumption increases about 15 percent in 1979 and about 8 percent in 1980, and the real exchange rate appreciates about 50 percent in the two years preceding the debt crisis.

[8]Real domestic credit exploded at a rate of 40 percent in 1980 and almost 50 percent in 1981, with foreign debt increasing to about 60 percent of GDP in 1982.

[9]For example, for Uruguay, real domestic credit increases on average 50 percent in the two years preceding the crisis and the real exchange rate appreciates about 40 percent since the stabilization program was implemented.

References

Diaz-Alejandro, C. 1985, "Good-Bye Financial Repression, Hello Financial Crash," *Journal of Development Economics*, Vol. 19.

International Monetary Fund, 1997, *International Capital Markets: Development, Prospects, and Key Policy Issues.*

Kaminsky, G. L. 1998, "Currency and Banking Crises: The Early Warnings of Distress," international Finance Discussion Paper No. 629, Board of Governors of the Federal Reserve System, October.

Kaminsky, G. L., and C. M. Reinhart. 1998a, "The Twin Crises: Causes of Banking and Balance-of-Payments Problems," Board of Governors of the Federal Reserve System, forthcoming in *American Economic Review.*

Kaminsky, G. L., and C. M. Reinhart. 1998b, "Financial Crises in Asia and Latin America: Then and Now," *American Economic Review,* Vol. 88, pp. 444–448.

Kaminsky, G. L., and C. M. Reinhart. 1998c, "On Crises, Contagion, and Confusion," George Washington University, mimeo.

Kaminsky, G. L., S. Lizondo, and C.M. Reinhart. 1998, "The Leading Indicators of Currency Crises," *Staff Papers*, International Monetary Fund, March.

Krugman, P. 1979, "A Model of Balance-of-Payments Crises," *Journal of Money, Credit, and Banking*, Vol. 11, 311–325.

McKinnon, R. I., and H. Pill. 1994, *Credible Liberalizations and International Capital Flows: the Overborrowing Syndrome,* Stanford: Stanford University.

Obstfeld, M. 1996, "Models of Currency Crises with Self-fulfilling Features," *European Economic Review.*

Chapter 28

The Inevitable Perils of a Precocious Giant

John A. Wing
Illinois Institute of Technology

In his classic of French literature, Francois Rabelais described the adventures of a picaresque father, Gargantua, and his son, Pantaguel. Both are robust and powerful giants. Because of their size, they went into the world at very young ages and were treated by others as adults. Sometimes their precociousness served them well; at other times, not. Sometimes the people with whom they came into contact were poorly served because of their failure to reflect on the giants' lack of maturity. The current problems of Asia are, in my mind, akin to the problems of Gargantua and Pantaguel. The West has confused economic size and power with legal and financial sophistication. Worse yet, the West appears surprised at the results of its confusion.

East Asia has become an economic giant but yet it is still a legal and financial adolescent. Like Gargantua and Pantaguel, it lacks the sophistication of a mature adult. For the sake of convenience, somewhat unfairly, I will treat Malaysia, Indonesia, Thailand, South Korea, Taiwan, and the Philippines as if they were a monolithic entity and call them the "East Asian Giants." While this treatment may be unfair in that it fails to recognize the considerable differences among these countries, for the purpose of my analysis, it is effectively accurate.

The so-called East Asian miracle of sustained high levels of economic growth and modest inflation was built on the four pillars of hard work, high savings rates, emphasis on education, and budgetary surpluses. These four pillars are cornerstones of capitalism. The economic Achilles' heel of the Asian giants is that their growth, while prodigious, was not to be unending. Growth driven by input factors always peaks while the more illusive "productivity gains" are hard to achieve in economies relying upon low labor costs for comparative advantage. Thus, embedded in the miracle of sustained growth, is the root of the Asian crisis.

The parentage of the Asian crisis is in some dispute. As is often the case with disasters, finger-pointing and blame-shifting are widespread. The only one of the usual suspects not rounded up in this crisis is the "macroeconomic policy-induced crisis." This form of crisis occurs when a central bank prints money to cover the budget deficits while trying to maintain pegged exchange rates. Usually, interest rates soar and the economy falters. The central bank finally begins to run low on the reserves necessary to hold the pegged price. The speculators come in, start shorting and there is a currency crash. Ultimately, the exchange rates float at a rate lower than the previously pegged rate. Net to net, it was a waste of money to the central bank and a windfall to the speculators.

The other usual suspects: (a) financial panic, (b) bubble collapse, (c) moral hazard crisis, and (d) disorderly workout procedures, all seem to own a meaningful piece of the responsibility in the East Asian crisis. Financial panic occurs when any set of investors attempt, usually for reasons not grounded in fundamental economics, to "get out" at the same time. In theory, financial panics could occur at any time. In practice, they seem to occur after there has been an asset bubble. Financial panic is usually the end game of "greater fool" investing, in which all the players realize prices are too dear but pay them anyway, thus creating an asset bubble. The reason they continue to play the game while knowing, or at least suspecting, they are paying too much is because thus far they have been able to pass the "bad penny" to a greater fool at a higher price. Then some event—the longer the game, the more trivial the event—spooks the players and they all run for the exits.

The trigger event in the Asian crisis is now alleged to be a modest slowing in the Thai economy. Given the input-driven nature of the growth and the lack of total production factor gains, this slowing was inevitable. The response of Japanese and other banks was to decline renewal of credits to the Asian Giants. The result was dramatic: a reversal of capital flow from plus \$89 billion in 1996 to minus \$12 billion in 1997. The largest change in capital flows came from net selling in the giants' stock markets (\$23 billion swing) and the reduction in credit to the giants' banks (\$76 billion swing).

However, in my view, the real music stopper was the recognition by Japanese financial authorities that Japanese banks had best circle the wagons around the Japanese economy and financial institutions. Given the problems at home, protecting the prosperity of others in their sphere of influence was no longer feasible or politically acceptable for Japan.

U.S. and U.K. portfolio managers, like most stock investors, were quite familiar with psychologically induced volatility and were quick to push the panic button. Equity portfolio managers punish missteps as small as missing a quarterly earning estimate by two cents with merciless abandonment. The slowing of the whole Thai economy seemed like an obvious and excellent reason to panic—before everyone else did.

It is well to remember that the portfolio managers had sold emerging markets investing to their best institutional clients as desirable co-variance reduction through global diversification. While I know co-variance reduction is a sound idea and widely accepted, it is a slim reed on which to hold at the apparent onset of a monsoon. Portfolio management is a business in which failure in relative performance is neither taken lightly nor forgiven quickly. I think the lessons to be learned from an asset bubble-financial panics scenario is that foreign investors, particularly if they themselves have uncertain footing on the slippery slope of seeking marginal risk adjusted returns, are likely, after a long run of profits, to hit the panic button at the first hint of a severe downturn.

The "moral hazard crisis" was more a domestic problem than an international one. In the U.S. savings and loan scandal, the assets of federally insured depositors were imprudently risked by dewey-eyed or villainous executives of mutual savings and loan associations in which the executives had no significant economic investment. In the East Asian crisis, most of the depository institutions had such high debt equity ratios that the owner/fiduciary aspects of managerial decision-making had been marginalized. It takes both fear and greed to make capitalism work; it is unwise to eliminate fear and to rely solely upon greed. The risk/reward analysis of bankers tolerating very high gearing ratios, both for themselves and for their clients, reflected fearlessness.

The failure to have comprehensive bank supervisory and inspection procedures, as well as an established procedure for closing insolvent banks, added to the Asian giants' problems in the creation of the crisis and equally as important, in its resolution. When the IMF seemingly unwisely determined that the Asian giants should raise interest rates and reduce government spending, the increased rates only further spooked the panic stricken foreign banks and further inflamed the currency speculators. The foreign banks' response was to more aggressively reduce credit exposures, and the currency traders' response was adding to their short position. Regrettably, there was no systematic way to deal with the resulting increase in the number of insolvent banks. It is clear that the workout procedures were not well suited to the circumstances.

Was this all predictable? No, but I think it was inevitable. Given that ... "in the long run we all are dead" ... predictions without, dates, aren't very helpful. It seems reasonably clear from my analysis of the economic and financial market data that the timing of the crisis was not predictable by conventional analytical means—until it was well underway. Rating agencies have been pilloried for not predicting the crisis. I think this criticism is quite unfair. The criticism arises from a misunderstanding of the role of investors' due diligence versus the role of rating agencies. Rating agencies should not attempt to predict panics lest their prophecies become self-fulfilling. I believe they did a reasonable job of alerting the investor to the potential for panic. For rating agencies to do more than suggest the potential for panic is inappropriate and unwise. Predicting the panic would only have accelerated, and possibly exacerbated, the crisis.

That not one investment banks' public research reports even alluded to the potential for the panic is a little more interesting. While I have no evidence, my personal experience in investment banking causes me to wonder if the desire of the investment bankers for positive relations with sovereign and corporate debt issuers might not have effectively suppressed the research department's willingness to speculate about the possibility of a panic. This sometimes happens in the U.S. with respect to potentially negative reports on corporate clients. In any event, the bottom line is that the crisis seemingly came as a great surprise.

Nevertheless, these fundamental problems might have been solved without a panic-induced crisis. There is no question that the panic arose in part from the reaction to slowing growth by the foreign lenders and investors. Periods of slowing growth are understandable and predictable. However, there are additional problems inherent to the East Asian Giants that made the panic inevitable, if not predictable. These problems are the lack of transparency, disclosure and hardnosed analysis.

The quality of bank's credit analysis is importantly a function of the quality of accounting procedures. The internal and external accounting procedures prevalent in both the government and corporate sectors in East Asia were significantly less rigorous than the norms in North America or Western Europe. Quarterly reporting, independence and adherence to some version of GAAP are not the general practices in East Asia. As a result, bankers will admit that the quality of bank credit analysis in East Asia was far below world standards. In East Asia, bank lending was viewed as more reputational than analytic. While knowing the customer is probably the most important ingredient in good credit decisions, the absence of a stream of reliable financial data is unsettling in times of unrest. An additional problem in emerging market investing is that Western debt and equity investors appear to have "bought" overall economic scenario stories buttressed by financial ratings. This is not what Graham & Dodd had in mind when they wrote "Security Analysis." This kind of surface analysis tends to minimize the confidence of the investors in periods of extreme price volatility.

The history of U.S. and world capitalism reflects continuous progress toward the recognition of the value of transparency in markets, disclosure of financial results and avoidance of commercial bribery and cronyism. Initially, executives tended to resist disclosure. The legal power of securities laws and exchange listing standards were required to obtain grudging acceptance. In the early phase, disclosure was viewed by corporate executives as revealing privileged information not appropriate for the public investors, and worse yet, helpful to competitors. In the U.S., the recognition that business executives and politicians should avoid the temptation of bribery, reciprocity and cronyism has required thirty or forty years of criminal convictions. In the U.S., we are nearing the end of the first phase and beginning a new phase in which executives accept the reality that full disclosure and arms-length dealings are good business. They are good business because they reduce borrowing costs, increase price earnings ratios and, most importantly, reduce the likelihood of investor panic. The East Asian giants are still in the less mature phase in which accurate and complete disclosure and puritanical aversion to corruption are not the norm. Until this paradigm shift occurs, there will be periodic panics because there will be disheartening revelations and ugly surprises.

A cultural revolution will be required to cause the paradigm shift to full disclosure, arm's length dealings, and market transparency. Thus, we now must focus on what should be done to avoid future panics and to ameliorate the one they have. I have six recommendations, which I believe would help.

1. Establish banking and securities laws with significant power of inspection and supervision by an independent agency of the government with the capability and willingness to impose harsh remedial sanctions as well as to recommend criminal prosecution with severe sentences for those convicted.

2. Convert a significant portion of the bonds and short-term debt in the corporate sector into equity.

3. Implore Western portfolio managers to abandon the "greater fool" theory of investing and to engage in detailed financial analyzes of all emerging market investments.

4. Implore bankers to insist on receiving a stream of reliable financial data from borrowers as a required part of the credit process.

5. Set up industrial banks or other forms of venture capital funds with long investment horizons, without daily pricing and not permitting regular redemption. These institutions should take on the job of making long-term, arms-length equity investments in productive enterprises.

6. Establish a legal framework for equitable and procedurally efficient bankruptcy proceedings, lien enforcement, and asset securitization.

When most or all of these measures are adopted, the precocious Asian Giants may have the maturity to participate in global capital markets without the periodic need for remediation and resuscitation. Remember, just because a young person is large and strong does not mean he has the experience and wisdom to react prudently to adversity. Treating such persons as mature is, at the very least, negligent entrustment and, depending on the circumstances, possibly a crime. The West must resist the temptation to over-invest and overburden the fragile infrastructure of the young Asian giants until they have developed the maturity to cope with the procedural, disclosure and transparency demands of the global capital markets.

Chapter 29

Banks and the Asian Crisis

Martin Mayer
Brookings Institution

For me, the papers in this session skirt around the central lesson of the Asian crisis: that banks still matter, enormously. In the United States, the capital markets dominate the credit markets, and only twenty-two percent of the indebtedness of American enterprise is to banks. In Asia, eighty percent or more of the indebtedness of enterprise is to the banks. The United States suffered a recession when banks were afraid to lend in 1990–91; for Asia, the disabling of the banks means the dismantling of the economy.

The IMF Capital Markets report (Adams, Mathieson, Schinasi and Chadha, 1998, p. 79) argues that one of the weaknesses of the Asian economies was "excessive reliance on banks as the primary source of financial intermediation." But it is difficult for a developing country to create financial markets that replace its banks as a primary source of financing, especially in an era of regulatory liberalization, when banks are both traders and the objects of trading. Neither Japan nor Germany has yet managed to make this work. In the United States, though the stocks of a few large financial corporations that owned banks were listed in the 1920s, bank stocks per se were not traded to a significant degree until the 1960s; until the 1930s, indeed, bank shares carried a liability for the remaining fifty percent of paid-in capital if anything awful happened to the bank.

It is all very well to talk about transparency, but the fact is that banks even in industrialized countries are blind pools of assets, and the certainty that those assets are sufficient to cover the liabilities is certified by the regulatory authorities under cover of bank secrecy. The world has changed in America because suppliers of funds to banks now feel, correctly or otherwise, that they have enough information to make their own judgment on the condition of the asset portfolio. So the need for the supervisors to certify that the bank can meet its obligations becomes an invitation, usually accepted, to moral hazard. In their hearts—and indeed in their heads, if not the mouthpart—banking supervisors agree with Lowell Bryan that "market discipline by depositors is another name for bank panics." (Bryan, 1991, p. 225) On Monday we advocate transparency; on Tuesday we speak of bilateral netting of derivatives and we fight against mark-to-market. When I hear a bank supervisor talk about transparency, I fear, I think of John Randolph's comment about a Senate colleague that the word honor in the mouth of Daniel Webster was like the word love in the mouth of a whore.

Moreover, if you can look through the mirror instead of into it, the question is not one of too-big-to-fail. LTCM is classic too-big-to-fail, moral hazard American style (the fear being not of a market collapse from liquidation, but of exposure of sloppy practice both by the banks and by their supervisor, which would *really* spook the markets). What happened in the South Korea, by contrast, is an expression of unavoidable if implicit claims on the taxpayer by creditors of failed banks chartered, regulated and supervised by the government that represents that taxpayer. Few economies can withstand the shock of a disruption to the payments system, and the money supply of the country is, after all, created mostly by the banks. To quote Andrew Sheng, "[A] central problem in the global banking system is that, irrespective of public or private ownership of banks, commercial bank losses in excess of capital have become de facto quasi-fiscal deficits." (Sheng, 1996, p. 9) Then, if the bubble bursts, the capacity of the government and the central bank to direct lending by their banks is largely lost, because taxpayers recognize that additional loans are on their marker, and they don't like it. Viz, not only Japan, but our own S&L crisis. I think Mr. Fons is right that a perception of transparency (mayhap, we should say "honesty") leads to cheaper funding—but only when the truth is more encouraging than previously believed.

The genie of market pricing cannot be put back in the bottle, and it probably must be given more wishes to execute. And markets do demand transparency; indeed, it is the clash of tectonic plates between the information systems of the markets and the information systems of banking that makes the earthquake. In a world where people don't believe central banks, and have reason not to believe central banks, commercial banks must be much more heavily capitalized: if the market demands twelve percent to fifteen percent from GE Capital in America, banks operating in less developed countries, multinational or local, must show *at least* that much. The cost to the borrower of reduced leverage in the lender should be less than the savings from the bank's ability to fund itself at lower risk premia. (Though it is important right now to see the cognitive dissonance of appeals for the private sector to return to lending to developing and transition economies, while accepting in advance that haircuts to its positions and "precommitments" will be taken even in well-structured loans if the country involved gets in trouble.)

Moreover, as the reaction to the failure of Long Term Capital Management has shown, neither LDC banks nor multinational Western banks can afford to carry contingent liabilities of the size implied by "total return" swaps, long-dated currency options and other leveraged bespoke derivative contracts. The fact that the banking industry has sold its customers, its regulators and its academicians on the proposition that custom-made derivatives are risk-reducing does not mean that the proposition is true. Tony Terraciano asked me a few years ago why I thought banks stepped on a rake every few years, and I had to say I didn't know the answer, and Alan Greenspan has now said that he doesn't know the answer either. But turning over risk management to people who step on rakes is not good governance.

Because I think the banking system is the key, I agree that disaster forecasting is most likely to be accurate if it emphasizes too-rapid growth of bank assets, as in Calomiris and to a lesser degree in Kaminsky. Assuming that the banks are made to recognize bad loans, growth in scheduled assets, to use an old-fashioned phrase, should be an excellent predictor of trouble—currency trouble, too, because the issuance of bank liabilities to fund non-performing assets is the functional equivalent of printing money. That, it seems to me, is the real reason to demand good supervision: the good supervisor prevents evergreening and forces banks to admit that loans have gone sour. What reduces risk premia below the danger level is the willingness to roll over and even increase the loans of companies that are not earning their debt service—what Hy Minsky called Ponzi finance. This gives a record of greatly reduced loan losses, which was one of the things the Fed kept citing in its goldilocks economy evaluations, and permits lending officers to shave terms and conditions.

Understanding the disaster in Asia begins, it seems to me, with the realization that there were real losses to be allocated, and no system for allocating them. Everybody plays *sauve que peut*, and the banks have more *peut*, especially the foreign banks, so the market takes the worst hit. Because there is no system for protecting bondholders (let alone stockholders, who are of course residual claimants), and because derivative instruments link debt paper in different countries, both psychology and mathematics become vectors of contagion. The newly issued UNCTAD Trade and Development Report for 1998 contains a very intelligent summary of what happened in the Asian countries after confidence fled, but it is flawed by the hopeful assumption that if only everybody could have held on a little longer, the values represented by the paper would have risen enough to make all the lenders whole. This was not true; indeed, the banking systems in all three countries where the IMF intervened were so seriously undercapitalized that compound interest was working against them.

I have suggested that one prophylactic against the return of these conditions is the separation of the lending function from the payments system function, which will permit central banks to get out of the business of guaranteeing the par value of deposit liabilities. (Mayer, 1998, p. 34) But we need time for that. Time will be needed also for the creation of a viable standstill process. In the interim, the two most useful steps would be increasing the capital requirements for banks engaged in international lending *or borrowing* and a change in the law to treat cash-settled OTC derivative contracts as the gaming instruments they usually are, making them unenforceable in American courts.

References

Adams, Charles, Donald J. Mathieson, Garry Schinasi and Bankim Chadha. 1998, *International Capital Markets.* International Monetary Fund.

Bryan, Lowell. 1991, *Bankrupt*, New York: Harper/Collins Books.

Martin, Mayer. 1998, *The Asian Disease,* Levy Institute, Bard College.

Sheng, Andrew. 1996, *Bank Restructuring,* Washington: World Bank.

Chapter 30

The Signals Approach to Early Warning of Currency Crisis: Does It Work and Is There a Better Way?

Andrew Berg and Catherine Pattillo
International Monetary Fund

Abstract: In recent years, a number of researchers have claimed success in systematically predicting which countries are more likely to suffer currency crises, most notably Kaminsky, Lizondo, and Reinhart (1998) and its extension in Kaminsky (1998). In this note, we assess the success of this approach, emphasizing out-of-sample testing. First, we try to answer the question: If we had been using the KLR model in late 1996, how well armed would we have been to predict the Asia crisis? Second, we analyze a more general probit-based model for predicting currency crises. In the process, we test several basic assumptions underlying the signals approach.

1. INTRODUCTION

In recent years, a number of researchers have claimed success in systematically predicting which countries are more likely to suffer currency crises. Perhaps the most prominent model for predicting currency crises is the signals approach of Kaminsky, Lizondo, and Reinhart (1998) (hereafter KLR), who monitor a large set of monthly indicators that signal a crisis whenever they cross a certain threshold.

Most recent claims of success in predicting crises have focussed on in-sample prediction, that is on formulating and estimating a model using data on a set of crises, then judging success by the plausibility of the estimated parameters and the size of the prediction errors for this set of crises. The key test is not, however, the ability to fit a set of observations after the fact, but the prediction of future crises.

Kaminsky (1998) is an important paper for at least two reasons. First, she makes substantial methodological advances compared to KLR in aggregating information from the various indicators into a composite estimate of probability of crisis. Second, she applies this approach to the 1997 crises in an out-of-sample fashion, that is using pre-1997 data to estimate the model. However, while she presents out-of-sample estimates of the probability of currency crisis, she does not provide tests of whether these forecasts are better than, for example, guesswork.

In this note, we assess the success of the KLR approach and its extension in Kaminsky (1998), emphasizing out-of-sample testing.[1] First, we address the question: If we had been using the KLR model in late 1996, how well armed would we have been to predict the Asia crisis? Second, we estimate a set of alternative models (BP probit-based models) using the data and crisis definition of the KLR method but with a different approach to generating crisis probabilities from the data. In the process, we test several basic assumptions underlying the signals approach. These BP models did not exist prior to the crises they attempt to predict and to that extent do not generate pure out-of-sample forecasts. However, the methodological innovations were not inspired by events in 1997, nor did we use success or failure in predicting 1997 outcomes to aid in the specification of the alternative models.

2. PREDICTING 1997 WITH THE ORIGINAL KLR MODEL

We can, following Kaminsky (1998), calculate the weighted-sum-based probabilities of crisis.[2] This produces a series of estimated probabilities of crisis for each country.[3] How good are these forecasts? Kaminsky (1998) concentrates on plots of these probabilities against actual crisis dates. Clearly, some crises are called and some are missed, but beyond that it is difficult to draw conclusions from these figures.[4] More generally, one of the challenges in assessing the predictive success of the model is that the estimated probability of crisis cannot be compared with the unobservable actual probability of crisis, but only with the occurrence or not of a crisis. For zero/one dependent variables, it is natural to ask what fraction of the observations are "correctly called." First, a cut-off level for the predicted probability of crisis is defined such that a crisis is predicted if the predicted probability is above this threshold. An observation is then correctly called if either (i) the predicted probability of crisis is above the threshold (an alarm is issued) and a crisis in fact follows within twenty-four months, or (ii) the probability of crisis is below the threshold and no crisis in fact ensues. A false alarm occurs when the estimated probability is above the threshold and there is no crisis within twenty-four months. Such "goodness-of-fit" data are shown in the first two columns of Table 1 for two cutoffs: fifty percent and twenty-five percent.

What can we conclude? A natural question is whether the estimated probability of crisis is above fifty percent prior to actual crises. The goodness-of-fit rows show that only four percent of the time was the predicted probability of crisis above fifty percent in cases when there was a crisis within the next twenty-four months, during the 1995:5 to 1997:12 period.[5]

If we are more interested in predicting crises than predicting tranquil periods and are not so worried about calling too many crises, we may want to consider an alarm to be issued when the estimated probability of crisis is above a lower cutoff. Table 1 shows that the Kaminsky (1998) probability estimates are above twenty-five percent in twenty-five percent of the precrisis observations. Even with only one quarter of the crisis observations correctly called, sixty-three percent of alarms are false, in that no crisis in fact ensues within twenty-four months. We also generate weighted-sum based probabilities drawing on the fifteen KLR variables augmented with two additional variables, the level of M2 to reserves and the ratio of the current account to GDP.[6] The addition of these variables improves out-of-sample performance slightly, as shown in the second column. In particular, thirty-two percent of the precrisis observations are called correctly. Most alarms, however, are still false.

This may sound like poor performance. It is worth noting, though, that these forecasts are significantly better than random guesses, both economically and statistically. The forecasts from the augmented KLR model in column (2), for example, suggest that the probability of a crisis within twenty-four months conditional on an alarm (using the twenty-five percent cut-off) is forty percent, which is somewhat higher than the unconditional probability of twenty-seven percent. A Pesaran-Timmermann test rejects, at the one percent level of significance, the hypothesis that the forecasts are no better than guesses based on the unconditional probability of crisis in the sample.

So far we have examined the ability of the models to predict the approximate *timing* of crises for each country. We can also evaluate the

Table 1 Comparing Predictive Power of Alternative Composite Indicators—Out-of-Sample

	KLR-Based Weighted-Sum Probabilities		Alternative Probit Models		
	Original Specification	Augmented with Current Account And level of M2/reserves	Indicator	Linear	Piecewise linear
Accuracy and Calibration Scores:					
Quadratic Probability Score	0.402	0.398	0.325	0.281	0.299
Log Probability Score	0.606	0.596	0.501	0.433	0.452
Global Squared Bias	0.01774	0.01946	0.02987	0.00581	0.01256
Goodness-of-Fit: (cut-off probability of 50 percent)					
Percent of observations correctly called	74	73	78	78	78
Percent of pre-crisis periods correctly called[1]	4	0	2	0	5
Percent of tranquil periods correctly called[2]	100	100	99	100	98
False alarms as percent of total alarms[3]	17	no crisis called	50	no crisis called	56
Goodness-of-Fit: (cut-off probability of 25 percent)					
Percent of observations correctly called	69	69	76	79	76
Percent of pre-crisis periods correctly called[1]	25	32	16	80	48
Percent of tranquil periods correctly called[2]	85	83	93	79	84
False alarms as percent of total alarms[3]	63	60	61	49	54

[1]A pre-crisis period of correctly called when the estimated probability of crisis is above the cut-off probability and a crisis ensues within 24 months.

[2]A tranquil period is correctly called when the estimated probability of crisis is below the cut-off probability and no crisis ensues within 24 months.

[3]A false alarm is an observation with an estimated probability of crisis above the cut-off (an alarm) not followed by a crisis ensues within 24 months.

Table 2 Correlation of Actual and Predicted Rankings based on KLR Approach

	Actual		KLR Weighted-Sum of Indicators[2]			
	Crisis Index[1]	Rank	Original Specification		Augmented[3]	
Country			Probability	Rank	Probability	Rank
Thailand	10.19	1	12.42	16	20.31	7
Korea	9.52	2	25.27	4	22.76	5
Indonesia	4.48	3	11.18	18	15.77	11
Malaysia	4.42	4	17.27	8	14.58	13
Zimbabwe	4.40	5	32.25	3	25.95	3
Taiwan Province of China	3.37	6	22.69	5	23.92	4
Colombia	3.01	7	16.91	9	15.46	12
Philippines	2.68	8	40.58	1	34.52	1
Brazil	0.82	9	36.67	2	32.08	2
Turkey	0.65	10	17.37	7	15.91	10
Venezuela	0.62	11	14.49	14	14.89	16
Pakistan	0.57	12	15.49	10	16.56	9
South Africa	0.52	13	21.78	6	18.98	8
Jordan	0.45	14	14.08	15	13.83	18
India	0.39	15	10.77	20	10.12	21
Sri Lanka	0.36	16	12.01	17	11.51	19
Chile	0.24	17	11.18	18	10.58	20
Bolivia	0.18	18	10.77	20	10.12	21
Argentina	0.15	19	14.82	12	13.84	17
Mexico	0.15	20	14.49	13	14.30	14
Peru	0.12	21	14.90	11	20.41	6
Uruguay	-0.02	22	10.77	20	10.12	21
Israel	-0.11	23	10.77	20	14.27	15
Correlation[5]				0.543		0.600
P-value				0.007		0.003
R^2				0.284		0.359

Table 2 Correlation of Actual and Predicted Rankings based on KLR Approach (con't.)

	BP Probit Models[4]					
	Indicator		Linear		Piecewise Linear	
Country	Probability	Rank	Probability	Rank	Probability	Rank
Thailand	0.20	4	0.38	2	0.25	6
Korea	0.28	3	0.26	9	0.31	4
Indonesia	0.15	8	0.26	8	0.24	7
Malaysia	0.20	5	0.38	1	0.32	3
Zimbabwe						
Taiwan Province of China	0.19	6	0.30	5	0.19	12
Colombia	0.17	7	0.36	4	0.35	2
Philippines	0.29	2	0.22	12	0.21	10
Brazil	0.38	1	0.25	10	0.46	1
Turkey	0.10	13	0.14	18	0.16	13
Venezuela	0.10	13	0.09	20	0.08	20
Pakistan	0.14	11	0.28	6	0.24	9
South Africa	0.12	12	0.23	11	0.21	11
Jordan	0.10	13	0.21	13	0.15	15
India	0.10	13	0.14	19	0.15	14
Sri Lanka	0.10	13	0.19	14	0.14	16
Chile	0.10	13	0.18	15	0.12	17
Bolivia	0.10	13	0.07	21	0.05	22
Argentina	0.10	13	0.15	17	0.10	19
Mexico	0.10	13	0.06	22	0.05	21
Peru	0.14	10	0.27	7	0.24	8
Uruguay	0.10	13	0.18	16	0.11	18
Israel	0.15	9	0.37	3	0.29	5
Correlation[5]		0.666		0.474		0.566
P-value		0.001		0.026		0.006
R^2		0.475		0.233		0.327

[1]The KLR crisis index (a weighted average of percentage changes in the exchange rate and reserves) is standardized by subtracting the mean and dividing by the standard deviation. Values above three are defined as a crisis and are shown in bold.

[2]Based on average of noise-to-signal weighted probabilities from during 1996:I-12, using out-of-sample estimates.

[3]Augmented with the inclusion of the current account and M2/reserves in levels.

[4]All probit models probabilities are average predicted probabilities for 1996:I-12, where model was estimated up to 1995:4.

[5]Spearman Rank Correlation of the fitted values and the actual crisis index and its p-value. The R2 is from a regressio of fitted values on actual values.

cross-sectional success of the models' predictions in identifying which countries are vulnerable in a period of global financial turmoil such as 1997. The question here is whether the models assign higher predicted probabilities of crisis to those countries that had the biggest crises. Forecasting performance can be evaluated in this manner by comparing rankings of countries based on the predicted and actual crisis indices. Table 2 shows countries' actual crisis index and predicted probability of crisis in 1997 for the various different forecasting methods.[7] The table also shows the Spearman correlation between the actual and predicted rankings and its associated p-value, as well as the R^2 from a bivariate regression of the actual rankings on the predictions.

The KLR-based forecasts are clearly somewhat successful at ranking countries by severity of crisis. The actual rankings of countries in 1997 by their crisis index are significantly correlated with forecasts from the weighted-sum of indicators-based probabilities. With the original KLR variables, twenty-eight percent of the variance is explained. The addition of the current account and the level of M2/reserves brings the R^2 up to thirty-six percent.

In sum, the KLR approach shows some promise. In particular, the fitted probabilities from the weighted-sum of indicators are significant predictors of crisis probability in 1997. This suggests the model may be useful in identifying which countries are vulnerable in a period following a global financial shock. Still, the overall explanatory power is fairly low. In addition, the overall goodness-of-fit for the out-of-sample predictions illustrate the low predictive power of the weighted-sum-based probabilities in predicting the timing of crisis. Although the model does significantly better than guesses based on the unconditional probability of crisis, most crisis are still missed and most alarms are false.

3. A PROBIT-BASED ALTERNATIVE MODEL

3.1 Methodology

In this section, we depart from the entire "signals" methodology that looks for discrete thresholds and calculates noise-to-signal ratios. Instead, we apply a probit regression technique to the same data and crisis definition as in KLR. In the process we test some of the basic assumptions of the KLR approach. Specifically, we embed the KLR approach in a multivariate probit framework in which the independent variable takes a value of one if there is a crisis in the subsequent twenty-four months and zero otherwise. This has three advantages: we can test the usefulness of the threshold concept; we can aggregate predictive variables more satisfactorily into a composite index, taking account of correlations among different variables; and we can easily test for the statistical significance of individual variables and the constancy of coefficients across time and countries.

KLR assume that the probability of crisis in the subsequent twenty-four months is a step function of the value of the indicator, equal to zero when the indicator variable is below the threshold and one at or above the threshold. They assume, for example, that when the real exchange rate continues to appreciate after it is already above the threshold, this does not increase the probability of crisis. In general, the relationship between a given indicator variable and the probability of crisis could take many more forms than a simple step function. Figure 1 presents various possible relationships between the probability of crisis (on the vertical axis) and the value of a variable *P*, measured as in KLR in percentiles (on the horizontal axis).[8] The KLR assumption, in terms of Figure 1, is that α_1 and α_3 are zero while α_2 is equal to 1. Other possibilities are also plausible. For example if α_1 is non-zero and equal to α_3, while α_2 is equal to zero, then there is a linear relationship between the indicator measured in percentiles and the probability of a crisis. That is, to continue the example, increases in the degree of overvaluation increase the risk no matter how overvalued the exchange rate already is.

We propose to let the data resolve the question of whether a step-function is in fact a reasonable description of the relationship between indicator

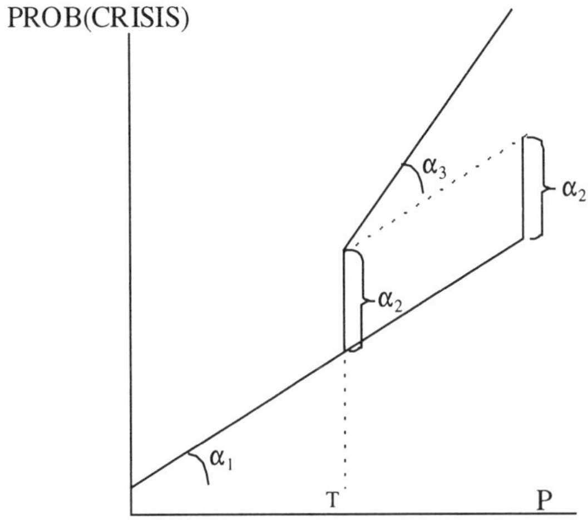

Figure 1. Relationship Between Predictive Variable and Probability of Crisis

variables and the probability of a crisis. To this end, we run bivariate probit regressions on the pooled panel in which the dependent variable is the KLR variable that takes a value of one if there is a crisis in the subsequent twenty-four months and zero otherwise. For each indicator we estimate equations of the form:

$$\text{prob}(c24 = 1) = f(\alpha_0 + \alpha_1 p(x) + \alpha_2 I + \alpha_3 I(p(x) - T)), \qquad (1)$$

where c24 = 1 if there is a crisis in the next twenty-four months, p(x) = the percentile of the variable x, and I = 1 if the percentile is above some threshold T and zero otherwise. Thus, α_1, α_2, and α_3 in equation 1 correspond to the α's in Figure 1. We use the thresholds T calculated from the KLR algorithm, since we are interested primarily in testing their approach against a more general alternative.[9]

Figure 2 graphs these estimates for three important predictive variables: deviations of the real exchange rate (RER) from trend, the current account deficit as a share of GDP, and the growth rate of the ration of M2/reserves. Consider, for example, the RER. The first panel of Figure 2 gives a richer view of the relationship between overvaluation and the probability of crisis. The choppy line in this figure presents the fraction of times the observation of a given percentile for RER deviations is followed within twenty-four

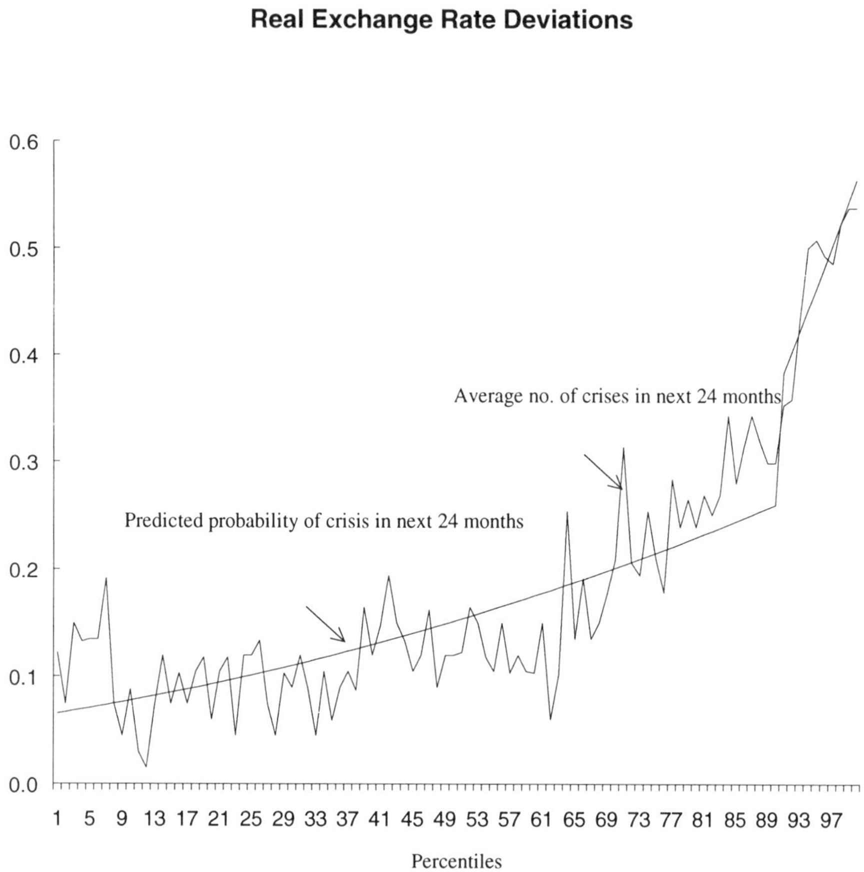

Figure 2. Average No. of Crises in Next 24 Months by Percentile of Variable

Current Account as Percent of GDP

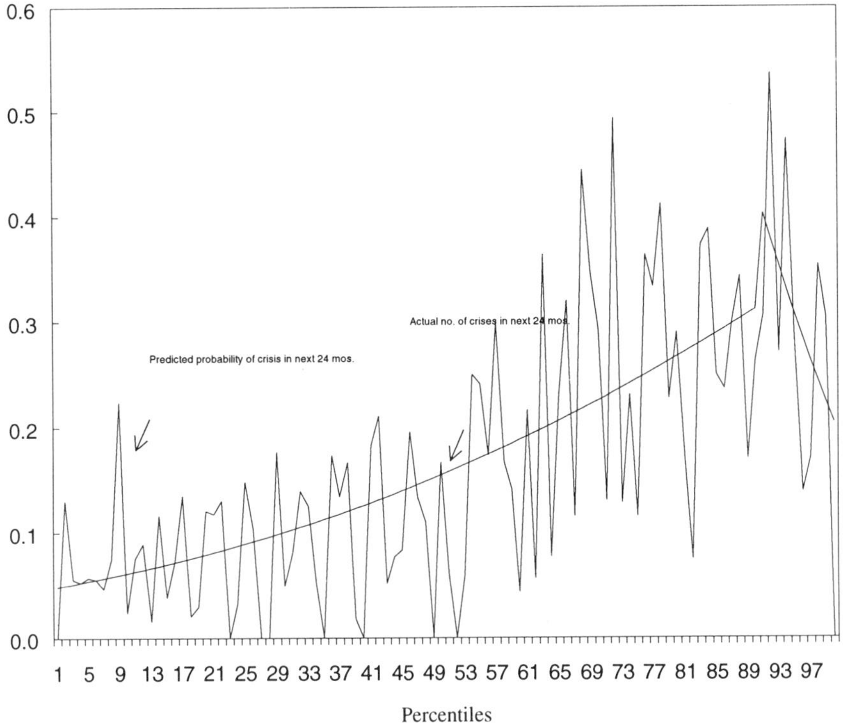

M2/Reserves Growth Rate

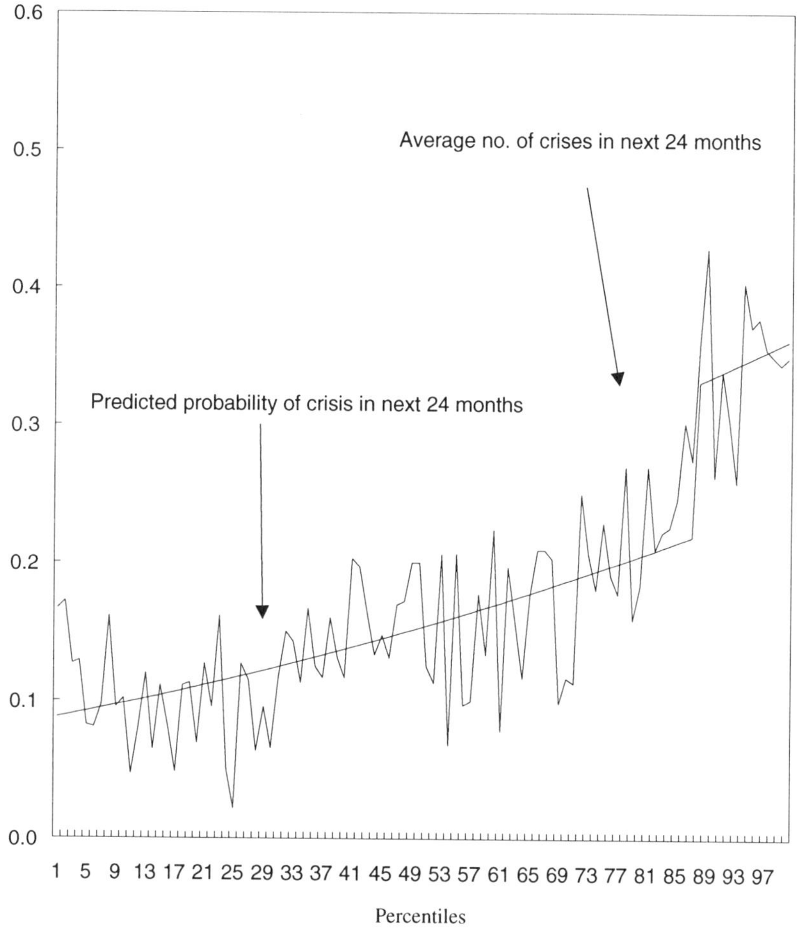

months by a crisis in the pooled data. The other line represents the estimated relationship discussed above. The message of this figure is that while the jump at the threshold is significant, it does not capture an important part of the variation in the probability of crisis as a function of RER deviations.

Although the outcome of this analysis varies somewhat across indicators, the general lesson is that although the jump in probability of crisis at the threshold is often statistically significant, the underlying percentile variable is usually also important in explaining the variation in crisis probability.

Multivariate probits are the natural extension to the bivariate probits discussed so far. We have estimated three types of probit models that explain whether a crisis occurs in the next twenty-four months (hereafter designated BP models). Model 1 uses the indicator form of the variables, where the indicator equals 1 above the threshold and zero otherwise. In Model 2 the variables enter linearly, expressed as percentiles of the country-specific distribution of observations. Model 3 is the result of a simplification starting with the most general piecewise-linear specification for all the variables. From a starting point that allowed the estimation, for each variable, of the slope below the threshold, the jump at the threshold, and the slope above the threshold, we used a general-to-specific procedure to simplify to the most parsimonious representation of the data.

The results show that in Model 1 the probability of crisis is increased when the following variables exceed their thresholds: RER deviations, the current account, reserve growth, export growth, and both the level and growth rate of M2/Reserves. These variables also increase the probability of crisis when entered linearly in Model 2, except for the growth rate of M2/reserves, while reserve growth itself is now significant. In the simplified piecewise-linear Model 3, two variables (RER deviations and current account) enter with a significant slope below the threshold, a jump at the threshold, and a steeper slope above the threshold; two variables enter linearly (reserve and export growth); and for two variables (M2/reserves and M2/reserve growth) only the jump at the threshold is significant.

3.2 Predicting 1997 with the BP Models

To test the various probit models out-of-sample, we use data through 1995:4 to estimate the regression coefficients, then extend the explanatory variables to generate predictions for the period 1995:5–1997:12. The estimated probabilities can be evaluated using the probability scores and goodness-of-fit measures discussed above.

Table 1 shows that on all the scoring measures,[10] the probits perform better than the probabilities based on the weighted-sum of indicators signaling. The linear model has the best scores, though the piecewise-linear model is close behind. Using the standard whereby a probability of crisis above twenty-five percent is considered an alarm, the linear and piecewise-linear probits perform well, much better than the weighted-sum based probabilities. The linear probit generates a probability of crisis above twenty-five percent in eighty percent of the periods that precede a crisis. Reflecting their greater prediction success, the probit models have a lower share of false alarms (crisis calls not followed by a crisis as a share of total crisis calls), as low as forty-nine percent for the linear model. Putting it slightly differently, for this model the probability of crisis within twenty-four months conditional on an alarm (using the twenty-five percent cutoff) is fifty-one percent, much higher than the unconditional probability of twenty-two percent.[11]

The linear model performs much better out-of-sample than the more general piecewise-linear model that includes a role for discrete jumps in the risk of crisis at the KLR thresholds. This suggests that the threshold and indicator concept add little to the explanatory power of the simple linear model in predicting crisis timing, at least for 1997. The worse out-of-sample performance of the indicator and piecewise-linear models (and similar or better in-sample performance) is consistent with the greater risk of data-mining in the indicator and piecewise-linear approaches.

As with the KLR models, we can also evaluate the performance of the probit models in predicting the cross-country incidence of crisis in 1997. Table 2 shows that country rankings based on all the probit forecasts are significantly correlated with actual crisis rankings in 1997. Forecasts based on the indicator probit rank countries more accurately than the weighted-sum of indicators-based forecasts, with an R^2 close to one half. This superior performance is consistent with previous results that the KLR weighted-sum-of-indicators forecasts are outperformed by the analogous probit model. Somewhat anomalously, the other two probit models perform worse than the indicator probit. In particular, the ranking based on the linear model that had the best goodness-of-fit has the lowest, though still significant, correlation with the actual ranking.[12]

4. CONCLUSION

This paper has examined the extent to which the KLR signals model, originally formulated and estimated prior to 1997, would have helped predict the 1997 currency crises. The KLR-based probabilities of crisis perform fairly well out-of-sample. When this model issued an alarm (predicted probability above twenty-five percent) during the 1995:5 to 1996:12 period, a crisis would actually have followed in 1997 thirty-seven percent of the time. This compares to a twenty-seven percent unconditional probability of crisis in 1997. Moreover, its forecasted cross-country ranking of severity of crisis is a significant predictor of the actual ranking, with an R^2 of twenty-eight percent. The addition of two variables to the KLR model, the level of the current account and M2/reserves, improves performance somewhat.

We have also compared the predictions of this model with a probit-based alternative, which we dub the BP model. The KLR forecasts perform better than some of the probits on a few of the measures, so this comparison is not unambiguous. Overall, though, the BP probit models provide generally better forecasts than the KLR models. Moreover, in contrasting the BP probit methodology with the KLR probabilities, the most direct comparison involves the indicator probit, as it also uses indicator predictive variables. Here in particular the probit generally outperforms. We also examine other probit specifications that do not embody the KLR indicators assumption and find that, while the results are not unambiguous, the linear model is the most successful.[13]

The testing performed here may give insight into the nature and causes of these crises independent of the value of the models as predictors.

- Both models make significant out-of-sample predictions despite the omission of some heavily emphasized phenomena such as poor banking supervision and weak corporate governance.
- The alternative method reproduces most of the KLR conclusions regarding which variables are important predictors of crisis. In particular, both approaches demonstrate that the probability of a currency crisis increases when the bilateral real exchange rate is overvalued relative to trend, reserve growth and export growth are low, and the growth of M2/reserves is high. Our analysis suggests, in addition to KLR, that a large current account deficit and a high ratio of M2 to reserves are important risk factors.

The out-of-sample comparison of different approaches provides some insight into important issues in the empirical modeling of currency crises. Most importantly, the data do not clearly support one of the basic ideas of the KLR indicator approach: that it is useful to interpret predictive variables in terms of discrete thresholds, the crossing of which is particularly significant for signaling a crisis. Both direct statistical tests and the generally superior performance of the BP linear model suggest that a better simple assumption is that the probability of crisis goes up linearly with changes in the predictive variables. There is, however, some evidence for nonlinearities of the sort assumed in KLR.

Notes

[1]For ease of exposition, in this note we refer to both Kaminsky, Lizondo, and Reinhart (1998) and Kaminsky (1998) as the KLR approach.

[2]The probabilities are based on a weighted average of the indicators with the weights based on the noise-to-signal ratios of each indicator. Note that in assessing the usefulness of individual indicators in predicting crises, our results are broadly similar to KLR both when we replicate their sample and for a modified sample (omitting the five European countries and adding other emerging market economies). The discussion in this note is based on a twenty-three country sample comprised Argentina, Bolivia, Brazil, Chile, Colombia, Indonesia, Israel, Jordan, Malaysia, Mexico, Pakistan, Peru, Philippines, South Africa, Sri Lanka, Taiwan, Thailand, Turkey, Uruguay, Venezuela, and Zimbabwe.

[3]We use data through 1995:4 to estimate the weighted-sum based composite indices, then extend the explanatory variables to generate out-of-sample crisis probabilities for the 1995:5-1997:12 period. Unlike Kaminsky (1998), we use only the good indicators, i.e., those with noise-to-signal ratio less than one.

[4]Kaminsky (1998) also reports various scores measuring the overall size of the errors, analogous to the mean-squared error measure (not specifically reported for the out-of-sample forecasts, however). These are more helpful for comparing different models than for assessing how well a given model works in an absolute sense.

[5]At the time of collection (April 1998), data were not available for December 1997 for all countries. More recent analysis has confirmed that the results reported here both for the KLR and BP models are not significantly affected by the addition of complete data for 1997 (some partial exceptions are noted below).

[6]Both are highly informative indicators, with noise-to-signal ratios less than one.

[7]The predicted crisis probability is the average of the probabilities during 1996:1–12, using the out-of-sample estimates. Averaging over for example 1996:1 to 1996:6 gives

somewhat different results. The actual crisis index used to rank the countries for 1997 is the maximum value of the monthly crisis index for each country during 1997.

[8]*P* is measured in percentiles in that the observations on the underlying predictive variable for a given country, for example twelve-month percent changes in real domestic credit, are expressed in terms of percentiles of the distribution of that variable for the country in question.

[9]This procedure is biased in favor of finding significant jump coefficients. Since we use the data itself to identify the biggest jump (through the KLR method), the subsequent tests will tend to find that the jumps we have found are unusually large. The tests we perform thus overestimate the statistical significance of the jump coefficient α_2.

[10]Probability forecasts can also be evaluated with accuracy and calibration scores that are analogs of a mean-squared error measure. Lower numbers indicate better performance. See Kaminsky (1998) and Berg and Pattillo (1998) for more discussion.

[11]These predictions are also statistically significantly better than guesses based on the unconditional probability at the one percent level.

[12]The contrast between the results of the rankings and goodness-of-fit comparisons is somewhat surprising but not inexplicable. The two measures are somewhat different and they need not correspond. The goodness-of-fit measure examines only whether crisis calls are correct or not and ignores the size of errors. The rankings comparison considers whether the highest probabilities of crisis are associated with the *largest* crises; the magnitude of the crisis, however, as distinct from whether or not there is a crisis, is not a factor in any of the models. These results are sensitive to the exact sample of countries involved in the ranking comparison. For example, eliminating Israel (one of the largest outliers) from the sample increases the R^2 of the rankings predictions of the percentile probit model from twenty-three to forty-two percent. The addition of December 1997 data (not available as of April 1998 when the data for these results were collected) reverses the order of the ranking correlations, with the linear BP model performing somewhat better than KLR.

[13]Performance of both the BP and KLR models is somewhat better in-sample than out-of-sample. In terms of relative performance of the different models, the conclusions drawn from the out-of-sample experience remain, except that the piecewise-linear probit model tends to perform somewhat better than the others in-sample. This result is not surprising given that it is a generalization of the other probit models. Its relatively greater degradation in out-of-sample performance is also not surprising in light of the greater risk of overfitting inherent in the more general specification.

References

Berg, Andrew, and Catherine Pattillo. 1998, "Are Currency Crises Predictable? A Test," IMF, working paper, No. 98/154.

Kaminsky, Graciela. 1989, "Currency and Banking Crises: A Composite Leading Indicator," George Washington University, unpublished, September.

Kaminsky, Graciela, and M. Carmen. 1996, "The Twin Crises: The Causes of Banking and Balance-of-Payments Problems," Board of the Governors of the Federal Reserve System, International Finance, discussion paper, No. 544 March.

Kaminsky, Graciela, Lizondo, and Carmen Reinhart. 1998, "Leading Indicators of Currency Crises," *Staff Papers,* Washington: International Monetary Fund, Vol. 45, March, pp. 1–48.

Pesaran, M. H., and A. Timmermann. 1992, "A Simple Nonparametric Test of Predictive Performance," *Journal of Business and Economic Statistics*, Vol. 10, pp. 461–465.

Chapter 31

Will Greater Disclosure and Transparency Prevent the Next Banking Crisis?

Eric Rosengren
Federal Reserve Bank of Boston

Abstract: Greater transparency and disclosure of the bank activities will not prevent future banking crises unless appropriate monetary, fiscal, and regulatory policies are also adopted. Nonetheless, greater disclosure of banking problems can reduce the costs of banking crises, even if transparency is not a panacea for preventing banking crises.

Countries around the world have been experiencing serious banking problems, often resulting in slower economic growth and large taxpayer bailouts (Caprio and Klingebiel 1996, 1997). The most recent string of banking problems is occurring in Asia, where troubled banks are compounding difficulties from exchange rate crises (Kaminsky and Reinhart 1998; Kaminsky 1999). The Asian banking problems have been complicated by the lack of transparency and disclosure in the banking system, making it difficult to gauge the severity of the situation or propose timely solutions (Goldstein 1998, 1999). As a result, a common policy recommendation by the International Monetary Fund, the World Bank, the U.S. Treasury, and leading academics has been to adopt greater transparency and disclosure in the banking system.

Few would deny that a more open and transparent banking system would have moderated current problems in Asia and improved the chances of a more rapid resolution, but the benefits of transparency should not be oversold. Transparency can ameliorate problems but it cannot prevent them. So long as banks continue to be intermediaries that transform assets by taking short-term demand deposits and investing in longer-term loans, they will be susceptible to large macroeconomic fluctuations. Intermediation serves a highly useful role in linking savings and investment, and the solution is not to prevent banks from playing this role. Rather, the solution to these problems requires measures that extend well beyond improving the financial information disseminated by financial intermediaries, since the failure of a banking system, as opposed to the failure of a few banks, reflects more serious macroeconomic problems.

The next section will briefly discuss what is meant by greater transparency in the context of banking operations. The second section will discuss why transparency is likely to reduce the costs of bank failures but not to prevent them. The third section will provide some recent evidence on the benefits of transparency, and the final section will provide some conclusions.

1. DEFINING TRANSPARENCY

While "transparency" is often discussed, only rarely is it clearly defined. This is unfortunate, because an accounting and management information system cannot be isolated from the purposes the information is to serve. By carefully examining what is meant by a transparent banking system, the paper by Jerry Fons (1999) makes a substantial contribution. Its primary focus is an examination of the association between countries with a pattern of corruption and countries with particularly opaque banking systems. Fons finds that countries where corruption is endemic are also countries with little transparency in their banking systems. A troubling implication, if this were to be viewed causally, would be that transparent banking systems could not be achieved until the pattern of corruption was broken. Such societal changes would likely be quite difficult to implement.

The association between banking transparency and corruption is useful in understanding why transparency is often difficult to achieve, but transparency requires more than a society with a willingness to obey rules. Many Northern European countries are viewed as having very little corruption; nonetheless, their banking systems are far from transparent. For example, the exposure of many of these banking systems to problem loans in emerging markets is impossible to deduce with current levels of disclosure. This is because disclosure and market discipline have not been the foundation of bank regulation in these countries.

A low level of corruption is also not a sufficient condition for avoiding banking crises. The Scandinavian countries appear to have among the lowest levels of corruption. Nonetheless, banking systems in several Scandinavian countries experienced widespread failures at the beginning of this decade. Thus, while many corrupt countries have poor transparency in banking, a low level of corruption is not sufficient for achieving a transparent banking system or avoiding serious banking problems.

Rather than defining transparency by association, I would prefer to define banking transparency by the information I would want available: in particular, three types of information critical to evaluating the financial condition of banks. First, are loans that fail to make payment of principal and interest classified and disclosed as nonperforming loans? Many countries in Asia did not disclose nonperforming loans, or used such restrictive definitions as to render the disclosure meaningless. Nonperforming loans should include "evergreened" loans, loans transferred to subsidiaries or affiliates, and direct and indirect loan exposures to failing companies.

Second, does reported capital closely reflect economic capital? Not only is this frequently not the case, but Japan, in the midst of a banking crisis, has chosen to move further from this standard. Japanese accounting rules have been changed to allow equity holdings to reflect book rather than market values; the netting of assets and liabilities to reduce the level of risky assets; bank management discretion in evaluating the value of real property; and capital infusions by the government. Such accounting gimmickry greatly reduces the value of international capital adequacy guidelines.

Third, can bank risks and strategies be determined from publicly available information? While most Asian countries fail to meet this criterion, so do most accounting systems in the developed world. Country exposures, industry exposures, hedge fund exposures, derivatives exposures, all are examples of information that would be useful in evaluating the financial condition of a bank but is rarely fully disclosed. In reality, few banks provide sufficient data for an outside monitor to be able to evaluate worst-case scenarios.

2. ARE THE ROLES OF BANKS INCONSISTENT WITH FULL TRANSPARENCY?

While disclosure is woefully inadequate in most banking systems, how compatible is transparency with the vital economic role banks play? One critical aspect of banking is the fact that banks utilize private information to make credit decisions. Part of a bank's value added is its ability to monitor and evaluate difficult-to-value assets. Thus, it is likely to be impossible for outsiders, with no access to loan files and no ability to monitor financial contracts, to accurately evaluate the bank. This is why any banking system, to be transparent, must also have reliable bank supervision. Bank supervisors have the knowledge and authority to monitor the management information system to verify that the private information is accurately portrayed in the financial statements. Thus, a condition for a truly transparent banking system must be the resources and human capital to provide adequate bank supervision.

A second critical aspect of banking is the fact that banks transform assets, and to intermediate requires taking risks. Any institution with liquid liabilities and illiquid assets is taking on risks. This transformation of assets provides a valuable service to the economy, by better linking saving and investment. However, the societal cost of these services is that the banking system becomes susceptible to large unanticipated shocks.

An example is the experience in the United States in the late 1980s and early 1990s. The United States has been a market leader in disclosure and transparency in its banking system. Yet, in New England, without any dramatic decline in exchange rates or unprecedented movements in interest rates, seventy-nine of the 509 banks there failed. A large drop in real estate prices was sufficient to cause fourteen percent of the banks in New England to fail, even though bank real estate exposures, nonperforming loans, and real estate prices had all been disclosed. The reason is clear from the table. When collateral values drop, bank capital can disappear quickly. Among the seventy-nine banks that failed, twenty-two had a drop of more than ten percentage points in their leverage capital ratio in a single year, and all but three of the failed banks experienced a one-year decline of more than three percentage points. That such large and rapid declines in bank capital can occur, in a country with substantial transparency and relatively stable macroeconomic policies, suggests the possibility of much greater losses in countries whose economy, interest rates, and exchange rates are far more volatile.

Any institution that provides substantial intermediation services may be endangered if macroeconomic policies are mismanaged. Large and unanticipated exchange rate declines, inflation rate increases, or collapses in collateral values are likely to bankrupt even well managed intermediaries. While intermediaries can adjust to mismanaged economic policies, they do so by "gaming" the system, by ceasing to provide standard intermediation services. Thus, banks did not disappear during the Brazilian hyperinflation, but they no longer provided the transformation of assets that is possible in economies with more stable monetary and fiscal policy. Even with perfect transparency, intermediaries will not survive with inappropriate monetary, fiscal, and regulatory policies.

3. THE BENEFITS OF GREATER TRANSPARENCY AND DISCLOSURE

Disclosure can reduce the probability of a banking crisis and aid in the recovery, however. Transparency did not prevent the widespread failure of banks in New England, but disclosure did force prompt realization of losses, the transfer of assets to new owners, and quick recovery in the real estate markets. In contrast, the Japanese banks have delayed disclosure, allowing the banks and the government to remain in control of assets that would be better utilized after quick and efficient transfer to new owners.

Disclosure also forces the closure of clearly insolvent institutions. This reduces moral hazard problems and removes overcapacity in the market. Weakened banks with poor underwriting policies can affect the lending environment for stronger banks. Failing banks in New England were closed, allowing healthier banks to recapitalize quickly. In contrast, the failure to disclose has allowed insolvent Japanese banks to remain in operation, deferring necessary consolidation.

Even with such limited disclosure, however, market pressures are forcing Japanese banks to take unpopular actions. This can best be seen in the effect of increases in the "Japan premium" (Peek and Rosengren, 1999). The Japan premium emerged in August 1995, coinciding with the failure of Hyogo Bank and the Kizu Credit Union. As the premium has widened, Japanese banks have been forced out of low-margin business, reducing their exposure in Hong Kong and Singapore and pulling out of markets in Europe and the United States. The large Japan premium has exacerbated pressures already created by capital constraints (Peek and Rosengren, 1997). As Japanese banks have had trouble getting international funding, many have been forced to withdraw from international operations and focus on domestic banking. Thus, pressure created by the Japan premium has encouraged Japanese banks to reduce their dollar exposures and avoid expanding further into Asia. This pressure has also forced banks to adopt strategies of looking for opportunities for higher returns and reducing assets and the number of branches and subsidiaries, in order to better accommodate their reduced capital. The Japan premium has also placed pressure on government officials to adopt bank bailout plans more quickly and encourage greater consolidation of the banking industry.

4. CONCLUSION

Disclosure and transparency are not a panacea, but they can reduce the costs of banking problems. Financial markets are quick to react to problems in institutions with large exposures to troubled sectors. This provides an incentive to limit exposure in any one area, and to quickly reduce exposure as problems emerge. Disclosure of problems can force banking consolidation, transfer of problem assets, and closure of insolvent institutions—necessary conditions for quick recovery of a troubled banking sector. The lessons from the United States and Japan indicate that other Asian economies may be better off following the U.S. rather than the Japanese model. While the resolution of banking problems in the United States was controversial and unpopular, it resulted in a rapid resolution. In contrast, Japanese banks, by failing to disclose problems and not being transparent, have delayed their recovery and exacerbated their difficulties

Acknowledgment: The views expressed are those of the author and do not necessarily reflect official positions of the Federal Reserve Bank of Boston or the Federal Reserve System.

References

Caprio, Gerald, and Daniela Klingebiel. 1996, "Bank Insolvencies: Cross-Country Experience," World Bank, policy research working paper, No. 1620.

Caprio, Gerald, and Kaniela Klingebiel. 1997, "Bank Insolvencies: Bad Luck, Bad Policy, or Bad Banking?," *Annual World, Bank Conference on Development Economics,* pp. 79–04.

Fons, Jerome S. 1999, "Improving Transparency in Asian Banking Systems."

Goldstein, Morris. 1998, "Comments on Early Warning Indicators of Financial Crises in Emerging Economies," in Federal Reserve Bank of Kansas City, *Maintaining Financial Stability in a Global Economy* forthcoming.

Goldstein, Morris. 1999, "Early Warning Indicators and the Asian Financial Crisis," *The Asian Crisis: Origins, Implications, and Solutions*, Kluwer Press.

Kaminsky, Graciela L. 1999. "Currency and Banking Crises: The Early Warnings of Distress," *The Asian Conflict: Origins, Implications, and Solutions*, Kluwer Press.

Kaminsky, Graciela L., and Carmen M. Reinhart. 1998, "Financial Crises in Asia and Latin America: Then and Now," *The American Economic Review Papers and Proceedings,* Vol. 88, pp. 444–448.

Peek, Joseph, and Eric S. Rosengren. 1997, "The International Transmission of Financial Shocks: The Case of Japan," *The American Economic Review*, Vol. 87, pp. 495–505.

Peek, Joseph, Eric S. Rosengren. 1998. "Determinants of the Japan Premium: Actions Speak Louder than Words," Federal Reserve Bank of Boston, manuscript.

Wing, Jack. 1998, "The Inevitable Perils of a Precocious Giant," *The Asian Conflict: Origins, Implications, and Solutions*, Kluwer Press.

Table 1. Largest one-Year Decline in the Leverage Ratio at Each New England Bank, 1988:I to 1996:IV

Percentage Point Decline	Banks That Did Not Fail	Failed Banks
Less than 1	149	
1 to 2	110	1
2 to 3	66	2
3 to 4	41	7
4 to 5	25	12
5 to 6	18	13
6 to 8	15	13
8 to 10	3	9
Larger than 10	3	22
Total	430	79

PART VII

MORAL HAZARD AND THE ROLE OF INTERNATIONAL RESCUE PROGRAMS

Chapter 32

Moral Hazard is Avoidable

Charles W. Calomiris
Columbia University

The international financial system is at a crossroads. We can conclude from the recent crises that markets do not work and that more government interventions, capital controls, and bailouts are needed, or we can conclude (correctly) that the incentive problems fostered by government and International Monetary Fund protection of banks and conglomerates, an absence of basic rule of law in many countries, and other core weaknesses of government policy are at the heart of recent financial fragility (Calomiris, 1998a). The latter approach is the more difficult path, since it implies a need for fundamental reform that will be politically difficult.

I want to discuss my admittedly ambitious proposal for reform of the so-called global financial architecture, and the IMF in particular (Calomiris, 1998b). I offer an economist's perspective on the central issue of the current policy debate: Can we provide preventative and responsive liquidity protection without undermining the core incentives of the market economy, as we have been doing with bailouts? I argue that even if we begin with an encompassing definition of "liquidity" problems, we can design institutions that resolve those liquidity problems without giving rise to the social costs that come from counterproductive bailouts of insolvent banks by domestic governments and the IMF.

It is not difficult to construct a set of mechanisms that resolve at the same time problems of illiquidity (by providing a responsive international lender of last resort facility alongside a domestic deposit insurance system) while avoiding the governance and incentive problems attendant to counterproductive bailouts of risk takers by ensuring credible market discipline of financial institutions. The hurdles that must be overcome in designing an appropriate financial architecture, then, are not those posed by economics, but rather by politics. The challenge is to get those with vested interest in the current allocation of political power—including bankers, developing country oligarchs, and the U.S. Treasury—to relinquish some of the power they currently wield in order to make the global financial system more efficient, competitive, and democratic.

My proposal focuses on the need to restore proper incentives in banking systems as a prerequisite to providing liquidity protection. Many others talk about the need for proper "transparency" or improved government supervision of banks. But I place my faith in private incentives. All the information in the world about bank risk is useless if there is no incentive to use it properly to rein in bank risk taking. And government supervision, while certainly necessary, is not a dependable alternative to private discipline, as the behavior of supervisors has illustrated now in scores of cases of banking system collapse. Furthermore, credible market discipline is a lever for other reforms. It will create a strong constituency for transparency and reforms to legal systems, and market signals about bank quality can limit politically motivated supervisory forbearance. The key to real reform is to place market discipline at the top of the list.

In tackling the moral hazard problem the biggest challenge we must confront is the lack of discipline over bank risk choices. Banks are allowed, and often encouraged, to increase their risk, particularly in response to adverse macroeconomic shocks. Before banks were protected by government safety nets, economic downturns produced immediate contractions of bank credit supply and cuts in bank dividends, as banks scrambled to reassure depositors that bank loan losses would not result in losses for depositors (Calomiris and Wilson, 1998).

Safety net protection has removed that important disciplinary check on bank behavior. Safety net protection (ultimately, taxpayer protection of banks and their claimants) relaxes market discipline on bank risk taking and subsidizes higher risk in banks. This effect is especially pronounced after banks experience initial losses to the value of their assets. In the wake of such losses, safety net protection encourages banks to consciously increase their asset risk. Those increases in risk often take the form of increased default risk and exchange rate risk after banks have already seen severe depletion of their capital.

Without a reliable means of bringing credible market discipline to bear on banks, to provide strong incentives for prudent risk management, government deposit insurance and IMF lending will spur excessive risk taking, financial collapse, and it attendant costs. But in the presence of credible market discipline, deposit insurance and IMF lending (if structured properly) can strengthen the financial system by helping to avoid liquidity crises, which result either from problems of asymmetric information or self-fulfilling expectations.

The two most important liquidity problems are (1) banking panics that result from temporary confusion on the part of bank debt holders about the incidence within the banking sector of losses resulting from observable macroshocks, and (2) self-fulfilling collapses of currencies that result from government illiquidity. To solve the first problem, I propose a set of banking regulations that together would remove the threat of banking panics—including (1) capital standards founded on market discipline, achieved through a requirement that banks maintain a minimal proportion of uninsured, junior (or subordinated) debt with a maximum credit risk spread; (2) credible deposit insurance for other bank debt claims; (3) a twenty percent cash (or equivalents) reserve requirement for banks; (4) a twenty percent "global securities" requirement for banks; (5) free entry by domestic and foreign competitors into banking; and (6) limitations on other government assistance to banks.

It is important to emphasize that a broad consensus has emerged on the need to add some form of subordinated debt requirement to the Basle capital standards as the best means to ensure credible market discipline of banks. Advocates of such a requirement now include: The Bankers' Roundtable, the U.S. Treasury, several Federal Reserve Bank Presidents, at least one Fed Governor, some members of Congress, and the Shadow Financial Regulatory Committee. I congratulate the Federal Reserve Board on assembling a task force to explore the question of how best to design and implement a subordinated debt requirement.

The combination of domestic deposit insurance and market discipline (which prevents the abuse of deposit insurance) can resolve the threat of banking panics that result either from confusion about the incidence of shocks, or self-fulfilling concerns about he insufficiency of bank reserves. The IMF's role would be mainly to address the other liquidity problem—liquidity crises that face member governments as the result of unwarranted speculative pressure on exchange rates. This was the original intent of the IMF's founders, and it remains a legitimate objective of IMF policy.

Recent studies that emphasize the value of IMF liquidity protection argue that the current form of IMF assistance is inadequate—it is too little, too late, and with too many conditions and delays to be effective in short-circuiting self-fulfilling runs on currencies or government debt. But how does one provide effective liquidity protection without encouraging counterproductive bailouts of banks and/or governments?

My plan (which in many respects mirrors the recent reform proposal of Meltzer, 1998) is to replace the current IMF and Exchange Stabilization Fund with a new IMF, which would offer a discount window lending facility. That facility would only be available to IMF members—and membership would require adherence to the aforementioned banking regulations, as well as some additional rules regarding government debt management, and (if a fixed exchange rate is maintained) a twenty-five percent minimum reserve requirement for the central bank and a requirement that banks offer accounts denominated in both domestic and foreign currency. By restricting access to the IMF window to members in good standing who conform to a few, simple, and easily verified rules, the IMF avoids free-riding on liquidity protection, and the hazard of unwittingly financing bank bailout in the guise of liquidity protection.

The rules governing the discount window follow Walter Bagehot's classic principles for ensuring liquidity, while avoiding free riding: lend freely on good collateral at a penalty rate. The specifics of membership rules, limits on collateral, and penalty lending rates (summarized in Table 1) encourage member countries' central banks (like their commercial banks) to reduce the risk of their securities portfolios and maintain adequate liquid reserves. If a member is in good standing, loans are made available on good collateral using one-week-old prices to value collateral. The loan interest rate is set at two percent above the value-weighted yield to maturity on the collateral offered. That provides a fast and effective means to short-circuit a self-fulfilling "bad equilibrium."

In implementing reform, the devil is in the details, hence my emphasis on "blueprints" (specific concrete proposals) rather than simply organizing principles. Slight differences in details can make the difference between a reform agenda that achieves both liquidity and proper incentives toward risk taking, and one that achieves neither.

Table 1
Elements of the Reform Plan

Membership Criteria for the IMF

Bank regulations:
Basle standards (but without restrictions on subordinated debt/tier 2 capital)
2 percent subordinated debt requirement (with rules on maturities, holders, and yields)
20 percent cash reserve requirement
20 percent "global securities" requirement
Free entry by domestic and foreign investors into banking
Bank recapitalizations are permitted, but strict guidelines must be met
(and must follow pre-established rules, as in preferred stock matching program)
Domestic lenders of last resort avoid bank bailouts by following Bagehotian principles

Other membership criteria:
Limits on short-term government securities issues
If fixed exchange rate, 25 percent minimum central bank reserve requirement
If fixed exchange rate, banks offer accounts in domestic and foreign currencies

IMF Lending Rules

Loans are provided only to members in good standing (those following above rules)
If a member defaults, it may not borrow for 5 years, and then only after arrears paid
Loans are for 90 days
Supernumerary majority of members required to roll over loans for another 90 days
Loans are collateralized by 125 percent of value of loan in government securities
25 percent of the 125 percent collateral must be in foreign government securities
The interest rate on the loan is set at 2 percent above the value-weighted yield on the collateral
observed one week prior to the loan request
The IMF reserves the right to refuse a loan to a member
No conditions are attached to IMF loans

IMF Funding

The IMF borrows from the discount windows of the Fed and other central banks
IMF borrowings from central banks are 100 percent collateralized by government securities
issued by the government of the lending central bank
Government securities that serve as collateral for IMF borrowings from central banks
are lent to the IMF by its member countries

Other Emergency Lending

IMF, World Bank, IDB, and others would make no other emergency lending available
The Exchange Stabilization Fund would be abolished

References

Calomiris, Charles W. 1998a, "The IMF's Imprudent Role As Lender of Last Resort," *The Cato Journal,* 17 Winter: 275–294.

Calomiris, Charles W. 1998b, "Blueprints for a New Global Financial Architecture," *American Enterprise Institute*, October.

Calomiris, Charles W., and Berry Wilson. 1998, "Bank Capital and Portfolio Management: The 1930s 'Capital Crunch' and Scramble to Shed Risk," NBER, working paper, No. 6649, July.

Meltzer, Allan H. 1998, "What's Wrong with the IMF? What Would Be Better?," Carnegie-Mellon University.

Chapter 33

Moral Hazard

Michael Mussa
International Monetary Fund

Moral hazard is a great sounding topic. Whenever I think of it, a picture of Monica Lewinsky and Linda Tripp comes to mind. However, moral hazard has really very little to do with morality and is not, indeed, a topic that is more appropriate for Geraldo than for a Chicago Fed Conference. Moral hazard is actually a technical economic concept, and there are literally hundreds of examples in the economic literature of the concept of moral hazard applied both to private business arrangements, and to public sector intervention.

It is important to understand that if our objective was to eliminate virtually every instance in which moral hazard was at all an issue, we would certainly have to abolish the IMF, abolish the World Bank, abolish the Federal Reserve, and abolish the U.S. government. Indeed, we would have to abolish most of our gross domestic product, if we wanted to be certain to get it all. So I think we want to restrict our attention, given that understanding, to circumstances in which moral hazard is really a significant problem that does need to be seriously addressed.

Now there are several things that I want to comment on in this regard.

First, the potential moral hazard directly generated by international support packages, sponsored by the IMF is certainly far less than the moral hazard problems that are typically associated with interventions by national governments. The IMF gives loans that it firmly expects to be repaid. It does not make gifts.

I found it ironic that, at the same time congressmen were complaining about the moral hazard potentially associated with the approval of the IMF quota increase, they were busily passing yet another bill to spend $4 billion bailing out farmers in the United States and continuing our policy of supporting that sector of the economy. Such support may be justified for a variety of reasons, but there is no doubt that it generates moral hazard. Meanwhile, the German government is generously spending $1 trillion in this decade to smooth transition of 18-million citizens of the eastern Länder into the greater Germany. There is surely moral hazard being generated in all that spending.

In contrast, as Charles pointed out, the subsidy on IMF lending is quite modest. But the suggestion is made, nevertheless, that the IMF facilitates moral hazard because the IMF support for Korea made it possible and legitimized the bailout of foreign banks that had lent money to Korean banks. Now, suppose that the Korean government had an additional $50 billion worth of reserves last December, it could then have done the bailout on its own without coming to the international community or the fund. Thus, while the Korean government created a moral hazard problem when it guaranteed the flows through Korean banks, the availability of liquidity support when the government faced liquidity problems, was not the fundamental source of that moral hazard problem.

Now you could say that it would be useful if the IMF and others were more forceful in seeking to have a system in which national governments were less generous and predictable in supporting weak banks and their creditors. I think that is right. But it is not just the IMF that could be doing that; also the BIS, the OECD, and the whole range of the economics profession should be doing it. I do not think that denying liquidity support, and forcing an even larger economic disaster on Korea than is already befalling it can plausibly be recommended as a rational way of dealing with this issue.

Second, lessening the true economic damage associated with economic crises, and thereby lessening the perceived hazard of damage associated with such crises, does not necessarily imply the creation of moral hazard. The objective is not to make a crisis as large and costly as possible so that we can discourage all risk taking. We do not want to have central bankers that will create big recessions because that will make people be more cautious in their investments. To the extent that international support packages do reduce the true economic damage associated with economic crises, that is a good thing. And to the extent that people therefore perceive less risk that is also a good thing. It only becomes a moral hazard problem to the extent that we are inducing people to undertake economically inappropriate risk, not to the extent that we are diminishing true risk.

Third, and this was a point raised by John Lipsky, when we look at the problems besetting the international financial system today, the crisis of world liquidity, and when we look before that at the narrowing of spreads and the escalation of asset prices that occurred over the course of the 1990s, before this crisis started, these trends are not plausibly a problem of moral hazard generated either by the fund or by anybody else. The subsequent reversal of these trends is also not a problem of moral hazard.

Fourth, some amount of moral hazard is almost inevitably a consequence of international support packages. But the issue is a balancing one. As President Abraham Lincoln put it, "There are few things wholly evil or wholly good." Almost everything, especially government policy, is an inseparable combination of the two, so that our best judgment as to the preponderance between them is continually demanded." That subject of balance has never been addressed by many of the critics of the fund and the international support packages. Rather, they simply argue: moral hazard is bad; support packages contain moral hazards; therefore, the support packages are bad. But there is real hazard out there and real damage and one seeks legitimately to balance the containment of this damage against the concern that some moral hazard may be generated. In particular, while some moral hazard may have followed from the example set in the Mexican crisis, this must be weighed against the very real damage that was avoided with the aid of international support.

Further, it is important to distinguish among cases. If we look at Russia, I think there is no doubt that there was a perception in the private financial market that Russia was "too nuclear to fail," and that financial support would be provided to Russia on terms and conditions that were not justified by the economic situation and economic policies of Russia but rather for other reasons. That generated a problem of moral hazard by facilitating flows of capital that would not otherwise have gone to Russia. But in the case of Korea, I agree with John and Charles, moral hazard generated by expectations of fund support is simply not a plausible explanation of capital flows to Korea before the crisis. Money flowed to Korea because investors thought Korea was a strong economy or they thought that, if the Korean banks had problems, the Korean government would cover the damage. It did not flow there because there was any significant perception that Korea was likely to come to the IMF and get an inappropriate financial support package.

Next, I would like to address the suggestions on how to deal with the problems of moral hazard. One suggestion, in the context of moral hazard problems associated with the fund itself has been to raise interest rates on fund loans. I have always thought that was a good idea; the fund charges somewhat too little. That problem, however, is being addressed by the higher charges the fund now makes on some of its large support packages. The more serious problem is how we are going to address moral hazard that is created by the actions of national governments. Here, there have been a number of useful suggestions. John has one. Charles has one. This is an important issue and the international community as a whole, including the fund but including others as well, needs to work much harder and more effectively on this issue.

However, I disagree with the suggestions that, "If a country comes to the fund in order to get an international support package because it is experiencing economic difficulties, then as a condition of providing that package, its creditors should be required to take a haircut." In other words, the policy would say that coming to the fund means a country must default on its debt obligations. The nature of a debt contract says that the creditor is entitled to receive his interest and principal regardless of what happens. He is not an equity holder. Now, as a practical matter, it is not that simple. The creditor receives interest and principal payments provided things do not go too badly. But if we have a particularly adverse outcome, then the creditor may not get fully paid. He has then to find some way to negotiate with the debtor to find a solution to the problem. But debt contracts are not written in such a way that accepts that creditors regularly expect to take a haircut. We call the circumstances in which the creditor takes a haircut a default. And defaults, particularly by sovereign governments, should be very rare events. However, they will not be events that never occur. That is important to containing the problem of moral hazard.

I want to emphasize that this is necessarily done in a dichotomous way. It should not be the case that every country that has an external problem and comes to the fund will have to default. That would be senseless. On the other hand, there will be some cases in which even sovereign defaults will occur. That has been and remains a policy of the international community. In Mexico in the 1980s, the banks had to delay and write down their claims. They were not bailed out. In Mexico in the 1990s, the perception was it was a liquidity problem and the creditors of the Mexican sovereign got out whole. In Russia, they took substantial losses. In other words, we cannot, should not, and do not have a system in which in every case creditors are expected to take losses or a system where creditors never take losses. Either would be senseless.

Chapter 34

Moral Hazard and the Role of International Rescue Programs

Pedro Pou
Central Bank of Argentina

I first want to make clear that in everything that follows, there are two very specific assumptions. First, that it is a high priority to maintain capital account convertibility, and second that I will be referring specifically to emerging economies, where emerging is defined as economies that do not have permanent access to international capital markets. This definition is very important to understand the line of reasoning that I will follow.

In my brief remarks, I would like to focus on the role of the IFI's and the trade-off between on, the one hand, reducing the probability of a liquidity shock, perhaps caused by some contagion effect, and, on the other hand, the problem of moral hazard.

However, before I get to the specifics we need to consider the appropriate overall policy stance of countries since the role of the IFI's should not substitute for good policies but rather to complement them.

In very broad terms, I would suggest that one precondition for this overall policy stance is of course sound macroeconomic policies where consistency between monetary, exchange rate and fiscal policy is a must. However, secondly I would suggest that to participate in world capital markets, emerging countries also need to have an appropriate financial policy.

This financial policy may consist of a number of elements including strong banking regulations regarding capital, provisioning and risk management. However, for emerging markets I would stress that it must also include a liquidity policy. These policies in the financial sector should be independent of the exchange rate regime in place. The general point is that as emerging economies tend to be subject to higher volatility they need a strong banking sector irrespective of their monetary arrangements.

However, as I mentioned in my definition, emerging markets, for reasons that I think we don't totally understand, may suddenly be cut off from international credit and government bond markets may simply dry up. This means that an emerging country has less degrees of freedom than say a typical G-10 country. For example, a G-10 country facing a liquidity problem in the banking sector can inject liquidity and at the same time sterilize that injection without jeopardizing monetary or exchange rate targets. An emerging country, whose government bond market has become illiquid does not have that option. Moreover, the monetary injection will not normally be accompanied by an increase in the demand for domestic liabilities and hence the exchange rate will instantly be put under pressure. Note that this also means that emerging countries have significantly less freedom to define their own monetary policy. Take an emerging economy that ostensibly has an independent monetary policy, let's say a flexible exchange rate, but no liquidity policy. If there is a liquidity shock and the Central Bank feels forced to inject liquidity into the banking sector then for the arguments I have given above this will most likely be reflected directly in the exchange rate so the independent monetary policy is really illusory. To put this another way, whatever macroeconomic rule an emerging economy adopts, whether this be an exchange rate, monetary or inflation target, then this rule may be put in severe jeopardy given a lack of access to international credit and insufficient liquidity. Of course an emerging country, which has no such rule, can claim greater "flexibility." However, "flexibility" in this context is really "instability."

Therefore, there is a need for a liquidity policy. I strongly believe that this policy should take into account the liabilities of both the private and public sector both in local and in foreign currency and with residents and nonresidents. In other words, what is required is an overall or Systemic Liquidity Policy. In recent crises, depending on the country context, we have seen liquidity problems in public debt, in bank debt, in other private sector debt and we have seen problems with foreign liabilities and with domestic liabilities. Our experience in Argentina, through with very different monetary and exchange rate arrangements, is that domestic residents run at least as fast as foreigners and that peso liabilities can be just as serious a problem as liabilities in dollars. I therefore would resist making strong distinctions between domestic and foreign or between resident and nonresident. I repeat, emerging countries may need to think about an overall or systemic liquidity policy.

Let me, as an example, refer more specifically to the banking sector where normally there will be an important concentration of liquidity risks. The instruments of a systemic liquidity policy can and probably should include (i) holding a specified proportion of liabilities in internationally liquid assets (i.e., foreign assets); (ii) developing internationally liquid instruments such as standardized mortgages, and securitized products; (iii) facilitating international contingent lines of credit for banks; (iv) holding significant international reserves of the central bank to provide liquidity lender of last resort support, and finally (v) arranging international contingent lines of credits for the central bank, to enhance those reserves.

Holding international reserves to back liabilities is clearly expensive, especially for emerging economies where the banking system is the largest component of the capital market. In economies where loans are a scarce good and where capital markets are underdeveloped there is a strong trade-off between a prudent liquidity policy and domestic credit creation. An extreme liquidity policy means narrow banking, and narrow in the strictest sense, i.e. banks holding only internationally liquid short-term papers (U.S. T-bills, for example). This policy implies no domestic credit in the normal way.

To enhance this trade-off between liquidity and credit formation the standard solution in the domestic context is the creation of a LOLR. This function is usually performed by the central bank, where the trade-off between the potential provision of liquidity, and hence control of the problems of "runs" and "contagion," versus the creation of a moral hazard has been well-understood since the last century. Indeed, we central bankers know very well the principles proposed by Bagehot in 1873, which try to define explicit rules that would allow an effective lender of last resort to operate but at the same time minimize the moral hazard created.

What I then see is a clear need for an informed debate of these issues but at the international rather than domestic level. We need a set of rules for an effective international lender of last resort to improve the trade-off between liquidity and credit but at the same time controlling the moral hazard.

I think we understand the moral hazard issue reasonably well now. Moral hazard occurs when creditors believe that, irrespective of the soundness of the investment being financed with their money, they are able to get somebody else to absorb the costs of their mistakes. That means that, in some of the recent crises, the mistakes are clearly shared by the borrower as well as by their creditors and also their supervisors. To the extent that private banks assumed that unlimited assistance to countries with problems was available—and to the extent that their supervisors did not require sufficient capital or provisions against those risky investments—then they must share the blame with the local authorities themselves.

I am not sure however that we fully understand the mechanisms, the depth nor the implications of contagion. Economists tend to focus on interesting but complicated explanations of contagion such as the low incentives for diversified fund managers to learn about individual countries, whereas market traders focus on more technical issues such as liquidity effects and the necessity to make margin calls and the effect of dynamic hedging strategies. In any event a serious topic for research is to understand the market microstructure issues which have led to this extremely indiscriminate sell-off of emerging market debt.

I am not sure either that we fully understand the depth nor the implications of this contagion. It is clear that most emerging countries are effectively cut off from world capital markets at current spreads. This obviously has a significant and self-fulfilling negative effect on those very same economies. The liquidity policy that I have described above is extremely important then to buy time. The best place to be when there is a huge storm is safely in the harbor and, with a strong liquidity policy, countries do not need to venture out to sea to place debt in these markets. However, this is only a partial solution. It does not solve the problems in these markets, it just buys time.

To solve the problem and so to preserve open capital accounts—which as I have said is an objective that I think we should keep as a high priority—then the international community needs to develop an international LOLR to protect countries from such storms. Such an institution would have to act with rules similar to those that apply to a central bank in relation to domestic banks. In a domestic context these include (i) strict monitoring so that the solvency of the bank is not in doubt and (ii) plenty of assistance to the financial system in general and especially to those banks that face the risk of contagion from the particular bank that is in difficulties.

Of course, this is easier said than done even in a domestic context. Central banks do not like to be too explicit about which banks would receive assistance and which would not. This policy has become known as constructive ambiguity. Whatever its merits in a domestic context, it is clear that in an international setting something more predetermined, less arbitrary, is needed, so that it is crystal clear that there are no political issues involved. The need for transparency in procedures and practices becomes paramount.

In fact I would advocate a two level approach. Countries that satisfy a set of criteria perhaps including a set of Maastricht type fiscal rules plus a set of financial criteria related to the soundness of their financial system should gain access to virtually unconditional lending to prevent them from being affected from other countries' problems. The conditionality in other words would be ex ante and not ex post and the idea is that this should then be a preemptive program such that everyone knows that the funds are available if required without conditions. In fact the IMF already does this although not quite in name. Argentina's EFF arrangement with the fund includes a substantial amount, which Argentina has chosen not to use, but is available just in case. What I am suggesting is in some sense only a formalization of these arrangements.

However, we must also realize that the nature of crises has changed. As stressed in the work of Michael Gavin and Andrew Powell, recent crises have reflected sharp disequilibria in financial stocks rather than the flow disequilibria typical of the 1970's balance of payments crisis. This has two strong implications. First, it means that the IFI's, whether they like it or not, are put in a very analogous position to a financial lender of last resort but second, the amounts of assistance required have grown considerably. The total sum committed for the packages to Mexico and Argentina in 1995, plus Thailand, Indonesia, Korea, and Russia amount to a staggering $185 billon dollars. We therefore need an effective lender of last resort which can commit significant quantities to countries that have satisfied a set of ex ante policy targets.

For countries that do not satisfy these policy targets but have some fundamental problems a different approach is then required corresponding closely to the more traditional operations of the IMF. In these cases, a substantial amount of policy dialogue and conditionality needs to be applied at the time of disbursement. Which countries are in the first group and which countries are in the second group obviously needs considerable research and may involve difficult political decisions. However, such an approach would clearly give a strong message to countries to get their houses in order.

In any event, I think we must also recognize that at some point we will reach the political limits of the amounts of official financing available. It is then both beneficial and necessary to "bail in" the private sector when it comes to crisis prevention and crisis resolution. My own view is that the IMF should probably focus on the arrangements I have just described but an entirely appropriate and complementary role for the MDB's (World Bank and IDB) would be to assist countries to set up private sector LOLR type facilities. As many of you know, in Argentina we have set up a private contingent liquidity rep. facility. We have also proposed that the unique status of the IDB and the World Bank implies that they have an extremely important role in complementing the private capital in this facility and that the presence of the multilaterals will significantly enhance the quality of this private lender of last resort arrangement.

This facility has a very important role in Argentina in helping to ensure that credit still flows to enterprises, and especially small and medium sized firms, in situations where banks suffer a liquidity problem from some totally external event. Anyone who thinks that this facility does not have a "productive purpose" should analyze the Tequila period in Argentina carefully, where a sharp liquidity crunch caused a severe recession and increased unemployment and poverty significantly. These ideas are general, they do not depend on our particular monetary arrangements and indeed several other countries have requested detailed information regarding the structure of our facility.

CONCLUSION

To conclude, I want to leave you with two main ideas. The first is that I still do not think that we understand well how contagion effects really occur. We also urgently need a much better understanding of the microstructure of international capital markets and specifically we need to analyze the behavior of hedge funds and mutual funds. For this we need information. As a first step I recommend that we gather position data on these funds and we analyze carefully the motivations for their actions. Just as the world has developed complex regulations for banks, which protect against systemic banking risk, it may be that their are particular characteristics of these markets which imply that we need regulations on world capital market players to protect the integrity of these markets. Having studied in Chicago, I am a firm believer in market processes but I think we must recognize that markets may function well or badly depending on the institutional settings. We need to be much better informed on how international markets actually function if we are to rely on these markets for countries' financing needs.

Second, we need to develop an effective lender of last resort. I know that there is resistance to these ideas, but it is very important to analyze the costs and benefits of action and inaction. The risk of action is that we might not get it exactly right from the beginning. However the question is whether action will improve on the current overall arrangements. The risk of inaction would be to leave the world as a very dangerous place in particular for emerging countries. Indeed it would run the enormous risk of going back in the process of opening of the capital account. Many may decide that the degree of volatility in capital markets is just too high to keep the capital account open.

Acknowledgment: I would like to thank the Federal Reserve Bank of Chicago for allowing me to comment on these very important topics in this excellent conference at this very opportune time.

Chapter 35

Moral Hazard and the Role of International Rescue Programs

Helmut Schieber
Deutsche Bundesbank

The problem of moral hazard has been at the center of the international financial crises of the past few years, stretching from Mexico via Asia and Russia to Latin America. The trend in the spreads for capital investments in emerging markets and other risky investments up to 1997 shows that the risk spreads declined constantly, even though the magnitude of the risks remained more or less unaltered, and that at the same time the willingness to make risky investments and the respective capital flows increased dramatically.

This trend was due to several factors. For example, attention should be drawn to the preference of many emerging market countries for fixed exchange rates, the intensifying competition among all kinds of institutional investors, an increasing international debate on the function of central banks and international organizations as "lenders of last resort," and the development of ever more sophisticated instruments for managing and diversifying risks. In the latter case, very often vague definitions of risks and "bold" proxy hedges were in evidence.

But the behaviour of the international financial institutions undoubtedly also played a role. Often encouraged and pressurized by the governments of the afflicted countries, they stepped into the breach with increasingly larger rescue programs whenever a new financial crisis arose, in some cases interpreting the statutes governing lending and the permissible range of operations very liberally.

The financing programs for Thailand, South Korea, Indonesia, and Russia illustrate this clearly. Private investors generally gained the impression that the considerable—if diminishing—spreads were a safe bet since. If things came to a head, international rescue programs would enable them to withdraw in good time from their investments, which had indeed been recognised as being risky from the outset. For example, talks with our German banks held during the Asian crisis showed that the credit analysts of these banks had in fact drawn their management board's attention to the precarious financial structure in the relevant countries, both regarding the currency denomination of the loans and the pattern of maturities. However, the boards nevertheless continued their expansive lending activities as they were convinced that the international community would not leave these countries, and thus also their creditors, in the lurch. This attitude constitutes the core of the moral hazard problem.

There can be no doubt that the situation has changed fundamentally in the meantime. Since it became clear that even the most extensive rescue programs can no longer cope with the potential for capital flight, which has increased drastically, investors' risk awareness has been aroused again owing to the painful experience made in Asia and Russia. This is illustrated by the trends in spreads at many levels, for example between industrial countries and emerging markets, between government and private sector bonds, even in interbank trade. In this respect, the moral hazard is receding, which, taken by itself, is a welcome development, even though the pace and the scope of this trend are contributing significantly to the current apprehensions.

Now I wish to deal specifically with the international rescue programs mentioned in the title by addressing three aspects: the role of the IMF in financial crises, the appropriate size of financial packages, and the appropriate conditionality of fund supported programs.

As far as *the role of the IMF* in managing financial crises is concerned, I would like to make one thing clear at the outset. The first choice should be no intervention in the markets. However, if—but only if—financial intervention is unavoidable, the IMF should be the "lead manager." The reasons:

1. The IMF has acquired an outstanding level of expertise in dealing with challenges to the international monetary system.

2. No other institution can better express the concerns and deliver policy recommendations. This remains true despite the fact that some of these recommendations are and should be the subject of a lively debate.

3. The past months have demonstrated once again that the fund is a very flexible institution and can act quickly when a crisis occurs.

Let me now turn to the second issue—*the size of IMF financial packages.* This issue is probably the most controversial one.

First, I do not share the view that extraordinarily large financial packages have automatically calming effects on financial markets.

- Neither in Asia nor in Russia did the announcement of large packages stop the capital outflows, either immediately or later, because—as mentioned—everyone could see that even these large packages were by far not large enough to finance all possible capital outflows.
- I suspect that such announcements may even intensify outflows. It is like "ringing the bell," thereby promoting the perception of an emergency. It indicates additionally that the exit door may be open only for some time.
- The situation was calmed only after crisis had made credible commitments to implement reforms and after the private sector had participated in finding a solution to the crisis.
- Large financial packages favor inevitably moral hazard and create the basis for the next crisis. Therefore:
- It is crucial for the fund to concentrate on its catalytic role and involve private creditors at an early stage. Concepts for sharing the burden of unavoidable losses are necessary. I know this raises a number of complex issues. The approach taken in Korea and—in a different way—in Indonesia, however, might provide a basis on which we can build.
- While advocating minimal intervention, I strongly prefer voluntary solutions. But if market participants cannot agree, additional means should be taken into consideration, for example a moratorium or a standstill.

I would like to turn now to my third and last issue: *the appropriate conditionality* of fund supported programs.

- I think the fund's two-pronged approach of macroeconomic adjustment and structural reforms is fundamentally appropriate.
- The sharp rise in interest rates was necessary—although not sufficient—to stop or at least reduce capital outflows.
- Fiscal austerity is in many cases appropriate to reduce current account deficits, and to finance to some degree the financial sector

restructuring. Anticyclical fiscal deficits to avoid or mend recession have to be handled very carefully.
- The IMF is doing well to insist that far-reaching financial sector reforms be carried out in order to correct these flaws.

In the context of the Asian and the Russian crisis, the fund had to act under extremely difficult economic and political circumstances. It found itself on the horns of a dilemma: it had to act quickly enough to prevent a deterioration of the crisis without acting prematurely. Fund-supported programs may be distorted by political shortcomings. To that extent, the outcome may not be optimal from an economic point of view.

Having said this, I conclude with two "footnotes." Firstly, we should also discuss the criticism from Martin Feldstein, who argued that some structural measures recommended in Asia look like being from the trade agenda of some member countries of the fund. In my view, unnecessary intervention in political sovereignty should be avoided. It may lead to a delay in seeking the help of the IMF in crisis situations. And that is exactly what we want to avoid.

Secondly, the incorporation of second lines of defence in international rescue programs ought to be dispensed with if—when it comes to the crunch—it turns out that they were not really meant seriously and were little more than "window-dressing." The credibility of international rescue programs is too valuable and too vulnerable to be jeopardized in that manner.

PART VIII

THE FUTURE ROLE OF THE INTERNATIONAL MONETARY FUND IN INTERNATIONAL RESCUE OPERATIONS

Chapter 36

Bailing in the Private Sector*

Barry Eichengreen
University of California, Berkeley

A particular concern of many critics of the existing international financial architecture is that official support has been used to bail out investors. In Mexico in 1995, Korea in 1997, and Russia in 1998, official funds were used to repurchase and retire short-term debt that private investors were unwilling to hold. Having benefited from high interest rates while their money was in place, creditors were effectively protected from capital losses when it came time to sell. The moral hazard thereby created provided an obvious incentive to engage in even less prudent lending, setting the stage for still larger crises and still larger bailouts. It would be better from a public-policy standpoint, the conclusion follows, were private investors and international banks in particular forced to "take a hit."

The Mexican crisis illustrates the problem. The government entered its crisis at the end of 1994 with some $28 billion of short-term foreign-currency-indexed government obligations (*tesobonos*) about to mature but only $6 billion of international reserves. Once confidence was lost, no investor had an incentive to make available additional foreign exchange. Had international assistance not been provided, Mexico would have been forced to suspend redemption of these debts, inflicting significant losses on its creditors and risking damage to its credit worthiness. Instead, the government used its U.S. and IMF loans to retire its tesobonos at full value as they matured.

---

*Some of the material in this section draw from my book, *Toward a New International Financial Architecture: A Practical Post-Asia Agenda* (Institute for International Economics, 1999), reproduced here by the permission of the Institute for International Economics.

In Korea the mechanism was more involved but the result was the same. Foreign creditors who had extended short-term loans to Korean banks attempted to withdraw their balances all at once. Those short-term credits far exceeded the government's foreign reserves. The Bank of Korea's reserves fell from $31 billion at end October 1997 to $21 billion at the end of December, and more than half of this latter amount was immobilized in the form of deposits with foreign branches of domestic banks.[1] Figures vary for the short-term foreign currency obligations of the Korean financial sector, but one seemingly reliable estimate puts them at about $26 billion in December.[2] Had no official assistance arrived, the Korean authorities would have been forced to declare a moratorium. Instead, the U.S.- and IMF-led loan enabled the government to inject more credit into the banking system, deposit more reserves at overseas branches of Korean banks, and keep interest rates lower than would have been feasible otherwise, while maturing foreign credits were paid back in full. The result was to replace a significant share of those foreign credits with official funds.[3]

One rationale for the Korean package sometimes heard in Washington, DC is that the Korean Peninsula is too important geopolitically for the South's economy to be left unaided. Similar arguments have been made about Indonesia, which sits astride some of the world's most important ocean-shipping lines. Russia being "Indonesia with nukes," the Korean and Indonesian precedents gave investors confidence that Russia would receive similar assistance. This rhetoric may seem exaggerated, but the fact of the matter is that in the wake of the IMF's Asian support programs the international bankers and others who poured money into Russia referred to positions in Russian GKO's (treasury bills) as the "moral-hazard play." There were sizable inflows into Russia in the months following the Asian rescue packages, followed by financial difficulties, a crisis, and an IMF package in the summer of 1998.[4]

In practice, of course, not all investors were shielded from losses. In Mexico, the prices of tesobonos tumbled before it became clear that the Mexican government would be able to retire them, and many investors who scrambled out of the market did so at a loss. In Mexico in 1994 and even more so in Asia in 1997, official support did not avert major declines in stock, bond and real estate prices, and investors in these markets incurred extensive losses. None of this is to deny that moral hazard is a problem and that existing arrangements for handling crises are deficient, but to caution that one should not exaggerate the extent to which investors have been shielded.

The real dilemma is presented by bank creditors. Foreign funding of domestic banks in the form of deposits and deposit-like instruments is highly liquid. Deposits have a fixed face value. Banks being key to the stability of a country's payments and credit system, governments are understandably reluctant to contemplate any treatment of these claims that might threaten their provision. These facts make it extremely difficult to write down foreign claims on domestic banks. It would be nice if foreign bank creditors could be made to "take a hit"—if they would agree to reschedule and write down their claims. But so long as they have the option of fleeing and bringing down the banking system in their wake, governments will contemplate this option only in extremis.[5]

If the tendency for official support to shield creditors from losses and to thereby encourage imprudent investor behavior was not sufficient grounds for concern, there is also the question of whether international assistance as currently constituted can protect the recipients from serious damage. All too often, IMF-led rescues are ineffective in containing a panic because the fund's resources are limited and doled out a drop at a time. Unlike a domestic lender of last resort, the IMF cannot print money, nor would its principal shareholders let it.[6] They are reluctant to do so because, compared to a government with regulatory powers dealing with a problem bank, the IMF has less ability to force corrective action on its members. Since the fund does not posses the other legal and supervisory powers of a government, in other words, it lacks the leverage to ensure that it will get its money back. This is why the IMF is endowed with fewer resources, why it lends less freely, and why it relies more heavily on continuing performance criteria when disbursing its funds. It is why the IMF hesitates to front-load its disbursements, requiring evidence that policy reforms are in train before it releases each additional bit of finance.[7]

For all these reasons, official support is generally less than meets the eye. The international community committed $57 billion to Korea, for example, but released only $13.2 billion by the time the crisis there reached its height.[8] As a result, countries receiving international assistance and trying to avoid a debt moratorium, standstill, or "pause" have to hike interest rates both to lure back foreign investors and to satisfy the fund.

Why are governments so willing to put their economies through the wringer? Why in particular do they hesitate to suspend payments and negotiate an agreement with the creditors to restructure the debt? Doing so would certainly discourage imprudent lending. More importantly from the domestic of view, governments could avoid putting their economies through the wrenching deflationary consequences of the adjustment required for the maintenance of external debt service.[9]

This option is shunned because governments and the international policy community regard the collateral damage as too severe. Countries that suspend payments and attempt to restructure find it difficult and costly to reach an agreement with their creditors. Their reputations are damaged. They find it harder to borrow on international capital markets subsequently.[10] However expedient the short-run policy, most governments regard the long-term consequences as unsupportable.[11]

Thus, "bailing in" the private sector—ensuring that private investors also "take a hit"—presupposes changes in institutional and contractual arrangements that make it palatable for governments to declare a moratorium and restructure their debts. It requires changes in the international financial architecture.

1. EX ANTE MEASURES

Two classes of measures can be considered under this heading: measures to discourage bank-to-bank lending, and the negotiation of international credit lines.

1.1 Discouraging short-term borrowing

The most direct way to avoid letting foreign creditors off scot free is not to borrow from them in the first place. This is not meant sarcastically. Short-term foreign credits, and the short-term foreign credits of domestic banks in particular, pose a special problem because they are so liquid, making it especially easy for those extending them to scramble for the exits. They pose a special problem because the institutions dependent on them are central to financial stability. The need to preserve the stability of the banking system thus makes it hard to impose on its creditors a share of the adjustment burden. This provides an argument for discouraging reliance on short-term foreign credits to the banking system in the first place. It is an argument for raising the Basle risk weights for foreign bank lending and for keying those weights to the source of banks' funding as well as the riskiness of their investments. In markets where political pressure prevents capital from being written down, it is an argument for taxes or quantitative ceilings on short-term foreign funding. And where nonfinancial firms can do the borrowing and pass the proceeds on to financial intermediaries, it is an argument for using measures like those employed by Chile, whose government, while applying a tax to all capital inflows, structures it so that it falls most heavily on short-term inflows. If administered successfully, such measures would increase foreign portfolio investors' reliance on stocks, bonds and other long-term instruments, on which they would automatically suffer capital losses in the event of a financial crisis.

1.2 Standby lines of credit

A second approach would be for governments to negotiate standby lines of credit. Foreign banks would agree to make these credit lines available in return for a commitment fee. Since foreign bank creditors would no longer be able to eliminate their exposure to the country in question, they would be more predisposed to negotiate a restructuring plan. From the standpoint of the borrowing countries, these credit lines would provide additional resources to insure against shocks to investor confidence. Both Argentina and Mexico have negotiated such agreements with foreign commercial banks despite the fact that neither country has an investment-grade sovereign credit rating. Notwithstanding, Mexico's recent tough negotiations to renew its credit lines, this suggests that other countries could do the same.[12]

The main weakness of these arrangements is that the banks will be able to hedge their exposure. At the same time they provide additional credits, they can contract to sell short government bills and bonds. The country will then have no additional financial resources for propping up its banking system and coping with the other consequences of the crisis.

This constraint can be relaxed were the IMF and the regional development banks to supplement the contingent facility.[13] Like the commercial banks, they too could make credit lines available to governments in return for a commitment fee and an interest charge. They could take guidance on the pricing of the facility from the banks, charging the same fees and requiring the same collateral. Only if a country qualified for a credit from the commercial banks would this be supplemented by the multilaterals. Thus, the conditionality would be negotiated ex ante, and the facility would available only to countries that had already taken reasonable steps to establish and preserve their credit worthiness.[14]

The Supplemental Reserve Facility (SRF) approved by the IMF's Executive Board in December 1997 is a step in this direction. The SRF is designed to provide financial assistance to a member suffering from a temporary loss of market confidence and exceptional balance of payments problems (presumably reflecting turbulence in other countries), and where there is the expectation that the problem can be corrected in short order. While access is not negotiated in advance, the idea is that these extra funds, sufficient to offset the impact on domestic markets of a sudden decline in market confidence, would be disbursed quickly (in conjunction with an existing standby or extended arrangement).[15]

The limitation of this approach is that the resources of the IMF and other multilaterals are small relative to those of the market and that they can be disbursed only following the negotiation of new conditionality.[16] The IMF cannot be transformed into a true lender of last resort that can provide unlimited resources to a financially distressed government; its principal shareholders would not let it borrow or print the money needed to underwrite intervention on this scale. Consequently, the fund is concerned to husband its limited resources and would be reluctant to agree to automatically disburse resources without attaching (and therefore having to negotiate) new conditions which maximized the probability of repayment.[17] Whether such funds can be disbursed with sufficient speed is therefore an open question. For all these reasons, these kinds of schemes can operate only at a limited scale and speed. They can provide only limited insurance financial shocks.

2. EX POST MEASURES

The most important changes that could be made to facilitate orderly workouts of international debts are the incorporation of new clauses into loan contracts. This section considers the cases of bonds and bank loans in turn. It then discusses IMF lending into arrears and the establishment of standing committees of creditors.

2.1 New provisions in sovereign bond covenants

Money center banks account for so much international lending because they have well-developed capacities to gather information about foreign borrowers and have cultivated long-term relationships with their clients which provide leverage when it comes time to collect on loans.[18] That said, changes in technology and market organization suggest that securitized instruments (bonds and derivative instruments based upon them) will account for a growing fraction of international lending over time. Improvements in information and communications technologies tend to undermine the informational advantage of banks. Advances in financial technology enable individual investors to unbundle and hedge credit and currency risks. Meanwhile, the growth of mutual funds, pension funds, hedge funds and other collective investment vehicles creates a demand for securitized investments. Securitization has made great strides in the advanced-industrial countries, where observers speak regularly of the shrinking market for banking services. International bonds are already accounting for a growing fraction of new commitments (bonds plus bank loans). One can confidently predict that bonds will account for a growing share of portfolio investments in emerging markets in years to come.

On balance, this technological revolution encouraging international lending to flow through bond markets rather than banks is probably a good thing. Insofar as it reflects improvements in the information environment, which render the market less dependent on banks as vehicles for surmounting informational obstacles, it implies a more efficient allocation of resources. And insofar as emerging market debt becomes less concentrated in the hands of the major money center banks, it leaves the latter less vulnerable to international debt crises.

But like many good things, the securitization of emerging market debt does not come without costs. Here the costs are additional problems at the renegotiation stage. Securitization means a significant increase in the number of creditors, small creditors in particular, multiplying collective-action problems.[19] Moreover, restructuring a sovereign bond issued in the United States (more precisely, under the legal provisions that govern bonds issued in that country) typically requires the unanimous consent of the bondholders, which can be a formidable hurdle. In the event of default, each bondholder has the right to sue the issuer, and no bondholder can be forced to agree to new terms by other bondholders. Unlike syndicated bank loans, there are no sharing clauses requiring individual bondholders to share any amount recovered with other bondholders and thereby discouraging recourse to lawsuits. There are no counterparts to the central banks and regulators that used their powers of moral suasion to encourage cooperative behavior by the members of commercial bank syndicates in the 1980s.[20] Neither do sovereign issuers have recourse to a bankruptcy filing, under which they would be protected from the threat of lawsuits and in the context of which terms could be imposed on minority creditors. Agreement being difficult to reach, issuers are understandably reluctant to contemplate restructuring.

In the event they do, "vultures" (offshore hedge funds or large individual investors) then have an incentive to purchase bonds from less patient investors and to threaten lawsuits designed to attach the debtor's assets. Wishing to avoid expensive and embarrassing litigation, the debtor may then feel compelled to buy them out at full price. Taken to the extreme, this suggests that maverick creditors will buy up all the defaulted debt and litigate to prevent sovereign issuers from settling for less than 100 cents on the dollar. Restructuring that involves writing down principal and interest will then be impossible.

One need not subscribe to this extreme version of the argument to see that the provisions governing the issuance of sovereign bonds complicate the process of renegotiation and restructuring.[21] It is hardly a mystery that, under present arrangements, governments are reluctant to go this route.

Fortunately, a solution is at hand, having been suggested two years ago by the G-10 in its report, *Resolving Sovereign Liquidity Crises* and now having been echoed by the G-22 in *The Report of the Working Group on International Financial Crises.* G-10 Deputies recommended making it easier to undertake negotiations by altering the provisions of loan contracts to include majority voting, sharing, and non-acceleration clauses.[22] This would prevent maverick creditors from resorting to lawsuits and other means of obstructing settlements beneficial to the debtor and the vast majority of creditors. (To their recommendations one might add the idea of minimum thresholds for creditor lawsuits, requiring that a certain minimum percentage of creditors, say ten or twenty-five percent, would be required in order to take legal action against the creditor.[23]) The addition of such clauses to bond contracts is the only practical way of creating an environment conducive to flexible restructuring negotiations. It is infinitely more realistic than advocating some kind of supernational bankruptcy court empowered to cram down settlement terms.

Some object that such provisions, by making it easier for developing countries to wriggle out of debt contracts, would only increase borrowing costs.[24] For those who believe that moral hazard and other market imperfections cause governments to rely excessively on foreign borrowing, this is not undesirable. Others question whether borrowing costs will in fact rise.[25] To be sure, majority-voting, sharing, and non-acceleration clauses make it easier to renegotiate defaulted debts, but if this permits a long deadlock to be avoided and renders the majority of investors better off, there is no reason why they might shun bonds with these features. Small bondholders, who lack the resources to sue, might be rendered better off if such clauses averted a long period when interest was not paid and bond prices were depressed while the government and maverick creditors fought their war of attrition. Institutional investors might be better off if, in the absence of this market-based solution, they came under pressure from their governments to cut a deal.

It is important to understand that the normal presumption that "if we see it, it must be optimal" is open to question in the present context. Those who argue that the prohibition on majority voting to restructure the terms of a loan is the market's way of strengthening the bonding role of debt are ignorant of the measure's history. In fact, the law was introduced not by proponents of the market but by individuals deeply suspicious of it. William O. Douglas championed the measure in the wake of the debt defaults of the early 1930s as one of a number of laws to protect small investors from victimization by securities houses. This peculiar history underscores that there is no necessary reason to retain these archaic measures. So does the fact that bonds issued under the provisions of the laws of Great Britain, a country lacking this one's populist tradition, have more renegotiation-friendly provisions. There, bondholders are represented by a trustee and cannot sue individually.[26] British bonds also provide for the binding of all bondholders by a majority vote at a bondholder meeting.

According to the G-10 report, new provisions are to be introduced into debt instruments through a "market-led process." Governments are to trumpet the virtues of new clauses but to otherwise take no action. They are to hope that the markets will see the light.

But if changes in contracts were so easily adopted, the markets would have done so already. That no progress has occurred in the intervening years suggests that there are significant obstacles to market-driven reform. One is the adverse signaling effect. If only some issuers include qualified-majority-voting clauses in their loan agreements, creditors may suspect that those debtors regard it as likely that they will have to restructure in the not-too-distant future. The qualified-majority-voting clause will be regarded as a negative signal that the borrower is less than fully committed to servicing his loan, much like a request for a prenuptial agreement. This can allow inefficient arrangements, put in place for historical reasons long past, to become locked in.[27]

The G-10 report, perhaps in a desire to look market friendly, says little about this dilemma. At one point it acknowledges the first-mover problem and suggests that official support for contractual innovation should be provided "as appropriate" but fails to elaborate. A more pro-active approach is now required. The IMF should urge all its members to adopt majority-representation, sharing, non-acceleration, minimum legal action threshold, and collective-representation clauses (where these last provisions make provision for an indenture trustee to represent and coordinate the bondholders). It should recommend that members require that all international bonds include such provisions as a condition for being admitted to domestic markets (including under Rule 144A).

To be sure, this is no panacea. Private placements would not be affected. New provisions could be added to existing loans only through a voluntary exchange of old bonds for new ones. Not only might some bondholders resist, but any one country that attempted to be the first to carry out the exchange might be seen as signaling that it was contemplating imminent default and precipitate a crisis.

All this means the incorporation of sharing, majority-voting and non-acceleration provisions into bond covenants will be slow. But slow progress is better than no progress.

2.2 New provisions for bank credits

Short-term credits extended by one bank to another are a more difficult case. Since interbank loans are not governed by formal contracts, renegotiation cannot be eased by altering contractual provisions. This can be gotten around if countries adopt laws limiting the terms and conditions under which short-term loans to their banks might be repatriated. Robert Litan and others urge countries to enact legislation imposing an automatic reduction of the principal of all foreign currency loans extended to banks in their countries that are not rolled over in the event of a crisis.[28] Foreign creditors could still get out, but only at a loss. The prospect of that loss would strengthen their incentive to stick around, to address their collective action problem, and to restructure the debt.

If this legislation is only passed when the crisis strikes, such initiatives have no advantage vis-á-vis current arrangements. Nothing now prevents countries from freezing or writing down foreign loans to their banks. In any case, governments' own behavior suggests that they fear action to freeze bank claims would provoke flight by other foreign and domestic creditors, forcing the imposition of across-the-board exchange controls.[29] They regard this as too damaging to their reputations for financial probity and to their countries' ability to borrow.

If the idea is that such legislation should be adopted in advance of any crisis, then the measure is likely to be much more demoralizing to lenders than the addition of majority voting clauses to bond covenants. If new clauses are added to bond covenants, the decision to halt interest payments will still be in the hands of the individual corporate, financial or governmental borrower. The write-down of principal will be determined on a case-by-case basis in negotiations between the debtor and its creditors. In contrast, the obligatory "haircut" for foreign bank creditors would apply across the board. Foreign creditors would be especially alarmed if, as is likely, the circumstances under which the new law was triggered were left to the government's discretion. Alternatively, if the trigger was the announcement of an IMF program, as some authors recommend, the merest hint that a government was exploring the possibility of obtaining help from the fund would provoke flight by its foreign bank creditors, precisely the outcome that the measure was intended to prevent. More generally, foreign bank creditors worried about a mandatory haircut will be tempted to flee at the first sign of trouble. Once the provision is triggered, of course, they will have an incentive to stay in, but imagine their incentive to get out before the trigger is pulled. This perverse effect has the potential to transform small crises into big ones. Then there is the familiar "after you, Alphonse" problem, that no country will want to be first to impose such legislation for fear of signaling that it is worried about a pending crisis. Finally, foreign banks are likely to respond to the measure by channeling their lending through the offshore branches of the debtor's banks. Creditors would then dispute the applicability of the developing-country law and appeal to their own courts in the effort to attach the assets of those offshore branches.

For all these reasons, the best way of dealing with the special problems created by short-term bank-to-bank lending is to discourage excessive reliance on this form of funding in the first place.

2.3 IMF lending into arrears

IMF policy through most of the 1980s was to lend to a country that had fallen into arrears on its external debts only after it had reached an agreement in principle with its creditors. The notion was that the fund should provide assistance only if commercial banks contributed to burden sharing by, in part, clearing away the country's arrears.[30] The debt crisis of the 1980s, a protracted affair, raised doubts about this approach. The banks, their balance sheets strengthening as they drew down their Latin American exposure, hardened their positions. Rather than the IMF using this policy as a lever to encourage burden sharing by the banks, the banks realized that they could use it as a club in their battle with governments. If countries refused to settle on favorable terms, the banks could veto new IMF money in addition to denying their own.

Consequently, in the late 1980s, in a departure from past practice, the IMF contributed to the pool of money used to retire nonperforming bank debts and replace them with Brady bonds. Since 1989 the fund has had a de facto policy of providing support for a member's adjustment efforts after the emergence of arrears but before an agreement had been reached between the debtor and its creditors, so long as the country in question was engaged in good-faith negotiations and making a serious effort to adjust. In more than three dozen instances the IMF has lent in support of adjustment programs before a member has cleared away its arrears to commercial banks. Lending into arrears can provide working capital for an economy that is making an adjustment effort and—analogous to the "debtor-in-possession" financing provided under U.S. corporate bankruptcy procedures—avert unnecessary damage to its economy. Insofar as collective-action problems, exacerbated by rules requiring the unanimous assent of creditors to the terms of any restructuring plan, render negotiations between governments and their creditors excessively protracted, IMF support to a country in arrears can help bring creditors to the bargaining table.[31] Insofar as sovereign debtors and the international community generally see the temporary suspension of payments, followed by negotiations to restructure, too difficult and costly to pursue, it may then be desirable for the IMF to tip the balance in this way, opening up debtor-creditor negotiations as a viable alternative to regular IMF rescues.

The G-10's 1996 report acknowledged that lending into arrears was a way for the IMF to expedite restructuring and asked the fund to contemplate extending the policy from commercial bank loans to bonded debts.[32] While the fund has not made lending into arrears standard policy, it seems prepared to move in this direction.[33]

The risk is that creditors might sue in an effort to attach the proceeds of the loan. While private debtors can seek shelter from a creditor lawsuit in the bankruptcy court, sovereign debtors have no such recourse. If the creditors are commercial banks, they will be subject to moral suasion by their central banks and regulators and are unlikely to seek to attach IMF assets in this way.[34] But if they are bondholders, as will increasingly become the case as securitization proceeds, the danger is greater. The fear if not yet the reality of lawsuits is real.

Perhaps IMF balances could be transferred from the fund's accounts to the central bank in question and the courts would recognize the central bank as a legally separate entity from the government and therefore not responsible for the latter's debts.[35] Perhaps attempts to attach the proceeds of the loan before the fund has disbursed them would be rejected by the courts on the grounds that its Articles of Agreement make the IMF immune from legal process.[36] Perhaps the courts could be swayed by a brief filed by a creditor-country government arguing against attaching IMF resources. Perhaps the creditors, knowing that they would have to do battle with the U.S. government and the IMF, would be reluctant to throw down the gauntlet.[37]

That said, what will happen is uncertain. This has prompted discussions of whether Article VIII.2(b) of the fund's articles of agreement should be amended to give official status to a country's standstill of payments and to shelter its government, and any IMF resources lent into arrears, from legal action. Article VIII.2(b) allows countries to apply exchange controls in response to balance-of-payments problems without violating their obligations to the IMF. That article would have to be given an authoritative reinterpretation by the fund's executive directors or more likely be amended with the consent of countries commanding eighty percent of the fund's voting power for it to give sanction to a standstill on external debt as opposed to the imposition of exchange controls.

It is unlikely that the requisite majority would agree to vest such powers in the hands of an international organization.[38] Not only would market participants oppose empowering the fund to interfere so extensively with private debt contracts, but the fund would not be seen as possessing the impartiality and detachment of a bankruptcy judge. Among other things, it might have made loans to the country itself. The idea of amending Article VIII.2(b) to empower the fund to declare a standstill would be rejected as soon as it was considered on Capitol Hill.[39]

Fortunately, there exist more practical alternatives. One is a limited amendment to the fund's articles of agreement in which its members agree to give immunity in their national courts to the fund's own disbursements and transactions. It is not obvious why, in order to achieve this limited goal, Article VIII.2(b) should have to be amended to give the fund the power to halt all legal action against a government. A complementary approach would be for countries to amend their own sovereign immunities laws to allow their courts to stay attempts to attach sovereign assets.[40] In the United States and United Kingdom, creditors are already prevented from attaching certain sovereign assets even when the sovereign has waived its immunity, as is commonly the practice when governments float international bonds. It would be desirable to clarify these provisions and for other countries to emulate them.

2.4 Standing committees of creditors

A final change in the international financial architecture to help bail in the private sector would be to create standing committees of creditors. Restructuring negotiations are most difficult and protracted when information is least complete. Where the preferences and capacities of all parties are common information, agreement should be immediate.[41] The more asymmetric the information environment, the more likely are debtors and creditors to fight a lengthy war of attrition. Establishing a standing committee of representatives of the various classes of creditors—bondholders, banks, and other institutional investors—that meets regularly with borrowers would open lines of communication and help to overcome information problems.[42]

A standing creditors' committee would also reduce transaction costs in times of crisis. When a crisis erupts and debt service is halted, negotiations cannot proceed until the creditors have been identified, which is time consuming when the process starts from scratch. The existence of a standing committee in continuous contact with its constituents would ease this difficulty. Next the debtor must decide with whom to negotiate—that is, who speaks for the creditors. The existence of a standing committee would answer this question in advance. Finally there is the need to gain the assent of a majority of creditors to the restructuring plan and to buy out those who refuse. The existence of a standing committee on which various classes of creditors interact regularly would create peer pressure for agreement and facilitate the extension of any required side payments. This last point is important: these committees would only offer nonbinding recommendations to the bondholders, who would then have the right to accept them or reject them. They would play much the same role as bank advisory committees in the syndicated bank debt crisis of the 1980s.

The difficulties created by the absence of these committees are evident in the recent experiences of South Korea and Russia. In Korea, the problem in the last week of 1997 was to get the banks to roll over their maturing short-term loans, to accept a delay in making interest payments, and to agree to the principle of converting those short-term credits into long-term loans. The Korean government and the banks reached that agreement by the skin of their teeth. With the help of Bill Rhodes' Rolodex the relevant bankers were located, pulled from their Christmas dinners, and thrust into negotiations.[43] Russia's experience in August 1998 following its suspension of payments further illustrates the confusion that can arise when there exists no committee of creditors.[44] First, the Russian authorities met with a small group of Russian and foreign banks to discuss the formation of a creditors' committee. Next, it was decided that the committee would be formed only after the authorities had somehow managed to draw up a full list of creditors. Finally, there were a variety of disagreements over the composition of the creditors' club.

To be sure, these arrangements will grow more complex with the shift from bank to bond finance. That shift will increase the number of interested parties and vest additional power in the hands of a class of creditors less susceptible to moral suasion by their central banks. But it will erode the effectiveness of Rhodes' Rolodex even more dramatically. What was possible in Korea will not be possible again. Standing committees will become essential.

One sometimes hears the objection that experience with corporate debt workouts suggests that committees of creditors can be quickly constituted if and when the time comes.[45] In fact, the situation for corporate bonds is quite different from that affecting sovereign debts. Most corporate bonds are issued in the United States through an indenture trustee. The indenture trustee is responsible for acting as a communications center to coordinate the bondholders. It must communicate with the bondholders and follow the instructions given by a majority. It is the bondholders' representative in negotiations with the debtor and the court. However, the Trust Indenture Act of 1939 exempts securities issued by foreign governments, their subdivisions and municipalities. Sovereign bonds are typically issued through a fiscal agent rather than an indenture trustee. The fiscal agent has a much more limited role, and its obligations are mainly to the issuer, not the bondholders. Its responsibilities do not extend to acting as a communications center or attempting to coordinate the bondholders.[46]

In fact, standing committees of creditors were the channel for disseminating information and organizing negotiations when bond finance was last important, from the late nineteenth century through World War II.[47] At first, ad-hoc bondholders' committees were formed in response to each interruption in debt-service payments. Predictably, these committees had trouble establishing contact with a majority of bondholders and opening lines of communication with foreign debtors. In Great Britain, the leading creditor country of the era, the situation was regularized in 1868 by the creation of the Corporation of Foreign Bondholders. Comprised initially of representatives of banking firms and brokerage houses, its governing body, the Council, was expanded in 1898 to include several individual bondholders and a representative of the London Chamber of Commerce. The Council became the recognized spokesman for the bondholders and their representative in negotiations, working closely with the underwriting banks and the London Stock Exchange. The same evolution occurred elsewhere with the establishment of standing bondholders committees in Paris, Amsterdam and Berlin before World War I and in the United States in the 1930s. These committees fell into disuse after World War II because the international capital market was slow to recover from the debt crisis of the 1930s and then because bond finance was superseded by syndicated bank loans. Now, however, bonds are back, and the creditors are more numerous and heterogeneous than when international lending was the domain of bank syndicates.

The idea of creditors' committees was resuscitated in the wake of the Mexican crisis by Rory Macmillan and by Richard Portes and myself.[48] To date, however, the investor community has been reluctant to act. It fears that standing committees would make it too easy for debtors to initiate restructuring negotiations, making it too tempting for them to suspend debt payments. It is better, in the narrow self interest of the creditors, for there to be no one on the other end of the line to pick up the phone.

For policy makers wishing to create a viable alternative to large-scale bailouts of crisis countries and for whom the difficulties of debtor-creditor negotiations render moratoria and restructuring unacceptably difficult and painful, standing committees of creditors are desirable precisely because they make it easier for debtors to initiate negotiations. Their formation is important for creating a viable alternative to ever-more-costly bailouts and disastrous Russian-style defaults, neither of which is an acceptable option.

The creation of such committees would require moral suasion and lobbying by G-7 governments, central banks, and the IMF. There would be nothing unprecedented about their involvement. The Corporation of Foreign Bondholders received a parliamentary charter and other forms of official support. Its U.S. equivalent, the Foreign Bondholders Protective Council, was formed only with the encouragement and support of the U.S. State Department.[49] These are precedents that should be followed. Specifically,

Rory Macmillan suggests the creation of two standing committees, a resurrected Foreign Bondholders Protective Council in New York to represent and coordinate the holders of government bonds issued under New York law and submitting to New York courts, and a resurrected Council of Foreign Bondholders to represent and coordinate holders of government bonds issued under English law. Because the vast majority of bonds are subject to either New York or English courts and law, two creditors councils would go a long way toward solving the problem.

3. CONCLUSION

Effectively bailing in the private sector requires changes in institutional and contractual arrangements to make it economically acceptable for governments to negotiate an orderly restructuring of their debts. For those who regard ever-larger IMF bailouts as undesirable because of their escalating cost and the moral hazard they create, but are also prepared to acknowledge that under present arrangements governments regard the costs of a unilateral moratorium as too severe, this is the only realistic alternative.

It is important to emphasize that there is unlikely to be a simple and wholly satisfactory solution to this problem. A moratorium on debt repayments ***should*** be unattractive; otherwise, the sanctity of loan contracts would be jeopardized. Contracts and institutional arrangements are structured to make the suspension of debt service painful precisely in order to keep borrowers from walking away from their debts. Were this too easy, the capital market would not function at all. Moreover, it is unrealistic to imagine the creation of an international bankruptcy court with the power to cram down settlement terms on debtors and creditors. And there are good reasons why the IMF cannot be transformed into a true international lender of last resort.

Notwithstanding these difficulties, steps can be taken. The most important of these include limiting short-term foreign-currency-denominated borrowing by banks (by, if necessary, placing a holding period tax on all portfolio capital inflows), adding sharing clauses to loan contracts, establishing creditors' committees, entertaining the possibility of IMF lending into arrears, and amending sovereign immunity laws. History shows that the market left to its own devices cannot provide a perfect solution to international debt problems, any more than the market can efficiently provide for the liquidation and reorganization of financially distressed domestic companies in the absence of an insolvency law. Markets, to operate efficiently, need institutional support. In the present context, the relevant institutional support must be provided by both governments and international organizations.

Notes

[1]See International Monetary Fund (1998), Box II.5.

[2]Shin and Hahm (1998), Table 1.7. Korean financial institutions had foreign currency denominated assets as well, since they were required to limit their open foreign exchange positions. But since their loans were of longer maturity than their liabilities, there was still the possibility of a very serious liquidity problem that the central bank was in no position to address.

[3]At that point, the number and exposure of the foreign bank creditors was reduced to the point where the Korean authorities were able to negotiate a restructuring with their bank creditors, in which the latter agreed to a temporary delay in payments and then to the conversion of their short-term assets into longer-term instruments.

[4]As events transpired, the IMF and the leading industrial countries refused to provide yet more money in the middle of August 1998, and the Russia government responded by devaluing and suspending service on most of its debts. But these actions came as a surprise to many investors, which is the point in the present context.

[5]Thus, the Korean negotiations at the end of 1997 are often cited as examples of how international banks should be "bailed in" during crisis negotiations. Again, however, the fact of the matter is that so long as the Korean government was reluctant to halt service on these and other external debts, the banks still had the option of exiting. Thus, the agreement reached with the government of Korea did not impose significant capital losses on the banks, which only agreed to a delay of service payments and, eventually, to the conversion of their short-term claims into longer-term obligations.

[6]As emphasized by Schwartz (1995).

[7]Unavoidably, the Fund must tranche its assistance rather than following Walter Bagehot's classic advice for a central bank acting as a lender of last resort, namely to lend freely at a penalty rate. This is the main problem with Meltzer's (1998) otherwise sound advice that the IMF should act more like a true lender of last resort by lending at a penalty rate. That it will not be able to lend *freely* at a penalty rate suggests lending at higher interest rates in order to limit moral hazard will not suffice to redress the crisis problem.

[8]Radelet and Sachs (1998), pp. 66–67.

[9]For clear statements of these arguments from authors with otherwise very different perspectives, see Meltzer (1998) and Radelet and Sachs (1998).

[10]In addition, there is the fear, well founded or not, that a standstill or moratorium will unleash contagion to other countries and threaten the stability of the international system.

[11]There are exceptions. These include Mexico in 1982, South Africa in 1985, Brazil in 1987, Venezuela in 1988, and Russia in 1998. Several distinctive aspects of the Russian situation help to explain the unusual outcome in this case. For one, the fact that Russia, unlike say Mexico and South Korea, did not show the resolve necessary to rein its budget deficit suggested that providing official funds to retire the existing short-term debt would not solve the problem, since additional debt would soon have to be issued. For another, the government's failure to make headway on its fiscal problems suggested that capital market access was in any case unlikely to be restored soon. Be that as it may, the aftermath of the Russian government's action, including full-fledge depositor panic, capital flight, and the suspension of foreign exchange trading, hardly reassured those worried that a government's unilateral suspension of payments could damage its credit worthiness and demoralize the markets.

[12]Argentina's contingent repurchase facility with thirteen commercial banks provides for $7 billion in standby credits, while Mexico's arrangement with thirty-one banks provides for $2.5 billion. Under the provisions of the former, the Argentine Central Bank can swap Argentine government securities for U.S. dollars up to the specified ceiling, at an effective interest rate of LIBOR plus 205 basis points. The commitment fee is 33 basis points. Loan length is two to five years, depending on the commercial bank involved. These agreements omit the no-adverse-material-change clause that would otherwise permit the banks to back out of their agreement in the event of a crisis.

[13]A similar idea is developed by Gavin and Hausmann (1998).

[14]Borrowers are expected to repay within one and a one half years of disbursement, and are charged 300 basis points above the rate on other IMF loans (with still higher rates charged if the loan is not repaid at the end of 18 months).

[15]That the IMF is reluctant to preapproval credits is not surprising. Like any lender, the fund would regret having preapproved a credit line were the economic policies and performance of the borrowing countries to suddenly turn for the worse. In addition, however, were the fund to then revoke its pre-approval, the market might take this as a strong negative signal, precipitating a crisis. For related discussion, see Goldstein and Calvo (1996), p. 271.

[16]The Clinton Administration has recently proposed establishing a new facility through which the IMF would extend standing lines of credit to qualifying countries. While this scheme might be practicable for countries like Argentina, which is relatively small relative to global financial markets and whose financial policies are exceptionally strong, there is reason to doubt that it could be used to meet the needs of countries like Brazil and South Korea, because the size of the requisite credits would outstrip available financial resources and because their costliness would lead the Fund to insist on additional conditions at the time of disbursement.

[17]There was some discussion in 1994 of the creation of a short-term financing facility under which the IMF would automatically disburse funds to countries experiencing temporary payments problems and whose eligibility had been determined in advance. But these

discussions were not informed by an appreciation of the magnitude of the funds that might have to be disbursed to restore confidence in private financial markets, given the rapid growth of the liquidity of the latter. Once the Mexican crisis revealed the extent of the commitments that could be required, the idea of automatic credit lines receded from view.

[18]Some observers would add that because banks are critical to financial stability, they can count on the support of the U.S. and other creditor-country governments in the event of debt-servicing difficulties.

[19]Stein's (1989) finding that bank creditors are more likely than bondholders to support corporate debt workouts negotiated in the shadow of the court is consistent with this implication. Miller and Zhang (1997) provide some theoretical and numerical exercises designed to show that this is precisely the consequence of the switch from bank to bond finance.

[20]To be sure, a non-negligible fraction of foreign bonds are held by commercial banks. And pension funds, mutual funds and insurance companies are also subject to regulatory oversight, if not always with the same intensity as banks. But institutional investors as a group hold only a fraction of the bonds outstanding, in contrast to the earlier situation with syndicated bank loans, rendering moral suasion less effective.

[21]Evidence against the extreme view can be drawn from four recent cases where countries succeeded in restructuring their sovereign bonds through unilateral exchange offers: Costa Rica in 1985, Nigeria in 1988, Guatemala in 1989, and Panama in 1993. In all these cases, the vast majority of bondholders, typically more than ninety percent, exchanged their old debt obligations for new ones rather than selling out to vultures (Pinon-Farah 1996). It can be questioned whether these cases are representative, however, since the terms of the exchange implied little reduction of interest or principal, only a grace period, longer maturities, and unbunching of payments.

[22]In the case of most international bonds, ten to twenty-five percent of the bondholders (more precisely, those holding ten to twenty-five percent of the principal) can vote to require immediate repayment of all principal and interest due in the event of default. In contrast, syndicated bank loans typically require fifty percent of creditors to vote for acceleration. This therefore raises the danger that even when a majority of bondholders prefer an orderly workout that will maximize the value of their claims, an impatient minority can trigger the clause requiring immediate repayment. The debtor would then have to reschedule not only interest payments and amounts due to be paid into a sinking fund but all principal as well.

[23]Note the parallel with the minimum percentages that already exist for activating acceleration clauses.

[24]Institute of International Finance (1996).

[25]At this point, there is little evidence of whether or not this is the case. While the Hong Kong Airport Authority is frequently invoked as an example of a borrower which has issued bonds with these provisions without obviously elevating its borrowing costs, but it is not a fully sovereign entity, rendering it a special case. A more systematic analysis of the pricing of

bonds issued under the British and American models (with and without the relevant provisions) is clearly called for.

[26]Although a specified minority holding a fifth to a quarter of principal can require the trustee to do so on their behalf.

[27]This path-dependence argument is a theme of Roe (1987).

[28]See Litan et al. (1998).

[29]Indeed, the market reaction to the Russian action freezing foreign credits on August 17, 1998, dried up all credit to the Russian financial system, provoked widespread capital flight, and forced the government to halt all foreign exchange trading several times in the final week of August.

[30]The traditional IMF position on lending into arrears was stated in an Executive Board decision in 1970. See Cline (1996).

[31]Goldstein (1996) argues that the fund's lending into arrears was critical for driving commercial bank creditors to the negotiating table in the second half of the 1980s and finally clearing away the Latin American debt crisis.

[32]Group of Ten (1996). Spokesmen for the creditors responded that lending into arrears may have been appropriate in the 1980s, when the existence of a generalized debt crisis justified the provision of public-sector enhancements to support debt reduction arrangements, but that it is not warranted in the "normalized" capital market conditions that exist today (Institute of International Finance 1996). Recent experience refutes this contention on two grounds: first, even "normalized" conditions can quickly become abnormal; and second, even if debt problems are limited in their geographical scope, the provision of the equivalent of debtor-in-possession financing by the IMF may be important for preventing the kind of complete economic breakdown that can set the stage for the contagious spread of the crisis, and it can help to expedite a negotiated agreement to restructure.

[33]See for example the comments of IMF Managing Director Michel Camdessus at his joint press conference with Philippe Maystadt, chairman of the Interim Committee, at IMF Headquarters, April 16, 1998, http://www.imf.org/external/np/tr/1998/TR980416.htm.

[34]During the debt crisis of the 1980s, when the principal creditors were international banks, lawsuits were consequently rare (except for precautionary suits filed merely to protect against expiration of the statute of limitations). However, when Argentina defaulted on some of its bonds in 1986, three bondholders sued successfully in U.S. courts. And when Panama defaulted in 1987, at least one bondholder pressed a lawsuit.

[35]When it is not waived, central bank reserves enjoy sovereign immunity in the major financial centers, most notably the United States and the United Kingdom.

[36]Under the provisions of Article IX.8(I). In addition, the fund's articles require it to deal only with members through their treasuries, central banks, and fiscal authorities. Thus, it

could argue that it cannot deal directly with a court-appointed receiver or with the creditors' fiscal agent.

[37]That there have been no attempts to date to attach fund disbursements is consistent with this view.

[38]In any case, member countries would have to pass domestic legislation ensuring that this measure had effect in their domestic courts.

[39]One need only recall congressional resistance to the dispute-panel provisions of the WTO agreement.

[40]As suggested by Hurlock (1995).

[41]This is a basic premise of bankruptcy theory: In a world of complete information and absent transactions costs, there is no need for a bankruptcy code or bankruptcy court, since debtors and creditors will be able to instantaneously adjust their contracts to any unanticipated contingencies.

[42]Some have suggested that such a committee, possibly with rotating membership, could also interface with the IMF and other official bodies. In practice, this would create more problems than it solved. For one thing, since membership on the committee would be selective, some in the markets would inevitably feel that other participants were getting preferential treatment from the IMF. And insofar as the real problem of information asymmetries arises in negotiations between the lenders and the borrowers, and not between the lenders and the IMF, it is with the debtor that the creditors' representatively most urgently need to interact. In instances where the IMF was negotiating the extension of financial assistance while the debtors and creditors were at the same time attempting to restructure outstanding debts, there might be occasion for exceptional discussions among the three parties, but it is not obvious why regular meetings between the creditors' committee and the official sector would be essential. And to the extent that there is a need for the fund and the financial community to exchange information in a time of crisis, this can be done more simply, by asking the central bank or national treasury in each of the creditor countries to identify a representative for their financial community.

[43]Or so the situation is described by Lee (1998). Rhodes is the vice-chairman of Citibank and a veteran of the debt crisis of the 1980s.

[44]See Reuters (1998).

[45]Thus, Institute of International Finance (1996) cites the case of AeroMexico as an example of how negotiations can proceed and be concluded swiftly in the absence of a bondholders' committee.

[46]Macmillan (1997), pp. 9–10.

[47]See Eichengreen and Portes (1989).

[48]See Macmillan (1995) and Eichengreen and Portes (1996).

[49]See Eichengreen and Portes (1989).

References

Cline, William R. 1996, "Crisis Management in Emerging Capital Markets," in *From Halifax to Lyons: What Has Been Done About Crisis Management?* Peter B. Kenen (ed.), *Essays in International Finance,* No. 200, International Finance Section, Department of Economics, Princeton University, October.

Eichengreen, Barry and Richard Portes. 1989, "After the Deluge: Default, Negotiation, and Readjustment During the Interwar Years," in *The International Debt Crisis in Historical Perspective*, Barry Eichengreen and Peter H. Lindert (ed.), Cambridge, MA.: MIT Press, pp. 12–47.

Eichengreen, Barry, and Richard Portes. 1996, *Crisis? What Crisis? Orderly Workouts for Sovereign Debtors,* London: Centre for Economic Policy Research.

Gavin, Michael, and Ricardo Hausmann. 1998, "A Contingent Facility to Promote Financial Stability and Strengthen Market Discipline," Office of the Chief Economist, Interamerican Development Bank, unpublished manuscript.

Goldstein, Morris. 1996, "Avoiding Future Mexicos: A Post-Halifax Scorecard on Crisis Prevention and Management," in *From Halifax to Lyons: What Has Been Done About Crisis Management?*," Peter B. Kenen (ed.), Essays in International Finance, No. 200, International Finance Section, Department of Economics, Princeton University, October, pp. 56–72

Goldstein, Morris, and Guillermo A. Calvo. 1996, "What Role for the Official Sector?," in *Private Capital Flows to Emerging Markets After the Mexican Crisis.* Guillermo A. Calvo, Morris Goldstein, and Eduard Hochreiter (eds.), Washington, DC: Institute for International Economics, pp. 233–282.

Group of Ten. 1996, *Resolving Sovereign Liquidity Crises*, Washington, DC: Group of Ten.

Group of Twenty-Two. 1998, *Report of the Working Group on International Financial Crises*, Washington, DC: Group of Twenty Two.

Hurlock, James. 1995, "The Way Ahead for Sovereign Debt," *Euromoney*, pp. 78–79.

Institute of International Finance. 1996, *Resolving Sovereign Financial Crises,* Washington, DC: Institute of International Finance.

International Monetary Fund. 1998, *International Capital Markets,* Washington, DC: International Monetary Fund.

Lee, Peter. 1998, "Korea Stares into the Abyss," *Euromoney* March, pp. 32–37.

Litan, Robert. et al. 1998, "Statement of the Shadow Financial Regulatory Committee on International Monetary Fund Assistance and International Crises," Statement No. 145, Shadow Financial Regulatory Committee.

Macmillan, Rory. 1995, "New Lease on Life for Bondholder Councils," *Financial Times*, August 15, p. 11.

Macmillan, Rory. 1997, "Towards a Sovereign Debt Work-out System," unpublished manuscript.

Meltzer, Alan. 1998, "Asian Problems and the IMF," Testimony Prepared for the Joint Economic Committee, U.S. Congress, February 24.

Miller, Marcus, and Lei Zhang. 1997, "A Bankruptcy Procedure for Sovereign States," Global Economic Institutions, working paper, No. 34, London: Economic and Social Research Council, August.

Pinon-Farah, Marco A. 1996, "Private Bond Restructurings: Lessons for the Case of Sovereign Debtors," IMF, working paper, WP/96/11.

Radelet, Steven, and Jeffrey Sachs. 1998, "The East Asian Financial Crisis: Diagnosis, Remedies, Prospects," *Brookings Papers on Economic Activity* 1, pp. 1–74.

Reuters. 1998, "Russia, Western Banks to Form Creditors Club." Monday, 24 August 8:25 am Eastern time, from the internet at http://biz.yahoo.com/finance/980824/russia_ban_1.html.

Roe, Mark. 1987, "The Voting Prohibition in Bond Workouts," *Yale Law Journal* 97, pp. 232–280.

Schwartz, Anna J. 1995, "G-7 Countries at Halifax Summit Repeat the Mexican Myth," Communique of the Shadow Open Market Committee, September 10–11.

Shin, Inseok, and Joon-Ho Hahm. 1998, "The Korean Crisis—Causes and Resolution," Korea Development Institute, unpublished manuscript, July.

Stein, Sol, 1989, *A Feast for Lawyers*, New York: M. Evans and Company.

Chapter 37

Does the IMF Have a Future? What Should It Be?

Robert E. Litan
Brookings Institution

It is not an understatement to say that the IMF—and indeed the entire world economy is currently facing its stiffest challenge since the fund was created after World War II. Many speakers at this conference have already addressed the crisis, the IMF's role in addressing it, and steps the fund should take in the future to prevent future crises.

In these remarks, I take on a higher-level issue: what should be done about the IMF itself. Does it have a future, and if so, what should it be?

Two years ago, such questions wouldn't even be asked in polite company. It was taken for granted that one of the world's largest international institutions, and certainly one of its most important, would forever be part of the economic and political landscape. Now, this isn't the case. The Congress has refused thus far to approve the Administration's request for $18 billion to help replenish the IMF's resources, which have been severely depleted by the various Asian rescue packages the fund arranged earlier this year. A shortage of resources is one reason (but certainly not the only one) why the fund didn't offer to provide Russia more money during late summer (after arranging a package in July). Even if the Congress eventually approves the $18 billion for this country's contribution to the quota increase. the acrimonius debate over the IMF's funding and future this time does not augur well for approval of additional funding in the future.[1]

I won't hold you in suspense. My bottom line is that the world has an important stake in giving a meaningful future to the IMF, not as a "lender of last resort" but as the "crisis and prevention manager" that it more realistically has been and should continue to be. In what follows, I address a number (but not all) of the recent criticisms of the fund. Some of the attacks are on target, but in my view, they justify reform of the fund, not its elimination. Nonetheless, at this writing, because limiting the fund to its current resources appears to be a possible near-term option, I attempt to guess what the world would be like if that outcome should come to pass. I conclude with a recommendation that the fund facilitate the rapid workout of the debt overhang in Southeast Asia in particular that is impeding economic recovery in the region.

1. IS THE IMF A LENDER OF LAST RESORT? SHOULD IT BE? CAN IT BE?

It is common to talk of the IMF as being an international lender of last resort (LLR), playing a role akin to the one played by central banks in a domestic context. I myself have used this analogy at times and I suspect many of those in this room have done so as well.

But the more I have thought about the subject, the more I have realized that the analogy falls short. In reality, while the IMF performs some functions that look like an LLR, it also differs from a domestic LLR in a number of important respects. Indeed, the differences are so fundamental—and so unlikely ever to be eliminated—that it is time we change the terminology of what the fund really does and should do in the future, assuming it should continue to exist.

Central banks within countries typically have three characteristics that enable them to function as lenders-of-last-resort:

- They can flood a troubled market with liquidity by printing money (which ordinarily lowers interest rates on government securities and thereby makes investments in riskier assets, such as loans, bonds and equity securities, relatively more attractive).
- They can provide *temporary* loans to specific *solvent* institutions, typically banks, that may find themselves short of liquidity in a crisis.
- They limit moral hazard by regulating potential borrowers (banks), and if they are following Walter Bagehot's rules, only provide loans at a penalty rate backed by good collateral.

The IMF differs from a domestic LLR, however, in the following important respects:

- First, although it has created a small amount of a kind of "world money" for central banks, or SDRs, the fund cannot act as the world's provider of liquidity. The resources of the fund are limited by the amount of currencies deposited by members. The fund cannot print money to lend to any worthy borrower like a central bank, but increasingly must husband its scarce resources, a topic I address in greater detail shortly.
- Second, while the fund can and does lend to individual countries in need of liquidity, its loans often have effective maturities that last for years.
- Third, I do not believe the distinction between "illiquidity" and insolvency" is useful in the international context. It is hard enough for a central bank, in the heat of a crisis, to distinguish whether any particular bank is illiquid or insolvent. But what would it even mean to say that a *country is* insolvent and not merely illiquid?. Sure, *governments* can and do default on their obligations. But are the *countries* "insolvent" when they do so, or are political leaders simply unwilling to pay the political and economic price of honoring the country's debts? Take Russia, as an example. Even though the government there has effectively defaulted on its loans, and caused the banks to do likewise, Russia remains very rich in resources and so is hardly "insolvent."
- Fourth, the fund does not regulate countries preemptively in the same way that central banks (or national supervisors) regulate their potential bank borrowers. To be sure, the fund has a carrot—money—to persuade countries that want to avoid a crisis by reforming their policies. But until countries ask for money, either in the absence or in the middle of a crisis, the fund has no ability to regulate their activities.
- With some exceptions, the fund does not charge a penalty rate on its loans, and in this sense the IMF looks very much like our Fed. At the same time, the fund's conditions on its loans seem to entail more micomanagement of its borrowers than would be the case even for a national bank supervisor of a troubled institution. But the fund imposes tough conditions because it cannot seize assets of countries, as can private creditors; or overthrow their leaders, as even U.S. regulators can now do in the case of weakly capitalized banks under the new "prompt corrective action" regime (to be precise, U.S. regulators can assume control of a weak, but still solvent bank, and sell it to others who can recapitalize and manage it).

- Sixth, unlike central banks that have an interest in immediately supplying such funds as may be necessary to stop a deposit run (consistent with prudent lending practices), the fund dribbles out the disbursement of its assistance in small doses. It does this because the prospect of handing over more money is its only real leverage to ensure that borrowing countries adhere to the fund's conditions. But gradualism has its costs as well, since countries can find it hard to stop a currency run when they are short of reserves on hand.
- Seventh, the IMF is governed by many different countries with different interests and must work by consensus. Its director does not have the power of, say, an Alan Greenspan to move the entire body, although recently the U.S. government (through the Treasury) has been well out in front in leading the IMF. However, the U.S. still only has an eighteen percent vote, and our influence inevitably must wane if we are not willing to provide the IMF with the additional resources it has requested.

In short, while I disagree with her recommendation that the IMF be dissolved, I could not agree more with Anna Schwartz when she concludes that the IMF is not like a domestic LLR. Furthermore, even when it had more funds to lend out relatively freely, the IMF's policy was to lend to *any of its members* willing to accept its conditions. The fund did not try to make a determination whether the country is merely illiquid rather than insolvent (nor, for reasons I have already outlined, would it have made sense to try). As the first article of the fund's Articles of Agreement makes clear, one of its major purposes is to "give confidence to members by making the general resources of the fund temporarily available to them under adequate safeguards, *thus providing them with opportunity to correct maladjustments in their balance of payments without resorting to measures destructive of national or international prosperity*" (emphasis added). In plain English, this means that the fund is there to help ensure that governments of countries don't do stupid things either that may *precipitate* a crisis that has spillover effects to other countries, or in the midst of a crisis, take steps to *aggravate* a crisis, to their own detriment and to the detriment of other countries.

It is more accurate, therefore, to say that the fund—it its emergency lending activities—is in the "crisis prevention and management" (CPM) business than to claim it is the international equivalent of a lender-of-last resort. The question the Asian-cum-Russia-cum potential Latin American crisis has put on the table, therefore, is whether the IMF should continue in this role, have its operations refined, changed, constrained or eliminated. It is useful to begin with the arguments for elimination first, for if the fund can't survive those, it doesn't make much sense to address the other options.

2. THE IMF AND FLEXIBLE EXCHANGE RATES

One alleged argument for dismantling the fund is built around the claim that it was created to support the Bretton Woods system of fixed (and only occasionally adjusted) exchange rates. Now that fixed rates are largely dead, it is said: it is time to sunset the IMF.

This argument is misplaced on several levels. As a threshold matter, even in the wake of the Asian crisis, not all countries have abandoned fixed rates, or their close cousins, currency bands or managed floating regimes. But more fundamentally, the main purpose for which the fund was created—to discourage countries from adopting economic policies in the heat of a balance of payments crisis that harm other economies in the process—is independent of the exchange rate regime that may be in place.

For example, events have shown that having a flexible exchange rate does not make it any easier for a country to manage a large "supply shock," such as a major jump in oil prices for oil importing nations or a sharp drop in commodity prices for exporting countries. In the former case, a jump in prices of a key import has a direct inflationary impact which is compounded by the drop in the exchange rate, which also makes other imports more expensive. The sharp currency depreciation that can follow a drop in world prices of important commodity exports can have a similar impact on exporting countries. If the affected countries also have sizeable foreign currency debts, then the sudden currency depreciation can generate a wave of bankruptcies that can further damage the economy, which may already be weakened by any attempts to fight the depreciation-induced inflation through restrictive macroeconomic policies.

By themselves, these familiar events may not justify IMF assistance. But as recent events have shown, foreign exchange markets are subject to contagion, which means that any initial currency depreciation can easily be magnified when domestic and foreign investors "run" to safe havens. If countries cannot borrow foreign currency to stop the run on their own reserves, then they may adopt any number of measures that restrict trade and capital in an effort to halt the inflationary impacts of their falling currencies. If only one or two countries take such counterproductive measures, the damage to the world may not be significant. But if many similarly situated countries follow a similar course, then the world economy suffers from a "tragedy of the commons" and many economies spiral downward together.

This is what happened in the 1930s. And it was what the IMF was created to prevent.

More sophisticated critics of the IMF may nonetheless respond that while the purposes of the fund theoretically may be appropriate in a world of flexible exchange rates, the availability of fund financing creates a kind of moral hazard—not the typical one I will discuss shortly—that discourages countries from adopting floating rates. These critics will (or should) point out that a major reason for the Asian crisis was that the countries in the region pegged their currencies to the dollar, encouraging local borrowers to engage in a massive arbitrage play: borrowing dollars at low interest rates with the aim of using the funds to earn much higher rates of return in local currency. Critics may point out that had the IMF not been in existence, and thus unavailable to provide liquidity in the event of a run on the currency, it is possible that the Asian countries never would have adopted the currency pegs that encouraged this arbitrage game.

It is impossible to know, of course, whether this would have been the case. But even if it were true, the "currency moral hazard" argument does not justify eliminating the fund. Although I personally believe that flexible rates should be the norm for most countries, fixed or managed rates may be useful in ending a hyperinflation by constraining the ability of centrals banks to pursue an overly expansionary monetary policy. Once inflation has been brought under control, then the case for pegging weakens. That should be a main lesson of the recent financial turmoil that the fund should be preaching to its members rather than any of the members calling for the downsizing or elimination of the fund.

3. THE IMF AND ITS WARTS

The criticisms of the fund extend far beyond issues about exchange rate regimes, of course. As I am about to briefly summarize, some of these attacks are partly valid. But to paraphrase the Clinton Administration's approach to affirmative action, the far better course is to "mend the fund, not to end it."

Moral Hazard: Let's begin with the better known "moral hazard" problem: that because IMF funds recently have been used to stabilize domestic banking systems, IMF rescues have the effect of insulating creditors of banks in borrowing countries against loss. This distorts the pricing of loans and encourages too much borrowing and lending at artificially suppressed interest rates.

IMF officials have acknowledged this problem, have urged attention be devoted to solving it, but at the same time, either have implicitly or explicitly suggested that this is a price that may have to be paid in order to prevent contagion. This view is far too pessimistic. In the United States, we heard similar objections to curtailing the ability of regulators to protect uninsured depositors during the 1980s and yet a law was enacted in 1991 (FDICIA) that does precisely that. In the international arena, the objective should be to establish a similar system, or at the very least, to adopt measures that have the effect of providing more market discipline. I will briefly discuss two steps that would move policy in this direction.

First, the Shadow Financial Regulatory Committee, of which I am a member, proposed last May and has just reiterated in September that future IMF emergency lending (or at the very least the interest rate on those loans) should be made conditional on borrowing countries having a mechanism that, with one caveat I am about to mention, imposes some kind of a haircut on foreign currency creditors of banks when such rescues are announced. The caveat is that the haircut not apply if the creditors keep their money in the banks—if they roll over their deposits or interbank loans (at no higher rate of interest) and keep their money in until the IMF loan is paid back. Furthermore, governments would be prohibited from guaranteeing any more than the principal amount of the interbank credits *minus the haircuts.* Such a system would *promote stability* because it penalizes lenders only if they *withdraw* their funds. It would also curtail moral hazard by encouraging lenders in the future to price their loans to reflect the possibility that they might have much longer effective maturities than anticipated or may suffer a haircut (lenders may also then be induced to purchase "catastrophe" insurance in the private market to protect them against suffering such losses).

I have heard it said that such a conditional haircut regime nonetheless would be destabilizing because it could encourage lenders who fear that an IMF rescue package is imminent to mount anticipatory runs on banks. I do not see this is as a drawback, but as a plus, provided the IMF has adequate funds to respond to crises when it is called upon to do so. As it is now, precisely because of the policy conditions the IMF imposes on its loans—the subjects I will turn to next—governments tend to put off going to the IMF until their currency reserves are nearly exhausted. If a conditional haircut system causes governments to adopt policy reforms sooner, then this is a clear advantage of the idea.

Another criticism of haircuts is that once they are imposed they allegedly would redline a country out of the international credit markets. The recent events in Russia might be cited as "proof" of this danger: it has been widely remarked within the financial community that, having effectively defaulted on its government debt and essentially wiped out the positions of foreign creditors of its banks, Russia has cut off itself off from foreign credit for years, if not decades. The Russian example is an extreme one, however: the Russian government didn't impose haircuts, but rather, *decapitation (creditors* will be lucky if they get ten cents on the dollar). Furthermore, given that Russia does not have anything close to a functioning market economy—nor is there a prospect that it will have one any time soon—it is hardly surprising that the financial community is saying that Russia has dealt itself out of world credit markets. A much better example for haircut critics to look at is the experience in Latin America following the issuance of Brady Bonds, which effectively guaranteed only the written-down portion of the original sovereign debt. This plan didn't redline Latin America out of credit markets; to the contrary, as economies in the region subsequently recovered, foreign capital returned.

Second, markets function best when all actors have up-to-date, accurate information, a condition that it is widely agreed was lacking before the Asian crisis and remains less than fully fulfilled today. Of course, even the best information will not be helpful if creditors know they will be bailed out of their mistakes, and that is why there is a need for some kind of conditional haircut for foreign currency creditors of banks. At the same time, if a haircut system is not to have the unintended side-effect of promoting contagion, it is vital that all financial actors have access to the best information about the financial condition of all countries—especially their currency reserves, net of forward obligations, and the amounts and maturity schedules of foreign currency debt (including debt of affiliates abroad)—so that they can distinguish the good from the not-so-good credits.

Fairly complete banking data are already published by the BIS, while the World Bank and the OECD provide other relevant financial information. Nonetheless, up-to-date, reliable information about *net* international reserves (gross reserves minus forward commitments) is still not available. The IMF should encourage all its member countries to collect and report data on net reserves and foreign currency debt (although even developed countries, including the United States, do not currently tabulate foreign currency debt of foreign affiliates, so this particular job will be a challenging one). The IMF can then post all of the information on its own Web site.

A more controversial question is whether the fund should provide to the public its Article IV *staff* evaluations of the economies of member countries (the of ficial Article IV evaluations for many countries are currently made public but these often read like committee-produced documents that are not as blunt as the staff reports). The case for doing so is that the IMF staff may be in a better position than outsiders to assess the real condition of a country's finances and the quality of its financial supervision, and that disclosing this information would enable the market to do what the fund as an institution may not be able to accomplish: to induce governments to follow constructive policies that avoid crises. The familiar arguments against release of the staff evaluations are that it could impede the fund's ability to gain confidential information from its client countries and may precipitate crises when none may be warranted, arguments that bank supervisors have long made about disclosing CAMEL ratings of the banks they supervise.

Morris Goldstein has suggested one possible way out of this box: *allow* countries themselves to publish their IMF staff evaluations, and hopefully a process of "competitive transparency" may induce other countries to follow. Countries that don't take this route would be pleading the financial equivalent of the fifth amendment from which the markets would draw adverse inferences. I don't know whether any countries would follow Goldstein's suggestion, but it certainly seems worth a try.

I am more dubious, however, of calls for the IMF or some other institution to become an "unbar-regulator," or regulator of the national financial regulators. For one thing, I'm not sure what such an international organization would or could actually do to countries that don't meet—some kind of minimum standard, other than publicize that fact. But this then gets back to the question of whether the unber-regulator will sacrifice its access to national regulators if it at the same time becomes a regulators' rating agency. I'll return to what I just said: let's try Goldstein's suggestion for voluntary disclosure first and hope that a process of "competitive transparency," as he calls it, will ensue.

Macro Policy Conditions Too Tough: The IMF has been attacked from both the right and the left for forcing too much macroeconomic austerity down the throats of the Asian countries, most of which were generally perceived to be following prudent macroeconomic policies before the crisis. In retrospect, the critics appear to be right about fiscal policy tightness and the IMF has since relaxed its deficit targets. Given the continued downward spiral of the Asian economies at the heart of the crisis, additional fiscal expansion—further tax cuts and selected infrastructure projects (schools, highways and the like)—seems warranted. (The same advice is not warranted for countries like Brazil that already have large fiscal deficits).

The IMF's prescription for tight money has been even more controversial. The conventional wisdom—which the IMF routinely follows in its rescues of countries experiencing currency runs—is that high interest rates are necessary to stabilize the currency. Things haven't worked out so neatly in Asia, however, because as World Bank Chief Economist Joseph Stiglitz has persuasively argued, applying the tight money remedy to economies with high initial levels of leverage can strangle the patient, sending the currency down even further. With 20/20 hindsight, this criticism looks persuasive, but in all fairness, it was not unreasonable for fund officials *at the time when the crisis first appeared* to have insisted on tight money, since without higher interest rates there was a real danger that the suddenly depegged currencies would have fallen even more sharply than they did. And there was no way of knowing at the time, back in the summer and fall of 1997, that the Asian crisis would be as severe and contagious as it has turned out to be.

In a recent piece in *The New Republic,* Paul Krugman argues otherwise, claiming that even in a crisis tight money runs counter to textbook wisdom, pointing to the decline of the U.S. dollar in 1985 as an example. Better he suggests to "roll with the punches", let the falling currency buoy exports and even cut interest rates to support aggregate demand. But as Krugman himself acknowledges, this "textbook" advice is not easily generalized to developing countries with large foreign currency debts that may be highly dependent on imports. As I have already suggested, in this situation, a sharply falling currency can trigger both uncomfortably higher inflation and a wave of domestic bankruptcies. Under these circumstances, it was not unreasonable *at the time of the initial crisis* (although it may subsequently have proved counterproductive) for the IMF to have insisted on tight money policies to stabilize falling currencies.

Nonetheless, given where the Asian economies *now* find themselves—flat on their backs—it may be appropriate for the countries there (with the IMF's permission) to run a Stiglitz-Krugman experiment by letting interest rates fall modestly and then watching what happens to both the economies and to the currencies. If Krugman and Stiglitz are right, then by stimulating the domestic economies, lower rates might help restore confidence in the currencies and not only brake their fall but perhaps give them a boost. If the experiment fails. then it is always possible to return to tighter money. At the very least, if the IMF is not willing to run the risks of doing this, it then ought to encourage the countries to move rapidly to reduce indebtedness of their private-sectors along the lines I outline shortly so that their economies would be better positioned to withstand any tight money policy that may be necessary to maintain the values of their currencies.

At the end of the day, however mistaken the IMF may have been in imposing its macroeconomic conditions in Asia—and there certainly is room for debate on that score—the presence of mistakes themselves does not justify dismantling the fund. The Federal Reserve made big mistakes in the 1930's, too, when it failed to fully discharge its role as a lender of last resort, but no one seriously considered abolishing the Fed. I realize I have earlier drawn a sharp distinction between the CPM role played by the fund and the LLR functions of domestic central banks. But the same logic holds. Mistakes don't justify execution.

Attacks on the IMF's Micro Conditions: The IMF has taken on a new role during and since the Asian crisis, defining conditionality to include not just macroeconomic belt-tightening but also a series of what can best be labeled "micro" reforms aimed at converting crony capitalism to something closer to Western-style capitalism, such as: improvements in financial regulation, adoption of bankruptcy regimes, cancellation of showy infrastructure projects, and improvements in disclosure. Critics have mounted three challenges to this new style of conditionality have mounted. Before considering each, I want to repeat in this context what I just suggested with respect to the fund's macro conditions: even if you believe that the conditions are unwise, it does not follow that the appropriate remedy is to eliminate the fund.

The first critique is that the micro fixes were not necessary to restore investors' confidence in the battered currencies, appropriate macro policy alone, it is asserted, would have done the trick. We'll never know whether this would have been true. Indeed, one of the best lessons from this crisis is that once confidence in a currency is lost, it is very difficult to know what can bring it back. In any event, even the critics must concede that financial supervision in these countries was weak and that too much money was allowed to chase the wrong projects. If the IMF had ignored these problems and handed out the money without addressing them, at the very least it would have been attacked for pouring good money after bad. After all, this in essence is the argument that has been leveled against the fund's loans to Russia. It seems to me to be equally valid with respect to the Asian economies.

Martin Feldstein and others have argued that a second major flaw of the IMF's micro conditions is that they intrude too strongly into the domestic affairs of borrowing countries and run the risk of exposing not only the fund, but the West as a whole, to a severe political backlash in the affected countries. In fact, even putting aside Malaysia, which didn't receive IMF assistance, evidence of a backlash has already surfaced, although it is difficult to sort out to what extent the complaints are made about IMF-directed micromanagement in particular or whether they represent deep (and understandable) frustration with the declining condition of the economies in the region. The truth is that we won't know for some time whether the political risks that imposing the conditions entailed ultimately outweighed the benefits of attempting to fix some of the underlying problems in these economies when the IMF's leverage was at its maximum.

Nonetheless, one way to minimize the political risks is for the IMF and the World Bank to encourage or even require borrowing countries to introduce Western style social safety nets, notably unemployment insurance, to cushion the deep pain now being felt in these countries. I recognize that the bank is giving attention to this subject; it may need more resources and much higher priority among the bank's many objectives.

A third attack on the micro conditions is that they require such a major change in the way borrowing country economies work that the IMF cannot reasonably expect the reforms to really "stick" within the time frame when the fund has leverage—that is, until the assistance it promises is fully delivered. This is a fair objection. We in the West should not expect entire cultural traditions to be overturned in a year or two, or even a decade. All we can reasonably expect is for the process of reform to begin and to hope it gradually seeps into the way the affected economies are run. But to claim that reform is not even worth trying because many years may pass before it takes hold is to give up before the game is even played.

4. A CONSTRAINED IMF?

Although the Congress may provide this round of extra money for the fund, it is entirely possible that this could be the last time. In the future, therefore, the fund could be significantly constrained. How might this effect the way it conducts business?

The most obvious implication is that much like an infantryman who is down to his last few bullets and doesn't want to waste any ammunition, a constrained fund will have to decide very carefully how it wants to use its limited resources. To some extent, of course, that is not a decision for the fund to make. Member countries have the right under the Articles of Agreement to take back a limited part of their quota. Only for borrowing above the automatically available part of the quotas would the IMF be able to pick and choose whom to lend to and on what conditions.

Two broad strategies in this far-from-first-best world are available: (1) intervene only to support large economies, such as Brazil, whose currency devaluations or depreciations could have systemic effects by triggering the decline of other major currencies; or (2) to support only smaller countries whose rescue packages wouldn't put great pressure on the fund's resources. If I were managing the fund, I'd pick the first strategy as the best of two undesirable alternatives, only because a primary purpose of the fund should be to prevent international systemic risk and this is most likely to occur when the currencies of larger countries are threatened. Over time, one might expect this strategy also to induce smaller countries in contiguous areas to form currency unions and thus generate economic blocks the size of which could become eligible for the IMF assistance if the need arose. Assuming the fund has any significant amount of resources by then, it would then be right back where it started: having to pick and choose its interventions very carefully.

So, in the end, there is no escaping the fact that a constrained fund lowers the likelihood that at some point particular countries or currency unions will become eligible for IMF lending assistance. fund critics will argue that this is a good thing: the prospect of not being rescued will encourage developing and emerging market economies to be more responsible in both their macroeconomic and microeconomic policies. They would make the same argument about developed country lenders and developing/emerging market country borrowers, all of whom would become more prudent.

The question, however, is: at what cost? For lenders and borrowers, the potential unavailability of fund assistance at some future point will mean that both will have to factor into their decisions the prospect of "contagion risk," or the possibility that events in other countries could through contagion effects suddenly and sharply change the value of any loan or investment. Foreign creditors and investors will therefore demand higher (probably much higher) rates of return, with the consequence that steady state capital flows to developing/emerging market countries may fall well below levels that otherwise would prevail. Indeed, in the wake of the ruble devaluation and effective default by the Russian government on its debt, global markets have priced emerging market country debt at double digit interest rate premiums over LIBOR. It is hardly a coincidence that this has occurred during a time when it has been plain for all to see that the resources of the fund may not stretch much further than a package for Brazil.

The contagion characterizing financial markets points to a second cost of failing to provide the IMF with additional resources. While more uncertainty about availability of IMF financing may indeed cause governments of all countries to behave more prudently, economic policy prudence cannot fully shelter countries from global economic turmoil. In the recent crisis, countries that have made progress toward improving their economic policies—as easured by Western standards—nonetheless have found their currencies under significant pressure by investors seeking safer havens during the storm. As Krugman has recently noted, smaller countries without the long record of economic success of developed economies, are always at risk of losing the confidence of investors, domestic and foreign.

It is entirely understandable, therefore, why some countries may be tempted in a world without a reliable crisis manager/safety net to shelter themselves from global economic turbulence by restricting trade and capital flows. Indeed, Malaysia (which is not under an IMF program but which easily could serve as an example to other countries in the future) has already imposed exchange and capital controls, while a number of Latin American countries reportedly are turning to import restrictions with the ostensible aim of improving their current account balances. There is a risk of much more of the same if the IMF remains effectively downsized.

This isn't to say that all self-help remedies are bad. As even the IMF has now conceded, it can be prudent for countries with weak banks and/or weak financial regulatory systems to discourage banks and other private actors from excessive borrowing in foreign currency, especially at shorter maturities. Chilean-style reserve requirements against such borrowings are one such device. Domestic taxes on such borrowings are another. Disincentives of this type do not entail the kind of spillover risks that the IMF was created to address; if anything, they tend to reduce them. The danger in a world with a constrained IMF is that countries will turn to more pernicious measures' cutting themselves off from the flow of equity investment (even short-term) and further curtailing trade, steps that would inhibit their long-term growth and that of the trading partners.

Another consequence of a limited IMF that I want to touch on is that it would encourage even more regionalism in economic affairs, about which I am ambivalent. On the one hand, there is a real danger that without the IMF as a reliable crisis manager, countries will turn to regional or even bilateral arrangements for financing: Southeast Asian countries to Japan; Mexico to the United States (as has already occurred), and so on. Over time, loyalty to multilateral solutions to economic problems could wane, while regional factions could grow. This pattern is already under way with the proliferation of regional trading arrangements—which need not be harmful to *world* trade if the arrangements do not raise barriers to outsiders and if they help set precedents of liberalization that can be copied on a global basis. Nonetheless, if married to the sentiment that restrictions on trade and capital are necessary to shelter economies from global economic turbulence, regional financial pacts—mini-IMFs, if you will—could further balkanize the world economy and threaten to undo the progress toward freer movement of goods and capital that has been made since World War II.

5. IMF AS WORKOUT ADVISER

The current financial crisis will not be resolved until the financial burdens borne by debtors in the affected countries are addressed quickly. This obviously is not a job for the IMF. It does not have the resources to serve as an international bankruptcy court or mediator of last resort to handle thousands, if not tens of thousands, of bankruptcies, nor should it usurp the role of national governments in this respect. However, the IMF can and should serve as a facilitator adviser in encouraging a rapid cleanup of outstanding debts in the short run, while in the long run the fund can help facilitate more orderly workouts by lending into arrears.

I begin with the immediate debt problem, where many thousands of firms all across Asia surely are bankrupt in the Western sense of the term: that is, when both assets and liabilities are marked to market, using current exchange rates. But by any long-term standard, exchange rates of Southeast Asian countries are also undervalued, victims of currency panic and a generalized loss of confidence since the crisis began last summer. At more reasonable exchange rates, many insolvent firms with foreign currency liabilities would not be insolvent and many other firms bordering on insolvency would be healthier. In addition, many fimns with large debts in domestic currency that may appear bankrupt now could nonetheless survive if the local economies recovered and they had the means to keep going until they did.

The Western, and pardon the expression "Chicago-school" approach, would be to let all these firms go. Let creditors pick up the pieces, and if they can't, better that the assets of the firms move into other hands. Of course, it would be best if the countries had functioning bankruptcy systems that sorted out the claims in an orderly fashion. But failing that, let the chips fall where they may.

All of this might be appropriate advice if there were functioning bankruptcy mechanisms in these countries and if the firms in trouble were few in number. But that is not the case in Asia (nor by the way does it appear to be the case in Japan). Bankruptcy processes are in their infancy and many, if not most, firms throughout the region are suffering. Most importantly, the continuing wave of bankruptcies or downsizings has sizeable macroeconomic consequences by causing consumers and businesses to save rather than consume and invest. Seemingly rational behavior at the individual level adds up to depression for the entire economy.

Last year, I wrote a short policy brief for Brookings suggesting a way out of this mess. I do not believe it is too late to try it. In brief, I recommended a three-part strategy of "rough justice" that each of the countries could follow and which the IMF could assist them in carrying out. This approach could be viewed as a temporary bridge eventually to having a more permanent and fully developed bankruptcy system. But given the current raging flood of macroeconomic distress, a temporary bridge seems to be called for:

- First, governments should establish a mechanism for performing "economic triage," separating the hopelessly insolvent firms from the survivable using an exchange rate somewhere between (half way would be a good compromise) the precrisis level and its current level.

- Second, subject all firms insolvent by some threshold margin using this exchange rate to a presumption of liquidation or forced merger, unless creditors quickly accept an equity for debt swap.
- Third, for all firms, arrange for "rough justice" equity-for-debt swaps. Shareholders of otherwise solvent firms using a longer-term exchange to value any debts would be treated more generously in these swap arrangements than firms that still would be marginally insolvent, but nonetheless treated as "survivable." To address national concerns about subjecting firms to fire-sales, existing shareholders or owners could be given an option to repurchase their equity at some premium within a set period, such as five years.

Although I didn't discuss this problem at the time I originally proposed this system, rough justice equity-for-debt swaps could pose special problems for one class of creditors: domestic banks. If the equity they received in the swaps were valued at less than the face value of the debt for which it is exchanged, then the combined value of the writedowns could easily push the capital levels of already troubled domestic banks under the regulatory minimum or even into insolvency.

One less than ideal solution to this problem would be to carry the equity without a writedown for some period, say five years, unless the debtors went out of business. The preferable alternative would be for national regulators to impose the writedowns and then clean up any banks that were then forced into insolvency by transferring the loans and related equity to a collection agency (like the American Resolution Trust Corporation), paying off the depositors and then selling the remaining "clean bank" to the highest bidder. National governments could finance the deposit payoff with a one-time bond issue and use the proceeds from the asset sales and gains on the equity positions held by the collection agent to help service and eventually retire some portion of the bonds. Assistance from the IMF and/or the G-7 countries would make it easier for countries with troubled banking systems to help make up any funding shortfalls.

The rough justice debt cleanup proposal would require legislation of some type in each of the countries. The IMF could also directly or through consultants be useful in providing advice on valuation and other details to the national authorities. But the aim would be to get the debt overhang out of the way quickly—admittedly with some mistakes along the way—so that consumers and businesses could begin to see the light at the end of the tunnel. A major side benefit of such a program is that it make it far easier to defend the currencies in the region because the debt service burdens of the private sector would be less onerous at any level of interest rates.

Finally, looking ahead, the IMF could facilitate more orderly workouts in the future if it adopted a policy of "lending into arrears"—that is, lending to countries that have adopted debt repayment standstills, debt writedowns or equity-for-debt swaps—as Goldstein and others have suggested. By reducing the ability of creditors to hold up an IMF rescue until they have arranged for repayment of their loans, such a policy would facilitate quicker resolution of debt problems in crisis situations.

6. CONCLUSION

It is time to not let the perfect be the enemy of the good. The IMF was and remains a good institution. Some of the ways it conducts business can and should be reformed. But the fund deserves a future and developed countries—the United States in particular—have a deep interested and an obligation to give it one.

Acknowledgments: I want to thank my Brookings colleagues George Akerloff, Ralph Bryant, and George Perry for helpful insights in developing these remarks, as well as my colleagues on the Shadow Financial Regulatory Committee from whom I have learned a great deal in our extensive conversations on this topic over the past year. Nonetheless, the views here remain my own, and are not necessarily those of the trustees, officers, or staff of the Brookings Institution.

Note

[1]At the time this speech was delivered, the outcome of the congressional debate over the $18 billion was in doubt. Since then, approval has followed, although with numerous conditions.

Chapter 38

Comment on "Bailing in the Private Sector" and "Does the IMF Have a Future"

Charles A. E. Goodhart
London School of Economics

In my view both Robert Litan and Barry Eichengreen draw too sharp a distinction between the lender of last resort functions of a central bank and the potential role of the International Monetary Fund. In most countries when a commercial bank seeks last resort assistance from its domestic central bank some credit risk will usually be involved in making such loans, especially if the central bank has raised the interest rate at which it will lend to the penal levels advocated by Allan Meltzer, since then the commercial bank will already have pledged its best assets as collateral on the open market. Whereas the central bank can theoretically monetize without limit, its capacity to incur credit risk is strictly limited by the relatively small size of its capital.

Consequently, in almost all countries support activities have taken the form either of the central bank acting as facilitator, organizer and whipper-in of a quasi-coordinated rescue mechanism, mostly involving finance from the private sector, or more commonly in recent years, of acting as a first line of defense until taxpayers' funds from government can be marshaled. Perhaps the locus classicus of last resort actions was the Bank of England's 1890 rescue of Barings; in fact the vast bulk of the pledged support funds came from the other commercial banks. LTCM is a case nicely in point, where in addition the comparative speed with which the central bank can act in a partial crisis was a relevant factor. In practice, however, globalization and enhanced competition have made it increasingly difficult to arrange such private sector support operations domestically, since the commercial banks will often demur on commercial, competitive and legalistic grounds, so the other route of government recapitalisation has become increasingly the norm in most countries from Scandinavia to Japan and many countries in between.

Seen in that light, as an independent and impartial facilitator of concerted private sector actions and as a similarly independent and impartial interlocutor between sovereign countries, do we need an institution like the IMF? The answer must be, resoundingly yes. If such impartial international facilitation and coordination is not done, then as Robert Litan rightly worries, the world is more likely to fragment into blocs with smaller countries seeking the direct protection of the core country within their bloc. I should perhaps add that one undercurrent of the ongoing crisis is that the fund has been widely perceived as so concerned about the Congressional vote on its own funding, and with other U.S. pressures, that its impartiality has been doubted, as Bob Johnson said and it has been sometimes characterized as being a cats-paw for U.S.-designed proposals and remedies. This perception even tarnishes good policy proposals such as allowing easier entry of foreign banks. In a crisis this is often perceived as allowing the foreign vultures to descend on the crippled chickens in the domestic financial farmyard. And I might just add further that the fund's political problems may become even harder yet when we move towards a more bipolar system between the euro and the dollar.

The problems of dealing with a financial crisis situation when the liabilities are denominated in *domestic* currency are hard enough, witness the problems in Japan. But the problems multiply when the liabilities are denominated in foreign currency (f.c.), usually in dollar form. The domestic authorities as a generality do not have the requisite f.c., otherwise there would be no such crisis. Both the scale, and the speed of disbursement, of the Fund's own resources are, as we have heard many times, limited. And the willingness and/or ability of foreign governments, notably in Washington and Bonn, to provide taxpayers' funds are strictly limited.

Under these considerable constraints, the past success of the fund in dealing with crises occasioned by *public sector* financial crises has in my view been remarkable. Using the analytical cookbook of recipes devised by Jacques Polak and Marcus Flemming in the early 1960s, they pretty successfully managed scores of such crises from the UK in 1968 and 1976 to Mexico in 1982 and 1995. My first function as a bank official in 1968 was to write an article explaining the concept of DCE, and, somewhat less convincingly, how we in the UK had come to think of it. I do not really regard the recent Russian episode as a major blot on the escutcheon. The problem lay with a combination of the severe internal governance problems of Russia itself, and with U.S. geopolitical pressures, not with the fund's advice or policies.

The particular problem of the recent Asian crisis was that the indebtedness burden was primarily in the private, not the public sector, and here the tried-and-true cookbook turned out to be insufficient and in some respects inappropriate. A concern that I have with Barry Eichengreen's paper is that most of his constructive proposals on bond contracts, creditors' committees, sovereign immunity laws, etc., while all worthy of consideration and discussion, relate primarily, in a few cases solely, to government sovereign indebtedness, and in all cases to bond, securitized, debts, whereas the crucial problem was how to handle *private sector* f.c. indebtedness, mainly to foreign banks.

Indeed the best advice of both Robert and Barry is to prevent any prior build-up of such large short-term f.c. private sector debt positions in the first place. And I feel reasonably confident that the fund will not now place any obstacles in front of a potential recipient country attempting to do just that. But are there any active steps that the fund can, and should, take to limit the build-up of such positions? Perhaps the first step is to encourage countries to obtain and to disclose more information on the stock/flow foreign currency indebtedness of their private sector, in addition to more data on their public sector positions. The drip-feed of ever worsening data on such Korean positions was a negative factor in handling that event.

The main debate between Robert and Barry is whether IMF lending should be made conditional on countries having a mandatory haircut clause on foreign banks lending in foreign currency to debtors in the recipient country. My own feeling is to side with Robert, though gingerly and uncertainly, that such a clause might be advantageous if applied universally in all cases and in all countries, but to go with Barry that the chances of getting such a clause universally adopted, in the USA as in Burkina Faso, is approximately zero.

So what do you do if you are in the IMF and a private sector f.c. indebtedness crisis nevertheless strikes? One good maxim is to know your own limitations. Robert Litan noted correctly that, and I quote, "The current financial crisis will not be resolved until the financial burdens borne by the debtors in the affected countries are addressed quickly," but he went on to say that, "This obviously is not a job for the IMF." But if this latter is correct, did the fund have any useful role in these cases in the first place, or did its intervention delay and perhaps worsen the necessary process of reducing the burden of such private sector debt to manageable and feasible proportions?

In this context I would also note that increasing interest rates beyond a certain, but unknown, point will discourage potential lenders since the rising risk of insolvencies will come to outweigh the potential extra return, as in Stiglitz/Weiss. This is just as applicable internationally as it is domestically. I surely do not envy anyone in having to guesstimate where the supply curve of international capital becomes backwards bending, but, in my opinion and with the benefit of hindsight, that level was probably considerably surpassed, and in some cases may even now remain so, in several Asian countries.

Chapter 39

Less Is More in the New International Financial Architecture

Randall S. Kroszner
University of Chicago and Federal Reserve Bank of Chicago

Reforming the "international financial architecture" is one of the most important and pressing questions facing international policy-makers today. A sturdy structure will help to minimize the risk of collapse, but much disagreement exists about how best to lay a firm foundation. Eichengreen and Litan have provided impressive and extensive overviews of possible reforms of both the international capital markets and the IMF to achieve this goal. Their papers focus on international rescues operations, also known in less polite company as "bailouts." Both make a convincing case that the IMF cannot take on the deus ex machina role of an international lender of last resort, and I wholeheartedly concur.

Rather than try to summarize their wide-ranging and thoughtful proposals, I will elaborate a theme that emerges from their papers and that can be applied to three aspects of the new international financial architecture: less is more. I borrow this phrase from one of the greatest and most influential architects of the twentieth century Meis van der Rohe, whose steel and glass structures loom large on the skylines of cities such as Chicago. Less reliance on politicized domestic banking systems, less bailout capacity, and less inflexibility by creditors in debt renegotiation can lead to more stability and to a firmer foundation on which international financial markets and institutions can operate.

1. LESS RELIANCE ON POLITICIZED DOMESTIC BANKING SYSTEMS CAN REDUCE LIKELIHOOD AND SEVERITY OF CRISES

Banking tends to be a sector, which faces large political pressures. Since banks tend to be highly regulated and to have their fortunes tied directly to the operation of the central bank, politicians have the potential to exercise considerable control over banks and the allocation of credit. In many countries, the commercial banks are little more than off-balance-sheet fiscal arms of the government. Politicians may use banks to provide subsidized credit to various sectors, as a form of industrial policy, and to targeted groups to increase political support. In return, banks often receive protection from competition through regulation and subsidies from the central bank.

Since the government is so heavily involved in banking, it may be very difficult to have effective government regulation of the domestic banking and financial sector. In these circumstances, simply hiring more and better-trained supervisors and adopting good regulatory principles is not sufficient because the government may have little incentive to enforce rules of sound banking, either on state-owned banks or privately-owned banks. The co-dependence of the banks on the government and of the politicians on the banking industry allows problems to grow unchecked, as the depth of the banking troubles in the Asian currency crisis countries illustrates. These perverse incentives are not unique to developing countries, as the long delays in responding to the Savings and Loan crisis in the U.S. and the banking problems in Japan also show.

The collapses of the domestic banking systems have contributed to the severity of the economic crises (and perhaps were an initial cause) and have slowed recoveries. A key reform would be to open the domestic banking markets to foreign competition. An increase in foreign bank penetration in emerging markets can generate a virtuous circle in that foreign banks tend to be less politically connected and less likely to be able to "capture" and be captured by the regulatory authorities (Kroszner, 1998a). Foreign institutions are less likely to succumb to pressure for directed lending by the government. With capture less likely and fewer direct benefits to the politicians of bank regulation (e.g., through quid pro quos for directed lending), regulatory reform becomes more likely. In addition, given their weak current state, the local banks are less likely to be able to oppose greater openness (Kroszner and Strahan, 1998).

Foreign financial institutions provide an extremely valuable stabilizing force that will help emerging markets to recover more quickly following a negative shock and generally promote stable economic growth. The domestic banks in these countries tend to be very poorly diversified, with most of their assets tied to the local economy. The collapse of the domestic banking system can make it difficult for local businesspeople to raise funds for positive net present value projects, thereby slowing recovery. Foreign banks, however, are internationally diversified and can ease such credit squeezes. Breaking down international barriers to bank entry is analogous to the recent elimination of barriers to interstate bank competition in the U.S. Allowing entry by banks from other states has been shown to increase state economic growth (see Jayrantne and Strahan, 1996). Less reliance on politicized local banking systems thus can produce more stability and growth. Less is more.

2. LESS BAILOUT CAPACITY CAN PRODUCE MORE STABILITY

As Eichengreen and Litan note, the IMF cannot act as an international lender of last resort as it is now constituted. Unlike domestic central banks, the IMF does not have the ability to create dollars, euros, pesos, etc. and thereby lacks a key feature of credible and effective last resort lenders. Although few countries are likely to be willing to cede their monetary sovereignty to the IMF to permit it to have such powers, the question remains of whether the IMF should be restructured to take on this function. I believe that the members of this panel would agree that, regardless of political feasibility, it is not desirable for the IMF to take on this role.

Perhaps the most important problem is that of moral hazard. As is well understood, and has been illustrated in numerous domestic banking crises such as the U.S. Saving and Loan debacle, the potential for ex post bailouts undermines ex ante market discipline (e.g., Kroszner and Strahan, 1996 and Kaufman and Kroszner, 1997). If there is an expectation of implicit insurance from the IMF, foreign investors will not exercise sufficient care in determining whether a country's debt is sound before investing. The mere existence of the moral hazard problem, however, does not mean that all forms of last resort lending are undesirable and that markets will inevitably lose their disciplinary role in a blind-faith reliance on bailouts. All forms of insurance involve some degree of moral hazard but that does not imply the existence of insurance companies is destabilizing or contrary to market discipline.

The extent of the moral hazard problem thus is the important issue, but its magnitude is an empirical question that is extremely difficult answer, particularly ex ante. As Litan notes, many market participants characterized the purchase of Russian debt in the spring and summer of 1998 as a "moral hazard play" because Russia was considered too important (some would say too nuclear) to fail. The ability of Russia to continue to raise funds internationally in the late summer was in large part due to the expectation that the IMF (and major Western governments) would provide some protection for investors. The IMF, however, did not. Russia defaulted on its debt, the ruble collapsed, and many of the world's most sophisticated investors lost billions.

The silver lining in the dark cloud of the Russian currency and financial crisis is the lesson that the IMF cannot be relied upon to bailout investors even in strategically important countries such as Russia. Perhaps the Russian crisis can be seen as the cost of the rescue package for Mexico in the mid-1990s, that is, the price that had to be paid in order to unlearn the apparent lesson from the Mexican bailout that international investors would be protected. The IMF did not have the resources to generate a credible rescue package for Russia and other governments were not willing to provide further funding at that time.

The constraint on the financial capacity of the IMF, thus, provides the benefit of mitigating the moral hazard problem. Additional funding for the IMF without steps to reign in the potential for moral hazard, however, relaxes the constraint and diminishes this benefit. Increasing the financial capacity of the IMF and moving the IMF in the direction of an implicit international lender of last resort may undo the hard-learned lessons of the Russian crisis. A less potent and less generously funded IMF could provide more stability in the international markets. Less is more.

3. CREDITORS WHO DEMAND LESS MAY RECEIVE MORE

The difficulties of debt renegotiation after a country falls into distress and the lack of clear and enforceable bankruptcy rules for international debt are identified by both authors as important targets for reform. Eichengreen details a number of specific changes to international debt contracts to reduce ex post coordination and bargaining costs and draws on historical experiences to consider the formation of active creditor committees to streamline the work-out process. Others, such as Sachs (1989) and Krugman (1998), have emphasized the distorted incentives that can occur when a country suddenly is overburdened with debt, because the debt overhang can act as tax on potential new investment projects. There may exist a debt "Laffer Curve" in which partial debt forgiveness can improve the welfare of the country by reducing the overhang and simultaneously leading to a better ultimate pay-off to bondholders.

While there has been much discussion of debt relief, almost no empirical work exists to determine whether countries ever are on the "wrong side" of the debt Laffer Curve. The extent of devaluations and debt overhangs in Asia and Russia have few precedents, but an instructive parallel can be drawn with the experiences of countries abandoning the gold standard during the Great Depression. The U.S. dollar, for example, declined sharply and suddenly against the French Franc and British Sterling soon after Roosevelt took office, and the gold content of the dollar was then officially devalued by sixty-nine percent with respect to the old gold parity. (Keynes characterized this period of high volatility of the U.S. dollar as a "gold standard on booze.") Since mid-1997, the devaluation of the Asian and Russian currencies with respect to the dollar has been between forty and eighty percent.

Until the Great Depression, most long-term debt contracts in the U.S. (both public and private) included a gold indexation clause, allowing creditors to demand repayment in dollars valued at the old exchange rate. If this clause had been enforced, debt payments thus would have increased by sixty-nine percent. Since there was roughly $100 billion of gold-clause debt outstanding and GDP was roughly $60 billion, enforcement of the gold clause would have increased the debt burden by more than GDP. Similarly, when the Asian currencies fell in value, the burden of their dollar-denominated debt rose. Following the devaluations, the external debt to GDP ratios increased sharply to exceed one in some cases.

Rather than allow many firms to be pushed into bankruptcy, in 1933 the U.S. government declared that it would not permit these clauses to be enforced, which was upheld in a landmark five-four Supreme Court decision. An examination of assets prices responses to the announcement of this debt relief shows that not only corporate equity but also corporate debt rises in value (see Kroszner, 1998b, for details). The equity and debt of low-rated and heavily-indebted firms experience the greatest increase, so firms closest to bankruptcy benefited the most from the decision. Government bonds with the gold clause, however, fall in value. These results suggest that the expected costs of financial distress and distorted incentives due to debt overhang were sufficiently high that the country was on the wrong side of the "debt Laffer curve."

In such circumstances, it may indeed be better to forgive than to receive. Asking for less can result in receiving more while also making the distressed country better off. While we cannot conclude from this historical episode that debt forgiveness today would improve the welfare of holders the currency crisis countries' debt, the parallels suggest that this is plausible possibility. New provisions in international debt contracts and new structures to coordinate debt renegotiation and relief thus are worthy of further investigation. Once again, less can be more.

References

Eichengreen, Barry. 1999, "Bailing in the Private Sector," *The Asian Financial Crisis: Origins, Implications and Solutions*, Kluwer Press.

Jayaratne, Jith and Philip E. Strahan. 1996, "The Finance-Growth Nexus: Evidence from Bank Branch Deregulation," *Quarterly Journal of Economics*, 101:1 639–70.

Kaufman, George, and Randall Kroszner. 1997, "How Should Financial Institutions and Markets be Structured?," in *Safe and Sound Financial Systems: What Works for Latin America?*, Liliana Rojas-Suarez (ed.), Washington: Inter-American Development Bank pp. 97–122.

Kroszner, Randall S. 1998a, "The Political Economy of Banking and Financial Regulatory Reform in Emerging Markets," *Research in Financial Services*, 10.

Kroszner, Randall S. 1998b, "Is It Better to Forgive than to Receive? Repudiation of the Gold Indexation Clause in Long-term Debt Contracts during the Great Depression," University of Chicago, Graduate School of Business, working paper.

Kroszner, Randall S., and Philip Strahan. 1986, "Regulatory Incentives and the Thrift Crisis: Dividends, Mutual-to-Stock Conversions, and Financial Distress," *Journal of Finance*, 51 September: 1285–1320.

Kroszner, Randall S., and Philip Strahan. 1998, "What Drives Deregulation? Economics and Politics of the Relaxation of Bank Branching Restrictions in the United States," National Bureau of Economic Research, working paper, June.

Kroszner, Randall, and Thomas Stratmann. 1998, "Interest Group Competition and the Organization of Congress: Theory and Evidence from Financial Services Political Action Committees," *American Economic Review*, 88 December.

Krugman, Paul. 1998 "Financing versus Forgiving a Debt Overhang," *Journal of Development Economics*, 29 November: 253–68.

Litan, Robert. 1999, "Does the IMF Have a Future? What Should It Be," *The Asian Financial Crisis: Origins, Implications, and Solutions*, Kluwer Press.

Sachs, Jeffrey. 1989, "The Debt Overhang of Developing Countries," in *Debt, Stabilization, and Development: Essays in Memory of Carlos Diaz-Alejandro*, Guillermo Calvo and Ronald Findlay (eds.), Oxford: Blackwell.

Chapter 40

Assessing IMF's Crisis Prevention and Management Record

Anna J. Schwartz
National Bureau of Economic Research

According to Robert Litan, the IMF is in the crisis prevention and management business.[1] He does not, however, say anything about whether it has in fact prevented any activity or practice of its clients that would otherwise end in a crisis. And when it comes to crisis management, Litan does not dispute the IMF's warts that critics have noted, including moral hazard and unwise macro and microeconomic conditions that it has imposed. Nevertheless, he argues that presence of mistakes does not warrant dismantling the fund. He draws an analogy with the Federal Reserve, which was not abolished, despite its big mistakes in the 1930s. The Federal Reserve may not have been eliminated after 1933, but it was subsequently stripped of policymaking power (even allowing for the 1937–38 increase in reserve requirements—the one break in system passivity) by the two-decade predominance of the Treasury in monetary matters. What happened to the Federal Reserve between 1933 and the 1950s may be a good example to follow were the IMF to be shorn of its delusions of global indispensability, given its sorry record of crisis prevention and management.

I shall first discuss the record, and then question the belief that there is no desirable alternative to the role the IMF has assumed since 1995.

1. RECORD OF PREVENTION AND MANAGEMENT

At least two features of the prelude to the Asian crises called for steps to limit what was in train. One was excessive credit expansion that capital inflows fueled by increasing liquidity. Another was the magnitude of short-term debt in foreign currencies that the private sector assumed.

To deal with the rapid expansion of credit that breeds banking crises, the IMF could have urged Asian central banks to neutralize the capital inflow. The central banks should have sold their notes to the market, offsetting the rise in liquidity. The Asian countries did indeed try, relying on unsuccessful measures, to reduce the liquidity of their monetary systems, but there is no evidence in IMF publications that it offered intellectual support for their efforts, particularly central bank sales to the money market of its own notes.

Short-term foreign loans denominated in a hard currency become a problem when a domestic currency is devalued. The domestic currency burden of the debt then escalates. Barry Eichengreen proposes that limits be imposed on short-term foreign-currency denominated borrowing by banks.[2] There is no indication, however, that the IMF expressed concerns about this feature of the Asian boom years. Limiting foreign claims on domestic banks is Eichengreen's choice of a policy to replace government's reluctance "to suspend payments and negotiate an agreement with creditors to restructure the debt." He notes all the procedural problems that currently exist and offers solutions that would help bring creditors to the bargaining table should borrowers seek to restructure a loan.

I question the assumption that underlies Eichengreen's proposal. Are governments in fact reluctant to default, and would they not do so except for IMF intervention to bail out the lenders? The foreign lenders to Asian banks should have had reason to worry about default on their loans but Mexico's experience with tesobonos taught them otherwise. Were there IMF warnings to the Asian borrowers that they were incurring growing risks from their exposure? The foreign lenders should have been warned that no bailouts were in prospect.

If the IMF did not bail out either the debtor or the creditor, market discipline would restrain cross-border lending by Americans and others and the willingness of borrowers to assume debts.

Eichengreen believes that the reason governments oppose writing down foreign claims on domestic banks is that governments seek to protect their domestic banks from the flight of foreign funds. The Latin American defaults of the 1980s tell a different story. It was the lenders' money center banks that the lender governments sought to protect. Restructuring would not have been so protracted except for their delaying tactics.

The IMF's discussions with its clients are confidential, so there is no public record of the advice it gives. The IMF has, however, pleaded, after the onset of a crisis for which critics have faulted its performance, that it gave good advice, but the clients rejected its advice, hence the crisis. The question that follows is, what qualifies the IMF to be in the crisis prevention and management business if it lacks the moral authority to win the respect of its clients for the advice it gives?

If there is a lesson to learn from the Asian crises, it is that prevention is preferable to post-crisis conditionality. Prevention should be a responsibility of a country's central bank.

2. SUPPOSE THERE WERE NO IMF CRISIS MANAGER

Supporters of the IMF give a scare-mongering response to this suggestion. One such response is the threat of contagion. If the IMF fails to bail out investors in one emerging country's markets, it is said, there will be a *tequila* effect on other emerging markets, so investors will abandon those markets as well. Pure contagion, however, would occur only in circumstances in which other emerging countries were free of the problems facing the first emerging country. No evidence exists of pure contagion. Brazil is currently assumed to be the innocent victim of crises in Asia and Russia, when investors are clearly disturbed by Brazil's well-known economic policy mistakes. Transmission is different from contagion. Shocks to one country will spill over to other countries through trade and the capital accounts. When investors withdraw their capital from countries with the same problems as were present in the first such country, this is a demonstration effect, not contagion.

There is still another scare story supporters of the IMF invoke. Absent the IMF, they say, the world financial system would revert to the 1930s. For this transformation to occur, the United States would have to endure three years of bank runs, which the Federal Reserve would take no action to halt, a one-third decline in the money stock, a decline of one half in national income, a deflation of prices by one-quarter to one-third, and unemployment would have to reach twenty-five percent. The rest of the world would have to cling to a gold exchange standard that was enforcing deflation and depression until individual countries abandoned it. The advanced industrialized countries would have to embrace protectionism and controls on capital movements. Does anyone truly believe that the world of the 1930s would reappear if the IMF would no longer bail out newly emerging countries that have mismanaged their economies? Let me counter with an alternative scenario.

A country engulfed by a financial crisis has a recourse that excludes an IMF bailout. That recourse is today's world of deep capital markets that are ready to lend to liquidity-constrained countries at interest rates that reflect true credit risk. A country that offers collateral, as Mexico did in 1995 by pledging oil revenue to the Federal Reserve and the ESF, and is willing to pay a market rate of interest that included a credit risk premium, as when it borrowed from German banks to repay its U.S. loans, can find a welcome in capital markets. The market evaluates borrowers on the basis of their financial prospects, not on the basis of subsidized IMF bailouts.

The IMF is said to be preparing a $30 billion package for Brazil. So long as Brazil can obtain these funds at a subsidized interest rate, why would it consider seeking a loan from commercial sources? But if the IMF were not in the picture, capital markets would not rebuff Brazil. It can offer collateral, and pay an interest charge that covers credit and exchange rate risk. The interest rate will be lower than the rate Brazil currently is prepared to pay to defend the *real.* The market will impose covenants on the loan that will require Brazil to rein in its fiscal deficit.

Someone will object that a country may lack collateral and may find a market rate of interest onerous. My answer is that the country should not be a borrower. Charles Calomiris would recreate the IMF as a lender only to countries that meet stringent criteria.[3] Countries, which fall short of the standard he sets, may require outright grants, not loans.

A financial crisis can have several elements: a current account deficit, a problem of debt service and amortization of international debts, and an undercapitalized banking system with a portfolio of nonperforming loans. The capital market can provide a short-term loan to deal with the current account deficit. The private parties involved in the loan contract, not the IMF, must negotiate restructuring the original terms of the loan. Eichengreen's suggestions for improving the process may be helpful. The government will need to adopt measures to repair the banking system. It is not the IMF but a country's government that has to put its house in order.

An IMF austerity program is not needed. Market forces themselves would impose belt-tightening in a country with an unsustainable current account deficit because it had borrowed too much and not made prudent use of the capital inflow.

We tend to forget that the IMF role as crisis manager is barely four years old. Relieving the IMF of that role does not mean that the international financial system will be imperiled. Before the 1990s, rescue loans were made in an attempt to prevent devaluation or abandonment of a pegged exchange rate by the core industrialized countries. They were temporary loans, at commercial market interest rates, limited in magnitude, but sufficient to offset a current account deficit. No taxpayer money was involved. Loans in the past accompanied a package of remedial policies.

Loans in this decade have been extended to newly emerging countries *after* their attempt to defend a peg has failed. The loans have been multiples of the amounts that were granted in the past. The recent loans are designed to offset a capital account outflow, the effect of which was to endanger repayment of the lenders. The size of the loan is large enough to provide the wherewithal to repay foreign and domestic lenders. A wealth transfer from taxpayers to wealthy recipients is involved.

A pervasive problem in the past as well as present times has been pegged exchange rates. Foreign commercial banks and other private lenders in recent crises extended loans at interest rates that did not take into account exchange risk, based on the incorrect belief that adherence to the peg was durable and credible. This experience supports floating exchange rates to avoid speculative attacks on pegs. If countries maintain floating exchange rates, capital markets should be able to handle any exigencies of both private and public finance.

Notes

[1]Robert E. Litan, 1998, "Does the IMF Have A Future? What Should It Be?," paper given at this conference.

[2]Barry Eichengreen, 1998, "Bailing In the Private Sector," paper given at this conference.

[3]Charles Calomiris, 1998, "Blueprints for a New Global Financial Architecture," paper given at this conference.

PART IX

LESSONS FROM THE CRISIS FOR THE INTERNATIONAL FINANCIAL SYSTEM

Chapter 41

Lessons for the International Financial System

Manuel Guitián
International Monetary Fund

1. INTRODUCTION

The currency turmoil in Asia–which now has extended to Russia as well–has been aggravated by a confidence crisis feeding on itself in a self-reinforcing and destructive way. Financial market "animal spirits" can be sensitive and fickle–which, I hasten to add, is not the same as saying that financial markets are irrational. And the nature of currency crises is such that they mutate over time, much like a virus. These factors make it extraordinarily difficult to predict crises. The initial triggers in a few countries like Thailand may have been reasonably visible, but the depth, timing, speed and spread of the events that followed were not foreseen.

At the broadest level, a key lesson from the latest crisis–common to earlier ones–is that we have to work hard in shaping both national and international efforts to contain their recurrence; needless to say, we are unlikely to be able to prevent them entirely, but we must find ways to minimize their severity and contagiousness. In both of these respects, a clear message from the ongoing crises is that sound financial markets and institutions, including their underlying legal, governance and accounting infrastructures, are critical. The speed, magnitude and flexibility of capital flows make international financial markets a strict taskmaster at the best of times; but, if we needed another reminder, recent events have demonstrated again that, in combination with significant weaknesses in domestic financial systems and their infrastructure, the effects of confidence shocks can be wide-ranging and debilitating.

The answer, however, does not lie in trying to turn back the clock by reverting to isolationism. Except perhaps in emergencies, a return to controls on international capital movements would be neither desirable nor effective. A distinction can be made here between cases of countries where controls have been maintained for some time, but the general direction of movement in the medium to long term is towards liberalization, and cases where countries have already liberalized, but try to backtrack on their previous policy direction. Such policy reversal is likely to be much more damaging, not only to the country itself but also to other countries engaged in liberalization efforts. Economies taking this route can impose a substantial negative externality on other countries by raising the perceived convertibility or transfer risk premium applied to them, and by increasing market nervousness. Current events in the international economy provide clear evidence of just this sort of negative externality.

Rather than backtracking on moves to a market-friendly environment, the dual objective of preventing crises and, when they do occur, minimizing their severity and spillovers are better served by mutually reinforcing actions in three main areas:

- *Improving the environment in which private markets function,* to help them distinguish accurately between different situations and react more smoothly to both good and bad developments.
- *Equipping national authorities with the capacity to operate in an increasingly global environment*, bearing in mind in particular that policy certainty and consistency are essential for stable financial markets.
- *Improving the surveillance capacity of the IMF and enhancing its contributions to the management and resolution of crises.*

Progress in these three areas will require measures at both the national and the international, multilateral levels. Given the scope for domestic currency crises to spill over internationally, it will be important for the multilateral framework to provide an appropriate incentive structure for national authorities. While clearly much remains to be settled, there is a reasonable degree of consensus about many of the central aspects involved.

2. IMPROVING THE ENVIRONMENT IN WHICH MARKETS OPERATE

Improving the environment in which financial markets operate will require that greater attention be given to several areas. First, *national financial systems and their legal and regulatory infrastructure need to be strengthened resolutely*, both to support sound market development and to keep up with the risk management implications of market innovations. Where key financial institutions themselves have accumulated substantial balance sheet problems, these need to be dealt with promptly and in a fashion that provides strong incentives for avoiding relapses. Supervision and regulation of key financial institutions, deposit insurance schemes, and the operation and legal structure of payments systems, all need to underpin market and internal corporate incentives to help ensure that credit and other risks—not least currency and liquidity risks—are recognized and well managed. Beyond the financial institutions per se, bankruptcy and debt recovery laws, as well as the judiciary process that enforces them, need to work effectively and transparently. And internal governance structures need to provide for an appropriate separation between the corporate sector, the financial system, and the state.

Second, *the quality and quantity of information available on financial markets often needs to be improved.* Financial markets require good information flows to adjust smoothly to positive or negative developments, and to distinguish well between different countries in different situations. Transparency of the financial sector's own conditions is critical here, as is qualitative information about the nature of the strengths and weaknesses of the infrastructure within which financial institutions operate. Clear, internationally comparable accounting standards, both for financial institutions and corporates are also required, along with appropriate public disclosure practices.

Third, and for related reasons, *macroeconomic policy transparency also needs to be encouraged.* Financial markets, and the public at large, will react particularly adversely when bad news about the economic and financial outlook, and the policy environment in particular, comes as a surprise. The temptation to conceal bad news can be strong. But it is out of tune with today's global financial environment, which, in the context of crisis prevention, requires a *precommitment mechanism.* Governments and financial institutions need to commit to an ongoing arrangement to provide disclosure and transparency, so that if *future* deterioration occurs, it becomes visible at an early stage, thus providing an incentive for policymakers and financial institutions to address problems at an early date.

Fourth, besides transparency and disclosure, there is a need for comparability among countries. This is behind current interest in the development and promulgation of various *standards and codes of good practice.* In areas outside its expertise, the IMF has been helping in the dissemination and encouraging the adoption of norms developed by other international organizations, as in the case of accounting standards, and good practices in the domain of financial sector supervision and regulation. This role is discussed in the fund's report *Towards a Framework for Financial Stability*, which includes the Basle Committee's *Core Principles*, the development and dissemination of which the IMF has actively supported. Similar action to cooperate, as appropriate, with the work of the international groupings of securities (IOSCO) and insurance (IAIS) regulators is under way. The areas of monetary and exchange rate policy, and fiscal policy, have always been core areas of the fund's mandate, and here we have taken the initiative to develop codes of good practice that would help ensure the transparency of members' policy frameworks. We have recently completed a fiscal policy transparency code, and work is well underway on a code for monetary and financial policy transparency.

3. IMPROVING THE CAPACITY TO WORK WITH GLOBALIZED CAPITAL FLOWS

Catering to financial markets' need for transparency and certainty are key parts of any broader strategy to balance the benefits and risks of participating in international financial markets, as are strengthening national financial systems and their legal, supervisory and judicial infrastructure. For many countries, however, the issue is *how far and how fast to open their capital accounts to international financial markets, and how to prepare for such a liberalization.* It is common knowledge that capital account liberalization in any specific case calls for careful attention to the pace and sequencing of policies and reforms. I do not believe there is a one-size-fits-all plan for an optimum speed and sequencing of capital account liberalization. But it is worth stressing that many of the reforms that would support capital account liberalization are likely to be highly desirable in their own right, irrespective of capital account liberalization; in turn, the discipline imposed by the latter may actually be helpful in encouraging the supporting measures to be taken. It is, therefore, more helpful to think of capital account liberalization as one part of a broader, mutually reinforcing reform process than as its end point.

In this regard, there are some key basic principles. Sound and well supervised financial sectors are clearly critical for a sustainable liberalization of the capital account; in particular, sound prudential frameworks are required to avoid excessive risk taking by financial institutions and corporates, especially in the form of short-term bank borrowing in foreign currencies. As already indicated, this includes aspects such as robust payments systems, good accounting and disclosure standards, workable insolvency and debt recovery processes, an effective corporate and financial sector governance process, and a well-designed and transparent boundary between the political world and the market, including one that minimizes moral hazard problems. Equally important are appropriately firm, consistent and coherent as well as transparent fiscal, monetary and exchange rate policies. Sooner or later, liberalized capital flows are likely to punish severely any real or perceived policy inadequacies or inconsistencies, like those related to attempts to pursue multiple objectives through single or insufficient policy instruments.

The complexity of the issues that need to be addressed to assure sustainable liberalization suggests that a simple linear approach to sequencing of capital account liberalization is unlikely to be adequate. This indicates that perhaps the single most important precondition for a successful and sustainable liberalization is a political willingness to recognize and deal determinedly with any weaknesses in the structure of the financial sector and the macroeconomic policy framework.

4. IMPROVING THE SURVEILLANCE CAPACITY OF THE IMF

The issues I have covered have important implications for the IMF's surveillance, financial and technical assistance roles in general and point to the need to broaden the institution's oversight over capital account liberalization, in particular. IMF surveillance will continue to play a crucial role in crisis prevention, and multilateral surveillance of broad international financial market trends will become even more important as a regular and ongoing aspect of its work.

The IMF's traditional role has been in respect of macroeconomic policies, together with key structural measures to support stabilization and effective macroeconomic management. In this context, we have been providing technical assistance to member countries for many years on financial sector issues, and have been moving actively towards an integration of macro policy issues and financial sector issues since the early 1990s. The Asian crisis gives heightened emphasis and urgency to these issues, and this trend in IMF work with its member countries will be further intensified.

Apart from the moves to improve data quality, enhance transparency and disseminate international standards and guidelines in coordination with other international agencies, the IMF's own surveillance of members is itself being broadened to look more specifically and directly into financial sector soundness issues. This is part of the broader global effort underway to strengthen financial systems worldwide. Where weaknesses are identified, technical assistance from the IMF and other international financial institutions can make an important contribution to rectifying deficiencies. Collaboration between the IMF and other multilateral institutions, especially the World Bank, is being intensified through a number of initiatives, aimed at both assisting in avoiding crises, and in dealing with crises effectively and efficiently if they arise. I need hardly mention that adequate funding of the IMF and other organizations is critical for crisis resolution.

Given the IMF's existing mandate and its broad membership, the institution is uniquely positioned to oversee and advise on the capital account liberalization process in member countries. But its ability to get into meaningful discussions with members on capital account reform issues has been limited to date, because it has been outside the fund's formal remit to look in depth at the kinds of capital flows a country is attracting, and whether the risks being assumed are well managed. Yet, the centrality of such issues to exchange rates and overall economic performance of individual members is obvious. Perhaps even more important are the multilateral aspects of countries' actions; as we have amply seen of late, capital liberalizations that are inadequately supported by other policies, and liberalizations that are reversed can have very serious adverse spillovers on other countries. Recent developments thus strengthen the need for an appropriate extension of IMF jurisdiction to the capital account, as a means to promote prudent, orderly and sustainable liberalization.

Chapter 42

Lessons from the Crisis

Everardo Elizondo
Banco de Mexico

There is a saying that not so long ago, an important Chinese official arrived in Paris and a reporter asked him his opinion about the French Revolution. The diplomat answered: "It is too soon to tell."

The Asian crisis has not been solved yet so it may be premature to draw "lessons" from it for the international financial system. Indeed, "it is too soon to tell."

However, what we have observed as of today, could be sufficient to derive some good advice. Manuel Guitián has already presented an excellent exercise in this respect.

I think that a comparison between the Mexican and Asian crises, in a couple of aspects, could be of some interest.

First, we have to recall that the Mexican economy suffered a severe depression in 1995, but then starting the following year it recovered at a speed that surprised all analysts (see Figure 1).

This recovery was undoubtedly related to two important factors: a vigorous American economy, and capital inflows from abroad.

Indeed, aggregate demand expansion in the United States allowed for an acceleration in the growth of Mexican exports, particularly in manufactured goods. This factor was the main engine of initial recovery. It is worth mentioning that in spite of the crisis, external credit lines for Mexican exporters continued to be available throughout this period.

Afterwards, domestic demand took over the role of impelling growth—stimulated, among other things, by the easing of the financial burden on debtors, due to the implementation of specific support programs. Recovery was also favored by the creation of new financial circuits; for instance, the granting of credit for the acquisition of durable consumption goods (i.e. automobiles) by foreign manufacturing firms. The evolution of the Mexican economy exhibited a "V"-shaped path.

Additionally, it is clear that the most difficult period of the depression was associated with a heavy fall in total foreign investment, although direct investment (almost) maintained its level. By contrast, portfolio investment registered notable declines from the fourth quarter of 1994 to the end of 1995. However, it showed a rapid and strong comeback. There is a clear association between the path of the flow of external resources and the evolution of GDP.

The mix of these favorable factors has been absent in the case of the Asian crisis. Specifically, since some time ago, the Japanese economy shows recessive conditions. And, in general, capital inflows have not resumed. Consequently, the usual evolution of the affected economies looks like an "L"-shaped path. The prolonged deterioration has hurt the financial system through several channels, which in turn has translated itself into an additional contraction of capital flows. The result has been a crisis without precedent for the last fifty years, as it was recently and appropriately defined by the president of the Federal Reserve Bank of New York.

From these differences, two very simple "lessons" can be derived: i) the "exit" of the Asian crisis goes, of course, through the reanimation of the Japanese economy, the region's "locomotive;" and ii) the abrupt contraction of the flow of external resources is a perfect recipe for a generalized disaster.

Would it be too much to say that "*without a Japanese recovery, non-Japan Asia will not recover at all ?*"

Another distinct aspect of the Mexican crisis, the fragility of the banking system, was repeated in the Asian case, with some variations in appearance but not in essence. As causal factors of the crisis (among others), one usually accepts the following list: the inadequate condition of prudential regulation; the weakness of official supervision; and the existence of government guarantees—implicit and explicit—for banking activities. This combination, among other things, explains the excessive risk-taking by credit managers.

This diagnosis is commonplace among analysts. However, recent difficulties in various financial institutions in developed countries proves that deficient regulation and supervision are not features only of developing nations. It also shows that the existence of moral hazard conditions is also not a peculiarity of premodern countries.

Moreover, these incidents have another common characteristic: they reveal a worrisome over-leveraged condition, or to say it in other words, an evident insufficiency of capital in diverse financial institutions.

So, another "lesson" to be drawn from the current crisis is that structural reforms are a pending task in all latitudes. As long as this process is not fully carried out, we will continue to hear calls in favor of controls of capital movements across boundaries. If such calls are heeded—and the foreseeable economic and political circumstances favor such attitude—we would be facing a regrettable step backwards.

Figure 1. GDP Growth: Mexico and U.S

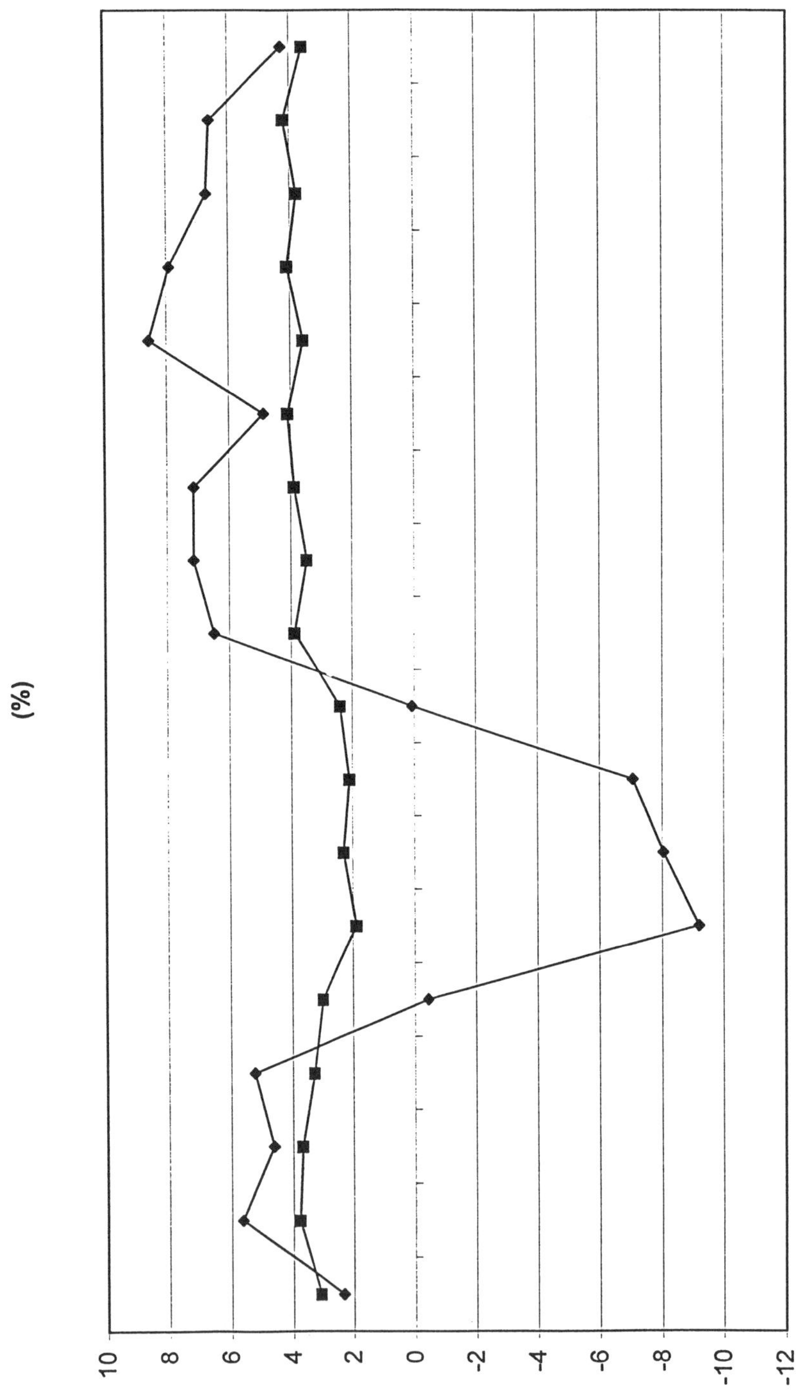

Chapter 43

An Analysis of Financial Crisis: Lessons for the International Financial System

Richard Portes
London Business School and Centre for Economic Policy Research

1. ALL CRISES ARE THE SAME

A financial crisis is a disturbance to financial markets that disrupts the market's capacity to allocate capital—financial intermediation and hence investment come to a halt.

Investors should take risks, and risks mean that some proportion of investments will fail. This is why we have domestic bankruptcy laws that provide for orderly workouts when investments and the firms that made them do fail. Similarly, if the international capital markets are functioning well, mistakes will be made. Then one or another country (or its private sector borrowers) will fail: a crisis. History records many. We should not expect or even wish to prevent them all. That would be at the cost of insufficient, excessively risk-averse investment. So such crises will always recur—but capital markets forget

The term "financial crisis" is used too loosely, often to denote either a banking crisis, or a debt crisis, or a foreign exchange market crisis. It is perhaps preferable to invoke it only for the "big one": a generalized, international financial crisis. This is a nexus of foreign exchange market disturbances, debt defaults (sovereign or private), and banking system failures: a triple crisis, in which the interactions are the key to causality, depth, and persistence (Eichengreen and Portes, 1987).

The widespread securitization of debt in recent years has not changed the picture—after all, one of the major historical examples is the 1930s crisis of defaults on sovereign bonds. Nor has it diminished the importance of banking sector fragility in provoking and exacerbating financial crises.

All crises are "crises of success" (Portes and Vines, 1997). The initial capital inflow that ultimately proves unsustainable (and perhaps unprofitable) is both a sign and—for a time—a cause of economic promise and success. But we have not yet learned how best to cope with the capital inflows, so success may lead to failure.

All crises raise the problem of distinguishing between insolvency and illiquidity. Today, some say that the "Asian miracle" economies are actually "hollowed out," "zombie" economies; all that investment just went into creating excess capacity or driving up real estate prices. Others argue that the growth was real, that these economies should still come top in the World Competitiveness Report, and their problem is simply overvalued exchange rates and the classical "run"—a self-fulfilling crisis of liquidation of short-term loans. We will not know for some time which view is correct.

Because crises will always recur and because their causation is so complex, we shall never arrive at an international financial system—whatever its "architecture"—that can dispense with mechanisms for the resolution of financial crises. "Better information," "early warning" and "preventive measures" will not remove the need for *orderly workouts*, whatever the source(s) of the crisis

2. ALL CRISES ARE DIFFERENT

The Asian macroeconomic fundamentals are good. And the Asian crises are primarily private-sector ones, in economies with high aggregate savings, sound fiscal positions, open and outward-looking policies, and relatively low sovereign debt. Rather than high inflation, the serious feature of the crises is debt deflation, or the bursting of a bubble. So this is very different from Mexico. In Russia, on the other hand, the key feature is fiscal imbalance—the inability of the tax system to provide an essential minimum level of government revenue.

The economies in crisis do have weak banking systems, and most started with somewhat overvalued exchange rates (some but not all pegged). Those are common features of financial crises. But the causes and current appearance of these crises are different from previous episodes. Common factors are de facto exchange rate pegs to the dollar, which resulted in overvaluation and large current account deficits, and excessive private sector foreign borrowing.

But the idiosyncratic factors are at least as important: Thailand's central bank took forward positions that depleted net foreign reserves, and its finance companies accumulated massive nonperforming loans; Indonesian industrial structures favor a particular political force but are inefficient; Korean banks borrowed too much abroad on short maturities; and the Korean industrial sector is exceptionally highly leveraged.

Thus financial crises differ across a wide range of features:

- The role of "fundamentals"
- The relative importance of bank and securitized debt
- The relative importance of private and sovereign debt
- Exchange rate regimes and history
- Underlying structure and dynamics

3. TYPES OF FINANCIAL CRISES

A taxonomy of financial crises is helpful (Radelet and Sachs, 1998). We can distinguish among the following features, which are perhaps best regarded as the proximate or initial causes of financial crises:

- A speculative attack on the exchange rate—here we must distinguish between attacks based on deteriorating "fundamentals" and those that exhibit self-fulfilling expectations;
- A "financial panic"—a bank run or its international analogue—in this case, no degree of "transparency" or better information will eliminate herd behavior, which is based on a collective action problem;
- The collapse of an asset price bubble;
- A crisis induced by moral hazard (implicit or explicit guarantees of bailout); and
- The recognition of a "debt overhang," followed by a *disorderly* workout.

Again, the key obstacle to foreseeing, preventing and indeed to resolving international financial crises is that they typically exhibit several of these features. There is no credible unicausal story, and in each crisis the nature of the interaction among the factors listed here is itself unique. In particular, we cannot simply regard the Asian financial crisis as a "financial panic" without recognizing the important roles of excessive nominal exchange rate rigidity, real estate price bubbles, and moral hazard that led to reckless behavior by lenders. Nor was the evident contagion that followed the initial crisis in Thailand just financial panic. There were common features in the economies that were hit, and there were significant links among them.

4. POLICY: EXCHANGE RATES

Contemporary policymakers are finally coming to understand what researchers (and the architects of Bretton Woods) recognized long ago: Fixed but adjustable pegs are simply unworkable with full capital mobility. Nevertheless, countries do introduce exchange-rate pegs for macroeconomic stabilization and subsequently cannot or will not "flexibilize" them soon enough to forestall speculative attacks. What policies are advisable when the attack materializes? Typically, financial fragility will make the interest rate defence ultimately infeasible, and intervention whether in spot or forward markets just feeds the speculators.

Thus if attacked, it is almost always best to save the reserves and let the exchange rate go. With appropriate monetary policies and adequate remaining reserves, it may be possible to bring the rate back to a reasonable and stable level fairly soon (e.g. France 1993, Czech Republic 1997). This is of course essential: a violent, uncontrolled depreciation will make it impossible to distinguish among "good" and "bad" domestic assets, in view of the high degree of foreign currency exposure that tends to arise in economies with pegged rates. It will only be possible to tell which assets are "good" when the exchange rate returns closer to "equilibrium"—and that is likely to take much longer if the defense of an indefensible peg has gone on too long.

The fashion for currency boards has already gone too far. A currency board is likely ultimately to fail—with potentially disastrous consequences—if the banking system or political discipline are weak and foreign exchange reserves are low.

5. POLICY: THE IMF AS INTERNATIONAL LENDER OF LAST RESORT

The International Monetary Fund cannot be a true international lender of last resort. It cannot fulfill the essential ILLR role, because it cannot create money. Moreover, it has no recourse to a fiscal authority that can provide the resources to fill the gaps in balance sheets, when "liquidity crises" turn out to be "solvency crisesl."

The sequence of events since summer 1997 demonstrates that in a world of full capital mobility, no "bailout package" can be sufficient if the markets are unconvinced—and even very large packages may not convince them. Moreover, the focus on foreign indebtedness, whether to banks or in securitized form, ignores the major role of domestic capital flight in most of the crises that we have observed. No feasible package will suffice to finance conversion of the entire domestic money supply (not just the monetary base) into foreign exchange.

Although the fund is conscious of contagion effects and systemic risk, its constitution and procedures require that it act country-by-country. In a systemic crisis, however, the domestic lender of last resort simply creates liquidity—"defends the money supply." That function is not possible under the current international financial system. And the IMF cannot follow the Bagehot rules for additional important reasons: it cannot take collateral that would be immune to sovereign repudiation; and it may be impossible to value financial asset collateral in a case of global systemic crisis.

6. PRINCIPLES FOR ORDERLY WORKOUTS

How to pick up the pieces once a crisis occurs will vary greatly from case to case. But there are some general principles (Eichengreen and Portes, 1995), some of which require action before any crisis hits.

Typically, an orderly workout of international debt will require both rescheduling and restructuring: partly the lengthening of maturities, partly conversion of debt into equity. It may also require writing off substantial amounts of debt—this has been well understood since the nineteenth century, however much creditors may resist it. The workout should not be a bailout of the creditors: implementation should put a high priority on minimizing moral hazard (the consequences of the Mexican bailout are still underestimated) and avoiding nationalization of private debt (an unfortunate feature of several of the Asian cases).

We have made several recommendations for contractual and institutional innovations to promote cooperation among holders of securitized debt (Eichengreen and Portes, 1995), and it is encouraging to see that these have been taken up seriously in the report of Working Group Three of the G-22. I would stress the importance of collective action clauses and other *ex ante* commitments in debt contracts (e.g. to give seniority to new loans). I am confident that these would be worthwhile even if, as market participants claim, they would entail larger spreads (less favorable lending terms) and indeed lower levels of capital flows—although I believe this claim is much exaggerated. Still, if it were correct, that would suggest that the terms have been improperly and unsustainably favorable to borrowers.

Any new architecture should make explicit provision for temporary payments standstills (requiring exchange controls or other restrictions on capital outflows) and IMF lending into arrears on either bank lending or securitized debt. It is important, too, that there be a better codified institutional framework for workouts. The complicated interaction among the fund, the London Club and the Paris Club is time-consuming and in practice hinders the restructuring and writeoffs that are ultimately necessary.

7. PROBLEMS, OBJECTIONS, AND OBSTACLES

There is a long list of obstacles to the construction of an agreed framework for orderly workouts. Most of them should be ignored, some of them can be avoided, and some must simply be regarded as inescapable costs of what will on balance be a much better system for dealing with financial crises.

i. It will always be desirable to have a "voluntary," "consensual" suspension of payments and debt restructuring, but what if the creditors simply will not accept that? Then there must be some "mandatory" element. Here the fund or another agency may play a key role in achieving better behavior on the part of both debtors and creditors.
ii. Borrower countries may resist provisions for orderly workouts (e.g. qualified majority clauses in debt contracts), because they believe that having such provisions in place ex ante will worsen their market terms. An initiative by the G7 to include such clauses in their own sovereign debt contracts would set a good example.
iii. Lender institutions will doubtless resist any such provisions—market participants blocked any implementation of the recommendations of the G10 Deputies (Rey) Report of 1996. They should be ignored.
iv. Defining the scope of any suspension of payments may differ from case to case, and the extent and nature of the exchange controls or other restrictions on capital mobility will have to be tailored to each case too.

v. Any selective suspension raises problems, e.g.: would there be a run on debts not covered? What about cross-default clauses?
vi. It may be difficult to enforce the capital controls required for a standstill (but their duration should not bc too long, if thc managcmcnt of the workout is expeditious).
vii. Offering seniority to new credits may encounter obstacles in existing *pari passu* clauses in loan contracts.
viii. It is claimed that no workout could be fully "orderly," because trade credit would freeze up—but that has happened anyway in the Asian crisis countries.
ix. Market participants claim that any orderly workout provisions would pose a threat to the international interbank market. But the evidence for this threat is unclear.
x. Critics of any workout involving debt reduction claim that this would indefinitely postpone the debtor's return to capital market access. But when Mexico went to the market in mid-1995, after its "successful" bailout that kept creditors whole, it got no better terms than did Poland at exactly the same time, although Poland had only six months previously agreed to a fifty percent writeoff with the London and Paris Clubs. And Poland did better than Hungary, too, although the latter had been punctually faithful on its exceptionally heavy debt service.

8. MULTIPLE, INCONSISTENT ROLES FOR THE IMF

Finally, it is important to recognise that the IMF already fulfills an excessive set of roles in the international financial system—"excessive" because they involve potential conflicts of interest and counterproductive overlapping. That problem would be exacerbated by giving the fund additional responsibilities in debt workouts. Here we may just list the various functions—it is evident how they may conflict in practice:

- Surveillance and analysis: macro and micro,
- Policy recommendations,
- Monitoring compliance with financial regulation and standards,
- SDDS,
- Providing information to the markets,
- Possibly administering contingent credit facilities,

- Other decisions on lending and conditionality,
- Status as priority creditor,
- Adjudicating on standstills,
- Intermediating between creditor and debtor in debt restructuring, and
- Certifying country adjustment programs for the Paris Club.

It is unfortunate that responses to the international financial crisis of 1997–98 have brought proposals to expand the range of the fund's responsibilities and activities. The existing set is already conflictual and dysfunctional.

References

Eichengreen, B., and R. Portes. 1987, "The Anatomy of Financial Crises," in *Threats to International Financial Stability,* R. Portes and A. Swoboda (eds.), Cambridge University Cambridge Press, pp. 10–58.

Eichengreen, B., and R. Portes.1995, *Crisis? What Crisis? Orderly Workouts for Sovereign Debtors*, London: CEPR.

Portes, R., and D. Vines. 1997, "Coping with Capital Inflows," Commonwealth Secretariat, London, economic paper No. 30.

Radelet, S., and J. Sachs. 1998, "The East Asian financial crisis: diagnosis, remedies, prospects," *Brookings Papers on Economic Activity*, 1, pp. 1–74.

Chapter 44

Lessons from the Asian Crisis

Edwin M. Truman
Board of Governors of the Federal Reserve System

It has been a great pleasure to participate in this conference for the past two days. I congratulate the Federal Reserve Bank of Chicago and the International Monetary Fund for putting it on. We should remember that this type of open dialogue is part of a process of transparency and accountability and, perhaps, adjust our rhetoric accordingly.

My remarks are in two parts: introductory comments on the topic of the conference and more specific comments on the topic of this roundtable.

First, six general comments. It is premature and naive to think on October 10, 1998 that we can have learned all the "lessons" of the Asian Financial Crisis because that crisis and its global ramifications are not over yet. A lesson prematurely learned may be the wrong lesson. We do not have a full accounting or even reasonable estimates of the costs and benefits of many of the potential or proposed remedies. All remedies impose costs; if they were costless, they would have been applied years ago.

Second, we should recognize that lessons from this crisis have two dimensions: for the longer term and for ongoing short-term crisis management. The latter dimension requires ad hoc remedies that we hope will not be counter productive to the structure we would like to build over the longer term. Moreover, we need to be sensitive to the fact that locking in new long-term solutions in the middle of a crisis suggests that mistakes will be made. Successful generals do not normally abruptly change their longer-term strategies in the middle of a battle.

Third, for both the short term and long term we are dealing with decision making under uncertainty. If we knew in August 1997 how the Asian crisis would evolve, no doubt different decisions would have been taken. Similarly, constructing a rigid and absolutist structure for the handling of future crises based on an incomplete model of this crisis strikes me as methodologically unsound.

Fourth, I like to distinguish between the international *monetary* system that governs reactions among sovereign nations with the IMF at the center and the much broader international *financial* system—Eichengreen's environment in which actors public and private make their decisions. In this crisis, the two have been intertwined, perhaps they always are in crises, but they are not in the same manner on each occasion.

Fifth, the objective of the IMF, at least in my view, is not to act as a lender of last resort to the international financial system. It is to maximize the welfare of all the citizens of countries participating in the international monetary system by, inter alia, preventing the adoption of antisocial policies though the mechanism or inducement of the provision of financial resources to member governments and through the promotion of positive collective responses, see Bob Litan's proposals at this conference.

Finally, all international financial crises do not involve national banking crises and vice versa. In Graciela Kaminsky's database, she identifies eighty-nine separate crises. Only half (thirteen) of her twenty-six banking crises involved external financial crises, and most of the other seventy-plus countries that have had banking crises over the past fifteen years have also not had associated external financial crises—the United States, the United Kingdom, and Japan to name three. It is reasonable to ask why. Moreover, only two of the joint banking and external financing crises ultimately involved IMF lending programs. At the same time, less than a twenty percent (thirteen) of Kaminsky's seventy-six external financial crises involved banking crises. Moreover, only a quarter of those crises (twenty-three) involved IMF programs. I conclude from these facts that it would probably be a mistake to hard wire the solutions to these two types of crises.

That having been said, I'd like to offer some thoughts on fourteen lessons for the international financial system from the Asian crises. I divide them into two tranches. Tranche I involves points where we can say with some confidence that the benefits of applying the lesson clearly outweigh the costs. Tranche II involves points where the jury is still out on whether the benefits outweigh the costs; we don't yet know enough about either.

I have identified eight reasonably clear lessons:

First, national authorities must have a well-articulated and consistently pursued vision of the role of the financial system in their economies. I associate this lesson with Jerry Corrigan. The point is that such a vision helps to guide policies moving forward and to avoid the mistakes of the past.

Second, there is little or no scope for the Asian model of finance in today's world, i.e., there is no place today for insider trading and lending directed by the government toward its chosen projects and activities. Asian leaders, in particular Japanese leaders, may not accept this lesson but most of the rest of the world does.

Third, supervisory systems need to be strengthened. The place to start is with the Basle Core Principles of Effective Banking Supervision, but that is not the place to end. This involves more than "regulating," "monitoring," and "supervising" the banking system. The establishment of a sound credit culture is required. But success should not be associated with the prevention of all bank failures; it should be measured by fewer failures and reduced economic and financial effects of those that occur.

Fourth, the legal infrastructure surrounding the financial system needs to be strengthened, i.e., bankruptcy laws, their unbiased application, and their prompt enforcement.

Fifth, more generally, what is needed is a culture of credit where lenders and investors make informed and rational judgments on the extension of credit and are prepared to take the consequences as well as reap the rewards of their decisions. All this takes time, just to get started. For example, Thailand was expected in its program that was endorsed by the IMF in late August 1997 to come up with a robust comprehensive program of banking system reforms in a few months. Instead, the first real plan was released on August 14, 1998! Some feel it is less than perfect. But all this is the easy stuff, i.e., establishing the plan for a new regime. The more difficult challenges lie in the consistent implementation of a sound plan.

Sixth, an important element of this process is the establishment of a transparent scheme of less than universal deposit insurance and associated standards with respect to structured early intervention to deal with the problems of financial institutions, as well as with respect to insolvency regimes. A decade ago this proposition would not have been agreed to internationally. Today we have learned that the national and international costs of de facto 100 percent deposit insurance outweigh any benefits with respect to increased financial stability. While progress will be slow, there is a clear need for common standards in this area as was called for in the report of the Working Group on Strengthening Financial Systems that was releasted on October 5.

Seven, more attention needs to be paid to the development of national bond markets and the associated infrastructures (such as accounting and disclosure practices) supporting both bond and equity markets. Again, this takes time. Much has been done in this area, especially in the Western Hemisphere, but more remains to be done if we are to avoid the frequent repetion of crises of the Asian type.

Finally, a related point, the authorities need to be alert to the excesses associated with credit booms. This is also easier said then done, but the place to start is with a countercyclical rather than a pro-cyclical supervisory policies.

In tranche II, I have six candidate lessons to suggest.

First, when a crisis emerges in the financial system, especially if it is systemic in nature, the first requirement is to apply a comprehensive solution. This is one of the messages delivered at this conference by the former governor of the Central Bank of Thailand, Mr. Chaiyawat. If this lesson is accepted, it implies the need for dramatic action closing institutions and, if needed, effectively nationalizing the remainder, imposing high prices on shareholders and managements. The ad hoc, piecemeal approach is more clostly in terms of the real economy and taxpayers' funds. My reading of the Chilian and Scandinavian experiences is consistent with support for this lesson. To apply this approach effectively, however, one needs strong ex ante supervision and reporting and clear legal structures and instruments.

If this lesson is not agreed, we need to understand why. Is it because of a concern with the health of the real economy, as in Japan? Or is it because of a view that time will cure all? The latter solution is difficult to achieve in a noninflationary environment.

Second, once a country has a serious domestic banking crisis, it is likely that any recovery in the real growth of bank credit will take years, which means it is all the more important to explore other means to de-leverage the economy. Mexico is an example where real bank credit declined for three years following its 1994 crisis. Abrupt action flies in the face of the Asian consensus model, but it is consistent with the model of arm's-length dealing.

Third, sequencing is important, but there does not appear to be consensus, including at this conference, about whether one should first restructure the financial system and later turn to the nonfinancial corporate sector or vice versa. One view that we heard from Curt Hunter was that one should start with the financial sector because the aim is to decouple it from the corporate sector; moreover, restructuring the nonfinancial corporate sector will take time, and meanwhile the economy needs a functional financial system. The alternative view that we heard at this conference from Yung Chul Park is that the reconstruction of the corporate sector must come first. Bank claims must be written down and converted to equity; until this is done it makes little sense to pretend that the banking system is strong. There is a middle way: buy out the banks claims on the nonfinancial sector as part of the banking system's restructuring. I conclude that we have no agreement on this point.

Fourth, another controversial issue is whether the authorities should place restrictions on the operations in foreign currency of domestic financial institutions. There is a clear need to weigh costs and benefits in this area, which involves many complicated issues. Should this be done by home country authorities? If so, on what basis: assets, liabilities, net positions? If so, through what means: guidelines, reserves, restrictions, capital charges? Should this be done by host countries? If so, should restrictions be imposed on foreign establishments? If so, through capital charges on lending institutions?

Fifth, what role should foreign investment in the financial system play? Again this is a controversial question despite Charles Calomiris's categorical positive answer. Do the gains from having a national banking/financial system outweigh the costs? The costs are clear: potential liability to shareholders, costs of administration, etc. What are the gains once we agree on the need for a genuine culture of credit?

Finally, what role should the various international organizations (e.g., the IMF, IBRD, and regional development banks, or even the WTO) play in all this, and what should be the relative roles of the international and regional groupings of national supervisors? For example, in setting standards, monitoring compliance, providing technical assistance and imposing solutions, where does the comparative advantage and the international interest lie? The IMF's role should not be zero, and a great deal is being done by the IMF, but there is less than complete consensus on how to build on the IMF's current activities going forward. For example, to the extent that the IMF is to play a major role monitoring compliance with international standards, are we concerned about (1) a lack of IMF expertise, and (2) the moral-hazard implications of country's financial system receiving a clean bill of health from the IMF? Concern about this second consideration has led some of us to think about an independent process of assessment of national financial systems and their supervisory structures. One suggested model is the accreditation process used in the United States for hospitals and educational institutions. Whatever is done in a prevention mode, the IMF clearly will be involved in crisis situations. But where does that leave the activities of other international financial institutions?

By way of conclusion, I believe we have come a long way and learned a great deal about this crisis, but we still have a lot to learn, in part, because this crisis is not over. My congratulations to the IMF and the Federal Reserve Bank of Chicago for helping us move forward.

Acknowledgment: The views expressed are solely my responsibility and should not be interpreted as reflecting the views of the Board of Governors of the Federal Reserve System or of any other person associated with it.

Chapter 45

An Analysis of Financial Crisis

Delano Villanueva
The SEACEN Center

Abstract: Adverse shift in investors' confidence in Asia was associated with weak fundamentals, particularly those pertaining to the external and financial sectors. Lessons from the crisis include strengthening those fundamentals, creating a large liquidity fund, and designing loss-sharing arrangements involving private lenders and borrowers.

The Asian financial crisis, beginning with the collapse of the Thai currency in July 1997 has generated much discussion worldwide. The SEACEN Seminar on Financial Crisis in the Asian Region held in Kuala Lumpur on June 23–25, 1998 marked an occasion for policy makers from the affected countries to put forth their views, share their experiences and insights as well as update one another on latest developments. The experiences of Indonesia, Korea, Malaysia, Philippines, Taiwan, and Thailand were thoroughly discussed.

1. OVERVIEW OF THE CRISIS

A common conclusion was that the cause of the crisis cannot be pinned down to just a few factors. There were "trigger" and "augmenting" factors. The most important trigger factor was the shift in investors' confidence after a build-up of massive short-term capital inflows to finance current account deficits. The sudden and drastic slowdown of exports in 1996 was mainly responsible for this shift in investors' sentiment, leading to capital flight and a free fall of currencies. The augmenting factors included, among others, structural weaknesses and inappropriate macroeconomic policies such as a rigid nominal exchange rate policy, a weak regulatory and supervisory framework, and a fragile financial system. These problems were compounded by ineffective handling of short-term capital inflows, which were invested mainly in the property and share markets. Another important augmenting factor was the contagion effect that fanned the crisis quickly across the region, even to countries seemingly not related to the origin of the crisis. To some extent, the different effects of the crisis on the individual countries reflected the respective country's resilience owing to its economic structure, sociopolitical factors and ability to manage the crisis.

To the Asian policymakers, the crisis was viewed as a result of collective actions of many parties—the private sector, policymakers, international investors, hedge funds, international rating agencies, and multilateral institutions. Although foreign investors ignited capital flight, fanned by domestic investors, the real panic began only when domestic investors moved capital out of the country after the crisis "threshold" was reached. Given the large resources that hedge funds commanded and their profit-maximizing objective, hedge funds also contributed to the crisis as can be observed from the patterns and sizes of their transactions during the height of the crisis.

2. LESSONS FOR THE INTERNATIONAL FINANCIAL SYSTEM

- The crisis has underscored the urgent need to overhaul the international financial system that had not kept pace with financial markets' rapid development and progress. In this respect, the following issues were emphasized: moral hazard of international rescue operations; prudential standards and incentives for compliance; greater transparency and disclosures; role of the IMF in surveillance and liquidity provision; risk management systems of private investors and financial institutions; and harmonization of bankruptcy laws. In addition, the crisis highlighted a danger of unregulated influx of short-term capital, especially when a country does not have adequate absorptive capacity and stringent regulatory-supervisory framework to efficiently intermediate such capital flows. To some extent, the crisis could be traced to a premature liberalization of the capital account, aggravated by a rigid exchange rate regime and (explicit or implicit) government guarantees of bailouts. On hindsight, there was a view that the affected countries could have done better by imposing some forms of price control/regulation on short-term capital inflows. The crisis has also shown that a country cannot liberalize the capital account while simultaneously maintaining a fixed exchange rate and pursuing an independent monetary policy.

- Financial assistance to the banking system, including restructuring of loans extended by foreign banks and other creditors, should have been the top priority. Otherwise, any multilateral or bilateral rescue package, whatever the amount, would not work; it would just flow out to pay domestic banks' debts to foreign banks.
- There is an urgent need for a swift and orderly international bankruptcy procedures in which private creditors lose some of the money they lent while debtors still have to repay some of the borrowed amounts, perhaps on easier terms and longer maturity. There was a felt need for an equivalent of the U.S. bankruptcy laws, in which a filing by a debtor is all that is needed to initiate the bankruptcy process (reorganization or outright liquidation). There is no coerced restructuring on private creditors and debtors, because they fully know in advance and in a transparent way the legally accepted procedures even before loans are made. Voluntary arrangements will not do, because international banks will just wait and wait until multilateral and bilateral rescue packages are worked out and implemented so that maturing debts are fully paid out of the loan disbursements—a far better arrangement for international creditors. But why should private creditors not lose money for mistakes in their lending decisions?
- Another important lesson learned was that it is crucial to always keep a sound financial sector. A breakdown of the financial sector's intermediary role and loss of confidence impacted severely on the real sector, transforming a financial crisis to a full-blown economic recession. In an era of global financial liberalization, emphasis must be placed on strong prudential regulation and supervision while ensuring good governance, transparency and public disclosure of the financial conditions of both banks and corporates. A country with inadequate regulatory framework and supervisory machinery may need to impose capital adequacy ratios much higher than the levels recommended by the BIS. However, higher capital adequacy ratios must be implemented gradually amidst major macroeconomic

imbalances and great uncertainties. In addition, the legal framework for orderly exit of insolvent banks and corporates must be improved to avoid panic and minimize the high cost of financial rescue operations. A blanket guarantee of bank deposits should be replaced by a limited deposit insurance scheme with "prompt-corrective action" features, like the current FDIC of the United States. Government guarantees on foreign borrowing should be avoided and private creditors should be made to bear the consequences of any mistakes on lending decisions. On the issue of transparency and disclosure, information from the market should also be as forthcoming as that from official sources, while a mechanism to ensure that official information is interpreted correctly should be in place.

- The Asian financial crisis has illustrated the herd behavior of investors during a boom–bust cycle: excessive capital flows followed by rapid and massive capital outflows. To some extent, this reflects an individual investor strategy not to be left behind with a relatively higher risk than others. It also showed shortcomings of the international financial system and lack of adequate legal infrastructure to handle the crisis effectively at both country and international levels. An effective way to deal with herd behavior is through transparency and disclosure, good governance and consistent macroeconomic policies. Private investors were always on the lookout for opportunities arising from inconsistent policies. Orderly procedures to deal with liquidity and solvency problems will also help facilitate swift negotiation among international creditors and debtors in times of crisis. Given the economic size of the affected countries, a close regional cooperation will bring in substantial benefits, both in preventing and resolving the crisis. These include bilateral arrangements to share information, enhance liquidity during the crisis, and other agreements concerning trade and payments. In this connection, there is an ASEAN Manila Framework to restore stability in the region's financial markets by identifying measures to enhance and complement the IMF's role in preventing and responding to the crisis, including regional surveillance and early warning systems. The ADB is heavily involved in this initiative.

3. THE CASE OF TAIWAN

The reasons why Taiwan came out of the crisis in relatively better shape were discussed. First, Taiwan had been enjoying current account surpluses since the 1980s. Such a prolonged period of surpluses, together with a precautionary attitude since Taiwan (a non-member of IMF) cannot draw on the IMF resources for its liquidity needs during emergency, permitted Taiwan to accumulate large international reserves. Second, Taiwanese firms have not been as highly leveraged as those in other countries as they prefer equity to debt financing. This minimized foreign borrowing and improved the resilience of the private sector. Third, like the Philippines, Taiwan had just recovered from its own asset price bubble crisis in the late 1980s, which caused a severe correction in the stock and real estate markets. The adjustments that followed help to strengthen the financial system as the authorities enforced stricter prudential regulation and supervision while banks had become more cautious toward lending backed by real estate or shares. For instance, the banking sector's exposure to loans backed by shares only accounted for 2 percent of total bank lending. Finally, the government's cautious stance in liberalizing the financial and capital markets helped to insulate the domestic sector from volatile international capital movements.

The case of Taiwan illustrates a general point about the careful liberalization of the capital account when the country was not in a position to channel the large influx of capital to productive sectors and when supervision and regulation of financial institutions were weak. There were four virtues that helped Taiwan weather the financial storm: large foreign exchange reserves and a timely introduction of a flexible exchange rate; a strong and sound banking system; low debt-equity ratio in the corporate sector; sound monetary and fiscal policies; and a well-diversified export sector.

Chapter 46

Lessons from the Asian Crisis for the International Financial System

Yukio Yoshimura
International Monetary Fund

One of the criticisms of the International Monetary Fund programs for the Asian crisis countries that is often heard concerns the very high interest rates the programs demand. The Asian countries complain that these high interest rates seriously depressed the regional economy. I will begin by commenting on the pros and cons of the very high interest rate policy, especially in relation to the management of the exchange rate. I will then move on to measures to overcome the dilemma between monetary policy easing and exchange rate stability.

1. THE DEFENSE OF THE EXCHANGE RATE

The IMF advised the Asian countries to sharply raise their interest rates in order to defend their exchange rates during the currency crisis. A fundamental question in this regard is whether a very rigid exchange rate regime, such as a fixed rate, was appropriate. The crisis has taught us a very important lesson about exchange rate regimes. It now seems that a majority of us do not support rigid exchange rate regimes for emerging market countries, except for the currency board arrangement. In the case of the currency board arrangement, it is recognized that certain strict conditions should be met. Generally speaking, a flexible exchange rate arrangement has merit for emerging market countries as it does not expose their currencies to the risk of a one-sided bet by speculators.

If the Asian countries had moved to a flexible exchange rate regime before the crisis, their stake in defending a specific level of exchange rate would not have become so high, and the interest rates might not have had to be raised so much. However, while flexibility in exchange rate management is desirable, a large and rapid depreciation of the currency is devastating for a country. As was widely seen during the Asian crisis, the rapid depreciation of currencies caused a large expansion of the external debt of banks and corporations, and a number of them failed. As Stanley Fischer says, "while the burdens imposed by higher interest rates were temporary, those caused by bigger devaluations would have been permanent."[1] I will go back to the issue of prolonged high interest rates later.

On balance, I think we can conclude that a certain amount of stability of exchange rate is an essential element of a sound economic framework. A sharp rise in interest rates is a necessary tool to defend a currency. When a currency is heavily attacked, a sharp rise in interest rates is necessary, or confidence in the currency could collapse. As the Asian countries were not generally accustomed to very tight monetary policy, their interest rates did not rise quickly and long enough to stabilize their currencies, especially in the early stages of the crisis.

However, in order to defend currencies, other effective tools should also be mobilized. Official market intervention can be effective especially when market sentiment is diverse, and it would strengthen tight monetary policy if the intervention is not sterilized. It is true that some Asian countries wasted a large amount of their foreign reserves vainly trying just to maintain the fixed rates. And it was strongly felt that official market intervention would not have been useful for these countries. This view also strengthened the belief that currencies should be defended solely through raising interest rates. But, the use of official market intervention should not have been ruled out.

2. VERY HIGH INTEREST RATES FOR A PROLONGED PERIOD OR FOR AN ENTIRE REGION

The next question is, if instability in foreign exchange markets does not abate, should very high interest rates be maintained for a prolonged period of time. This is a special concern for Asian countries, because their corporations generally borrow heavily relative to their equity capital, and very high interest rates would eat up their profits. It can be argued that such a corporate financing structure should be changed. However, this is a long-term agenda item for the Asian economies: it is not something that can be done overnight. A more acute issue in the short run is to avoid widespread corporate failures, as these would further depress the economy and increase social tension.

Concern about very high interest rates will increase if a crisis spreads beyond a particular country. Then the tight monetary policy of one country would adversely affect the economic conditions of others, and vice versa. If interest rates are very high, the interplay among the countries in the region would seriously affect the regional economy as a whole. For an individual country, tight fiscal and monetary policies are usually the right response to a currency crisis. However, if an entire region is in crisis, and if each country pursues tight economic policies, the region may become trapped in a depression, and no country will be able to escape from the crisis. This is a fallacy of composition.

As the current crisis is spreading to Latin America and to large investors in the industrial countries, it could now threaten the stability of the global economy. Reflecting the growing concern about global deflationary pressure, global easing of monetary policy is being widely suggested. Why could we not have promoted such reflationary measures when the crisis began to spread throughout Asia? Certainly, a key player in the Asian region is Japan, and Japan's continued recession is very disappointing. But, could the other countries of the region have taken a reflationary stance by reducing their interest rates? Regrettably, the answer is no, since the easing of monetary policy in one country would have led to a depreciation of its currency and, in a regional context, the depreciation of one currency would have provoked others to follow suit, and the fear of competitive devaluation would quickly have grown. This is another kind of fallacy of composition.

3. OPTIONS OTHER THAN CAPITAL CONTROLS

Thus, if we stick to the present policy framework we end up with no solutions. That is why Paul Krugman proposed a change of policy framework from plan A—the orthodox policies which are the current IMF prescription—to plan B—capital controls.[2] He rightly argues that the free movement of short-term capital hampers the easing of monetary policy, which is necessary in order to avoid prolonged economic depression. However, before jumping to capital controls, we had better check carefully whether other approaches really are useless.

3.1 Private creditor involvement

In this context, the issue of earlier involvement of private creditors in crisis situations is something that could be considered. In the case of Korea, when private creditors accepted a voluntary roll over of short-term lending and the rescheduling of debt repayments at the end of last year, the outflow of funds subsided significantly. The Korean situation had improved by then, and the exchange rate has started to rise. If we had undertaken a bailing-in operation of private creditors earlier in the crisis, the amount of outflow could have been much smaller. We were hesitant to ask private creditors to take on the burden, however, as it would have changed their relationship with debtors away from the status of "business as usual." In reality, however, the business as usual status could not be maintained as the crisis had already begun.

The issue of private sector involvement is a very complicated one, and there are many questions that have to be answered from the legal, technical, and practical standpoints. We have to study further in order to maximize the benefits and find a practical and workable solution. I would point out that private sector involvement could also have some side effects. For debtors, it could lesson their motivation to make their scheduled repayments, if they expect there will be semi-automatic refinancing or rescheduling in crisis situations. For creditors, it could hamper the provision of new money if they expect refinancing or rescheduling at an earlier stage. In essence, by formalizing the early bailing-in of private creditors, the constructive ambiguity of the creditors' and debtors' status could be lost.

3.2 Regional approach

Another approach is to explore more coherent policies region-wide as soon as a crisis becomes regional. Of course, regional surveillance is one vehicle for this purpose. In the case of Asia, many meetings have been held for the purpose of regional surveillance, but we can strengthen the surveillance by making our regional policy discussion more substantive. While we have had many discussions on individual countries, there has not been sufficient analysis of economic linkage and aggregate policy effects in the region. The discussion on policies and strategy for the economic recovery of the region as a whole should be pursued vigorously, reflecting the recent shift in global policy thinking from inflation prevention to fostering growth. A recent Japanese proposal, the so-called Miyazawa Plan, will contribute to regional recovery along these lines.

In this connection, I should like to comment on the controversial idea of an Asian regional financing mechanism, which was informally but actively discussed one year ago. If a crisis in one or two countries in a region appears likely to extend to the region as a whole, the injection of massive liquidity would help greatly avoid a region-wide crisis. If international financial institutions cannot provide the necessary liquidity because of limited resources, such a regional financing mechanism would be very useful in preventing contagion and mitigating a credit crunch. What needs to be discussed is how much liquidity is needed and how much could be provided by the region itself. When we discussed the idea of a regional financing mechanism for Asia last year, both the proponents and the opponents forgot to focus on the issue of liquidity, and unfortunately the discussion was confused by various geopolitical considerations.

4. CAPITAL CONTROLS

Finally, I would like to touch upon the issue of capital controls. What has been amazing in recent weeks is the shift in the financial community's opinion of capital controls. Once it was taboo to even mention capital controls. But now it seems that many of us, albeit reluctantly, accept the idea of capital controls in extreme circumstances, provided measures are not taken unilaterally. It is surprising when we remember that even rather modest controls on capital inflow, as in Chile, were not universally accepted when we discussed the issue several months ago. The recent crisis in some hedge funds, and its serious adverse impact on leading private financial institutions, must have changed the financial community's perceptions. To cope with the current very unusual circumstances, it is probably necessary to consider very unusual measures.

That said, our knowledge and analysis of capital controls are insufficient since this was for so long a taboo subject. We need more analysis on what kind of controls on capital movements would be most effective. We also need to look at possible economic and social distortions resulting from capital controls. Open discussion on this subject should be welcomed, as it would clarify the merits and limits of this unorthodox measure.

Acknowledgment The views expressed are those of the author and not necessarily those of the Japanese government or the IMF.

Notes

[1]Stanley Fischer, 1998, " Lesson from a Crisis," *The Economist*, October 3, pp. 23–27.

[2]Paul Krugman, 1998, " Saving Asia," *Fortune Magazine*, September 7, pp. 75–80.

PART X

SUMMARY

Chapter 47

Conference Summary

George G. Kaufman
Loyola University Chicago and Federal Reserve Bank of Chicago

I also had the honor of summarizing last year's conference on "Preventing Bank Crises," which the Federal Reserve Bank of Chicago co-sponsored with the World Bank and the proceedings of which were just published (Caprio et al., 1998). I found that conference considerably easier to summarize. There was far less disagreement than at this year's conference. Last year's conference took place just before the outbreak of the Korean and South East Asian crises and focused primarily on the problems in Latin America in 1994–1995 and in the transition economies of Eastern Europe and the former USSR. Even before the current crises, the IMF had reported banking crises in some 130 of its 180-plus member countries. There was almost a universal agreement among the participants at last year's conference on the causes and solutions of these banking crises. I might repeat these conclusions as they were pretty much noted again this year and by now appear old hat and almost a mandatory mantra:

- Encourage market discipline to supplement regulatory discipline;
- Increase the accuracy and timeliness of reporting;
- Improve transparency;
- Make bank regulation independent of political influence;
- Require sufficient bank capital to absorb both regular losses and adverse macroeconomic shocks;
- Privatize state-owned banks and reduce or remove altogether government influence from state-controlled banks;
- Permit foreign ownership of banks;
- Improve the legal system, particularly bankruptcy and property rights laws; and

- Improve bank infrastructure, including increasing the sophistication of both bankers and bank regulators and supervisors.

Even if these conditions were satisfied, there would still be market failures, but exit would be orderly. What these conditions should prevent is disorderly exit. There appeared to be far less agreement among this year's participants on "now what," particularly as the new crises are both banking and currency (balance of payments) crises, and on "where do we go from here," particularly with respect to the form and shape of the design of any new architecture for the international financial system.

Nevertheless, there appeared to be some underlying agreement on a number of issues:

- Fragility and insolvency of banking and financial systems were a major cause of the current crises in East Asia and most of these systems require appropriate recapitalization, including the use of public funds to reduce any negative net worth's, as soon as possible to both speed recovery from the current crisis and to prevent future crises. Some individual institutions may not be worth recapitalizing and should be merged or liquidated, but the banking system as a whole needs to regain economic solvency.
- Although we cannot identify the precise straw that broke the camel's back or the last card that brought the house down, we can recognize, particularly ex-post and also to some extent, in the case of unduly fragile banking systems combined with fixed exchange rates, ex-ante, underlying conditions that are likely to cause crises and represent "accidents waiting to happen." Unfortunately, reliable early warning systems directed at predicting the precise timing of the breakdowns have not been successfully developed, either among researchers or private credit rating agencies, and the necessary research is still in its infancy. As a result, ex-post workout provisions for bank and other foreign debt obligations are important and need to be perfected.
- The East Asian crises have had deeper and more lasting adverse effects on the macroeconomies than initially believed. Indeed, a number of speakers were almost prophets of doom and gloom, emphasizing the parallels with the long-lasting LDC problems of the 1980s rather than with the much briefer Mexican and Argentinean problems of the mid-1990s. But it may be that, just as we tended to be late in predicting or recognizing the seriousness of the current problems, we may be late in recognizing a bottoming out of the crises. At least some cheery news of sightings of possible recoveries

was reported for South Korea and Thailand and of no significant further deterioration elsewhere. Russia is a special case, although it effects other countries through portfolio rebalancing and a general "flight to safety" by large international investors. A key to Asian recovery remains Japan.

The major area of heated debate and disagreement was on the past and potential future role of the IMF. A number of speakers mentioned the old medical adage "do no harm," but there was no agreement on whether the IMF had achieved this. The high interest rates that the IMF encouraged assisted countries to attempt to prevent further deterioration in their exchange rates came in for particular criticism. No one argued that the IMF had acted perfectly in the past and many IMF speakers appeared more open and candid about its past weaknesses and current problems than before. They recommended a number of changes in their own procedures to improve their future performance. Many of these focused on more timely and transparent information and reducing the moral hazard responses by banks, bank depositors, particularly foreign depositors, and investors in assisted countries.

But this did not satisfy everyone. Some believed that the IMF had often done more harm than good in the past and that it should be greatly overhauled and its activities curtailed, if not abolished altogether. World private capital markets could and would provide liquidity but not insolvency assistance with fewer adverse moral hazard consequences. Is the fact that Taiwan has largely escaped the recent Asian flu attributable to it not being a member of the IMF and therefore subject to stronger market discipline? Other participants called for the continuation of the IMF (possibly combined with the World Bank) to provide credit on a more limited and better defined basis for true liquidity problems, although some doubted whether it is possible to distinguish between liquidity and solvency problems for sovereign countries. They argue that "less is more" and that the IMF should be resurrected to concentrate solely on crisis prevention and management.

On the other polar extreme were those who preferred a larger and more powerful institution that is effectively a global lender of last resort. Such an institution would require greater funding as international financial problems are now becoming much larger, particularly as transitional capital flows continue to increase in magnitude and speed of reversibility and to dominate current account imbalances in affecting exchange rates. As a result, the IMF needs to act before crises begin (be more proactive) rather than after crises have started (be less proactive). Others argued that either this is not feasible as a true lender of last resort needs to be able to print money without limit, something the IMF can not now and is never likely to be permitted to do, or that a true Bagehotian lender of last resort operating on a fully collateralized penalty rate basis would be a very small and hardly used institution.

If one could peel back the layers of disagreement in orderly fashion and examine one issue at a time, I believe that even on this issue considerable agreement could be reached. That is, there is more smoke than fire in many of the arguments. But some fires do exist and it will take time to work out agreements on the new architecture. Judging from the substance of the disagreements voiced at this conference, to separate the smoke from the fire and focus only on the fire, future discussions need to be held in open forums and include academics and practitioners as well as current policy makers. The cost of failing to discover and correct as many potential weaknesses as possible is too high to justify omitting any critics from the table.

In the meantime, what can we do now? We probably did not schedule sufficient time for this. Crisis management is as likely to be ad hoc in the near future as not and arguments will continue to focus on important issues, such as whether the IMF recommended increases in interest rates in East Asia were useful or not in preventing further depreciations in exchange rates and should be recommended again. In the longer run, agreement existed on the need for more stable macroeconomic policies and higher private capital levels for banks that could absorb the even larger shocks that are likely to occur in the future, particularly from greater and more volatile international capital flows. Because this final recommendation is one that I have vocally favored for many years, this is a good point for me to stop.

Reference

Caprio, Gerard, Jr., William C. Hunter, George G. Kaufman, and Danny M. Leipziger. 1998, *Preventing Bank Crises: Lessons From Recent Global Bank Failures*, Washington, DC: World Bank and Federal Reserve Bank of Chicago.

CONFERENCE PROGRAM

Thursday, October 8

WELCOMING REMARKS

Michael H. Moskow, President, Federal Reserve Bank of Chicago

SESSION 1: Origins of the Asian Crisis
CHAIR:
Gregory F. Taylor, International Monetary Fund

SPEAKERS:
Craig Burnside, Hoover Institution, Martin Eichenbaum, Northwestern University and Federal Reserve Bank of Chicago, and Sergio Rebelo, Northwestern University
Michael P. Dooley, University of California, Santa Cruz and Board of Governors of the Federal Reserve System
Reuven Glick, Federal Reserve Bank of San Francisco

DISCUSSANTS:
Roberto Chang, Federal Reserve Bank of Atlanta
David D. Hale, Zurich Group

ROUNDTABLE 1:
Causes and Implications of the Asian Crisis
The Role of the Financial Sector, Domestic Policies, and Contagion
CHAIR:
Jack B. Evans, Hall-Perrine Foundation

PANELISTS:
Joseph R. Bisignano, Bank for International Settlements
J. Soedradjad Djiwandono, formerly Bank of Indonesia
William C. Hunter, Federal Reserve Bank of Chicago
Desmond Lachman, Salomon Smith Barney
Flemming Larsen, International Monetary Fund
Kazuo Ueda, Bank of Japan
Chaiyawat Wibulswasdi, formely Bank of Thailand

DINNER PROGRAM
CHAIR:
Robert J. Darnall, Chairman, President and CEO, Inland Steel Industries, Inc.

KEYNOTE SPEAKER
Karin Lissakers, Executive Director, International Monetary Fund

Friday, October 9

SESSION 2: Response to the Crisis – Overview and Case Studies
CHAIR:
Danny Leipziger, World Bank

SPEAKERS:
Overview: Bijan B. Aghevli, International Monetary Fund
Korea: Stijn Claessens, World Bank
Thailand: Yoshihiro Iwasaki, Asian Development Bank

DISCUSSANTS:
Richard J. Herring, University of Pennsylvania
Yung Chul Park, Korea Institute of Finance
Robert Townsend, University of Chicago and Federal Reserve Bank of Chicago

SESSION 3: Containing the Risks of Future Crisis—Strenghening the Regulatory Framework
CHAIR:
Verne G. Istock, First Chicago NBD

SPEAKERS:
Allan H. Meltzer, Carnegie Mellon University
Tom de Swaan, ABN AMRO Bank, N.V.

DISCUSSANTS:
George J. Benston, Emory University
Anil K. Kashyap, University of Chicago and Federal Reserve Bank of Chicago
Carl-Johan Lindgren, International Monetary Fund

LUNCHEON PROGRAM
CHAIR:
Lester H. McKeever, Jr., Washington, Pittman, and McKeever and Director, Federal Reserve Bank of Chicago

KEYNOTE SPEAKER
Robert A. Johnson, formerly Moore Capital Management

SESSION 4: Early Warning Indicators, Transparency, and Market Response
CHAIR:
Zhang Zhixiang, International Monetary Fund

SPEAKERS:
Jerome S. Fons, Moody's Investors Service
Morris Goldstein, Institute for International Economics
Graciela L. Kaminsky, George Washington University
John A. Wing, Illinois Institute of Technology and ABN AMRO

DISCUSSANTS:
Martin Mayer, Brookings Institution
Catherine Pattillo, International Monetary Fund
Eric Rosengren, Federal Reserve Bank of Boston

ROUNDTABLE 2: Moral Hazard and the Role of International Rescue Programs
CHAIR:
Norman R. Bobins, LaSalle National Bank

PANELISTS:
Charles W. Calomiris, Columbia University
Charles H. Dallara, Institute of International Finance
John Lipsky, Chase Manhattan Bank
Michael Mussa, International Monetary Fund
Pedro Pou, Central Bank of Argentina—presented by José A. Costa, International Monetary Fund
Helmut Schieber, Deutsche Bundesbank

DINNER PROGRAM
CHAIR:
Michael H. Moskow, President, Federal Reserve Bank of Chicago

KEYNOTE SPEAKER
Stanley Fischer, First Deputy Managing Director, International Monetary Fund

SESSION 5: The Future Role of the International Monetary Fund in International Rescue Operations
CHAIR:
David Marshall, Federal Reserve Bank of Chicago

SPEAKERS:
Barry Eichengreen, University of California, Berkeley
Robert Litan, Brookings Institute

DISCUSSANTS:
Charles A. E. Goodhart, London School of Economics and Bank of England
Randall S. Kroszner, University of Chicago and Federal Reserve Bank of Chicago
Anna J. Schwartz, National Bureau of Economic Research

ROUNDTABLE 3: Lessons from the Crisis for the International Financial System
CHAIR:
Raghuram Rajan, University of Chicago

PANELISTS:
Manuel Guitian, International Monetary Fund
Everardo Elizondo, Banco de Mexico
Richard Portes, London Business School and Centre for Economic Policy Research
Edwin M. Truman, Board of Governors of the Federal Reserve Bank of System
Delano Villanueva, South East Asian Central Banks
Yukio Yoshimura, International Monetary Fund

CONFERENCE SUMMARY
George G. Kaufman, Loyola University, Chicago and Federal Reserve Bank of Chicago
Michael H. Moskow, Federal Reserve Bank of Chicago

Contributors

BIJAN B. AGHEVLI is the deputy director in the Asia and Pacific Department at the International Monetary Fund. He was previously a senior advisor in the research department in charge of managing the department's research program on developing countries. He also spent two years as a research fellow at the London School of Economics. He has worked extensively on Asian countries, including Japan and the Asian crisis countries, and has published papers in the general area of international and monetary economics.

GEORGE J. BENSTON is the John H. Harland Professor of Finance, Accounting, and Economics in the Goizueta Business School and professor of economics in the College of Arts and Sciences of Emory University and honorary visiting professor at City University (London). Before coming to Emory in 1987, he was on the faculties of the University of Rochester and the University of Chicago and has been the John M. Olin Distinguished Visiting Fellow at Oxford University and a visiting professor at the London School of Economics, the London Graduate School of Business Studies, Hebrew University, and the University of California, Berkeley. Mr. Benston has published extensively on accounting, banking, and other economic subjects. He received his B.A. from Queens College, M.B.A. from New York University, and Ph.D. from the University of Chicago.

JOSEPH R. BISIGNANO is the deputy director of the Monetary and Economic Department of the Bank for International Settlements. Prior to his current position, Mr. Bisignano was senior vice president and director of research at the Federal Reserve Bank of San Francisco. He has served as a visiting professor of economics at Stanford University as well as assistant professor of economics at Rutgers University. Mr. Bisignano holds an M.A. and Ph.D. in economics from Stanford University, an M.B.A. in finance from Columbia University, and a B.S. from the University of Buffalo.

NORMAN R. BOBINS is president and chief executive officer of LaSalle National Bank and LaSalle National Corporation. He is also chairman of LaSalle Bank NI and LaSalle Bank N.A., and the head of Midwest Commercial Banking for ABN AMRO North America, Inc., the parent of the LaSalle Banks. Mr. Bobins joined The Exchange National Bank of Chicago in April 1981 as senior executive vice president and chief lending officer. The Exchange was acquired by LaSalle National Corporation in 1990. He came to the Exchange from American National Bank and Trust Company where he was senior vice president, holding various commercial lending positions over fourteen years. In June 1995, Mayor Richard M. Daley named him to Chicago's School Reform Board of Trustees. In addition, Mr. Bobins is a trustee of DePaul University, the Public School Teachers' Pension and Retirement Fund of Chicago, and the University of Chicago Hospitals. He is past president of The Bankers Club of Chicago, chairman of the board of directors of the Chicago Clearing House Association, and a board member of Spertus College. He is a member of the Bankers Roundtable, the Chicago Committee, the Commercial Club of Chicago, the Leadership Council for Metropolitan Open Communities, and Northwestern University Associates. Mr. Bobins earned his B.S. from the University of Wisconsin in 1964 and his M.B.A. from the University of Chicago in 1967.

CRAIG BURNSIDE is a national fellow of the Hoover Institution at Stanford University, currently on leave from his position as an economist for the World Bank. Mr. Burnside has been an assistant professor at the University of Pittsburgh as well as a lecturer and assistant professor at Queen's University. Mr. Burnside has extensive publications, including papers, short articles, and book chapters. He holds a B.A. in economics from the University of British Columbia and an M.A. and Ph.D. in economics from Northwestern University.

CHARLES W. CALOMIRIS is the Paul M. Montrone Professor of Finance and Economics and Director of the Program in Financial Institutions at the Columbia University Graduate School of Business. He also directs the Project on Financial Deregulation at the American Enterprise Institute. Mr. Calomiris has published widely in journals and books, including the

American Economic Review, the *Quarterly Journal of Economics*, the *Journal of Business*, the *Journal of Money, Credit, and Banking*, and the *Oxford Economic Papers*. Mr. Calomiris is the recipient of research grants or awards from the National Science Foundation, the World Bank, the Japanese Government, the Herbert V. Prochnow Foundation, and the Garn Institute of Finance. In 1995 he was named a university scholar at the University of Illinois at Urbana-Champaign, where he served as associate professor of finance and co-director of the Office for Banking Research. He is a member of four editorial boards, a research associate at the National Bureau of Economic Research, a visiting fellow at the American Enterprise Institute, and a consultant for the World Bank and the St. Louis and the New York Federal Reserve Banks. He has been a visiting scholar at the Federal Reserve Board of Governors, the Federal Reserve Banks of Chicago and St. Louis, and an advisor to the governments of Mexico, Argentina, and El Salvador on banking reform. Mr. Calomiris received a B.A. in economics from Yale University in 1979 and a Ph.D. in economics from Stanford University in 1985.

ROBERTO CHANG is a research officer with the Federal Reserve Bank of Atlanta. Prior to joining the Bank in 1993, he was an assistant professor of economics at New York University. He has also worked as an economist at the Central Bank of Peru. Mr. Chang is a member of the American Economic Association. He is an associate editor of the *Journal of International Economics*. His research has been published in many journals, including the *Journal of Monetary Economics* and the *Journal of Economic Theory*. He has received several honors, including a research grant from the National Science Foundation. A native of Lima, Peru, he received his Bachelor's degree from the Universidad Catolica del Peru and his Ph.D. in economics from the University of Pennsylvania.

STIJN CLAESSENS is a principal economist in the Financial Economics Group of the Financial Sector Practice of the World Bank. Prior to coming to the bank, Mr. Claessens taught at New York University. He has also worked in the World Bank's finance complex, Chief Economist's Office, the Debt and International Financial Division, the Finance and Private Sector Development Division for the Europe, Central Asia, Middle-East and North Africa Regions, and the East Asia and Pacific Region. He holds a Ph.D. and Master's in business economics from the Wharton School of the University of Pennsylvania and a Master's in business economics from Erasmus University, the Netherlands.

CHARLES H. DALLARA became third managing director of the Institute of International Finance in July 1993. As the institute's chief executive officer, he is responsible for developing and executing the institute's programs under the guidance of the Board of Directors. From June 1991 to July 1993, Mr. Dallara was a managing director at J.P. Morgan & Company, heading Morgan's investment and commercial banking business in Eastern Europe and the C.I.S., the Middle East, Southeastern Europe, Africa, and India. Mr. Dallara earned a B.S. degree in economics from the University of South Carolina. He received an M.A. and a Ph.D. from the Fletcher School of Law and Diplomacy, Tufts University.

ROBERT J. DARNALL is chairman, president, and chief executive officer of Inland Steel Industries, Inc., and has been associated with Inland Steel since 1979. He has been chairman, president, and chief executive officer since 1992. He is also a member of the Board of Directors of the Federal Reserve Bank of Chicago. Mr. Darnall is a member of the Boards of Directors of the International Iron and Steel Institute, Cummins Engine Company, Inc., and Household International, Inc. He received a B.A. degree in mathematics in 1960 from DePauw University, a B.S. degree in civil engineering in 1962 from Columbia University, and an M.B.A. degree in 1973 from the University of Chicago.

TOM de SWAAN is a member of the Managing Board of ABN AMRO Bank N.V., which he joined in 1998. He also serves as chairman of the Basle Committee on Banking Supervision. Beginning in 1992, he assumed responsibility for the supervision of credit institutions and mutual funds in the Netherlands. During this period, he served as chairman of the Joint Forum on Financial Conglomerates and the Banking Supervisory Committee of the European Monetary Institute. In 1986 he became a member of the Governing Board of De Nederlandsche Bank in charge of payment systems and IT. Mr. de Swaan started his professional career at De Nederlandsche Bank (the Netherlands Central Bank). He holds a master's degree in economics from the University of Amsterdam.

J. SOEDRADJAD DJIWANDONO is a noted economist and policymaker in Indonesia. After starting his career as a reseacher in the National Institute for Economics and Social Research of the Indonesian Institute for Sciences (LIPI) in 1963, he rose to head its economics division in 1968. He was special assistant to the Minister of Trade in Indonesia from 1969 to 1972. In 1972, he became the head of the Bureau of Monetary and State Finance in the National Development and Planning Agency (BAPPENAS) and in 1984, assistant minister coordinator for economics, finance, and industry. From 1988 to 1993, Mr. Djiwandono served as the state minister for trade of the Republic of Indonesia and served as the governor of Bank Indonesia, Indonesia's central bank, from 1993 until February 1998. He has also been associated with the University of Indonesia since 1978 and is currently a professor of economics. He has written a number of books and articles on monetary policies, finance, and international trade-related issues. He holds a B.A. in economics from Gajah Mada University, an M.Sc. in economics from the University of Wisconsin-Madison, and an M.A. in political economics from Boston University. He also received a Ph.D. in economics from Boston University.

MICHAEL P. DOOLEY is an economist in the Division of International Finance at the Board of Governors of the Federal Reserve on leave from the University of California, Santa Cruz. He is a research associate at the National Bureau of Economic Research and an editor of the *International Journal of Finance and Economics*. He has served on the staff of the Board of Governors and the Research Department of the International Monetary Fund. His research deals with exchange rate determination, international capital movements, capital controls, debt management policy, and issues associated with sovereign debt.

MARTIN EICHENBAUM is a professor of economics at Northwestern University and a consultant to the Federal Reserve Bank of Chicago. Before coming to Northwestern, Mr. Eichenbaum was visiting associate professor of economics at the Graduate School of Business at the University of Chicago as well as an assistant, then associate professor of economics at Carnegie Mellon University. He has published widely on issues of macroeconomic equilibria and markets. Mr. Eichenbaum holds a Bachelor's degree in economics from McGill University and a Ph.D. in economics from the University of Minnesota.

BARRY EICHENGREEN is the John L. Simpson Professor of Economics and Political Science at the University of California, Berkeley, research associate of the National Bureau of Economic Research, and research fellow of the Center for Economic Policy Research. His most recent book is *Globalizing Capital: A History of the International Monetary System*, just reissued by Princeton University Press in paperback with new material on the Asian crisis.

EVERARDO ELIZONDO is the vice governor of Banco de México. Prior to his appointment, he was chief economist at Bancomer, S.A. from 1992 to 1997, and director of the Instituto Quantum, also in 1992.

From 1983 to 1992, Mr. Elizondo was president, index, of Economia Aplicada, S.A. From 1982 to 1983, he was a visiting scholar at the University of Texas, Austin. He served as chief economist and vice president of Grupo Industrial ALFA, S.A. from 1974 to 1982. Mr. Elizondo began his career as chief economist at Grupo Serfin, S.A. He received a B.A. in economics from Universidad de Nuevo León, an M.Sc. in economics from University of Wisconsin, Madison, and a diploma from the International Tax Program at Harvard Law School.

JACK B. EVANS is president of the Hall-Perrine Foundation, a private philanthropic corporation located in Cedar Rapids, Iowa. He has been president since January 1996. He is also a member of the Board of Directors of the Federal Reserve Bank of Chicago. From 1972 to 1995, he held various positions with the SCI Financial Group, Inc., a regional financial services firm, including vice president of research, executive vice president, and president and chief operating officer. Mr. Evans also owns and manages three grain farms in Iowa. He is chairman of the Board of Trustees of Coe College and a board member of the Cedar Rapids Gazette Company, Priority One (past chairman), and the Hall-Perrine Foundation. He is also vice chairman and board member of the United Fire & Casualty Company. Mr. Evans received a B.A. degree in business administration from Coe College in 1970 and an M.B.A. degree in finance and investments from the University of Iowa in 1972.

STANLEY FISCHER is the first deputy managing director of the International Monetary Fund, a post he assumed in September 1994. Prior to joining the Fund, Mr. Fischer was the Killian Professor and head of the Department of Economics at Massachusetts Institute of Technology (MIT). He was assistant professor of economics at the University of Chicago until 1973, when he returned to the MIT Department of Economics as an associate professor. He became professor of economics in 1977. He has held visiting positions at the Hebrew University, Jerusalem, and at the Hoover Institution at Stanford. From January 1988 to August 1990 he served as vice president, development economics and chief economist at the World Bank. He has also held consulting appointments with the U.S. State Department, the U.S. Treasury, the World Bank, the International Monetary Fund, and the Bank of Israel. Mr. Fischer is the author or editor of numerous books. From 1986 to 1994 he was editor of the *NBER Macroeconomics Annual*; he has also served as associate editor of other economics journals. He has published extensively in the professional journals. He received a B.Sc in economics and an M.Sc. in economics at the London School of Economics and obtained his Ph.D. in economics at MIT.

JEROME S. FONS is a managing director in the Banking and Sovereign Group at Moody's Investors Service in New York. From 1990 through 1994, Mr. Fons was the principal author of Moody's corporate bond and commercial paper default studies and has published widely in the field of credit risk. Prior to joining Moody's, Mr. Fons was an economic advisor at Chemical Bank and an economist with the Federal Reserve Banks of New York and Cleveland. Mr. Fons holds a Ph.D. in economics from the University of California, San Diego.

REUVEN GLICK is vice president in charge of the International Studies Section of the Economic Research Department at the Federal Reserve Bank of San Francisco and director of the Bank's Center for Pacific Basin Monetary and Economic Studies. Mr. Glick is the author of many articles in the area of international macroeconomic policy and Pacific Basin financial developments. He was formerly on the faculty of the Graduate School of Business at New York University and a consultant to the World Bank on international debt issues. Mr. Glick received a B.A. degree in economics from the University of Chicago and a Ph.D. degree in economics from Princeton University.

MORRIS GOLDSTEIN is the Dennis Weatherstone Senior Fellow in International Finance at the Institute for International Economics. He has held the position of deputy director of the International Monetary Fund Research Department as well as serving as senior technical advisor at the U.S. Treasury, a visiting research associate at the London School of Economics, and as Baker-Weeks Research Fellow at the Brookings Institution. He has published widely in the field of international economics. Mr. Goldstein received an B.A. in economics from Rutgers College and a Ph.D. in economics from New York University.

CHARLES A. E. GOODHART is the Norman Sosnow Professor of Banking and Finance at the London School of Economics (LSE). In 1997 he was appointed one of the outside independent members of the Bank of England's new Monetary Policy Committee. Before joining the LSE in 1985, he worked as an adviser at the Bank of England, becoming a chief adviser in 1980. Earlier he had taught at Cambridge. Besides numerous articles, he has written books on monetary history and a graduate monetary textbook.

MANUEL GUITIÁN is director of the Monetary and Exchange Affairs Department at the International Monetary Fund. After working on conditionality and other IMF policy issues early in his career, Mr. Guitián participated actively in the process of accession to Fund membership of the countries in transition from central planning to market-based economic regimes and led missions to the European members of the G-7 as well as to countries in transition and in the process of structural reform. He is the author of numerous articles on international monetary matters and on balance of payments, exchange rate, and external debt issues. Mr. Guitián graduated in law from the University of Santiago de Compostela and in economics from the Compulutense University of Madrid. He also holds a Ph.D. in economics from the University of Chicago.

DAVID D. HALE is the global chief economist for the Zurich Group and its investment affiliates. He joined the group following its acquisition of Kemper Corporation, where he had served as chief economist for many years. Since 1990, he has also been a consultant to the U.S. Department of Defense on how changes in the global economy are affecting U.S. security relationships. In addition to his responsibilities at Zurich, Mr. Hale is a member of a variety of government and private sector economic policy research groups in Washington, Tokyo, and Bonn. Mr. Hale holds a B.Sc. degree in international economic affairs from the Georgetown University School of Foreign Service and an M.Sc. degree in economics from the London School of Economics.

RICHARD J. HERRING is the Jacob Safra Professor of International Banking and vice dean and director of the Undergraduate Division at the Wharton School of the University of Pennsylvania. He has served as advisor to the Federal Reserve Board, the Council of Economic Advisers, the U.S. Treasury, the Central Bank of New Zealand, the International Monetary Fund, and the World Bank. Before his current position at Wharton, Mr. Herring taught at Princeton University. He received his A.B. from Oberlin College and his M.A. and Ph.D. from Princeton University.

WILLIAM C. HUNTER is senior vice president and director of research at the Federal Reserve Bank of Chicago. Prior to his current position, he was a vice president and head of the financial markets and banking sections in the Research Department of the Federal Reserve Bank of Atlanta. He has held the position of associate professor of finance at Emory University and has held faculty positions at Atlanta University, the University of Georgia, Chicago State University, and Northwestern University. He was a visiting scholar with the Board of Governors of the Federal Reserve System. Mr. Hunter received his B.S. in business and economics from Hampton Institute (now Hampton University) and holds an

M.B.A. in finance and a Ph.D. in finance and environment from Northwestern University.

VERN G. ISTOCK is chairman, president, and chief executive officer of First Chicago NBD Corporation. Mr. Istock joined NBD in 1963 as a credit analyst trainee, and took on increasing responsibilities over time, becoming a group head in the Metropolitan Corporate Division in 1971. In 1977, Mr. Istock was appointed head of the United States Division. In 1982, he was named an executive vice president with responsibility for all corporate banking divisions. He was elected vice chairman and director of NBD Bancorp and NBD Bank in 1985. He was named chairman and chief executive officer on January 1, 1994. Upon the merger of NBD and First Chicago Corporation on December 1, 1995, Mr. Istock became president and chief executive officer of the new corporation, First Chicago NBD Corporation, and was elected chairman on May 10, 1996. Mr. Istock is also a member of the Board of Directors of the Federal Reserve Bank of Chicago. He is a director of the Bankers Roundtable, a director of the International Monetary Conference, and has served on the Board of Directors of the Michigan State Chamber of Commerce and the Business Attraction and Expansion Council of the Greater Detroit Chamber of Commerce.

YOSHIHIRO IWASAKI is chief of the Strategy and Policy Office (SPO) of the Asian Development Bank. Prior to his appointment as the head of SPO in November 1997, he served for three years as manager of the Programs Department (West) covering Bangladesh, Bhutan, India, and Nepal. From 1983 to 1990, Mr. Iwasaki served as economist/senior economist at the Economics Office and the Programs Department (West). From 1991 to 1994 he worked for the International Monetary Fund as senior economist, Central Asia Department. He has also served as a visiting professor at the University of the Philippines' School of Economics. Prior to 1983, Mr. Iwasaki's experience included four years of consultancy work on trade and development for the Institute of Developing Economies and the International Development Center of Japan in Tokyo, five years in the export–import business of machinery and petrochemical plants, and the development of a natural gas project for C. Itoh & Co. He has a doctorate degree in economics (development) from Stanford University. He received his master's and bachelor's degrees in economics from Keio University, Tokyo.

ROBERT A. JOHNSON was an investment manager at Moore Capital Management from 1995 to 1996 before taking a sabbatical to work on charitable activities. He is currently the president of the National

Scholastic Chess Foundation, which promotes using the game of chess in the curriculum of schools in poverty stricken urban areas. He is also an active member of the board of directors of the Shake A Leg Foundation, which focuses on the rehabilitation of people with spinal cord injuries. Before joining Moore Capital, Mr. Johnson was a managing director at Soros Funds Management in New York City. His fund was very involved in the emerging markets of Asia and Latin America. Prior to joining Soros Fund Management, Mr. Johnson was a member of the proprietary trading team at Bankers Trust Company, and he managed an exotic currency fund for the Bankers Trust Company's Funds Management Division. Mr. Johnson was the chief economist of the Senate Banking Committee under William Proximire from 1987 to 1989. Mr. Johnson worked concurrently as a consultant to the Robert Strauss-Drew Lewis led Bipartisan National Economic Commission on the fiscal implications of the resolution of the Savings and Loan situation. Mr. Johnson also worked as a senior economist of the Senate Budget Committee under Pete Domenici from 1986 to 1987, and was a research economist in the Division of International Finance at the Federal Reserve Board from May of 1984 until early 1986. Mr. Johnson received his Ph.D. in economics from Princeton University in 1986 and B.S. degrees in electrical engineering an din economics from the Massachusetts Institute of Technology.

GRACIELA L. KAMINSKY is currently a professor of economics at George Washington University. She has been a consultant and visiting scholar at the International Monetary Fund and World Bank. She has worked in the Division of Monetary Affairs at the Board of Governors of the Federal Reserve System and was an assistant professor of economics at the University of California, San Diego. Ms. Kaminsky has published extensively on issues of open economy macroeconomics. She received her Ph.D. from the Massachusetts Institute of Technology.

ANIL K. KASHYAP is a professor of economics at the University of Chicago's Graduate School of Business. Mr. Kashyap joined the faculty in 1991. He is a consultant to the Federal Reserve Bank of Chicago's Research Department and serves on the Advisory Council to the Japan External Trade Organization. Previously he served as a staff economist for the Board of Governors of the Federal Reserve System. He earned his Ph.D. in economics in 1989 from the Massachusetts Institute of Technology and his Bachelor's degree in 1982 in economics and statistics from the University of California, Davis.

GEORGE G. KAUFMAN is the John F. Smith, Jr., Professor of Economics and Finance at Loyola University, Chicago and a consultant to the Federal Reserve Bank of Chicago. From 1959 to 1970 he was at the Federal Reserve Bank of Chicago, and after teaching for ten years at the University of Oregon, he returned as a consultant to the Bank in 1981. Mr. Kaufman's teaching and research interests are in financial economics, institutions, and markets. He is co-chair of the Shadow Financial Regulatory Committee. Mr. Kaufman received a B.A. from Oberlin College, an M.A. from the University of Michigan, and a Ph.D. in economics from the University of Iowa.

RANDALL S. KROSZNER is associate professor of business economics at the University of Chicago's Graduate School of Business and a consultant to the Federal Reserve Bank of Chicago. Mr. Kroszner has been a visiting professor at the Stockholm School of Economics, the Institute for International Economic Studies at the University of Stockholm, and the Free University of Berlin. Mr. Kroszner graduated magna cum laude from Brown University and received his Ph.D. from the economics department of Harvard University in 1990.

THOMAS H. KRUEGER is division chief of the Southern I section of EU1 at the International Monetary Fund. Mr. Krueger joined the IMF in 1988 as an economist. He has served in various capacities at the IMF including as senior economist and deputy division chief. Mr. Krueger completed his undergraduate studies in economics in 1982 at the University of Freiburg. He received an M.A. in economics in 1985 and a Ph.D. in economics in 1988, both from the University of Chicago.

DESMOND LACHMAN is the managing director for Salomon Smith Barney's emerging market economic research. Previous to his current position, he was global coordinator, then head, of global emerging market research. Prior to joining Salomon, Mr. Lachman was deputy director in the Policy and Review Department at the International Monetary Fund. He also served as senior advisor in its European department. Mr. Lachman holds a bachelor of commerce degree from the University of Wiwatersrand, South Africa, and a Ph.D. from Cambridge University.

FLEMMING LARSEN is deputy director of research at the International Monetary Fund, Washington, DC. Since 1992, he has had the senior responsibility for the IMF's World Economic Outlook, the Fund's flagship publication and one of the most authoritative surveys of global economic trends and policy issues. In 1990–92 (while on leave from the

IMF), Mr. Larsen was division chief in the European Commission, with responsibility for international monetary affairs. Before joining the IMF in 1985, he was director of forecasting at Wharton Econometrics in Philadelphia and senior economist at the Organization for Economic Cooperation and Development in Paris. Mr. Larsen holds degrees from the University of Aarhus, Denmark, and the College of Europe in Bruges.

DANNY LEIPZIGER is director for finance, private sector, and infrastructure for Latin America and the Caribbean at the World Bank. Mr. Leipziger led the team negotiating the World Bank's $3 billion emergency loan to Korea in December 1997. Since joining the World Bank in 1981, he has been lead economist for country groups in East Asia and Latin America and senior manager of the Economic Development Institute. Mr. Leipziger led the team negotiating emergency bank restructuring operations in Argentina in 1995 and the renewal of bank lending and advisory work in Vietnam in 1989 to 1990. He served previously at USAID and the Economic Bureau and Policy Planning Staff of the State Department. Among his recent publications are Lessons of East Asia and Distribution of Income and Wealth in Korea. Mr. Leipziger edited the World Bank's *East Asia Country Studies* series in 1993 and has published widely on development economics. Mr. Leipziger holds a Ph.D. from Brown University.

CARL-JOHAN LINDGREN is senior advisor of the International Monetary Fund's Monetary and Exchange Affairs Department (MAE) with responsibility for financial sector issues. He formerly headed MAE's Banking Supervision and Regulation Division for several years and spearheaded the IMF's work on banking soundness and bank restructuring issues as well as on the dual relationship between macroeconomic and financial sector developments and policies. He is one of the principal authors of various published IMF policy papers on financial sector issues including bank soundness and macroeconomic policy, systemic bank restructuring and macroeconomic policy, and toward a framework for financial stability. Mr. Lindgren has participated in various international working parties dealing with strategies for strengthening financial sectors in emerging market economies. Since the middle of last year, he has been heavily involved in the financial sector crises in Asia. Mr. Lindgren has been a staff member of the IMF since 1970, serving first as an economist in the Latin American region, later advising central banks worldwide on monetary management and money market development issues, and in the 1990s focusing on financial sector issues. Mr. Lindgren is a graduate of the Swedish School of Economics in Helsinki.

JOHN LIPSKY is the chief economist of the Chase Manhattan Bank. He also serves as the director of research of Chase's Global Bank. A managing director of the bank, Mr. Lipsky was appointed a member of the Chase Manhattan Corporation's Policy Council, the senior policymaking organization. Previously, Mr. Lipsky had been chief economist of Salomon Brothers, Inc., a position he had occupied since 1992. From 1989 to 1992, Mr. Lipsky was based in London, where he directed Salomon Brothers' European Research Group. He joined Salomon Brothers in 1984, following a decade at the International Monetary Fund, where he helped to direct the Fund's exchange rate surveillance and tracked international capital market developments and spent 1978 to 1980 as the fund's resident representative in Chile. Mr. Lipsky's professional affiliations include the Board of Directors of the National Bureau of Economic Research and of the American Council on Germany. Mr. Lipsky received a Bachelor's degree in economics from Wesleyan University and an M.A. and a Ph.D. in economics from Stanford University.

KARIN LISSAKERS is the executive director for the United States at the International Monetary Fund. Her previous positions include lecturer in international banking at Columbia University, senior associate at the Carnegie Endowment for International Peace, as well as staff director for the Senate Subcommittee on Foreign Economic Policy. She has authored a book and several articles on international banking issues. Ms. Lissakers holds a B.A. from Ohio State University and an M.A. from John Hopkins University.

ROBERT E. LITAN is the director of the Economic Studies Program and the Cabot Family Chair in Economics at the Brookings Institution, where he served as a senior fellow from 1984 to 1993 and as director of two research centers in the program from 1987 to 1993. From 1993 to 1995, he was deputy assistant Attorney General at the Department of Justice. During 1995 and 1996, he was associate director of the Office of Management and Budget. Mr. Litan has practiced at two Washington law firms. He received his B.S. in economics from the Wharton School of Finance, University of Pennsylvania, his J.D. from Yale Law School, and both his M.Phil. and Ph.D. in economics from Yale University.

DAVID MARSHALL is economic advisor and senior financial economist at the Federal Reserve Bank of Chicago and adjunct professor of finance at the University of Chicago. Before coming to the Federal Reserve System, he was on the faculty of the Kellogg Graduate School of Management at Northwestern University. His research focuses on linkages between financial markets, financial institutions, and macroeconomic performance. He has had papers published in *Econometrica,* the *Journal of Finance,* the *Journal of Financial Economics,* the *Journal of Monetary Economics*, the *Journal of Money, Credit, and Banking*, and *Macroeconomic Dynamics*. Mr. Marshall received a B.A. from Yale University, and an M.S. and Ph.D. in economics from Carnegie-Mellon University.

MARTIN MAYER is a guest scholar at the Brookings Institution. He is the author of three novels and thirty nonfiction books, about half of them about business and financial subjects, most recently *The Bankers: The Next Generation.* He has been a consultant to the American Council of Learned Societies in the 1960s, a member of the President's Panel on Educational Research and Development for Presidents Kennedy and Johnson, and a member of the President's Commission on Housing for President Reagan. Mr. Mayer is a graduate of Harvard.

LESTER H. McKEEVER, JR. is the managing partner and head of Washington, Pittman & McKeever, a Chicago-based CPA and consulting firm. He has been affiliated with the firm for over thirty-five years, and has been managing partner since 1976. He is also chairman of the Board of Directors of the Federal Reserve Bank of Chicago. Mr. McKeever is a director of Worldwide Broadcasting, Inc., Printing Specialties, Inc., the Castlerock Group, Inc., the Neighborhood Institute Development Corporation, and the MBIA Insurance Corporation of Illinois. He also is an active member of the American Institute of Certified Public Accountants and the Illinois Society of Certified Public Accountants. Mr. McKeever is a board member of the American and Chicago Bar Associations, as well as the Government Finance Officers Association and the American Association of Attorneys to CPA's. Mr. McKeever received a bachelor's degree in accounting from the University of Illinois at Urbana-Champaign, and a J.D. from the IIT-Chicago Kent College of Law. He is a CPA, with credentials for Illinois, Michigan, and Wisconsin, and has been admitted to the Bar in Illinois, U.S. District Courts, and U.S. Tax Courts.

ALLAN H. MELTZER is the Allan H. Meltzer University Professor of Political Economy and Public Policy at Carnegie Mellon University and visiting scholar at the American Enterprise Institute. He has been a visiting professor at Harvard, the University of Chicago, the University of Rochester, the Yugoslav Institute for Economic Research, the Austrian Institute for Advanced Study, the Getulio Vargas Foundation in Rio de Janeiro, and the City University, London. He has served as a consultant for several government as well as foreign agencies. Mr. Meltzer's writings have appeared in numerous journals and he is the author of several books. He is a director emeritus of Cooper Tire and Rubber company and a director of the Sarah Scaife Foundation, the Commonwealth Foundation, the Advanced Materials Group, and Stillhalter Vision.

MICHAEL H. MOSKOW is president of the Federal Reserve Bank of Chicago. Appointed in 1994, he serves as the Bank's chief officer and rotates as a voting member of the Federal Open Market Committee, the Federal Reserve System's most important monetary policymaking body. He began his career teaching economics, labor relations, and management at Temple University, Lafayette College, and Drexel University. From 1969 to 1977, he held a number of senior positions with the U.S. government, including under secretary of labor at the U.S. Department of Labor, director of the Council on Wage and Price Stability, assistant secretary for policy development and research at the U.S. Department of Housing and Urban Development, and senior staff economist with the Council of Economic Advisors. In 1977, Mr. Moskow joined the private sector as vice president of corporate development and planing at Esmark, Inc. and was named executive vice president of Estronics, Inc., its wholly-owned subsidiary in 1980. He later served as president and chief executive officer of Velsicol Chemical Corporation, vice president of corporate development for Dart and Kraft, Inc. and vice president of strategy and business development for Premark International, Inc. In 1991, President Bush appointed Mr. Moskow Deputy United States Trade Representative, with the rank of Ambassador. Mr. Moskow joined the faculty of the J.L. Kellogg Graduate School of Management at Northwestern University in 1993. Mr. Moskow is the author of seven books and more than twenty articles. He received a B.A. in economics from Lafayette College in Easton, Pennsylvania, in 1959, and an M.A. in economics in 1962 and a Ph.D. in business and applied economics from the University of Pennsylvania in 1965.

MICHAEL MUSSA is the economic counselor and the director of the Department of Research at the International Monetary Fund. Before joining the staff of the fund, Mr. Mussa was a long time member of the faculty of the Graduate School of Business of the University of Chicago, starting as an associate professor in 1976 and being promoted to the William H. Abbott Professorship of International Business in 1980. From 1971 to 1976, he was on the faculty of the Department of Economics at the University of Rochester. During this period, he also served as a visiting faculty member at the Graduate Center of the City University of New York, the London School of Economics, and the Graduate Institute of International Studies in Geneva, Switzerland.

YUNG CHUL PARK is a professor of economics at Korea University, Seoul. He is also chairman of the Deliberation Committee for Financial Development at the Ministry of Finance and Economy and is currently overseeing the merger of Korea's two largest commercial banks as chairman of the CBK-Hanil Bank Merger Committee. He previously served as the chief economic adviser to Doo Hwan Chun, president of the Korea Development Institute and to the president of the Korea Institute of Finance. He was also a member of the Bank of Korea's Monetary Board. He was the director of the Institute of Economic Research at Korea University, taught at Harvard and Boston Universities as a visiting professor, and worked for the International Monetary Fund. After completing undergraduate work at Seoul National University, he received his Ph.D. from the University of Minnesota.

CATHERINE PATTILLO is an economist in the Research Department of the International Monetary Fund. Prior to joining the IMF, she held a research post at the Center for the Study of African Economies, Oxford University, and was an economics fellow at St. Antony's College. During graduate school she interned at the World Bank, Federal Reserve Board, and the Federal Reserve Bank of New York. She has also worked for the United States Agency for International Development (USAID) in Kenya, Tanzania, and Uganda. She received her B.A. from Harvard University and her Ph.D. from Yale University.

RICHARD PORTES is president of the Centre for Economic Policy Research, which he founded, professor of economics at the London Business School, and directeur d'Études at the École des Hautes Études en Sciences Sociales in Paris. He was a Rhodes Scholar and a fellow of Balliol College, Oxford, and has also taught at Princeton and Harvard (as a Guggenheim Fellow). He was founding professor of the department of economics at Birkbeck College (University of London). Mr. Portes is a fellow of the Econometric Society and secretary-general of the Royal Economic Society. He has written extensively on sovereign borrowing and debt, European monetary issues, international monetary economics, centrally planned economies and transition, macroeconomic disequilibrium, and European integration.

PEDRO POU is president of the Central Bank of the Republic of Argentina. He has served as an international economics professor at various universities, as a director of investigations at the Center of Latin American Monetary Studies (Centro de Estudios Monetarios Latinoamericanos), director of the Center for Macroeconomic Studies of Argentina (Centro de

Estudios Macroeconomicos de Argentina), and aid consultant on various projects. Mr. Pou's public sector appointments include adviser to the secretary of Economic Programming (1975), economics minister of the Buenos Aires Province (1981–83), and director (1991–94) and vice president (1994–96) of the central bank. Mr. Pou holds an agricultural engineering degree from the National University in Argentina and a Ph.D. in economics from the University of Chicago.

RAGHURAM RAJAN is the Joseph L. Gidwitz Professor of Finance at the Graduate School of Business, University of Chicago. Rajan received his Ph.D. in 1991 from the Sloan School of Management at M.I.T. He has taught courses on corporate finance and financial institutions. His research interests include organizational behavior, corporate financial policy, financial intermediation, regulation, and comparative financial systems. His articles have appeared in academic journals, books, and newspapers. Rajan has been a consultant for various financial institutions, the Bertil Danielsson visiting Professor of Banking at the Stockholm School of Economics, and visiting Professor of Finance at the J.L. Kellogg Graduate School of Management, Northwestern University. He is the Director of the Research Program in Corporate Finance at the National Bureau of Economic Research and is an associate editor of a number of finance and banking journals.

SERGIO REBELO is the Tokai Bank Distinguished Professor of International Finance at the J.L. Kellogg Graduate School of Management of Northwestern University. Prior to joining Kellogg, Mr. Rebelo taught at the University of Rochester and at the Portuguese Catholic University. He has served as a consultant to the World Bank, to the International Monetary Fund, and to the Board of Governors of the Federal Reserve System. He is currently affiliated with two research networks: the Center for Economic Policy Research and the National Bureau of Economic Research. Mr. Rebelo serves as an associate editor of the *American Economic Review, Journal of Monetary Economics*, *European Economic Review*, *and Journal of Economic Growth*. He is on the Advisory Board of the Carnegie-Rochester Conference on Economic Policy and has served on the panel of Economic Policy. Mr. Rebelo is working on a chapter for the *Handbook of Macroeconomics*. His papers have been published in *the American Economic Review*, the *Journal of Political Economy*, the *Journal of Monetary Economics*, the *Journal of Economic Dynamics and Control*, and the *European Economic Review*. His research has been financed by the National Foundation. He received a Sloan Fellowship for his dissertation work and has been awarded an Olin Fellowship by the National Bureau of Economic Research.

ERIC ROSENGREN is a vice president and economist at the Federal Reserve Bank of Boston. He heads the Banking Monetary Policy Section of the Research Department. He has written numerous articles on financial markets, corporate control, and banking. His most recent articles have appeared in or are forthcoming in the *American Economic Review*, *Quarterly Journal of Economics*, *Journal of Finance*, and *Journal of Money, Credit, and Banking*. After graduating summa cum laude from Colby College he received a Ph.D. in economics from the University of Wisconsin-Madison in 1986.

HELMUT SCHIEBER is a member of the board of the Deutsche Bundesbank responsible for international tasks and relations. Prior to his current position, he held the posts of vice president; senior director for credit, securities, and the central portfolio; head of the training division; and personal assistant to the president of the Land Central Bank.

ANNA J. SCHWARTZ is a member of the research staff at the National Bureau of Economic Research, a distinguished fellow of the American Economic Association, and a past president of the Western Economic Association. She has served as staff director of the U.S. Gold Commission. She is the author of numerous articles on monetary economics and several books. Ms. Schwartz has served on the board of editors of the *American Economic Review* and is currently a member of the editorial boards of the *Journal of Monetary Economics, the Journal of Financial Services Research*, and the *Journal of Money, Credit, and Banking*. She holds a Ph.D. in economics from Columbia University.

GREGORY F. TAYLOR is the executive director for Australia, Kiribati, Korea, the Marshall Islands, Mongolia, New Zealand, Papua New Guinea, the Philippines, Seychelles, Solomon Islands, Vanuatu, and Western Samoa region for the International Monetary Fund. Mr. Taylor has held a number of governmental posts, including secretary of three governmental departments: the Department of Industry, Science, and Tourism, the Department of Primary Industries and Energy, and the Department of Employment, Education, and Training. He began his career in public service in 1966 as an economist in the Australian Department of the Treasury. He then served as a technical assistant in the Office of the Executive Director of the International Monetary Fund. From 1977 to 1979, he was the financial minister in the Australian delegation to the Organization for Economic Cooperation and Development. From 1980 to 1982, he was assistant secretary in the Financial Institutions Division of the Australian Department of the Treasury. He has also been deputy secretary to the Department of the Prime Minister and Cabinet and chairman of the Industries Association. Mr. Taylor received a B.Ec. with honors from the University of Adelaide.

ROBERT TOWNSEND is the Charles E. Merriam Distinguished Service Professor of Economics in the Department of Economics and research associate at NORC at the University of Chicago. He is also a consultant to the Federal Reserve Bank of Chicago. He began his teaching and research at Carnegie Mellon University. He is a member of the Econometric Society and the American Academy of Arts and Sciences and has served as editor of the *Journal of Political Economy* and panel member in economics for the National Science Foundation. With grants from NICHD and NSF, Mr. Townsend has done research in Thailand for over ten years. He received his B.A. from Duke University and his Ph.D. from the University of Minnesota.

EDWIN M. TRUMAN is staff director of the Division of International Finance, Board of Governors of the Federal Reserve System. He joined the staff of the division in 1972 and has served in a number of areas. He is a member of the Euro-Currency Committee of the G-10 Central Bank Governors and attends meetings of the Working Party Three of the OECD's Economic Policy Committee. His publications include works on European economic integration, international monetary economics, economic development, and international debt problems. He is a former associate professor of economics at Yale University, where he also received his Ph.D. in economics. He received his B.A. from Amherst College and an L.L.D. (hon.) from Amherst College.

KAZUO UEDA is a member of the Policy Board of the Bank of Japan. Previous to his current position, Mr. Ueda was a professor at the University of Tokyo where he held an assistant professorship. Other assistant professorships included Osaka University and British Columbia University. Mr. Ueda holds a Ph.D. in economics from the Massachusetts Institute of Technology.

DELANO VILLANUEVA is deputy director for research at The SEACEN Center of the International Monetary Fund where he has served in multiple areas including Central Banking (now the Monetary and Exchange Affairs Department), Asian, Research, Middle Eastern, and IMF Institute. He has published extensively in the areas of monetary and growth economics, his work appearing in numerous journals. Mr. Villaneuva joined the IMF after earning his Ph.D. in economics from the University of Wisconsin.

CHAIYAWAT WIBULSWASDI is the former governor of the Bank of Thailand. Before his appointment to the Bank of Thailand in 1997, Mr. Wibulswadi was the deputy minister of finance and the minister of finance. From 1995 to 1996, he was an economic advisor to the Prime Minister. He has also been a trustee for the Thailand Development Research Institute, a university council member for the National Institute for Development Administration, and vice president and acting president of the Economic Society of Thailand. He received a B.A. from Williams College and a Ph.D. from Massachusetts Institute of Technology.

JOHN A. WING is the Frank Wakely Gunsaulus Professor of Law and Finance at the Illinois Institute of Technology and director of its Center for the Study of Law and Financial Markets. He joined the school in July 1998. Mr. Wing is also chairman of ABN AMRO Sage Corporation, of ABN AMRO Mutual Funds, and of the investment committee of ABN AMRO Private Equity Partnerships. Prior to joining the staff of IIT, Mr. Wing was chairman of the board and chief executive officer of ABN AMRO Incorporated, formerly the Chicago Corporation. From 1975 to 1980, Mr. Wing was president of A.G. Becker, a subsidiary of The Becker Warburg Paribas Group. Mr. Wing holds a B.A. in economics from Urban College and an L.L.B. from George Washington University Law School.

YUKIO YOSHIMURA is the International Monetary Fund executive director for Japan. Previous to his current role he was the deputy director general at the Ministry of Finance of Japan, held several positions at the Ministries of Finance and Foreign Affairs, was executive director of the Inter-American Investment Corporation, and worked as an alternate executive director at the World Bank. He has served as a member of the Group of Ten Working Party on Electronic Money. Mr. Yoshimura received a B.A. in economics from Tokyo University.

ZHANG ZHIXIANG is executive director for China at the International Monetary Fund. Mr. Zhang assumed this position in 1996. Previously he was alternate executive director. Before joining the IMF, he held various positions at the People's Bank of China, including director of the International Department from 1994 to 1996 and chief representative, Representative Office for Europe, London, from 1992 to 1994. Mr. Zhang holds a B.A from Beijing Foreign Language Institute and an M.I.P.P. degree from Johns Hopkins University.